The Uses of Idolatry

The Oxford Handbook

The Uses of Idolatry

WILLIAM T. CAVANAUGH

OXFORD
UNIVERSITY PRESS

OXFORD
UNIVERSITY PRESS

Oxford University Press is a department of the University of Oxford. It furthers
the University's objective of excellence in research, scholarship, and education
by publishing worldwide. Oxford is a registered trade mark of Oxford University
Press in the UK and certain other countries.

Published in the United States of America by Oxford University Press
198 Madison Avenue, New York, NY 10016, United States of America.

CIP data is on file at the Library of Congress
ISBN 978–0–19–767905–0 (pbk.)
ISBN 978–0–19–767904–3 (hbk.)

DOI: 10.1093/oso/9780197679043.001.0001

Paperback printed by Marquis Book Printing, Canada
Hardback printed by Bridgeport National Bindery, Inc., United States of America

MIX
Paper from
responsible sources
FSC® C103567

Contents

Acknowledgments

Interdisciplinary work is always a risk. Ranging widely over disciplines invites justifiable complaints about the brevity of the discussion of any one subject, the vast areas of the iceberg of scholarship left untouched, and shortcomings in the treatment of the iceberg's tip. I was nevertheless encouraged to take this risk by the Notre Dame Institute for Advanced Study, where I began this book as a Fellow in the fall of 2018. The NDIAS fosters research into big questions that affect our ability to lead meaningful lives, research that requires transgressing narrow disciplinary boundaries. For one wonderful semester I shared seminars and more informal conversations with colleagues from disciplines ranging from political science to quantum computing. Thanks to Fredrik Albritton Jonsson, Karl Ameriks, Gary Anderson, Kim Belcher, John Betz, John Deak, Daniel Hinshaw, Andrey Ivanov, Clare Kim, Ulrich Lehner, Gerry McKenny, Lisa Mueller, Jean Porter, Raphael Mary Salzillo, Laura Dassow Walls, and Alexandre Zagoskin for rich conversations about my project during my time at Notre Dame. Special thanks to Brad Gregory, who was then director of the NDIAS, for his friendship and helpful feedback as this book project was getting off the ground. I also want to thank the NDIAS staff, Kristian Olsen and Carolyn Sherman, for their kind hospitality, and my student research assistants, Chris Enabnit and Mark Florig, for their library sleuthing and helpful feedback on drafts of the first two chapters.

In 2019 I was privileged to present drafts of the first three chapters of this book at a symposium entitled "Many Old Gods" sponsored by the Institute for Ethics and Society at the University of Notre Dame Australia in Sydney, where I was a visiting professor for a ten-day stay. I am grateful to my respondents Renée Köhler-Ryan, Joel Harrison, Rachelle Gilmour, and Matt Tan for their insightful comments and criticisms that have undoubtedly made the book better than it would have been. Thanks as well to Tim Smartt and Annette Pierdziwol for their hospitality and hard work making the symposium happen.

In September 2022 I presented the substance of chapters 1, 2, 3, 6, 7, and 8 in four lectures for the faculty of St. Meinrad Seminary and School of Theology in Indiana. I want to thank Kevin Schemenauer for arranging my visit, and all his fellow faculty for their stimulating feedback and helpful comments and suggestions, many of which made their way into the final manuscript in some form.

So many people have enhanced this book with their insights and critiques that I fear leaving someone out. It is nevertheless a great pleasure to think back and thank the people whose generosity has made the road I have walked. For reading parts of the manuscript and commenting on them I am extremely grateful to Stanley Hauerwas, Johannes Hoff, Vincent Lloyd, Scott Moringiello, Chris Ryan, and Paul Tyson. I have presented parts of the argument of this book in lectures at many different venues: Victoria University in New Zealand, Radboud University Nijmegen, Netherlands, Örebro School of Theology in Sweden, University of St. Thomas in Minnesota, Malone University in Ohio, Wycliffe and Regis Colleges at the University of Toronto, Trinity College, Dublin, University of Chicago, University of Gothenburg in Sweden, Spring Arbor University in Michigan, Sun Yat-Sen University in Zhuhai, China, Northern Seminary in Illinois, the Crossroads Cultural Center in New York, the University of Mary in North Dakota, University of Public Service of Budapest, Edith Stein Philosophy Institute of Granada, Spain, the Center for Catholic-Jewish Studies of Saint Leo University in Florida, Institut Catholique in Paris, International Congress of the Sociedade de Teologia e Ciências da Religião in Belo Horizonte, Brazil, Catholic University of Eastern Africa in Nairobi, and the Notre Dame–Newman Centre for Faith and Reason in Dublin. A regrettably partial list of people to thank for the above invitations—and the accompanying hospitality and conversations that have helped hone my thinking—includes Stephen Adubato, Pablo Baisotti, John Berkman, Jeff Bilbro, Maria Clara Bingemer, Ryan Boettcher, Sylvain Brison, Con Casey, Gary Chamberland, Jan Eckerdal, David Fitch, Shawn Floyd, Joel Halldorf, Michael Kirwan, Cesar Kuzma, Allister Lane, Joe Mangina, Chris Marshall, François Moog, Michael Morris, Michael Naughton, Tamás Nyirkos, Arne Rasmusson, Fáinche Ryan, Jared Schumacher, Ola Sigurdson, Dan Sportiello, Mátyás Szalay, Matthew Tapie, Stephan van Erp, Scott Waalkes, and Fredrik Wenell.

At DePaul, I am so privileged to count on the support of my dean, Guillermo Vásquez de Velasco, and my colleagues in the Catholic Studies Department. Special thanks to my colleagues in the Center for World Catholicism and Intercultural Theology. Mike Budde has been my friend for many years, a never-ending source of acute scholarly insights and gallows humor. Stan Chu Ilo is one of the most simultaneously talented and holy people I know; I am praying that that combination will prevent him from being named a bishop somewhere so that I can continue to work alongside him. Karen Kraft and Marlon Aguilar are the backbone of the CWCIT, not only running it but exemplifying the hospitality and communion that the global church aspires to.

I want to thank my editor Theo Calderara for once again making Oxford University Press a pleasure to work with.

Chapter 2 of this book appeared in abbreviated form as "Enchantment: Charles Taylor's Naïveté," in the journal *New Polity* 1, no. 3 (November 2020): 3–23. Thanks to Marc Barnes and Andrew Jones at *New Polity*. Portions of chapter 6 appeared in my article "The Splendid Idolatry of Nationalism," in *Pro Publico Bono* 9, no. 2 (2021): 4–25, for which I have Tamás Nyirkos to thank.

Finally, thanks to my family, especially my wife, Tracy, and our boys—Finnian, Declan, and Eamon—for living good lives and bringing me joy. I dedicate this book to my brother Dan, who has—as the liturgy says—gone before us marked with the sign of faith, but whose goodness, faithfulness, and adventurous spirit continue to inspire me.

Introduction

Everybody Worships

In his famous Kenyon College commencement address in 2005, novelist
David Foster Wallace told the graduates:

> [I]n the day-to day trenches of adult life, there is actually no such thing as
> atheism. There is no such thing as not worshipping. Everybody worships.
> The only choice we get is what to worship. And the compelling reason for
> maybe choosing some sort of god or spiritual-type thing to worship . . . is
> that pretty much anything else you worship will eat you alive.[1]

Worship money and you'll never have enough. Worship your body and you
will always feel ugly. Worship power and you will always feel weak and afraid.
Worship your intellect and you will end up feeling stupid. Worship of this
kind is not so much a conscious decision as our default setting. We live in
a world that encourages and profits from our misdirected worship: "the so-
called real world of men and money and power hums merrily along in a pool
of fear and anger and frustration and craving and worship of self."[2]

This book is an attempt to work out the novelist's insight in a scholarly
register. The empirical argument of this book is that worship has not receded
in a supposedly "secular" world, but has rather migrated from the explicit
worship of God to the implicit worship of things of human creation. The normative theological argument is that this migration has not necessarily been
a step forward. At the same time, however, I want to avoid nostalgia; if it is
true that we all worship, it is also true that we have always worshiped badly.
While attempting to suggest how to worship less badly, I also want to recognize sympathetically that the ubiquity of worship indicates a deep longing in
the human heart for the transformation of our lives.

To make these kinds of arguments is to question some of the most prevalent stories modern Western people like to tell about ourselves, especially the
self-congratulatory ones about having left the foolishness and dependency

The Uses of Idolatry. William T. Cavanaugh, Oxford University Press. © Oxford University Press 2024.
DOI: 10.1093/oso/9780197679043.003.0001

2 THE USES OF IDOLATRY

of worship behind. We have learned to describe our present age as "secular" and "disenchanted." Previous ages took the presence of God and spirits and ancestors and more for granted; we moderns, nourished by a more scientific worldview, have moved beyond such beliefs and embraced a more rational point of view, devoid of worship and devoid of overarching narratives of meaning. According to this story, where religious belief survives in the West it is marginalized from public discourse; what remains of Western religion has been internally secularized, concerned more with this world than something that transcends it. The public/private dichotomy tracks a whole series of other binaries with which we have learned to describe our world: disenchanted/enchanted, secular/religious, nonbelievers/believers, natural/supernatural, mundane/otherworldly, immanent/transcendent, modern/premodern, and so on. These binaries are part of the narrative construction of "the West," and we have learned to describe the relationship between the West and the rest of world also in binary terms. Paul Gifford, for example, contrasts the "pervasive 'enchanted religious imagination'" of Africa with the West's "completely 'disenchanted' Christianity—one thoroughly in keeping with the surrounding milieu."[3]

The present book explores the uses of such binaries and argues that they are more ideological than empirical: what characterizes the modern West is not disenchantment but rather the condition of having learned to describe ourselves as disenchanted. The point is not that there is no difference between modern and premodern, or between the United States and Africa; a Fourth of July parade is not the same thing as a Corpus Christi procession, and collecting sports memorabilia is not the same thing as witchcraft. But we need to be clearer about what is different and what is not. The above binaries accentuate the differences but obscure the similarities. What has diminished in the West is explicit worship of the Jewish and Christian God; what has not diminished is worship. The idea of a disenchanted, secular, and this-worldly West is complicated by—among many other things, some positive, some not—the prevalence of commodity fetishism, ritualized nationalism, and faith in the "invisible hand" of the market to lead us to the promised land. American shoppers run frenzied for discounted electronics at the stroke of midnight during the yearly ritual of Black Friday; to describe them as disenchanted is to miss something crucial. And that might be precisely why we in the West find such binaries so appealing: they license a more flattering self-image of the modern Westerner as scientific, sober, mundane, and focused on the real world. But self-flattery is rarely the way to wisdom.

The present book can be understood as a continuation of the argument of my book *The Myth of Religious Violence*.[4] In that book, I contend that there is no good reason to think that there is a set of "religious" ideologies and institutions with a peculiar tendency toward violence not shared by their "secular" counterparts. People kill for all sorts of things: gods, flags, freedom, ethnicity, oil, nations, the workers' revolution, the free market, and many other ideologies and practices that people treat as ultimate. Through an extensive genealogy of the religious/secular distinction, I show that the distinction is a modern Western construct, a product of church-state struggles in early modern Europe, subsequently exported to the rest of the world through the process of colonization. The religious/secular distinction is not a neutral set of descriptive categories, and the idea that religion has a greater tendency than the secular to promote violence is not a commonsense observation about the world. Both are ideological constructs that privilege certain Western secularist arrangements. I show how the myth of religious violence is used, in domestic policy and law, to justify the marginalization of what is labeled "religion," and is used, in foreign policy, to justify violence against "religious"—especially Muslim—social orders.

Although there is hardly any explicit theology in *The Myth of Religious Violence*, I have told audiences for years that it is really a book about idolatry, inordinate devotion to what is not God. It is a basic biblical insight that people have a tendency to worship all sorts of things that are not God, and to sacrifice both themselves and other people for the things they worship. In the present book, I seek to make that analysis explicit. The idea that worship has not receded but migrated to other objects besides God is not a new insight; for example, Jamie Smith's brilliant three-volume *Cultural Liturgies* series explores the nature of humans as worshiping creatures and the ways in which worship forms us; Eugene McCarraher's *Enchantments of Mammon* uncovers in fascinating detail capitalism as the "religion" of modernity.[5] The charge of idolatry more specifically is thrown around rather freely in the contemporary world. Pope Francis, for example, rarely talks about the world economy without calling it idolatrous. When one looks for a systematic and interdisciplinary treatment of idolatry in the contemporary world, however, one finds very little. There are many scholarly examinations of idolatry in the biblical texts, but they tend to draw connections to the contemporary world rather briefly and tentatively. Studies of idolatry tend to treat it as a "religious" problem, but if, as I argue, idolatry critique transcends the religious/secular distinction—because the worship of anything, not only gods, can be idolatry—then an analysis of idolatry must extend beyond religious studies and theology and be fully interdisciplinary. In this book, I attempt a synthetic study of idolatry—and the related ideas of enchantment and sacrament—over a wide range of disciplines: sociology (Max Weber and Émile Durkheim), philosophy (Charles Taylor and Jean-Luc Marion), political science (Ernest Gellner and Anthony D. Smith), economic history (Karl Marx and Sut Jhally), and theology (Augustine and the Bible). I hope to show that work from disparate fields—for example, Weber on enchantment, Smith on nationalism as religion, Marx on commodity fetishism—can best be understood under the theological rubric of idolatry.

Idolatry critique is dangerous because of its ready association with chauvinism: *you* don't worship like *we* do, and therefore you must be shunned or destroyed. The Bible and colonial history offer many examples of the destruction of "idolaters" and the subjugation of "heathens." I argue nevertheless that idolatry critique can be useful because it helps to overcome some of the binaries that I call into question in *The Myth of Religious Violence*. Idolatry critique questions the religious/secular dichotomy, because worship is not confined to gods but applies to all sorts of realities commonly labeled "political" or "economic." Idolatry critique calls into question substantivist definitions of "religion," because it recognizes that what matters is not what people say they believe but what their behavior reveals about their implicit beliefs. If someone claims to believe in the Christian God but never darkens the door of a church and spends all their waking hours obsessing about the stock market, the colloquial idea that money is their god and capitalism their religion captures something important about how their world is structured.

Idolatry critique also helps express the negative consequences of many types of misdirected worship. Idolatry is ultimately a form of narcissism, an attempt at aggrandizing the self. This self-love, however, is a type of entrapment or self-isolation from God and from other people; it results in self-diminishment. The Bible and David Foster Wallace make the same salient point: worshiping money, the nation, and other such mundane things will ultimately eat you alive. We come to be dominated by our own creations. I work out this point on a theoretical level through Weber and the Christian theological tradition, and at an empirical level through detailed analyses of nationalism and consumer culture. I chose these two examples because they operate beyond our private obsessions, acting as public, organizing, and unifying idolatries, godlike systems in which we are embedded. They are gods that are given, not chosen. Individuals cannot simply decide not to be nationalistic or consumeristic; idolatry in this sense is about how the whole social world is structured.

Nevertheless, I want to get beyond jeremiads against idolatry. The title of this book, *The Uses of Idolatry*, has a double sense, indicating, on the one hand, how idolatry is used to constitute the unjust structures of this world and, on the other hand, how the concept of idolatry is useful for bridging the supposed divide between believers and nonbelievers. I want, in a way, to present idolatry in a sympathetic light. As St. Paul tells the Athenians in Acts 17, their proclivity to worship is evidence that they are groping for God, and may still find God. Idolatry critique helps to overcome the binary of believers/nonbelievers by showing that we all believe in something; we are spontaneously worshiping creatures whose devotion alights on all sorts of things, in part because we are material creatures, and the material world is beautiful. Following an invisible God is hard for material creatures, so we fixate on things that are closer to hand. Idolatry critique applies equally to those who profess belief in God and those who don't. We all worship, and we all worship badly, to greater and lesser degrees. Idolatry critique is therefore best understood first and foremost as self-critique, an exercise in cultivating the virtue of humility. I am not so much interested in "idolatry" as a stable and univocal master category by which we can critique others and get our own worship in order; the only remedy for idolatry is ultimately an unmanageable encounter with the living God, one that throws all of our lives into question.

Beyond the critique of idolatry, I provide a theological account of sacrament as a way of healing idolatry. Any attempt to overcome idolatry cannot simply pit God against the world and opt for the former. As material creatures, we live and move and have our being in the material world and in God simultaneously. What is needed is a practice of sacramentality that sees and uses things in the light of their being in God. I attempt to sketch an aesthetic and an ethic of immersion in material creation that neither elevates material realities into gods nor lowers human beings into instruments to be dominated, but rather participates in divine life through the material realities that God sustains in being. The Incarnation—the pouring out of God into the flesh of the poor man Jesus of Nazareth—is crucial to this participation. The best remedy for idolatry is an uncontrollable encounter with the incarnate God in the chaos and vulnerability of those who are marginalized by the idolatrous systems that eat people alive.

I would like this book to address two different audiences and to suggest that perhaps they are not so starkly different after all. The first audience is those who claim to believe in God, primarily but not exclusively the Christian community. To claim to believe in God is not necessarily to worship God in reality. I hope that this book will help Christians and others to think more deeply about our own practical idolatries and to seek God's help in remedying them and healing a broken world. The second audience is those who claim not to believe in God. I hope that the theoretical and empirical work of this book might demonstrate that the supposed divide between "believers" and "nonbelievers" is perhaps not so wide as is often assumed. In this regard, my argument has affinities with the political theology that has followed in the wake of Carl Schmitt's famous observation that modern political concepts are in fact secularized theological concepts; the sovereignty of God has been replaced with the sovereignty of the state, the miracle with the state of exception, and so on.[6]

Political theology, however, is largely bifurcated into two camps: those (mostly Christian) theologians who explore political matters in the light of the reality of God, and those "secular" thinkers who regard God as a fiction that has serious political consequences. In the latter camp are figures like Paul Kahn, whose book *Political Theology* explores the way that nation-states like the United States have taken on the aura of the sacred, especially in war and its emphasis on sacrifice. For Kahn, political theology is a tool for unmasking the persistence of theology in supposedly "secular" regimes, but it cannot be a way of making normative judgments based on convictions about some transcendent God who actually exists. "In a godless world, that is, a world with no normative significance whatsoever, there is nothing that nature has to teach us in thinking about how to order the political, except that it is entirely up to us."[7] Christian political theology therefore differs as night from day from what Kahn considers political theology. "The latter is an entirely secular field of inquiry, while the former expresses a sectarian endeavor that is no longer possible in the West."[8] Robert Yelle's book *Sovereignty and the Sacred* similarly challenges the religious/secular and politics/theology distinctions, only to buttress them by dismissing the possibility of normative theology that posits the existence of a real God: "The idea of an absolutely sovereign god or king is a projection of human agency."[9] Yelle's book is an exploration of "exit signs" from the suffocating hegemony of law, bureaucracy, and debt, the application of "the same flat, rationalizing level to everything."[10] He explores antinomian theological practices like pardon, Jubilee, and monastic economies, but ends up concluding that they are only utopian, temporary, and symbolic. Because God is just a human projection, escape from the dialectic of sovereignty and law is only a "liminal moment."[11] Both Kahn and Yelle seem to open the door to theology only to slam it shut again.

If we really are to challenge the politics/theology and secular/religious dichotomies, I don't share the anxious compulsion to exclude God-talk from serious intellectual inquiry, which only ends up reinforcing those dichotomies. Barring the possibility of God rules out our exit from the "same flat, rationalizing level" and traps us in an immanent box of our own making. Some might consider my invocation of God in this book to be mere special pleading by a Christian theologian, but I want to suggest that the existence of God solves a problem raised by political theology. Neither Kahn nor Yelle gives an account of *why* the sacred continues to occupy what is in reality a God-shaped hole left by the migration of the holy from the church to the state and market. It may be that the most economical explanation for the need to worship something that transcends ourselves is the existence of something that transcends ourselves. It is, of course, always possible to dismiss evidence of the ubiquity of worship in human experience and in the human heart by concluding, in a Sartrian vein, that the longing for God we experience is absurd, a cosmic joke played on us by a universe in which no God actually exists. Nevertheless, I want to suggest that the reason there is a God-shaped desire in human experience is that it corresponds in some way to a God who actually exists and bends the arc of the moral universe toward love. The present book is not an attempt to prove this. I do, however, point to what I encounter in the world, the longing for transcendence in human experience, and point to indications of a God who corresponds to and fulfills that longing. If the universe is not a joke but a comedy, not a tragedy but a drama in which love has the final word, then something like the God revealed in Jesus Christ might be worth considering.

I want to be clear, at the same time, that Christ is not an answer that Christians have but a person who puts our lives into question. If I tell the story of a world that continues to be Christ-haunted, it is not meant to be a triumphalistic vindication of the Christian past over the grand errors of modernity but rather an unsettling search for a God who has escaped our attempts to bring the divine under human control. I am trying both to invite those who think they know nothing of God to see God manifest in creation and in the longings of the human heart, and to invite those who think they know something of God to relinquish our attempts to grasp hold of God and engineer divinity in our own image.

This book consists of eight chapters. The first two chapters examine the idea that the modern West is disenchanted and devoid of gods. Chapters 3 through 5 offer an account of idolatry using scripture, theology, and phenomenology, respectively. Chapters 6 and 7 each examine a modern instance of idolatry. Chapter 8 presents an account of incarnation and sacrament as a remedy for idolatry. The book is intended as a synthetic interpretation of a theme, not a comprehensive history of ideas; I make no attempt to survey every major thinker (Luther, Barth, Ellul, et al.) who has written on idolatry. I have no doubt that the insights of such thinkers would have enriched my analysis, as well as lengthened an already lengthy book. I also make no attempt to analyze every major manifestation of idolatry in the contemporary era. I devote a chapter apiece to nationalism and consumer culture as two of the most prevalent and publicly accepted examples, while recognizing that many other possible topics (racism, technology, and celebrity, to give a few examples) could be explored. I can only acknowledge that much work remains to be done, most of it by scholars other than me.

Chapter 1 is a reinterpretation of Max Weber's work. Weber is famous for declaring that the modern secular world is disenchanted, and this idea has been both accepted by many and contested by others who argue that modernity has its own types of enchantment. In this chapter I argue that Weber himself did not really buy the disenchantment narrative. He was conflicted on this question and saw how rationalization produces its own types of irrationality. Through a detailed analysis of Weber's work, I explore his unthought, his inability to escape the conclusion that disenchantment is not the disappearance of the sacred but the migration of the sacred from the "religious" to the "secular." Weber declared that, in modernity, "[m]any old gods ascend from their graves."[12] Weber worried furthermore that such gods of our own making—especially the bureaucratic state and capital—have come to dominate us, making escape impossible. I argue that disenchantment is not the condition of modernity but the way we have learned to describe the condition of modernity. I argue that we need to overcome the dichotomy of enchanted/disenchanted and, rather than try to determine whether or not we are actually disenchanted, look at the kinds of power that are buttressed by the enchanted/disenchanted dichotomy.

In chapter 2, I examine a more contemporary account of secularization that adopts the disenchantment of the modern West as a given. Charles Taylor's account of the secular age accepts a wide gap between us in the modern West on the one hand and those who came before us or live outside the West on the other: "A race of humans has arisen which has managed to experience its world entirely as immanent."[13] This secular exceptionalism is based in a series of binaries that play crucial roles in Taylor's analysis: West/non-West, modern/premodern, secular/religious, nonbelievers/believers, immanence/transcendence, natural/supernatural, disenchantment/enchantment, and so on. In every case, Taylor tries to bring the two poles closer together, but I argue that he does not do enough to question the terms under which the binaries are given in the first place. I argue, however, that—as with Weber—resources to question these binaries can be found in Taylor's work itself. Taylor states that consumerism is "almost" a stronger form of magic, that art is "putatively" religious, that scientific naturalism can be a piety that "verges on" religion. These hedge words keep the religious/secular dichotomy—and the other dichotomies as well—intact, but I explore why Taylor thinks he needs these dichotomies and what would happen if he reconfigured or abandoned them. At one point Taylor claims that those who confine themselves to the immanent frame in fact are "responding to transcendent reality, but misrecognizing it."[14] To be true to this insight, I argue, Taylor—the Catholic philosopher—needs a theology of idolatry. There is no "race" of humans who experience the world entirely as immanent; there is rather a set of people in the West who have learned—for various reasons having to do with how power is distributed in Western societies—to describe their world as immanent and disenchanted, while they are still involved in all sorts of worship. In other words, there is a gap between our descriptions of the world as disenchanted and the way we actually behave, and we need a theology of idolatry to address this gap.

I explore the theme of idolatry in the Christian scriptures, both Old and New Testaments, in chapter 3. I first consider the biblical idea that humans are inherently worshiping creatures. Then I explore some themes in biblical treatments of idolatry and show how they question some modern binaries: enchanted/disenchanted, religious/secular, believers/nonbelievers, worshipers and non-worshipers. The Bible expands the concept of idolatry to include more than the explicit worship of other named gods besides YHWH. Idolatry includes greed, reliance on military power, attachment to material things, and other kinds of devotion to what is not God. Idolatry is not so much a metaphysical error as it is misplaced loyalty; idolatry is about behavior, not simply belief. Idolatry is also usually a matter of degree, of inordinate devotion to one or another of the goods of this life; when it crosses the line from ordinate to inordinate is often hard to discern. From these reflections, I move to consider the place of images in the biblical material. I argue that Israelite aniconism still leaves room for a kind of sacramental seeking of God through the material world. In the next section of the chapter, I consider the negative consequences of idolatry, most notably the theme, found in Weber, that we are oppressed by gods of our own making. The prophets identify an exchange by which life is imputed to mute material images while life is drained away from their human makers. This theme anticipates Marx's analysis of commodity fetishism by several millennia. Finally, the last section of the chapter examines self-critique and sympathy. Idolatry critique in the Bible is most commonly self-critique, the prophetic calling back of the people of God to true worship. There are also moments of sympathy in biblical critiques of idolatry, as in Wisdom 13:6–7: "Yet these people are little to be blamed, for perhaps they go astray while seeking God and desiring to find him. For while they live among his works, they keep searching, and they trust in what they see, because the things that are seen are beautiful." My theological reading of the biblical material provides a basis for questioning the narrative of secularization as disenchantment, and for doing so without resorting to mere jeremiad.

I turn to Augustine in chapter 4 for a Christian theological account of idolatry. For Augustine, idolatry—despite its outward appearance as dedication to something other than the self—is rooted in a kind of self-love, though one that paradoxically results in self-dissolution. I begin by examining Augustine's analysis of the Roman creation of gods as a manifestation of self-love, the desire to have gods who serve them rather than they serving God. The result is paradoxically a slavish domination of humans by their own creations. For Augustine, the explicit worship of pagan gods is part of a broader critique of the worship of created things instead of God. I then consider Augustine's attitude toward temporal things. I show that Augustine has sympathy for us material creatures who cling to material things both from delight at their beauty and from fatigue caused by the flux of time. We seek rest in temporal things, though they cannot stop death or satisfy our eternal longings. I analyze Augustine's distinction between use and enjoyment and show that inordinate attachment to created things instead of to their Creator is a reduction of people and things to means toward which the end is the self. In the following section, I show how Augustine regards idolatry as a kind of narcissism or self-worship, despite its appearance of worshiping an

Other. In an act of self-assertion, people make their own gods, but then, obeying the law of their nature, bow down and worship them. Thus does autonomy become heteronomy, and self-love becomes domination by one's own inventions. To return to God is simultaneously to return to one's true, unalienated self. In the final section of this chapter, I consider Augustine's view of material images. Augustine shares a generally biblical and Platonic suspicion of graven images, but allows for a nonidolatrous sacramental practice of images insofar as they participate in the Image of God, Jesus Christ. Augustine thus reverses the dynamic of idolatry we explored in the previous chapter; rather than life being drained from humans by their conforming to the idols they make, conforming to the sacramental objects that point to God can give humans participation in the fullness of divine life.

In chapter 5 I examine Jean-Luc Marion's phenomenology of the idol, perhaps the most intensive exploration of idolatry from a Christian thinker in the contemporary context. For Marion, like Augustine, idolatry is ultimately a form of narcissism, but Marion develops a more sympathetic account of idolatry as an authentic expression of the human experience of the divine. First, I show how Marion's critique of idolatry fits into his attack on ontotheology and the attempt to reduce God to human concepts. I then examine three stages of Marion's treatment of the idol. In the first stage, Marion regards the idol theologically. In its search for God, the self becomes fatigued and lets its gaze come to rest on material objects that dazzle it. The idol is a mirror to the self rather than a window to the divine; God is cut to the measure of the self. In the second stage, Marion considers the idol phenomenologically in the form of human-made art; the self is overwhelmed by the idol as a saturated phenomenon. In both these stages, Marion regards the idolater with sympathy; though cut to human measure, idols are a genuine, but limited, experience of the divine. In his third stage, Marion returns to theology in his exploration of Augustine. Here, idolatry is the resistance the self offers to the truth; the truth, not the idol, is the saturated phenomenon that overcomes me with its power. Idolatry is not so much true-but-limited, but rather tries to substitute what it loves for the real truth. Finally, I explore Marion's passing reference to a "splendid idolatry," the giving over of the self to something larger than the self. Marion wonders if we moderns have lost our ability for such a splendid idolatry, but also gives hints that that might not be the case.

Using these themes from Augustine's and Marion's work, chapter 6 explores nationalism as a kind of splendid idolatry dedicated to the service of something larger than the self but ultimately coming down to a type of collective narcissism. Nationalism calls forth real virtues of self-sacrifice for ideals and people beyond the individual self, while simultaneously directing lethal levels of devotion toward what is not God. Once again we become subject to gods of our own making, gods that are constituted by the mirrors we hold up to our collective self. In the first section of this chapter, I explore theories of nationalism as "religion," in figures such as Durkheim, Carlton Hayes, Robert Bellah, Carolyn Marvin, and Atalia Omer. In the second section, I look at theories about the origins of nationalism, especially those of Ernest Gellner and Anthony D. Smith, and argue that Western forms of nationalism appropriated the sacred from the old Christian order. Next, I give a sympathetic account of the splendid virtues of nationalism, which share the matter but not the same end as the Christian virtues. I examine two Catholic attempts to distinguish nationalism from patriotism and to defend a virtuous, though limited, devotion to the nation-state. I argue that many nation-states cannot survive with such limited devotion, which is why they need nationalism to become a "religion." I then explore the vices of nationalism, particularly collective narcissism, the worship of the collective "we," which results in racism and the willingness to kill for the nation-state. Nationalism tends toward idolatry, incompatible with the worship of God. In the final section of the chapter, I consider whether there are other types of collective belonging that are compatible with the worship of God, exploring the biblical theme of the people of God.

In chapter 7 I investigate a more apparently "unsplendid" type of idolatry, consumer culture, which seems fixated on stuffing the self with things instead of aspiring to serve something greater than the self. Before critiquing consumerism, however, I build on the sympathetic approach to idolatry in chapters 3 through 5 and the notion of idolatry as the search for meaning in created things. As Augustine puts it, we are called to delight in God's material creation insofar as its beauty aids us in our journey back to God. Nevertheless, in the process of "misrecognition," to use Taylor's word, the pursuit of material things becomes an end in itself. In the first section of the chapter, I use the work of anthropologists Mary Douglas and Daniel Miller to explore the way people necessarily use material goods to communicate their deepest meanings. In the next section, I consult studies of consumer behavior as religion, with related themes of magic, the sacred, transcendence, liturgy, animism, and fetishism in consumer culture. In the following section, I consider how and why this investing of divinity in things is accompanied by the exploitation of labor. Here I examine Marx's analysis of commodity fetishism, the personalization of commodities and the depersonalization of human workers. I show how this dynamic pervades online shopping, in which only products appear while human workers remain invisible and subject to stringent discipline. As anticipated in the biblical critique of idolatry discussed in chapter 3, material things take on life, while life is drained away from human persons. The magic of commodities is the flip side of the ruthless rationalization of human labor. I update Marx's analysis by showing how more recent developments in capitalism—the deskilling of labor, globalization, financialization and the growth of debt, the ubiquity of marketing, surveillance capitalism, and the commodification of the self—in every case illustrate the twinned dynamic of the personification of commodities and capital on the one hand and the instrumentalization of human beings on the other. Consumer culture embodies one of the principal dynamics of idolatry: oppression by the products of human making. Finally, I examine the dynamics of narcissism in consumer culture, using Augustine and Marion as my guide.

In chapter 8 I point toward a nonidolatrous practice of the material world. I first consider the question of sacramentality, the notion that divinity is found in creation. If the problem were disenchantment, then seeing divinity in all things might suffice to counter it. Given that the problem, as Eugene McCarraher puts it, is "misenchantment,"[15] however, the question *Which divinity?* must be addressed. In the second section of the chapter I address that question with a consideration of the Incarnation of God in Jesus Christ as an antidote to idolatry. Idolatry attempts to reach up and seize divinity, to bring it within human grasp; the Incarnation is God's self-emptying descent into creation, offering communal participation in God's life as a gift to be received. I then turn to Marion's contrast of the icon to the idol. While idols serve as mirrors to the self, the icon serves as a portal to participation in God. Marion's analysis of the icon cannot remain mere aesthetics; the point for us is to become a living icon of charity. I explore this theme in the practice of the sacraments, especially the Eucharist, acknowledging that there are idolatrous practices of the Eucharist as well as those that heal our idolatry. The Eucharist cannot be reduced to ethics, but it must be lived out in a way that counters idolatries like nationalism and consumerism. I contrast the divinized "we" of nationalism and the divinized "we" of the body of Christ, and contrast the consumption of others with the self-offering of being consumed in Christ's body. Idolatry can be healed only by encounter with the living God, an encounter—unprogrammable according to our ethical criteria—that takes place most especially in the unmanageable encounter with Christ in those who are marginalized by our idolatrous practices.

One way to understand the normative theological argument of this book as a whole is to say that if everybody worships, we might as well try to worship a true God instead of a false one. Wallace puts this conclusion negatively: false gods will eat you alive. I want to put this conclusion more positively: to worship the true God is to encounter joy, a profound connection with our fellow creatures and with the God who transcends but permeates them all. To be healed of idolatry is to break through the zero-sum competition between me and you, between us and them, and between me and God. To resist divinization of the self and of its possessions is simultaneously to participate in divinity, the joyful and ecstatic opening of the small self to communion with all things and with the God who is love.

1

Max Weber's Polytheism

If you bought this book—as opposed to begging, borrowing, or stealing it—
there is a good chance that you bought it from Amazon, which has made
the purchase of nearly anything fantastically easy. You simply make a few
clicks in a virtual environment, and the product appears on your doorstep,
like magic, within a day or two. If you have the money, almost anything from
anywhere in the world can be summoned out of thin air to materialize at
your home.

The material world can be experienced thus as magical, but this experience is hard to square with even a cursory examination of the ruthlessly efficient international network necessary to make such deliveries work. When
Max Weber wrote about the rationalization of modern Western society over
a hundred years ago, he could not have foreseen the lengths to which such rationalization has been taken in an Amazon warehouse, or "fulfillment center."
There poorly paid "associates," who are often temporary workers with few
benefits, scurry among the bins retrieving and packing just about anything
that can be imagined. A handheld device keeps track of their movements.
It directs them to the next item to pick, and a timer starts: fourteen seconds
to scan in the next item four aisles over, for example. The device warns
them if they are falling behind and keeps track of their pick rate. Falling behind, calling in sick, and other offenses can cost a worker their job, so some
"associates" have resorted to urinating in bottles to avoid taking bathroom
breaks.[1] In January 2018 Amazon received patents on a wristband that can
track a warehouse worker's arm movements. Responding to the negative
reaction, an Amazon spokesperson presented the wristband as a liberating
boon for workers: "The speculation about this patent is misguided. . . . This
idea, if implemented in the future, would improve the process for our fulfillment associates. By moving equipment to associates' wrists, we could free
up their hands from scanners and their eyes from computer screens."[2] In the
Amazon warehouse, Weber's melancholy description of the "iron cage"—a
heartlessly efficient mechanized modernity—seems fully vindicated.

The Uses of Idolatry. William T. Cavanaugh, Oxford University Press. © Oxford University Press 2024.
DOI: 10.1093/oso/9780197679043.003.0002

Weber famously described the modern, secularized world as disenchanted, which means several interrelated things: devoid of divine or demonic spirits, devoid of mystery, and devoid of an ordered meaning.[3] Weber's word *Entzauberung* is customarily rendered "disenchantment," but there is no precise English equivalent. Talcott Parsons's famous translation of the revised version of Weber's classic *The Protestant Ethic and the Spirit of Capitalism* renders the phrase *Entzauberung der Welt* as "elimination of magic from the world," which is closer to the meaning in German. *Zauber* is "magic"; *Entzauberung der Welt* is literally "the un-magic-ing of the world." Something about the idea of disenchantment or elimination of magic seems to capture a reality of the modern secularized world, in which Amazon warehouses have replaced cathedrals as the large buildings toward which civic authorities direct public subsidies and pride. And yet the idea that the modern world is disenchanted has not gone uncontested. The magical deliveries that Amazon pulls off by way of treating human beings as robots[4] suggest that magic comes in many forms and continues to haunt our world.

In this first chapter, I analyze Weber's concept of disenchantment and show that, in Weber's own writings, enchantment and disenchantment are not as easily kept separate as is usually supposed. I want to expose the "unthought" in Weber's own thought: the notion that rationalization produces its own type of irrationality that it cannot suppress or avoid. In so doing, I want to pull apart the enchantment/disenchantment dichotomy on which arguments since Weber have depended. I do not wish simply to accept the enchantment/disenchantment divide and argue that modernity either is or is not enchanted. My task is rather to examine the disenchantment narrative, beginning with Weber, and argue that disenchantment is not the condition of modernity but the way we have learned to describe the condition of modernity, a description that authorizes the exercise of certain kinds of power. I will examine the work that the enchanted/disenchanted dichotomy does for us in what has come to be called the modern West.

In the first section, I examine four types of discourses of disenchantment in scholarly thought since Weber and argue for a type that consistently questions the antinomies upon which most debates on disenchantment are based. In the second section, I lay out the historical narrative that Weber tells about rationalization and disenchantment, showing how rationalization is based in belief in gods, then sends the gods to their graves, then demands that the old gods rise from the dead. In the third section, I explore Weber's unthought, his inability to escape the conclusion that disenchantment is not the disappearance of the sacred but the migration of the sacred from the "religious" to the "secular." We do not in fact cease to worship, but we are now subject to gods of our own making. In the fourth and concluding section, I ask what kind of work the enchanted/disenchanted distinction is doing in the modern context, and I briefly suggest some ways the discourse of disenchantment functions in the economic and political realms.

1.1. Discourses of Disenchantment

The phrase *Entzauberung der Welt* predates Weber (1864–1920) and is traceable back to the 1830s.[5] Weber made the phrase and idea famous, though his writings contain only a few scattered mentions of *Entzauberung*, which he uses rather impressionistically. One searches in vain for a systematic treatment of the concept in Weber's corpus of work; it is more a suggestive term than a finely honed analytical concept.[6] The discourse on disenchantment has nevertheless mushroomed far beyond the scope of Weber's treatment of it. On the one hand, Weber's idea of the modern world as disenchanted has achieved hegemonic status. Charles Taylor has confidently written, "Everyone can agree that one of the big differences between us and our ancestors of 500 years ago is that they lived in an 'enchanted' world and we do not."[7] On the other hand, a significant body of literature has pushed back on this hegemony, arguing that enchantment has not been marginalized in the modern world.

Joshua Landy and Michael Saler identify three different types of scholarly discourse on enchantment and disenchantment. The first—and by far the most prevalent, as the Taylor quote indicates—is the notion that the modern world is disenchanted. Landy and Saler call this type "binary." Belief in gods and other unseen spirits, ghosts, and demons that are responsible for various interventions in people's lives has been replaced by the rationalization of social processes and scientific explanations of phenomena. Any lingering enchantment in Western society must be an atavism, a relic of premodern society or the creation of a coping mechanism to deal with the reality of disenchantment. Belief in wonders and miracles and divine intervention is relegated to ghettoes of popular culture and associated primarily with "primitives," minorities, immigrants from the Global South, women, children, the poorly educated, and the poorly paid. Those elites who rebel against the iron cage and seek refuge in art, neopaganism, the triumph of the irrational will, and Eastern mysticism tend to be seen as reactionary antimodernists who have turned their back on reality.[8] In the binary approach, the disenchantment of the modern world can be celebrated or lamented, but it is accepted as a fact.

The second type in Landy and Saler's typology—the "dialectical" approach—rejects the idea that modernity is disenchanted and argues that, on the contrary, the modern world is enchanted, though in a deceptive and dangerous way. This idea is found already in Karl Marx's theory of commodity fetishism, in which mere products of human making are endowed with an autonomy of their own, and the merely material is mistaken for animate life.[9] Landy and Saler's primary example of the dialectical approach is Max Horkheimer and Theodor Adorno's classic *Dialectic of Enlightenment*, first published in 1947 in the wake of World War II. Horkheimer and Adorno set themselves to figure out how the most "enlightened" of societies could have devolved into such barbarism. They argue that such barbarism is not a departure from the Enlightenment but is inherent in the Enlightenment's very project of demythologization.

According to Horkheimer and Adorno, "The program of the Enlightenment was the disenchantment of the world; the dissolution of myths and the substitution of knowledge for fancy."[10] In the pursuit of scientific knowledge, the search for meaning in matter is abandoned.[11] Matter is furthermore stripped of divinity: "The disenchantment of the world is the extirpation of animism,"[12] that is, a world populated by supernatural beings. For the Enlightenment, deities are but replicas of the human beings who produced them; "the supernatural, spirits and demons, are mirror images of men who allow themselves to be frightened by natural phenomena."[13] There is, in other words, a type of idolatry critique inherent in the Enlightenment, though Horkheimer and Adorno do not use that term. The problem is that myth returns as now human beings take the place of gods in their attempt to control and give meaning to nature.[14] Francis Bacon's supposed equation of knowledge with power set the Enlightenment on this path: "What men want to learn from nature is how to use it in order wholly to dominate it and other men. That is the only aim."[15] But in that aim is revealed the same fear that produced myth:

Man imagines himself free from fear when there is no longer anything unknown. That determines the course of demythologization, of enlightenment, which compounds the animate with the inanimate just as myth compounds the inanimate with the animate. Enlightenment is mythic fear turned radical. The pure immanence of positivism, its ultimate product, is no more than a so to speak universal taboo. Nothing at all may remain outside, because the mere idea of outsideness is the very source of fear.[16]

Horkheimer and Adorno nevertheless do not give up on the project of enlightenment, which they see as separable from the Enlightenment. The former is salvageable through self-criticism. That they continue to see enlightenment as an advance over myth is apparent in their view of modern mythology as recidivism, a "reversal universally apparent today," a "retreat from enlightenment into mythology." They remain convinced that "social freedom is inseparable from enlightened thought."[17] But they think that such thought must become self-critical: "If enlightenment does not accommodate reflection on this recidivist element, then it seals its own fate."[18]

Insofar as myth remains a pejorative term for Horkheimer and Adorno, enchantment and disenchantment remain opposing terms. Both the "binary" and the "dialectical" approaches, in Landy and Saler's typology, are either/or propositions, the first contending that modernity is disenchanted, the second arguing that it is still enchanted. To both of these, Landy and Saler oppose a third option, which they label the "antinomial" type. This approach sees modernity as embracing antinomies, seemingly contradictory positions, both rationality and wonder, secularism and a type of faith. Postcolonial scholars, for example, have explored the ways that non-Western cultures have negotiated modernization in complex and messy ways, beyond a mere binary choice between the rational West and the mystical East. Work on "alternative modernities" has problematized oppositions such as those between science and religion, and religion and rationality.[19] Landy and Saler's own edited volume, *The Re-enchantment of the World*, brings together scholars who explore, for example, the way that modern science is as likely to restore a sense of mystery as to extirpate it, or the way that people create alternative mental worlds through poetry or find "secular epiphanies" as spectators at sporting events. Such

antinomial theorists of modernity are at last able to put on display a set of enchantments that are *voluntary*, being chosen (*pace* Adorno) by autonomous agents rather than insidiously imposed by power structures, *respectable*, compatible as they are (*pace* Weber) with secular rationality, and *multiple*, being replacements, each one in its own way, for a polymorphous God.[20]

This third type, according to Landy and Saler, is "the modern enchantment *par excellence*: one which simultaneously enchants and disenchants, which delights but does not delude."[21] Contemporary people allow their reason and imagination to be delighted, but "without the transcendent meanings and purposes of a religious world view";[22] "wonders have become interiorized and are enjoyed with a certain ironic distance,"[23] which is compatible with secular reason.

I think that all three of these approaches to disenchantment in Landy and Saler's typology are problematic. I reject the "binary" approach, as will become apparent in my analysis of Weber. I will argue that Weber cannot keep enchantment and disenchantment divided into separate categories in the way that many think he can. The very categories of enchanted and disenchanted are not neutral descriptive terms; the enchanted/disenchanted dichotomy is itself a central tool in the ideological apparatus of Western modernity, and it is all the more powerful because it masquerades as a descriptive rather than a normative distinction. But for the same reason, my analysis of Weber is simultaneously a critique of the "dialectical" approach. The enchanted/disenchanted binary is no more innocent in Horkheimer and Adorno's use of it. There is a great deal of value in their critique of the Promethean temptation at the heart of the Enlightenment and in their analysis of the boundary around "pure immanence" that ends up reproducing a kind of primitive taboo. Their dialectical approach is helpful in pointing out some of the continuities between modernity and the enchanted and mythical societies that modernity has supposedly relegated to the past. Their goal remains, nevertheless, an enlightenment purified of myth, a yet more rigorous self-criticism that guards ever more vigilantly against the return of myth and enchantment. The dichotomy between enchantment and disenchantment, if confused in current practice, remains as rigid as ever in theory.

For similar reasons, my critique of Weber is simultaneously a critique of Landy and Saler's preferred alternative to both the binary and the dialectical approaches. It is true that Landy and Saler helpfully question the salience of the either/or choice between enchantment and disenchantment. They point the way to a more historical reading of this divide that sees it not as two alternatives embedded in the nature of things, nor as a neutral tool for describing different people and societies, but as a contingent way of dividing up societies and time periods that provides cover for certain types of power. Nevertheless, the types of reenchantment they highlight still conform to many of the same dichotomies that have helped to construct Western modernity. The term "secular epiphanies," for example, is used to distinguish subjective experiences from "religious" epiphanies. The enchanted/disenchanted binary may be called into question, but the religious/secular binary remains firmly in place, despite all of the scholarship that has been done over the past few decades showing that the religious/secular distinction is a very contingent modern and Western distinction, one that is constantly being made and remade, and one that is not innocent of association with Western power, especially in colonial contexts.[24]

As Landy and Saler state in the block quote above, the modern enchantments that they offer must be "respectable," which they define as "compatible . . . with secular rationality." Despite acknowledging the "messy" nature of modernity,[25] on the very same page we are allowed only "respectable" enchantments, those that conform to some given standard of "secular rationality" that does not delude. Such enchantments are "replacements" for God; belief in God has apparently been declared *verboten* by the Enchantment Police. While rightly calling into question the vulgar supersessionist narrative, whereby enchantment has been sequentially replaced by disenchantment and there is no turning back, Landy and Saler nevertheless succumb to a kind of vulgar secularist narrative in which belief in God is simply no longer possible, and Christianity and the like need replacement by more "rational" enchantments. In introducing the final chapter in the volume, Landy and Saler write, "When it comes to individual redemption, one could be forgiven for thinking that there is simply no hope of its rational replacement. As R. Lanier Anderson shows, however, not only can the Christian concept be replaced, but the replacement actually turns out to be superior to the original."[26] The replacement is Nietzsche's "eternal recurrence," which is not only free from metaphysical baggage but more effective than its Christian counterpart.[27] Landy and Saler also apparently think that their belief in "autonomous agents" that voluntarily choose their enchantments is both free of any metaphysical commitments and free of any debt to Western constructions of the autonomous rational self. "Secular rationality" is just rationality as such, not a unique type of Western rationality, and there is no need to apply to it the same kind of historical and ideological critique to which other Western concepts like disenchantment are subjected.

All three of these approaches to disenchantment suffer from some version of the same defect: the perceived need to police the borders established by Western thought, either between enchantment and disenchantment or between secular rationality and other inferior kinds of thought. But Landy and Saler's typology is incomplete. It is unfair to subsume all those who question the enchanted/disenchanted binary under their "antinomial" type, at least as they have described it. Given their parameters for modern enchantments— that they be voluntary, respectable, and multiple—there are some scholars who question the narrative of disenchantment who fit this category. In addition to the contributors to their volume, one might name Jane Bennett, whose *Enchantment of Modern Life* aims at an "enchanted materialism" which restricts itself to operating within a putative purely immanent space marked out by the material.[28] Such projects remain thoroughly Western, despite calling the enchanted/disenchanted boundary into question, as they leave the material/spiritual and immanent/transcendent dichotomies untouched. But many postcolonial scholars are much more thoroughgoing in their critique of these Western categories. They do not respond to the same anxiety to color within the lines that the secular/religious and related binaries have imposed upon us.

I will offer just a couple of examples, out of many possible, of this fourth kind of approach. Margaret Wiener's contribution to the volume *Magic and Modernity* analyzes an incident in Bali under Dutch rule in 1921. Colonial authorities accused a local figure named Nang Mukanis of disturbing the peace by performing various public rituals invoking the intervention of gods on behalf of throngs of people who came to seek his help. The governor, Henri Damsté, ordered Nang Mukanis arrested, and all of his ritual items and clothing were burned before the eyes of the local people. Damsté then summoned the local Balinese authorities and berated them for failing to protect their people from "stupid tricks." Damsté reported that these authorities looked appropriately ashamed of themselves and "disenchanted." As Wiener argues, the opposition of magic to Western thought is deeply embedded in Western ideology, but magic and Western thought are inextricably intertwined within that ideology. Wiener comments, "Colonialism *required* native magic, as its foil and ground."[29] The irrationality of the natives demonstrated the rationality of European science and government and the need to bring such benefits to the local people: "Indeed, there are grounds to argue that 'magic' was a ghostly product of the project of modernity itself."[30]

Here Wiener invokes Bruno Latour's dual concept of translation and purification, both of which typify what we have learned to call "modern."[31] The work of purification in colonialism involves the strenuous efforts to separate the European from the non-European and culture from nature. Through science, Europeans claim direct access to nature, unmediated by culture, fact untainted by belief, reason untainted by magic. At the same time, however, purification is inseparable from translation or mediation, which creates mixtures and hybrids. Latour argues that the dual processes of translation and purification are inseparable and mutually implicated. Without translation, purification would be unnecessary; without purification, translation would be ruled out.[32] Using Latour, Wiener argues that the burning of Nang Mukanis's belongings was simultaneously a purification and a hybridization. Damsté assumed that the public incineration of the objects was a lesson in disenchantment imparted to the local populace: the objects were burned, and the gods did not come to Nang Mukanis's defense. But the natives did not lose their belief in magic, and the Dutch were perplexed. A contemporary (1921) commentator in the *Police Guide* lamented that the Dutch conquest of Balinese warriors armed with charms and fetishes had not brought them to reason: "However often the effect of Netherlands bullets already brought disenchantment in a bloody way and proved the invalidity of such hocus pocus notions with facts, the unshakeable belief in a more possible way to obtain invulnerability continually re-emerged again."[33] According to Wiener, it is no surprise that the public burning of Nang Makunis's belongings did not achieve its intended effect. Destroying someone's power by destroying the objects that represent that power is a common type of magic, and would have reinforced the locals' belief in the power of ritual items. And the expressive and symbolic aspects of magic are illustrated precisely in the attempt to overawe the natives by the public pyre. Such magic is inherent in colonial rule: "How else could a handful of Europeans—even with technologically efficient weapons—have controlled millions of natives if not through practices entailing illusion and delusion?"[34] But, crucially, the natives are not the only ones deluded: "[T]ricking themselves was as important as duping the natives. These dramas, in other words, might better be seen as directed toward Europeans than toward subject populations. They constituted spectacular occasions on which Europeans could convince themselves once again of their inherent superiority."[35]

Wiener is not merely arguing that the Europeans are as enchanted as the natives, or that there are crossings of the border between enchantment and disenchantment. She wants, rather, to "challenge the boundary formation on which the construction of modernity depended."[36] She does not appear to be interested in defending any border separating respectable from disreputable. This does not mean, of course, that there is no such border; the point is rather that the border is as contingent and artificial as the one separating Mexico from the United States, though belief in it likewise has very real consequences, not all of which are happy. Examining the power relations inscribed in treating the border as if it were a natural thing helps to reveal the illusions under which a supposedly disillusioned society lives.

A second example of this fourth approach to disenchantment is Jason Josephson-Storm's more recent book *The Myth of Disenchantment*. Josephson-Storm gathers a wealth of evidence that magic exists and always has in the center of a Western world that has supposedly been disenchanted. He begins with polling data showing that 73% of contemporary Americans report believing in at least one of a list of paranormal phenomena: psychic healing, ESP, ghosts, telepathy, extraterrestrials, necromancy, witches, and so on.[37] One's first reaction might be to attribute such beliefs to the relatively high level of "religious" belief in the United States, but data show that those Americans who define themselves as religious are less likely to believe in paranormal phenomena than those who define themselves as not religious.[38] Furthermore, data show that in Europe, where belief in God is much less popular than in the United States, belief in the paranormal is about the same as in the United States. In Britain, more people believe in ghosts than believe in God.[39] What this suggests to Josephson-Storm is that secularization is not the same as disenchantment and that ghosts and spirits have rushed in to fill the vacuum left by the death of God in European culture.[40] From this brief and suggestive look at contemporary belief, Josephson-Storm then goes back to the roots of Western science, beginning in early modernity, and unearths, in chapter after chapter, the occult beliefs of the great Western scientists: Bacon was an alchemist and magician, Giordano Bruno wrote a treatise on magic, Descartes was a Rosicrucian, Newton was fascinated by alchemy, Marie Curie attended séances, Oppenheimer was into Oriental mysticisim, and the list goes on. Even dour old Max Weber spent two long springs of rest and recuperation (1913 and 1914) at the Monte Verità commune in Ascona, Switzerland, where members dabbled in nudism, Taoism, palm reading, séances, free love, and Ouija boards. Weber did not partake, but Josephson-Storm makes the case that the experience informed his views of Eastern religion and his attraction to mysticism, which he admired ambivalently but did not think was an option he could take.[41]

Josephson-Storm explains scientists' fascination with magic in terms of the triangular relationships among what came to be called science, religion, and magic. Both science and religion were defined over against magic and superstition. At the same time, science and religion defined themselves over against each other. The idea that science and religion are two universal—that is, transhistorical and transcultural—ways of reading the world that are locked in perpetual struggle, a struggle finally ended with the victory of science in modernity, was a nineteenth-century myth projected backward[42] onto, for example, the Galileo case.[43] Josephson-Storm cites Peter Harrison's impressive body of work, which demonstrates that what we call simply "science" emerged from an epistemic basis in Christian theology but gained coherence by defining itself against the irrationality of "religion," which became the negative image of science.[44] Magic, Josephson-Storm argues, was conceptualized as a third term in this relationship and became both threatening and appealing. On the one hand, magic threatened to destabilize the boundaries around both science and religion. On the other, many saw magic as an opportunity to repair the breach between science and religion.[45]

By exploring the complex relationships among these three terms, Josephson-Storm is trying to get beyond the simple binary of enchanted/disenchanted. In doing so he wants to be rid of the idea that the West ever was disenchanted. As he puts it, "The tyranny of reason or instrumental rationality never occurred."[46] He does not thereby want to argue that in fact the modern world is enchanted. He thinks that the enchantment/disenchantment binary is itself part of the power apparatus that defines modernity. Unlike Landy and Saler, he does not appear to be invested in defending any of modernity's other defining binaries: secular/religious, reason/faith, and so on. Indeed, Josephson-Storm questions, following Latour and Hans Robert Jauss,[47] the very concept of modernity, which implies rupture and novelty. It is not that nothing has changed from what we call medieval to modern times. But those changes are distorted if they are described as the loss of myth or the move from myth to reason. Modernity, according to the myth of disenchantment, is the first society that has left myth behind. So Josephson-Storm frames his study as a genealogy of the "myth of a mythless society."[48] He writes, "I am interested in the process by which Christendom increasingly exchanged its claim to be the unique bearer of divine revelation for the assertion that it uniquely apprehended an unmediated cosmos and did so with the sparkling clarity of universal rationality."[49] What this implies is what I have elsewhere called the *migration* of the holy, not the loss of myth but its recon-stitution in other forms.[50]

The term "myth" has different shades of meaning in different contexts. Though we sometimes use it to mean (1) a belief that is simply false, Weber and others use it more precisely to mean (2) a primitive form of symbolic thought that will eventually give way to reason. There is another use of "myth," however, that is not pejorative, but rather names (3) the irreducibly narrative nature of human thought and meaning; here myth and symbol can never simply be reduced to a universal reason. "Myth" can also be used to denote (4) those background beliefs that achieve hegemonic status in a given society, such that they are assumed without question. When Josephson-Storm calls out the "myth of a mythless society," he appears to be claiming that the idea that we can reduce myth to reason (2) is both part of our hege-monic belief system in the modern West (4) and false (1). We live and move and have our being in an irreducibly narrative world (3). Josephson-Storm does not state what stories he lives by, but at the end of the book he rejects the idea of a mythless future and avers that we have no reason to flee from myth (3). He also indicates that some myths are better than others: "Criticism may imply demythologization, but we merely exchange one tale for another, albeit hopefully, a better one."[51] He does not say what tale he thinks is better or best, or which, if any, he thinks are true.

There are limitations to professing the need for myth. At some point, judgments are required about what myths—or to use a word that sounds less pejorative, narratives—are better or truer than others. Another limita-tion to Josephson-Storm's book is that it emphasizes belief over behavior. The polling data are based on what people say they believe, and the case studies of scientists are based on their esoteric beliefs. All of this is fascinating and relevant but incomplete, for what people think and say they believe is only part of the picture. I will argue that it is possible for people who claim to have no beliefs of any kind to behave toward merely material realities in ways we normally associate with enchantment. The burden of my chapters on idolatry will be to try to move beyond both these limitations. It is for these reasons that I think idolatry is a key concept. Nevertheless, I take Josephson-Storm's and Wiener's approaches to questioning the binaries on which the myth of modernity depends as exemplary for my analysis of disenchantment.

The task now is not to decide whether or not a given state of affairs is enchanted or disenchanted, but rather to ask, *What work is the enchantment/*

disenchantment divide doing in any given context? Changing the discourse on disenchantment will take the work of many scholars over time, doing empirical observation and interrogating texts and practices both in the West and in the Global South, where the colonial project still shows its effects. In later chapters I will contribute to that work by examining some practices of late modern Western societies that both depend upon and threaten these binaries: enchanted/disenchanted, transcendent/immanent, religious/secular, believers/nonbelievers, and so on. For now, however, I want to pick up where Josephson-Storm's book leaves off, with his discussion of myth. He contends that we have no choice but to choose a myth. I will now turn to another scholar who thought the same thing. His name is Max Weber.

1.2. Disenchantment and Rationalization in Weber

To make our way to this choice in Weber we will have to follow through his analysis of the restriction of choice; to get to myth, we will have to go through rationalization, for as with all binaries in Weber, they are mutually implicated and depend upon each other. Though the term *Entzauberung* appears only relatively late in Weber's work—the first use is 1913, seven years before his death—the attention it has received is really a matter of felicitous branding rather than a new product. As Peter Ghosh puts it, "*Entzauberung* was not a new idea in 1913, but an extension of an old one, rationalization."[52] Weber opposes rationalization to magic; *Entzauberung* is a significant part of what he means by rationalization:

> To measure the stage of rationalization that a religion represents, there are above all two criteria, which furthermore are inwardly connected in many ways. First, the degree to which it has stripped away *magic*. Then the degree of systematic unity into which it has brought the relationship of God and the world and, accordingly, into its own ethical relation with the world.[53]

The identification of rationalization with the diminishment of magic is complicated, however, by the fact that Weber identifies different senses of rationalization:

> We have to remind ourselves in advance that "rationalism" may mean very different things. It means one thing if we think of the kind of rationalization

the systematic thinker performs on the image of the world: an increasing theoretical mastery of reality by means of increasingly precise and abstract concepts. Rationalism means another thing if we think of the methodical attainment of a definitely given and practical end by means of an increasingly precise calculation of adequate means. These types of rationalism are very different, in spite of the fact that ultimately they belong inseparately together.[54]

After recognizing this distinction between theoretical and practical/instrumental reason, Weber continues on to recognize minimally that "'rational' may also mean a 'systematic arrangement,'" in which case even "methods of mortificatory or of magical asceticism"[55] qualify as rational, insofar as they are methodical. Here, at least, magic and rationalization are not opposed. Elsewhere Weber identifies "value rationality" (*Wertrationalität*), an example of which would be "the actions of persons who, regardless of possible cost to themselves, act to put into practice their convictions."[56] One can also find in Weber a kind of institutionalized or formalized rationality, where norms and procedures are followed simply because they have been institutionalized; this is the rationalization inherent in bureaucracy, where things are done because "that's the way things are done around here."[57]

The sense in which magic is opposed to rationalization is further complicated by the ill-defined nature of the concept of magic in Weber. For Weber, magic characterizes an early stage of history before the development of "higher" salvation religions, but he never explicitly defines magic, nor does he consistently differentiate magic from religion. Magic is rather a primitive stage in the evolution of religion. The matter is confused at the beginning of *The Sociology of Religion* when Weber writes, "The most elementary forms of behavior motivated by religious or magical factors are oriented to *this* world."[58] Although it seems that Weber is using the terms "religious" and "magical" interchangeably here, it is more likely that he intends religion to be the more inclusive term, with magic as a primitive stage in the development of religion.[59] Although Weber regards magic as something primitive, it nevertheless survives in the modern world as an atavism in the peasantry, of whom Weber writes somewhat contemptuously, "*Peasants* have been inclined towards magic. Their whole economic existence has been specifically bound to nature and has made them dependent upon elemental forces. They readily believe in a compelling sorcery directed against spirits who rule over or through natural forces, or they believe in simply buying divine benevolence."[60] In this quote can be seen many of the characteristic features of magic for Weber. Magic is associated with naturalism, concrete and this-worldly, relating immediately to the material world, before symbolization and mental abstraction. The spirits that exist operate through nature; God or the gods have not yet been removed from the world as in the great religions of the Axial Age. The relationship of magic to the spirits of nature is also transactional rather than ethical. As the quote indicates, he considers magic to be a kind of bribery, an attempt not to appease the divine wrath with good intentions and behavior but rather to suborn the powers that be into delivering this-worldly benefits. The motivation of magic is simple: "The pervasive and central theme is: *do ut des*,"[61] literally "I give so that you give" or, to use a more familiar Latin phrase, *quid pro quo*. There is a kind of "primitive rationalism" here; where we might tend to associate magic with fantasy and hocus pocus, Weber emphasizes the concrete practicality of techniques designed to deliver quotidian this-worldly benefits.

Weber describes the evolution from magic to more advanced salvation religions in terms of stages of increasing abstraction. There is abstraction already at the most primitive stage of religious activity, in that people believe in spirits that are in some sense concealed "behind" objects in the natural world. These are not yet personal gods that operate independently of objects. According to Weber, belief in spirits is more advanced when there are certain persons who possess charismatic magical powers capable of manipulating the spirits in various ways. At the next stage of abstraction, the spirits attain a kind of independence from objects; they no longer inhabit objects or processes continuously, but can possess things, events, or people temporarily. This is a step toward the highest stage of abstraction, in which "spirits may be regarded as invisible essences that follow their own laws, and are merely 'symbolized by' concrete objects."[62] There results the rise of the soul on the one hand, and the rise of gods, demons, and other independent supernatural powers on the other, "the ordering of whose relations to man constitutes the realm of religious behavior."[63] According to Weber, "mythological thinking" is the term that describes "the pattern of thought which is the basis of the fully developed circle of symbolic concepts."[64]

The replacement of the original naturalism with symbolism is an important watershed for Weber, but his use of the term "magical symbolism"[65] indicates that the key indicator of magical activity is not naturalism as such. The difference between "magic" and "religion" is hard to pin down in the absence of a clear definition of either term. Though he begins his treatise on the sociology of religion with a refusal to define "religion,"[66] he comes close when he writes, "The relationships of men to supernatural forces which take the forms of prayer, sacrifice and worship may be termed 'cult' and 'religion,' as distinguished from 'sorcery,' which is magical coercion."[67] Here it is coercive manipulation of the spirits or gods that seems to define magic. Indeed, Weber writes provocatively, "Whoever possesses the requisite charisma for employing the proper means is stronger even than the god, whom he can compel to do his will. In these cases, religious behavior is not worship of the god but rather coercion of the god, and invocation is not prayer but rather the exercise of magical formulae."[68] Here again, magic and religion are not entirely separate things; magic seems to be a primitive stage of religion in which the gods are manipulated, and Weber makes clear that magical elements continue to be employed even in more advanced religions everywhere they are practiced. Catholic priests, for example, continue to exercise such magical powers.[69]

Magic is opposed to rationality, but only to a particular kind of rationality. Weber writes, "[R]eligiously or magically motivated behavior is relatively rational behavior, especially in its earliest manifestations. It follows rules of experience, though it is not necessarily action in accordance with a means-end schema."[70] By "rules of experience" Weber seems to mean, for example, that if it rained not long after we did a particular dance, then we should do the same dance in the same way if we want it to rain again. This is not exactly what Weber has called "increasingly precise calculation of adequate means."[71] Today we can distinguish a scientific account of causality from magic: "Only we, judging from the standpoint of our modern views of nature, can distinguish objectively in such behavior those attributions of causality which are 'correct' from those which are 'fallacious,' and then designate the fallacious attributions of causality as irrational, and the corresponding acts as 'magic.' "[72] But in terms of the *goal* of such behavior, there is a sense in which magic is more rational than more advanced salvation religions because it is more focused on this world:

> On the one hand, there is an ever-broadening rational systematization of the god concept and of the thinking concerning the possible relationships of man to the divine. On the other hand, there ensues a characteristic recession of the original, practical and calculating rationalism. As such primitive rationalism recedes, the significance of distinctively religious behavior is sought less and less in the purely external advantages of everyday economic

success. Thus, the goal of religious behavior is successively "irrationalized" until finally otherworldly non-economic goals come to represent what is distinctive in religious behavior.[73]

Weber describes how there "develops a hope for salvation as an irrational yearning to be able to be good for its own sake."[74] The rationalization process in religion is accompanied by an increasingly irrational, because otherworldly, goal of religious behavior.

Weber gives different explanations for the process of rationalization and abstraction in religion. In *Sociology of Religion*, written as part of his massive *Wirtschaft und Gesellschaft* (*Economy and Society*), Weber emphasizes the order and regularity that universal gods bring to economic activity and the structures of society that support it. According to Weber, rationalization favors the cults of gods who exert influence over universal natural and social phenomena—like the motion of the stars and planets or the sacred terrestrial social order—over merely local spirits whose influence is more particular.[75] Upon the former type of gods "depend both rational economic practice and the secure, regulated hegemony of sacred norms in the social community."[76] With these types of gods come also increased ethical demands on individual human subjects, "making it possible to calculate what the conduct of a given person may be."[77] This has enormous repercussions for the regular functioning of economy and society.

In Weber's introduction to his series of articles titled "Die Wirtschaftsethik der Weltreligionen" ("The Economic Ethic of the World Religions"), the order necessary for a functioning economy is important, but here the emphasis is on intellectual order, that is, on the need humans have for coherent meaning. There are many varieties of belief in salvation. "Behind them always lies a stand towards something in the actual world which is experienced as specifically 'senseless.' Thus, the demand has been implied: that the world order in its totality is, could, and should somehow be a meaningful 'cosmos.' This quest, the core of genuine religious rationalism, has been borne precisely by strata of intellectuals."[78] According to Weber, the most important thing humans encountered as senseless was suffering. Primitive ways of dealing with suffering were to blame it on either possession by a demon or the wrath of an offended god. The alleviation of suffering was at first a matter of performing the proper rituals; the worldly benefit of such magic was obvious. Key steps in the rationalization of religion with regard to suffering were the development of the myth of a savior and the development of ethical religions, where the gods could punish the unjust and reward the righteous. Since so often in this life the righteous suffered and the unjust prospered, explanations .were sought outside of the life of the present world. Present suffering was explained by sin committed in a former life or by one's ancestors, or belief in the afterlife was posited to ensure that the guilty were punished and the righteous rewarded. In both cases a satisfactory theodicy necessitated appeal to a world beyond the present world as we know it.[79]

The rationalization of religious ethics necessarily accompanies this theodicy. Individuals must try to follow the correct ethical path in order to assure themselves that they are among the righteous who will be rewarded. The goal is a permanent state of holiness that makes the subject "inwardly safe against suffering."[80] Crucially for Weber, this puts salvation religions in a state of permanent tension with the world. The more the religions have been true religions of salvation, and the more rationalized they are, the greater this tension has been. Rationalization has moved religion from a direct, magic, ritual encounter with the external world and toward inward sacred values as the source of salvation. This has produced a strong tension between ethical salvation religion and the things of this world.[81] The inner and the outer worlds stand in tension over against one another, as they did not in the immediate, magical relation of the person to the external world.

In his essay "Zwischenbetrachtung," translated by Gerth and Mills as "Religious Rejections of the World and Their Directions,"[82] Weber addresses different "spheres" of modern life—family, economics, politics, aesthetics, sex, and intellectual life—and argues that in each case salvation religion has produced tension between religion and the world, which has also had the effect of augmenting the "*internal and lawful autonomy* of the individual spheres."[83] In the sphere of family relations, for example, it is taken for granted that the follower of the savior should stand closer to the savior and to the "brother in the faith" than to one's natural family. Those who do not hate father and mother, wife and children, cannot be Jesus's disciples (Luke 14:26).[84] In the economic sphere, magic always promised material prosperity, but rationalized salvation religions have warned against attachment to worldly goods. Disinterested agapic love in religion has ironically been mirrored by the depersonalization of economic life in the modern capitalist economy, where money "is the most abstract and 'impersonal' element of human life."[85] The more rational and impersonal capitalism becomes, the less reconcilable it is with a "religious ethic of brotherliness."[86] The same dynamic holds in the political sphere. "Magic religiosity" entertained tribal gods, but universalist salvation religions broke the barriers of such local loyalties. As in economics, however, this rationalization was met with a parallel rationalization in politics, leading to the modern impersonal state, where bureaucrats neither hate nor love. "The state's absolute end is to safeguard (or to change) the external and internal distribution of power; ultimately, this end must seem meaningless to any universalist religion of salvation."[87] The state must uphold the orderly distribution of power through the threat and use of violence, which stands in obvious tension with the Sermon on the Mount.[88]

So far Weber has emphasized the way that rationalization has produced the mutual alienation of religion from the different spheres. When he comes onto the question of violence, however, he veers into discussing the similarity between religion and war: "The mutual strangeness of religion and politics, when they are both completely rationalized, is all the more the case because, in contrast to economics, politics may come into direct competition with religious ethics at decisive points."[89] The most decisive point is in war, which "makes for an unconditionally devoted and sacrificial community among the combatants and releases an active mass compassion and love for those who are in need," which feelings break down natural boundaries of family, region, and class.[90] Moreover, war makes the soldier "experience a consecrated meaning of death," in which he believes that he is dying for a sacred cause.[91] "The very extraordinary quality of brotherliness of war, and of death in war, is shared with sacred charisma and the experience of the communion with God."[92] After thus temporarily collapsing the gap between religion and politics, Weber hastens to argue that the brotherliness of war is bound to seem devalued, mere fratricide, in the view of religions of salvation. He thereby attempts to subsume this discussion of war into his overall narrative of the mutual estrangement of religion from the other spheres of life. But Weber's brief foray into this area where the boundaries between religion and politics, enchantment and disenchantment, meaning and meaninglessness, suddenly dissolve is significant, because it indicates the difficulty he has in policing the boundaries between the two terms of some of his most essential binaries. I will have more to say about this further on.

According to Weber, the very similarity of war and religion raises the tension to its greatest height. He then turns to address how this tension can be alleviated: "As in economics, the only two consistent solutions of this tension are those of puritanism and mysticism."[93] Mysticism is the inward flight from the world. The mystic does not necessarily remove himself physically from the world, but effects an inward renunciation of violence and of worldly goods. The mystic refuses to participate in the violence necessary to the political order and will give his coat to any needy person who comes by, "not for man's sake, but purely for devotion's sake."[94] Puritanism is Weber's favorite historical example of what he more broadly calls "inner-worldly asceticism." While the mystic proves themselves against the world, the inner-worldly ascetic proves themselves through the world, that is, by active engagement with the world, while maintaining an inward distance from entanglement in the world.[95] Though puritanism regards the violence of the world as depraved, it accepts the necessity of using that violence as a means toward making God's commandments known. Similarly, puritanism accepts the "routinization of the economic cosmos" because it views the material things of this world as valuable only insofar as they are the raw material through which the believer fulfills their duty and tests the state of their soul.[96] Mysticism and inner-worldly asceticism do not prevent the splitting of religion from the world but rather allow believers to live in the world, convinced that they have resolved the tension inwardly. Weber writes, "Both inner-worldly asceticism and mysticism ultimately condemn the social world to absolute meaninglessness, or at least they hold that God's aims concerning the social world are utterly incomprehensible."[97]

In the intellectual sphere, this question of meaning is the focal point of the tension between religion and the world. "The tension between religion and intellectual knowledge definitely comes to the fore wherever rational, empirical knowledge has consistently worked through to the disenchantment of the world and its transformation into a causal mechanism. For then science encounters the claims of the ethical postulate that the world is a God-ordained, and hence somehow *meaningfully* and ethically oriented, cosmos."[98] Here the disenchantment of the world is the scientific reduction of the world to meaningless matter. According to Weber, the empirical method rules out *in principle* any rational assignment of meaning to the world.[99] "Every increase of rationalism in empirical science increasingly pushes religion from the rational into the irrational realm; but only today does religion become *the* irrational or anti-rational supra-human power."[100] Religion is irrational today as the result of a long process of rationalization in which religion itself was instrumental. Religion takes shape in the attempt to provide a rational explanation of the world in the light of unjust suffering, but this leads to the devaluation of the world, since no inner-worldly solution can be found. The more theodicy tries to solve the problem of unjust suffering, and thus rationalize the world, the more the door is opened for the only logical solution to the problem, which is that the world has no meaning. More generally, Weber writes that the more religion centered on rational explanation and doctrine, the more it encouraged rational lay thought, which became free of priestly control and led eventually to the skeptics and philosophers and scientists who were hostile to faith. Religion tried to protect itself from the self-sufficient intellect by claiming that religious knowledge operates in a different sphere than intellectual knowledge, through a direct grasp of the world's meaning "by virtue of a charisma of illumination." But this served only to isolate religion further, to push it further into the realm of the irrational.[101] Weber concludes:

> Viewed from a purely ethical point of view, the world has to appear fragmentary and devalued in all those instances when judged in the light of the religious postulate of a divine "meaning" of existence. This devaluation results from the conflict between the rational claim and reality, between the rational ethic and the partly rational, and partly irrational values. With every construction of the specific nature of each special sphere existing in the world, this conflict has seemed to come to the fore ever more sharply and more insolubly. The need for "salvation" responds to this devaluation by becoming more other-worldly, more alienated from all structured forms of life and, in exact parallel, by confining itself to the specific religious essence. This reaction is the stronger the more systematic the thinking about the "meaning" of the universe becomes, the more the external organization of the world is rationalized, the more the conscious experience of the world's irrational content is sublimated. And not only theoretical thought, disenchanting the world, led to this course, but also the very attempt of religious ethics practically and ethically to rationalize the world.[102]

Weber works out this thesis of the disenchantment of the world by religion most thoroughly and famously in his analysis of the Protestant Reformation, especially its Calvinist variant. His narrative in *The Protestant Ethic and the Spirit of Capitalism* is an extension of the consistent narrative of rationalization that he has traced from the rise of salvation religions to his own stage of modernity. Religion is both the protagonist and the victim of the rationalization process. The Puritanism that develops out of Calvin's thought is Weber's prime historical example of the way that inner-worldly asceticism leads to disenchantment. According to Weber, the inscrutability of God's will, brought to its extreme in the doctrine of predestination, left the individual with a feeling of "inner loneliness." No priest, no church, no sacraments could save them. It is precisely in this context of the desacramentalization of the world that the only three instances of the phrase *Entzauberung der Welt* appear in Weber's most famous work, and only in the 1920 edition. In Puritanism, "[t]hat great historic process in the development of religions, the elimination of magic from the world [*Entzauberung der Welt*] which had begun with the old Hebrew prophets and, in conjunction with Hellenistic scientific thought, had repudiated all magical means to salvation as superstition and sin, came here to its logical conclusion."[103] According to Weber, "The rationalization of the world, the elimination of magic as a means to salvation, the Catholics had not carried nearly so far as the Puritans (and before them the Jews) had done."[104] Weber refers to the Catholic priest as a "magician" who performs the miracle of transubstantiation and holds the keys to atonement through the confessional.[105] The Puritans considered such external means idolatrous and, like the ancient Hebrew prophets, wanted to sweep the world clean of idols, so that God could be all in all. Weber's picture of disenchanted Puritans is rather hard to square with the Salem witch trials.[106] But for Weber, the Puritan attitude—combining God's absolute transcendence with a suspicion of all things fleshly—could only result in an extreme devaluation of the world.[107]

In medieval Catholicism, such an attitude would lead to the monastery, a flight from the world. But the Reformation saw monastic life as unbiblical and smacking of works-righteousness. Now, every Christian would be a monk, seeking perfect inward holiness, but doing so in the world.[108] As Weber puts it, "The radical elimination of magic from the world allowed no other psychological course than the practice of worldly asceticism."[109] According to Weber's famous thesis, the anxiety a Calvinist must feel over their own salvation could be relieved not—as for a Lutheran—with inward emotional assurance but only by "objective results." Believers must throw themselves into "intense worldly activity," which, for the Puritans, among others, meant business. Worldly success could never be the means of attaining salvation but was rather the indispensable "sign of election."[110] And since there was no room for a Catholic "magical" cycle of sin, repentance, confession, absolution, and then more sin, good works had to be rationalized: "The God of Calvinism demanded of his believers not single good works, but a life of good works combined into a unified system."[111] The discipline of monastic asceticism had left the world unchanged. "Now it strode into the market-place of life, slammed the door of the monastery behind it, and undertook to penetrate just that daily routine of life with its methodicalness, to fashion it into a life in the world, but neither of nor for this world."[112]

The result, in Weber's tale, is capitalism, which is both the child of religion and one of the primary forces behind the marginalization of religion in the modern world. The inscrutability of the Calvinist God means that the Puritan inner-worldly ascetic, when acting in the world, must embrace "a sort of happy stupidity" about the meaning of the world, and concentrate only on their calling in the world.[113] In Weber's scheme, the Puritan is a bridge between salvation religion and capitalism; the businessman, like the Puritan, is concerned only with fulfilling his calling to make money, and gives no thought to the meaning of the world. According to Weber, the Protestant revolution was to bring the notion of "vocation" out of its medieval confinement to vowed religious life and into everyday life, but in trying thus to address the world, Christianity became worldly. "Then the intensity of the search for the Kingdom of God commenced gradually to pass over into sober economic virtue; the religious roots died out slowly, giving way to utilitarian worldliness."[114] The rise of capitalism through Calvinism is an important part of Weber's overall narrative of rationalization both through and against religion. In capitalism as in other spheres, religion would play an important role in rationalization, which split apart the rational from the irrational. On one side of this chasm stands capitalism, the ruthless and all-encompassing "cosmos" of machine production, "which has, through the subordination of the process of production to scientific points of view, relieved it from its dependence upon the natural organic limitations of the human individual."[115] On the other side of the chasm religion is stranded, fading and irrelevant to the life of the disenchanted world that it helped to build.[116]

And so, as we have seen, in sphere after sphere of life, the process of rationalization and disenchantment has separated cold fact and technique from the meaning of the world. What is to be done under these circumstances? To come finally to Weber's answer to this question, I will turn to his lecture "Science as a Vocation," where he addresses the question directly. For Weber, the split between fact and meaning or value is both a fact and a serious problem, because we urgently want to know what the meaning of our lives actually is. Weber quotes Tolstoy approvingly: "Science is meaningless, because it gives no answer to our question, the only question important for us: 'What shall we do and how shall we live?'"[117]

According to Weber, scientific progress and the process of rationalization put us moderns at something of a disadvantage in comparison to more "primitive" people. Rationalization as technical progress has in one sense removed us from the material world; the vast majority of us know little to nothing about the way things in our life work. How the streetcars we ride work, why paper money is exchangeable for goods, and why prices fluctuate—these things and much more are mysteries to most of us. American Indians or Hottentots, Weber says, know incomparably more about their tools. Rationalization does not mean increased knowledge:

> It means something else, namely, the knowledge or belief that if one but wished one *could* learn it at any time. Hence, it means that principally there are no mysterious incalculable forces that come into play, but rather that one can, in principle, master all things by calculation. This means that the world is disenchanted. One need no longer have recourse to magical means in order to master or implore the spirits, as did the savage, for whom such mysterious powers existed.[118]

It is worth noting that Weber in this passage seems undecided whether the principle of calculability is "knowledge or belief." He is certain, however, that it is not the kind of knowledge or belief that can deliver meaning. Weber follows this passage by asking if "the process of disenchantment . . . and, in general, this 'progress,' to which science belongs,"[119] have any meanings beyond the purely practical and technical. He surveys some of the hopes for a comprehensive scientific path to true being or true art or true nature or true God or true happiness that have captured people's attention since Plato and concludes that such hopes have been abandoned: "Who—aside from certain big children who are indeed found in the natural sciences—still believes that the findings of astronomy, biology, physics, or chemistry could teach us anything about the *meaning* of the world?"[120] Science delivers facts; religion is the realm of value and meaning.

The problem is that, as we have seen, Weber regards the need for meaning to be a fundamental fact about human beings, though he makes no attempt to demonstrate this fact through scientific means. Indeed, as Ghosh comments, the fundamental human need for meaning is "the *only* explicit a priori commitment on which [Weber's] thinking relies."[121] The question of meaning is—as in Weber's quote from Tolstoy—"the only question important for us," and yet it is the only question that science cannot answer, and therefore the only question we cannot answer with knowledge.

Science further presupposes that what is yielded by scientific work is important in the sense that it is "worth being known." In this, obviously, are contained all our problems. For this presupposition cannot be proved by scientific means. It can only be *interpreted* with reference to its ultimate meaning, which we must reject or accept according to our ultimate position toward life.[122]

The loss of meaning may be the source of "all *our* problems," but when Weber says that we must assign meaning according to "*our* ultimate position toward life," he really means "*my* ultimate position toward life." Disenchantment does not mean the complete loss of meaning in the world, but rather its individualization and interiorization. As Weber writes, "The fate of our times is characterized by rationalization and intellectualization and, above all, by the 'disenchantment of the world.' Precisely the ultimate and most sublime values have retreated from public life either into the transcendental realm of mystic life or into the brotherliness of direct and personal human relations."[123] The search for meaning withdraws from the public to the private and interior realm.

Answering "the only question important for us" is the task of each individual, and there are different roads to take. Weber mentions and dismisses the romantic option, popular among German youth, which would eschew the scientific approach as desiccated and abstract and strive instead for artistic and religious experience as the path toward a new mythopoesis. Weber rejects such irrationalism.[124] Great art, he declares, is today intimate and not monumental. As for a return to religion, he appears to think it suited only to those who are not manly enough to face reality: "To the person who cannot bear the fate of the times like a man, one must say: may he rather return silently, without the usual publicity build-up of renegades, but simply and plainly. The arms of the old churches are opened widely and compassionately for him."[125] Such a return to religion requires an intellectual sacrifice, but Weber promises not to rebuke the one who gives it. Weber holds those who clarify their ultimate standpoint in higher regard than those who lack the courage to do so.[126]

How, then, does the manly man[127] confront the problem of meaning? On the one hand, Weber thinks that even those who still seek some kind of religious experience must face the fact of a godless world: "The inward interest of a truly religiously 'musical' man can never be served by veiling to him and to others the fundamental fact that he is destined to live in a godless and prophetless time by giving him the *ersatz* of armchair prophecy."[128] On the other hand, Weber characterizes the situation of the present day not as atheism but as "polytheism."[129] He translates Tolstoy's question "What shall we do, and, how shall we arrange our lives?" into "Which of the warring gods should we serve? Or should we serve perhaps an entirely different god, and who is he?"[130] Polytheism is a direct consequence of the process of rationalization. The absolute divorce between fact and value means that "the various value spheres of the world stand in irreconcilable conflict with each other,"[131] with no factual basis for adjudicating their rival claims. Such conflicts can be decided only by nonrational means. The final product of the long process of disenchantment and rationalization is not an entirely rationalized world but a world in which the rational is haunted by the irrational from which it has been sundered:

> We live as did the ancients when their world was not yet disenchanted of its gods and demons, only we live in a different sense. As Hellenic man at times sacrificed to Aphrodite and at other times to Apollo, and, above all, as everybody sacrificed to the gods of his city, so do we still nowadays, only the bearing of man has been disenchanted and denuded of its mystical but inwardly genuine plasticity.[132]

Here it is important to note that Weber seems to observe no difference in the empirically observable behavior of ancient versus modern people. The difference lies in the presence or absence of some "mystical but inwardly genuine plasticity" to which Weber mysteriously claims access.

Weber writes, "Today the routines of everyday life challenge religion. Many old gods ascend from their graves; they are disenchanted and hence take the form of impersonal forces. They strive to gain power over our lives and again they resume their eternal struggle with one another."[133] We misunderstand Weber's purpose here if we think he is merely pointing out that consensus has broken down and people believe in all sorts of things. He appears to be using the term "gods" metaphorically, for the presence of "disenchanted gods" is something of an oxymoron, but the word "gods" is really essential here for Weber. He is not saying that people value all sorts of different things, so who's to judge? Plurality of values does not lead to pluralism, to resignation, or to a Richard Rorty type of irony; it leads to clashes of values, because people remain wholly committed to them. Our need for meaning is both plural and absolute.[134] Values are not easily disposable consumer goods;

instead they "strive to gain power over our lives." This is why "gods" is more than a casual metaphor. Gods are jealous, which is why "they resume their eternal struggle with one another." Elsewhere Weber comments, "It is really a question not only of alternatives between values but of an irreconcilable death-struggle, like that between 'God' and the 'Devil.' Between these, neither relativization nor compromise is possible."[135]

Another important detail to note about this passage is that the gods are not new ones but "old gods" resurrected. This is a curious choice of words, given the way we normally associate Weber with the view of modernity as rupture with the past. Weber is trying to explain to his audience an entirely new situation, unprecedented in human history. We live in a disenchanted world, as none of our ancestors did. Why not, at minimum, *new* gods for a new situation? Is disenchantment really nothing more than a change of name, for example, from "Apollo" to "capitalism"? Is the world truly disenchanted if the human person is still subject to external "forces," the only difference being that they have become "impersonal"? The difference between an enchanted world and a disenchanted one becomes hazy at this point.

The key difference for Weber seems to be that premodern people simply found themselves subject to forces beyond their control, whereas the modern person is forced to make a sheer groundless choice among the various value systems or "gods." Weber begins from

one fundamental fact, that so long as life remains immanent and is interpreted in its own terms, it knows only of an unceasing struggle of these gods with one another. Or speaking directly, the ultimately possible attitudes toward life are irreconcilable, and hence their struggle can never be brought to a final conclusion. Thus it is necessary to make a decisive choice.[136]

The manly man is the one who makes this absolute choice, knowing that it is a sheer choice, with no given facts, no revelation, to guide it. It is not a mere choice, as one chooses a salad dressing; it is a "decisive choice." Nevertheless, if appeal to a transcendent ground for choice has been cut off, then the purely immanent rationalization that characterizes the modern world necessitates the purely irrational choice of one or more of the gods that continue to haunt modernity. Weber's use of the word "gods" here is not casual but very deliberate; he cannot seem to escape the realization that rationalization carries within it an irreducible moment of irrationality. The old gods cannot rest in their graves. Weber thinks that, unlike "primitive" people, we moderns are, or should be, fully conscious of this irrational moment. But we seem to be back where Josephson-Storm left off: the need to choose a myth to live by.

1.3. Weber's Unthought

Weber is not unaware of the paradox of irrationality as the product of rationalization. For Weber, however, the difference between an enchanted world and our own is that the gods have become a conscious choice. Universal religious meaning has broken down. Meaning does not belong to the cosmos, but has been internalized. As Weber writes, "The fate of an epoch which has eaten of the tree of knowledge is that it must know that we cannot learn the *meaning* of the world from the results of its analysis, be it ever so perfect; it must rather be in a position to create this meaning itself."[137] Meaning now resides in the mind, and we now know that we are making it all up. Some commentators see Weber as a kind of existentialist who finds the dignity of modern individuals precisely in their freedom to create meaning for themselves. According to Alkis Kontos, for example, Weber admired the Greeks because they had to choose among many gods, and this pluralism made them better. What mattered was not making the right choice; what mattered was the choosing. Such freedom of choice is what makes human life worth living, and the Greeks, unlike the barbarians, were conscious of this.[138] Such courage and integrity is still possible on the other side of centuries of Christian dominance of the West. After the collapse of Christendom, we can now finally recover the true human essence, which we find in the making of free existential decisions. The ethic of responsibility becomes the ethic of ultimate ends. This is a new type of enchantment.[139]

I do not find this reading of Weber very persuasive. Making the right choice was clearly not a matter of indifference to him—why else would the gods struggle among themselves? The gods were not easygoing liberals who tolerated each other's presence. The fact that making the right choice of meaning could not be done scientifically *bothered* Weber. As Susan Hekman points out, unlike Enlightenment figures Weber did not think that ethics could be a science, but like Enlightenment figures he believed in objectivity enough to lament the irrationality of ethics.[140] One needed to face this lamentable fact "like a man." The best that could be done was to make this irrational choice and then, as the conclusion to "Science as a Vocation" makes clear, *obey*: "We shall set to work and meet the 'demands of the day,' in human relations as well as in our vocation. This, however, is plain and simple, if each finds and obeys the demon (*daimon*) who holds the fibers of his very life."[141]

Weber is less like the liberated, god-shopping pagan and more like the Calvinist whose interior life he describes in detail and with such confident familiarity in *The Protestant Ethic and the Spirit of Capitalism*. Just as, for the Calvinist, the meaning of God's ways with history and the individual's fate were unknowable, revealed only in the form of decrees by the *deus absconditus*, so was the meaning of life unavailable to Weber and to the mortal individual in modernity. And just as the Calvinist therefore lived in a state of inner loneliness and remoteness from God, so did Weber describe himself. As Ghosh comments, "Weber steers clear of the language and thinking of secularization, with its assumption that there had been a qualitative change from a godly to a godless state, just as he personally (but privately) described himself not as 'godless' (*gottlos*), but as 'alien' or 'remote from God' (*gottfremd, gottfern*): '*wholly and utterly remote from God*, one lives *against* God, *wholly and utterly* alone.'"[142] The fact that Weber deliberately avoided the language of atheism and the death of God or gods in favor of "polytheism" indicates that he was not merely unhappy to be living in a disenchanted world, but perhaps that he intuited that the border between enchanted and disenchanted was not so easy to guard.

Weber clearly believed that the human individual has the freedom to make a decisive choice among the various gods on offer. Indeed, the decisive choice is arguably for Weber a remnant of magical charisma in the modern world.[143] But the reason this charismatic moment is precious for Weber is that it stands out against the backdrop of the dreary constraints under which such a choice is made.[144] The gods that can be chosen must struggle not only against each other but against the gods that are simply *given* to us. The famous final paragraphs of *The Protestant Ethic and the Spirit of Capitalism* give an important clue to the reason Weber cannot shake his sense that the old gods have not yet left us. His images of force, determinism, fate, and the "iron cage" need to be read in light of his conviction that the gods still "strive to gain power over our lives." In concluding his tale of unintended consequences, Weber writes of how Puritan asceticism

> did its part in building the tremendous cosmos of the modern economic order. This order is now bound to the technical and economic conditions of machine production which to-day determine the lives of all the individuals

who are born into this mechanism, not only those directly concerned with economic acquisition, with irresistible force. Perhaps it will so determine them until the last ton of fossilized coal is burnt. In Baxter's view the care for external goods should only lie on the shoulders of the "saint like a light cloak, which can be thrown aside at any moment." But fate decreed that the cloak should become an iron cage [*stahlhartes Gehäuse*].[145]

Weber continues, "Since asceticism undertook to remodel the world and to work out its ideals in the world, material goods have gained an increasing and finally an inexorable power over the lives of men as at no previous period in history."[146] The language of "power over the lives of men" echoes what Weber said about the old gods *redivivi*; we must obey the *daimon* who holds the fibers of our very lives. The language of coercion likewise echoes the use of force among the gods in their *Kampf der Götter*, and both are a logical consequence of the divide between rationality and ethics: if there is no universal ethical standard of truth, then all that remains to persuade one another is force.

The idea that there is no universal truth—no God, no natural law, no universal reason that discovers an inherent, meaningful order to the world— raised hopes among some nineteenth-century thinkers for a definitive liberation of humanity from its shackles. Marx and Nietzsche, for example, regarded the death of God and gods as the moment when humanity would finally take the reins of its own destiny in hand and bring radical and liberating change. A countertradition developed, however, that Eyal Chowers calls "entrapment imagination." Entrapment thinkers, among whom Chowers situates Weber, emphasized the power and inertia of large, complex social institutions and the fragmented nature of human meaning, such that profound transformations would be nearly impossible. Most interesting about such thinking is that its pessimism issues from the same source as the optimism of Marx and Nietzsche: the notion that there is no pregiven order, that we humans are making it all up. There is a kind of mirroring effect in which collective institutions become humanity's "great double." We now look to the sky for meaning and order, but all we see is ourselves; there is no one or no foundation or no principle there to save us from ourselves.[147] Chowers reads Mary Shelley's *Frankenstein* (1818) as an early warning of the dangers of this doubling. Shelley's human characters reflect the wide divide between reason and ethics; human reason produced the monster—a marvel of science— but humans refused to accept him into their community. Human technical prowess produces wonders, but we come to be dominated by our own creations, which are made in our own image and likeness. The creations of humanity are unpredictable and ungovernable precisely because there is no inherent order to the cosmos. And so humans come to fear being controlled by our own artifacts. As the monster says to Dr. Frankenstein, "You are my creator, but I am your master; obey!"[148]

Obeying our demons does not have the same shade of horror for Weber that it has for Shelley, because the *daimon* that Weber has in mind is the life-giving commitment one makes to an ethical ideal of meaning, not the deadening capitulation to the capitalist and state machine. Weber is not as pessimistic, as he persists in identifying a moment of true freedom in our decisive choice among the gods. Though he writes, "Everywhere the cage for the new serfdom is ready,"[149] he leaves open the possibility that the honest and responsible subject will not settle into life behind bars. The modern person must choose an ethical path to follow, but this is not an arbitrary decisionism; it is obedience to a calling, a vocation. The human person strives for coherence and consistency of meaning, which Weber calls "personality."[150] The irony is that the same search for consistent meaning, as we have seen, ends up, through the long process of rationalization, draining the world of meaning and of coherence, as fact is separated from meaning, and the value spheres fragment. There develops in modernity, then, a disciplined self that is governed by the rules of the modern bureaucratic matrix—the factory, the government ministry, the school, and more.

Gilbert Germain has contrasted Weber's treatment of human freedom with that of Jacques Ellul's critique of technological society. According to Germain, although Weber argues that ends have been largely subsumed by means in modernity, there remains the individual's freedom to choose a different end. Weber still hopes for a different future in the choices of heroic individuals. If we keep means and ends separate, we can clear the way for authentic acts of the valuation of ends, most especially in the realm of politics.[151] Ellul is more pessimistic. He does not think that means and ends can be kept separate. Ellul argues that technique has become both means and end,[152] and individuals are not simply free to choose another end. Politics is just another domain subjected to technique. Technique in fact has taken on an aura of the sacred; it is omnipresent and omnipotent, "a god which brings salvation" and commands unwavering respect for delivering present marvels—like Amazon packages to our doorstep—and promising future freedoms. We even revere

technique when its power turns against us, blaming ourselves for misman-
agement. Technique enthralls and enchants us.[153]

Germain's argument is valuable, but it seems to me that what is found
in Ellul—specifically the concerns about the inescapability of technique,
about our own creations turning against us, about the divinization of the
products of rationalization, and about the collapsing of means and ends—
can be found in Weber himself. For Weber the self chooses in a situation
of constraint, with no hope of radically transforming the institutions that
confine the self. In Weber's words, "Once it is fully established, bureaucracy is among those social structures which are the hardest to destroy."[154]
Bureaucracy is not only hard to destroy as a whole, but the individual also
finds it "escape-proof." Ancient patrimonial bureaucracies, as in China,
Egypt, Rome, and Byzantium, established the pattern, but they were still
"highly irrational." "In contrast to these older forms, modern bureaucracy
has one characteristic which makes its 'escape-proof' nature much more
definite: rational specialization and training."[155] This training produces a
disciplined self that obeys external commands, not the ideal self-creation
of the personality. The disciplined self only chooses instrumental means to
ends that are given by others. The disciplined self "is only a single cog in an
ever-moving mechanism which prescribes to him an essentially fixed route
of march."[156]

Although Weber chides Marx with his comment "It is the dictatorship of
the official, not that of the worker, which, at present anyway, is on the advance,"[157] the official is not really in charge either. The whole institutional
mechanism, which is a product of human ingenuity, is beyond human control. According to Weber, "When fully developed, bureaucracy also stands,
in a specific sense, under the principle of *sine ira ac studio*. Its specific nature,
which is welcomed by capitalism, develops the more perfectly the more the
bureaucracy is 'dehumanized,' the more completely it succeeds in eliminating
from official business love, hatred, and all purely personal, irrational, and
emotional elements which escape calculation."[158] On the one hand, this dehumanization can be seen as a degradation, a lowering of human activity to
subhuman status. On the other hand, however, this dehumanization can be
seen as an exaltation of this human creation to god-like status; bureaucracy is
dehumanized precisely to the extent that it transcends human control and instead takes control of its human subjects. Here we see a kind of Feuerbachian
projection of the inventions of the human mind to the status of gods.[159]
While Marx was concerned with the subjection of humans to the material

objects they produced (commodity fetishism), Weber was concerned with a similar mystification of the institutions that humans create:[160]

> An inanimate machine is mind objectified. Only this provides it with the power to force men into its service and to dominate their everyday working life as completely as is actually the case in the factory. Objectified intelligence [*geronnener Geist*] is also that animated machine [*lebende Maschine*], the bureaucratic organization, with its specialization of trained skills, its division of jurisdiction, its rules and hierarchical relations of authority. Together with the inanimate machine it is busy fabricating the shell of bondage which men will perhaps be forced to inhabit some day, as powerless as the fellahs of ancient Egypt.[161]

The products of the human mind have taken life and—either now or in the near future—rule over us like gods. We stand in the same position as the ancient Egyptian peasant before the gods and pharaohs, except that rationalization is closing off our escape routes more efficiently.

At the same time that machines have taken life, however, the gods have been reduced to "impersonal forces."[162] An exchange has taken place, whereby God has been depersonalized, reduced to merely immanent and impersonal forces of human creation, while the most mundane and rational processes and institutions have been divinized. Because they are merely human creations, there is no appeal to them for mercy. No single individual can change their predestined fate as determined by the inscrutable will of the modern *deus absconditus*. So the modern individual must proclaim their own freedom to invent their own god and devote themselves to it. At the same time, other gods are not simply offering themselves up to human choice but rather imposing themselves with irresistible force upon the individual. Weber tells the story of fragmentation and plurality of meaning and values at the same time that he tells the story of a stifling uniformity. Plurality and uniformity may simply be two sides of the same coin of modernity. Likewise, enchantment and disenchantment are inextricably entangled. Rationalization has clearly not done away with irrationality, and disenchantment has not put the gods to bed. In every case, the two sides of these binaries seem to need and depend upon each other.

Weber's description of impersonal and irresistible bureaucracy will resonate with anyone who has been subjected to assessment, compliance, and training exercises at the twenty-first-century university, but the extent to which Weber's empirical description of modernity is accurate is not central to my argument here. I will take a more empirical approach to the current realities of nation-state and market in later chapters. What matters now is to see that in Weber's own thought, despite his best efforts, he cannot keep the poles of enchantment and disenchantment apart. The basic human need for meaning has driven a process of rationalization that first produced gods and then, by the same process, eliminated them from the realm of fact. The search for meaning produced the rationalization that pushed the question of meaning into an irrational sphere, alienated from the factual realm. In neither of the two opposing realms, however—fact/meaning, public/private, rational/irrational, objective/subjective—have the gods been put to rest. In the subjective realm, the individual must assert their freedom by making the essentially irrational choice to obey one of the gods who will give meaning to one's life. In the objective realm, the same individual is confronted with the products of the human mind that have become a *lebende Maschine*, a living machine, dehumanized and divinized, and now exercise a power over humans that is beyond human control. The fact that the gods are now impersonal forces does not appear to make much difference; the personal gods, Weber thought, were always likewise the product of human ingenuity.

By Weber's own account, rationalization and disenchantment have not eliminated the irrational and the enchanted elements from the modern polity and economy. Indeed, in some respects, rationalization has produced a more intense form of irrationality. Consider, for example, the importance of violence in Weber's account of rationalization in the political sphere. Resort to violence has always been essential for the protection of the tribe and polity, Weber explains. It is only with the rise of rationalized salvation religions that this necessity has been called into question, for such universalist religions, gathered around the worship of a God of universal love, reject violence as a compromise with the world. Weber contrasts the Sermon on the Mount and its injunction to resist no evil with the state's imperative to claim a monopoly on the legitimate use of violence, which is the very essence of the state, and to employ violence to do justice within its borders and protect its borders from attack from without:

> According to the inescapable pragmatism of all action, however, force and the threat of force unavoidably breed more force. "Reasons of state" thus follow their own external and internal laws. The very success of force, or of the threat of force, depends ultimately upon power relations and not on

ethical "right," even were one to believe it possible to discover objective criteria for such "right."[163]

Here we see the split between the objective and the subjective, fact and ethics, rational and irrational. The more rationalized religion becomes, the more it is pushed into the irrational sphere of ethics. Politics and religion come into conflict because while, in this case, Christianity tries to cling to its love command from the mouth of God and reject violence, the rationalized state must do what everyone but the most otherworldly mystic acknowledges that it needs to do, which is to employ the threat and use of violence on a purely pragmatic and nonethical basis. Violence is here a mere means to the end of protecting the polity.

The same pragmatic logic dictates, however, that violence will unavoidably breed more violence, according to Weber. Not only this, but violence becomes an end in itself. The modern polity, precisely in and through the logic of violence, will come to resemble the religious community:

> As the consummated threat of violence among modern polities, war creates a pathos and a sentiment of community. War thereby makes for an unconditionally devoted and sacrificial community among the combatants and releases an active mass compassion and love for those who are in need. And, as a mass phenomenon, these feelings break down all the naturally given barriers of association. In general, religions can show comparable achievements only in heroic communities professing an ethic of brotherliness.[164]

As this last line makes clear, the state at war out-religions religion; the state at war offers the sense of unconditional brotherly love that is achieved by religion only in monastic communities. Weber continues on to argue that the state does a better job than religion at giving meaning to death. Ordinary death is inscrutable; it is a fate that befalls everyone, but no one can say why it comes to any individual precisely when and why and in what manner it does. Death in war offers a meaningful death—the soldier believes he is dying *for* something:

> The why and the wherefore of his facing death can, as a rule, be so indubitable to him that the problem of the "meaning" of death does not even occur to him. At least there may be no presuppositions for the emergence of the

problem in its universal significance, which is the form in which religions of salvation are impelled to be concerned with the meaning of death. Only those who perish "in their callings" are in the same situation as the soldier who faces death on the battlefield.[165]

Once again, the state at war out-religions religion. Salvation religions will see this kind of "inner-worldly consecration" in a negative light, as merely glorifying fratricide. Nevertheless, Weber says, "[t]he very extraordinary quality of brotherliness of war, and of death in war, is shared with sacred charisma and the experience of the communion with God, and this fact raises the competition between the brotherliness of religion and of the warrior community to its extreme height."[166]

Religion and the modern state are in direct competition with one another only because of the similarities between them. Both are the products of a long process of rationalization that, in different ways, issues from the same source: the human search for meaning. And both address that search for meaning in remarkably similar ways: by gathering people into loving communion, consecrating life in this world to a sacred cause, offering the sacrifice of that life unto death, and solving the problem of the meaning of death. At the same time, Weber's contrast between an ethic of responsibility and an ethic of ultimate ends guarantees that the state will win this competition. Precisely because "the decisive means for politics is violence," religion must withdraw from politics to preserve the purity of its devotion to an ethic of universal love from compromise with the world.[167] I think this means that the sacred has not been drained out of the modern world; it has migrated from the church to the state and market. This is Weber's unthought. Weber's own discussion of war indicates that disenchantment as a historical process is more of a dislocation than a quantitative diminution. Indeed, sacred violence escalates in modernity on Weber's account. Of course, there are many qualitative differences; the holy changes when it migrates. But the main point is that in Weber's account of political violence, the two terms in each of his antinomies—rational/irrational, disenchanted/enchanted, fact/value, politics/religion, and so on—mirror each other to such an extent that the antinomies themselves threaten to break down.

There is a similar instability to Weber's categories in the sphere of economics. As we have seen, Weber points to the similarity between the depersonalization of the love ethic in religions of salvation—one loves everyone, regardless of who they are—and the depersonalization of economic transactions in modern capitalism. Money is not simply impersonal but "the most abstract and 'impersonal' element that exists in human life."[168] According to Weber, capitalism is impersonal precisely insofar as it is rational. By "impersonal," Weber does not just mean cold and lacking compassion, but primarily lacking personnel: "For this reason one speaks of the rule of 'capital' and not that of capitalists."[169] Humans are not in charge, but are being ruled by a god of their own making. As is the case with all forms of bureaucracy, the element of dehumanization is key for Weber. And this dehumanization can be read not as a degradation to the subhuman but as an exaltation to the divine. As Ghosh notes, Weber thought that Christianity in the West has been replaced by capitalism, "an order that is ultimately as *irrational* in its foundation as Calvinist religion, because capital like the Calvinist god is an impersonal power ruling over the individual person according to its logic and not theirs."[170]

In conjunction with his overarching narrative of rationalization, Weber frequently points to the irrationality of the capitalist economic order. In *The Protestant Ethic*, for example, he describes the way that business has replaced church for the German bourgeoisie, and that their expressed motive of "providing for [their] family" has in fact been replaced with business as an end in itself. "That is in fact the only possible motivation, but it at the same time expresses what is, seen from the view-point of personal happiness, so irrational about this sort of life, where a man exists for the sake of his business, instead of the reverse."[171] This is what has become of the Protestant notion of a "calling" or "vocation." Weber notes that there is no hedonistic or even eudaimonistic motivation here; the business person does not make money as a means to enjoy life. "Earning more and more money" is the *summum bonum*:

> It is thought of so purely as an end in itself, that from the point of view of the happiness of, or utility to, the single individual, it appears entirely transcendental and absolutely irrational. Man is dominated by the making of money, by acquisition as the ultimate purpose of his life. Economic acquisition is no longer subordinated to man as the means for the satisfaction of his material needs. This reversal of what we should call the natural relationship, so irrational from a naïve point of view, is evidently as definitely a leading principle of capitalism as it is foreign to all peoples not under capitalistic influence.[172]

There are two things worth underscoring in this passage. The first is the theme of transcendence. Capitalism has not apparently reduced all to the merely immanent and mundane. The fact that the making of money has become an end in itself means that the capitalist is the very opposite of a materialist. The capitalist's focus is not on the material things that they can buy with money, but on money itself, which, as Weber has said, is the most immaterial and abstract element in modern life. When Weber says at the end of *The Protestant Ethic* that "material goods have gained an increasing and finally an inexorable power over the lives of men as at no previous period in history,"[173] he does not seem to have in mind a Marxist critique of commodity fetishism. Weber's subjects are not focused on material goods themselves, except as a means to the making of money. This end is "entirely transcendental" both in the sense of its immateriality—the way that it goes beyond merely immanent and mundane reality—and in the sense that it is the object of the capitalist's devotion. Just as the Calvinist God was the end that must be served for God's own sake, so money is the end toward which human activity must be directed. Like the Calvinist before God, humans are "dominated" by money-making, "subordinated" to acquisition. Weber makes clear that this is not a conscious ethical choice by individuals: "The capitalistic economy of the present day is an immense cosmos into which the individual is born, and which presents itself to him, at least as an individual, as an unalterable order of things in which he must live."[174] This capitalistic "cosmos," like the earlier Christian cosmos, transcends the individual and subordinates them to its inscrutable providence. As Ghosh comments, "Transcendence was ever-present in [Weber's] eyes (even if it was by no means an unmixed blessing), and again we see why to describe the historical movement he portrays as secularization, with its implications of radical qualitative change, would be deeply misleading."[175]

The second thing worth underscoring about the above passage is the absolute irrationality at the core of the capitalist order. Weber does not shy away from pointing to the elements of irrationality at the heart of rationalization.[176] On his visit to Chicago, for example, Weber noted that the streetcar company calculated that its indemnities for four hundred deaths and injuries per year cost less than the measures necessary to prevent accidents, so it introduced no safety measures.[177] In other contexts, Weber associated charisma—which is closely linked to magic in his account of rationalization—with the capitalist entrepreneur.[178] What is crucial to note, however, is not the mere juxtaposition of rationality and irrationality in Weber, but the fluidity of the very categories themselves. In a footnote to the above passage in the 1920–1 edition of *The Protestant Ethic*, Weber responds to Lujo Brentano's critique of the 1904–5 version. Brentano finds Weber incoherent in this passage, insofar as rationalization leads to an irrational form of life. Weber responds:

> He is, in fact, quite correct. A thing is never irrational in itself, but only from a particular rational point of view. For the unbeliever every religious way of life is irrational, for the hedonist every ascetic standard, no matter whether, measured with respect to its particular basic values, that opposing asceticism is a rationalization. If this essay makes any contribution at all, may it be to bring out the complexity of the only superficially simple concept of the rational.[179]

It would be inaccurate to depict Weber as a kind of relativist on the basis of this passage. But his comment on the complexity of the concept of the rational indicates that he was not unaware of the instability of the antinomies on which so much of his thought is built.

I began my exploration of Weber's work with the suggestion that he, like Josephson-Storm, thinks we need to choose a myth to believe in. I showed how Weber makes room in his analysis for a decisive choice among the gods on offer. Josephson-Storm argues that there have always been many gods on offer, and this means that "we have never been disenchanted." To Alan Jacobs, critiquing Josephson-Storm, this "does not mean that 'we have never been disenchanted,' but that we *have*, and sometimes we hate it."[180] Building on Jacobs's critique, L. M. Sacasas argues that, though people continue to seek enchantment, the sacred canopy of a meaningful cosmos has collapsed; the search for enchantment is a symptom of that collapse. Premodern people had meaning given to them. "Modern individuals, considered as a type, assume that what meaning is to be had, they must supply." So they make their own enchantments. "As hungry for meaning as the modern individual may be, they will be unlikely to cede their autonomy to the idea of an order that exists independently of their own will and desires."[181] If my analysis is correct, however, even Weber was not so sure that a shared sense of the sacred had simply collapsed in modernity. It had rather migrated from the churches to the state and the market. In Weber's account, the sacrificial violence of war for the state produced a community of shared meaning that traditional religion could only envy. And the capitalist economic order was an overarching cosmos into which one was born and in which one learned to obey money, the most perfect—because the most abstract and ubiquitous—of gods. It is true that Weber did hold out the hope that those willing to face modernity "like a man" could assert their freedom and submit to a god of their own choosing. But any such god would be hemmed in by other gods, most especially the gods of state and market which—from the individual's point of view—were not chosen but were *given*, whether the individual acknowledged them or not. Any autonomy of which Sacasas writes was for Weber exercised only amid severe restraint: "The Puritan wanted to work in a calling; we are forced to do so."[182] Weber would regard the notion that there is in fact no "order that exists independently of their own will and desires" as childish fantasy. Any freedom we have must be exercised within the limits imposed by the gods of human creation.

Weber clearly thought that modern people are disenchanted because they believe that, in principle, a scientific explanation can be given for natural phenomena, with no need for recourse to magical means to invoke spirits or gods. As an explanation of the natural world, Weber thought that science was replacing religion, and empirical fact was replacing belief. But Weber is interested not simply in theoretical knowledge but also in practical knowledge. In other words, Weber was interested in much more than what people say they believe, and he was interested in more than explanations of the natural world; he was interested above all in how people act, and most especially in how society is structured and scripted to reflect and inform the way that people act and what they say they believe. It is not that Weber thought belief was unimportant; it is rather that the *form* of belief is relatively independent of the *content* of the belief. Weber therefore emphasizes the way that the transition from a religious to a nonreligious belief system does not necessarily mark a sharp break in the way people actually behave. The transition from a Christian to a modern social order is a clear example. Calvinism has the determinism of predestination:

> There is a non-religious counterpart of this religious evaluation, one based on a mundane determinism. It is that distinctive type of guilt and, so to speak, godless feeling of sin which characterizes modern man precisely as a consequence of his organization of ethics in the direction of a system based on an inner religious state, *regardless of the metaphysical basis upon which the system was originally erected*. It is not that he is guilty of having done any particular act, but that by virtue of his unalterable idiosyncrasy he "is" as he is, so that he is compelled to perform the act in spite of himself, as it were— this is the secret anguish that modern man bears.[183]

It is the structural features of society and the way they create a certain kind of interiority—here compelling the person to act, despite themselves—that matter to Weber. The actual content of the metaphysical belief, or lack thereof, in God is of secondary relevance at best. This is why it is possible for Weber, in "Science as a Vocation," to describe the modern person as simultaneously disenchanted, having no recourse to gods to explain the natural world, and yet still sacrificing to the gods that strive to gain power over our lives. In the social and institutional sense, Weber did not seem to think that the world was disenchanted but rather that the old gods had merely changed names.[184]

1.4. The Myth of Having No Myth

I have been exploring some of the ambiguities in Weber's thought, the mirroring of opposites, the places where he acknowledges or half-acknowledges that the disenchantment of the modern world is still haunted by enchantment and indeed can be told as the story not of the twilight of the gods but of the exchange of one set of gods for another. Weber is commonly referred to as if he were a quintessentially modern figure, one who sees the Enlightenment as a fundamental break with the past. Modernity is the sign of rupture, the moment in history when Western rationality broke with the irrationality of its Christian past, when history overcame myth, knowledge supplanted faith, science replaced tradition, and the state superseded the church. In this view, Weber is perhaps melancholy about living in a disenchanted world, but he did not question that disenchantment was a fact and a radical departure from the past. But I hope to have shown some ways in which Weber doubted this narrative, or at least opened up avenues for doubt.

Weber clearly believed that modernity is something new: modern science has unlocked truths about the material world to which the ancients and the medievals did not have access; machine production has created a proliferation of objects for consumption unimaginable before; and the very reality of a transcendent realm beyond the mundane has come to be questioned as never before. For Weber, there are indeed certain watershed moments in history—especially the so-called Axial Age and the Protestant Reformation—that introduced new and unprecedented social imaginaries that have far-reaching consequences. Historians have criticized Weber for exaggerating the novelty of the Reformation; there is a large and growing body of work arguing that Protestants were not as disenchanted, nor medieval Catholics as enchanted, as Weber supposed.[185] What often goes unremarked about Weber, however, is his simultaneous emphasis on the continuity of history. The process of rationalization is not an invention of the Enlightenment but something that began among ancient priests. It proceeded through the Reformation, and Weber again and again emphasizes the continuity between religious and postreligious motivations: religious vocation becomes a calling in business, belief in predestination becomes "mundane determinism" and a "godless feeling of sin which characterizes modern man,"[186] and so on. Likewise, that the products of human ingenuity have come to rule us is nothing new—the gods have always been human creations. Rather than seeing the modern "impersonal forces" as new gods, Weber calls them old gods that have ascended from their graves, albeit with a modern twist. Weber's thoroughgoing historical sensibilities would not allow the appearance of something completely new under the sun. Weber does not in any simple way embrace the idea of the Enlightenment as a radical break with the past. Rather than seeing Weber as an untroubled heir of the Enlightenment legacy, Asher Horowitz and Terry Maley's comment is more accurate: "Max Weber's work is exemplary in expressing and at least partially articulating the moment at which the Enlightenment becomes irreversibly reflective concerning its own reason."[187]

The myth of disenchantment as a radical break with the past dies hard, however, because it is so useful. The self-congratulatory idea that we moderns occupy the adulthood—or in Weber's gendered term, the manhood—of the human race, as opposed to the primitives who occupy premodern times and non-Western spaces or the weaklings who take refuge in the open arms of the churches, is immensely appealing. Here "myth" does not mean simply a story that is not true but rather a story that cannot be questioned without paying some kind of social price—the fourth sense of myth I identified above. In this sense a myth is not a story that can be chosen but an overarching narrative so embedded in the power structures of a society that it becomes invisible, like water to a fish. Alison Stone's pithy definition of a myth as "a publicly given horizon of meaning which we are powerless to criticize"[188] is useful in this context. If free market capitalism, for example, is the end product of a process of rationalization, if it operates on objective principles which limit the merely subjective and personal to the realm of consumer choice, then it becomes simply inevitable and natural and therefore not something with which we can interfere. We might lament the working conditions in an Amazon warehouse, but to intervene with laws and regulations would be a crime against nature. We must put our trust in the invisible hand of the market to sort the matter out rationally and impersonally.

In politics, the myth of disenchantment, as already mentioned, has been used to legitimize European colonization, to oppose the rationality of the West with the superstition and primitive enchantment of non-Western cultures.[189] Within the West, viewing the nation-state as disenchanted helps to obscure the theological basis of the state, which has decided advantages for secular power. It keeps those labeled "religious" from interjecting "irrational" considerations into the smooth functioning of the state. The separation of religion from secular politics, and the ideal privatization of the former, allows those who claim to believe in the Sermon on the Mount to support and participate in war, which is considered indispensable to a rational politics. It also authorizes war against other kinds of social orders—Muslim, especially—that are considered irrational because they do not separate religion from politics in the way that the West does. Such social orders are prone to fanaticism, a threat to rational and peacemaking Western social orders, and so we have felt obliged to bomb the irrationality out of them. Our violence is rational and secular; their violence is irrational and religious.

For Weber, disenchantment means, among other things, the exclusion of miracles from public space. In the political realm disenchantment means the bureaucratic attempt to eliminate the exception from law, to reduce the governance of people by people to a depersonalized and rational process of management. Modernity regards itself, as Robert Yelle puts it, as the exception to end all exceptions.[190] Disenchantment, though not without antecedents, had come to its logical and apparently irreversible conclusion only in Western modernity. For Carl Schmitt, on the other hand, it was impossible to reduce politics to the mechanical application of statutes in order to make the world predictable. As Yelle argues, Schmitt's decisionism was his response to the narrative of the disenchantment of the world. For Schmitt, miracles had merely migrated from theology to jurisprudence, from God to the state. In Schmitt's oft-quoted words:

All significant concepts of the modern theory of the state are secularized theological concepts not only because of their historical development— in which they were transferred from theology to the theory of the state, whereby, for example, the omnipotent God became the omnipotent lawgiver—but also because of their systematic structure, the recognition of which is necessary for a sociological consideration of these concepts. The exception in jurisprudence is analogous to the miracle in theology.[191]

Weber regarded the separation of charism from law to be a part of the rationalization process. Schmitt regarded this aspect of Weber's thought as "the most striking example of a new political theology for both theologians and non-theologians,"[192] one derived from Protestant theological sources. The modern closure of political theology, as the subtitle of Schmitt's *Political Theology II* indicates, is a "myth," as is the idea that we live in a world devoid of enchantment. As Yelle notes, although Schmitt's own project was fraught with pathologies of its own, he was right that liberalism had repressed any awareness of its own implicit theology, and Yelle concludes, "It requires an act of repression, of misrecognition if not outright hypocrisy, to enforce an absolute divide between the theological and the secular."[193]

The key question, then, is not whether or not modernity is disenchanted but rather what kind of work is being done, in any given context, by labeling things either enchanted or disenchanted. In other words, whom and what does the enchanted/disenchanted distinction authorize, and whom and what does it marginalize? My analysis of Weber shows not that we are now in fact enchanted rather than disenchanted, nor merely that there are many crossings of the border between enchantment and disenchantment, but that the categories themselves are unstable and prescriptive, not merely descriptive. Weber himself did not regard these categories—and other antinomies of modernity, like rational/irrational, secular/religious, and immanent/transcendent—as fixed and clearly differentiated from each other, or at least he did not do so without a troubled conscience. What we see in Weber's work is how the binaries around which his work is built are constantly mirroring and turning into their opposites. Belief in the gods breeds rationalization, which sends the gods to their graves; the ingenuity of human reason clamps humans into the iron cage, while the old gods are set free from their icy tombs.

The revival of the old gods calls the tale of secularization—at least as usually told—into question. In the next chapter, I will examine a more contemporary version of the disenchantment and secularization narrative, that of Charles Taylor, and argue similarly that the differences between modern and premodern are not as great as we usually assume.

2

Charles Taylor's Naïveté

Charles Taylor is one of the world's eminent philosophers, and he is also a Catholic from Quebec. This biographical detail is important for explaining Taylor's abiding interest in the process of secularization in the West. It is only a small exaggeration to say that the five-hundred-year process that Taylor describes in his landmark book, *A Secular Age*, was compressed into just a few years in his home province. Along with the French language, Catholicism was one of the principal ways with which Quebecois marked their identity over against the rest of Canada. The Catholic Church and the civil government were densely intertwined for much of the history of Quebec, and by the twentieth century the Church was deeply implicated in the everyday lives of the people of the province. The official Church controlled education, healthcare, the regulation of marriage, and most charitable activities, and was deeply involved in labor organizing, cooperatives, and other aspects of economic life. As late as 1960, 80% of Quebecois went to Mass at least once a month. And then they stopped. Seemingly overnight in the decade of the 1960s, the Quiet Revolution brought an end to Church hegemony in Quebec society, and the active practice of Catholicism went into steep decline. What took its place is what Taylor calls a "closed secularism" that is often hostile to any appearance of faith in public. Within a short time frame, Quebec went from one of the most Catholic to one of the most militantly secularist places on earth.

One Quebecker who did not give up on practicing his Catholic faith was Charles Taylor.[1] He has, however, been careful in his professional life to keep his personal convictions out of direct application to his philosophical work. Taylor's faith nevertheless lurks at the borders of his work and is clearly one of the main motivators for his inquiries into the secular. Taylor wants to understand what happened in Quebec, and in the Western world more generally. How did we go from a situation—five hundred years ago in Europe, more recently in Quebec—in which belief in God was taken for granted to one in which belief in God is entirely optional and increasingly unpopular? One common assumption is that the discoveries of science have made religious

The Uses of Idolatry. William T. Cavanaugh, Oxford University Press. © Oxford University Press 2024.
DOI: 10.1093/oso/9780197679043.003.0003

belief untenable or unnecessary, but what happened in Quebec had nothing to do with scientific discoveries, and Taylor thinks that the same holds true more broadly in the West. Like Weber, Taylor thinks that what happened to religion in the West had its origins not in science but in Christian reform efforts. Also like Weber, Taylor describes these changes in terms of disenchantment: "Everyone can agree that one of the big differences between us and our ancestors of 500 years ago is that they lived in an 'enchanted' world and we do not."[2]

Taylor's work on secularity begins from this notion of a big difference between "us" and everyone else. The first paragraph of *A Secular Age* remarks on this yawning gap, both across space and across time. Taylor notes how secularity makes "the 'we' who live in the West" different from "almost all other contemporary societies (e.g. Islamic countries, India, Africa), on the one hand; and with the rest of human history, Atlantic or otherwise, on the other."[3] This secular exceptionalism is based in a series of binaries that play crucial roles in Taylor's analysis: West/non-West, modern/premodern, secular/religious, nonbelievers/believers, immanence/transcendence, natural/supernatural, disenchantment/enchantment, and so on. In every case, Taylor tries to bring the two poles closer together, to argue that those who stand on the opposing sides of these dichotomies have more in common than they think they do and more to say to one another than is usually supposed. But Taylor begins from these dichotomies and assumes that they describe the world as currently structured; though he acknowledges, in most cases, that there is nothing historically inevitable about them, he does think that, now that it has taken place, "the process of disenchantment is irreversible."[4] There is no crossing back over the gap between enchantment and disenchantment once the gap has been opened. Though Taylor's purpose is irenic, he begins from the fact of the big difference between the people who stand on either side of these divides—modern and premodern, Western and non-Western, nonbelievers and believers: "A race of humans has arisen which has managed to experience its world entirely as immanent. In some respects, we may judge this achievement as a victory for darkness, but it is a remarkable achievement nonetheless."[5]

In this chapter, I will argue that this language of different "races" of humans—nonbelievers and believers—is not simply exaggerated but deeply misleading. The differences between the people on the opposing sides of these binaries are not in the way they act in the world but in the way they have learned to describe the world. There are not two races of people, those who have beliefs and those who have no beliefs but only facts; what marks secularity is rather the condition under which we have been taught to separate people into believers and nonbelievers. Although in every case Taylor wants to bring the two terms in these binaries closer together, I will argue that he does not do enough to question the terms under which the binaries are given in the first place. I do think, however, that in many cases the resources to question these binaries can be found in Taylor's work itself. As with Weber, there is a troublesome unthought in Taylor's work that needs to be made explicit in order to tackle the problems that Taylor is trying to address.

In the first section of this chapter, I will lay out Taylor's updating of Weber's historical tale of secularization. In the second section, I will parse Taylor's description of the modern secular world he says we live in. In the third section, I will examine some of the ways Taylor describes the modern world and argue that they distort our description of what is going on. I will conclude that there is a gap between our descriptions of the world as secular and the way we actually behave, and that we need a theology of idolatry to address this gap.

2.1. How We Got Here

Charles Taylor starts his historical tale of disenchantment, much like Weber does, in the so-called Axial Age, a term invented after Weber by Karl Jaspers under the influence of Weber's work on "world religions."[6] Until the Axial Age, roughly the eighth to the third century BC, the human person was subject to a triple embeddedness. In what Taylor calls "early religion"—before the Axial Age—the person is first embedded in society, and "religious life is inseparably linked with social life."[7] Spiritual forces are ubiquitous, and society is structured around relations with them. The person relates to such spiritual forces and beings as a member of the social group; the group, or a representative of the group, is the primary protagonist of transactions with the gods. Ritual action is collective. There is no equivalent of a personal relationship with Jesus, nor would it be thinkable for a person within such a context to imagine opting out, emigrating to another social group, or ceasing to believe in or propitiate the gods of the group. The second embedding in early religion is of spiritual forces in the cosmos. The gods do not transcend the material world but are embedded within it, in totems and sacred places. The third form of embedding—and most crucial for Taylor's thesis—has to do with human flourishing: it does not go beyond mundane goods. People implore the gods and spirits for health, prosperity, fertility, and long life, all inner-worldly things.[8] "There is a certain understanding of human flourishing here which . . . seems to us quite 'natural.' "[9] There is as yet no appeal to "supernatural" goods like life after death.

The Axial Age marks the beginning of the road to disenchantment precisely insofar as it marks a disembedding in the above senses. The new "higher" religions—brought into being in vastly different civilizations by such founding figures as Confucius, Gautama, Socrates, and the Hebrew prophets—introduced the differentiation of the individual from the social group, the transcendence of the cosmos by the gods, and the questioning of merely mundane flourishing either by a conception of salvation from the world or an imperative to change the world for the better.[10] Though "rationalization" plays a somewhat smaller role in Taylor's narrative, he is clearly drawing on Weber's account of the emergence of "salvation religions" out of the attempts by practitioners of "magic" to coerce mundane goods out of a recalcitrant nature.[11] As in Weber, the Hebrew prophets' critique of idolatry plays a significant part in disenchantment. Taylor cites Elijah's contest with the prophets of Baal on Mount Carmel to illustrate a world in which enchantment has been banished. Rather than counter bad magic with good magic, Elijah shows that the transcendent God alone has power over nature, and the supposed magic of Baal's prophets is nothing at all. The world is emptied of enchantment, and all power resides with God in heaven.[12] As in Weber, however, the disenchantment process begun in the Axial Age took a long time to come to fruition. The old-time religion retained much of its hold on the people, especially the peasants, even after the Axial religions gained official status in their societies. The individualism latent in Axial spirituality, for example, was practiced by elites such as monks.[13] It would take reform movements in late medieval Christianity to move the disembedding process forward, precisely in their attempts to bring the fullness of Christian practice out of the monasteries and into the everyday lives of rank-and-file lay Christians.

Weber's story of this decisive move centers on the Protestant Reformation, most especially Calvinism, but Taylor picks up the story of disenchantment before the Reformation, in the late medieval efforts that he calls "Reform," which predated Protestantism. Reform indicates a deep sense of dissatisfaction with the two-tiered ethic that characterized medieval Catholicism: perfection for those in the vowed religious life, lower standards for the laity.

Periodic reform movements had always existed to try to convert some of the laity to a higher standard of Christian practice. But what characterized Reform was an attempt to delegitimize the two-tiered system itself and elevate all Christians to a higher standard. Reform was pushed from below by lay movements that cultivated intensely personal devotions to, for example, the suffering humanity of Christ. Reform was pushed from above by the clergy and eventually by civil authorities, who came to understand their task as the Christianization of the common people, which would, not coincidentally, produce disciplined and orderly citizens. Whether from above or from below, Reform, according to Taylor, moved the central locus of the practice of the faith from external ritual to the interior of the human person. Meditation on the Five Wounds of Christ, for example, was meant to produce intense feelings of identification with the suffering of Christ. The crucial effect was on the human heart rather than on the material world.[14]

In the enchanted medieval world, material things could be what Taylor calls "charged" objects, bearers of power that he calls "magical."[15] Such objects could be used to ward off illness or bad weather. Except in heretical movements like the Waldensians and the Lollards, Reform did not attack the Catholic sacramental system until the Reformation broke out. The attack on sacraments and the whole gamut of Catholic rituals and sacramentals—pilgrimages, relics, rosaries, holy water, and so on—was theologically motivated. Reformers rejected the confinement of God to merely material objects; such materialization of God's power was an affront to the transcendence of God over all creation. It was also a distraction from the spiritual life; Erasmus chided his fellow Catholics for venerating the bones of St. Paul without paying attention to his teachings.[16] The attack on what Taylor calls the Church's "white magic" thus reinforced a barrier between the spiritual and the material that would come to play a significant role in the disenchantment and secularization of the world.

In the Reformation, Taylor's narrative dovetails with parts of Weber's again. The Calvinists play a key role for Taylor, in two ways. The first is in the disenchantment of religious life, in the precise sense of the elimination of magic from the world. Central to Calvin's thought is the utter depravity of human beings and our complete helplessness to surmount that depravity by our own power. It is idolatrous to think that manipulating sacraments and sacramentals could affect our salvation. The Eucharist is important to Calvin, but the effect is interior, dependent upon God's act of faith within the human person. What Calvin "can't admit is that God could have released something of his saving efficacy out there into the world, at the mercy of human action, because that is the cost of really sanctifying creatures like us which are bodily, social, historical. . . . So we disenchant the world; we reject the sacramentals; all the elements of 'magic' in the old religion."[17] The second important effect of Calvinism on the eventual rise of secularization lies in its drive to reform not only the Church but the entire secular order. As does Weber, Taylor emphasizes the tension between renunciation of the world to love God, and the demand to affirm ordinary human life and flourishing in work, family, and civic life. The attempts by Calvin's Geneva and by the Puritans to bring the Gospel to bear on every aspect of daily life, vanquishing all vices, had the effect in the long term of validating worldly life. The attempt to transform the world for God became, in the long run, a kind of worldliness. The more the Calvinists built an orderly society for the glory of God alone, the more they became confident in their own abilities to impose order on the world. The theological conviction that they were helpless sinners was eventually hollowed out by their own success.[18] In these moves—the removal of God from the material world and the confident embrace of mundane life—Taylor sees a "double movement towards immanence."[19]

The development of a full-blown exclusive humanism is still a long way off, but Taylor sees an interiorization of the Christian life in Reform more generally and the Reformation more particularly. The eventual evacuation of God from the world was prepared by the movement of God to the interior life of the human person. Taylor describes the difference between medieval and modern selves in terms of the permeability of the boundaries between the self and the world. He contrasts the modern world with the enchanted medieval world,

> the world of spirits, demons, moral forces which our predecessors acknowledged. The process of disenchantment is the disappearance of this world, and the substitution of what we live today: a world in which the only locus of thoughts, feelings, spiritual élan is what we call minds; the only minds in the cosmos are those of humans . . . and minds are bounded, so that these thoughts, feelings, etc., are situated "within" them.[20]

In the enchanted world, power resided not only in human minds, for there were other spirits and demons and saints in heaven that had their own personal agency. Power furthermore resided not only in minds but in the external world of things, such as holy relics, which had the power to impact not only minds but the material world by curing illness or saving ships from being wrecked, for example. "Thus in the enchanted world, charged things can impose meanings."[21] This type of power, says Taylor, shows how the line between personal agency and impersonal force was blurred in the medieval world, because the cure was equally attributable to the relic itself and the saint it belonged to. At the same time, the boundary between mind and world was also hazy; events in the physical world like bumper harvests or famines were acts of personal agents, be they saints or demons, and not just the result of exceptionless physical laws. More crucially, the mind/world boundary is blurred because power and meaning can overwhelm the mind from without. The person can become possessed by a spirit or fall under the influence of a spell or be taken over by melancholy. Meaning here is neither simply within nor simply outside of the mind; "we think of this meaning as including us, or perhaps penetrating us."[22] In such a world, selves are "porous."[23]

The disenchanted world, by way of contrast, is inhabited by "buffered selves," for whom the boundaries between mind and world are clear and distinct. Meaning resides in the mind, so that the effect of prayer or even veneration of a relic is on the interior of the person, and not on the material world outside the person. Meaning is furthermore under the control of the mind, at least to a certain extent. The buffered self can still become overwhelmed with feelings of depression and melancholy. But one can be told that it is just a matter of body chemistry, and thus take some distance from the bad feelings. The meaning of depression is at least partially defined by one's response to it. For the porous self, on the other hand, there is no such recourse. In the medieval period, black bile is not simply the cause of melancholy; it *is* melancholy. Once one is in the grips of melancholy, one can only pray that another external force, like the intervention of a saint, will offer relief.[24]

Taylor's historical narrative, like that of Weber, is centered on two crucial turning points—the Axial Age and the age of Reform—but Taylor adds a wealth of detail in bringing the tale of secularization up to the present. Political elites play an important role in the early modern period, moving to ban carnivals, dancing in cemeteries, and a host of other unruly popular practices that Taylor regards as "enchanted." In coordination with church authorities, the civil powers in the nascent state became increasingly interventionist, attempting to uniformize and homogenize the populace, eliminating marginal populations and educating the masses to speak and act more like their social betters. Such attempts, writes Taylor, are "rationalizing" in Weber's dual sense of using instrumental reason and in ordering society by a set of values (*Wertrationalität*).[25] These efforts serve to focus attention on this world, as opposed to the next. Philosophers and theologians play a role in Taylor's narrative as well. The nominalists helped disenchant the world by collapsing the analogy of being into univocity; God is sheer will confronting the world rather than revealing Godself through the world in signs and symbols. Intrinsic teleology is expelled from nature, resulting in nature as a mechanism.[26] Descartes brings this mechanistic view of the material universe to completion, instituting the most rigorous mind/body and mind/world dualism, relegating all meaning to the intra-mental. Descartes's agent is "super-buffered."[27] The Romantics reacted against the reduction of human life to rational control,[28] but although Romanticism pushed back against disenchantment, in some crucial ways Romanticism moved the process of secularization forward by anticipating the kind of expressive individualism that breaks into a mass phenomenon in the West after World War II. Taylor calls this the Age of Authenticity: each of us has our own way to realize our humanity, and we need to be true to our interior self, not conform to what society or the previous generation or religious or political authority expects of us. This individualism coincides with a breakdown of communities like churches, and also produces a "nova effect" of extreme plurality, the availability of myriad choices of what to believe and how to live. Through all these shifts and more, Taylor argues, secularity advances in the contemporary West in three different senses: (1) reference to God or religion is removed from public spaces, such as the state, the market, and educational institutions; (2) religious belief and practice decline; and (3) religious belief becomes optional. According to Taylor, what it means to live in a secular age is that some people believe and some do not, but *all of us* live in the condition where belief is just one option among others.[29]

2.2. Where We Are

This brief summary does not do justice to the rich historical detail Taylor lays out across hundreds of pages of text and notes in *A Secular Age*. I am primarily interested, however, in Taylor's description of the world we live in now. After laying out his historical narrative in the first four parts of the book, Taylor begins part 5 with a condensed description of "where we are . . . the spiritual shape of the present age."[30] Taylor begins with disenchantment, specifically its "inner" side, the movement from porous to buffered selves. This is accompanied by interiorization, by which Taylor means not only the division between mind and world and the epistemologies—from Descartes to Richard Rorty—that promote it, but also the development of the idea that there is a rich inner life of thought and feeling to be explored. "We might even say that the depths which were previously located in the cosmos, the enchanted world, are now more readily placed within."[31] With interiority comes discipline, self-control, and a concern for intimacy to be carried out in private spaces. Interiority also presupposes individualism, the idea that society is made up of and constructed by individuals, rather than seeing the social group as the primary given reality, the person as embedded in that group, and the group as embedded in the cosmos. The obverse of individualism is the atrophy of ideas of cosmic order and teleology. Such a diminishment Taylor calls "another facet of disenchantment,"[32] the outer side of that phenomenon. Finally, Taylor remarks on the movement from reference to a "higher time," an epoch of cosmic fulfillment, to secular time, measured instrumentally by the homogeneous modality of clock readings. In summary of this description of our world, Taylor writes:

> So the buffered identity of the disciplined individual moves in a constructed social space, where instrumental rationality is a key value, and time is pervasively secular. All of this makes up what I want to call "the immanent frame." There remains to add just one background idea: that this frame constitutes a "natural" order, to be contrasted to a "supernatural" one, an "immanent" world, over against a possible "transcendent" one.[33]

In these few pages many of the most important analytical terms Taylor uses are on display, and they come in binaries: enchantment/disenchantment, exterior/interior, transcendent/immanent, religious/secular, supernatural/natural. In each case, the first term pertains to the premodern, and the second to the modern. Though the first terms are intimately related to each other, and the second terms to each other as well, the terms within each group are not simply synonymous. Taylor argues, for example, that religion and enchantment are not the same thing. Disenchantment is sometimes confused with the end of religion, and the terms are often used synonymously. As Taylor points out, even Weber sometimes uses the term in this way. "But I have been using the word here in a narrower sense: disenchantment is the dissolution of the 'enchanted' world, the world of spirits and meaningful causal forces, of wood sprites and relics."[34] Taylor says that enchantment is essential to some forms of religion, but not to others, such as Christianity that has gone through Reform, in both its Protestant and Catholic varieties. Such kinds of religion have gone from being more embodied to being more in the mind; they have changed but not disappeared.[35] Part of what Taylor is trying to rebut here is the idea that scientific views of the natural world inevitably lead to the decline of religion, as if religion has become superfluous because we no longer think that saints control lightning.[36]

For Taylor, the process of disenchantment achieved a "sorting out" of the transcendent from the immanent, and the supernatural from the natural, not only in theory but in the experience of Western Christians. This sorting was at first fully compatible with belief in God, and in fact was pushed forward by a more intense dedication to God and a zeal to extirpate all forms of idolatry in the early modern period. This "rage for order" wanted both to sort out God from the world, so that God would be all in all, and to bring God into all aspects of daily life, as in Luther's idea that every Christian, not just those called to vowed religious life, has a vocation. According to Taylor, this dual process invests the immanent with a new kind of significance and solidity that would eventually lead to the possibility of living in a purely immanent world, with no reference to the transcendent.[37]

Taylor uses "immanence" and "transcendence" to denote what pertains to this world and what goes "beyond" it. The key question, as Taylor puts it, is "[D]oes the highest, the best life involve our seeking, or acknowledging, or serving a good which is beyond, in the sense of independent of human flourishing?"[38] For a Christian, the answer is yes; worshiping God is the ultimate end, and even though God wills human flourishing, worshiping God is not contingent on this fact. "The injunction 'Thy will be done' isn't equivalent to 'Let humans flourish,' even though we know that God wills human flourishing."[39] Buddhism also goes beyond human flourishing, but in a very different way. In one sense, the Buddha can be construed as directing us toward true human bliss, but "it is clear that the understanding of the conditions of bliss is so 'revisionist' that it amounts to a departure from what we normally understand as human flourishing."[40] In both Christianity and Buddhism, believers are called to detach themselves from their own flourishing. Renunciation cannot simply be redefined as flourishing, according to Taylor, because the ultimate goal remains something beyond one's own flourishing and that of other humans.[41] In the Christian case, those who are open to transcendence, this "beyond," live it in three dimensions: the sense of a higher good beyond human flourishing, belief in a transcendent higher

power that makes this higher good intelligible, and belief that our lives extend beyond this mundane life between natural birth and death.[42]

Taylor contrasts this transcendence—or what he sometimes calls "transformation"—perspective with the "immanence perspective,"[43] which is
"a humanism accepting no final goals beyond human flourishing, nor any
allegiance to anything else beyond this flourishing."[44] This is what Taylor
calls a "self-sufficient" humanism. Before modernity, humans were in "an
order where we were not at the top."[45] Now, for the first time in history, a
self-sufficient, purely immanent humanism is a widely available option.[46]
Taylor offers a "one-line description of the difference between earlier times
and the secular age: a secular age is one in which the eclipse of all goals beyond human flourishing becomes conceivable; or better, it falls within the
range of an imaginable life for masses of people."[47] Such a purely immanent
humanism needs to be distinguished from what Taylor calls the "immanent
frame," which encapsulates both religious people and exclusive humanists.
The immanent frame creates buffered selves living within a society seen as rationally constructed by human hands and subject to secular time; it contrasts
the immanent and the transcendent, but it does not *necessarily* do away with
the transcendent. "What I have been describing as the immanent frame is
common to all of us in the modern West, or at least that is what I am trying
to portray. Some of us want to live it as open to something beyond; some
live it as closed. It is something which permits closure, without demanding
it."[48] The immanent frame means that being open to transcendence is now
optional.

Though religious people in modernity live in the immanent frame, they
are open to something beyond it. In telling the story of the secular age, Taylor
makes extensive use of the opposite term to "secular," which is "religious." But
what is "religion"? Taylor says the term "famously defies definition, largely
because the phenomena we are tempted to call religious are so tremendously
varied in human life."[49] It is a daunting task to determine what is common
between archaic societies where "religion is everywhere" and the "clearly
demarcated" beliefs, practices, and institutions in our society that we call "religion." Taylor plainly thinks that "religion" is a transhistorical and transcultural phenomenon, present both today and in ancient societies.

But if we are prudent (or perhaps cowardly), and reflect that we are trying to
understand a set of forms and changes which have arisen in one particular
civilization, that of the modern West—or in an earlier incarnation, Latin

Christendom—we see to our relief that we don't need to forge a definition which covers everything "religious" in all human societies in all ages.[50]

The change that matters in the West is the movement from "a world in which the place of fullness was understood as unproblematically outside of or 'beyond' human life" to an age in which some contest this understanding and place it "'within' human life."[51] "In other words, a reading of 'religion' in terms of the distinction transcendent/immanent is going to serve our purposes here. This is the beauty of the prudent (or cowardly) move I'm proposing here."[52] Taylor acknowledges that this will not do for a definition of "religion in general," but it will do for a definition of religion in the West, which invented an immanent order in nature that does not *necessarily* require reference to the transcendent.[53]

Taylor thinks that this concept of religion gives him a handle on what has declined as the secular has advanced. He engages with secularization theorists and partially agrees and partially disagrees with their description of where we are and how we got here. He agrees that we need a definition of religion that allows us to see that something has changed; it will not do to cast the definition of religion so broadly—as one's "ultimate concern," for example—that we can simply claim that, since everyone holds some sort of value in their lives as ultimate, people are still as religious as ever.[54] Taylor thereby rules out functionalist, Durkheimian definitions of religion, at least for his purposes. Taylor accepts Steve Bruce's definition of religion as "actions, beliefs and institutions predicated upon the assumption of the existence of either supernatural entities with powers of agency, or impersonal powers or processes possessed of moral purpose, which have the capacity to set the conditions of, or to intervene in, human affairs."[55] Taylor acknowledges that we could cavil about the details of this definition. There are some "spiritual" outlooks that do not seem to invoke the supernatural, but it is hard to say in many cases, and sharp lines elude most definitions. The natural/supernatural divide is furthermore a Western concept, which would be a problem, says Taylor, if he were not limiting himself to the West. Taylor does, however, appreciate Bruce's inclusion of "impersonal powers" because it recalls what Taylor calls "moral forces" in our enchanted past.[56] And so Taylor accepts Bruce's definition, writing, "Plainly something important has happened; there has been a decline in something very significant, which most people recognize under the term 'religion.' We don't have to follow the masses in our use of this term, but we need *some* word if we are to try to understand the significance of this decline, and 'religion' is certainly the handiest one."[57] Taylor continues:

> With this definition in mind, I can agree with Bruce on the crucial phenomenon: "Although it is possible to conceptualize it in other ways, secularization primarily refers to the beliefs of people. The core of what we mean when we talk of this society being more 'secular' than that is that the lives of fewer people in the former than in the latter are influenced by religious beliefs."[58]

Defining secularization in terms of beliefs is noteworthy here. Although Bruce's definition of religion includes actions and institutions along with beliefs, the actions and institutions are defined by their reference to a certain kind of belief, the assumption of the existence of supernatural entities or impersonal forces possessed of moral purpose. Bruce's definition is substantivist, that is, based on the substance of what people claim to believe, which helps to restrict the definition of religion to the usual suspects: Christianity, Judaism, Islam, Hinduism, Buddhism, and a few others. Functionalists, on the other hand, are more interested in what people do than in what they claim to believe. As Peter Clarke and Peter Byrne put it, "Functionalists prefer to define 'religion' not in terms of *what* is believed by the religious but in terms of *how* they believe it (that is in terms of the role belief plays in people's lives). Certain individual or social needs are specified and religion is identified as any system whose beliefs, practices or symbols serve to meet those needs."[59] So secular nationalism, for example, can be considered a religion under this definition. Taylor's endorsement of religion and secularization as a matter of belief seems designed to head off any such expansive, functionalist view of religion. He is trying to explain what has changed in Western society and thinks it is unhelpful to use a functionalist definition of religion to claim that nothing has changed; for example, nationalism proves we are just as religious as ever. He does acknowledge, in a footnote, that a broader definition of religion can be useful for other kinds of reflection: "Sometimes it helps in understanding our society to bring out the common elements between different outlooks, which straddle what we normally see as the secular/religious divide. But for my purposes here, I need the narrower concept."[60]

What declines in secularization is religion, but Taylor adds to Bruce's definition that it is not only belief in supernatural entities and impersonal powers that fades but also the belief that Taylor calls the "transformation perspective,"[61] that is, that the goal of life is beyond human flourishing. So far Taylor and standard secularization theorists like Bruce agree, though the latter do not focus on "transformation" as such. But Taylor goes on to argue that the standard secularization thesis—that religion is on a trajectory of terminal decline in modern societies—is flawed. Taylor rejects the tendencies among secularization theorists to equate religion with enchantment, such that religion declines inevitably as technology advances, and to see religion as merely epiphenomenal, a symptom of underlying economic or political or social or psychological dynamics. Taylor suggests instead that the demand for religion is a perennial human need,[62] though it is also in our society cross-pressured by resistance to it, for the historically contingent, that is, not inevitable, reasons that he has laid out. Taylor agrees with secularization theorists on many of these reasons—factors like urbanization, mobility, and so on. But he does not think the process of secularization is linear, nor does he think that these factors simply lead to a loss of religion. While traditional religion has been challenged, these factors did not bring about "an atrophy of independent religious motivation."[63] Instead, the breakdown of traditional religious forms in modernity has led to the formation of new forms: new religious orders in post-Revolution France, the identification of God with the nation in imperial Britain, the proliferation of denominations in the United States, and so on.[64] Religion has declined in the West, but Taylor thinks the more interesting story is the explosion of different forms of religion in modernity, its fragmentation. There is now a tremendous plurality of outlooks, not only religious but also nonreligious and antireligious.[65] Of his three types of secularity, Taylor points most especially to the third, optionality. What is most interesting about the present situation is not simply the decline in religious belief but the change in the conditions of belief. Now, as never before, belief in God is optional. Optionality, not simply loss, is the heart of Taylor's narrative of secularization.

Optionality describes for Taylor the change in the past five hundred years from a society in which it was virtually impossible not to believe in God to a society in which belief in God is just one of the available options. Pluralism describes the fact that there are many options, both of types of supernatural entities in which to believe and of forms of disbelief. Taylor describes the shift in Western society by means of another binary: naïve/reflective. Medieval Christians experienced God naïvely, as an immediate certainty. Atheism was simply not an option for the overwhelming majority of people. We live now in a reflective society, one in which—no matter how strong one's own convictions—virtually all are aware that there are other options available. It may be that, in some milieux, certain options are the default; a small town in Utah might have one default position on God, a sociology department at a state university might have another. But all are aware that other options are out there, even though it might take a radical break with one's own context to embrace them. Secularization is the process by which the spaces in which unbelief is the default option expand, but more important for Taylor, it is the process by which faith in God becomes optional. By this, Taylor does not mean *merely* optional, as if God were an item on a menu. The option of choosing belief or unbelief is generally not taken lightly. But optionality means that we recognize there are others who take different options, and they are not necessarily subhuman savages or morally blind.[66] This is what it means to live in a reflective society. The medieval tacit, taken-for-granted background of belief in God is simply gone. "The frameworks of yesterday and today are related as 'naïve' and 'reflective,' because the latter has opened a question which had been foreclosed in the former by the unacknowledged shape of the background."[67] Furthermore, while naïveté achieved hegemonic status in premodern society, reflectivity has achieved hegemonic status in the present.

> The main feature of this new context is that it puts an end to the naïve acknowledgement of the transcendent, or of goals or claims which go beyond human flourishing. But this is quite unlike religious turnovers of the past, where one naïve horizon ends up replacing another, or the two fuse syncretistically—as with, say, the conversion of Asia Minor from Christianity to Islam in the wake of the Turkish conquest. Naïveté is now unavailable to anyone, believer or unbeliever alike.[68]

2.3. Misrecognition

So far I have laid out Taylor's account of how "we" modern Westerners got to be secular and what being secular entails. For Taylor, secularity means reflectivity, optionality, disenchantment, the decline of transcendence, and the decline of religion. I want now to examine each of these aspects of secularity and question whether they in fact describe how our world actually works. I will use Taylor's concept of misrecognition to query his descriptive account of our secular age.

2.3.1. Reflectivity

A few pages after declaring the end of naïveté in modernity, Taylor begins talking about what we moderns perceive naïvely. We are convinced that the only locus of thoughts, feelings, and spiritual élan is within the mind; we have the possibility of introspective self-awareness, even though we also believe that some things in the mind are unconscious and cannot be brought to consciousness. Taylor calls this modern view "radical reflexivity":[69] "What I am trying to describe here is not a theory. Rather my target is our contemporary lived understanding; that is, the way we naïvely take things to be. We might say: the construal we just live in, without ever being aware of it as a construal, or—for most of us—without ever even formulating it."[70] Taylor is not thereby opting for a particular theory of the relationship of body and mind, Cartesian or otherwise. He is trying to describe a naïve, taken-for-granted background assumption that even very untheoretically inclined moderns live in, without articulating it. Here he is interested not in what people believe, but how they believe; not in what people say they believe, but how their actions and words express implicit beliefs:

> I am interested in the naïve understanding, because my claim will be that a fundamental shift has occurred in naïve understanding in the move to disenchantment. This is unlike what I said above on the issue of the existence of God and other spiritual creatures. There we have moved from a naïve acceptance of their reality, to a sense that either to affirm or deny them is to enter a disputed terrain; there are no more naïve theists, just as there are no naïve atheists. But underlying this change is the one I am now talking about in our sense of the world, from one in which spirits were just unproblematically there, impinging on us, to one in which they are no longer so, and indeed, in which many of the ways they were there have become inconceivable. Their not so impinging is what we experience naïvely.[71]

So the move from taking God for granted to disputing God's existence is a move from naïve to reflective, from a position where one set of options is precluded to a position where that set of options is fully available. Underlying that move, however, is the move from porous to buffered selves, and that is a move from naïve to naïve. It is, in other words, a move from a position where one set of options is precluded to a position where another set of options is precluded.

At first glance Taylor's use of "naïve" and "reflective" seems to fit with the standard Enlightenment narrative of modernity as maturity, as the move from childish credulity to full adult awareness. But Taylor's continued use of "naïve" for our modern understanding of the self names the possibility that modernity has its own forms of credulity. Taylor does not mean "naïve" as a pejorative term; every society necessarily has its own forms of taken-for-granted understandings. The real question is not whether premodern and modern societies have such unarticulated background understandings, but whether or not those understandings really differ from each other as much as Taylor seems to believe they do. Taylor presents optionality as a qualitatively different kind of naïveté; optionality implies awareness, a heightened mindfulness of many options. But what if optionality is not optional? What if there is a gap between belief and behavior even in a so-called reflective society that has shed its "naïveté"? If optionality has become our naïveté, as Taylor himself indicates, then our descriptions of our own beliefs and behaviors will unavoidably be structured by a larger political context that escapes our notice. Hent de Vries asks:

> Does the tacit character of background framing—the "taken-for-granted" of which Taylor speaks—differ significantly in the two (naïve and reflective) ages? Or does any belief, any engagement, imply that I immediately blot out the very background, precisely since the moment we hold any view or adopt any course of action, however habitualized, we must take for granted at least some things—indeed, a vast majority of things—even if we can never attain the level of explicitness that a meaningful use of "reflection" or "optionality" would require?[72]

As de Vries comments, if optionality cannot be rejected, then

> [p]aradoxically, secular optionality would be somewhat of a naïveté—the very myth and opinion, superstition and dogma, credulity and fideism—of our time. In any case, its regime of possibilities would not be something about which we can reflectively—or, more precisely, discursively—think and live or act upon as such or throughout. That is to say, if there were ever such a thing as optionality, then it could never leave behind a certain level of implicitness, an unthought and lack of choice, of sorts. Its eventual expression could never satisfy our need for discursive articulation and conceptual explicitness.[73]

The problem here is not that there are background understandings that never rise to explicit consciousness. We need many such assumptions in order to function in any world. As de Vries points out, we need to take for granted a "vast majority of things" in daily life. The problem for Taylor is that his description of the new regime of optionality and choice implies a level of explicitness that can never be attained. The problem is not in the "fact" of optionality but in the ideology of optionality. We are convinced that we live in a regime of choice, whereas in fact we cannot opt out of seeing ourselves essentially as choosers. Taylor himself describes this new situation as a new naïveté, but he thinks that it is a qualitatively different kind of naïveté that decisively separates us from our ancestors; we are reflective as they were not. But if reflectivity is our new naïveté, then perhaps the difference is not as great as Taylor would have it. Reflectivity implies that we modern Westerners have closed or at least narrowed the gap between what is and our descriptions of what is. But Taylor himself at points indicates that the difference between us and our ancestors might not be as great as we suppose.

In order to get to the bottom of this puzzle, we need to examine Taylor's notion of "social imaginary." Taylor uses this term to describe the background frameworks of our thought and action, not the explicit beliefs or intellectual schemes with which people explain their world, but something broader and deeper that Taylor sometimes calls the "conditions of belief." The social imaginary is the way people "imagine their social existence, how they fit together with others, how things go on between them and their fellows, the expectations which are normally met, and the deeper normative notions and images which underlie these expectations."[74] Social imaginary differs from social theory because the former is often expressed not in theoretical terms but in images and narratives; it is not an elite exercise but is shared by large groups of people, even the whole society; and it is "that common understanding which makes possible common practices, and a widely shared sense of legitimacy."[75] Sometimes a social imaginary starts out as an elite theory and eventually comes to be held by the whole society; Taylor thinks this is what happened with the theories of Grotius and Locke.[76] A social imaginary is not opposed to theory, but it can never be adequately expressed in theory; what makes it what it is its taken-for-granted and unarticulated nature across a whole society. In this sense, a social imaginary is like the fourth sense of the word "myth" that I outlined in the first chapter.

A social imaginary, according to Taylor, is "both factual and 'normative'"; we have a sense of the way things are and the way things ought to go and what practices violate those norms.[77] A social imaginary is deeper and wider than practices; it includes a notion of the ideal behind actual practices and some sense of a "moral or metaphysical order" beyond the ideal that helps make sense of it. This background understanding makes the practice possible, but the practice largely "carries" the understanding. There is a mutual influence between understanding and practice that allows for changes over time. In the change from the medieval to the modern, says Taylor, "the modern theory of moral order gradually infiltrates and transforms our social imaginary. In this process, what is originally just an idealization grows into a complex imaginary through being taken up and associated with social practices, in part traditional ones but often transformed by the contact."[78]

Taylor's concept of the "social imaginary" is behind his repeated claims that the transition from, for example, porous to buffered selves "has to be seen as a fact of *experience*, not a matter of 'theory,' or 'belief.'"[79] What Taylor means here is that, whether or not medieval or modern people would be able to come up with a theoretical understanding of the self as either porous or buffered, they experience the self in one of these ways. Taylor repeatedly emphasizes that the difference between then and now is not just that we give two different descriptions of the same experience, as two people might have the same sore throat but give different etiologies for it. In the case of porous and buffered selves, different interpretations mean different experiences: "Because the meaning is integral to, it is constituent of the experience."[80] And this is the case not only with the experience of the self, but with the experience of the world. The cosmos in modernity is no longer experienced as ordered according to an antecedent plan.

> I'm not talking about what people believe. Many still hold that the universe is created by God, that in some sense it is governed by his Providence. What I am talking about is the way the universe is spontaneously imagined, and therefore experienced. It is no longer usual to sense the universe immediately and unproblematically as purposefully ordered, although reflection, meditation, spiritual development may lead one to see it this way.[81]

Taylor makes clear that when he talks about "experience," he does not mean merely subjective feelings independent both of the object experienced and of changes in our dispositions and the bent of our lives. Such individual "experiences," distinct from both object and agent, are "quintessentially modern" and spring from the influence of Descartes and others.[82] What

Taylor means by "experience" is not interior and individual but rather a so-cial production, affecting the individual person but formed by the images and practices of the social imaginary.

Taylor's concept of social imaginary is not deterministic; he thinks that, with some effort, we can see things differently from what is given by the social imaginary. With reflection, a modern Western person can see the universe as ordered by divine Providence; with some philosophical study, one can come to reject the quintessentially modern, Cartesian view of the subject and its subjective experiences. Despite saying that "the immanent frame is common to all of us in the modern West"[83]—though some live it as open to something beyond, and others as closed—Taylor begins his final chapter with stories of "some of those who broke out of the immanent frame."[84] To break out of the dominant social imaginary, however, takes effort, training, and maybe some luck; most of us will be unable to resist the gravitational pull of the spontaneous, naïve view of reality, whether in premodern or modern Western society. In the modern West, this does not necessarily mean it is extraordinarily difficult to believe in God; rather, it means that it is hard not to see belief in God as one option among many. Hard, perhaps, but not impossible. Taylor's language of "breaking out" of the immanent frame indicates that the social imaginary is not all in all. Social imaginaries are contingent, they change over time and across space, and the individual person is never entirely determined by any given social imaginary.

All of this opens up the possibility of a gap between the way we imagine and describe the world and the way it actually is, between the social imag-inary and what Taylor in places calls "reality." When Taylor says, "A race of humans has arisen which has managed to experience its world entirely as immanent,"[85] he does not mean that God is really dead or that reality is what-ever a social imaginary says it is. When Taylor collapses description and in-terpretation into experience, he does not mean that the world is entirely the product of the human imagination. The fact that we experience the world in a certain way does not necessarily mean it really is that way. Although Taylor mostly tries to stay on the descriptive level throughout *A Secular Age*, there are a few places where he lets show his normative convictions about what re-ally is. For example, he thinks that those who experience the world entirely as immanent are subject to a deleterious "spin," a judgment which he says is not as harsh as Weber's accusation of intellectual dishonesty against those un-manly men who take refuge in churches.[86] "My concept of spin here involves something of this kind, but much less dramatic and insulting; it implies that one's thinking is clouded or cramped by a powerful picture which prevents one seeing important aspects of reality. I want to argue that those who think the closed reading of immanence is 'natural' and obvious are suffering from this kind of disability."[87] It must be the case, then, that there are true and false social imaginaries, or at least truer and falser, or better and worse. Likewise, in the last pages of *A Secular Age*, Taylor tips his hand as a believing Christian. In opposition to those who think "religious, transcendent views" are erroneous and will fade over time, Taylor writes:

> In our religious lives we are responding to a transcendent reality. We all have some sense of this, which emerges in our identifying and recognizing some mode of what I have called fullness, and seeking to attain it. Modes of fullness recognized by exclusive humanisms, and others that remain within the immanent frame, are therefore responding to transcendent reality, but misrecognizing it.[88]

This notion of "misrecognizing" reality raises some intriguing possibilities for Taylor's description of the modern Western world. There are clearly some aspects of the modern social imaginary that Taylor thinks are misrecognizing reality. For example, he objects to the sharp modern distinction between the natural and the supernatural that creates a view of nature as hermetically sealed and closed off from any reality beyond it: "Indeed, what may have to be challenged here is the very distinction nature/supernature itself."[89] There are other aspects of the modern social imaginary, however, that Taylor seems to accept as accurate representations of reality. For Taylor, the differences between naïve and reflective, conformity and optionality, enchantment and disenchantment, religious and secular, premodern and modern, and so on, seem to capture something important about the modern world. I would like to probe further into some of these binaries and ask if they are not themselves part of the misrecognition that Taylor would like to challenge.

2.3.2. Optionality

As we have already seen, optionality is closely bound up with reflectivity in Taylor's thought. I have just discussed Taylor's concepts of reflectivity and social imagination as he grapples with what we know and what we know we know in both premodern and modern societies. Now I would like to probe further into the choices we are free to make. For Taylor, the Age of Authenticity—which he dates from the 1960s—is marked by a plurality of choices in the matter of religion, over against the conformity of previous eras. The 1960s accelerated the modern process of individuation, the social imaginary that insists each individual must follow their own path in life and not conform to the crowd.

What strikes Taylor most about modern Western society is not that it has made us all into materialists and foreclosed the religious option. The most important fact is that modernity has created a "free space" in which people can wander amid a plurality of options without having to remain definitively in any one.[90] In an earlier dispensation, what Taylor dubs the "paleo-Durkheimian," one's connection to the holy involved belonging to a church, which was coextensive with society. In the neo-Durkheimian dispensation, the primary locus of the sacred is the nation-state, though one still belonged to a denomination of one's choice. The post-Durkheimian Age of Authenticity, which Taylor dates from the middle of the twentieth century, has elevated individual freedom of choice as its primary value; one must always be true to whatever rings true to one's inner self. What the individual finds meaningful has no necessary embedding in either church or state.[91] The story of this dispensation is, of course, intertwined with the rise of consumerism.

When Taylor comes to discuss consumer culture in this context, however, his analysis is in tension with his narrative of optionality. Taylor does not present consumer culture as simply offering us more options; in fact, it functions more like a premodern religion, linking people through branding and mutual display to each other and to a higher meaning. And behind the retail choice of consumerism lies wholesale manipulation:

> Now consumer culture, expressivism and spaces of mutual display connect
> in our world to produce their own kind of synergy. Commodities become
> vehicles of individual expression, even the self-definition of identity. But
> however this may be ideologically presented, this doesn't amount to some
> declaration of real individual autonomy. The language of self-definition is
> defined in the spaces of mutual display, which have now gone meta-topical;
> they relate us to prestigious centres of style-creation, usually in rich and
> powerful nations and milieux. And this language is the object of constant
> attempted manipulation by large corporations.[92]

Taylor himself thus questions whether what we have in this situation is "real individual autonomy." The possibility of misrecognition here explains his reference a few pages earlier to "this new (at least seeming) individuation."[93] What seems does not necessarily line up with what is. For Taylor, individuation is in fact a new form of relationality; rather than the common action of the Age of Mobilization, what we have in the Age of Authenticity is mutual display, individuals expressing their individuality to each other through the purchase and use of consumer products.

What Taylor means by "mutual display" is illustrated by individuals who identify themselves with a brand, and therefore brand themselves; they purchase Nike shoes, and thereby display themselves as those who "just do it," joining themselves imaginatively to a pantheon of sports heroes and other consumers, all of whom are expressing their individuality in the same way. Taylor calls this "linking myself to some higher world, the locus of stars and heroes, which is largely a construct of fantasy."[94] The notion of a "higher world" seems to link these practices with transcendence, though Taylor does not make this explicit. His language of "higher" and "lower" here is hard to miss, however. Modern consumer society "link[s] us through commodities to an imagined higher existence elsewhere."[95] Taylor notes that, for many people today, identification with a brand or style has tended to "displace" belonging to traditional collective agencies like church, state, and political party.[96]

This displacement (migration?) is usually narrated as liberation, but Taylor notes the coercive effects that produce it and that it produces. The post-Durkheimian dispensation either had the effect of gradually releasing people into the fragmented world or, where consumer culture has taken over, "explosively expelling" people into it. "For, while remaining aware of the attractions of the new culture, we must never underestimate the ways in which one can also be forced into it: the village community disintegrates, the local factory closes, jobs disappear in 'downsizing,' the immense weight of social approval and opprobrium begins to tell on the side of the new individualism."[97] This is one of the few places in Taylor's massive book where he hints at the role that capitalism plays in the story of secularization. In this respect, he is very unlike Weber, for whom capitalism occupies a central role. Taylor does, however, at least show signs of sympathy with Weber's verdict that "material goods have gained an increasing and finally an inexorable power over the lives of men as at no previous period in history."[98] Taylor notes both the power of branding in creating meaning and the discipline that corporations exert on both workers and consumers. He might be more sanguine than Weber about the possibility of escaping the iron cage: "a more genuine search for authenticity begins only where one can break out of the Logo-centric language generated by trans-national corporations."[99] But Taylor also notes that the people who have lately rebelled against church and sexual mores and an ethic of self-sacrifice in their personal lives have remained rigidly disciplined in their work life.[100] This is one of the few places where Taylor at least tacitly acknowledges that capitalism has managed to shake loose attachments to family and community that might interfere with the flexibility and malleability of consumers and workers, while simultaneously augmenting their responsiveness to the corporation. Being a rebel consumer in private life while being a cog in a cubicle at work is not a contradiction, since both keep the wheels of production moving.

"But all this conformity and alienation may nevertheless feel like choice and self-determination."[101] Here Taylor notes a gap not only between the ideology of choice and real autonomy (as in the last block quote above) but between the experience—what it feels like—and the reality, the conformity and alienation to which the person is actually subjected. Taylor's analysis raises the possibility that the way we have learned to name the modern era—as a regime of unbridled freedom of choice—does not match up with reality. Taylor does not think that this is the only story to tell about expressive individualism. He thinks that metatopical spaces of mutual display can unite people around genuine issues.[102] He acknowledges that there have been gains and losses in the post-Durkheimian dispensation, and judges that the gains have outweighed the losses. Taylor rejects the *ideology* of choice—the notion that more choice always makes us happier and authority is inherently suspect—but seems to accept the *fact* that we have more options than ever.[103] His comments on conformity and coercion in consumer culture and the generation of new forms of "imagined higher existence" through commodities, however, cut against the overarching tale of optionality, plurality, and secularity that he is trying to tell.

Taylor wisely tries to avoid any narrative that ends in resentful nostalgia for an age that is not coming back and was not that great to begin with. The dismantling of traditional societies' rigid conformity to gender, family, social, and economic roles has been a significant gain. And the problems with consumer society must not be caricatured into some kind of totalitarian regime. Since the 1980s there has been a reaction against earlier critiques of consumerism that present consumers as mindless dupes being controlled by corporations. More recent critics have shown how consumers are active agents at the micro level, shaping their own identities and meanings through acts of consumption without regard to status. Such studies are an important correction to previous work, but as Juliet Schor has argued, they often ignore the macro level, or conflate the micro and macro levels. Such analyses tend to be depoliticized and unable to account for the power that producers wield in the marketplace. At the micro level, consumers may be conscious and active, but at the macro level they reproduce predictable class-based outcomes, outcomes that are in part anticipated and engineered by producers. As corporate power has grown to dominate not just "economic" space but also politics and the informational and symbolic systems of society, consumer choice operates within the very construction of the person as consumer. Schor writes:

> If we accept the view that individual agency is now central to the operation of consumer society (in contrast to an earlier era in which there was more overt social conformity), it is the companies who figure out how to successfully sell agency to consumers that thrive. In this formulation, subjectivity does not exist prior to the market (à la neoclassical economics) but is a product of it. This does not make subjectivity "false" as in earlier critiques, but it does imply that subjectivity is constrained and market driven. After all, only certain forms of subjectivity are profitable. So while consumers have gained one kind of power (market innovations begin with them), they have lost the power to reject consumption as a way of life. They are trained from the earliest ages to be consumers, and it becomes nearly impossible to construct identity outside the consumer marketplace.[104]

The problem again is precisely that optionality is our new naïveté. On the micro level we have plenty of choices, but we cannot opt out of a particular kind of anthropology that constructs the subject as consumer. Consumerism functions as a myth, an unquestionable ideology. Thus, not just the ideology but even the "fact" of choice is questioned. If optionality is not optional, then perhaps the "fact" of choice is itself an ideology; we do have plenty of choices on the micro level, but on the macro level we cannot choose not to be a chooser, to define the self as an autonomous "god" that creates its own world through choice. It is not just the commodities themselves, as in "commodity fetishism," that exert power over us; the fetishism of the self as chooser blinds us to real authenticity. If optionality is our new naïveté, then we can never

bring it to explicit consciousness. If this is the case, then optionality is something that has power over us. The hegemony that optionality exerts is in part
due to our inability to see and name that power. It is a power that always
operates behind our backs. As in Weber, we become subject to the power of
gods of our own making. Because this is the new naïveté, it is nearly impossible to name that power as anything other than freedom.

Taylor is not unaware of this dynamic, as we have seen. His general approach is to appreciate the freedoms that modernity has made possible while
warning against the new unfreedoms that it has spawned. Taylor favors
"open secularism," in which religion is welcome as an option in public discourse, over "closed secularism," which tries to exclude religion from public
expression, as in France. In an interview, Taylor suggests that closed secularism is more prevalent in Europe than in the United States because of
the legacy of confessional states in the former: "[H]ard secularists like the
Jacobins couldn't envision any other structure. So they had to swap one
total society for another. . . . How can we run a society if we don't agree on
these fundamental things? . . . In some sense, closed secularism is still in the
mindset of confessional states, only we change the confession."[105] Taylor thus
rejects closed secularism, but his comments on individuation in the age of
consumerism open the possibility of seeing something "confessional" about
open secularism as well. If one cannot escape the regime in which religion is
a consumer choice, then perhaps the nova effect masks a more fundamental
uniformity.

2.3.3. Disenchantment

Taylor nevertheless believes that there is a qualitative difference in the kind
of naïve subjectivity experienced by premodern and postmodern Westerners
that is captured by the term "disenchantment." In a response to responses
to *A Secular Age*, Taylor identifies disenchantment as one of two large
developments that explain how we got to the place where faith is considered
optional.[106] He thinks the disenchantment of the modern world is something
on which everyone can agree.[107] As we saw in chapter 1, however, everyone
does not agree that the modern world is disenchanted; Landy and Saler point
to all kinds of immanent reenchantments, and Josephson-Storm thinks there
is no reenchantment because the modern world was never disenchanted in
the first place. Why does Taylor think everyone can agree that the modern

world is disenchanted, and why does he think that description does neces-sary work?

Taylor himself, in responding to questions on his concept of disenchant-ment, has identified it as one of his "fuzzy areas, which I'm still having trouble working out."[108] He tries to confine the concept to a "narrow corral": "The 'enchanted' world which disenchantment brought to an end was a world full of spirits, and moral forces embedded in things, like relics or love potions."[109] But he admits that "[d]isenchantment (Weber's 'Entzauberung') is a concept which has trouble staying in place. It regularly escapes the corral of exact definition."[110] Taylor thinks he knows why it won't stay put: "It is widely felt that the modern training and discipline which has made us 'buffered' has excluded too much."[111] Movements like Romanticism see disenchantment as a loss and call for reenchantment, living in attunement with the natural world and the cosmos. Taylor thinks this is something different from the narrow sense of disenchantment as experience of wood sprites and so forth, which cannot be reconstituted in modernity. But he says:

> So I want to retain my narrow, "corralled" concept of disenchantment, but I understand why the horse keeps jumping the fence; and am even partly reconciled to it. The issues of "re-enchantment" that many people want to debate today are intertwined causally and conceptually with "disenchant-ment" in the narrow sense, and clearly defining the difference between what was at stake in earlier "disenchantment," and what is at issue in "re-enchantment" today, is so difficult, that keeping the horse in the corral will be next to impossible.[112]

In a footnote Taylor takes solace in the fact that Weber's horse also jumped the fence; Weber began with a notion of disenchantment as the extirpation of "magic," but then expanded the notion to include the sidelining of religion itself.[113]

Insofar as disenchantment is identified with a general decline in encounters with wood sprites and seeking cures through relics, then, Taylor's thesis is fairly uncontroversial (although the polling data Josephson-Storm cites on modern Western belief in ghosts, demons, witches, etc., should give us pause even here).[114] Insofar as it is uncontroversial, however, it is also not very interesting. Taylor clearly wants the concept of disenchantment to say more about the world we inhabit than simply that most people no longer believe in fairies.[115] With the Romantics, on whose side he puts himself,[116]

Taylor experiences disenchantment as a more general loss in Western modernity.[117] He clearly thinks there are gains that come with the loss, but there is a loss nonetheless. But a loss of what? Taylor does not miss wood sprites but rather "kinship with the universe" and "attunement with the world," which he calls a "profound human need/aspiration."[118] Taylor seems to buy the Romantic idea—found in a different form in Weber—that Western modernity threatens to subject human existence to the soulless march of instrumental rationality. Sometimes disenchantment means decline in encounters with fairies and the like, but sometimes for Taylor it means a much more general sense of the deadening of the world, the reduction of encounters with the material universe to instrumental attempts to manipulate mere matter.[119] This is the usual way the trope of disenchantment has been used to describe Western modernity, both by those who celebrate the decline of superstition and irrationality and by those who mourn the loss of a deeper connection to the natural world. Taylor has not been able to resist the gravitational pull of this common story that modern Westerners tell about themselves.

But is this description true? Taylor clearly does not think that it is true in the sense that it corresponds to the way the universe actually is. He does not believe in fairies, but he does believe that the universe is in fact infused with the presence of God. Those who describe the world as mere matter, closed to any contact with something beyond mere matter, are misdescribing the universe. But there is another sense in which we can challenge the story of disenchantment: we can doubt whether it accurately describes the way that modern Western people actually experience the world. Perhaps even those who would deny that the modern West is enchanted experience it as enchanted. To argue this, one would have to posit a possible gap between the way people experience the world and the way they describe that experience.

Taylor himself hints at this possibility in his discussion of the Age of Authenticity, specifically in the rise of consumer culture. He cites Yves Lambert's study of Breton village life, where "since time out of mind" a modest subsistence economy was densely intertwined with ritual communal life centered around the local Catholic church. After World War II, the advent of consumer society turned people very quickly toward the pursuit of personal prosperity. Lambert quotes a local: "We no longer have time to care about that [religion]. One seeks money, comfort, and all that; everyone is now into that, and the rest, bah!"[120] The tight community life fragmented into individualism and a plurality of options. But it was the way that different aspects of community life—what we would call religious and economic—were so closely united that caused the fragmentation. Otherworldly salvation and inner-worldly material well-being had been so tied together in Breton Catholicism that any change in the one would necessarily affect the other. Another local: "Why would I go to mass, they say to themselves, when my next-door neighbour is doing as well as me, perhaps even better, and he doesn't go."[121] Taylor comments, "It is almost as though the 'conversion' was a response to a stronger form of magic, as earlier conversions had been."[122]

The single word "almost" here keeps Taylor's thesis about the disenchantment of the modern Western world from unraveling. Taylor recognizes a strong similarity between premodern and modern forms of society, but then pulls back; it is almost there, but not quite. What if we removed that "almost" and explored the unthought behind Taylor's insight here? What if modern consumer culture really is a form of magic, indeed a "stronger form of magic," *Zauber*, than the Catholicism which had structured Breton life since time out of mind? Magic, as Taylor uses the term, is associated with the "moral forces embedded in things" that is part of his definition of enchantment. By pointing to a stronger form of magic in consumer culture, Taylor indicates that consumer culture is responding to material things as if they were invested with moral force, the ability to deliver happiness, comfort, salvation. Material objects are not at all dead matter for the Bretons and for Westerners more generally. They are rather the totems around which so much of social life is structured. Taylor's insight here is not exactly new; Marx identified the fetishism of commodities long before consumer culture came to dominate Western society. I will explore these matters in depth in chapter 7. For now, it is important to note that Taylor himself raises the possibility that magic still pervades contemporary culture, and that his own analysis of the disenchantment of modernity would come apart if the "almost" were removed.

To see consumer culture as a form of magic, we would need to refuse the idea that modern Westerners *experience* their world as disenchanted, even if they still describe it as such. We would need to allow for a gap between experience and description. To do so would call into question the usefulness of the enchantment/disenchantment divide as a purely descriptive tool. Taylor is flummoxed by the fuzziness of the concept of disenchantment: "It regularly escapes the corral of exact definition."[123] Perhaps it is better to see it not as a purely descriptive tool; the enchantment/disenchantment binary is instead prescriptive, a rhetorical device that helps make the world in a certain way.[124] As Courtney Bender puts it, "[T]he secular is marked not by disenchantment, but by an *oft-repeated claim* that we have been disenchanted."[125]

The interesting question is why we have been taught to describe the modern Western world as disenchanted even though we might not experience it that way. One way of answering that question is to acknowledge that the enchantment/disenchantment binary is most commonly used to drive a wedge between "us" and "them," between us moderns and either our ancestors or non-Westerners. The terms are most commonly used either to dismiss practices and beliefs we don't like as superstitious or primitive, or to bemoan the soullessness of the modern world. As descriptive terms, they are incoherent and misleading. The key question, to restate one of the main points of chapter 1, is not whether modernity is disenchanted, but rather what kind of work is being done, in any given context, by labeling things either enchanted or disenchanted? In other words, whom and what does the enchanted/disenchanted distinction authorize, and whom and what does it marginalize?

To remove the "almost" from Taylor's comment on consumer culture would also help Taylor make sense of his Romantic and Christian conviction that "living in attunement with the world is a profound human need/aspiration."[126] If this profound need to encounter transcendent reality in material things is in fact hardwired into human existence, even though we are capable of misrecognizing it, then it must go somewhere other than simply going away when it is suppressed. Removing the "almost" allows us to see consumer culture as a different way of dealing with this basic human need. The holy in this case has not simply disappeared from things but has migrated to other kinds of things and taken on different modalities. The formal similarities between Catholicism and consumerism—between sacramentality and the fetishization of material goods especially[127]—help explain how the transition in Breton culture could take place so quickly, so thoroughly, and without much resistance. This explaining the transition by way of formal similarity is an extension of Taylor's own comment about the deep connection between salvation and material well-being in the predecessor culture, except that the connection remains, *mutatis mutandis*, in Breton culture *after* the transition as well. The locus of salvation has simply migrated to consumer goods. Perhaps the people lined up at the Best Buy on Thanksgiving, waiting to burst into the store at midnight and run frenzied for the discounted televisions, are not "buffered" selves after all. William Desmond has written on the "ontological porosity" of the human person—visible in human responses to touch, music, laughter, and other common experiences—by which we find (or lose) ourselves by surrendering to what is beyond ourselves. Desmond insists that we are never simply buffered, and that porosity does not fade away with

Western modernity.[128] Seeing the translation of devotion from relics to consumer goods as a migration, and not simply as a loss of "magic," would help reinforce Taylor's claim at the conclusion of his final chapter: "The account I'm offering here has no place for unproblematic breaks with a past which is simply left behind us." Taylor quotes Robert Bellah: "[N]othing is ever lost."[129] The sense of the holy may take different, even perverse and idolatrous forms, but if Taylor is right about perennial human needs and aspirations,[130] it does not simply disappear.

2.3.4. Decline of Transcendence

One of the most significant changes in the social imaginary of the West, according to Taylor, has been the sorting out of transcendence from immanence and the relative decline of belief in the former. Taylor defines transcendence as that which takes people beyond human flourishing, and contends that there now exists, for the first time in history, a race of people who experience their world as purely immanent, as purely to do with human flourishing. Defining religion in terms of transcendence, and not simply in terms of belief in God, allows Taylor to include Buddhism and other nontheistic belief systems in his category of religion, and allows him to distinguish Christians and Buddhists on the one hand from exclusive humanists on the other.

There are multiple problems with this categorization. Whether or not the transcendent/immanent divide really makes sense in Buddhism is a difficult question. The distinction between transcendence and immanence comes from the Judeo-Christian context, with its distinction between a Creator God and creation, a distinction that Buddhism does not have. In order to make Buddhism fit the transcendent/immanent paradigm, transcendence has to be given a very broad and nonspecific sense. Taylor locates the distinction within Buddhism through his distinction between mere human flourishing and goals that go beyond human flourishing. Both Buddhism and Christianity, according to Taylor, offer renunciation of normal human flourishing; both serve goals that are "independent of human flourishing."[131] There are at least two problems here. One is in his characterization of Christian renunciation.[132] The eternal goal of Christian life is not independent of human flourishing. The gift of self in Christian renunciation is simultaneously the receiving of one's true self, which is described as *theosis*, the deification of the human person. The created order, furthermore, is not met with mere detachment but is integral to the process of *theosis*. Human flourishing in communion with God, other people, and the material order is a foretaste of the eschaton, which is not just the entry of the individual into heaven after death but the re-creation of the material order, a new heaven and a new earth (Is. 65:17; II Peter 3:13). The relationship between Christian renunciation and human flourishing is at least more complicated than Taylor makes it out to be.[133] The second problem is that Taylor struggles to distinguish "religious" renunciation from other kinds of renunciation, such as that of the Stoics. According to Taylor, Christian and Buddhist renunciation is out of compassion for others, whereas Socrates's death—"utterly different" from Christ's—is "leaving this condition for a better one."[134] Why the "better condition" is not "beyond human flourishing" is unclear to me. Taylor seems to be working too hard here to get Christianity and Buddhism to stay on one side of the divide and Stoicism and exclusive humanism to stay on the other.

If this battle is unwinnable, Taylor can fall back to his "prudent (or cowardly)" claim that the transcendent/immanent divide needs to work only within modern Western culture, for it is only here that the formerly interpenetrating realms of transcendence and immanence became "watertight," to use his term, in modernity.[135] Even within Western culture, however, the distinction is hard to maintain with anything like watertight clarity. William Connolly, for example, has responded to Taylor by distinguishing between two types of transcendence, radical and mundane. Connolly does not believe in God (radical transcendence), but he does believe in experiences outside of conscious awareness or full representation that interact with actuality in fecund ways (mundane transcendence).[136] Connolly identifies himself with other immanent naturalists who project an open temporal horizon that is irreducible to either closed naturalism or radical transcendence.[137] Martha Nussbaum likewise distinguishes between two different types of transcendence: external, which she rejects, and transcendence that is internal to human life, which she accepts.[138] Then there are philosophers of immanence who prefer to do away with the transcendent/immanent distinction altogether. For such philosophers, the very distinction perpetuates the traditional problem of seeing immanence as negatively related to transcendence. Immanence remains transcendence minus something, a remainder when transcendence is sealed off. Immanence in the presence of transcendence remains something fallen, incomplete, limited, and inferior. For Gilles Deleuze, for example, there is nothing but pure immanence; the creativity formerly assigned to transcendence is an effect of immanence. There is no negativity within immanence, no differencing from what something is not. The positivity within immanence is only a *temporal* "going beyond" into an open future, a dynamic process of ceaseless becoming new. It is not expressed in *spatial* "upper" or "lower" terms.[139]

What does Taylor make of such attempts to scramble the transcendence/immanence binary? Taylor responds to Nussbaum in the pages of *A Secular Age*. He tries to make sense of what distinguishes internal from external transcendence; perhaps external means any transformation that would render certain human goods impossible for us. Ruling out external transcendence would then mean rejecting Plato's denigration of erotic love, but would we not then also have to declare a universal and decentered ethical concern for others forbidden? Taylor concludes, "All this underscores how problematic are the distinctions, not only between internal and external transcendence, but even transcendence/immanence itself." Nevertheless, Taylor goes on to say, "Of course, I want to retain the notion of transcendence, along the lines of my original distinction between exclusive and inclusive humanisms, for the purposes of my principal thesis."[140] Does the kind of internal or mundane transcendence of certain humanisms count as real transcendence for Taylor? Ruth Abbey says it does; she thinks Taylor accepts "deep ecology," for example, as a kind of transcendence without traditional religion, thus denying traditional religion any monopoly on transcendence.[141] Peter Gordon disagrees; for Taylor naturalistic experiences of mystery in nature do not count as "actual transcendence" but are ultimately reducible to exclusive humanism.[142]

Which interpretation of Taylor is correct? As with disenchantment, Taylor tries to distinguish between a broad sense and a narrow sense of transcendence, recognizing aspirations to transcendence in Nussbaum's "broader sense," but adding, "I have normally been using the term in a narrower sense in this book."[143] He does not do so consistently, however. When he needs to find transcendence in nontheistic Buddhism in order to count Buddhism as a religion, Taylor uses transcendence in a broad and nonspecific sense. When he needs to locate nontheistic humanisms on the immanent side of the dichotomy, he uses transcendence in a narrow sense. Taylor sees in the "immanent transcendence" of the heirs of Nietzsche a restlessness "at the barriers of the human sphere."[144] But he is unwilling to abandon the barrier that separates the transcendent from the merely human. He expresses doubt that a fully adequate account of transcendence or "upper" language can be given in purely immanent or "lower" terms.[145] Nevertheless, there are many borderline cases. Festive events like rock concerts, Taylor says, are "plainly 'non-religious'; and yet they also sit uneasily in the secular, disenchanted world. . . . The festive remains a niche in our world, where the (putatively) transcendent can erupt into our lives, however well we have organized them around immanent understandings of order."[146] Here Taylor's use of "disenchantment" has clearly jumped the fence, and the only thing keeping transcendence in his narrower corral is the word "putatively" in parenthesis, which operates like the "almost" in his discussion of consumerism—as a hastily erected bit of fencing to protect the binaries that Taylor thinks he needs.

Part of the difficulty for Taylor is that he is trying to use the transcendence/immanence binary in a general way to divide modern Westerners into two categories, "believers" and "nonbelievers," rather than examining the binary's specific usefulness, or lack thereof, in any particular context. The transcendence/immanence binary has a very specific set of uses within the Christian tradition that may or may not be helpful when applied to other contexts. Even within the Christian tradition, transcendence/immanence is much more complex than simply distinguishing God who is "beyond" human life from what remains "within" human flourishing. The original context of the concept "immanence" in Christian thought was the inner *perichoresis* of the three persons of the divine Trinity, in which "all varieties of divine being and every divine person who is so by relating to the other, must necessarily be fully contained in the other."[147] The relationship of transcendence and immanence in Christian thought is further complexified by the Incarnation, which makes the transcendent God visible in immanent form without thereby reducing God to something created.[148] In the Christian tradition, appealing to divine transcendence can support the integrity and intrinsic worth of material creation because God's creative act allows things to exist for their own sake. It is precisely because God is wholly other, entirely transcendent to creation, that God is also entirely immanent in creation, "in all things, and innermostly," as Aquinas says.[149] The relationship of transcendence to immanence in the Christian tradition is not spatial, as Taylor often portrays it; transcendent does not mean "over there" as opposed to immanence's "in here."[150] Precisely because God is wholly transcendent and not a thing in the universe, God does not compete with things or absorb them into God, but causes them to exist for their own sake. God does not take the place of something else, but invites difference to happen. As I will argue in the final chapter, the result of such a sacramental view of the world is a more satisfying materialism, a true immanent transcendence.

Taylor will object that he is not talking about transcendence and immanence in theory but about the social imaginary of the modern West. Transcendence and immanence were experienced as mutually interpenetrating until the modern secular age made them "watertight."[151] Taylor thinks that his definition of religion in terms of transcendence needs to fit only the modern West. But in responding to critiques of his use of "transcendence," he has also said that he needs it as a general term that applies universally.[152] What reasons can he give for using such a fraught term? "Well, one was that I wanted to say something general, something not just about Christians. In the end, I think there is a point one could make about the insufficiency of human flourishing as the unique focus of our lives, which recurs throughout all of human history and cultures, albeit in very different ways."[153] When Taylor needs a term that will include both Christianity and nontheistic Buddhism, he uses "transcendence" in a broad and quite vague sense. When he needs a term that will include Christianity and exclude nontheistic types of humanism, he uses "transcendence" in a narrow sense. He wants to be inclusive, but not so inclusive that any experience of fullness counts as transcendent.

Why not allow that rock concerts are more than the "putative" eruption of transcendence in our lives? Because Taylor thinks that what we ultimately need is not rock concerts, but God. When Taylor says, "Modes of fullness recognized by exclusive humanisms, and others that remain within the immanent frame, are therefore responding to transcendent reality, but misrecognizing it," he does not really think they are responding to "transcendent reality"; he thinks they are responding to God. Taylor is a believing Christian, and he believes that God is a reality, the most real reality.[154] This, of course, does not mean that Christians have a monopoly on understanding God, nor on encountering God. Misrecognition means that God is active in all of reality, even if people don't acknowledge it. And this means as well that people do need rock concerts and good art and the beauty of nature and all the sacramental encounters with God in material reality; it is misrecognition only if we fail to see that the true source of being and beauty is somehow more than the merely material.[155]

This, I think, is what Taylor really wants to say, but his status as a philosopher and his secular audience make him reticent to say it. What has declined in the modern West is not belief in transcendence; what has declined is belief in God. But if Taylor is right that humans have an inherent desire for God, then those longings will appear in all kinds of places, including rock concerts and consumer goods, even if they are misrecognized as such.

2.3.5. Decline of Religion

The idea that the holy migrates and is not simply lost or foreclosed would help Taylor tell his story of secularization as a new way of describing the world, but not necessarily as a completely new way of experiencing the world. As it is, Taylor's contention on page 772 that nothing is ever lost stands in tension with his assertion on page 1 that secularity makes us modern Westerners different from "anything else in human history." Taylor is trying to give a balanced account of what has and has not changed in the transition from premodern to modern societies. His most urgent task, however, is to explain what has changed; he did not write a massive book on the secular age in order to say *Nothing to see here folks. Move along.* His emphasis is on how peculiar we are. And the religious/secular distinction is key to his entire narrative.[156] If we live in a secular age, we must be able to answer the question *Secular, as opposed to what?* The other side of the binary from secular is "religious." As we have already seen, Taylor rejects functionalist definitions of religion that would spread the meaning of the term broadly, to cover, for example, nationalism or Marxism. He is afraid that if we allow such Durkheimian definitions, we will be able to claim that nothing has really changed, that we moderns are still as religious as ever. Something has clearly changed, and Taylor defines that change in terms of a decline in religion: "[T]he proportion of belief is smaller and that of unbelief is larger than ever before; and this is even more clearly the case, if you define religion in terms of the transformation perspective. Thus my own view of 'secularization' . . . is that there has certainly been a 'decline' of religion."[157]

Nevertheless, Taylor is more nuanced than typical theorists of secularization in describing this decline. Although he accepts that there has been a decline of religion, he rejects the idea that such a decline is a linear process made inevitable by advances in human understanding. He also thinks that religion does not simply go away; it mutates and takes new forms. Those forms, however, remain within what a substantivist would regard as "religion." In the paleo-Durkheimian ancien régime, my connection to the sacred consists in belonging to the church, which is coextensive with society, which is ruled by a king. The sacred is embedded in a hierarchical cosmos to which one simply belongs. This order preexists the people who inhabit it since time out of mind. In the neo-Durkheimian Age of Mobilization, roughly 1800–1950, citizens see themselves as coming together as equals to form a political entity, which has a providential role to play in God's design. I belong to the denomination of my choice, but I am still connected to what Taylor calls "the broader, over-arching 'church,'" which is identified with the political entity.[158] "In both these cases, there was a link between adhering to God and belonging to the state—hence my epithet 'Durkheimian.'"[159] The point that Taylor is trying to make here is that the neo-Durkheimian dispensation is a change in, but not simply a diminishment of, religion. Where there is "religiously-defined political identity-mobilization . . . a potential decline in belief and practice is retarded or fails to occur."[160] Taylor's point is similar with regard to the post-Durkheimian Age of Authenticity. Although religion in the West has declined, one should not read the precipitous drop in church attendance in some European countries as a sign of the end of religion. Expressivist individualism has fragmented religious identities, but the quest for transcendence lives on, and even in decidedly post-Christian places, people "may retain an attachment to a perspective of transformation which they are not presently acting on."[161] Large-scale disasters bring even Swedes out to churches for memorial services.

So Taylor agrees that religion has declined, but he pushes back against the secularization thesis that religion is in terminal decline in the modern West. Taylor, as we have seen, nevertheless accepts the secularization theorists' substantivist definition of religion as about beliefs, not function, and more specifically about beliefs in transcendence, something beyond the immanent world. Though they share the same definition of religion, Taylor thinks that the secularization theorists miss the continued salience of religious belief in our world. He continues to define religion, however, in terms of things that look like Christianity. So he acknowledges that everyone, believer and non-believer, has their own version of "fullness," a perspective in which this life looks good and whole and as it should. Even a militant atheist like Richard Dawkins has a naturalistic "piety of belonging" and a sense of wonder; Taylor even comments that "the piety verges perhaps on the 'religious.'"[162] But they are not religious in Taylor's definition of the term. Here "verges," "perhaps," and the scare quotes around the word "religious" serve the same purpose that Taylor's "almost" serves in his discussion of the stronger form of magic. They serve to maintain the definitional boundary that Taylor thinks he needs, even though the boundary gets quite fuzzy at this point.

Do we really need this boundary? Why accept the substantivist definition of religion as about belief in transcendence? Taylor thinks he needs such a definition in order to keep his subject matter properly delimited; if nationalism were a religion, then the whole religious/secular distinction would get thrown into confusion. But there might be good reasons to question this distinction. The distinction has come under increasing scrutiny from scholars who view the religious/secular distinction as both historically constructed and politically motivated. In other words, the religious/secular distinction is a modern Western invention and does not simply identify a natural kind "out there" in the world called religion that one bumps into in all times and places. And the religious/secular distinction is constructed in different ways according to different political purposes that need to be interrogated.[163]

Taylor thinks he can avoid the problem of the historicity of the religious/secular distinction by making the "prudent (or cowardly) move" of limiting his concept of religion to the modern West. What he means by "religion" is what "we modern Westerners" mean by religion: belief in God or something transcendent. Taylor has been criticized for ignoring the ways that the non-Western world has been deeply implicated in the West's self-definition, including in its construction of the religious/secular divide.[164] But also problematic is the fact that Taylor does *not* consistently limit his use of "religion" to the modern West; he discusses "early religion" in the pre-Axial age, where "religion is everywhere" and is inextricably linked with social life,[165] he discusses "higher" post-Axial religions,[166] and he continues to use the term "religion" to describe what is going on in medieval Christendom.[167] What makes these very different phenomena "religious" is not a matter of belief in God; in assessing the "common human religious capacity" exhibited by "early religion," Taylor is struck by

> first, the ubiquity of something like a relation to spirits, or forces, or powers, which are recognized as being in some sense higher, not the ordinary forces and animals of everyday; and second, how differently these forces and powers are conceived and related to. This is more than just a difference of "theory" or "belief"; it is reflected in a striking difference of capacities and experience; in the repertory of ways of living religion.[168]

Taylor does not explain why religious experience is not merely a matter of belief for ancient peoples, but it is for us modern Westerners. If the "common human religious capacity" is not a matter of belief but about how one relates to "forces or powers" in the world, it is not clear why the sacred nationalism that Taylor describes in the neo-Durkheimian dispensation or the "stronger form of magic" that Taylor discovers in modern consumerism cannot count as religion, even if modern Westerners have learned to call these phenomena "secular."

I have already discussed Taylor's views of consumerism. Let's look at his analysis of "religion" in the neo-Durkheimian dispensation. Taylor invokes Durkheim here for the latter's idea that religion and society are deeply intertwined. For Durkheim, the real object of religion is society; religion is the way that a society represents itself to itself. According to Durkheim, "a religion is a unified system of beliefs and practices relative to sacred things, that is to say, things set apart and surrounded by prohibitions."[169] What is sacred and what is not, however, is not defined by the content of belief. For Durkheim, anything can be regarded by a society as sacred. It does not matter if the national flag is explicitly believed to be a representation of a god or not; what matters is the function that such separation of the sacred from the profane serves in any given society. The social order is reinforced or contested by the symbolization of communal solidarity among the members of society. There is no essential difference between the rituals and taboos surrounding the flag and those having to do with God or gods; both represent a society's symbolization of itself to itself. For Durkheim, all religion, insofar as it does not make explicit the reference to the society itself, is a kind of misrecognition. Durkheim thought that origin of this misrecognition lay in the complexity of society itself. People experience the constraints of social forces beyond the individual's control, but since these forces are too complex for any individual to understand, they give rise to mythological accounts and ritual practices that pay homage to these forces.[170]

Taylor's use of Durkheim seems limited to a general sense that, in some dispensations, religion and group belonging are closely related. Taylor thinks that only paleo- and neo-Durkheimian societies behave as Durkheim thinks all societies do. Taylor also defines religion differently than Durkheim does. Taylor does not think that the real object of religion is society itself; instead he defines religion as belief in the transcendent. So in the neo-Durkheimian dispensation, Taylor defines religion in Western society as still meaning almost exclusively belief in God, but he describes how such religious belief becomes thoroughly intertwined with the new sense of nationalism, as in Britain or Poland or the United States. What he cannot allow is Durkheim's suggestion that nationalism is itself a kind of religion, that devotion to the nation is not essentially different from devotion to God, that nationalism is a kind of self-worship that reinforces social belonging and social order by the sacralization of the group itself. Taylor comes close to doing so in his suggestion that religion does not simply go away in modernity but takes on other forms. He comes close in his suggestions that national identity becomes a new sort of "church" in the neo-Durkheimian dispensation. He comes close in his extension of the neo-Durkheimian category even to virulently antireligious forms of nationalism like those of revolutionary and republican France.[171] But ultimately such forms of piety can only *verge on* religion, can only be *almost* religion, can only be *putative* religion if Taylor's tale of secularization as the decline of religion is to hold up.

My point here is not to defend Durkheim's reduction of all forms of worship to society's worship of itself; as will become clear in the next chapter, I accept the basic biblical distinction between a true God and false gods. Nor am I interested in defending Durkheim's functionalist definition of religion over against substantivist definitions. As I have argued at length previously,[172] any attempt to define "religion" once and for all times and places—whether a more restrictive substantivist attempt or a more expansive functionalist attempt—will get bogged down in anachronism and the imposition of a Western invention on non-Western contexts. There is an extensive and ever-growing corpus of scholarly work showing that the religious/secular distinction is a modern Western invention, one that was invented for very particular political purposes in early modern Europe and then exported to the rest of the world in the process of colonization.[173] In Europe, the distinction accompanied the rise of the state and divided the responsibility of the church from that of the state; in Europe's colonies, the distinction divided local culture from the tasks of rule. Given the malleable and politically inflected ways that religion has been defined, the most sensible approach seems to be neither substantivist nor functionalist but constructivist: in any given context, one should ask why certain things get labeled "religion" and other things do not. What work is the distinction doing in any particular setting? Why did late nineteenth-century Western scholars consider Confucianism a religion, while Chinese scholars rejected that designation? Why do some consider American nationalism a civil religion, while others insist it is secular? Why is godless Theravada Buddhism considered a religion, but godless Marxism is not? In Durkheim's case, John Bossy shows how he could not relate "religion" to "society" in the way he does without the simultaneous and mutually implicated invention of both concepts in early modern Europe.[174] Even within the modern West, we should examine the work that such concepts are doing, and not simply treat them as neutral descriptors.

Taylor is not unaware that the term "religion" is fraught, but, as we have seen, he thinks the reason it defies definition is that its different manifestations are so diverse. But how do we know that these different manifestations are all "religion" to begin with? Taylor says "the phenomena we are tempted to call religious are so tremendously varied in human life."[175] But why are we "tempted" to call them all religious if they are so varied? More to the point, why do we want to call some things religious and some other, very similar things nonreligious? What makes nontheistic Buddhist rituals "religious," by Taylor own reckoning, but rituals surrounding the proper treatment of the American flag—very precise rules for folding, displaying, venerating, and keeping it from touching the ground or being otherwise "desecrated"—are not? Taylor uses "religion" broadly when he wants to include Buddhism, but narrowly when he wants to exclude nationalism.[176] He hopes that his "prudent (or cowardly)" move to restrict "religion" to the way the term is usually used in the West will solve the problem, but it doesn't. It merely casts a fog of legitimacy on the way we usually use the religious/secular distinction and makes sure that the way the distinction works in our society goes unquestioned. But the rise of the religious/secular distinction is part of the story of the changes in Western society that Taylor is trying to tell. Secularization, in other words, is not merely the waxing of the secular and the waning of the religious in the West; secularization is the very invention of the religious/secular binary and the process by which certain things got labeled religious and other things did not. And that process is a matter of the redistribution of power in the West, including the transfer of power from the church to the state. Indeed, the word "secularization" was originally used in the early modern period to denote the transfer of goods from ecclesiastical to civil control.[177] What the church was left with in this process is "religion," which comes to be seen as inherently private; the state, being secular, is public. We can agree with Taylor that the removal of coercive power from the church is a gain. But we might be more able to see the problems with the transfer of violence from the church to the state if we could name that violence as sacred, not secular. This is what Durkheim helps us to do, and it is what the religious/secular distinction helps cover up.[178]

Taylor recognizes the continuation of Durkheimian rituals in the secular world but thinks that they are essentially distinct from religious rituals as experienced in premodern societies.

Of course, we go on having rituals—we salute the flag, we sing the national anthem, we solemnly rededicate ourselves to the cause—but the efficacy here is inner; we are, in the best case, "transformed" psychologically; we come out feeling more dedicated.... The "symbol" now invokes in the sense that it awakens the thought of the meaning in us. We are no longer dealing with a real presence. We can now speak of an act as "only symbolic."[179]

I think Taylor is right that we certainly do speak this way. But I don't think he is sufficiently attentive to why we speak this way now. It may be that we are not simply using new categories to describe a new kind of experience; it may be that the categories themselves help to shape the description, and therefore the experience itself. In other words, the description of patriotic ritual as "only symbolic" might not be merely descriptive but prescriptive; it might be doing some political work. To recognize patriotic ritual as "religious," as more than only symbolic, puts it on the same level as "traditional religions" such as Christianity and Judaism, and thereby sets up a confrontation between church and state over idolatry. To deny that patriotic ritual is religious, to call it "only symbolic," is to preserve Western political arrangements from challenge.

Taylor's account relies too heavily on people's descriptions of their own beliefs, and not on their empirically observable behaviors. People may fully recognize that the nation is not a god, that the flag is just a piece of cloth, that the cause to which they are dedicating themselves is a temporal one, but what really matters is what they do with their bodies. If they are willing to kill and die for something they would describe as "only symbolic," then their dedication to the cause is manifestly *not* something whose "efficacy here is inner," as Taylor puts it. It is not only that Taylor's account of internalization is itself too internalized. It is that the modern trope of internalization is itself an effect of external, political arrangements of power. To say that my ritual patriotic actions are "only symbolic" allows me to be a good Christian and a good American soldier at the same time.

Consider Taylor's account of ritual sacrifice among the Dinka:

On one hand, the major agents of the sacrifice, the "masters of the fishing spear," were in a sense "functionaries," acting for the whole society; while on the other, the whole community becomes involved, repeating the invocations of the masters, until everyone's attention is focussed and concentrated on the single ritual action. It was at the climax "that those attending the ceremony are most palpably members of a single undifferentiated body." This participation often takes the form of possession by the Divinity being invoked.[180]

Compare this to Mark Twain's account of his fellow citizens' behavior during wartime:

> The loud little handful—as usual—will shout for the war. The pulpit will—warily and cautiously—object . . . at first. The great, big, dull bulk of the nation will rub its sleepy eyes and try to make out why there should be a war, and will say, earnestly and indignantly, "It is unjust and dishonorable, and there is no necessity for it." Then the handful will shout louder. A few fair men on the other side will argue and reason against the war with speech and pen, and at first will have a hearing and be applauded, but it will not last long; those others will outshout them, and presently the antiwar audiences will thin out and lose popularity. Before long, you will see this curious thing: the speakers stoned from the platform, and free speech strangled by hordes of furious men. . . . Next the statesmen will invent cheap lies, putting the blame upon the nation that is attacked, and every man will be glad of those conscience-soothing falsities, and will diligently study them, and refuse to examine any refutations of them; and thus he will by and by convince himself that the war is just, and will thank God for the better sleep he enjoys after this process of grotesque self-deception.[181]

Do we not here too see the whole community repeating the invocations of the masters, becoming possessed by a kind of divine force, and acting as a single body to prosecute the blood sacrifice? What Twain describes is not the action of "buffered selves," and the religious/secular dichotomy applied to these two examples would only obscure rather than illuminate what is going on. And that may be precisely why it is used.

2.4. Conclusion

This kind of obscuration is of course not Taylor's intention. Insofar as Taylor tries to explain how modern Westerners came to think about the world the way we do, his account is brilliant and largely successful. He is aware of the ambiguities of some of the dichotomies he employs, and in every case he tries to bring the two sides closer together, arguing that most everyone, believer and nonbeliever, feels "cross-pressured," pulled by different forces in both directions. Taylor's intention is irenic, to divest believers of fear and resentment of nonbelievers and disabuse nonbelievers of the tendency to see believers as credulous and backward.

Despite his intentions, however, Taylor's dichotomies in some cases unnecessarily reinforce the divisions. I am not simply arguing that a society that claims to be reflective, pluralistic, disenchanted, immanent, and secular is in fact naïve, hegemonic, enchanted, transcendent, and religious. I am arguing that these very dichotomies undermine attempts to get our descriptions of the world right, because they are not neutral descriptors but in fact carry prescriptive power. The key question, again, is not whether or not our society is enchanted or secular but what kind of work those terms are doing when they are used. To say that we live in a secular age is really to say that we live in an age in which we use the religious/secular distinction the way we do, along with the other binaries Taylor employs. In a "secular" society these binaries are used to separate two "races" of people, believers and nonbelievers, when the real question is *Belief in what?* Everyone believes in something; you tell me what you believe, I'll tell you what I believe, and then let's have a conversation.[182] It is not belief that has declined in the modern West, but belief in the biblical God. It is not religion that has declined in the modern West, but Christianity (and maybe Judaism as well). These are real and important changes, but they are not adequately described as shifts from belief to unbelief, from naïveté to reflectivity, from enchantment to disenchantment, from transcendence to immanence.

The question of explicit belief, however, is only part of what is really happening. If we are going to get our descriptions of the world right, we need to attend not only to what people say they believe but to their actions, which may express implicit beliefs. Taylor ultimately wants to tell a story of misrecognition; God is still there, but we have been disciplined to ignore this fact. Instead of acknowledging God, we attempt to find fullness in material objects and social processes. At some point, Taylor—or at least those who think that Taylor is right on this crucial point—will need to do theology, that is, discuss God and why and how it is that God is misrecognized. The theological concept that corresponds to this misrecognition is idolatry. I will take up the analysis of idolatry in the next chapter.

3

Idolatry in the Scriptures

So far we have found reasons even within Max Weber's and Charles Taylor's own work to question the notion that we in the modern West live in a disenchanted world. Weber thinks that the search for meaning is a fundamental feature of human life and that, as a result, humans create gods to which we are then subjected. Taylor thinks that all people have an inherent desire for fullness, and those who try to confine that search for fullness to a purely immanent frame are really responding to God but misrecognizing the reality of God. In this and following chapters, I would like to explore these suggestions from a theological point of view, through the lens of the concept of idolatry, starting with the Bible. Although he was not himself a Christian or a theist of any kind, Weber's notion that humans are oppressed by gods of their own making is captured precisely in biblical notions of idolatry. And Taylor's conviction that humans are responding to transcendent reality but misrecognizing it overlaps with the biblical idea that human beings are spontaneously worshiping creatures whose devotion alights on all sorts of created things that are not God.

According to the book of Exodus, the Israelites could stand only a little less than six weeks of Moses's absence (24:18) before they demanded new gods to worship: "When the people saw that Moses delayed to come down from the mountain, the people gathered around Aaron, and said to him, 'Come, make gods for us, who shall go before us'" (32:1). The story of the Golden Calf that Aaron made is a story not only of the fickleness of the human heart and our capacity for self-deception but also of the longing for worship that often appears in the Bible as a basic anthropological datum. A theological conception of idolatry rooted in the scriptures seems to imply that human beings have an inherent need to worship, one that is often misdirected. If this is not just a characteristic of ancient people but a characteristic of the human person that is relatively constant over time, then a secular society, as Taylor intuits, cannot be characterized by the mere loss of worship, the sloughing off of any devotion to something that exceeds a closed immanent frame. Within the notion of idolatry, in other words, lies a challenge to the common

The Uses of Idolatry. William T. Cavanaugh, Oxford University Press. © Oxford University Press 2024.
DOI: 10.1093/oso/9780197679043.003.0004

narratives of secularization that see it as the turn to the merely mundane. Beginning in this chapter I will explore the idea that some people may have ceased to worship God, but they have not ceased to worship, even if the gods now, as Weber intimated, have new names.

An analysis of idolatry may not seem like a very promising place to go because of its ready association with chauvinism. Idolatry critique is based in an exclusive type of claim, that only one God is to be worshiped. Idolatry critique is furthermore often associated with a rigorist critique of the many ways that worship can go wrong, leaving the acceptable paths to true worship few and fraught with peril. Idolatry critique is prone to a kind of narcissism: *you* don't worship like *we* do, and so you must be wrong. The potential for violence is clear; if we think that God is jealous of other gods, then we may be tempted to anticipate what we assume will be God's judgment upon those who follow them. For some good reasons, the sensibilities of the contemporary age have turned away from the language of idolatry. The Second Vatican Council, for example—famous for its embrace of the world and its turn away from the anathemas of the previous century—abandoned idolatry critique almost entirely. In the thousand pages of official documents from Vatican II, language about idols or idolatry occurs only three times.[1]

And yet the concept of idolatry seems to capture something important about the contemporary scene that cannot be completely left behind. Even though Pope Francis is regarded by many as the very embodiment of the spirit of Vatican II in his optimism and love for all, he has made frequent recourse to the language of idolatry. The terms "idol(s)" or "idolatry" appear fourteen times in Francis's first encyclical, *Lumen fidei*. There he states that the opposite of faith is not a simple lack of belief but idolatry. When one stops believing in God, one does not simply stop believing; rather one believes in all sorts of things, "an aimless passing from one lord to another.... Those who choose not to put their trust in God must hear the din of countless idols crying out: 'Put your trust in me!' "[2] Francis has repeatedly used the language of idolatry when describing the contemporary economic system. For example, "We have created new idols. The worship of the ancient golden calf (cf. *Ex* 32:1–35) has returned in a new and ruthless guise in the idolatry of money and the dictatorship of an impersonal economy lacking a truly human purpose."[3] Francis has likely been influenced by Latin American liberation theologians, for whom in the 1970s and 1980s the concept of idolatry was key to opposing the brutal marginalization and oppression of millions by regimes that combined neoliberal economics with military rule.[4] Such theologians saw in neoliberal economics a process not of rationalization but rather of irrationality, in which, as Eduardo Galeano put it, "[p]eople were in prison so that prices could be free."[5] The concept of idolatry captures something important here: the notion that people are not simply prone to imperfect decision-making but in fact are sacrificed to false gods that may be merely human fabrications but nevertheless hold people in their thrall.

Beyond the usefulness of the concept of idolatry in the contemporary context, from a Christian theological point of view it hardly seems possible to do away with the notion of idolatry. From a Christian point of view, there exists a good God independent of our conceptions of God, who created everything from nothing and is therefore wholly other than any created thing. God is unique, beyond genus, and indeed not a thing in the universe at all. To treat anything in the same way that one treats God is therefore a very serious problem. The result is not only a metaphysical error but a distorted way of living in the world, for God alone is the source of good and the guide for a good life. To follow what is created *instead of* the Creator is to cut off the created from the source of good and to establish rival gods, with all that such rivalry implies for violence and injustice. For this reason, Genesis 3:5 identifies the primordial sin as the desire to be "like God"—or, as others translate it, "like gods." Usurping the position of the one God leads directly to rivalry and the first murder, in Genesis 4. By chapter 6, the narrator ruefully reports that "the earth was filled with violence" (6:11). The prohibition of idolatry is an unavoidable and salutary corollary of ethical monotheism. If there is a good Creator God, then substituting the worship of created realities has serious consequences.

Idolatry critique, nevertheless, is easily turned toward violence; it is used to establish boundaries not merely between the true God and false gods but between us and them, between *us* who have worship sorted out properly and *you* idolaters who offend with every breath you take. But idolatry is a flexible and multivalent concept with a varied history, and its value can be determined only in its use. Is there a way of deploying idolatry critique that is not violent? Is there a way of distinguishing truth from falsehood and thus establishing protocols for the avoidance of idolatry that does not imply the coercion of others? Can idolatry critique be understood irenically as a way of blurring the boundaries between believers and nonbelievers by recognizing that we all worship? Can idolatry critique be deployed as a form of self-critique that blurs the boundaries between idolaters and nonidolaters by recognizing that we all worship badly?

In this chapter, I begin to develop a Christian theological conception of idolatry grounded in the biblical sources. I first explore the scriptural idea that humans are inherently worshiping creatures. In the second section, I explore some themes in biblical treatments of idolatry and show how they question some modern binaries: enchanted/disenchanted, religious/secular, believers/nonbelievers, worshipers/nonworshipers. The third section is an exploration of the proper and improper uses of material images in the Bible. In the fourth section, I spell out the consequences of idolatry in the domination of humans by gods of their own making. Finally, I explore how the Bible in places allows for a sympathetic understanding of the need for worship, and how the boundaries between idolaters and true believers are often blurred. The present chapter is not by any means meant to be an exhaustive treatment of the theme of idolatry in the Bible. It is also not meant to imply that there is one biblical approach to idolatry; there is a diversity of approaches in the Bible, and idolatry is a more significant theme for some authors and editors of canonical material than for others. The present chapter is meant, nevertheless, to provide a theological reading of biblical treatments of idolatry that can challenge the modern notion that we live in a secular age.

3.1. *Homo liturgicus*

We have examined Weber's basic conviction that human beings are meaning-seeking creatures whose quest leads them to the manufacture of gods to worship. As a Christian, Taylor does not share Weber's belief that all gods are of human making, but he does share the same basic anthropology that sees the human being as a seeker after some higher synthesis, what Taylor labels "fullness." For Taylor, God is real, but misrecognized by humans, whose devotion falls on all sorts of created things. This basic anthropology of the human being as a worshiping creature—*homo liturgicus*, to use James K. A. Smith's phrase—is profoundly biblical and is implicit in many treatments of idolatry in the Bible.

Smith's "Cultural Liturgies" series draws on Taylor's notion of "social imaginaries" to argue that

> liturgies—whether "sacred" or "secular"—shape and constitute our identities by forming our most fundamental desires and our most basic attunement to the world. In short, liturgies make us certain kinds of people,

and what defines us is what we *love*. They do this because we are the sorts of animals whose orientation to the world is shaped from the body up more than from the head down.[6]

What Smith calls "liturgies" are the ritual enactments of our ultimate loves in daily life, whether a church service or singing the national anthem, hand over heart. The search for meaning is not so much about what we *think* we are doing as about the images that order our world, either consciously or not. We are driven by pictures, stories, myths, and narratives more than by concepts. We are desiring creatures who are pulled toward many different created things; these are our loves, what gets us out of bed in the morning. We are "teleological creatures," as Smith says.[7] More than simply personal preferences, our desires are embedded in *social* imaginaries, communal stories and images that help to shape our loves. We develop pictures of what human flourishing would look like and what threatens human flourishing, and these pictures are inevitably communal because they picture an entire social world necessary for individual happiness.[8]

Smith goes beyond Taylor in labeling our ultimate loves that which we "worship." More than simply things to which we are attracted, our ultimate loves are those things to which we pledge allegiance, though not necessarily consciously. Worship implies some kind of ultimate loyalty; liturgies are "rituals of ultimate concern."[9] Unlike Taylor, Smith does not think that such rituals can be "only symbolic," whose "efficacy here is inner."[10] And, as in the block quote above, whether these kinds of worship are labeled "sacred" or "secular" matters little. Indeed, the attempt to separate "sacred" from "secular" often obscures the basic similarity in the way that all people's lives are ordered. We miss the similarities between what goes on in a cathedral and what goes on in a shopping mall when we try to separate them into "religious" and "secular" categories.[11] For this reason, Smith imports the term "worship" into Taylor's notion of social imaginaries, because it helpfully blurs the lines between "religious" and "social" life in the modern West. The term "worship" gets across the seriousness of the kind of loyalties that people still hold in a supposedly disenchanted world. Worship indicates that our loves are not simply reflected but are *shaped* by the kind of rituals in which we participate.[12] Worship is furthermore *exclusive*; loves that are ultimate are jealous, and they "want their particular vision of what really matters to supersede or trump all other competing practices."[13] This does not necessarily mean that each person has only one ultimate love; it is more the case that our various loyalties are in tension. As Weber says, the gods do not tolerate each other's presence, but war among themselves. It is worth noting that Weber's language of "gods" for our ultimate value commitments anticipates Smith's intuition that "religious" language is necessary to convey the ultimacy of the loyalties and devotions that even "secular" people find unavoidable.

In constructing his account of *homo liturgicus*, Smith relies primarily on Heidegger, Taylor, and his own phenomenological reading of the ubiquity of worship in contemporary society. Only after constructing a philosophical anthropology of humans as worshiping creatures does Smith turn to the Bible, when he begins to discuss the particularities of Christian worship.[14] If we examine the scriptures, however, we see that the anthropology of humans as *homo liturgicus* is already embedded in biblical critiques of idolatry. The recurrent biblical concern with idolatry is itself a recognition that the human person has a need to worship, a need that is commonly worked out in and through the created material world.[15]

The picture of humans as desiring creatures comes across clearly from the opening chapters of Genesis. In the first creation account in Genesis 1 (26, 28), good things are created by God, until humans are created and given dominion over these good things. Humans are created with hunger, but God provides for the satisfaction of that hunger. "God said, 'See, I have given you every plant yielding seed that is upon the face of all the earth, and every tree with seed in its fruit; you shall have them for food'" (1:29). In Genesis 2 (20–5), we learn that the humans are created with sexual desire, flesh calling out to flesh, and the man and the woman are created to cling to one another. In addition to desire for created things, it is implied that humans are created with a desire for God, because they are created in the image of God (1:26–7). Humans stand poised somewhere between God and the rest of creation. They desire created things, but those desires are satisfied by the free gift of God. As Alexander Schmemann writes, "All that exists is God's gift to man and it exists to make God known to man, to make man's life communion with God."[16] Desire for created things is part of God's good creation.

When this communion with God and with the rest of creation is shattered in Genesis 3, it again is worked through the mechanism of human desire. The Fall happens because "the woman saw that the tree was good for food, and that it was a delight to the eyes, and that the tree was to be desired to make one wise" (3:6). There is no indication that these desires as such are evil. The Fall comes about because the humans have sought to "reach out [their] hand and take" (3:22) rather than receive from the hand of God. Humans are created as receptive creatures receiving from the provision of God, but the original harmony of this creation is disrupted when they become grasping creatures who take what is not given to them.[17] The serpent promises that they will "be like God" (3:5) if they take and eat the fruit that has not been given to them. The text implies that the root of sin is the inordinate desire for created things and the simultaneous usurpation of God's position. Desire itself, however, is not evil, but a basic anthropological datum. People desire created things, and that desire is entwined with their desire for communion with God. That desire is capable of being distorted, however, and desire for God can be supplanted by or confused with desire for created things. The path is open for the proper worship of God to be displaced by the worship of creation—idolatry, in other words.

The book of Wisdom explains idolatry in terms of this common human tendency to confuse creator and creation. God the creator is present in God's creation: "For your immortal spirit is in all things" (12:1). People should be able to look through created things and see the one who created them:

> If through delight in the beauty of these things people assumed them to be gods, let them know how much better than these is their Lord, for the author of beauty created them. And if people were amazed at their power and working, let them perceive from them how much more powerful is the one who formed them. For from the greatness and beauty of created things comes a corresponding perception of their Creator. (13:3–5)

Unfortunately, people deify the creation, and thus show their ignorance. The text goes on to condemn in harsh language the foolishness of idolatry: praying to a lifeless and helpless bit of wood (13:10–9), relying on a piece of wood much more fragile than one's wooden boat to ensure a safe journey on the sea (14:1–4), honoring as a god the image of a mere mortal human being (14:15–7). The result is all manner of violence and debauchery and oppression: "For the worship of idols not to be named is the beginning and cause and end of every evil" (14:27). But before condemning idolatry in this way, the text considers a more sympathetic take: "Yet these people are little to be blamed, for perhaps they go astray while seeking God and desiring to find him. For while they live among his works, they keep searching, and they trust in what they see, because the things that are seen are beautiful" (13:6–7). Idolatry is common because of the basic human condition of living among beautiful things. The existence of beautiful things gives people enough intimation of the existence of God to search for God. But precisely because the existence of God is evident through the beautiful things that God created, there is also a tendency to confuse God with the beautiful things themselves. The basic dynamic of desire found in the creation and Fall account of Genesis is found here as well.[18] Desire for God is intertwined with desire for created things, and the two are easily confounded, with dire consequences. Unlike the developmental account of religion on which Weber and Taylor rely, from primitive animism to a "higher" monotheism, here we find a degenerative account, from the worship of YHWH to the scattered worship of divinity in myriad created things.

The same theme is carried through in the New Testament. As Stephen Fowl notes, "In many respects Romans 1:18–32 offers a condensed version of Wisdom's much longer discussion."[19] The passage reads, in part:

> For the wrath of God is revealed from heaven against all ungodliness and wickedness of those who by their wickedness suppress the truth. For what can be known about God is plain to them, because God has shown it to them. Ever since the creation of the world his eternal power and divine nature, invisible though they are, have been understood and seen through the things he has made. So they are without excuse; for though they knew God, they did not honor him as God or give thanks to him, but they became futile in their thinking, and their senseless minds were darkened. Claiming to be wise, they became fools; and they exchanged the glory of the immortal God for images resembling a mortal human being or birds or four-footed animals or reptiles.
>
> Therefore God gave them up in the lusts of their hearts to impurity, to the degrading of their bodies among themselves, because they exchanged the truth about God for a lie and worshipped and served the creature rather than the Creator, who is blessed for ever! Amen. (Rom. 1:18–25)

Paul continues on to spell out the manifestations and consequences of idolatry[20] in all manner of immorality, violence, and wickedness (1:26–32). The root cause of idolatry, as in Wisdom, is the failure to enter into communion with God through God's creation. The failure, however, is not simply a metaphysical error but is more a failure to give honor and worship to God, "for though they knew God, they did not honor him as God or give thanks to him." They became lost in images reflecting aspects of the creation, and they "worshipped and served the creature rather than the Creator."

Fowl notes that both of these passages are directed against "nonbelievers," that is, non-Jews and non-Christians, respectively. For this reason, Fowl thinks they will be of limited use for understanding the idolatry of believers. In the case of Romans, Fowl argues, Paul emphasizes that being baptized transfers a person's allegiance from the realm of sin to the reign of Christ:

> Indeed, the entire point of the argument in 6:1–14 is that believers have left the realm of Sin behind. Although they may and will transgress from time to time, they and their situation cannot be characterized in the same way Paul characterizes the pagan world in chapter 1. Although it is the case that believers might supplant worship of the creator for worship of the creature, the reasons for this would have to be different from those that characterize pagans outside of Christ. Rather than a failure to know God at all, the idolatry of believers reflects a failure of attention and a failure to embody those things entailed in belief in the God of Jesus Christ.[21]

Although clearly Paul thinks that Christ is the remedy for sin, I think that Fowl exaggerates the gap between the idolatry of believers and nonbelievers. For Fowl, the difference begins with the fact that Christians know God and pagans don't. But Paul says of the pagans, "[F]or though they knew God, they did not honor him as God or give thanks to him" (Rom. 1:21). The problem is less about knowledge than about allegiance. The fact that Christians claim to "know" that Jesus is Lord does not solve the basic human tendency to become distracted by the things of the world and worship and serve creatures rather than the Creator.

It is not hard to find evidence that the "believers" are as spontaneously idolatrous as the "nonbelievers." The narrator of the second book of Kings, for example, explains the Assyrian conquest of Israel as punishment for worshiping other gods and following the customs of the peoples the Israelites had conquered:

> The people of Israel secretly did things that were not right against the Lord their God. They built for themselves high places at all their towns, from watch-tower to fortified city; they set up for themselves pillars and sacred poles on every high hill and under every green tree; there they made offerings on all the high places, as the nations did whom the Lord carried away before them. They did wicked things, provoking the Lord to anger; they served idols, of which the Lord had said to them, "You shall not do this." (II Kings 17:9–12)

The Israelites' error was not metaphysical. They do not appear to have denied the existence of the LORD. They heard the word of the LORD forbidding them to serve idols, which is why they did what they did "secretly" (17:9). But their need to worship drives them to worship all sorts of things and in all sorts of places, "on every high hill and under every green tree."

The passage continues on to say that the prophets warned them, but "[t]hey would not listen but were stubborn, as their ancestors had been, who did not believe in the Lord their God. They despised his statutes, and his covenant that he made with their ancestors, and the warnings that he gave them. They went after false idols and became false; they followed the nations that were around them, concerning whom the Lord had commanded them that they should not do as they did" (II Kings 17:14–5). The passage says both that their ancestors "did not believe in" the LORD and that they made a covenant with the LORD. Here again their failure does not seem to be a metaphysical denial of the existence of the LORD but rather a stubborn refusal of their exclusive loyalty to the God of Israel. The narrator continues listing their deviations: they made cast images of two calves and a sacred pole, they worshiped "all the host of heaven," they served Baal, and they used divination and augury (17:16–7). The Israelites were exiled as punishment, but the people dwelling in the land continued to worship promiscuously: "So they worshiped the LORD but also served their own gods" (17:33; also 17:41).

The urgent need manifested in the episode of the Golden Calf (Ex. 32) for something to worship is matched by the pervasiveness of idolatry among the people of God. Isaiah 2 announces that the house of Jacob is "full of diviners from the east and of soothsayers like the Philistines" (2:6); "Their land is filled with idols; they bow down to the work of their hands" (2:8). Jeremiah (25:4–7) complains that the warnings of the prophets against serving and worshiping other gods have not been heeded. Tobit (1:5–6) declares that all his kindred and ancestral house sacrificed to King Jeroboam's calf, but Tobit alone went to Jerusalem to offer proper sacrifice to the LORD.[22] The frequency of idolatry among the Israelites is hardly different from the regularity of idolatry among the nations (see Jer. 10, for example). And given the explanation of the origins of idolatry in both Wisdom and Romans, we should not be surprised. The ubiquity of idolatry is a corollary of the ubiquity of worship, the attraction of the human person as desiring creature to the beautiful things of the creation. Worship, in this sense, is simply a condition of being human, a desiring, teleological creature. We are meant to see through the beautiful things to the Creator of them all; this, in the biblical view, is true worship. But the manifestation of God in creation lends itself to the confusion of God with creation, the root of idolatry. Some such anthropology of the human person as *Homo liturgicus* is necessary to explain the sheer ubiquity of worship—including false worship—in the Bible, as well as the sheer ubiquity of worship in contemporary society, as we will discuss in subsequent chapters.

3.2. Breaking Down Binaries

One potential problem with seeing worship and idolatry as ubiquitous is that the concepts will cease to pick out anything in particular. If worship is everywhere, then it is nowhere. Fowl worries that "idolatry" in the hands of Tertullian and some modern commentators becomes just another name for sin.[23] For Brian Rosner, this is both the strength and the weakness of an expansive concept of idolatry: it can be applied to almost anything, but for that very reason it lacks explanatory power. It does not do justice to the complexity and subtlety of the Bible's treatment of the many different forms of sin.[24] So Rosner, in his book *Greed as Idolatry,* insists that the Pauline contention in Colossians 3:5 and Ephesians 5:5 that greed is idolatry is a metaphor. He thinks that understanding greed as idolatry helps us to resist the ways in which money can distract us from devotion to God. But he insists that it is only a metaphor in order to keep the concept of idolatry from becoming too expansive and too general.

According to Rosner, "The most obvious comment about the utterance 'greed is idolatry' is that it is a metaphor: greed is not literally idolatry. The greedy do not bow down before their possessions or set up altars to them."[25] The literal sense of idolatry to which Rosner appeals here appears to be restricted to worshiping divine beings, bowing down to or setting up altars to them. We will need a settled, literal definition of idolatry and another of greed if we are to have a metaphor, for " 'man is a wolf,' for example, relies on both the speaker and the hearer 'having a body of shared knowledge or assumptions about the nature of men and the nature of wolves.' "[26] For a metaphor to work, there must be some overlap between the attributes of the two terms—both men and wolves are cruel and cunning, for example—but in a metaphor they will share only a few attributes. The point of a metaphor, according to Rosner, is to put together two incongruous things to shock us into a new way of thinking.[27]

In order to see greed and idolatry as two incongruous things, and thus to maintain the boundary between a metaphorical and a literal understanding of the Pauline dictum, Rosner needs a definition of idolatry that highlights its "religious" aspect, as opposed to greed, which deals with the "secular" matters of money and possessions. Bowing down and building altars are properly religious gestures, and they are not performed as a manifestation of greed. Rosner considers greed an "implicit religion," a category prevalent in some circles of sociology since the 1980s. Implicit religions are those things like sports fanaticism, nationalism, and politics that are "rather like but not quite like religion, or while they may not appear to be religion on the surface, they reveal themselves to be so on closer inspection."[28] Rosner rejects this idea, saying that such things are not "'objectively religious,'" in scare quotes, without saying what "objectively religious" means. The most that can be said, Rosner allows, is that greed "resembles religion in certain ways."[29] The crucial factor in separating religion from nonreligion is self-understanding, that is, practitioners' own conviction that they either are or are not religious. Greed cannot be said to be a religion, because the greedy lack "religious self-understanding,"[30] that is, the *belief* that greed is a religion.

Rosner is trying to be precise in building bridges between greed and idolatry. In an attempt to keep the concept of idolatry from getting too expansive, however, he feels obliged to reinforce a set of binaries: metaphorical/literal, religious/secular, idolaters/nonidolaters, belief/behavior. I do not think the biblical text supports these binaries, and in the end I don't think Rosner is sure either. He delays giving a formal definition of idolatry until chapter 9 of his book, and then he relies heavily on Moshe Halbertal's and Avishai Margalit's book on idolatry. While acknowledging that "Halbertal and Margalit are adamant that idolatry is too complex a notion to be distilled in a single definition," Rosner nonetheless forges ahead to give his own definition: "*idolatry is an attack on God's exclusive right to our love and trust.*"[31] The problem with this definition is that it contradicts his earlier statement of the literal sense of idolatry as meaning worship by bowing down or setting up altars to gods. Rosner has ended up with as broad a definition of idolatry as those he criticized for being too expansive. Under this definition, the Pauline idea of greed as idolatry is not a metaphor at all. If greed is defined as Rosner defines it—"*the greedy are those with a strong desire to acquire and keep for themselves more and more money and possessions, because they love, trust, and obey wealth rather than God*"[32]—then greed is literally, not metaphorically, "*an attack on God's exclusive right to our love and trust.*"

Maintaining the distinction between a literal and a metaphorical use of "idolatry" requires a fairly tightly circumscribed term. But the term does not appear in the Old Testament at all, and appears only sparingly in the New. We who assume that the Old Testament[33] is filled with accusations of idolatry are surprised to find that there is no single word in the Old Testament that corresponds. The English word comes from the Greek term *eidōlolatria*, a combination of *eidōlon* (image) and *latria* (worship). The Pauline literature uses the word *eidōlolatria* (e.g., I Cor. 10:14; Col. 3:5), but it does not appear in the Greek version of the Old Testament, with which Paul was familiar. The Septuagint employs the word *eidōlon*, but uses it to translate many different Hebrew terms. In the Septuagint Pentateuch, for example, *eidōlon* is not used in the episode of the Golden Calf—often considered the quintessential example of idolatry—but it is used elsewhere, and for seven different Hebrew expressions. In the Septuagint as a whole, sometimes the term *eidōlon* is used for Hebrew terms such as *pesel* and *tselem* (e.g., Is. 44:10–20; Dan. 3:1) that correspond fairly closely to the root meaning of *eidōlon* as "image" or "likeness," though *tselem* can also mean "shadow," an imperfect likeness, and it is rendered "statue" in many translations of Daniel. Sometimes the plural *eidōlois* is used to translate *elohim*, which simply means "gods" (e.g., I Kings 11:8). Sometimes *eidōlois* is used for *teraphim*, cultic objects used in divination.[34] Sometimes *eidōlois* translates *hevel* (e.g., Deut. 32:21) which means "vapor" or "breath" and indicates the insubstantiality and nothingness of idols. Sometimes *eidōlois* is used to translate *gillulim* (e.g., Lev. 26:30), a strongly pejorative term meaning "filth," "dung," "defilement."[35] I could continue with more examples; both the Greek *eidōlon* and the English "idol" are used to translate multiple Hebrew words. One Bible dictionary in English lists eighteen different Hebrew words in the Old Testament that are rendered by "idol."[36]

The complexity of the concept of idolatry in the Old Testament, however, does not mean it is not important. To the contrary, the prohibition on worshiping other gods is the very first of the Ten Commandments: "I am the Lord your God, who brought you out of the land of Egypt, out of the house of slavery; you shall have no other gods before me" (Ex. 20:2–3). The complexity of the concept does give clues, however, as to why idolatry could come to be identified with more than the explicit worship of Baal and other named gods. We will be able to understand how idolatry comes to have such an expansive meaning only if we can see that biblical texts are concerned with more than metaphysical belief in other gods. The

prohibition on images not only of false gods but of the true God as well
indicates that the biblical texts are concerned with the proper disposition
and behavior of people toward both God and creation, with making sure
that the Creator is not confused with or improperly mixed up in material
creation. What comes to be called "idolatry" goes beyond the explicit worship of deities that are falsely believed to exist and has to do with the entirety of human attitudes and practices with regard to created realities. In
the Bible, the boundaries we would construct between belief and behavior,
religion and secular life, are blurred. The command to follow the LORD
alone was to be worked out in all areas of the life of the community, not
simply worship on the Sabbath.

There is no question that the Old Testament is concerned with drawing
boundaries between the worship of the God of Abraham, Isaac, and Jacob
on the one hand, and the worship of the gods of the surrounding peoples
on the other hand. The Golden Calf, for example, can be read as a reference
to the worship of other gods; in Egypt, whence the Israelites had recently
been liberated according to the Exodus narrative, there were popular cults
of gods—Ptah, Re, Osiris, and Apis—who appeared in the shape of a bull.
The text seems to warn of the sin of syncretism, though there is some ambiguity whether the "gods" (*elohim*) of Exodus 32:8—"These are your gods,
O Israel, who brought you up out of the land of Egypt!"— refers to pagan
deities or the representation of YHWH by a pagan image.[37] In either case,
the text draws boundaries between YHWH and false gods, and drawing
boundaries between gods could result in violence. The Golden Calf is frequently invoked today, such as by Pope Francis, to condemn ideologies of
exclusion and violence. If one reads to the end of the story in Exodus 32,
however, it is Moses's violence in response to the Golden Calf that is most
shocking:

Moses stood in the gate of the camp, and said, "Who is on the LORD's side?
Come to me!" And all the sons of Levi gathered around him. He said to
them, "Thus says the LORD, the God of Israel, 'Put your sword on your side,
each of you! Go back and forth from gate to gate throughout the camp, and
each of you kill your brother, your friend, and your neighbor.'" The sons
of Levi did as Moses commanded, and about three thousand of the people
fell on that day. Moses said, "Today you have ordained yourselves for the
service of the LORD, each one at the cost of a son or a brother, and so have
brought a blessing on yourselves this day." (Ex. 32:26–9)

A few verses later we are told "Then the LORD sent a plague on the people, because they made the calf" (32:35), in case the slaughter of three thousand did not get the point across.

How is a modern reader—especially one who regards this text as sacred scripture—supposed to make sense of this extreme reaction? Christians and Jews have many different hermeneutical strategies for rejecting the violence of such passages: reading them allegorically, situating them in their historical context, attributing the violence to human authorship, seeing the scriptures as a long pedagogy in which such passages represent a primitive stage, and so on. But even if the violence can be separated from the ban on idolatry, how can we make sense of such a strong condemnation of those who follow other gods? We now consider religious liberty to be one of the signal achievements of modernity. After centuries of warning that freedom of belief leads to the sin of "indifferentism," the Catholic Church embraced the principle of religious liberty in *Dignitatis humanae*, one of the crowning documents of Vatican II. How can the condemnation of idolatry be reconciled with the freedom of each human being to worship according to their own conscience?

We must first be clear that *Dignitatis humanae* rejected any form of coercion of religious belief, but did not thereby declare that all gods are equal. The document holds to the truth of God revealed in Christ.[38] When looking at the biblical accounts of idolatry, however, we are addressing a different issue from what we call "religious belief." What we modern Westerners call "religion" was not separable from "secular" realities like politics and economics in Israelite thought and practice. And belief as a mental process of assent to certain metaphysical doctrines about God or gods was not the primary issue in the condemnation of idolatry. We moderns tend to think that criticizing each other's politics and economics is fair game, but criticizing another's religion is off limits. Politics and economics are public matters that bear on everyone in concrete, material, bodily ways. Religion, on the other hand, is interior and private. Religious belief goes on between one's ears, and although that belief often results in bodily practices, these take place in semi-private associations on weekends, with which coercive laws must, as far as possible, not interfere. Religious belief should be tolerated, no matter how wacky, because, as Thomas Jefferson put it, "it does me no injury for my neighbour to say there are twenty gods, or no god. It neither picks my pocket nor breaks my leg."[39] The divide between belief and behavior is clear in Jefferson's dictum.

This is far from the dominant biblical view. The Bible consistently confounds modern belief/behavior and religious/secular binaries. Consider the famous contest in I Kings 18 between Elijah and the prophets of Baal. In the middle of a three-year drought, the desperate Israelite people and their king Ahab have been vacillating between the worship of YHWH and the cult of Baal. Ahab's queen, Jezebel, has encouraged the worship of Baal and Asherah and has had the Yahwist prophets killed. Elijah alone remains. Before the gathered Israelites at Mount Carmel, he challenges 450 prophets of Baal to call down fire from heaven on a bull prepared on an altar. The prophets beseech Baal all day long, to no avail. Elijah then calls upon the LORD, who sends fire from heaven to consume Elijah's bull. The spectacle convinces the Israelites that the LORD is the true God. Elijah orders all the prophets of Baal killed. Then the drought breaks.

Though the text does not use the language of idols or idolatry, the issue here is straightforwardly the worship of other gods. The reader is meant to cheer the Israelite God's triumph over the false gods. The modern reader, however, is appalled by the intolerance and violence. As Timothy Gorringe puts it, channeling the modern reader, "What Elijah ought to have done was set up a dialogue programme and affirmed the best in the Ba'al religion seeing what he, as a Yahwist, could learn from it. Why take this absolutist way?"[40]

To answer this question, we need to see that there is much more going on in this text than a contest over "religious belief." The rival gods represent two rival systems of rule and rival systems of property. As Gorringe points out, the name Baal means "owner." The Baalist kings had absolute power, and property was an alienable commodity under Canaanite law. For the Israelites, by contrast, the king was subject to the monarchy of God, and property was inalienable. Each family had their *nachalah*, their share of property.[41] Ahab violates this arrangement. He wants Naboth's vineyard to extend his palace garden, but Naboth refuses to sell, which would be a violation of Israelite law: "The LORD forbid that I should give you my ancestral inheritance" (I Kings 21:3). Jezebel, the chief promoter of the cult of Baal, is indignant that some yokel is standing in the way of the king. She has Naboth killed and presents his vineyard to Ahab. The LORD is displeased, and sends Elijah to Ahab: "Thus says the LORD: Have you killed, and also taken possession?" (21:19). Elijah pronounces judgment and doom on the house of Ahab: "Indeed, there was no one like Ahab, who sold himself to do what was evil in the sight of the Lord, urged on by his wife Jezebel. He acted most abominably in going after idols, as the Amorites had done, whom the Lord drove out before the Israelites" (21:25–6).

The contest between the LORD and Baal is not simply about what we would call "religious belief," but is also about what we would call "economics" and "politics." In the biblical text, there are no such distinctions. The text is simply about the God of life versus the gods that kill and take possession, which is the hallmark of idolatry. The text needs to be read in light of tensions in the ninth century BC between a traditional peasant tribal culture and an urbanized elite influenced by Baalism. Such a historical reading helps us to avoid the anachronism of seeing the issue of idolatry as limited to "religious belief," but it is more than an exercise in getting the history right. For Gorringe, drawing on the work of Ton Veerkamp, the issue of idolatry is the key to assessing our current economic system because the fundamental justification of ownership rights in any society is a theological question. There is always a "god" in this sense, whether or not people express explicit belief in the existence of such a being:[42] "Every generation will be confronted with its own Ba'als, their own strange gods, who grab power over them and seek to devour them."[43] For Gorringe, as for Pope Francis, our market economy is such a strange god, a god of death opposed to the true God of life.

One might object at this point that "god" is being used metaphorically here, whereas the text of I Kings refers to actual belief in the existence of gods. This objection is correct; the biblical text is clearly using "gods" differently than are Gorringe and Veerkamp. But the wider point—that idolatry is not just a "religious" matter—is the viewpoint of the biblical text itself and not a retrospective eisegesis.[44] Indeed, treating the issue as one of "religious belief" is anachronistic, because it imposes modern categories on an ancient text. When the Pauline letters use the term "idolatry" (*eidōlolatria*), it can apply nonmetaphorically to greed because the boundary between "religion" and "economics" had yet to be constructed. We tend to think that economic systems, like capitalism or Marxism, can be critiqued, but religions are to be tolerated and accepted. But the difference on display in I Kings is not between religion and economics; it is between a good way of life and a lousy one.

The work of Mark S. Smith is helpful in this regard, because he argues that the exclusivity of Israelite monotheism was a response to the imperialism suffered at the hands of the Assyrians and the Babylonians. In its early stages, argues Smith, there was a considerable degree of "translatability" in Israelite thought, that is, the recognition of the deities of other cultures as was common in the ancient Near East.[45] Assyrian and Babylonian empire-building, however, included a kind of theological imperialism, whereby the chief god—Assur for the Assyrians, Marduk for the Babylonians—subsumed the functions of other gods. In response, the Israelites asserted the omnipotence and independence of YHWH, who is not one of the subordinate gods but the one God to whom the Israelites owed worship. Again, "religion" and "politics" are not two distinct matters. In Deuteronomy, written during the Assyrian Empire, the existence of other gods is not necessarily denied, but exclusive loyalty to YHWH is commanded. The text calls for violence against the Canaanites and their gods, but the Canaanite nations are in actuality long past. The polemic is meant to invoke not violence against others but resistance to empire; idolatry critique is meant to keep the Israelites from following the gods of the empire.[46] Violence, argues Smith, "is not a function of theism, whether polytheism or monotheism; it is a function of power and the capacity to wield it."[47] This does not by any means indicate that the Israelites were innocent of violence; it does mean that idolatry critique, especially from the point of view of a people subjected to empire, is not inherently violent but can be used as resistance against violence.

Walter Brueggemann's study of Israelite liturgy confirms the connection between idolatry critique and resistance to oppression. For Brueggemann, liturgy is not merely a religious rite but a constitutive, world-making activity. Reality is socially constructed, in the sense that the stories that are enacted liturgically shape the way we perceive and interact with the world.[48] Brueggemann's notion of social construction is close to Taylor's "social imaginary," which I discussed in the previous chapter: there is a mostly unarticulated set of background assumptions in a culture that shape reality by imagining it to be a certain way. Brueggemann, however, emphasizes bodily ritual action as that which creates and perpetuates reality, and he does not restrict "liturgy" to what happens within a temple or church. The liturgy of the temple or church is already a political act, and politics has its own liturgies that attempt to form the world in a certain way.[49] Brueggemann emphasizes the multiplicity of such world-making liturgies on offer in any given culture. According to Brueggemann, there are a lot of liturgies out there that create different worlds; the important question is which one is true.[50]

For Brueggemann, the praise of God enacted in true liturgy is not a response to a world already established and fixed but is rather a participation in the ongoing building of the world which is decreed by God.[51] True liturgy, in other words, has a time-filled and eschatological dimension. As he examines Israelite liturgy, however, Brueggemann notes how liturgy can be co-opted by the powerful as a means of reinforcing the status quo, as a mere hallowing of the way things are, giving divine sanction to the way things have already been arranged to the benefit of the few. He regards such liturgies of the status quo as idolatrous because he defines idolatry as the worship of "a god who has no history and will not act."[52] The status quo is reinforced by the worship of gods who do nothing, gods who will not disturb or critique or change the way things are. Idols do not act because they are nothing; they are *hevel*, mere vapor, emptiness. As Jeremiah 10:3–5 makes clear:

> For the customs of the peoples are false: a tree from the forest is cut down, and worked with an ax by the hands of an artisan; people deck it with silver and gold; they fasten it with hammer and nails so that it cannot move. Their idols are like scarecrows in a cucumber field, and they cannot speak; they have to be carried, for they cannot walk. Do not be afraid of them, for they cannot do evil, nor is it in them to do good.

Idols are gods who cannot move, cannot speak, cannot walk, cannot act, and cannot have any effect on the status quo.

The injustice that Jeremiah confronts among the Israelites in Jerusalem is a mixture of the worship of gods with other names (7:9, 7:18) and the explicit worship of the LORD without its having any positive effect (7:4, 8:8). According to Brueggemann, the ideology Jeremiah encountered in Jerusalem as the invasion of the Babylonians drew near was "a royal-political-economic system which said 'peace, peace' when there was no peace (6:14, 8:11). The idolatry he had to meet was the self-deceiving worship of an indifferent god who provided cover, security, and rationalization for covenant breakers (7:8–11)."[53] For Jeremiah, breaking the covenant was not simply a matter of offering prayers to a god with the wrong name. It was a matter of not acting justly with one another, oppressing the alien, the orphan, and the widow (7:5), stealing, murdering, committing adultery (7:8), oppressing the poor, and being deceitful (9:4–6).

For Second Isaiah, writing after the Babylonian conquest, breaking the covenant was the temptation to give in to the seductions of the empire and its inert gods. The prophet's mockery of idolatry is not "religious intolerance" in modern terms, not the simple chauvinism of one who says *My religion is right, and yours is stupid*. The critique of idolatry in Second Isaiah can be understood only against the political context of the exile. The gods of human creation are inert and cannot rescue the people from their bondage:

All who make idols are nothing, and the things they delight in do not profit; their witnesses neither see nor know. And so they will be put to shame. Who would fashion a god or cast an image that can do no good? Look, all its devotees shall be put to shame; the artisans too are merely human. . . . The carpenter stretches a line, marks it out with a stylus, fashions it with planes, and marks it with a compass; he makes it in human form, with human beauty, to be set up in a shrine. He cuts down cedars or chooses a holm tree or an oak and lets it grow strong among the trees of the forest. He plants a cedar and the rain nourishes it. Then it can be used as fuel. Part of it he takes and warms himself; he kindles a fire and bakes bread. Then he makes a god and worships it, makes it a carved image and bows down before it. Half of it he burns in the fire; over this half he roasts meat, eats it, and is satisfied. He also warms himself and says, "Ah, I am warm, I can feel the fire!" The rest of it he makes into a god, his idol, bows down to it, and worships it; he prays to it and says, "Save me, for you are my god!" They do not know, nor do they comprehend; for their eyes are shut, so that they cannot see, and their minds as well, so that they cannot understand. No one considers, nor is there knowledge or discernment to say, "Half of it I burned in the fire; I also baked bread on its coals, I roasted meat and have eaten. Now shall I make the rest of it an abomination? Shall I fall down before a block of wood?" (Is. 44:9–11, 13–9)

The inert muteness of wooden gods (46:7) is contrasted with the power of the true God's word: "[S]o shall my word be that goes out from my mouth; it shall not return to me empty, but it shall accomplish that which I purpose" (55:11). God's purpose in Second Isaiah is a new exodus (43), not salvation in the next world but deliverance from bondage in this one. Both Jeremiah and Second Isaiah oppose false worship to a true liturgy, a true form of world-making that participates in the activity of the living God. Writes Brueggemann, "Both Jeremiah and Second Isaiah by their poetry invite Israel *to depart* the false world of royal-imperial construction and *to enter* the world of Yahweh, a world of grief embraced and new possibility enacted."[54]

If in the Old Testament idolatry is not simply a matter of worshiping gods with other names, and if idolatry is not purely a matter of "religious" belief, then it becomes possible to extend the notion of idolatry to the modern context. Brueggemann, writing in the United States in the late 1980s, believes that a nation in which the explicit worship of the God of the

Bible still predominates is in fact in a similar situation to that of Jeremiah's Jerusalem: we worship a false, inert god that justifies the status quo, in our case one of consumerism and the arms race and oppression of the poor and marginalized. We have lost the memory of a God who liberates. "The outcome, surely, is an idol, an immobilizing transcendence, a god so secure, so established, so allied with the American dream that there is no space left for anguish, ambiguity, uncertainty, hurt beyond guilt."[55] Brueggemann blames the lack of true worship on both the religious right, with its fearful support for American militarism, and the religious left, with its excessive self-confidence in its own problem-solving capacity. "I submit that our pastoral situation is precisely one of idolatry—of a god who has everything settled, has sanctioned the proper positions, and has sorted everyone out."[56]

The main point that we should note from this is that idolatry in the Old Testament is not primarily a matter of belief alone but of behavior. The key question underlying the matter of idolatry is not what people believe about the metaphysical status of gods but how people organize their lives and loves around what they worship. Idolatry is primarily a matter not of error but of betrayal. Indeed, the metaphysical status of other gods in the biblical text is murky; it is not always clear that the command to worship God alone necessarily entails the denial of the existence of other gods. Exodus 15:11, for example, asks, "Who is like you, O LORD, among the gods?" Many scholars see a lingering henotheism or monolatry in some strata of the Old Testament, that is, the recognition that other gods may exist, but there is only one that the faithful of Israel should worship. Jan Assmann goes so far as to argue that the ban on idolatry is based in a kind of jealousy that presupposes the existence of other gods. God can be jealous only, Assmann contends, if there exist other potential objects of love and worship. Jealousy is a characteristic of monolatry, not monotheism, so the Bible—at least in its early material—must presuppose the existence of other gods. Only in the later writings, such as Second Isaiah, is the Bible strictly monotheistic.[57]

I don't think that Assmann is right to claim that monolatry is a logical consequence of God's jealousy. If "jealousy" simply means that God does not want people to worship other gods, it does not follow that God or the authors of the biblical texts must necessarily think that such gods are real. God's jealousy could just as easily be provoked by the worship of nonexistent gods. Halbertal and Margalit take a more sensible approach, it seems to me, to the presence of monolatry or henotheism in the Bible. They point to passages like Psalm 82:1, which declares, "God has taken his place in the divine council;

in the midst of the gods he holds judgment." Such material points to henotheism rather than monotheism, but Halbertal and Margalit point out that
the metaphysical gap between the two is perhaps not so great, since there
are versions of monotheism that make room for a host of subordinate divine
beings that accompany the one high God, as a king or queen is surrounded
by a court.[58] Regardless of whether the existence of other gods is affirmed or
denied, however, Halbertal and Margalit argue that idolatry in the Bible is
not primarily identified with the cognitive error of believing that other gods
exist. Even where the Bible appears to believe that a cognitive error has been
made, the error is not the sin itself but only the condition for the possibility
of the sin, which is the worship of another god.[59] The main difficulty with
idolatry is not metaphysical error but disloyalty. Idolatry is not primarily
stupidity but betrayal. To be clear, this does not mean that beliefs are irrelevant. It means rather that belief and behavior are inseparable, such that what
people actually believe is more accurately reflected by what they do than by
what they claim to believe.

The importance of loyalty to God in the Old Testament is based on the
personal relationship that God has established with the Israelites. This God
is not a metaphysical abstraction but the God of Abraham, Isaac, and Jacob,
who has brought the Israelites out of slavery in Egypt. The Decalogue begins
with God reminding the Israelites of God's saving action; the ban on idolatry flows directly from that event: "I am the Lord your God, who brought
you out of the land of Egypt, out of the house of slavery; you shall have
no other gods before me" (Ex. 20:2–3). As Brueggemann has emphasized,
YHWH is an active God, a God who is present in history to shape events according to a liberating plan. Idols are inert, inactive. Halbertal and Margalit
concur: "The denunciation of idolatry in the Bible is often accompanied
by the expression 'other gods that you have not known.' In other words,
what is lacking between those divinities and Israel is 'knowledge,' yedi'ah,
a term used to denote a personal and intimate relationship."[60] YHWH is a
personal God who interacts in history with the Israelites and requires re-
membrance of that history and that relationship. Idolatry is a form of for-
getfulness, of fickleness and disloyalty.

Just as "knowledge" is used as a euphemism for sexual relations (e.g.,
Gen. 4:1), so the primary image the prophets use for idolatry is unfaithful-
ness between husband and wife. God orders Hosea (1:2) to marry a "wife of
whoredom" to symbolize the relationship between God and Israel, which
is constantly whoring after other gods. Ezekiel (16) and Jeremiah (2:1–3:5)

develop the same basic metaphor, often with erotic detail.[61] For Ezekiel (16:34), Israel's idolatry is more like nymphomania than prostitution, for she did not even accept payment. As Halbertal and Margalit point out, the metaphor depends on a quite anthropomorphic portrayal of God; although anthropomorphism is often frowned upon because of its association with idolatry, in the scriptures anthropomorphism is often a basis for idolatry critique. It is the personal relationship between God and human beings that gives idolatry its power to offend. What distinguishes YHWH from other gods is not being more abstract than they are.[62] On the contrary, what distinguishes the God of the Bible is precisely the personal relationship in history that God establishes with the Israelites. At the same time, however, God does not act as humans act. Though an adulterous wife is to be put to death according to the law governing human relations, God acts at variance from human law by continually taking Israel back, despite the people's infidelity. God will remember the covenant made with the Israelites even when they have forgotten, and they will remember when God has forgiven them (Ezek. 16:60–3).

Another important anthropomorphic image of God in the Bible is that of God as king. Just as disloyalty within the marital relationship is used as a metaphor for idolatry, so disloyalty within a political framework marks idolatry as well (e.g., I Sam. 15:22–3). Not only is God frequently described as king (e.g., Ps. 93, 95–9), but the covenants God makes with the Israelites are thought to be modeled after agreements between kings and their vassals in the ancient Near East. The connection between idolatry and kingship was an obvious one to the biblical writers, not only because God was king but because the kings of the surrounding nations were regarded as gods. This is clearly the case in Egypt, where the pharaohs themselves were divinized, as would the Roman emperors later be. In Mesopotamia, the kings were the gods' representatives on earth, and sometimes their incarnation.[63] The worship of other nations' gods was thus intimately linked with political loyalties, and the attribution of godly qualities to earthly kings was seen in Israel as a usurpation of the true God's kingship. Ezekiel (28:1–2, 7) addresses the word of the LORD to the prince of Tyre:

> Because your heart is proud and you have said, 'I am a god; I sit in the seat of the gods, in the heart of the seas,' yet you are but a mortal, and no god, though you compare your mind with the mind of a god. . . . I will bring strangers against you, the most terrible of the nations; they shall draw their swords against the beauty of your wisdom and defile your splendor.

In the book of Isaiah, the LORD similarly strikes down the pretensions of those foreign kings who set themselves up as gods. The Babylonian king, the "Day Star" who announces, "I will ascend to heaven; I will raise my throne above the stars of God" (14:12–3), is struck low by God's mighty power. The Assyrian king Sennacherib proclaims the superiority of his might over the gods of other nations, including the Holy One of Israel, boasting, "I dried up with the sole of my foot all the streams of Egypt" (37:25), only to be vanquished by the LORD. The true God is the only king who is a deity, and the only God who is a king.[64]

In all these cases, the idolatrous elevation of mere mortals to the status of gods is associated with economic and political oppression. In Ezekiel, the prince of Tyre has become proud by amassing great wealth through trade (28:5), and the trade of the king of Tyre is associated with violence and injustice: "In the abundance of your trade you were filled with violence, and you sinned. . . . By the multitude of your iniquities, in the unrighteousness of your trade, you profaned your sanctuaries" (28:16, 18). Isaiah foresees the day when the king of Babylon, "who made the world like a desert and overthrew its cities" (14:17), will be greeted with the taunt "How the oppressor has ceased!" (14:3). Sennacherib, heir to "the kings of Assyria [who] have laid waste all the nations and their lands" (37:18), meets a similar defeat at the hands of the living God.

It is not only or even principally the Egyptians', Babylonians', and Assyrians' rulers that are the targets of prophetic attacks on idolatry; the Israelites' alliances with such rulers incur the prophets' wrath: "Alas for those who go down to Egypt for help and who rely on horses, who trust in chariots because they are many and in horsemen because they are very strong, but do not look to the Holy One of Israel or consult the Lord!" (Is. 31:1). Here Isaiah condemns trust in the Egyptians and in the mundane means of military might as a rejection of God and indeed a false deification of the Egyptians and their technology: "The Egyptians are human, and not God; their horses are flesh, and not spirit. When the Lord stretches out his hand, the helper will stumble, and the one helped will fall, and they will all perish together" (31:3). It is the LORD himself who will come down to fight on Mount Zion and defend Jerusalem (31:4–5). Isaiah therefore admonishes the people, "Turn back to him whom you have deeply betrayed, O people of Israel. For on that day all of you shall throw away your idols of silver and idols of gold, which your hands have sinfully made for you. Then the Assyrian shall fall by a sword, not of mortals; and a sword, not of humans, shall devour him" (31:6–8).[65] Here the worship of idols is not only associated with the Israelites' alliance with foreign rulers and reliance on military might; Isaiah implies that the Israelite dalliances with other types of power is itself a form of idolatry because it is a rejection of God and a raising of mere flesh to the status of gods.

This prophetic stance is not limited to Isaiah; Hosea (14:3) similarly links his critique of Israelite idolatry with foreign alliances: "Assyria shall not save us; we will not ride upon horses; we will say no more, 'Our God,' to the work of our hands." Ezekiel (16:26–8) likewise condemns the Israelites who have "played the whore" with the Egyptians and the Assyrians, thus linking the marital and the political images of idolatry. Jeremiah (2:11, 17–8)also regards alliances with foreign rulers as a betrayal of God:

> Has a nation changed its gods, even though they are no gods? But my people have changed their glory for something that does not profit. . . . Have you not brought this upon yourself by forsaking the Lord your God, while he led you in the way? What then do you gain by going to Egypt, to drink the waters of the Nile? Or what do you gain by going to Assyria, to drink the waters of the Euphrates?

Like Ezekiel, Jeremiah (2:24) links the Israelite alliances with adultery, likening the house of Israel to a wild ass, sniffing the wind for lovers in unrestrained lust:

> But you said, "It is hopeless, for I have loved strangers, and after them I will go." As a thief is shamed when caught, so the house of Israel shall be shamed—they, their kings, their officials, their priests, and their prophets, who say to a tree, "You are my father," and to a stone, "You gave me birth." . . . But where are your gods that you made for yourself? Let them come, if they can save you, in your time of trouble. (2:25–8)

But of course they cannot, "for the Lord has rejected those in whom you trust, and you will not prosper through them" (2:37). The essential issue is one of trust and the betrayal of that trust. It does not matter much if the people put their trust in other nations, in the gods of other nations, or in the most advanced military means of the time. As long as they do not put their trust in God, they are idolaters.[66]

There is an important difference, however, between the marital and political images of idolatry. Marriage is much more exclusive than political loyalty. In a monogamous relationship, one can have only one spouse, and the relationship is not divisible or transferable to another party. There can be no stand-in for one's spouse, nor can a spouse be shared with another person.[67] Political authority, by way of contrast, is divisible among many different levels of authority, and one's loyalty can belong simultaneously to several different levels of government. Such loyalties are mediated by various representatives as well.[68] And so in the Bible, God the king also sanctions the authority of a human king who stands in as partially, but not fully, representative of God's authority on earth. Kingship in other ancient Near Eastern nations was embedded in the cosmic order; the king participated in divinity and was responsible not only for social order but often for the natural order as well.[69] Scripture presents kingship among the Israelites, on the other hand, as a contingent arrangement, not part of the way things are but God's rather grudging concession to Israelite pleas. Israel is allowed a king, but only on the condition that the king is understood as God's agent and not a rival to God's power. God accedes to Israelite demands for a king, but only with a great deal of ambivalence, precisely because the temptation to idolatry will be ever present.

The first book of Samuel presents the Israelites' request for a king as a desire to be "like other nations" (I Sam. 8:5). Their reasons are largely military ones: "[W]e are determined to have a king over us, so that we also may be like other nations, and that our king may govern us and go out before us and fight our battles" (8:19–20). The LORD's response to Samuel puts the request in the context of idolatry:

> Listen to the voice of the people in all that they say to you; for they have not rejected you, but they have rejected me from being king over them. Just as they have done to me, from the day I brought them up out of Egypt to this day, forsaking me and serving other gods, so also they are doing to you. Now then, listen to their voice; only—you shall solemnly warn them, and show them the ways of the king who shall reign over them. (8:7–9)[70]

Samuel tells them what to expect from a human king (8:10–8): he will take your sons for his armies and to make weapons and to keep the royal household well-provisioned; he will take your daughters as perfumers and cooks and bakers to keep him living luxuriously; he will confiscate some of your land and your harvest and your slaves and your animals for the benefit of himself and his courtiers; finally, "you shall be his slaves. And in that day you will cry out because of your king, whom you have chosen for yourselves; but the LORD will not answer you in that day" (8:17–8). Samuel thus makes plain that a king, like any other idol, is a creation of human desires, and like most idols it will come to rule over the people that made it, with bitter consequences.[71]

God nevertheless allows the Israelites to have a king and to direct their loyalty to the king, but only insofar as it is clear that the king is not God. The biblical text puts limits on the power of the king. In Deuteronomy 17:14–5, the LORD anticipates the Israelite desire for a king: "When you have come into the land that the Lord your God is giving you, and have taken possession of it and settled in it, and you say, 'I will set a king over me, like all the nations that are around me,' you may indeed set over you a king whom the Lord your God will choose." Kingship may be a creation of human desires, but God remains in charge of the whole process and chooses who will occupy the throne. The LORD furthermore puts limits on the king's power and wealth:

> Even so, he must not acquire many horses for himself, or return the people to Egypt in order to acquire more horses, since the Lord has said to you, "You must never return that way again." And he must not acquire many wives for himself, or else his heart will turn away; also silver and gold he must not acquire in great quantity for himself. (17:16–7)

As in Isaiah, the king must rely on God, not on military might and wealth. These passages have an arresting parallel in Judges 7. Gideon is about to go to battle against the Midianites with thirty-two thousand troops at his command. But the LORD says to Gideon, "The troops with you are too many for me to give the Midianites into their hand. Israel would only take the credit away from me, saying, 'My own hand has delivered me' " (7:2). Gideon sends more than two-thirds of his troops home, but there are still too many for the LORD. By the time the LORD pronounces them ready to go to battle, Gideon has only three hundred soldiers left; the LORD has dismissed the rest. In the ensuing engagement, there is no question to whom credit for the victory belongs. Modern people are scandalized by the image of a warrior God, but ignore the lesson: the people that is *least well-prepared* militarily is the one that follows God.[72]

For my purposes, the point of these passages is that idolatry in the Old Testament is not limited to belief in other explicitly named gods besides the God of Abraham, Isaac, and Jacob. Although following other gods is clearly a concern, putting one's trust in created things is regarded as the functional equivalent of the explicit worship of other gods. Old Testament texts call into question the belief/behavior and religious/secular binaries. It is not surprising, therefore, that when idolatry is treated in the New Testament, the concept is expanded beyond the explicit worship of pagan gods.

The Gospels do not use the term *eidōlolatria* or its cognates. There are only a few occasions when the Gospels use terminology directly associated with idolatry in the Septuagint. Jesus is reported to have spoken of the Temple in Jerusalem as "made with hands" (*cheiropoiēton*; Mk. 14:58), an Old Testament expression for idols (e.g., Ps. 115:4; Is. 44:9–20). Jesus also asks whose image (*eikōn*) is on the coin used for paying taxes to Caesar (Mk. 12:16; Matt. 22:20; Lk. 20:24). The trap set by his questioners here clearly invokes questions about idolatry. Jesus's attitude toward paying tribute to Caesar is subtle and ambiguous, cleverly eluding the trap set for him by not saying a simple yes or no. Some commentators see in Jesus's response a nonchalance regarding the presence of potentially idolatrous coins in the Temple precincts.[73] Other commentators emphasize the idolatrous inscription on the coin divinizing the Roman emperor—Tiberius Caesar, son of the divine Augustus (*divi Augusti filius Augustus*)—and see revolution in Jesus's response: if you give to God what is God's, there is nothing left for Caesar.[74] What seems clear, however, is that the Pharisees' question could only be a trap if affirming the payment of taxes to Caesar was potentially offensive to the Jews. Idolatry in this case is most closely associated with images of a foreign god—Caesar— but also involves issues of loyalty to the governing authorities and the use of money, issues that are not purely "religious" but are political and economic as well. The question is set up as a test of loyalty to either the God of Israel or the deified Roman emperor. Although modern people commonly read Jesus's response as an affirmation of the separation of church and state, such readings are highly anachronistic in a context in which the emperor was also a god. They also ignore the immediate textual context surrounding this incident in the Gospels, a context of mounting conflict between Jesus and the authorities as Jesus nears his death in Jerusalem. The idea that this episode provides an irenic interlude in which Jesus recognizes a legitimate division of labor between God and Caesar is implausible.[75] No Jew would recognize the legitimacy of loyalty divided between God and Caesar.[76]

The contest between loyalty to God and loyalty to other earthly things is expressed most directly in Jesus's warning in the Sermon on the Mount about the dangers of money: "No one can serve two masters; for a slave will either hate the one and love the other, or be devoted to the one and despise the other. You cannot serve God and wealth" (Matt. 6:24). The word translated by the NRSV as "wealth" is *mamōna,* a Greek rendering of an Aramaic word. The fact that the Greek text leaves the Aramaic word untranslated has led other translations, such as the King James Version, to render the word "Mammon" as well. The word untranslated lends itself to the personification of Mammon as a god or demon, a tradition dating back at least to John Chrysostom in the fourth century.[77] Such a personification is consistent with Jesus's depiction of wealth as a master, one that calls forth a stark choice between love and hate. Jesus offers no middle ground between being devoted to money and despising it. Jesus's saying is rightly understood in the context of idolatry, the contest between rival gods. The saying is embedded in a whole series of Jesus's exhortations in Matthew 6:19–34 that do not simply oppose the true God to material possessions but rather admonish his listeners to rely on God to provide for their material needs. Jesus does not deprecate people's desires for food and clothing but wants them to recognize that it is the Creator God who provides for all their needs. Jesus implies that idolatry is grasping at what is not given—eat of this and "you will be like God" (Gen. 3:5)—and the opposite of idolatry is the grateful reception of God's beneficence.

Perhaps the most direct reference to idolatry in the Gospels is contained in the temptation sequence in Matthew 4, where the devil offers Jesus all the kingdoms of the world if he will fall down and worship him. Jesus's response, "Worship the Lord your God, and serve only him" (4:10), quotes Deuteronomy 6:13, which is followed by "Do not follow other gods, any of the gods of the peoples who are all around you, because the LORD your God, who is present with you, is a jealous God" (6:14–5). To fall down and worship the devil is unambiguously idolatry, but the text implies that there is a subtler kind of idolatry in bread. The devil's first temptation is for the hungry Jesus to turn stones to bread, to which Jesus also responds with Deuteronomy: "One does not live by bread alone, but by every word that comes from the mouth of God" (Matt. 4:4, quoting Deut. 8:3). Idolatry again is not limited to the explicit worship of gods or demons but includes the prioritizing of worldly material goods over the word of God.

Though direct references to idolatry are few in the Gospels, the issue of idolatry becomes more acute in the rest of the New Testament. As Stephen Barton notes, the increasing engagement of Jews with Gentiles among the early followers of Jesus necessitated a greater focus on the avoidance of idolatrous situations.[78] Paul notably provides detailed and complex instructions to the Christians in Corinth for dealing with food that had come into contact with idols. But the Pauline concept of idolatry extends beyond pagan worship of other gods and encompasses a broader category of behaviors toward material things, as we have already seen in our discussion of Romans 1. For example, Paul warns the Philippians (3:18–9), "For many live as enemies of the cross of Christ; I have often told you of them, and now I tell you even with tears. Their end is destruction; their god is the belly; and their glory is in their shame; their minds are set on earthly things." Paul may be referring to Jewish dietary restrictions here, but more likely he is referring to general self-indulgence, as in Romans 16:18, where he describes those causing dissent and offense: "For such people do not serve our Lord Christ, but their own appetites." The word translated "appetites" here in the NRSV is the same one translated "belly" in Philippians 3:19: *koilia*. When Paul says their god is their *koilia*, he is clearly using "god" metaphorically; the enemies of Christ's cross do not literally worship their bellies. But the implied idolatry is not merely metaphorical; as in Romans 1, the source of idolatry is fixating on earthly, created things, to the distraction from or exclusion of heavenly things. Paul goes on in Philippians 3:20 to declare that the Christian's citizenship is in heaven, thus contrasting the devotion to created things with the devotion to the Creator.

This passage in Philippians is thus similar to the passage in Colossians (3:5) where greed is identified not metaphorically but literally as idolatry: "Put to death, therefore, whatever in you is earthly: fornication, impurity, passion, evil desire, and greed (which is idolatry)." Once again the contrast between earthly and heavenly draws the boundary between idolatry and proper worship. This passage is closely echoed by Ephesians 5:5, where the greedy person is identified as an idolater: "Be sure of this, that no fornicator or impure person, or one who is greedy (that is, an idolater), has any inheritance in the kingdom of Christ and of God." As Rosner points out, these passages are not isolated but build on Old Testament associations of greed with idolatry. The incident of the Golden Calf, the paradigmatic example of idolatry in the scriptures, forges a link between gold and idolatry and between idolatry and disordered desire, as Paul makes plain in I Corinthians 10:6–13. Psalm 10:3 sees material possessions as a substitute for God: "[T]hose greedy for gain curse and renounce the Lord." Job 31:24–8l inks putting trust in gold with being unfaithful to God. In Proverbs 30:8–9, the narrator asks God for neither poverty nor riches, but only for daily sustenance, "or I shall be full, and deny you, and say, 'Who is the Lord?'"[79] Hosea 10:1 links economic abundance to the worship of other gods: "Israel is a luxuriant vine that yields its fruit. The more his fruit increased, the more altars he built."

The lines between poverty, daily sustenance, and riches are difficult in practice to discern, and this raises an interesting problem in describing idolatry. If some material things are necessary for life, but material things can also become substitutes for God, at what point does possession of material things shade into idolatry? How much is too much? Fowl wisely suggests that the question cannot be answered merely quantitatively. The common idea that greed is pursuing more than one is due requires a societal standard of what each is due that eludes most societies, especially our own. Fowl appeals instead to the creation and Fall account in the opening chapters of Genesis. There we are owed nothing, but all is the free gift of a gracious God. We have only to gratefully receive what God has given. Greed, on the other hand, is the grasping at something that God has not given. The Fall is this grasping at the fruit of the tree that was not offered. It is idolatry because it is the denial of God, and the attempt instead to "be like God" (Gen. 3:5). If greed is merely grasping at more than what we are owed, it is hard to see it as idolatry. If it is, instead, the attempt to usurp God's position and deify ourselves, then the notion that greed is idolatry makes sense.[80] Discerning when the normal human desire for material things has become greed, however, remains elusive. Idolatry here as elsewhere is on a continuum of more or less. This does not, however, mean that greed is not really idolatry.

We do well to remember that idolatry is not a tightly circumscribed concept in the Bible. The word "idolatry" has no equivalent in the Hebrew text, and the word "idol" translates a host of quite different Hebrew terms. An exact definition of idolatry in the Bible may not be feasible; the way the term "idolatry" is used marks out a varied set of protocols for determining when the exclusivity of one's devotion to the LORD has been breached. As we have discussed them so far, those protocols can be identified in part by what they are not. Idolatry is, first, not primarily about belief, if belief is understood as the mental sorting out of ideas about what exists and what does not. The Old Testament is inconclusive about the metaphysical status of other gods, and the sin of idolatry does not seem to depend on what one believes about the existence of such gods. Idolatry is more about behavior than belief alone; it is about the worship, devotion, loyalty, and trust directed at things other than God. And because it is about devotion to other things, idolatry is, second, not merely a matter of what we would call "religion." The worship of God or gods is intimately tied with economic and political practices. The worship of YHWH is inseparable, as we have seen, from a system of inalienable property rights, care for widows, orphans, and aliens, limited government, avoidance of excessive wealth, and a deep suspicion of reliance on military might. The rejection of any of these things by means of economic or political oppression is intertwined with the rejection of God and devotion to something or someone else. Idolatry is, third, then, not exclusively about the explicit worship of other named gods besides the LORD. Idolatry does not necessarily mean worshiping the Egyptians' gods; it could mean relying on the Egyptians' horses and chariots, instead of the LORD, to keep one safe. Idolatry could mean reliance on oneself or on any created thing instead of God for one's security and well-being.

If idolatry is given such an expansive meaning, however, then we need to be clear that idolatry exists on a continuum of more and less. The adultery metaphor for idolatry is exclusive; the difference between having sex with one's spouse and having sex with someone who is not one's spouse is easy to mark. But the political image of idolatry is more complex. If God the king allows a human king, at what point does loyalty to the human king shade into disloyalty to God? How much wealth is required to sap one's dependence on God? How many troops are too many troops? Gideon probably thought he was taking a tremendous leap of faith when he sent twenty-two thousand of his thirty-two thousand home. God thought otherwise, but why stop at three hundred? Would not a victory with only one hundred have shown God's might even more clearly? Idolatry is clearest when an Israelite is sacrificing a bull to Baal, and there is no question that the prophets were very concerned with such practices. The identification of a pharaoh as a god would be equally clearly idolatrous, but material cooperation with such a pharaoh by means of a military alliance is at a greater remove from the explicit worship of a rival god. Things get murkier when the issue is offering overt worship to YHWH while disobeying God's law by oppressing the poor, as in Brueggemann's analysis, or stockpiling wealth or relying on military might. To say that things get murky does not necessarily mean that the sin of idolatry is less severe in such cases; it just becomes harder to discern, which may make it more pernicious. Such discernment is the vocation of the prophet: to reveal to the people important truths that are difficult to see. What all these cases have in common is a turn away from God to place one's hope in something created. The temptation to idolatry is ever-present, and is in many ways a condition of being human, a creature immersed in creation and endowed with the God-like powers of choice. In this sense, the story of the Fall in Genesis 3 is the story of idolatry as the primordial sin: "when you eat of it your eyes will be opened, and you will be like God" (3:5). Insofar as all humans share in this primordial sin, we are all idolaters. And so the Bible itself calls into question the idolaters/nonidolaters binary.

What we have seen so far of idolatry in the Bible indicates that idolatry critique can indeed be used to draw boundaries between those who worship the true God and those who worship false gods. Such boundaries can be used to promote violence against those who are labeled idolaters. Insofar as idolatry is a constant temptation for those who live in the condition of creatures on the earth, however, idolatry critique can also be used to blur boundaries, in two ways. Idolatry critique can, first, be a recognition that we all worship, that humans are spontaneously worshiping creatures whose devotion alights on all sorts of created things. Idolatry critique is also practiced in the Bible, second, as a prophetic form of self-critique, a denunciation of the Israelites as being "like other nations," thus blurring the boundaries between the Israelites and the idolaters outside of the community. We all worship, and we all worship badly.

3.3. No Graven Images

Determining the relationship between the first clause of the Decalogue, "I am the Lord your God, who brought you out of the land of Egypt, out of the house of slavery; you shall have no other gods before me" (Ex. 20:2–3), and the second, "You shall not make for yourself an idol, whether in the form of anything that is in heaven above, or that is on the earth beneath, or that is in the water under the earth" (20:4), is complicated. The Hebrew word here translated "idol" is *pesel*, a graven or carved image, rendered as *eidōlon* by the Septuagint; the parallel passage in Deuteronomy 5:8 uses the same term. The ban on images bears a complex relationship to the ban on worshiping other gods, because the ban on images refers not only to images of false gods but to images of the true God, YHWH, as well. Since the LORD does not show himself, Moses commands the people not to present the LORD in visible form:

> Then the Lord spoke to you out of the fire. You heard the sound of words but saw no form; there was only a voice. . . . Since you saw no form when the Lord spoke to you at Horeb out of the fire, take care and watch yourselves closely, so that you do not act corruptly by making an idol for yourselves,

in the form of any figure—the likeness of male or female, the likeness of any animal that is on the earth, the likeness of any winged bird that flies in the air, the likeness of anything that creeps on the ground, the likeness of any fish that is in the water under the earth. And when you look up to the heavens and see the sun, the moon, and the stars, all the host of heaven, do not be led astray and bow down to them and serve them, things that the Lord your God has allotted to all the peoples everywhere under heaven. (Deut. 4:12, 15–9)

Here we see again that the underlying issue is not simply the explicit worship of gods with other names but the attitude of the worshiper to creation. Images are dangerous because they threaten to confuse the Creator with creation and thus direct the devotion of the worshiper away from God. At the same time, however, humans often feel that images are necessary for sensual creatures to make contact with the divine.

Although Israelite worship is known for its aniconism, the reality on the ground is more complex. There appears to have been a range of different positions on images among the Israelites, both in practice and in the scriptures. At one extreme, some scholars argue that there was a cult statue of YHWH in the First Temple.[81] Others argue that there was a divine image in the Holy of Holies even in the Second Temple period, removed only by the Hasmoneans in the second century BC.[82] Herbert Niehr has argued that the biblical polemics against cult statues and divine images presuppose their existence and use among the Israelites.[83] Stuart Weeks is not alone in casting a skeptical eye on such strong and speculative claims,[84] but he does acknowledge that there are places in the Old Testament itself where the use of cult images in the worship of YHWH is noted without polemic, as in the story of Micah in Judges 17–8, who installs a silver idol in a shrine in his house. Weeks argues that the Israelites shared in the standard ancient Near Eastern sense that cult objects could be bearers of the divine presence in a way that was not merely symbolic. The Bread of the Presence, set before Yahweh as a meal in the Tabernacle, would be evidence of this sense from within Israelite worship. Weeks also notes that the Ark of the Covenant indicates that Israelite worship shared with its neighbors a sense that the divine presence could be localizable without being confined to any location.[85] Karel van der Toorn has similarly argued that veneration of the Torah scroll—carried by the devout on their persons in miniature and ritually transported in the Ark of the Covenant—was analogous to practices of other Near Eastern people that have long been denigrated as fetishistic.[86] Nevertheless, the Ark is not an artificial body in the image of Yahweh; it is meant rather to provide a seat for the divine presence (Ex. 25:17–22) or a footstool for God (e.g., I Chron. 28:2).[87] This unique approach to the divine presence, Weeks thinks, is evidence for the centrality of aniconism in Israelite worship. God was understood to have physical form, but that form was to be described only verbally, not represented iconographically. Images were associated with other people's gods and were therefore forbidden to Israelites as a form of apostasy, but the Pentateuch and historical writings assumed the same concept of divine presence that the surrounding peoples did. Only in later prophetic writings do polemics against idolatry attempt to prove the superiority of Yahweh over other gods by denigrating their images as devoid of divine presence, and thereby questioning the power and divinity of those gods themselves (e.g., Jer. 10:1–16; Is. 44:9–20).[88]

Benjamin Sommers has argued that different theologies of the relationship between God and material creation can be correlated with different sources of the Hebrew scriptures. According to Sommers, the earliest sources of the Pentateuch (JE) operate on a "fluid" model of God's presence in which God is both close and transcendent at the same time. The "God with many bodies" is both vulnerable and omnipotent, capable of walking in the garden (Gen. 3:8) and being present in heaven simultaneously. Critique of graven images is muted in this material, because part of God's transcendence is a certain freedom to move in and out of material things.[89] The lines become sharper in the Deuteronomic materials, in which God's body is "located exclusively in heaven."[90] God's name, not presence, is in the temple in Jerusalem, and the critique of graven images takes on urgency. In the later and more fully developed Priestly materials, the Ark of the Covenant is God's footstool, and God is present in the Tabernacle.[91] God nevertheless maintains radical otherness and meets any attempt to control or manipulate the divine presence with violence, as in the story of Nadab and Abihu in Leviticus 10:1–3. In the Priestly material, there is little explicit critique of images because materiality is given a tightly regulated role in holiness through strict binaries of holy/profane and clean/unclean.

What this range of approaches implies is that there is indeed a strong aniconic tendency in Israelite worship, but Israelite aniconism is not simply the disenchantment of the world, at least not in the sense of the elimination of what Charles Taylor calls "charged objects" from the world.[92] The difference can be seen in the account of the Golden Calf in Exodus 32–34, generally attributed to JE, which is spliced into the Priestly account of the construction of the Tabernacle, along with the Ark of the Covenant and the table for the Bread of the Presence (25–31, 35–40). In Exodus 25–31, the LORD gives detailed instructions for the construction of a place for him to dwell among the people. Exodus 32 recounts the incident of the Golden Calf, the people's sin and punishment. In Exodus 33, as a further consequence of the building of the Calf, the LORD announces that he will withhold his presence from the people as they go up to the Promised Land: "Go up to a land flowing with milk and honey; but I will not go up among you, or I would consume you on the way, for you are a stiff-necked people" (33:3). But Moses intercedes, and the LORD relents: "My presence will go with you, and I will give you rest" (33:14). In Exodus 34 the covenant is renewed, and in 35–40 the Tabernacle and all its furnishings, including the Ark and the table of the Bread of the Presence, are finally constructed. In Nathan MacDonald's reading, the contrast between the graven image of the Golden Calf and the seat for the invisible presence of God in the Tabernacle is a matter of control of the divine presence. The construction of the visible image for God is an attempt to *ensure* the divine presence; the Tabernacle, by contrast, offers hospitality for God to abide freely among the people. The construction of the Golden Calf is therefore also an act of political rebellion, both against Moses's leadership and ultimately against waiting on the presence of God.[93]

Israelite aniconism stood in contrast to the surrounding cultures, for whom images provided a fixed point of access to the deities being invoked. Cults of gods were often transactional: sacrifices in exchange for a good harvest, for example. The localization of the spirit of the deity in a statue or other kind of image made the presence of the god accessible and at least somewhat manipulable, given that it was tied in some way to a concrete material object. Israelite aniconism is meant, at least in part, to guard against the attempt to control God, to fix God in place and ensure God's presence. The absolute and inviolable holiness of God—the otherness of God—needed to be respected.[94] Here we return again to some of the foundational themes evident in the opening chapters of Genesis. There is an absolute distinction between Creator and creation; the Creator is free, and creation is wholly dependent for its being on the Creator. There can be no attempt to tie the Creator to creation, or confuse Creator and creation. All such attempts to grasp and control are manifestations of the primordial sin: to grasp what is not given, and to thereby aspire to become like God.

The fear that God will be subjected to human control by the fashioning of visible images of God is just one of the possible sources of the ban on divine images. The preference for verbal description over pictorial representation could be due to the fear that the worshiper will mistake the representation for what is being represented, thus blurring the lines between God and the world.[95] The mistaking of a statue for the god itself was probably rare in the ancient world.[96] More common would have been the fear of misrepresentation, that the image would communicate misleading or inappropriate ideas about God. Some layers of the Old Testament are open to the idea that God has physical form: God has a face, though no one can see it and live (Ex. 33:20); God walks in the garden (Gen. 3:8), eats and drinks with the elders of the people (Ex. 24:11), sits on a throne (Is. 6:1), and so on. But any visible depiction of God would be inevitably misleading. All such representations would violate the ineffability of God and threaten to blur the absolute distinction between God and creatures, with potentially serious consequences.[97] Perhaps thanks to Michelangelo, Westerners have a tendency to think of God as an elderly white man with a white beard. How much distortion in Christian views of race and gender has resulted? One more possible motive for rejecting images has to do not so much with distorting our ideas about God as with forgetting God and becoming immersed in the attractions of creation. Instead of being a medium through which we establish contact with God, images become ends in themselves. The worshiper's gaze ceases to move through the image toward God; instead it comes to a stop in the image and becomes fascinated by it. Rather than establishing contact with God, idols block communication with God. As Assmann comments, "To the aniconists, this happiness with and within the world as it is seems like blind entanglement. Idolatry, they declare, is *Weltverstrickung*—entanglement within the world, addiction to the visible and the material."[98]

What all of these different motives for the ban on divine images have in common is a concern to prevent the muddling of Creator with creation. This concern is not alien to the concern to prevent the worship of other gods. What precisely is the relationship between the ban on worshiping other gods and the ban on images? This has been a matter of dispute among Christians. Catholics and Lutherans treat the two clauses together as the first commandment of the Decalogue; Reformed and Orthodox Christians regard them as two separate commandments. According to Assmann, reading the two clauses together makes the ban on images a commentary on the prohibition of other gods. The message is that one should not make images because images are powerful and have a tendency to become other gods, that is, other objects of devotion. Assmann calls this reading "political" because it has to do with loyalty to the one true God. Reading the clauses as separate commandments renders a different emphasis. The ban on images is not about worshiping the wrong gods but worshiping the right God in the wrong way. This reading Assmann calls "theological" because it is about the unrepresentability of God. Ultimately, however, Assmann thinks that both readings are about loyalty:

> We must not forget, however, that on both readings the prohibition of images is given a political commentary that explains it by reference to God's jealousy and his distinction between friend and foe. "You shall not bow down to them or serve them, for I the LORD your God am a jealous God, visiting the iniquity of the fathers on the children to the third and the fourth generation of those who hate me, but showing steadfast love to thousands of those who love me and keep my commandments" (Exod. 20:5–6; Deut. 5:9–10). God resents the making of images for it is an act of defection and apostasy. This shows that the political meaning was, at least originally, the dominant interpretation.[99]

Another way of putting this is that what unites the two prohibitions is the concern that people will betray God by becoming unduly attached to created things instead of to the Creator. And it is precisely this concern that allows for the expansion of the concept of idolatry beyond the explicit worship of other named gods and beyond the attempt to depict YHWH in visible form.

As we have seen, there are good theological reasons for the Israelite ban on images, but the fact that Israelite aniconism was not absolute—that the Israelites continued to represent the presence of God in the Bread of the Presence, the Ark of the Covenant, and the Temple itself—indicates that securing the divide between Creator and creation is complex and admits of many different nuances. On the one hand, God is not God if God is entangled in creation. On the other hand, humans are not humans if they do not try to reach out to God in ways that are accessible to the senses. We are material creatures and therefore need some kind of material representation to make contact with the divine. Any attempt to worship the invisible God must somehow bridge the unbridgeable gap between Creator and creation. The scriptures tacitly acknowledge this human need by presenting God in all sorts of anthropomorphic ways: God speaks, feels, walks, and emotes.

God furthermore engages the human senses, letting God's own presence be known in the burning bush and the pillar of fire. Exodus 3 achieves a delicate balance between immanence and transcendence in that the bush burns but is not consumed; the episode combines what is within common human experience with what transcends it. We can think and speak of God only in terms of such images. But all such images fall short, and the danger of creating false gods is ever present. Nevertheless, one cannot help but feel a certain sympathy with the people who grew impatient with the absence of Moses and the absence of God. Following an invisible God is hard; it exhausts the human capacity to be patient and to live with uncertainty and a lack of signs that appeal to our material nature.[100]

The delicate interplay between transcendence and immanence takes on a new dimension in the New Testament, where Jesus Christ is claimed to be the very "image of the invisible God" (Col. 1:15; also II Cor. 4:4). I will have more to say about this in the final chapter of the book. For now it is important to note how the Christian view of Jesus Christ as the *eikōn* of God is in continuity with the aniconism of the Old Testament. In I Corinthians 8, Paul seems to address the objection that Christian belief is idolatrous when he contrasts idolatry, with its "many gods and many lords" (8:5), with Christian belief: "[F]or us there is one God, the Father, from whom are all things and for whom we exist, and one Lord, Jesus Christ, through whom are all things and through whom we exist" (8:6). Somehow the Jewish belief in the oneness of God is not compromised by confessing Jesus as Lord. The conclusion of I John likewise contrasts idolatry with Jesus Christ, the true God and the bearer of eternal life. Unlike the pagan idols, which are constantly pilloried in the Old Testament as mute and frozen and lifeless, Jesus is a living person who manifests the being of God.[101] Kavin Rowe notes that in using the term *eikōn* for Jesus, the Pauline literature transfers to Christ a term used for pagan idols, as in Romans 1:23. While false gods fail to come to life in idols, the true God, though invisible, is made visible in God's human image, Jesus Christ.[102] Joel Marcus adds:

> [S]ince Paul elsewhere uses *eikōn* for the image of Christ and of God that is borne, at least *in nuce*, and as an eschatological pledge, by the believer (Rom. 8:29; I Cor. 11:7; 15:49; II Cor. 3:18), the implication would seem to be that Paul's addressees are to seek God's likeness not in the religious statuary that crowds their world but in the moveable icons that are their Christian brothers and sisters, "whom he . . . predestined to be conformed to the image of his Son" (Rom. 8:29).[103]

In other words, humans are prohibited from making images of God because we are images of God.[104] What prevents this from becoming an idolatrous elevation of humans to divine status is explained in the difference between being made in the image and likeness of God (Gen. 1:26–7) and being like God (3:5). In the former, human beings are a manifestation of God's goodness and creative power, having received their being from God and having their continued being completely dependent on God's grace. In the latter, likeness to God is not received but is rather grasped at, with the intent not to manifest God but to replace God. Both aspire to bridge the gap between humanity and divinity. But idolatry attempts to do so by human initiative, to render gods in the image of humans and thereby put humans in God's place; the *theosis* that Christ consummates is by God's initiative, to complete the rendering of humans in the image of God and thus make God known among humanity.

If the Incarnation is in continuity with the Old Testament witness in this way, it displays significant discontinuities with paganism. Paul's speech to the Athenians in Acts 17 is often seen as exploring common ground with pagan philosophy; some, like Martin Dibelius, go so far as to attribute the main ideas of the speech to Stoicism rather than to Paul's or Luke's Christian worldview.[105] And there certainly is an irenic tone to Paul's speech. But Paul's take on material images marks a significant difference from pagan practice:

Then Paul stood in front of the Areopagus and said, "Athenians, I see how extremely religious you are in every way. For as I went through the city and looked carefully at the objects of your worship, I found among them an altar with the inscription, 'To an unknown god.' What therefore you worship as unknown, this I proclaim to you. The God who made the world and everything in it, he who is Lord of heaven and earth, does not live in shrines made by human hands, nor is he served by human hands, as though he needed anything, since he himself gives to all mortals life and breath and all things. From one ancestor he made all nations to inhabit the whole earth, and he allotted the times of their existence and the boundaries of the places where they would live, so that they would search for God and perhaps grope for him and find him—though indeed he is not far from each one of us. For 'In him we live and move and have our being'; as even some of your own poets have said, 'For we too are his offspring.' Since we are God's offspring, we ought not to think that the deity is like gold, or silver, or stone, an image formed by the art and imagination of mortals. While God has overlooked the times of human ignorance, now he commands all people everywhere to repent, because he has fixed a day on which he will have the world judged in righteousness by a man whom he has appointed, and of this he has given assurance to all by raising him from the dead." (Acts 17:22–31)

In this passage, Paul finds *homo liturgicus* hard at work, the "extremely religious" Athenians worshiping gods by use of altars and images. They have even found it necessary to erect an altar to an unknown god, just to make sure that all gods are covered. The Athenians are searching for the divine in material things "made by human hands," and yet they still haven't found what they are looking for; the visible images do not produce knowledge of the divine. Luke's Paul inverts their expectations, proclaiming that the God who is invisible is known, in and through God's own creations, not the creations of humans. God gives life to all living things; humans cannot give life to images. The images formed by the art and imagination of mortals furthermore produce only ignorance of God, not knowledge. But God nevertheless overlooks human ignorance and is manifest in God's own creation, so that people may grope and find God in the beautiful things God has made.

The image of God in humans plays an important role in inverting the Athenian worldview. As Rowe puts it, the pagan error is to assume that because we are the offspring of divinity, we can read god off the face of humanity. Paul's speech implies that precisely because we are the living offspring of the living God, we cannot image God, that is, "we cannot refract the notion of divinity through our humanity."[106] The problem again is one of direction; Christianity moves from God to humanity, whereas idolatry moves from humanity toward the divine. The image of God restored in humanity by Jesus Christ is a gift of God, not a ladder which we can climb to attain God. A proper theology of nature can never be a way of obviating the revelation of God in Jesus Christ, as if we can simply read God off of the creation. The Incarnation, in other words, is a statement about how God has chosen to use material reality to reveal Godself, not a statement about the intrinsic revelatory nature of material reality as such.[107]

Although there are discontinuities with paganism, the ban on images—like the ban on worshiping other gods—can be deployed both for draw boundaries between us and them and for blur those boundaries, in two ways. First, just as Jeremiah's idolatry critique can be directed against the Israelites for fabricating their own "other gods" while claiming to worship YHWH, so the ban on images can be a rigorous form of internal critique that locates the impulse to idolatry not simply "over there" but within the heart of the Israelites' attempts to make contact with God. As Halbertal and Margalit point out, the ban on images opens the way for ever more rigorous self-critique, because even verbal and mental images fall short of God.[108] Negative theology—the negation of language about God as inevitably misleading, since any attempt to render God in human language violates God's ineffability—is an extension of idolatry critique, and it serves to discipline our own efforts to reach God as much as, if not more than, it works to negate others' language about God. The more rigorous the critique of images, the more we are all cast as idolaters, and the playing field is leveled. We all worship, and we all worship badly. Second, though, as we have seen, any attempt to ban images entirely is going to run up against the reality of human beings as sensual creatures who need to make contact with the Creator through the creation of which we are a part. Even in the Old Testament, there is a recognized need for a sacramental presence of God, in the Ark, in the Bread of the Presence, and in the anthropomorphic images of God in language. God cannot be found *in* creation, but there is a constant negotiation of proper and improper ways of finding God *through* creation. And this negotiation opens a way of empathy even with idolaters who are groping for God in the creation. I will have more to say about this in the final chapter, on sacrament. For now, the point is that the Bible's critique of idolatry is not as one-sided as it sometimes appears, and the boundaries drawn are often also blurred.

3.4. The Consequences of Idolatry

Despite this sympathy for the human condition, the Bible leaves no doubt that idolatry is a problem with serious consequences for human life. Idolatry, as we have seen, is linked with the primordial sin of Genesis 3:5: pride, or the willful attempt of the human creature to "be like God." The story of the Golden Calf is often seen as Israel's "original sin," an act of rebellion against the covenant with YHWH.[109] Pride is the root sin underlying idolatry. In Psalm 81, for example, the people refuse to listen to YHWH's admonition against "strange" and "foreign" gods (81:9), "So I gave them over to their stubborn hearts, to follow their own counsels" (81:12). Likewise Deuteronomy frequently links forgetting God and serving other gods with self-exaltation, especially in treating possessions as if they were due to one's own achievement and not gifts received from God:

When you have eaten your fill and have built fine houses and live in them, and when your herds and flocks have multiplied, and your silver and gold is multiplied, and all that you have is multiplied, then do not exalt yourself, forgetting the Lord your God, who brought you out of the land of Egypt, out of the house of slavery. . . . Do not say to yourself, "My power and the might of my own hand have gained me this wealth." But remember the Lord your God, for it is he who gives you power to get wealth, so that he may confirm his covenant that he swore to your ancestors, as he is doing today. If you do forget the Lord your God and follow other gods to serve and worship them, I solemnly warn you today that you shall surely perish. (8:12–4, 17–9; see also 6:10–4, 11:13–6, 31:20, and 32:15–8)

As Fowl notes, it is not immediately obvious to the reader of such passages in Deuteronomy why self-exaltation and the forgetting of our dependence on God leads to the following of other gods. Why does contentment with material abundance not lead to self-sufficiency and the forgetting of gods altogether?[110]

I want to observe that this question suggests the extent to which the biblical authors assumed that humans are *homo liturgicus*; they cannot simply go without something to worship, even if that desire is rooted in self-aggrandizement. To answer why other gods are preferable to YHWH, Fowl suggests we consider the possibility that other gods are more easily controlled than the living God of Abraham, Isaac, and Jacob. Other gods are less demanding and more easily manipulated. Fowl points to Zephaniah 1:12, where the LORD promises to punish "the people who rest complacently on their dregs, those who say in their hearts, 'The Lord will not do good, nor will he do harm.'" The complacency of wealth has led them to conclude that God will not act. As in Brueggemann's analysis, false worship creates gods that do nothing. People can follow idols because idols ask so little of them. People can claim to follow them without having to change their lives. As for the benefits, Fowl writes, "Sacrifices to such gods may work like a weak form of insurance."[111] People get status and some help fulfilling their wishes from gods that are more like Santa Claus than like the LORD, who enforces a rigorous ethical code.

As Fowl suggests in passing, however, the idea that we can control our idols may be nothing but self-deception. The gods may be more demanding than we think.[112] Fetishes are usually so called when they are believed to have some power over those who worship them.[113] The theme we uncovered in

Max Weber's work—that we are oppressed by gods of our own making—is a profoundly biblical theme.

We have already seen this theme worked out in the warnings of the prophets. In I Samuel 8, the rejection of God as king, equated with serving other gods, leads to dire consequences: the king-god will take your sons and daughters, your land and harvest, your slaves and flocks, and "you shall be his slaves" (8:17). Samuel's warning comes true in the story of King Ahab's confiscation of Naboth's vineyard, among many other instances. The gods of human making reinforce an unjust status quo either by directly sanctioning unjust human relations, as in the story of Ahab and Naboth, or by their inability to do either good or evil, as in Jeremiah. The emptiness of the false gods in Jeremiah and Isaiah is not harmless, however; as long as people follow them instead of following the true God, the people will be alienated, cut off from the source of their well-being and redemption, and subject to all manner of injustice. Only when the people turn away from gods of human creation to the true God who made them (Is. 44:24) will the bars of Babylon be broken down (43:14) and Jerusalem be rebuilt (44:26–8).

Wisdom 14 spells out the consequences of both kings and idols representing kings. The author derives the origin of idols from absence: a man carves an image to honor his deceased son, or an artisan carves an image of the king who lives far away. In the latter case, the ambition of the artisan to please the ruler causes him to make the image exceedingly beautiful, and the people, "attracted by the charm of his work," began to worship a mere human being as a god (14:15–20). "And this became a hidden trap for humankind, because people, in bondage to misfortune or to royal authority, bestowed on objects of stone or wood the name that ought not to be shared" (14:21). The passage then proceeds to detail the consequences of this human bondage to idols of our own creation:

> For whether they kill children in their initiations, or celebrate secret mysteries, or hold frenzied revels with strange customs, they no longer keep either their lives or their marriages pure, but they either treacherously kill one another, or grieve one another by adultery, and all is a raging riot of blood and murder, theft and deceit, corruption, faithlessness, tumult, perjury, confusion over what is good, forgetfulness of favors, defiling of souls, sexual perversion, disorder in marriages, adultery, and debauchery. For the worship of idols not to be named is the beginning and cause and end of every evil. (14:23–7)

Because the people "trust in lifeless idols," they imagine that they will suffer no harm. But all of these woes befall them, the passage stresses, not because of "the power of the things by which people swear" but because of the justice of God (14:28–31). In the list of what goes wrong in 14:23–7, it is hard to separate sin from punishment. The passage implies not only that the punishment is a direct response to the sin but that the punishment is the sin itself.

The idea that idols of human creation will come to oppress their makers is a common theme in the Old Testament. Psalm 106, for example, presents the idols as a "snare" and as devourers of children:

> They served their idols,
>> which became a snare to them.
> They sacrificed their sons
>> and their daughters to the demons;
> they poured out innocent blood,
>> the blood of their sons and daughters,
> whom they sacrificed to the idols of Canaan;
>> and the land was polluted with blood (106:36–8)

As a consequence of their idol worship, the psalmist continues,

> [the LORD] gave them into the hand of the nations,
>> so that those who hated them ruled over them.
> Their enemies oppressed them,
>> and they were brought into subjection under their power. (106:41–2)

This idea that, because of their idol worship, the LORD hands the Israelites over to their enemies to oppress them is found throughout the Old Testament. In Judges 2, for example, the people "abandoned the LORD, the God of their ancestors, who had brought them out of the land of Egypt; they followed other gods, from among the gods of the peoples who were all around them, and bowed down to them" (2:12). As a consequence, "the anger of the Lord was kindled against Israel, and he gave them over to plunderers who plundered them, and he sold them into the power of their enemies all around, so that they could no longer withstand their enemies" (2:14). Here the liberation that the LORD has brought them in the exodus is contrasted with the oppression in store when they serve other gods. As in Psalm 106, there is a sense in which the punishment is not extrinsic to the offense but a direct consequence of abandoning the God who liberates for gods who demand the blood of children.

This theme is clear in Jeremiah, for example, where the LORD warns:

> Because the people have forsaken me, and have profaned this place by making offerings in it to other gods whom neither they nor their ancestors nor the kings of Judah have known, and because they have filled this place with the blood of the innocent, and gone on building the high places of Baal to burn their children in the fire as burnt-offerings to Baal, which I did not command or decree, nor did it enter my mind; therefore the days are surely coming, says the Lord, when this place shall no more be called Topheth, or the valley of the son of Hinnom, but the valley of Slaughter. (19:4–6)

The people will fall by the sword to their enemies, the city will become a horror for others to hiss at, and "I will make them eat the flesh of their sons and the flesh of their daughters, and all shall eat the flesh of their neighbors in the siege" (19:9). The people are devoured by their own false gods. The punishment comes through the will of God, but there is a sense in which it is a direct and logical consequence of their own idolatry: because they sacrifice their children to Baal, they will have to eat their own children. In Jeremiah 5, the LORD contemplates punishment for those who have committed idolatry. Despite having fed them to the full, "Your children have forsaken me, and have sworn by those who are no gods" (5:7). Such gods are nullities, mere inventions of human imagination. The worship of such gods will nevertheless have dire consequences for the Israelites. The LORD will hand them over to foreign enemies. "They shall eat up your harvest and your food; they shall eat up your sons and your daughters; they shall eat up your flocks and your herds; they shall eat up your vines and your fig trees; they shall destroy with the sword your fortified cities in which you trust" (5:17). Once again, their children will be devoured because of their idolatry, because they put their trust in their own fortifications and not in the LORD. And the punishment will fit the crime: "And when your people say, 'Why has the Lord our God done all these things to us?' you shall say to them, 'As you have forsaken me and served foreign gods in your land, so you shall serve strangers in a land that is not yours'" (5:19). If the people want to serve other masters, let them serve other masters. The sin and the punishment are the same thing: the people have made for themselves false gods, gods of death instead of the Lord of life. The people put their trust in their own creations and bowed down to serve them. And so they shall; they shall be servants of their own creations, and their own creations will make them pay. Once again, there is no separation of "religion" from "politics"; service to false gods is inseparable from service to foreign rulers.

There is a notable exchange in the Bible's presentation of idolatry, whereby the projection of life by humans onto lifeless human creations—"no gods"—takes life away from living human beings. We have already seen this to be true in the violent consequences of idolatry. There is also a persistent biblical theme in which the worship of idols of metal and stone turns the worshiper into a similarly lifeless object. This mirroring effect is explicitly stated in Psalm 115:3–8:

Our God is in the heavens; he does whatever he pleases. Their idols are silver and gold, the work of human hands. They have mouths, but do not speak; eyes, but do not see. They have ears, but do not hear; noses, but do not smell. They have hands, but do not feel; feet, but do not walk; they make no sound in their throats. Those who make them are like them; so are all who trust in them.

This language is repeated almost identically in Psalm 135:15–8. The God of life is contrasted with the lifeless gods made by human hands out of metal. Those who make such idols or trust in them will become as lifeless as they are. In chapter 7, I explore Marx's exposition of the exchange of life and lifelessness between alienated workers and animated commodities: as commodities take on life and relate to one another as exchange values, life is drained away from those who make them. For now, it is worth noting that this exchange is found in the Bible, long before it was identified by Marx.

The lifelessness of idolaters in the Bible is most commonly expressed in terms of human body parts that do not function as they would in a living person. This theme is common is Isaiah's critique of idolatry: "They shall be turned back and utterly put to shame—those who trust in carved images, who say to cast images, 'You are our gods'" (42:17). Idolaters are regarded as deaf and blind (42:18–9). The idolater "sees many things, but does not observe them; his ears are open, but he does not hear" (42:20). In the following chapter, Isaiah again associates "the people who are blind, yet have eyes, who are deaf, yet have ears!" (43:8) with those who form "no god" (43:10). In the next chapter, Isaiah mocks the man who uses half a piece of wood to cook dinner and the other half to make an idol to worship. The man becomes as lifeless, blind, and stupid as the block of wood: "All who make idols are nothing, and the things they delight in do not profit; their witnesses neither see nor know. . . . They do not know, nor do they comprehend; for their eyes are shut, so that they cannot see, and their minds as well, so that they cannot understand" (44:9, 18; cf. 6:9–10). What G. K. Beale calls "sensory-organ-malfunction" is associated with idolatry also in Ezekiel (12:2) and Jeremiah (5:21, 7:24–6, 11:8, 25:4, 35:15, 44:5).[114]

The exchange of human life for the lifelessness of idols is expressed in other ways in the Bible as well. II Kings 17:15 says of the Israelites, "They went after false idols and became false." Jeremiah 2:5, 11 proclaims, "Thus says the Lord: What wrong did your ancestors find in me that they went far from me, and went after worthless things, and became worthless themselves? . . . Has a nation changed its gods, even though they are no gods? But my people have changed their glory for something that does not profit." Hosea 9:10-1 reports, "But they came to Baal-peor, and consecrated themselves to a thing of shame, and became detestable like the thing they loved. Ephraim's glory shall fly away like a bird—no birth, no pregnancy, no conception!" In both Jeremiah and Hosea, "glory" is not only that of God but God's glory as reflected in Israel. Glory is a property of the Israelites as long as they worship the LORD, whose glory is reflected in those who truly follow the true God. (See Hosea 4:7: "The more they increased, the more they sinned against me; they changed their glory into shame.") Given this background, it is reasonable to posit that the theme of Israel's glory is echoed as well in Psalm 106:19–20: "They made a calf at Horeb and worshipped a cast image. They exchanged the glory of God for the image of an ox that eats grass." Beale suggests that here "glory" refers not only to the LORD but to the reflection of the LORD's glory in human beings.[115] The implication is that as long as the Israelites worship and follow the LORD, they reflect the LORD's glory. When they turn to idols, on the other hand, an exchange takes place in which they forfeit the glory of God and instead become as false, worthless, detestable, shameful, and bovine as the idols they worship. In imputing life to lifeless inanimate things, the people take on the lifelessness of the "no gods" they worship.

This reading is affirmed by the same theme in Romans 1, where Paul explains idolatry as a form of exchange: people failed to see God in material things, and so "they exchanged the truth about God for a lie and worshipped and served the creature rather than the Creator" (1:25). Paul echoes the Old Testament language of glory, alluding to Psalm 106:20: "Claiming to be wise, they became fools; and they exchanged the glory of the immortal God for images resembling a mortal human being or birds or four-footed animals or reptiles" (Rom. 1:22–3). The glory referenced here is certainly God's glory, but as Paul spells out the consequences for human beings, it is clear that exchanging God's glory for material images (*eikonos*) perverts the glory of God as reflected in human beings. Their minds are darkened (1:21) and debased (1:28), and their bodies are degraded (1:24). They become subject to all manner of vices and violence, as Paul catalogs in the following verses (1:26–31). The implication is that humans are icons (*eikonos*) of what they worship, for good or for ill. This mirroring mechanism is affirmed in II Corinthians 3:18, where Paul writes, "And all of us, with unveiled faces, seeing the glory of the Lord as though reflected in a mirror, are being transformed into the same image [*eikona*] from one degree of glory to another; for this comes from the Lord, the Spirit." This verse is the conclusion of Paul's observations on the glory of Moses's face in contrast to the idolaters in Exodus 32–4.[116]

In Luke's presentation of Paul's speech on idolatry to the Athenians in Acts 17, we can see a similar dynamic of reflection. Paul contrasts the living God who gives life to humans with the inert gods that are made by human hands: "The God who made the world and everything in it, he who is Lord of heaven and earth, does not live in shrines made by human hands, nor is he served by human hands, as though he needed anything, since he himself gives to all mortals life and breath and all things" (Acts 17:24–5). Some commentators think that Paul's reference to God in whom "we live and move and have our being" (17:28) is part of his polemic against idols, which—as we have seen in Old Testament polemics—do not live or move or have any real existence as gods.[117] Paul continues, "Since we are God's offspring, we ought not to think that the deity is like gold, or silver, or stone, an image formed by the art and imagination of mortals" (17:29). The glory of the living God cannot be reflected by inanimate objects. By implication, only living human beings can be reflections of God's glory. The lifelessness of idols reflected in their followers is then contrasted with the resurrection of Jesus—who is the Temple not made with human hands (Mk. 14:58)—and the resurrection of the dead that Jesus offers those who follow the living God (Acts 17:30–2; cf. II Cor. 5:1).[118]

Beale sums up the evidence in this way:

[P]eople resemble what they revere, either for ruin or restoration. God has made all people to reflect, to be imaging beings. People will always reflect something, whether it be God's character or some feature of the world. If

people are committed to God, they will become like him; if they are committed to something other than God, they will become like that thing, always spiritually inanimate and empty like the lifeless and vain aspect of
creation to which they have committed themselves.[119]

I will spell out the implications of this aspect of the biblical critique of idolatry
in subsequent chapters. At this point it is worth noting the similarity between
the Bible and Weber's analysis, discussed in chapter 1, of the "many old gods"
that ascend from their graves and "strive to gain power over our lives."[120] The
biblical critique of idolatry likewise warns of the consequences of the human
creation of gods out of created realities: we come to be dominated by our
own creations, "enslaved to beings that by nature are not gods" (Gal. 4:8), and
there is a type of exchange whereby the attribution of life to lifeless objects
and processes—Weber's *lebende Maschine*, living machine—in turn drains
the life away from those living persons subjected to them.

3.5. Self-Critique and Sympathy

Weber was much more pessimistic than Marx or Nietzsche about the possibility that humans would be able to cast off their propensity for making
gods to rule over them. For Weber, *pace* Marx and Nietzsche, the modern
"discovery" that all gods are human inventions was not good news. If there
is no pregiven order, if we are making it all up, Weber thought we were
fated to project our own dysfunction onto the gods. The mirroring function that the Bible describes works to our detriment; we look to the sky and
see nothing but ourselves, and so the institutions we create can only be our
own doppelgangers. Because there is no inherent order to the universe,
our creations are ungovernable. There is no one out there to save us from
ourselves.

The biblical story is ultimately a comedy and not a tragedy precisely because, besides all the false, human-made gods, there is a true God, who is
good. In Weber's world, there can be no idolatry critique because there is
nothing but idols. Besides some gestures toward heroic individual human
choice, there is no way out of false worship because there is no true God. The
Bible sees things differently. Despite pervasive idolatry, true worship is possible. Indeed, the pervasiveness of idolatry is in some way an affirmation of
the human need to worship that is instilled in the creation by the act of the

Creator. Idolatry exists because there is a real God against which to measure false worship, but precisely because there is a real God who is good, true worship is always a possibility.

If we turn once more to Acts 17, we can see how Luke's Paul weaves idolatry critique together with a sympathetic understanding of the kind of worship that humans spontaneously engage in. Paul is, first, "deeply distressed to see that the city was full of idols" (17:16). He enters into debate with the Athenians and first addresses them by noting how *deisidaimonesterous* they are (17:22). The King James Version translates the word as "too superstitious," but the NRSV renders it as "extremely religious." The ambiguity of the term might be deliberate, allowing Paul to be both critical of and sympathetic to the ubiquity of worship among the Athenians.[121] Paul remarks on the local altar dedicated to "an unknown god." The Athenians appear to be covering all their bases by erecting an altar to any god they might not have heard of yet: just in case there is another god out there that we don't know, we will worship that god too.[122] Paul regards the Athenians' worship as, to use Charles Taylor's word, "misrecognition." "What therefore you worship as unknown, this I proclaim to you" (17:23). God is the Creator of all things and gives life to all living things, so God does not live in shrines "made by human hands" (17:24–5):

> From one ancestor he made all nations to inhabit the whole earth, and he allotted the times of their existence and the boundaries of the places where they would live, so that they would search for God and perhaps grope for him and find him—though indeed he is not far from each one of us. For "In him we live and move and have our being"; as even some of your own poets have said, "For we too are his offspring." (17:26–8)

There is here at least the possibility of reading the Athenians' idolatry sympathetically. They have such a need for worship that they will leave no god without honor. But they seek the divine in things made by human hands. In this, they are not far from the true God, who gives Godself to be found in the beauties of creation.[123] Here Luke's Paul is not far from the Paul of Romans 1:19–20, who writes, "For what can be known about God is plain to them, because God has shown it to them. Ever since the creation of the world his eternal power and divine nature, invisible though they are, have been understood and seen through the things he has made." In his speech to the Athenians, Paul seems to appreciate the earnestness with which they are searching for God, and he holds out hope that they will continue to "grope for him and find him," for God is near to each thing God has created, including all human beings, God's own offspring, who derive life and being from God, and are immersed in God. God can be found by those who earnestly seek the invisible God in God's creation; the Athenians' mistake is to identify divinity with visible, created things. Paul's sympathetic reading here is an echo of the Wisdom of Solomon: "Yet these people are little to be blamed, for perhaps they go astray while seeking God and desiring to find him. For while they live among his works, they keep searching, and they trust in what they see, because the things that are seen are beautiful" (13:6–7).

In each of these passages, the suggestion of sympathy is immediately qualified, if not rejected. Both Wisdom and Romans declare that the very availability of the invisible God in visible creation leaves people with no excuse for not finding God (Wis. 13:8–9; Rom. 1:20). In his Areopagus speech in Acts 17, Paul declares that God has excused such earnest idolatry in the past, but no more, now that the Messiah has come: "While God has overlooked the times of human ignorance, now he commands all people everywhere to repent" (17:30). There is no question that the Bible draws a sharp line between the true God and the many idols available in the material world. Nevertheless, the absolute divide between the one Creator God and God's creation can itself mean that the lines between those who worship and those who do not, or between those who worship rightly and those who worship wrongly, are not absolute. The twin ideas that the true Creator God is available in all of God's beautiful creation and that the human person is a spontaneously worshiping creature allows for the possibility of a sympathetic approach to idolatry. It is precisely because there is one true God who created all things and continues to be present in them that idolatry is so difficult to uproot. I will have much more to say about the relationship between the invisible God and visible creation in the final chapter, on sacrament. But for now it is important to note that even in the Bible itself, idolatry critique has the potential to blur the lines between idolaters and nonidolaters, those who worship and those who do not. The Bible does not seem to recognize a distinction between worshipers and nonworshipers, and thus the distinction between religious and secular would appear to be a misrecognition of the human condition. We all worship.

It is apparent as well that idolatry critique in the Bible is predominantly self-critique. We all worship, and we all worship badly. The passages I have been examining that deal with pagan idolatry are dwarfed by the number of passages that deal with the idolatry of the people of God. As Fowl writes:

The bulk of the prophetic writings identify and call the people of Israel away from their idolatrous ways. It must be said, however, that the prophets do not have a great record of success in turning people away from idolatry. Indeed, one thing you can be pretty sure of is that when a prophet comes on the scene to denounce idolatry, things are already in a pretty bad way. Unless we contemporary believers are radically different from our forebears in the faith, when a prophet denounces our idolatrous ways, we are not likely to recognize the charges laid against us; we will be stubbornly unwilling to change our ways, and we will be deaf and blind to the voices and signs God sends our way.[124]

There is a sharp distinction between the true God and false gods, and between God and creation. The distinction between believers in that God and nonbelievers in that God is not so sharp, however, because of the phenomenon of idolatry, which, as we have seen, is less a matter of what people say they believe and more a matter of behavior. This does not at all mean that beliefs are unimportant, but rather that beliefs and practices are inseparable. For better and for worse, people's implicit beliefs are embedded in their behaviors. What people say they believe is sometimes betrayed by their actions; what people actually believe, their beliefs implicit in their actions, are sometimes at variance with their explicit beliefs, what they claim to believe.[125] The people of God are meant to be a "priestly kingdom and holy nation" (Ex. 19:6) but are in practice thoroughly idolatrous. In the Old Testament, the retribution of God falls mostly on the Israelites, not on other nations. Other nations who serve other gods are primarily used as means to accomplish God's retribution on Israel.[126]

The fact that many forms of idolatry are on a continuum of more and less, as we have observed, means that the boundaries between idolatry and right worship, and between idolaters and right worshipers, are also flexible and needing careful discernment. In I Corinthians 8–10, for example, Paul attempts to lay out rules for the Christian community who live in a context in which food offered to idols was an important part of social gatherings. Should the Christians eat such food if offered? Paul's response is complex. He begins by noting the nullity of idols: "Hence, as to the eating of food offered to idols, we know that 'no idol in the world really exists,' and that 'there is no God but one'" (8:4). This knowledge should give the Christian an attitude of freedom; since false gods do not really exist, "[w]e are no worse off if we do not eat, and no better off if we do" (8:8). If eating presents a stumbling block to those weaker members who do not understand that the false gods do not exist, however, then we should refrain (8:9–13). Paul goes on to proclaim that he will not use his freedom for his own benefit but will cross the boundaries between Jews and Greeks, and between the strong and the weak, in order to bring people to salvation: "To those outside the law I became as one outside the law (though I am not free from God's law but am under Christ's law) so that I might win those outside the law. To the weak I became weak, so that I might win the weak. I have become all things to all people, so that I might by any means save some" (9:21–2). Paul warns the community to flee from idols (10:7, 14) and to gather in fellowship around the Eucharist, not around food sacrificed to idols (10:16–22). Nevertheless, his instructions to the community are complex. Paul assumes that they must live among idolatry and idolaters; he does not suggest that they can or should withdraw from the surrounding society. So Paul instructs:

> Eat whatever is sold in the meat market without raising any question on the ground of conscience, for "the earth and its fullness are the Lord's." If an unbeliever invites you to a meal and you are disposed to go, eat whatever is set before you without raising any question on the ground of conscience. But if someone says to you, "This has been offered in sacrifice," then do not eat it, out of consideration for the one who informed you, and for the sake of conscience—I mean the other's conscience, not your own. For why should my liberty be subject to the judgement of someone else's conscience? If I partake with thankfulness, why should I be denounced because of that for which I give thanks? (10:25–30)

Paul is concerned with idolatry but leaves open a considerable range of possible interactions with idolaters. As David Horrell observes:

> There is in Paul a collocation of on the one hand a strong rhetoric of difference, with its stark contrasts between the idolatrous world and the pure *ekklesia*, which underpins a strong sense of group-identity and separation, and on the other hand a concern for accommodation and peaceful coexistence which permits a considerable degree of social integration and open interaction.[127]

For the early Christian community, the task was not retreating into an impossible place of purity but finding ways of "living *with* idols," as Christopher Rowland puts it, without serving them or taking up the lifestyle associated with them.[128] Idolatry was not limited to what modern people consider "religion." As Rowland notes, "It was not that the wider world outside pagan temples was somehow a neutral zone as far as idols and demons are concerned." The Christian life "meant wrestling principalities and powers on a continuous basis, and seeing in the everyday temptations to a life of covetousness, the temptation to idolatry (Col. 3:5)."[129] Such wrestling did not mean the refusal to use money but rather the careful discernment of how to use money without serving Mammon. The point at which the use of money becomes idolatrous is not marked by a sharp boundary, and so the boundary between idolatry and right worship tends to run right through the human heart. The line between idolaters and nonidolaters is not coterminous with the line between the visible church and the rest of the world. Though Christians confess with their tongues belief in the God of Jesus Christ, what they confess with their lives is a more complicated matter.

What I have tried to suggest in these first three chapters is that the modern binaries of enchantment and disenchantment, religious and secular, believers and nonbelievers, worshipers and nonworshipers are more ideological than empirical. They do not simply correspond to the way the world is. In the present chapter, I have explored a theology of idolatry grounded in the biblical texts as a way toward a more adequate description of human life, both ancient and modern. The various treatments of idolatry found in the biblical texts suggest that human beings are spontaneously worshiping creatures whose devotion is directed toward all sorts of created things. As Weber saw, people have a proclivity for making gods, either personal or impersonal, that come to rule over them, with often severe repercussions. The inanimate things to which we impute life drain the life away from us. This dynamic befalls both "believers" and "nonbelievers" because it is behavior, not what people claim to believe, that is decisive. In this sense, any sharp boundary between believers and nonbelievers is misleading. Rather than seeing the domination of humans by false gods as our inescapable fate, however, the Bible teaches that there is a true God among the countless false ones. The true God is often "misrecognized," in Taylor's language, but that observation is grounded in the hope that there is a true and good God who can lead us away from domination and into true freedom. The Christian hope is that, although the Kingdom of God is not yet fully consummated, God has reached out to us, taking on material form in the Incarnation, so that we might still grope and find God amid the things of this world. In the next chapter, I will examine another theological approach to that hope in the work of Augustine.

4

Augustine on Idolatry as Self-Worship

In exploring some of the dynamics of idolatry in the Bible in the previous chapter, we encountered a portrayal of the human person as a desiring creature whose many loves alight on all kinds of created things. The biblical writers recognize both the promise of such motivated seeking and its dangers: in the movement of the created person toward other created things, the source of creation can be neglected, and the self can attempt to usurp God's position. The human making of gods is an attempt to bring God down to a human level while elevating humans to a god-like level; we want to have gods that serve human desires rather than the other way around. Pride and idolatry are therefore intertwined. As idolatry is based on a falsehood—the elevation of the creature to the status of the Creator—the attempt at elevation inevitably fails; we think we can control the gods we make, but they end up dominating us. The violence humans suffer is self-inflicted. In idolatry, a kind of exchange takes place in which inanimate objects take on life, while life is drained away from human persons.

In the present chapter, I would like to build on the biblical material by exploring a theological understanding of idolatry through the writing of St. Augustine of Hippo. Rather than attempt a historical survey of theological reflections on idolatry throughout the centuries, I will explore the work of Augustine, who has had a formative influence on the Christian tradition of thinking about idolatry, desire, worship, and the human person's relationship to Creator and creation. For Augustine, idolatry—despite its outward appearance as dedication to something other than the self—is rooted in a kind of self-love, though one that paradoxically results in the dissolution of the self.

In the first section of this chapter, I examine Augustine's critique of pagan idolatry. In the second, I investigate his analysis of the human relationship to created things, and then, in the third, the perversion of that relationship by self-deification. In the fourth section, I consider Augustine's take on graven images and their relationship to sacraments. The reading of Augustine in this chapter helps provide the groundwork for later chapters that interpret

The Uses of Idolatry. William T. Cavanaugh, Oxford University Press. © Oxford University Press 2024.
DOI: 10.1093/oso/9780197679043.003.0005

contemporary social dynamics in terms of idolatrous self-worship, and for the final chapter that tries to imagine a sacramental alternative.

4.1. Augustine against the Gods

The kind of idolatry with which Augustine is most immediately concerned is the pagan worship of the gods of the Roman pantheon, which persists in the late Roman Empire, despite the widespread acceptance of Christianity. Augustine's *City of God* is in part a polemic against the worship of the Roman gods. In the face of charges that Rome's misfortunes in the early part of the fifth century could be laid at the feet of Christians—who had angered the gods by discouraging cults directed toward their appeasement—Augustine narrates Roman history as one long series of violence and calamities, from which the gods were powerless to protect the people. Such gods were no-gods, the mere inventions of human ingenuity. Violence was the natural consequence of pagan idolatry, for the gods were nothing more than de-monic constructs built from the self-aggrandizing desires of the Romans themselves.

Such polemics might seem rather remote from present affairs; there are very few people today for whom Jupiter worship is a live concern. But Augustine's attacks on pagan worship open onto some of his wider concerns with attachment to temporal things, human pride and self-love, and the eth-ical consequences of worshiping anything other than the true God. What matters to Augustine is not so much the specific characteristics of the Roman gods, though he does not spare them contempt (e.g., Priapus, "swelling in all his naked obscenity!").[1] The gods are nevertheless in some sense beneath contempt, because they do not exist. They are transparently the products of human creation. What matters to Augustine is the process of god-making and what that process says about human behavior and the dynamics of the human soul.

In book IV of the *City of God*, Augustine marvels at the sheer number and variety of gods to whom the Romans appealed. Augustine mocks the "crowd of tiny gods" (*turba minutorum deorum*), each with their own niche: the goddess Seia looked after the grain when it was sown, but Segetia took over when shoots began to appear, and Tutilina was in charge once the grain was reaped and stored.[2] Augustine gives example after example of the innumer-able but inconsistently distributed middle managers of the cosmos. There is one highest god, Jupiter, who is thought by some to "fill the universe," but at the same time he must endure the indignity of sharing his power with his wife Juno and countless other gods who claim different realms of geography or activity as their turf. Some pagans try to cover this dishonor by identifying all the many gods with Jupiter, but they then fail to explain why each of the other gods must be worshiped instead of simply worshiping one god.[3] In addition to marveling at the gods the Romans have, Augustine wonders why they have not found more. Why, for example, is "Foreign Injustice" not a god, when it has played such an important role in the expansion of the empire?[4] Why not "Temperance" and "Fortitude" and other virtues?[5] There seems to be no reasonable limit on the arbitrary multiplication of gods. For Augustine, the proliferation of gods is related to the rise of the Roman Empire, but not in the way the pagans seem to think. Rather than attributing Roman strength to the favor of the gods, Augustine seems to regard the proliferation of gods as just one more manifestation of restless Roman acquisitiveness.[6] The Romans acknowledged a goddess named Quies—tranquility—but put her temple outside the city gates and refused to adopt it as a national shrine. Was this, Augustine asks, a "symptom of an untranquil spirit?" Or was it rather that a people who worshiped a "mob of demons (for clearly they were not gods)" could not enjoy the tranquility to which Jesus, the true Physician, invites humanity?[7]

Much of the *City of God* can be read as Augustine's attempt to show the link between idolatry and the absence of peace in the history he tells. Book III tells the story of Rome as one long tale of blood in which the gods do not protect the Romans but rather feed their lust for domination that fuels war and conquest:

This "lust for domination" [*libido ista dominandi*] brings great evils to vex and exhaust the whole human race. Rome was conquered by this lust when she triumphed over the conquest of Alba, and to the popular acclaim of her crime she gave the name of "glory," since the sinner, as the Bible says, "is praised in the desires of his soul, and the man whose deeds are wicked is congratulated."[8]

Book IV then connects this lust for domination with the restless proliferation of gods. Book XVIII returns to this theme in telling the history of the Babylonian/Assyrian Empire, the forerunner to Rome, which Augustine calls the "second Babylon."[9] These two great empires exemplify the outworking of the earthly city in history, which is a tale of dominance and submission born of human pride. This sordid history of violence is densely intertwined with idolatry. As book IV does for Rome, book XVIII recounts the multiplication of gods under the Babylonians, Egyptians, and Greeks, including the deification of human kings. As Gregory Lee comments, "On Augustine's account . . . violence and idolatry are both symptoms of the same impulse: an inordinate desire for earthly goods coupled with a refusal to seek them from God."[10]

For Augustine, the gods are manufactured by humans out of their own desires. He closes book XVIII of the *City of God* by contrasting the two cities with regard to their respective positions on divinity and creation: "One of them, the earthly city, has created for herself such false gods as she wanted, from any source she chose—even creating them out of men—in order to worship them with sacrifices. The other city, the Heavenly City on pilgrimage in this world, does not create false gods. She herself is the creation of the true God, and she herself is to be his true sacrifice."[11] Augustine's description of the two cities here echoes his more famous summary at the end of book XIV, in which he contrasts the two cities in terms of two kinds of love: self-love (*amor sui*) and the love of God. There too Augustine links idolatry to human pride and the attempt to fulfill selfish desires rather than the will of God. Quoting Paul in Romans 1, Augustine writes that the earthly city does not honor God as God, but rather

exalting themselves in their wisdom, under the domination of pride [*superbia*]—"they became foolish, and changed the glory of the imperishable God into an image representing a perishable man, or birds or beasts or reptiles"—for in the adoration of idols [*simulacra*] of this kind they were either leaders or followers of the general public—"and they worshipped and served created things instead of the Creator, who is blessed for ever."[12]

At the root of both idolatry and pride is an inversion of the proper order of Creator and creation. Rather than acknowledging that they are creatures of the one Creator, humans become the creators of the gods. Some even celebrate this human power. Augustine quotes Hermes Trismegistus, who, though freely admitting that the ancestors "invented the art of creating gods," thinks (as would Nietzsche much later) that the human manufacture of gods is "wonderful," for "the miracle of miracles is that man has been able to discover the divine nature and to bring it into being."[13] For Hermes, god-making is an exercise of human power and nobility. Augustine, on the other hand, does not think that bowing down to a mere creature of human ingenuity can be ennobling. He is incredulous that Hermes would lament the passing of the gods "who, on his own showing, are the creations of men . . . as if there were any unhappier situation than that of a man under the domination of his own inventions."[14] Rather than exalting humans by making them creators of the gods, the human attempt to disturb the proper order—in which humans occupy a middle position between God and beasts—can only result in the lowering of humans to subhuman status. After again quoting Romans 1:21ff., as he does in many other places, Augustine writes:

> It is easier for a man to cease to be a man, by worshipping as gods things of his own creation, than it is for things of man's own creation to become gods as a result of his worship. It is more likely that "man who is in a position of honour and who does not realize it," should become "comparable to the beasts," than that the work of man's hands should be ranked above a work of God, created in God's image—that is, man himself. So it is just that man should be sundered from him who made him, when he puts above himself that which he has created.[15]

The vertical imagery here reflects that of the Fall, whereby grasping at what is higher—eat from the tree and "you will be like gods" (Gen. 3:5)—leads to the downward fall of humanity and the obscuring of the image of God in which we are made. Similarly, the self-elevation of humanity to the status of god-maker only lowers us to being subject to mere human artifacts.

For Augustine, the attempt to assert control over the divine leads directly to the loss of control, and the attempt to possess is but a symptom of being possessed by demons. "For the fact that man was the maker of his gods did not mean that he was not possessed by what he had made, for by worshipping them he was drawn into fellowship with them, and I do not mean fellowship with senseless idols [idolorum stolidorum], but with crafty demons."[16] Idols are mere material things, bereft of life; Augustine quotes Psalm 115: "They have eyes, but they do not see."[17] Idols nevertheless are possessed by "unclean spirits" (inmundi spiritus), which are "bound to these images by this wicked art" (eisdem simulacris arte illa nefaria conligati), and these spirits take their worshipers into captivity.[18] Human pride mirrors the pride of the demons, whose fall from their angelic state was "the just result of their turning away from him who supremely is, and their turning toward themselves, who do not exist in that supreme degree. What other name is there for this fault than pride [*superbia*]?"[19] Precisely in their turning away from God and toward themselves they lose themselves, and become captive to the will of an evil other. Pagan idolatry is not just full of unintended consequences; it is born not just of error but of deceit, the deception through which the demons enlist the earthly city to join their rebellion against God.[20]

This rebellion against God has the pernicious effect of confusing the relationship between divinity and material creation. The pagan gods represent the divinization of temporal activities and material creation which, being subject to change, cannot be the true God. Naturalists like Varro reduce the gods to symbolic representations of natural phenomena, and Augustine is almost ready to recognize a certain value in this, provided it "were at least congruous with the spirit of religion" and devoid of depraved practices and cults.[21] But in the end, Augustine regards this attempt to rescue the gods as blasphemous and evil, since it is wrong to worship anything, either material or spiritual, that is created instead of the Creator. If any element of creation is worshiped, it is an evil thing, not because creation is evil but because creation should be employed only in the worship of him to whom worship is due, the Creator of all.[22] Augustine has no patience for Varro's attempt to rescue the gods by referring them to the elements of the sky and the earth: "Even if the attempt succeeded, no truly religious person worships the world in place of the true God."[23] Elsewhere, in *De doctrina christiana*, Augustine similarly dismisses the suggestion that Neptune is not a god but is taken as a symbolical representation of the sea. It may be true that those who make gods of the works of humans are worse than those who make gods of the works of God— that is, natural elements of creation, like the sea—but both are still idolaters, for both render worship to the creation instead of to the Creator.[24]

When Augustine writes of idols and idolatry, his primary reference is to the worship of pagan gods and the sacred images of these gods. He writes in *De trinitate* that "they are called idolaters who pay to images that service which is due to God" (*idolatrae dicuntur qui simulacris eam seruitutem exhibent quae debetur deo*).[25] But for Augustine, the explicit worship of the images of pagan gods is part of a broader critique of the worship of created things instead of God. In the passage from *De trinitate* just cited, Augustine distinguishes between two senses of "service" in Greek: *douleúein*, by which we serve one another in love, and *latreúein*, a kind of service that belongs only to God. Idolaters render the latter to creatures.[26] Later in *De trinitate* Augustine discusses the "distinguished philosophers" of the nations who have been able "to discern the invisible things of God by those things which are made" but nevertheless have fallen into iniquity because they philosophize without Christ, the Mediator between the visible and the invisible:

> For placed as they were in these lowest things, they could not but seek for some means whereby they might reach those sublime things which they had understood; and so they fell into the power of these deceitful demons, who brought it about that they changed the glory of the incorruptible God into a likeness of the image of corruptible man [*in similitudinem imaginis corruptibilis hominis*], of birds, of four-footed beasts, and of serpents. For in such forms they even set up or worshiped idols [*idola*].[27]

Again, Romans 1 helps Augustine to establish a connection between pagan idolatry and the broader theme of undue attachment to the lower things of creation.

Augustine sounds the same theme in *De doctrina christiana*: "Among superstitious things is whatever has been instituted by men concerning the making and worshiping of idols [*idola*], or concerning the worshiping of any creature or any part of any creature as though it were God."[28] Through the connection between the worship of pagan gods and undue attachment to temporal things, Augustine makes clear that such attachments are not innocent. Indeed, he associates idolatry with demonic activity. Augustine quotes Paul's first letter to the Corinthians (10:19–20), agreeing with Paul that idols are nothing in themselves but are used in the worship of demons instead of God. Augustine continues:

> For what the Apostle says concerning idols and the sacrifices that are made in their honor should be understood concerning all imaginary signs which lead to the cult of idols or to the worship of a creature or its parts as God, or pertain to the concern for remedies and other observations which are not as it were publicly and divinely constituted for the love of God and of our neighbor but rather debauch the hearts of the wretched through their love for temporal things. With reference to all teachings of this kind, therefore, the society of demons is to be feared and avoided.[29]

For Augustine and ancient Christians more generally, demons are real spiritual powers invested with agency. Recognition of the nearness of demonic spirits has certainly diminished in the modern West—though not in many places in Africa and elsewhere—and in this limited sense the standard disenchantment narrative holds true. Augustine's world is not the same as ours in the West. But Augustine remains relevant because for him the worship of pagan gods is one particularly acute symptom of a more general "love for temporal things" which detracts from the love for God.

4.2. Created Things

To unpack Augustine's critique of idolatry, it is undoubtedly important to understand the historical context in which he writes. For Augustine, the primary valence of idolatry was the worship of the Roman gods and their images. It is equally important to recognize, however, that the *City of God*, while giving a detailed history of the Roman Empire and empires that preceded it, is meant to be a universal history not just of this or that people or empire but of the two cities with their two loves. The earthly and heavenly cities are manifested in history but are not limited to geographical places or times. They are instead two types of performances running through all times and places, marked either by love of self or love of God, by love of temporal things that pass away or love of eternal things that last. The history of the two cities begins with the angels' fall but continues through the life of every human person caught between worship of and rebellion against the one true God. To explore Augustine's critique of idolatry, then, we must move beyond his context in the late Roman Empire and consider his universal history of the human race as a history of the contradictory forces that tug at each human soul.

As we have seen, pagan idolatry for Augustine is one manifestation of a wider tendency in the earthly city to cling to perishable created things instead of to their Creator. What made the earthly city earthly was the futile attempt to drag divinity down to earth. The Roman quest for glory was an attempt to find eternity among things that pass away. So in book V of the *City of God*, Augustine writes:

Those Roman heroes belonged to an earthly city, and the aim set before them, in all their acts of duty for her, was the safety of their country, and a kingdom not in heaven, but on earth; not in life eternal, but in the process where the dying pass away and are succeeded by those who will die in their turn. What else was there for them to love save glory? For, through glory, they desired to have a kind of life after death on the lips of those who praised them.[30]

Though his presentation of early Roman heroes is not without admiration, for Augustine the Romans set out to conquer other nations not out of a kind of Nietzschean life-affirming will to power but rather out of a kind of desperate attempt to secure immortality amid the utter absence of hope for such. With no hope for eternal life, the Romans could only cling more fiercely to temporal things, despite the futility of such attachments in the face of death.

Augustine explores this theme at great depth in his *Confessions*. There the story he tells on a broad historical canvas in the *City of God* is told through a detailed examination of his own soul and his personal journey toward God. The death of his close friend in book IV of the *Confessions* provides an opportunity for him to reflect at length on the misery of "every soul overcome by friendship with mortal things and lacerated when they are lost."[31] The problem was not the friendship as such, but the fact that Augustine had loved "a person sure to die as if he would never die."[32] Augustine grapples with the reality of time, and the way that time eventually dooms our attachments to all temporal things. Things fall apart. Things die. *I myself* die, rendering all my attachments temporary, unstable, unfulfillable. Wherever the human soul turns, it is "fixed in sorrows" (*ad dolores figitur*) unless it is fixed upon God, who alone is eternal and does not die. Nothing has being unless it is summoned out of nothingness by God, who alone escapes the ravages of time.[33]

The perishable things that God has made are not without value; they can even be an aid to the worship of God:

Let these transient things be the ground on which my soul praises you (Ps. 145:2), "God creator of all." But let it not become stuck in them and glued to them with love [*amore*] through the physical senses. For these things pass along the path of things that move towards non-existence. They rend the soul with pestilential desires; for the soul loves to be in them and take its repose among the objects of its love. But in these things there is no point of rest: they lack permanence. . . . No one can fully grasp them even while they are present.[34]

The false attachment to material creation instead of the Creator is again the inability to deal with the reality of time. We get stuck, we seek rest, in the flux of time where there is no rest, no permanence. Augustine presents life on earth as a mixture of delight and weariness; we alight on material things both because they enchant our physical senses and because they offer some solace and repose on an arduous journey through time. Behind both delight and weariness stands the false promise of at least a temporary escape from the dread of our own mortality and that of the ones we love. Delight in transient things can become a distraction from having to face mortality; seeking rest seems to offer the opportunity to stop the relentless march of time toward death. When we become attached to things with love (*amore*), the soul is rent in two, pulled apart, one part longing to move toward God, to whom love is properly owed, the other part stuck in the present, fascinated by temporal things.

It is worth noticing that a kind of death comes not only to living creatures but to all temporal things. All things are on "the path of things that move towards non-existence": "Things rise and set: in their emerging they begin as it were to be, and grow to perfection; having reached perfection, they grow old and die. Not everything grows old, but everything dies. So when things rise and emerge into existence, the faster they grow to be, the quicker they rush towards non-being. That is the law limiting their being."[35] To say that only God is eternal is to say that all created things are marked for death, for nonexistence. To call them "temporal" things is to say there is no refuge from the movement of time toward death to be found in them. This is why "[n]o one can fully grasp them even while they are present." There is a movement in them toward absence that eludes our detection. Our physical senses regard things as fully present; our physical perception, Augustine says, is "slow" (*tardus est enim sensus carnis*).[36] We are fooled into attributing presence and permanence to temporal things that obey an unseen hastening toward nonexistence.

Despite this rather grim reckoning with death, Augustine does not think that earthly delight is mere illusion. The demonic is not absent from the *Confessions*, but the emphasis there is more on the goodness of all that is. In his rejection of Manichaeism in books V–VII, Augustine turns away from the view that material creation is evil. Following Genesis, he concludes that everything that is created by a good God must be good, and evil must be the mere privation of good, a falling away from an original ontological goodness. Evil is not a substance but "a perversity of will twisted away from the highest substance, you O God, towards inferior things, rejecting its own inner life and swelling with external matter."[37] But he continues on to explain that even the inferior things are a path to God. Quoting Romans 1 yet again, Augustine writes, "I was wholly certain that your invisible nature 'since the foundation of the world is understood from the things which are made, that is your eternal power and divinity.' "[38]

The beauty of created things nevertheless has an ambivalent position in Augustine's narrative. Augustine continually refers to the beauty in material creation, the "fleeting experience of beauty in these lowest of things."[39] At an early stage of his development, Augustine wrote a treatise on beauty in which he tried to determine what qualities inherent in things made them beautiful. He distinguished between beauty which is a kind of totality in itself and beauty which comes from a thing being well-adapted and fitting to another thing. He wrote, he says, two or three books on the subject; he cannot remember exactly, having long since relegated them to the trash bin.[40] At that stage he was searching for beauty as an inherent quality in things themselves. As he confesses to God in the famous passage in book X, "[Y]ou were within and I was in the external world and sought you there, and in my unlovely state I plunged into those lovely created things which you made." Although he says he sought God in external things, he does not seem to know yet that it was God that he was searching for. "You were with me, and I was not with you. The lovely things kept me far from you, though if they did not have their existence in you, they had no existence at all." God can be found in beautiful things, but it is only in retrospect that Augustine comes to call God "beauty so old and so new." Beauty is the presence of God shining *through* things, not a quality that has its origin *in* things. Until he realizes that beauty is not a quality that inheres in things themselves but is an epiphany of God in each beautiful thing, beauty is only a distraction for Augustine, one that entangles him in external things and keeps him far from both God and himself. For his self is also not a quality inhering in him but is a gift received from outside himself. Augustine's true self, he comes to realize, is summoned by the presence of God from outside him, while the false self, the ego, was lost in the world of things. The true self is summoned by God who creates him and calls to his creation: "You called and cried out loud and shattered my deafness. . . . You touched me, and I am set on fire to attain the peace which is yours."[41]

The apparent ambivalence of beauty comes not from an ambivalence in created things themselves but instead from an ambivalence in the human will, a wavering in the human power of judging and using things. According to Augustine, the fault is not with God's good creation: "[H]eaven and earth and everything in them on all sides tell me to love you. Nor do they cease to

tell everyone that 'they are without excuse' (Rom. 1:20)."[42] Augustine immediately mitigates the apparent harshness of Paul's words, citing a later passage
about God's mercy from the same letter of Paul to the Romans (9:15). It is
only the grace of God working in the person that can inspire them to refer
the beauty of creation to the love of God. Without God's inscrutable mercy,
creation's praise would be falling on deaf ears. Augustine is finally able to
hear it. He asks the earth and the sea and the sun and the moon and the living
creatures if they are the object of his love, and they respond, "We are not your
God, look beyond us." Augustine comments, "My question was the attention
I gave to them, and their response was their beauty."[43] And still some are able
to see the beauty and hear the praise and some are not. Augustine dismisses
the idea that the created order appears and speaks differently to different
people; to accept this idea would be to question the goodness of the created
order.[44] What varies is the quality of judgment within people which either
does or does not allow them to receive the truth of creation. Again citing
Romans 1:20, Augustine says that people can question creation and see the
invisible things of God through the visible things God has made: "Yet by love
[amore] of created things they are subdued by them, and being thus made
subject become incapable of exercising judgement. Moreover, created things
do not answer those who question them if power to judge is lost."[45] In other
words, the idolatry of improper attachment to created things is caused by
the person's response to those things, not by the things themselves. Created
things are not idols in and of themselves; idolatry arises in the relationship of
the person to the thing.

In this passage, it is love of created things that leads to the loss of a proper
relationship between human beings and things. Augustine clearly thinks that
love belongs to God, even though things, with their beauty, can be vehicles
for that love. But when Augustine asks what it is that he loves when he loves
God, he claims that he does not love physical beauty or temporal glory, the
brightness of light, the sweet melody of songs, the smell of flowers, the taste
of honey, or the embrace of bodies. He loves instead the interior light, sound,
smell, taste, and touch that cannot be touched by time or lost because of
physical limitations because they all reside in the eternal God.[46] This seems
like Augustine is deprecating material creation; things cannot be loved, and
only the spiritual senses, not the physical senses, are truly helpful. Augustine
does allow a positive role for physical pleasure, and allows for a kind of love
of created things in God: "If physical objects give you pleasure, praise God
for them and return love to their Maker lest, in the things that please you,

you displease him. If souls please you, they are being loved in God [*in deo amentur*]; for they also are mutable and acquire stability by being established in him."[47] Nevertheless, Augustine's acknowledgment of the goodness of creation here seems, at first glance, rather grudging. Physical pleasure in objects must be immediately returned to God, and love of other people gains integrity only if they are loved not for themselves but in God.

We will perhaps achieve clarity by examining Augustine's distinction between enjoyment and use (*fruitio* and *usus*),[48] but it is precisely here that some have accused Augustine of a distorted view of God's creatures. As Augustine posits in *De doctrina christiana*, "To enjoy something is to cling to it with love for its own sake. To use something, however, is to employ it in obtaining that which you love, provided that it is worthy of love."[49] Things to be enjoyed make us blessed, while things to be used help sustain us as we move toward blessedness.[50] Only things which are eternal and immutable are to be enjoyed;[51] God alone is to be enjoyed as an end in Godself.[52] Everything else, including human beings, are to be used so that we may enjoy God. We are commanded to love one another, but Augustine asks whether we are to love one another for our own sake or for the sake of something else. "If for his own sake, we enjoy him; if for the sake of something else, we use him. But I think that man is to be loved for the sake of something else."[53] By the same logic, Augustine concludes that we should not enjoy ourselves either. He employs the familiar metaphor of a journey home to explain the use/enjoyment distinction. Those who cannot live in blessedness anywhere but their native country will need vehicles for land and sea to get there. If we enjoyed the vehicles and other amenities of the journey, we might not wish to conclude the journey quickly, "and, entangled in a perverse sweetness, we should be alienated from our country, whose sweetness would make us blessed."[54] In this metaphor, all created things, including human beings, are vehicles for the journey to God. In his attempt to avoid idolizing created things, Augustine seems to instrumentalize things and even people as mere means to be used toward the end of enjoying God. There seems little that could be more selfish than using other people for the sake of one's own enjoyment, even if that enjoyment is of God.

Such critiques have been advanced most prominently by Anders Nygren and Oliver O'Donovan.[55] Nygren reads the *usus/fruitio* distinction through his dichotomy of *eros* and *agape*. Using the neighbor as a thing cannot conform to Nygren's *agape*, an altruistic neighbor-love that stands opposed to the self-absorbed and instrumentalizing *eros*.[56] O'Donovan distinguishes between an ontological employment of the *usus/fruitio* distinction and an eschatolog-ical one. According to O'Donovan, Augustine's distinction is an appropriate recognition of the ontological subordination of creatures to the Creator. Use-love is an appropriately subordinate love to the kind of love that is due to God. When put into Augustine's eschatological framework, however—exemplified by his metaphor of the journey—his distinction serves to instrumentalize human beings, to use them as a mere means toward an end. Created things are demoted to a means to attain heaven, something to be discarded when the end is attained. The journey motif, according to O'Donovan, reinforces an instrumentalized use of created things "in which the object of use is assumed merely temporarily and without commitment."[57] O'Donovan thinks that Augustine's use of the distinction and the metaphor most detrimentally instrumentalizes human beings and therefore stands in irreconcilable tension with Jesus's command that we love one another. O'Donovan regards the dis-tinction as a mistake that Augustine later wisely abandoned.

Such critiques of Augustine's distinctions have been rightly criticized for being insufficiently nuanced and unfair to his intent.[58] Augustine's use of *usus/fruitio* has been too easily assimilated to the Kantian means/end dis-tinction in the modern era. "Using someone" in modern English has an un-mitigated negative connotation, implying the selfish and callous disregard for the good of the person being used. In ancient Latin, on the other hand, the verb *uti* can have instrumental meanings, but can also mean "to have friendly relations or associate with." *Frui* conversely can mean "to delight in," but can also signify "to derive advantage from" or "profit by."[59] Helmut David Baer suggests we allow Augustine the same flexibility in his use of the terms. Rather than, as does O'Donovan, assume a rigidity in the *usus/fruitio* dis-tinction and then fault Augustine for inconsistency in its application,[60] we should recognize that Augustine is trying to invent a way of talking about the relationship of God and creatures that both recognizes the absolute di-vide between them and proclaims that that divide has been bridged by the figure of Jesus Christ. Augustine introduces the *usus/fruitio* distinction in I.3.3 of *De doctrina christiana* but does not begin to discuss neighbor-love until I.22.20, after he has discussed Christ and his Body, the Church. Christ, Augustine tells us, works through the "principle of contraries" by which in becoming mortal he freed us from mortality.[61] Christ's status as both divine and human—and human participation in Christ through the sacraments and acts of charity—disrupts any reading of *usus* as instrumentalizing others for selfish ends.

Christ bridges the *usus/fruitio* divide because Christ is both the goal of the journey, as God, and the vehicle or means by which humans attain the goal. "Thus He says, 'I am the way, and the truth, and the life'; that is, you are to come through me, to arrive at me, and to remain in me."[62] Or again, "Although He is our native country, He made Himself also the Way to that country."[63] Christ "wished to lay down Himself as a means for our return,"[64] and so we may say that Christ is among those things to be "used" to get to God. Augustine himself employs the language of use in his metaphor of Christ as the cure that heals our wounds:

> Just as a cure is the way to health, so also this Cure received sinners to heal and strengthen them. And just as physicians when they bind up wounds do not do so haphazardly but neatly so that a certain beauty accompanies the utility [*utilitatem*] of the bandages, so the medicine of Wisdom by taking on humanity is accommodated to our wounds, healing some by contraries and some by similar things.[65]

In this relationship, however, Christ is not a passive tool that the human person employs but is "at once the Physician and the Medicine."[66] God is the active agent who gives Godself to be used in Christ. God makes Godself useful to us in Christ so that we may enjoy blessedness with God in eternal life.

At the same time, Augustine contends that God uses human beings and does not enjoy them, but that use is part of God's love for us: "Therefore He does not enjoy us but uses us. For if He did neither, I cannot see how He could love us."[67] Augustine makes clear that the human way of using things and God's way of using things differ: "For we refer the things that we use to the enjoyment of the goodness of God; but God refers His use of us to His own good."[68] In other words, God's use refers to Godself, but human use is not self-referential. When a human person uses their neighbor, they refer the neighbor to God, not to themselves. To refer their neighbor to themselves would be to "enjoy" the neighbor, which would be a selfish act. The end of all human beings is God. As Baer remarks, "loving the neighbor for the sake of God means loving the neighbor in reference to her good; it means treating her with the respect she is due."[69] Using the neighbor is therefore the only way to respect the neighbor and help them toward their goal. To use the neighbor is to provide that neighbor with "refreshment" along the journey and to encourage them on their way home.[70]

Augustine asks, as Jesus was asked, "And who is my neighbor?" Jesus responds with the parable of the Good Samaritan. Augustine reads the wounded Jew in the parable as the neighbor, but broadens the category to include everyone—"every man is to be thought of as a neighbor"[71]—even including our enemies.[72] At the same time, Augustine identifies Christ with both the Samaritan and the recipient of the Samaritan's mercy, for "Our Lord God Himself wished to be called our neighbor."[73] For human persons the love of the neighbor will not only be densely intertwined with the love of God but will also be a kind of imitation of Christ, who is both Samaritan and neighbor. Neighbor-love is a kind of *usus* that participates in the way God uses us, which is also a way of making Godself useful for us so that we will achieve blessedness. In Christ, the barriers between God and humans, and between individuals and their neighbors, become blurred or even erased. The individual does not use the neighbor for selfish gain, to achieve the goal of getting admitted to heaven. All of the different streams of love flow together:

> But whatever else appeals to the mind as being lovable should be directed into that channel into which the whole current of love flows. Whoever, therefore, justly loves his neighbor should so act toward him that he also loves God with his whole heart, with his whole soul, and with his whole mind. Thus, loving his neighbor as himself, he refers the love of both to that love of God which suffers no stream to be led away from it by which it might be diminished.[74]

If God is love, then love is a kind of ocean in which all the different currents of love are intermingled, referred to one another by being referred to God, their source. There is no "mine" and "thine" in the love of God.[75] Just as God uses us by becoming useful to us, so we become useful to other people, loving them toward their good. And as we participate in this circulation of self-giving love, so do we receive and find our own good:

> That use which God is said to make of us is made not to His utility but to ours [*non ad eius, sed ad nostram utilitatem*], and in so far as He is concerned refers only to His goodness. When we are merciful to anyone and assist him, we do so for his utility [*utilitatem*], which is our goal; but in a curious way our own utility follows as a consequence when God does not leave that compassion which we expend on one who needs it without reward. The

greatest reward is that we enjoy [*perfruamur*] Him and that all of us who enjoy [*fruimur*] Him may enjoy [*perfruamur*] one another in Him.[76]

This is perhaps the most important passage in book I of *De doctrina christiana*. Here Augustine runs together the utility of God, oneself, and the neighbor. The "goal" becomes not the self's own blessedness but the utility of the neighbor, in which one is blessed as well. *Usus*, meanwhile, seems to flow directly into *fruitio*, for we not only enjoy God but enjoy one another in God. So, after all, we do enjoy the neighbor, though we do so, as we do anything good, in God.[77]

So if human creatures are not to be instrumentalized, what about the rest of creation, that is, temporal goods? Does Augustine denigrate material creation, seeing temporal things as only potential means to the end of eternal life? On the one hand, Augustine makes clear that "[n]ot everything which is to be used is to be loved [*diligenda sunt*]"; among things to be used, only human beings, angels, and the human body are to be loved as such.[78] But Augustine also says that the entire "temporal dispensation" was made for our salvation, and "[w]e should use it, not with an abiding but with a transitory love and delight [*dilectione et delectatione*] like that in a road or in vehicles or in other instruments, or, if it may be expressed more accurately, so that we love [*diligamus*] those things by which we are carried along for the sake of that toward which we are carried."[79] The kind of loving normally associated with God (*amare*), pertains neither to humans nor to temporal goods, but both are allowed *diligere*, and humans can even delight (*delectare*) in temporal goods, provided it is a transitory love and delight.[80] Augustine is not simply a grump who is afraid that someone somewhere might be having a good time. If God's creation is beautiful, then it should incite our love and delight. The problem, as we have already seen, is when people put their hearts into their things, as if they were going to stop time and save them. Augustine is not without sympathy for those who do; he acknowledges there are times of great weariness on our journey when we desire rest.[81] We are delighted by things and seek a kind of permanence in them. We are entitled to love them and delight in them precisely insofar as they are aids to our journey home. They become problematic when we see them as the actual source of our happiness, and when that happiness is cut off from the happiness of others. If I use things only as a means to my own self-given ends and neglect the neighbors journeying with me, then any delight quickly turns into an obstacle to attaining our true end together.

Temporal things are problematic not simply because God is offended by the misdirection of love intended for God to other things. The problem is that temporal things—including other people—will inevitably fail to fulfill the kind of eternal longings that we invest in them. It is not only that God will be dissatisfied; humans themselves will be dissatisfied. "Between temporal and eternal things there is this difference: a temporal thing is loved more before we have it, and it begins to grow worthless when we gain it, for it does not satisfy the soul, whose true and certain rest is eternity; but the eternal is more ardently loved when it is acquired than when it is merely desired."[82] Just as the ardor of romantic love fades, just as the desire and delight associated with a new car dissipates like that new car smell, all our temporal attachments will inevitably disappoint if they are not oriented toward our eternal destiny. And our eternal destiny, as Augustine has made plain, is bound up with the destiny of other people. Seeking one's own pleasure and neglecting love for the neighbor stifles the circulation of self-giving love and frustrates our enjoyment of God and of one another in God.

The importance of Augustine's *usus/fruitio* distinction for our analysis of idolatry can now be stated plainly. In trying to avoid the idolization of created things, both people and material goods, Augustine has been accused of going to the other extreme, of denigrating creation and instrumentalizing it, so that both people and things are mere means to the end of eternal life. What should now be clear is that, as Sarah Stewart-Kroeker writes, "[t]he apparently opposite poles of idolatry and instrumentalisation betray a magnetic attraction: the problem with idolatry is precisely that it instrumentalises and objectifies what the self loves for its own pleasure and consumption."[83] What constitutes idolatry, understood as inordinate attachment to created things instead of to their Creator, is the use of created things for one's own self-given ends. Idolatry and instrumentalization are not opposites; both narcissistically reduce people and things to the measure of our own wants. Both idolatry and instrumentalization are a reduction of people and things to means toward which the end is the self.

4.3. Self-Love

It is not immediately obvious, however, that idolatry is reducible to self-love. Idolatry is a type of worship, and at least appears to be the worship of something besides the self, the bowing down to gods of some kind, or to people or other created things, anything but the self. For Augustine, however, all human history can be reduced to two kinds of love: either one loves the one true God, "carried as far as contempt of self," or one loves the self, "reaching the point of contempt for God."[84] In Augustine's scheme, insofar as idolatry turns away from the true God, then, idolatry must be a form of self-love. But idolatry is not always or even usually a kind of crass and obvious self-seeking. There are, as we have seen, moments of sympathy in Augustine for the kind of weariness of the journey and delight in beauty that causes people to attach themselves to created things. Temporal honor has its own beauty and harmony, and human friendship brings about a noble unity between souls.[85] Augustine allows that such attachments can take the form of moving beyond the self; he shows a certain respect for the pagan Roman statesmen and soldiers whose sense of duty to the empire, something greater than themselves, moved them to self-sacrifice: "They took no account of their own material interests compared with the common good, that is the commonwealth and the public purse; they resisted the temptations of avarice; they acted for their country's well-being with disinterested concern; they were guilty of no offence against the law; they succumbed to no sensual indulgence."[86] Though they were motivated by love of praise, Augustine cannot help but acknowledge their virtue, which checks greater vices. The fact that God allows such virtue the temporal reward of human glory, Augustine writes, should suppress the Christians' pride.[87]

Ultimately, however, if not done in God, such attachments are in fact reducible to self-love. Augustine sees idolatry as a prideful turning away from God and toward the desires of the self. In characterizing the two cities and their two kinds of love at the end of book XIV of the *City of God*, Augustine returns to Paul's account of idolatry in Romans 1, where the idolaters' foolishness is attributed not simply to a mistake or to human frailty but to a willful refusal to honor God and to give thanks to God. Book XIV is largely an investigation into the origin of sin. In chapter 13 of book XIV, Augustine anticipates the conclusion of the book, writing, "In one city love of God has been given first place, in the other, love of self [*amor sui*]," and then immediately turning to Genesis 3:5, "You will be like gods." The origin of sin is pride as an attempt at self-deification, the exaltation of the self over God. Deification in itself is not evil; it is the goal of human life. Being like God is what we aspire to. The trap that the Devil lays for humans is cunning precisely in its appeal to what is good. Had humans been willing to receive deification from its true source, they would have been exalted. "In fact they would have been better able to be like gods if they had in obedience adhered to the supreme and real ground of their being, if they had not in pride made themselves their own ground. For created gods are gods not in their own true nature but by participation in the true God. By aiming at more, a man is diminished, when he elects to be self-sufficient and defects from the one who is really sufficient for him."[88] Augustine continues on to identify this self-regard as the primordial sin: "This then is the original evil: man regards himself as his own light, and turns away from that light which would make man himself a light if he would set his heart on it."[89] By turning toward oneself, a creature created from nothing (*ex nihilo*), the human person becomes, not quite a nonentity, but descends toward nothingness (*nihilo propinquare*).[90]

In his anti-Pelagian tract *The Spirit and the Letter*, Augustine also connects pride and idolatry. The Pelagians attribute self-sufficiency to the human will; how could God reward good behavior with eternal life if humans were not the source of their own actions? Augustine, on the other hand, attributes human perfection to God's grace:

> [I]t will be thanklessness in the soul to attribute to itself that which comes to it from God—above all, to think of the works of righteousness as its own, as acquired by itself for itself. This is not the vulgar conceit of wealth or good looks or eloquence, or of any of those good things, of body, mind, or circumstance, which may equally be possessed by wicked men; it is a would-be superior pride in those goods which properly belong to the good. It is the fault which has caused even great men to fall away from the steadfastness of the divine being into the dishonour of idolatry.[91]

It is worth noting that here Augustine links idolatry not simply to vulgar attachment to temporal goods but to the pride with which righteous people attribute their own good deeds to themselves. Such self-inflation, however, has the opposite of the intended effect; instead of exalting people to the status of gods, they fall to the status of nonentities. Such people "have mounted themselves like blown-up bubbles into the empty air, and fallen down not to rest but to be shattered on the stones of idolatry."[92] Just as idols are nothing but vanity and wind, so "[e]mptiness is the peculiar disease of men who deceive themselves in the belief that they are something, when they are nothing."[93]

Although elsewhere Augustine certainly does attack the "vulgar conceit of wealth" and such attachments to temporal goods, it is significant that he tends to tie such attachments to the root sin of pride. In *De Genesi ad litteram*, for example, Augustine considers the relationship between two scripture passages that apparently offer differing etiologies of sin. Ecclesiasticus (Sirach) 10:13 says, "The beginning of all sin is pride," while I Timothy 6:10 says that the "love of money is the root of all evils." Augustine reads the latter passage in terms of an expansive understanding of avarice as "what goads people to go for anything more greedily than is right because of their superiority and a kind of love for their very own property." There is no conflict between the two scriptural explanations of the root of sin. The love of money is just a particular kind of pride, or "ruinous self-love," for "not even human beings, after all, would be lovers of money, unless they thought that the richer they were, the more superior they would be too."[94] This kind of self-love, Augustine says, is "puffed up" (referring to I Cor. 13:4), but at the same time diminishes the person, because it signals the withdrawal of the person from what is common into privacy, the concern for what belongs to one's own self. The very term "privacy" is fitting, says Augustine, because it indicates "loss rather than gain in value; every privation, after all, spells diminution."[95] Privacy is a kind of deprivation, a shrinking of the self. The intent, nevertheless, is the inflation of the self. Money is not idolized for its own sake, but rather as a means for the narcissistic aggrandizement of the self. Idolatry once again meets instrumentalization. They are different but related effects of self-love.

Richard Miller comments, "For Augustine, narcissism and idolatry are two sides of the same coin, forged together by the self as the reference point for conceiving of both God and neighbor."[96] As we have seen, book IV of *Confessions* contains an extensive commentary on idolatrous attachment to transitory created things, the principal one of which is his unnamed friend, whose death leaves Augustine distraught. Augustine describes his friend in terms of himself; they were identical in age, interests, and also beliefs, at least after Augustine had convinced him to think as he did.[97] He describes his friend as his "other self" (*ille alter eram*); they were "one soul in two bodies."[98] Augustine describes friends willing to die for one another and says that his friend's death produced the opposite effect in him; he was "tired of living and scared of dying."[99] Augustine mourned and was inconsolable in his grief. He describes himself as being more attached to his life of misery than to his deceased friend. He confesses that he should have turned to God in his grief; those who love another in God lose none who are dear to them, "for all are dear in the one who cannot be lost."[100] But he was so turned in upon himself that he could not turn to God. He writes in one and the same passage "My error was my god" and "I could not escape from myself."[101] The same narcissism that could see his friend only as a reflection of himself had trapped him inside himself and blocked his way to God. Augustine could not find rest except in his own bitterness.[102] The idolatry of inordinate attachment to a temporal good—his unnamed friend[103]—manifests in a narcissistic self-love. The friendship was not a true friendship, which Augustine defines as being bonded together in the gift of the Holy Spirit's love.[104] His friend was rather a mirror, in which Augustine could see only his own reflection. The love that the young Augustine professed for his friend was not really love at all, because it was unable to escape the confines of the self. It was self-love, not love of the other.

The relationship between self-love and idolatry needs further exploration, however, because idolatry implies the worship of an other, which self-love seems to negate. The way that Augustine presents self-love and the love of God as an absolute dichotomy could mislead us into overlooking the deep connection between self-love and worship. Worship seems to indicate self-sacrifice and self-giving, a certain kind of ascetic discipline by which the self shows its devotion to an other, a god of some kind, be it true or false. This would appear to be the opposite of self-love and pride. Idolatry is worship and obedience to an other; pride is excessive regard for the self. But Augustine makes two moves that undo this dichotomy. First, he presents the inflation of the self not simply as an opposition to God but as an imitation of God. Second, he contends that self-love, regardless of its attempt to magnify and serve the self alone, will inevitably turn autonomy into heteronomy, and the self will end up in abject servitude to its own inventions.

In considering the motives for his youthful theft of pears in book II of the *Confessions*, Augustine dismisses the idea that the beauty of temporal things was behind the act. He had nicer pears at home, and he and his friends hardly ate any they stole, throwing most of them away. He acknowledges that he would not have committed the theft alone, but he dismisses the idea that the act was motivated by a good like friendship.[105] He famously concludes that he had "no motive for my wickedness except wickedness itself";[106] he and his friends took pleasure in doing what was forbidden to them. What they really coveted was neither pears nor companionship but the power to live by their own rules. Augustine describes this as not only wanting to be free from God but as an imitation of God: "Pride imitates what is lofty; but you alone are God most high above all things. What does ambition seek but honour and glory? Yet you alone are worthy of honour and are glorious for eternity."[107]

Augustine continues: cruelty mimics God's power, avarice imitates God's possession of everything, ignorance emulates God's simplicity, and so on. Augustine concludes, "In their perverted way all humanity imitates you. Yet they put themselves at a distance from you and exalt themselves against you. But even by thus imitating you they acknowledge that you are the creator of all nature and so concede that there is no place where one can entirely escape from you."[108] Pride as Augustine understands it is more than simply a turn to the self and away from God. Self-love is not secularization, the kind of Copernican revolution by which some moderns think that society has become human-centered instead of God-centered, the illusions of theology having been replaced by a new humanism. For Augustine, a human-centered world is still a God-haunted world. Humans try to usurp God's position, but they cannot quite pull it off. In trying to become their own gods they can only imitate God, thus offering God a backhanded acknowledgment of God's grandeur and conceding that there is nowhere to run from the love of God. Even in self-love, Augustine suggests, there is an element of worship, albeit unintended, of God.

This begrudging and unintentional acknowledgment of God nevertheless still seems distant from the kind of imploring, praising, trembling, hoping, reverence, ritual, and devotion that we usually associate with worship. Worship seems the opposite of self-exaltation. As Augustine sees it, however, self-aggrandizement is an aspiration but never a reality. Self-love is petty and mean, an adolescent fist-shaking at God. "Was I acting like a prisoner with restricted liberty who does without punishment what is not permitted, thereby making an assertion of possessing a dim resemblance to omnipotence? Here is a runaway slave fleeing his master and pursuing a shadow (Job 7:2). What rottenness!"[109] The one who loves the self remains a slave, despite petulant gestures of rebellion and autonomy. Self-love can never serve as the ground of our being; we did not create ourselves and cannot rest in ourselves. You, God, "have made us for yourself, and our heart is restless until it rests in you."[110] This is simply reality, in Augustine's view; we are *homo liturgicus*, and the basic human need to worship God can be diverted and misdirected, but it cannot be eliminated. Because at some level we intuit that we can rest only in God, we clothe earthly things in an aura of divinity. If we will not worship God, despite our inherent need to worship God, then self-love will inevitably lead us to worship the products of the self.

There is a kind of mirroring effect here, and the ability to create one's own gods can be presented as a Promethean assertion of autonomy.

Augustine is not buying it. As we have already seen in his retort to Hermes Trismegistus, Augustine thinks that we inevitably become subject to the gods we create; rather than autonomy, we live in bondage to mere human inventions. The episode of the pears can be read not as an assertion of autonomy but as following the crowd. Without a real God to serve, self-love inevitably becomes servitude to the products of human pride. The theme of sin as bondage to one's own creations is a frequent theme in *Confessions* and elsewhere. Augustine describes himself before his conversion as "bound not by an iron imposed by anyone else but by the iron of my own choice."[111] The narcissistic mirroring effect of self-love is not liberation but captivity. Augustine follows the reasoning of Paul in Romans 1. Idolaters begin in self-assertion, the refusal to honor and thank God. They make their own gods and think themselves wise, but in fact they grow stupid. They exchange the glory of the immortal God for an imitation, and end up debasing themselves in the worship of mortal creatures like crawling things. In an act of self-assertion, people make their own gods, but then, obeying the law of their nature, bow down and worship them. Thus does autonomy become heteronomy, and self-love becomes domination by one's own inventions.

In this fashion, self-love as it is commonly understood is in fact self-hate. Paradoxically, those who want to preserve the self in its autonomy end up surrendering it (see Mark 8:35). In Sermon 90A, Augustine considers what the love of oneself truly entails. This is a crucial question, because Christ has commanded us both to love God and to "love your neighbor as yourself" (Matt. 22:39). Proper love of the neighbor, then, depends on the well-ordered love of oneself, which depends on the love of God. Augustine speculates that his listeners will think of self-love as taking care of one's own needs: "When I am hungry I feed my body, because I love myself. I don't want to be worn out with toil, because I love myself. I don't want to be trapped in poverty, because I love myself. . . . I don't want to feel pain, because I love myself."[112] And so on. Augustine declares that these seemingly innocent acts of self-care are in fact not self-love but self-hate. Why? Because such acts of self-preservation typify the brute animals below us. Humans, on the other hand, are made in the image of God above us, and we are meant to refer our actions to the love of God. Caring for our bodily needs is acceptable and good, for all creation is good, but they become iniquitous when the image of God is "worn down" by earthly desires and our attention becomes fixed on our own needs and wants. The self cannot be loved apart from the love of God; "if you lower your love down from there to yourself, you won't be in him, but in yourself; so that's when you will perish."[113]

Both the proper love of oneself and the proper love of the neighbor are rooted in the well-ordered love and worship of God, for God is the good that is common to all, "the good which belongs in its entirety to each and every one, however many more come to possess it."[114] This conception of God as the common good is crucial to Augustine, because it breaks down any zero-sum relationship posited among humans and between humans and God. The true God is not in competition with humans. The worship and love of God is not a subtraction from the goods enjoyed by human beings. The common good is not diminished by being shared; it is not exhausted no matter how many possess it in its entirety. In God the whole dichotomy of autonomy versus heteronomy is overcome, because God is not simply other to human beings, or rather, because God is so completely other—not another thing in the universe that competes with us for space, but the Creator of all who sustains all things in being, which is our common good—God is also not other to us, but *interior intimo meo*, "more inward than my most inward part."[115] To return to God is simultaneously to return to oneself. Deification is available to humans by participation in God, provided it is received and not grasped. The true love of oneself consists in finding the self in the other, recognizing one's part in the common good that is God along with other people. The true love of oneself can be expressed as exchanging the illusion of the small soul, the *pusilla anima*, for the great soul, the *magna anima*.

All that we have seen so far should be sufficient to cast doubt on Charles Taylor's genealogy of interiority in his *Sources of the Self*, which traces a direct line from Augustine's supposed "radical reflexivity" to Descartes's *cogito*. In actuality, for Augustine self-reflexivity is the dissolution of the soul, which is found truly only in God, not in some interior space.[116] John Cavadini points out that Augustine does not even have a Latin term that corresponds to the modern English "the self." Self-love is *amor sui*. The pronoun is reflexive; self-love is love reflected back on itself, not love of some separate thing called "the self." "If 'the self' corresponds to anything in Augustine, it is this reified structure of pride, an attractive illusion, but ultimately a self-contradiction, doomed to eternal incoherence."[117]

For Augustine, self-love becomes self-hate and autonomy becomes heteronomy as the self is divided against itself. In shrinking the soul down to its earthly desires, cutting it off from others, privatizing it, the soul is divided from the source of its being. The small self sees itself in competition with

God and with other people. Augustine continues in Sermon 90A to describe what happens when self-love is construed in zero-sum terms: "If you want to thrive on another person's misfortunes, if you want things to go badly with someone else so that they may go well with you," then you are "hating your own soul."[118] In *De doctrina christiana*, Augustine likewise describes what happens to the self when, through inordinate earthly desires, it seeks to usurp God's position and make other people serve it. The self that loves itself

> thinks it has gained much when it can also rule over its associates, who are other men. For it is the nature of the vicious spirit to desire greatly and to claim as its desert that which is properly due only to God. Such self-love [*sui dilectio*] is better called hate. For it is iniquitous for the spirit to wish those below it to serve it and to refuse at the same time to serve a superior, and it is said most justly, "He that loveth iniquity hateth his own soul."[119]

Narcissistic self-love is in fact not just self-diminution but self-negation. The self that cuts itself off from the source of its being slides back into the nothingness out of which it was summoned by God.[120] Creation *ex nihilo* is reversed, and the rebellion of humans against God renders them nullities, the empty "blown-up bubbles" whose idolatry deceives them into thinking they are something, when in fact they are nothing.[121] In this respect, Augustine echoes a theme we saw in the previous chapter. As Isaiah 44:9 declares, "All who make idols are nothing," for they imitate the nothingness of their gods. Idols are mere *hevel*, vapor or breath (e.g., Deut. 32:21); both idolaters and the images they make are nothing but empty wind (Is. 41:29).

4.4. Images

This relationship between people and the images they make needs further exploration. So far, I have been discussing Augustine's view of idolatry in terms of his stance toward the pagan gods, along with the broader themes of idolatry as attachment to creation over Creator and as self-deification. Now I want to discuss briefly Augustine's approach to "graven images," the kinds of artifacts that humans make for themselves. As we saw in the previous chapter, there is a complex relationship in the Bible between the ban on worshiping other gods and the ban on images. On the one hand, images threaten to attribute divinity to some aspect of material creation, and thus confuse Creator and creation. They can mislead the viewer as to the true nature of God, invite the viewer to get lost in the delights of human artifice, or subject access to God to human control. On the other hand, images can be sacramental and open sensual creatures to the reality of the divine. Images are bridges that allow traffic both ways between the divine and the human, and therein lies both their danger and their promise.

Augustine comes out of a broadly Platonic tradition of ambivalence about images. Human-made images are imperfect copies that may have some pedagogical use but are under suspicion because they exist at a distance from the truth. This is true not only of images of the gods but also of images of common objects. In the *Republic*, Socrates criticizes the painting of a bed because it is at two removes from the truth: the form of bedness is the truth, the carpenter must know that truth to make a particular bed, but the painter who makes a painting of that bed needs to know only the appearance of that particular bed.[122] The painting is a copy of a copy, and therefore unreliable. Images not only exist at a distance from the truth but also mask that difference; the better the copy, the more it can be mistaken for the real thing. Plato attempts to ban image-makers from his republic. God-made images—that is, the natural world—on the other hand, can be beneficial to those who contemplate their divine harmonies. According to Plato, the more the person contemplates those harmonies, the more they participate in those harmonies. In conforming the soul to those divine harmonies, god-made creation mediates the ascent of the human soul.[123]

Although Plotinus mitigated Plato's anxiety about human-made images, raising the possibility that they could function like god-made images, Augustine generally hews closer to Plato on this issue. Like Plato, Augustine lives in a world of images he regards as false. This includes not only statues and other images of pagan gods but also the theater, which Augustine links to idolatry.[124] In book III of his *Confessions*, for example, he says he was captivated by theatrical shows (*spectacula theatrica*), which are "*plena imaginibus miseriarum mearum*";[125] they are not only full of images but are full of images of his own miseries. The mirroring effect of idolatry is operative here. Miserable people go the theater to have their own miseries reflected back to them. They experience, Augustine says, a kind of pleasure in their own feelings of being compassionate to the characters on the stage. An audience member "if he feels pain . . . stays riveted in his seat enjoying himself."[126] Augustine thinks this is not true mercy but rather a kind of narcissism that is endemic to "fictional and theatrical inventions." One problem is the kind of shows the people enjoy, which invite them to feel pleasurable mercy for adulterous lovers rather than authentic compassion, which would want to see them healed of their sin. The deeper problem, however, seems to be the fictional nature of theatrical images. Such images offer passive entertainment that evokes feelings but does not move the audience to true mercy in action. "A member of the audience is not excited to offer help, but invited only to grieve."[127] Human-made images are false because they mimic real life but do not offer real participation in the drama. Fictional images are mere phantasms, an unreliable copy rather than reality. They only "scratch the surface" (*in superficie raderer*).[128] The participation of the audience is limited to a drama of feelings that takes place on the interior stage, closed within the self. At the same time, the feelings of compassion distract the audience member from the repair of their own miserable soul. As Natalie Carnes comments, for Augustine theatrical performances "simply wall one further into one's own inner life extending the self and bending it toward vice."[129] The problem with human-made images like theater is that they promote a kind of narcissism, in which we create images that reflect our own selves back to ourselves for our own pleasure, without offering a route out of the misery of our self-enclosure.

Augustine is more sanguine about God-made images, that is, created things in the natural order. Although, as we have seen, all created things can lead people astray if people become inordinately attached to them, created things can also reveal God, their maker. As Augustine explains in *De trinitate*, all things created by God the Father are created in the Son, who is the very Image of God and coequal with the Father and the Holy Spirit: "For if any image [*imago*] answers perfectly to that of which it is the image, then it is made equal to it, not the object to its own image."[130] The Image of God is not an unreliable copy but the real thing,[131] and something of that reality carries through to all created things, which participate in the beauty and order of the Trinity that permeates them and holds them in being. "Therefore all these things which are made by divine skill, show in themselves a certain unity, and form, and order. . . . When therefore we regard the Creator, who is understood by the things that are made we must needs understand the Trinity of whom there appear traces in the creature, as is fitting. For in that Trinity is the supreme source of all things, and the most perfect beauty, and the most blessed delight."[132]

Augustine thus shares Plato's preference for God-made over human-made images, but Augustine does not wish to banish images and image-makers altogether. He seems to recognize the importance of images as mediators between the human and the divine. If images are not to be idolatrous, however, they will have to be a participation in Jesus Christ, the Image of God (cf. Col. 1:15). In one of his sermons, Augustine looks out at the sparse crowd of churchgoers and recognizes that many who would ordinarily be there had gone to a series of spectacle entertainments that were being held locally. He proceeds to describe Christ as the true spectacle of God. Psalms foretold and the Gospel passion accounts described how Christ was stared at and mocked. Paul's first letter to the Corinthians exhorts Christians to follow Christ's example as the Body of Christ and become a "spectacle to the world" (4:9).[133] The way to participation in the spectacle of Christ is the Eucharistic liturgy, which is itself an alternative spectacle that replaces the spectacles of the false gods.[134] Christ the "true Mediator" is both priest and oblation. Christ has established the daily Eucharistic sacrifice of the Church to be the "sacramental symbol" through which the Church "learns to offer itself through him."[135]

This dynamic of participation in the spectacle makes the liturgy different from the passive consumption of images in the theater and in the games. The Eucharist, Augustine makes clear in another sermon, is not a reenactment of Christ's crucifixion, and Christians are not bloodthirsty spectators at this sacrifice. Christians at the Eucharist do not partake of the role of persecutor, as spectators at the games do. "In a word, our interest in one and the same spectacle is quite different from that of the persecutor. He was enjoying the martyr's punishment, we its cause; he was taking pleasure in what he was suffering, we in why he was suffering; he in his torments, we in his strength."[136] Augustine's comments on *spectacula theatrica* in the *Confessions* have a striking counterpart here. In the Eucharist Christians do not stand back from the spectacle and take pleasure in the suffering we witness. Christians are instead invited to enter into the drama and become a spectacle to the world as the very Body of Christ. The drama is not pulled into the interior of the spectator, reduced to the production of certain private pleasures and feelings; the participant in the Eucharist is rather drawn out of the confines of the small self into a larger Body and a public performance, pulled onto the stage, as it were. So Augustine, in another sermon, tells his congregation that in the Eucharist they themselves are on the altar in the form of the elements: "So if it's you that are the body of Christ and its members, it's the mystery meaning you that has been placed on the Lord's table; what you receive is the mystery that means you. It is to what you are that you reply Amen and by so replying you express your assent."[137] The Eucharist turns Christians into icons of

Christ in the world. Their performance of the Body of Christ demands not just cultivating certain feelings but loving their neighbors in action.

Augustine does not back away from images, but considers the sacramental images of bread and wine and water and more to be God-given and not simply human-made. Augustine in fact is rather earthy in his imagery of the ontological change that participation in the sacraments brings about. He tells his congregation that, like wheat is ground for bread,

> [i]n the same way you too were being ground and pounded, as it were, by the humiliation of fasting and the sacrament of exorcism. Then came baptism, and you were, in a manner of speaking, moistened with water in order to be shaped into bread. But it's not yet bread without fire to bake it. . . . So the Holy Spirit comes, fire after water, and you are baked into the bread which is the body of Christ.[138]

David Meconi shows how Augustine, despite his ambivalence about temporal things, consistently exhorts the faithful to become the inanimate objects revered by the Church: be gold, be valleys, be the altar, be chrism, be the temple of God, be God's living tree, be God's city, be the Sabbath, and so on.[139] Far from avoiding material images, Augustine urges Christians to become the things of God, to identify themselves with material things.

The context of such exhortations, typically taking place near the end of Augustine's sermons, is almost always the liturgy. They are part of what Meconi calls Augustine's "mystagogy of identification." As mystagogy, they are meant to lead the followers of Christ into a more active participation in the liturgical and ethical life of the Church. As identification, they are based in Augustine's ontology and epistemology, which see signs as participating in God's being, but as efficacious only when they are actively assimilated into people's lives. Augustine invites Christians not to be passive spectators of the liturgy or inactive consumers of the images found in scripture, but to be drawn into the drama of redemption enacted in the liturgy and into the daily exercise of charity, the love of God and neighbor. The things of this world are used, in Augustine's sense of *usus*, toward the ultimate goal of the participation of the human person in God.[140]

Augustine's use of images comes out of his iconic vision of the creation, explored above, in which all things speak of their Creator, for those who have ears to hear. Augustine comes out of a Platonic tradition for which the relationship between divinity and creation is participatory and not competitive.

God wills things to be like God. Because people can become conformed to the world of temporal things and thus worship the creature instead of the Creator, however, they need a pedagogy to lead them to God. That pedagogy is the charity rightly ordered by the Holy Spirit which loves God through love of the neighbor and creation and thereby is drawn into the very life of God. Participation in God is a matter of not becoming fixed on signs but rather seeing through them to their proper referent.[141] But this seeing through signs is not a way of overlooking them or discarding them as unnecessary hindrances to seeing directly. As carnal creatures, we have signs as our language, and we are to meet God in them, not bypass them. We are to become ourselves living signs that point beyond ourselves to God.

As in Plato, there is an assimilative logic at work here by which the soul is conformed to that which it contemplates. We are changed by the things we know through an intellectual sympathy. For Augustine, love is an especially important unifier of subject and object. Love is the longing to be united to the beloved. Love brings the lover and the beloved into union, and actually conforms the lover ontologically to what is beloved. So in Sermon 15 Augustine exhorts his congregants to look around them at the beautiful marble, gilded ceiling, and gold vessels in the basilica and to become true temples of God themselves. Augustine invites them to reflect on how difficult it sometimes is to find similar beauty in their neighbor. He tells his audience, "You have looked but not discovered what you were looking for because you have not become what you are looking for. Similarity finds unity with what is similar, that which is unlike repels the unlike."[142] They are to become beautiful like the liturgical vessels and decorations of the church, and then they will find beauty in their neighbor. This is not a merely aesthetic exercise; becoming the things of God must be enacted in active neighbor-love. And as we have already seen, for Augustine being united to the neighbor in love also unites us with God. The pedagogy moves from the beauty of material images to the beauty of the human soul to the source of all beauty, which is God. To become the things of God is to participate in God, "becoming gods by becoming God's," as the title of Meconi's article puts it.

How can Augustine preach becoming gods and preach becoming gold vessels to his fellow Christians while simultaneously rejecting the idolatry of the pagans, who make images of gods out of precious metals? He takes on this question directly in another sermon, where he contrasts the pagan gods made of silver and gold and wood to the gods made by the one "deifying God" (*Deus deificator*). What is better, Augustine asks, to make gods or to become gods? Those who make gods become less than earthly raw materials by trying to fashion them into gods, while those who allow earthly materials to be signs of the God who made them become assimilated to the divine life. Augustine admonishes the pagans not to become the wood they adore and thus become less than human, but then remarkably he invites his listeners to become the chrism oil used by the Church.[143] Augustine thus reverses the dynamic of idolatry we explored in the previous chapter; rather than life being drained from humans by their conforming to the idols they make, conforming to the sacramental objects that point to God can give humans participation in the fullness of divine life.

Material signs are clearly not idolatrous in and of themselves. All depends on the direction to which the signs point. Human-made images mire humans in creation; God-made images elevate humans to participation in the Creator. For Augustine, sacramental signs are not mere products of human creation but participate in the Incarnation, in which God takes on material creation. The most important God-made images of God, however, are human beings themselves. When they live as they are called to live in charity, they reflect God rather than see their own reflections in the images they create.

I will say more about sacrament as an antidote to idolatry in the final chapter. For now, I will simply note where Augustine has brought us so far in our attempt to understand idolatry theologically. For Augustine, the explicit worship of other gods is a manifestation of a broader turning away from God and toward creation. Creation can be read iconically as a window to the divine, but it can also be read as a mirror that narcissistically reflects our own wants and pleasures and fears back to us. The ethical consequences of such idolatry can be dire, including violence against the other for being other, and neglect of the needs of the other for falling beyond the purview of our own desires. Healing idolatry necessitates overcoming the dichotomy of self and other and participating in the circulation of love that includes oneself, one's neighbor, and God.

5

Marion on Idolatry as a Mirror to the Self

The present chapter in many ways builds on Augustine's analysis and brings it into the contemporary context. Jean-Luc Marion's phenomenology of the idol is perhaps the most intensive exploration of the idolatrous self from a Christian thinker today. Marion rarely touches on the larger societal dynamics of idolatry; instead, he focuses on the relationship of the self to the idol, and elaborates—over the course of many of his works—a phenomenology of the idol as mirror to the self. As we have seen, this same theme is at the heart of Augustine's reflections. Although Marion does not discuss Augustine in any depth in his work on the idol and the icon,[1] he does acknowledge his debt to Augustine in his book *In the Self's Place: The Approach of St. Augustine* (*Au lieu de soi: L'approche de Saint Augustin*). As the title hints, the book is an analysis of Augustine's deconstruction of the false self and his recognition that the true self must be received from God.[2]

Marion's phenomenology of the idol elaborates on the mirroring effect we found in Augustine and the basic contrast between grasping and receiving, trying—like Augustine—to overcome any zero-sum depiction of the relationship between God and the human person. Marion sees idolatry as cutting the divine to the measure of human experience, but Marion also develops a more sympathetic take on the idol as expressing something of genuine divinity. Rather than simply lament the "death of God" in the modern West, Marion explores opportunities to be rid of our idolatrous conceptions of "God" and deepen worship of the true God. At the same time, there are hints in Marion that the modern West might not be disenchanted, that there might still be a type of "splendid idolatry" that captures our attention.

In this chapter I follow the shifting analyses of idolatry over the course of Marion's work. The first section contrasts Marion's context with Augustine's, showing how Marion's reflections on idolatry are situated in his critique of post-Cartesian metaphysics. Sections 5.2 through 5.4 explore the idol in Marion's early work, the idol as saturated phenomenon in his work begun in the late 1990s, and idolatry in his more recent work on Augustine. Section 5.5 examines the relevance of Marion for the exploration of political and

The Uses of Idolatry. William T. Cavanaugh, Oxford University Press. © Oxford University Press 2024.
DOI: 10.1093/oso/9780197679043.003.0006

economic idolatries. Together, the Bible, Augustine, and Marion provide theological and phenomenological tools for the examination of contemporary idolatries in the next two chapters.

5.1. Marion against Metaphysics

Although Marion thinks with Augustine in his exploration of the idol, the contexts in which the two thinkers write are completely distinct and, in some respects, opposed. Augustine is concerned that his contemporaries worship too many gods; Marion writes in a secularized late-modern Europe where belief in God has atrophied and withdrawn from public life. Marion's project can be understood against the backdrop of the so-called death of God in Western culture. Two of Marion's primary interlocutors are Friedrich Nietzsche and Martin Heidegger, who have, respectively, proclaimed the death of God and the death of ontotheology. The confident speculative edifice built over centuries by Christian civilization on the foundation of Greek thought—whereby the presence of God was assumed and knowledge of God was carefully parsed—has collapsed, leaving us apparently with no access to the divine. While Augustine's pagan contemporaries bumped into gods in all aspects of their daily lives, Marion's contemporaries are seemingly bereft of such consolations.

Marion nevertheless wants to enlist Nietzsche and Heidegger in the fight against idolatry; the "death of God" is really just the death of the idolatrous god, or "God," as Marion indicates. What Marion means by "God" in quotation marks is the kind of God that is accessible by human initiative through concepts. We must be able to confine "God" within a concept if we are to declare that "God" does not exist. There must be a rigorously defined object denoted "God" if we are to subject that object to conceptual scrutiny. The proof offered by conceptual atheism—if "God" is x, while x is y (illusory, alienating, etc.), then "God" is y—is as valid as the concept of "God" it makes use of. But if "God" is limited to what we can conceive of God, then what we have rejected is only an idolatrous concept of God that reduces God to what can be grasped by human knowledge. As Marion puts it, " 'God' is dead only if 'God' can die."[3] What dies in the "death of God" is only "God," the shadow of God. And so Marion contends that believers in God can and should practice conceptual atheism as much as atheists can.[4] What dies in such atheism is only an idolatrous conception of "God." "As idol, the concept arranges a presence of the divine without distance, in a god who reflects back to us our experience or thought, with enough familiarity that we always master its play."[5]

For Nietzsche, the God that dies is Immanuel Kant's God, one who has been reduced to the measure of human morality in a religion trimmed to fit within the limits of reason alone. Although there is an apophatic moment in Kant—who relegates the essence of God to the noumenal, and thus the unknowable—and Kant demolishes metaphysical idols like proofs of the existence of God, Kant nevertheless reintroduces God to his scheme as the guarantor of the human moral law. For Nietzsche, the confines of such bourgeois morality prevent the "pantheistic affirmation of all things," and so the god of morality must die. "At bottom," Nietzsche writes, "it is only the moral god that has been overcome."[6] The transvaluation of values that Nietzsche espouses allows for the creation of new, life-affirming gods. As Marion notes, Nietzsche merely completes Feuerbach's unmasking of Kant's God as the projection of human moral perfection onto an illusory transcendent being. Both Kant's proof of God and Nietzsche's rejection of God rely on the same reduction of God to morality. "In both cases, human discourse determines God."[7] Proofs of the existence of God are inevitably idolatrous, and Nietzsche is right to reject them.

Marion finds that Nietzsche, however, does not succeed in escaping idolatry but falls into a different kind of idolatry. The new gods are the products of human creation. The gods have been liberated from subjection to morality, but then chained to the human will to power. In a way, Nietzsche simply embraces what Augustine turns away from in repugnance: the endless proliferation of small gods of human making, each made to reflect some aspect of the restlessly acquisitive *libido dominandi*. For Nietzsche, the moment of liberation comes from the realization that we are god-makers. Nietzsche writes:

For an individual to posit his own ideal and to derive from it his own law, joys and rights—that may well have been considered hitherto to be the most outrageous of human aberrations and idolatry itself. . . . The wonderful art and power of creating gods—polytheism—was that through which this drive could discharge itself, purify, perfect and ennoble itself. . . . Monotheism, in contrast, this rigid consequence of the teachings of a normal human type—that is, the belief in a normal god next to whom there are only false pseudo-gods—was perhaps the greatest danger to humanity so far.[8]

For Marion, Nietzsche has merely articulated the final extreme of the idolatrous process, which ends in banality, the endless proliferation of our own reflections, to the point of disgust. "The barbarous surging forward of terrible and trivial 'idols' (for we very rightly name them 'idols'), of which our nihilistic age ceaselessly increases the consumption, marks the exasperation of idolatry and not, to be sure, the survival of some natural—then delinquent—desire to see God."[9]

As with Nietzsche, Marion is both appreciative and critical of Heidegger. Marion adopts Heidegger's dismantling of metaphysics and ontotheology, the attempt to build a ladder through concepts in order to reach God. According to Marion, metaphysics—at least as it has typically been practiced since Descartes[10]—inevitably subjects the appearance of God to the limits of human thought. Positing God as the ground of being has the effect of reducing God to the status of a being in the world while simultaneously elevating human confidence in its ability to describe the attributes of God. Metaphysics thinks God starting from the *causa sui* and thus can think God only within the limits of the category of causality. Metaphysics is idolatry insofar as it subjects the divine to conditions set by human experience.[11] Heidegger's critique has the potential to free our thinking about God from such idolatry. Heidegger writes, "The god-less thinking which must abandon the God of philosophy, God as *causa sui*, is thus perhaps closer to the divine God."[12]

As with Nietzsche, however, Marion finds that Heidegger's liberation of God from one type of idolatry ends in subjecting God to another. In Heidegger's case, the attempt to think beyond beings to Being as such establishes the anteriority of the ontological question to the ontic question of "God." Once again, God is subjected to the conditions established by human thought, because the question of Being only appears as a question to *Dasein*.[13] For Heidegger, the question of God is only a subset of the question of Being; theology is about a human being's faith and is therefore a regional and limited concern, subordinate to phenomenology, which is about the more fundamental relationship of *Dasein* to being as such.[14] In order to reach a nonidolatrous thought of God, Marion contends, God will have to be thought outside of metaphysics; rather than thinking of God in terms of being, we must think God in terms of love. Only love gives itself; God does not wait to be grasped or comprehended. Love goes out of itself in self-abandon, without conditions.[15] Love even "imposes on itself a self-critique without end or reserve."[16]

In contrast to that of Augustine, then, Marion's analysis of idolatry is not set in terms of a polemic against the opponents of the true God. Marion recognizes the ills of his age, but also sees in the collapse of Christian civilization in the West an opportunity to deepen the worship of God beyond illusion and beyond idolatry. Marion's critique of idolatry contains self-critique as an essential, not an accidental, feature. In Marion's thought, furthermore, critique of one's own idolatry is requisite not only of any attempt to think God but also of any attempt to think or act at all in the world. Both theists and atheists are idolaters, and all must be opened to the gift of love.

5.2. The Idol as Mirror

Although Marion's primary concern is the idolatry of concepts that he identifies with metaphysics, conceptual idolatry is just one type of the broader phenomenon of idolatry. According to Marion, idols come in many forms, "whatever it may be, thing, man, woman, idea, or god."[17] The idol—and its opposite, the icon—is not a particular thing or class of things (or persons, ideas, gods, etc.). Rather, "[t]he icon and the idol determine two manners of being for beings, not two classes of beings."[18] As in Augustine, idolatry is in the subject's gaze, not in the object itself. The same being can be either an idol or an icon, and in fact can pass back and forth between the two, depending on the subject's gaze. In Marion's early work—primarily L'idole et la distance (1977) and Dieu sans l'etre (1982)—the idol is contrasted pejoratively with the icon. Idolatry is not simply the worship of false gods but includes false worship of the true God and more broadly a defective manner of being in the world toward things that signal the divine.[19]

Marion is vague, perhaps deliberately so, on what it means for a being to signal the divine. He wants to make clear that "not just any being can give rise to, still less demand, veneration."[20] As he lays out his phenomenology of the idol, he seems to have in mind a statue of Venus, and not a flat-screen TV. "The only works that can pretend to the contradictory status of idol and/ or icon are those that art has so worked that they no longer restrict their visibility to themselves (as in what are so rightly called the 'pleasurable arts' [arts d'agrément]), but as such and by thus remaining absolutely immanent in themselves, that they signal indissolubly toward another, still undetermined term."[21] This term may be undetermined, but Marion insists that it concerns the divine, though idol and icon are distinguishable in that they "signal in different ways." They are "two modes of apprehension of the divine in visibility."[22]

What distinguishes idolatry from iconicity is not stupidity. There is in Marion none of the kind of ridicule we found in Isaiah 44, where the narrator heaps scorn on the man who uses half a block of wood to cook his dinner and the other half to make an idol to worship. The person who constructs the idol, says Marion, knows perfectly well that the idol does not coincide with the god. The person makes the idol and asks the divine to invest it. What invests the idol in fact is an authentic experience of the divine. A human experience of the divine precedes the idol and establishes the idol by means of the human gaze upon the idol. We construct the idol and ask the divine, according to our own experience of the divine, to open up in the idol, to favor us and correct us. Marion writes, "We experience ourselves at our best in the divine,"[23] but he does not seem to mean a sanitized version of human experience. In life, death, peace, war, love, drunkenness, spirit, and beauty we experience what Marion calls the "panic capital of the divine," and we invest that capital in our idols. There is no trickery or stupidity here. Instead, idolatry "is characterized solely by the subjection of the divine to the human conditions for experience of the divine, concerning which nothing proves that it is not authentic."[24]

According to Marion, the idolater is not duped, but ravished. The first intention of the gaze is to aim at the divine. The gaze searches visible things, "transpiercing" them, seeing through them, as it were, seeing nothing, restlessly looking for the divine and not finding it. The gaze finally stops on an idol, something that presents itself as visible, splendid, and luminous enough to fill the gaze. Because it is completely visible, and to see it suffices to know it, the idol is not illusory. *Eidōlon* is that which is seen (*eidōn*). The gaze finds itself dazzled by the idol. The hitherto insatiable gaze that transpierced the visible now comes to rest on the idol, the "first visible," and the gaze is filled by its visibility.[25] When the gaze stops, its aim settles, and the not-aimed-at disappears. "If the idolatrous gaze exercises no criticism of its idol, this is because it no longer has the means to do so."[26] All else disappears, and the gaze stands ravished. When the gaze stops, Marion makes clear, it does not, "at least at first, arise from an ethical choice: it reveals a sort of essential fatigue."[27] As we noted with Augustine in the previous chapter, the journey is long, and belief in an invisible divinity is hard for a carnal being to sustain over the long haul. We long to see the divine, to feast on what our heart desires. Our gaze invests the idol with all these longings. We are not so much fooled as overwhelmed, by both weariness and longing.

The fact that we invest the idol with our longings and seek satisfaction in it indicates the essential mirroring function of the idol. Marion describes the gaze as a kind of radar signal that bounces off the idol and returns to the self, indicating its position relative to the idol. The idol does not resemble us but rather the divinity that we experience.[28] Because the idol subjects the divine to the conditions set by a human experience of the divine, the divine is cut to the measure of the human and mirrors back to the human its own experience: "the idol always culminates in a 'self-idolatry.'"[29] This is true equally of statues and ideas; conceptual idols capture the mental rather than physical gaze, dazzling it and returning it to the self. A conceptual idol is a picture not so much of the divine as of a person's or a culture's conception of the divine, limited by its time and place. As a mirror, it tells us more about those who formulated the concept than about God.

As in Augustine, idolatry is marked by a kind of self-worship, a narcissism that can only find its own desires and aspirations reflected back to it in its acts of veneration. Unlike in Augustine, however, Marion does not simply deny the presence of the divine in this experience, much less dismiss the idol as demonic. The idol, according to Marion, "presents a certain low-water mark of the divine."[30] Marion will not presume to deny the authenticity of the experience of the divine in idolatry. Because the divine has been cut to the measure of the human, the divine is truncated, reduced, distorted, but traces of the divine are not necessarily absent. "The idol: less a false or untrue image of the divine than a real, limited, and indefinitely variable function of *Dasein* considered in its aiming at the divine. The idol: the image of the divine that *Dasein* forms, hence that much less God than, in a more real way, a figure of the divine."[31] The idol is less God, more human experience of the divine, but perhaps not entirely devoid of some inchoate participation in the divine life. Marion seems to acknowledge that possibility in his response to a critique that regards his monotheism as "the point of view of those who declare false what would inspire in others the highest veneration." Marion replies, "[M]y personal attempt to *accede* to monotheism [implies no such thing, since] the theory of the idol that I outline has precisely no other consequence than to give legitimacy to other venerations and for that very reason to explain their multiplicity, hence to limit their dignity."[32] The italicized *accede* seems to indicate that a true encounter with God not cut to the measure of human experience is Marion's aspiration, but he has found no way to guarantee such access to God. His phenomenology of the icon, as we will see, tries only to establish the possibility that such a gift could be received. In a way that

Augustine does not, Marion recognizes the potential dignity, though limited, of venerations other than his own. At the same time, Marion recognizes the limits of his own, ostensibly Christian worship. The mere claim to believe in one God does not make one a monotheist in fact and does not settle the question of which god or gods one actually worships. As in the Bible, behavior, not mere belief, is decisive.

The image of the mirror in Marion evokes Narcissus, who fell in love with his own reflection. Part of what tempers the critique of the narcissism of idolatry in Marion, however, is the invisibility of the mirror. The idol saturates the gaze with visibility; it dazzles the gaze in the way that, if one were to look directly at the sun, the sun would very quickly fill the gaze and blot out every other thing from visibility. The idol masks its own mirror function. When the aim of the gaze settles, everything else that could be aimed at disappears; the aim is captured by the idol. The invisible mirror, along with everything else, becomes what Marion calls *invisable*, that which cannot be aimed at. The idol allows no invisible, both because it is fully visible and fills the gaze and because it simultaneously renders all else *invisable*. The "precise function" of the idol "consists in dividing the invisible into one part that is reduced to the visible and one part that is obfuscated as *invisable*."[33] This obfuscation is not trickery or deliberate illusion, nor is it stupidity. It is, nevertheless, obfuscation, the inability to maintain the proper invisibility of the divine or the proper visibility of creation. But this obfuscation for Marion does not merit the same ethical censure that Augustine directs at idolatry; it seems to be a function of human weakness more than of human vice, though the two may not be entirely separable.

The invisibility of the divine is also expressed in Marion's term "distance." The problem with idolatry is that it tries to overcome the distance between the divine and the human through human initiative. The aspiration toward unity with divinity is good and proper to human being. Idolatry, however, tries to grasp at divinity rather than receive it as a gift. Idolatry tries to pull the god close, to subject it to the conditions of human experience. Idolatry is a violation of God's distance, by which Marion means more than simply a spatial or ontological divide between God and creation. Distance is not simply the transcendence, the otherness, of God; it cannot be reduced to a simple absence of God. God is both transcendent and immanent; distance must be both maintained and traversed. Distance characterizes our relation to God. Distance is di-stance, the standing of two terms in relation to one another. Only distance allows relation: "only he can become my neighbor who remains forever outside of me and my doubles."[34] And yet God uniquely does not remain simply outside of me, but is also, and for the same reason, *interior intimo meo*. As Aquinas explains, precisely because God is Creator and therefore wholly other than creation, "it must be that God is in all things, and innermostly."[35] Or as Marion puts it, "God withdraws in the distance, unthinkable, unconditioned, and therefore infinitely closer."[36] God is not contained in the idol of ontological difference or Being, but expresses Godself as love. Marion follows Hans Urs von Balthasar in expressing distance as the *kenosis* of God, God's own self-emptying, the withdrawal of God from presence and representation, most especially in the concealment of God in the crucified Jesus of Nazareth.[37] The revelation of God is simultaneously the concealment of God. God gives Godself but reveals nothing but the gift without conditions. God loves those who do not love God, manifests Godself to those who turn away.[38] God is not the being on the other side of the gap defined by distance, but, as Robyn Horner points out, Marion personifies distance as God.[39] Distance is grace. Distance "engenders us," as Marion writes. "Distance, precisely because it remains the Ab-solute, delivers the space where it becomes possible for us to receive ourselves."[40] Distance does not separate us from God but defines the space in which we both receive ourselves from an Other and discover our intimacy with that Other through love. God's *kenosis*, the withdrawal of God into unthinkability and unrepresentability, is what makes us possible.[41] Idolatry is the attempt to reduce invisibility to visibility, to reduce distance to fit within a concept or a representation, and thus to reduce both divinity and humanity.

5.3. The Idol as Saturated Phenomenon

Beginning in the 1990s, Marion's treatments of the idol take on a different dimension than in his earlier works. The primarily negative, though not entirely unsympathetic, treatment of the idol found in *The Idol and Distance* and *God without Being* is supplemented by an appreciation of the idol as a "saturated phenomenon." Marion's analysis of the idol becomes framed less by theology and more by phenomenology. During this period, Marion is responding to criticisms that his work smuggles God into phenomenology. In some ways, Marion's nontheological study of the idol can be read in conjunction with his broader concern to show that his phenomenology is a rigorous first philosophy and not theology as such.[42]

Marion posits the category of saturated phenomena as part of his attempt to correct what he sees as shortcomings in Edmund Husserl's phenomenology. The original promise of phenomenology is that it would return to things themselves and how they appear, without the distorting mediation of metaphysics. According to Marion, Husserl deviates from the promise of phenomenology by focusing too heavily on intentionality and objects. The phenomena Husserl examines are objects, and the subject constitutes them as objects by intentionality.[43] For Marion, Husserl's subject is still in control of objects rather than allowing phenomena to give themselves. Some phenomena, says Marion, overpower our intention; we cannot grasp or control them. These are "saturated" phenomena because they saturate and overwhelm our capacity to understand and manage them. Saturated phenomena are not necessary or predictable, but contingent and excessive. Unlike "poor phenomena," we cannot master them or make them submit to our will. They are given, and we can only receive them (or not).[44]

Marion distinguishes four types of saturated phenomena: they can be saturated in terms of quantity (an immense event like World War II, too large to fully comprehend), quality (something too intense and brilliant to grasp, like a great work of art), relation (intimate experiences of the flesh, like pain and pleasure), and modality (like the face of another person, who can never be reduced to an object).[45] Marion treats the idol under the second type of saturated phenomenon. In his chapter of *In Excess* on saturation by quality, titled "The Idol or the Radiance of the Painting," Marion turns to human-made art, specifically painting, to exemplify the idol. Here the idol has lost any obvious connection to the divine; the paintings that Marion examines do not necessarily have any theological content, good or bad. The idol nevertheless retains many of the dynamics that Marion gave it in his early work. The idol as painting captures the gaze and dazzles it, overwhelming our sight with an excess of visibility.

In sharp contrast to Plato, Marion does not denigrate painting as a mere copy of a copy, at two removes from the original Form of the thing represented. On the contrary, the painting "steals" admiration from the original; it "provokes more vision" than the original, and thus overtakes it.[46] Great paintings do not merely deviate from the original but differ from them in order to call forth some vision of the artist that is more profound and more intense. To see what Marion means here, we can think of Van Gogh's painting *Bedroom in Arles*. The two-dimensional depiction of Van Gogh's bed departs from how we would see the bed on which the painting is based.

Plato's suspicion of human-made art comes to rest on that deviation from the original bed, which is itself a deviation from the ideal Form of bedness. But through Van Gogh's artistry, we now see more of the bed than we would if we were looking at his physical bed, or rather, not more of the bed itself but just *more*, in a way that is not graspable and reducible to concepts or to the perception of the bed as an object. As Marion puts it, "Admiration is therefore concentrated on the resemblance, precisely because it no longer resembles anything, but, drawing onto itself all the glory and confiscating it from everything else, it enters alone into pure semblance. The resemblance alone 'seems'—appears, shines, sparkles."[47] The resemblance becomes the original, phenomenologically speaking, and the original is forgotten, or seen as a mere sketch or precursor to the work of art.

Marion describes the way a painting captures the gaze in much the same way he has described the idol in his earlier work. He depicts the usual condition of our gaze as the "vagabond and aesthetically unfaithful sight," a loose child who passes from one spectacle to another without stopping. The common gaze sees through things, transpierces them, and moves on. When it encounters the painting, however, the gaze is arrested, fascinated, "swallowed up," "crushed," stopped. "Satisfied, it can no longer go to see any other thing elsewhere but is exhausted in going over it, in recognizing and assimilating it. . . . In this way the *idol* is accomplished: the first visible that sight cannot pierce and abandon, because it saturates it for the first time and hoards up all admiration in it."[48]

Already at this stage of the analysis, however, we can note differences between the way the gaze encounters the painting and Marion's earlier analysis of the idol. Here the gaze does not seem to settle on the idol out of fatigue from keeping up its endless aim. The exhaustion comes from going over the idol itself; the gaze is captured and then exhausted by sheer fascination, the need to keep looking at it, to see it again and again from fresh angles. Marion's emphasis here is also not on the active role of the gaze in making what is viewed either an idol or an icon, depending on how it is viewed. Although Marion does describe the idolater as "ravished" in *God without Being*, the idol there is more conditioned by the gaze: "The idol depends on the gaze that it satisfies, since if the gaze did not desire to satisfy itself in the idol, the idol would have no dignity for it."[49] Or again, "[T]he fabricated thing becomes an idol, that of a god, only from the moment when the gaze has decided to fall on it, has made of it the privileged fixed point of its own consideration."[50] In *In Excess*, the idol does not depend on the gaze, and the gaze does no deciding. The idol rather gives itself to the gaze in an irresistible way, compels the gaze, controls it. "The look cannot refrain from consecrating all its admiration and all its available power to these visibles that the painting imposes on it."[51] As a saturated phenomenon, the emphasis is on the way it imposes itself on the person, who cannot grasp it, control it, or assign meaning to it. The painting is excessive in its quality. It is not an object to be taken in by the master gaze but a phenomenon that foists itself upon the gaze.

Although the gaze does not make the idol, the idol retains the mirroring function that it had in Marion's earlier work. Until it encounters the idol, the gaze is not aware of its own capacity, what it is capable of seeing. The idol gives the measure of the gaze by overwhelming it with excess. The idol functions as an "invisible mirror":

> My idol defines what I can bear of phenomenality—the maximum of intuitive intensity that I can endure while keeping my look on a distinctly visible spectacle, all in transforming an intuition into a distinct and constituted visible, without weakening into confusion or blindness. In this way my idol exposes the span of all my aims—what I set my heart on seeing, and thus also want to see and do. In short, it denudes my desire and my hope. What I look at that is visible decides who I am. I am what I can look at. What I admire judges me.[52]

Or as Marion also says, "Name your idol, and you will know who you are."[53] Nevertheless, the mirroring function of the idol operates differently than it does in his earlier work. In that work he was primarily interested in how idolatry captures our experience of the divine and cuts God down to a human measure. Marion's main concern in both *The Idol and Distance* and *God without Being* is to counter the reduction of God to metaphysical categories that attempt to put God within human reach. In his work on saturated phenomena, the idol does not attempt to put anything within our grasp but rather overwhelms us with its power. Marion still uses divine language—the painting "consecrates" phenomenality[54]—but his main concern is phenomenological, not theological.

As in his earlier work, the idol as painting dazzles the gaze with an excess of visibility. An ordinary three-dimensional object always remains partially invisible to the gaze. At any one time, one can see only three sides of a six-sided box, for example. What cannot be seen at any time is what Husserl calls the "appresented." Physical objects never fully appear; they are both presented and appresented. In a two-dimensional painting, however, everything appears, and the appresented disappears. Cubism is an extreme example of this, in which all six sides of the box can be made to appear simultaneously to the gaze. But Marion does not restrict his analysis to cubist technique. In painting more generally, the artist strives "to present precisely those aspects that shine with a greater radiance,"[55] so that we are spared any curiosity about what is not presented. In Cézanne's *La Sainte-Victoire au grand pin*, we do not wonder what the other side of the mountain looks like. The painting "reduces the object to the presentable in it."[56] What is presented is more than enough to saturate my gaze; I am overwhelmed by the power of the visible, and what is not visible drops from my aim. In "great art," says Marion, "nothing is lost when something does not make itself seen."[57]

What the painting presents is not an object or a copy or representation of an object. What we see is the vision of the artist, not the objects of the artist's intention. Nothing is re-presented; the painter does not copy but rather produces a new thing never before seen. The idol adds a visible to the world which transcends the world. There is nothing absent from the painting; it is pure presence. The painting is a kind of non-physical space that eliminates the unseen and reduces the phenomenon to pure visibility. Here is "the visible elevated to the rank of idol."[58] As Marion presents it here, the idol truly is an elevation, not a diminution. This elevation seems to have social effects, not simply effects on the individual viewer: "The painter produces absolutely new phenomena, and what phenomena—idols! It is the idols that, in each era, reign over the natural visibles, over the appearance of constituted objects, and that oblige us to see everything starting from the paradigms their fascination imposes."[59] Here Marion presents idols as less a mirror of society and its desires in a given era and more that which sets the agenda for the society's vision.[60] For this reason, Marion says that art cannot avoid ethical responsibility. Art, in seeking to fascinate and satisfy the spectator's gaze, "plays with the other person."[61] Marion does not prejudge whether or not this play is ethical in any particular case; here he offers no negative evaluation of the idol as such. He merely says that art has an ethical responsibility that it cannot evade. The ethical responsibility issues from the power that art as saturated phenomenon holds over the viewer.

What the viewer sees in a painting in one sense is dependent upon the gaze. As Marion says, the idol exposes what the viewer is capable of seeing, the desires and hopes and limits of the viewer. In this sense, what is seen depends upon the gaze that sees. But the gaze does not master the painting or determine it. In fact, no gaze is adequate to the painting; we can never see a painting once and for all, but must continually re-see it. Unlike poor phenomena, ordinary objects that we can know how to use with one look, the painting always exceeds any single gaze. Each viewing offers the appearance of some new unseen; all is visible, but not all is seen, because the sheer visibility of the painting as saturated phenomenon always overwhelms the ability of any single gaze to see it all and comprehend it. The museum, therefore, is a necessary institution, one that allows coming back again and again to look. We have lost the ability, Marion writes, to construct churches and palaces, but a type of pilgrimage is still available through the museum, where a "remnant of veneration" survives, which is "worth more than blind barbarism."[62] The private collector has no right to restrict the viewing of art to one single gaze; no matter how refined, the private collector's gaze can never receive the excess of visibility that a great painting offers. Even the most educated gaze is inadequate to take in a painting on one visit, and it is different with every visit, which also means that the painting is different with every visit. The painting requires a multitude of looks "bouncing" off it. Even the groups of tourists shuffling through museums, ill-suited though they are to see, play an important role. Who is to say that one of them has not glimpsed and distinguished a splendor that no other, more educated gaze had yet received? Who is to say that the painting cannot educate certain looks? Who is to say that the apprehension of the painting's glory has not advanced under their vigil?[63]

We should note the traditional language of divinity that Marion uses here: church, pilgrimage, veneration, glory, vigil. As with his earlier analysis, there is something of the divine in the idol, which Marion describes as an expression of a human experience of the divine; in his analysis of the painting as saturated phenomenon, it is the vision of the artist which appears on the canvas. In his work on the painting, however, the appearance of the saturated phenomenon seems to overwhelm human experience rather than simply be cut to the measure of human experience. There is a sense in which great art is a kind of revelation, but a revelation not in the strictly theological sense. Marion treats revelation as a fifth, paradoxical type of saturated phenomenon, which transcends the other four categories because it is saturated in all four ways at the same time.[64] A painting might not be a revelation in this sense, but there is a way in which the painting participates in the divine. In its excess of visibility, the painting perhaps makes something of the divine accessible to the human gaze. But this accessibility is precisely what marks the painting as an idol because it threatens to bring God within human reach. What is visible threatens to destroy distance. This is why the painting is limited by its very excess of visibility.

At the end of his chapter on the idol and painting in *In Excess*, Marion acknowledges the ethical choice that Mark Rothko made in refusing to depict the human form. Rothko, according to Marion, knew that the human face cannot be reduced to visibility in the flatness of the painting. The painting is a façade that eliminates depth, a move which does no damage to the things of the world but distorts only the human figure, especially the face. The idol releases the gaze from the objectification of the world, but it is limited in that it cannot give the face. The painting as idol is dangerous because it offers the Other to the gaze in such a way that it can be mistaken for an object.[65] Here Marion draws on Emmanuel Lévinas's analysis of the face of the other as that which cannot be reduced to an object of visibility. The face of the other remains invisible and incomprehensible; to know or to grasp the other person is to violate them. I can only enter into relationship with the face of the other. Marion applies this analysis to the icon, which, instead of being seen, sees me. The icon reverses perspective, with the vanishing point in front of the painting, not behind the image. The icon does not give the visible, but rather the invisible by means of the visible. The viewer becomes vulnerable to the icon. Rather than functioning as a mirror which reflects my desires, the icon exposes me to the gaze of God and what God wants of me, while maintaining the invisibility of the divine, since I am not looking at God, but God is looking at me.[66]

I will say more about Marion's phenomenology and theology of the icon in the final chapter. For now, we see how the relationship between the idol and the icon shifts over the course of Marion's writings. In the early writings, idol and icon are opposed ways of approaching the divine, one inappropriate and the other more appropriate. In Marion's later work on the saturated phenomenon, however, idol and icon are more like two dimensions of the human approach to God. On the one hand, God is immanent, comes close to us and overwhelms us with a vision of God's plenitude. On the other hand, God is transcendent, withdraws from us and maintains the absolute distance between Creator and creation. Christina Gschwandtner sums up this dynamic in Marion: "The abundant vision of God overwhelms us with its immensity and grandeur, but it also blinds us, calls us out of ourselves, unsettles us, reorients us; it gives us nothing visible or tangible but instead calls us beyond ourselves."[67] God gives both too much and nothing of Godself. God is manifest, overwhelmingly, in God's creation and in the inklings of the divine that human artists, squinting in the overpowering and almost unbearable light, can expose to visibility. At the same time, God is invisible, beyond our grasp in a kenotic withdrawal, and yet beckoning us forward, vulnerable, into the dark. The idol gives hints of the divine in an inherently dangerous form that requires the chastening rigor of the icon.

Shane Mackinlay has critiqued what he considers to be the inconsistency between Marion's earlier accounts of the idol and those found later in his less theological work. In the earlier work, the gaze is active. Mackinlay quotes *The Crossing of the Visible*: "It [the painting] does not impose itself to be seen, since it is the look which imposes on it to appear as it appears, merely a representative of the desire to see or to make itself seen."[68] In *Being Given*, by contrast, the painting is a pure given that imposes itself on the gaze. The painting is not looked at, but seen.[69] Mackinlay thinks that Marion reduces the subject to pure passivity in the later work, and that such a position, without any hermeneutical intervention by the subject, is impossible to sustain. There is no phenomenon that gives itself absolutely and requires no interpretation by the one who receives the phenomenon. Mackinlay writes that "the richness and validity of saturated phenomena are not secured by dethroning absolute subjectivity, only to replace it with an objectivity or givenness that is equally absolute."[70] He thinks that Marion's own account of saturated phenomena as normative undermines the pure givenness of saturated phenomena. In *Being Given*, Marion acknowledges that saturated phenomena are unusual, but he denies that they are exceptional or extreme cases. It is poor phenomena that are exceptional, because they are the ones in which phenomenality is distorted. Everyday phenomena constituted by the sovereign ego appear as objects and therefore as something other than what they really are. They are a consequence of our objectifying approach to them. The saturated phenomenon, which appears truly, is the norm for all phenomena, according to Marion.[71] But if that is the case, Mackinlay asks, why are we not dazzled daily with saturated phenomena? The answer, Mackinlay posits, is that they do not impose themselves on us but require some sort of hermeneutical openness of the person in order to be seen. We must provide some interpretive framework that is capable of receiving such phenomena. There must be "an actively receptive stance that is prior to the appearance of phenomena . . . a hermeneutic space in which phenomenality becomes possible."[72] It is our objectifying gaze that prevents us from receiving phenomena as saturated.[73]

Mackinlay has brought attention to a significant tension in Marion's treatment of saturated phenomena, including the idol. The solution, Mackinlay thinks, is to see the appearance of saturated phenomena as a "middle-voiced" happening, with the receiver neither entirely passive nor entirely active. In theological terms, faith opens a space that makes the reception of revelation possible, but faith is a gift of God's grace; the person is neither entirely active nor merely passive.[74] Mackinlay acknowledges that Marion has responded to a similar critique; in a rejoinder to Marlène Zarader, Marion has written, "[T]here is not an over-simplified choice between 'activity' and 'passivity,' with no other option."[75] Mackinlay thinks that Marion has still not explained how the resistance to saturated phenomena can be squared with pure and absolute givenness. But Marion can be read as searching for precisely that middle voice. At times, Marion emphasizes the way the idol overwhelms the gaze to give the measure of the one who gazes. At other times, Marion emphasizes the way the gaze makes the object into an idol by its manner of looking. The gaze, however, is not the same as the subject; when Marion says that the gaze "decides," it is not necessarily the transcendental ego deciding, but the gaze that happens in the interaction between the two terms, the gazer and what is gazed at. The gaze is itself a kind of middle-voiced term between the one who gazes and what is gazed at. Likewise, Marion has in fact acknowledged the need for hermeneutics; in *In Excess* he writes, "One sees already that the banal interpretation of a phenomenon as given not only does not forbid hermeneutics but demands it."[76] The question is not about the necessity of hermeneutics but of what kind of hermeneutic, the "phenomenological legitimacies" of any hermeneutic. The saturated phenomenon as event is so excessive that it would demand a hermeneutic not under the control of the subject but one "deployed without end and in an indefinite network."[77] Such an open-ended network is itself a middle-voiced happening that takes place in the spaces between and among many different persons.

The point here is similar to what we found in Augustine's treatment of idolatry. For Augustine, idolatry is the refusal to receive both oneself and the world as gifts of God. Idolatry bifurcates the world into a sovereign self that attempts to manage the world as means to its own ends and a world of objects that serve as mirrors of the self rather than windows to their Creator who sustains them in being. The poverty of phenomena is the result of the objectifying gaze that sees created things as mere things, subsisting in themselves and not given, means to the end of the self and not "the ground on which my soul praises you," in Augustine's words. The poverty of the self lies in its privation, cutting itself off from the world in its objectification of the world, and cutting itself off from God in the futile gesture of narcissistic self-love. God is the love that happens in the distance between and among God, the neighbor, and oneself.

5.4. Marion on Augustine

We come, then, to Marion's treatment of idolatry in his more recent work, specifically in his only extensive direct engagement with Augustine. Although there are only scattered references to the idol in his book on Augustine, the idol nevertheless remains a key concept for Marion, and helps us to see how his work on idolatry is indebted to Augustine's portrayal of the idol as a kind of mirror to the self.

Marion enlists Augustine in his battle against the idolatrous metaphysical self that has typified modernity. He contrasts Augustine's view of the person as one who desires to Descartes's view of the person as one who knows. Descartes's *cogito* assures the knower of both the existence of the ego and its essence. For Augustine, we are first not knowers but desirers. I desire, therefore I am. But desire does not arise from within me; rather it imposes itself on me from without. I do not choose what I desire; desire identifies me. What I desire is not intentional and reflects better than my intentional thoughts who I really am. "Desire is enacted over me so immediately that it mirrors for me the first image that I will ever have of myself. More than mirror, it serves for me as idol."[78] Here Marion seems to use "idol" in a nonpejorative way; the idol is a mirror, reflecting back what the person desires and therefore is, but there is no judgment yet about the truth or falsehood of what the person desires. The diversity of desires simply identifies the diversity of people; show me what a person wants, and I will tell you who they are. If not quite *homo liturgicus*, then, Augustine identifies humans as *homo amans*, the human person as lover. From one of Augustine's sermons: "There is nobody who does not love. The only question is what does he love."[79] One has to be concerned not with knowing oneself but rather with identifying what is decisive for one, what one loves in truth. Marion comments, "More intimate to me than any equality of the *self* to itself thus turns out to be the distance of the lover to what he loves."[80]

This distance indicates that what one loves must be beyond the control of the lover. All the various loves, says Augustine, are symptoms of a single unconditional desire that possesses all people: the desire for a happy life, the *vita beata*. But the *vita beata* is something we neither possess nor know; we have an "absolutely certain desire for an absolutely unknown *vita beata*."[81] If what we love and want to make us happy is not marked by distance—is simply a mirror to the ego—then the ego folds in upon itself. If love is true *caritas*, then I discover that I do not possess a self but find it ecstatically in that to which I belong and to whom I must return. The *vita beata* is found in God, who is *caritas*. I am where I love, and if I love God, God appears in the place of the self. "And thus I am not from myself nor in myself because I am no longer essentially who I am but what I love—my distance to the place of [my] *self* is defined by my distance to what I love. The *cogito, sum* is carried away toward the *interior intimo meo*."[82] I discover myself not in discovering in the mirror of the idol what desires belong to me, but in finding the Love to whom I belong. Once again, the basic option is between self-love and the love of God.

From this analysis of desire, Marion moves to an examination of truth in Augustine, in a chapter titled "Truth, or the Saturated Phenomenon." The main problem, as in the phenomenological critique of metaphysics, arises when truth is seen as something to be grasped or mastered by the human subject. But here Marion treats the saturated phenomenon unapologetically through the lens of theology, not merely phenomenology. Desire is for God, but human desire is true only if it is oriented toward the true God. For Augustine, God is the "highest and more inward truth" (*summa et interiora veritas*). Heidegger accuses Augustine of subjecting truth to the control of theory. The search for the *vita beata* is reduced to the search for God and truth as objects of knowledge (*Objektwissen*), thus subjecting them to the idolatrous limits of metaphysics.[83] But Marion contends that Augustine's God is not an object of knowledge, and that desire does not need to know its object in order to desire it in the *vita beata*: "Desire does not here presuppose the knowledge of what it loves but precedes it."[84] One does not need theoretical knowledge of the existence and essence of the true God as a precondition of loving God. Loving God is a response to the desire of God that overcomes the person from outside of oneself.

Marion acknowledges that it seems strange for truth to be determined by desire, which we generally assume distorts the dispassionate and reasoned approach to finding what is true. But he rejects the reduction of all truth to theoretical truth, and instead posits a kind of nontheoretical truth that is not an object of knowledge but overwhelms the self with excess, truth as a saturated phenomenon. This is a truth that, rather than waiting to be grasped, imposes itself with such power that it becomes an ordeal, such that one "who should receive it can also, sometimes or even most often, not be sufficient for it."[85] The truth in this nontheoretical sense imposes a choice: either bear with the ordeal of its excess and risk being changed, or evade the truth and flee from its excess. This choice, Marion claims, does not always belong to ethics. In theory, the true and the false can be neatly separated. No one in theory prefers to believe the clearly false over the true, and even the one who chooses to do evil knows the difference between truth and falsehood. In the nontheoretical sense, on the other hand, the truth can be loved or hated. The truth in this sense does not, like theoretical truth, simply deliver a fact about the state of things but exercises a judgment about me, according to whether I accept or reject it.[86]

Here Marion draws on a passage from Augustine's *Confessions*, in which Augustine ponders why truth engenders hatred, despite the fact that everyone desires the *vita beata* which is grounded on truth:

> The answer must be this: their love for truth takes the form that they love something else and want this object of their love to be the truth; and because they do not wish to be deceived, they do not wish to be persuaded that they are mistaken. And so they hate the truth for the sake of the object which they love instead of the truth. They love truth for the light it sheds, but hate it when it shows them up as being wrong.[87]

No one wants to be deceived; everyone prefers the truth to falsehood. This is why people want what they love to be the truth, even if it is not. Idolaters do not deny the truth, but rather falsify it to retain the appearance of truth. They still love the truth, in their own way. But they love something and are attached to it so much that they desperately want it to be the truth, to the point that they turn against the real truth and hate it. "Far from renouncing the truth, the liar tries to make it such that what he prefers (the idol that he loves) to the truth holds precisely the place of truth."[88]

What Marion is describing here, however, is different from his previous descriptions of the idol, in which the viewer is simply ravished by the visibility of the idol, and all other truths are rendered *invisable*. Here the idol is that which provides resistance to the saturated phenomenon, which is the truth. The power of the truth has overcome the idolater, who sees himself accused and so hates the truth. The truth is a light that illuminates every deformity; "Here the light of God floods every man, therefore accuses him by manifesting his sin, and this manifestation cannot be obscured."[89] There is no choice of whether or not to let the light of truth accuse me. The only choice is either to bear it, to not deny my deformity, and thereby be free of it, or to try to hide from myself the fact that I cannot hide from it. The self is not passive before the saturated phenomenon, but actively mounts resistance to it.

Marion distinguishes four stages of this type of idolatry. The first is the excess of the light of truth that confronts the person, which he calls "bedaz-zlement." The second stage is the refusal of the ordeal, the pain caused by the violence of truth's splendor. The pain is caused by the weakness of the person's intention, their unwillingness to suffer exposure to the truth. The third stage is a measure of relief that comes from recoiling from the truth. The person gets some rest, not from fatigue, as in Marion's earlier accounts of the idol, but from the pain of facing one's own defects. The pleasure of avoiding the truth would, Marion says, be unbearable if it had to keep the awareness of the truth it fled, so the truth must be denied its status as truth. According to Marion, this flight is not first moral but purely phenomenolog-ical, because it results from powerlessness. Only at the fourth stage is a choice involved: either flee the pain or confront it, either refuse the truth and remain in my habitual self or accept the truth and become changed. The flight from truth does make truth not aimed at (*invisable*), but one can't help but see it (visible). Knowing the truth, however, is not enough; I must decide to bear the truth and change, or I will contradict my desire for the *vita beata*, and therefore contradict myself.[90] As in all forms of idolatry, self-love is merely the reverse side of self-hatred. "If . . . I love myself, however deformed, more than the light that accuses me, then I will have to hate it, since it will continue to accuse me, and I will also have to love myself as deformed. And in this way I will end up hating myself as much as I hate the truth."[91]

The narcissistic self negates itself by wanting to possess truth (and, Marion adds, beauty) rather than receive it from God. "The fault is committed most exactly when I want to make myself like God without however becoming so by him and on the basis of him, but by myself only."[92] This is a perverse imi-tation of God, without God. It is not a matter of loving only God, but loving all things in God, who sustains them in being. Only God can be enjoyed, but through enjoying God everything else becomes lovable.[93] Love in its truest sense is participation, not possession. If my aim is the possession of finite things apart from God, then they become my idols, and I, as in the biblical critiques of idols, become like them. "This is the law of idolatry: I always become what I intend and possess; if I intend less than God, I will become less than him, *therefore less than myself*."[94]

We have found three different, though interrelated, phases in Marion's thinking on idolatry. In the first phase, Marion considers the idol theologically. The human gaze, fatigued by its search for an invisible God, alights on certain objects—mostly pagan statues and metaphysical concepts—and is dazzled by them. The divine is cut to the—authentic, but limited—human experience of it. In the second phase, Marion considers the idol phenomenologically in the form of human-made art; the divine is not necessarily absent, but Marion brackets it from consideration. The idol still offers the self a mirror of its desires and aims, but here the accent is on the self overwhelmed by the idol as saturated phenomenon, not on the phenomenon cut to human measure. Again, the idol is true, but limited; it cannot give the human face to be seen. In the third phase, Marion returns to theology in his exploration of Augustine. Here he considers idolatry in terms of the metaphysical self, the love of the ego versus the love of God. Idolatry is the resistance the self offers to the truth; the truth, not the idol, is the saturated phenomenon that overcomes me with its power. In a way similar to his early accounts of idolatry, the self settles into idolatry out of weakness, here recoiling from the pain of the truth rather than from fatigue. In this account, however, idolatry is not so much true-but-limited; rather the self hates the truth and tries to substitute what it loves for the real truth.

As in his previous accounts, there is ambiguity in Marion's work on Augustine about where the self finds the power to become an idolater. Does the self determine the idol with its gaze, or is the self overwhelmed by the idol? From where does the idolater summon the gumption to refuse the truth while standing squinting in its blinding light? In his work on Augustine, Joeri Schrijvers writes, "Marion wants to be . . . Levinas and Heidegger at the same time,"[95] oscillating between a passive Levinasian subject which is always already turned toward the other and an active Heideggerian subject—with its *Jemeinigkeit*, or "ownness"—that must make a decisive choice with regard to the truth. As does Mackinlay, Schrijvers sees Marion oscillating between an active and a passive subject. Unlike Mackinlay, however, Schrijvers does not see this as a contradiction in Marion's thinking, but rather sees Marion as exploring the same contradictory self that Augustine explores in the *Confessions*. As in Augustine, the will is divided; it acknowledges the truth and yet does not will it. The only solution for Marion is a theological one: in the encounter with God, the self discovers what it cannot give. The person does not summon up all their resources and then make a decision for or against God. The one who belongs to Christ, according to Marion, receives their decision as a gift. Belonging to Christ is precisely to occupy that middle voice in which I both come to my humanity and participate in divinity; there is no zero-sum relationship between God and oneself.[96]

5.5. Contemporary Idolatries

Using Marion's analysis of idolatry to read the contemporary context is not a straightforward affair. Marion recognizes that the idol can be anything—thing, person, idea, god—and he recognizes that idols change over time as societies change. His studies of idols are selective, however, focusing mainly on ancient pagan statues, post-Cartesian metaphysics, and modern paintings. The exception is his discussion of idolatry in his Augustine book, which applies broadly to any human being confronted with the truth. Marion conducts his phenomenological reading of Augustine while bracketing history; the difference between Augustine's place and time and our own seems to make no difference to the analysis. Unlike Augustine himself, Marion makes no attempt to read history as the unfolding of God's interactions with humanity, and no attempt at a political reading of idolatry. For Augustine, especially in *City of God*, idolatry manifests in history through the Roman worship of false gods and the violent conquest of other peoples. Marion's reading of Augustine is focused on the *Confessions* and salvation from idolatry at the level of the individual soul.

Marion nevertheless does occasionally engage idolatry from a historical and political angle, and where he does his work is suggestive. In *God without Being*, Marion discusses the difference between the ancient gaze on idols and our own. He first distinguishes between the gaze of the artist and that of the spectator. The ancient sculptor of a *kouros*, for example, tries to capture in stone or wood what the artist has experienced of the divine, the point where a gaze froze. The spectator who views the idol is also captivated by the brilliance of the first visible, and the spectator's gaze is similarly arrested. The idol serves as a "materially fixed relay between different brilliancies produced by the same first visible," but only provided that the spectator adopt a "religious" attitude.[97] Idolatry depends on the gaze, and the idol itself cannot produce the gaze. Whether a statue is an idol or just art depends on the gaze of the spectator. "Because the idol allows the divine to occur only in man's measure, man can consign the idolatrous experience to art and thus keep it accessible, if not to all and at all times, at least to the worshipers of the god, and as long as the gods have not fled. Art no more produces the idol than the idol produces the gaze."[98]

So what happens if the gods have fled? What form does idolatry take in the contemporary world after the death of "God"? Here Marion seems to lament

the ease with which we desert idolatry, when our gaze takes off from work, visiting a particular temple or museum—to the extent that these visits lack the aim whose expectation could let itself be fulfilled and hence frozen, the signs of stone and color must wait, as mute gazes, for some animated eyes to reach them and be dazzled once again by the still-confined brilliance. Often we do not have, or no longer have, the means for such a splendid idolatry.[99]

From here, Marion turns to a different, apparently less splendid type of idolatry. If "we occidentals" have lost our aesthetic means for grasping the idols in human art, we have other options, most especially conceptual idolatry, by which the mind's gaze is frozen in a concept, and "God" is reduced to the measure of human knowledge.[100]

What does Marion mean by "splendid idolatry"? He does not develop this thought and does not come back to this phrase, but he seems to spy something vital in the hungry gaze searching for the divine, yearning to be filled, ready to give itself over to something other than itself. In a footnote to this passage he discusses Robert Walser's prose poem *Das Götzenbild*, in which the protagonist comes across a "dreadful image" from Africa in an ethnological museum and is frozen by it. Not just an aesthetic appreciation, the gaze elicits a desire in him to prostrate himself in front of the image and adore it.[101] To this profound and terrifying response, Marion juxtaposes us modern occidentals, wandering bored through museums, our gaze on holiday, our expectation focused more on getting selfies with the Venus de Milo and checking out the gift shop than connecting with the original brilliance the artist tried to capture. Marion strikes a different tone, as we have seen, in his discussion of painting in *In Excess*. There the tourists are depicted more sympathetically; Marion allows the possibility that they will glimpse some splendor, even be "educated" by a painting.[102] But despite the mirroring effect of the idol, or perhaps because of it, a splendid idolatry seems to demand something more of the person than the mere aesthetic consumption of images. Splendid idolatry demands worship, a kind of giving over of the self to something larger than the self, a bodily urge to drop to one's knees. There is something here both splendid and threatening.

In his chapter on vanity in *God without Being*, Marion considers the possibility of a contemporary gaze that is free of idols entirely because it adopts an attitude of boredom and detestation for the world that is incapable of either idolatry or *agape*. Marion uses Paul Valéry's character M. Teste to illustrate the gaze that transpierces everything, that is not captivated and arrested by anything. It sees and traverses everything "with the eye of the proprietor," but reduces everything it sees to nothing. The choice here, according to Marion, is not between an external idol and self-idolatry, since such a gaze has contempt for all idols, even itself. The choice, then, is between the icon and self-hate. The hatred of the idol flows back on the gaze itself; the gaze's ability to transpierce everything prohibits the gaze from ever encountering a gaze other than its own, so it ends in hatred of the self.[103] The icon, whose gaze would be able to save Teste from "drowning in his own obviousness," is ruled out. The gaze that goes beyond idols without receiving the icon is, Marion says, "both possible and actual every day: our own." Teste "shows us the rigor of our own situation." According to Marion, both he himself and his readers stand in the position of Teste: "We must ask, less of Teste, therefore, than of ourselves, how we manage in this way to maintain a gaze that does not see and does not let itself be seen, neither idolatrous nor iconic."[104] Here Marion appears to suggest that our current situation as Westerners after the death of "God" is typified by disenchantment, a movement beyond idolatry, splendid or otherwise. If not typical, such an attitude is at least "both possible and actual."

Has idolatry, splendid or otherwise, really receded? Do we modern Westerners really no longer have the means for it? Is there nothing analogous to the kind of bodily urge to self-sacrificial worship that Marion has pointed to as splendid idolatry? Occasionally, Marion hints that such idolatry continues in modern forms. In one passage in *The Idol and Distance*, he describes how political idols both terrorize and reassure by bridging the distance between the city and divinity:

> Hence its prodigious political effectiveness: it renders close, protective, and faithfully sworn the god who, identifying himself with the city, maintains an identity for it. This is indeed why politics always gives rise to idols, even after paganism; "Big Brother," the "Great Helmsman," the *Führer*, or the "Man we love best" must be divinized: made into gods, they conjure the

divine or, more vulgarly, destiny. Idolatry gives the cult of personality its true dignity—that of a familiar, tamed (and therefore undangerously terroristic) figure of the divine. Idolatrous temptation for ancient Israel always depended on political necessities. Conversely, it is to politics first that our time owes the fact that we are not lacking for new idols.[105]

The emphasis here—as in most of Marion's early work on idolatry—is on the taming of divinity, the overcoming of distance, bringing the god too close. But just after this passage Marion acknowledges a theme we have seen treated more extensively in Weber and in the Bible: the obedience and homage people pay to the gods they have produced and reduced. The idol, Marion writes, "delivers the divine to us to the point of enslaving it to us, just as much as it enslaves us to it."[106] The political idol appears here as a kind of saturated phenomenon that overwhelms us.

Marion continues on to explore the post-Enlightenment "twilight of the divine" as the logical endpoint of an idolatry that has brought the gods too close. The idol makes divinity too manipulable, too secure. "Everything is set up to allow a Feuerbachian reappropriation of the divine: since, like a mirror, the god reflects back to me my experience of the divine, why not reappropriate for myself what I attribute to the reflection of my own activity?"[107] Here Marion seems to suggest that the Feuerbachian moment has come to pass in the death of "God" and the desertion of idolatry. We have become conscious of our god-making and have therefore the means to cease being dazzled by idols of our own making. But Marion does not return to the political question, at least not in his treatment of the idol. Why, post-Feuerbach, are we still enslaved to idols of our own making? If distance has been overcome, why are humans not simply masters of our own destiny, but subject to new idols?

Perhaps the absorption of divinity into humanity has made humans into gods that are so much harder to shrug off and rebel against because they do not look like gods at all. Our obedience is assured because we believe that we are obeying ourselves. Political idolatry after Feuerbach is not limited to cults of personality, communism, fascism, and the deification of the state. Democratic nation-states call forth nationalistic fervor and self-sacrifice because we believe in us, the nation made up of no one but us mortals, guided by nothing but the will of the people. The mirror is now no longer invisible; we know that we are projecting our own will onto the nation, something larger than ourselves. We have consciously reappropriated to ourselves the reflection of our own activity. But if the mirror is no longer invisible, the idol is, as such, harder to see. Something similar may be going on in our economic activity as well. Our claim that we obey only our own desires erases our sense that we are obeying at all. The banality of consumer culture makes it easier to, like Teste, drown in our own obviousness.

Marion is useful for our analysis because he explores sympathetically the ways in which idolatry is reflective, generating a type of self-idolatry. Teste does not ultimately escape idolatry because self-hate is merely the obverse of self-love. Our attempts at autonomy from God turn into heteronomy, the subjugation of ourselves to the creations of our own will, a theme we have also explored in the Bible and Augustine. Marion is reticent to explore the broader political and social dynamics of idolatry in the contemporary context, but I think such exploration is necessary. Equipped with the theological and phenomenological tools I have developed in chapters 3 through 5, I will investigate the contemporary persistence of political and social idolatries, both splendid and unsplendid, in the next two chapters.

6

The Splendid Idolatry of Nationalism

In the previous chapter we saw how Jean-Luc Marion, like Augustine, treats idolatry primarily as a kind of narcissism, a mirror to the self. Marion, however, also makes room for a more sympathetic treatment of the idol, in which the idol calls forth a kind of worship and self-giving that breaks through the boredom and indifference of the contemporary self. Marion associates such a "splendid idolatry" with art, particularly pagan art, that seems to summon seriousness, dedication—perhaps virtue—which is real, though limited, not quite yet the summit of revealed virtue. Splendid idolatry contrasts with the contempt the modern gaze has for all idols, even itself, which does not release the self for true worship but leaves it dead-ended in boredom and self-hatred. Marion suggests that such a disenchanted condition, which refuses both idol and icon, is that of his own Western contemporaries, who no longer have "the means for such a splendid idolatry."[1]

In the present chapter, I will explore the possibility that we do still have the means for a different kind of splendid idolatry. I will explore this possibility through an examination of the phenomenon of nationalism. As we have seen, Marion himself largely avoids analyzing idolatry at any level except that of the self; he has produced a careful phenomenology of the self, as in Augustine's *Confessions*, but he has no counterpart to the *City of God*, where the contest between love of God and love of self is played out on the broad canvas of history and politics. But we do find a hint in Marion's early work that "it is to politics first that our time owes the fact that we are not lacking for new idols."[2]

Marion makes this remark in the 1970s in the context of comments on dictatorships and cults of personality. In his subsequent work over the next few decades, he may have assumed that the West, at least, was past the stage of such authoritarian idols. He may have assumed, along with nearly everyone else, that the fall of the Soviet Union, the stability of Western liberal democracies, and the success of the European Union had ushered in a postauthoritarian and postnational epoch of globalization and increasing liberalization.[3] In recent years, however, there has been a resurgence of

The Uses of Idolatry. William T. Cavanaugh, Oxford University Press. © Oxford University Press 2024.
DOI: 10.1093/oso/9780197679043.003.0007

nationalism in Western democracies and elsewhere; it has sometimes been accompanied by, but it is not dependent on, the idolization of authoritarian figures. Brexit did not depend on a cult of personality surrounding Boris Johnson, and Polish and French nationalisms have not depended on charismatic leaders. Where such leaders have arisen—Putin in Russia, Orbán in Hungary, Trump in the United States, Modi in India—they have drawn on a much deeper well of nationalist sentiment that long preceded them and will long survive them. The phenomenon of nationalism is much more entrenched and has longer historical roots than modern authoritarianism, and nationalism is compatible with, but does not depend on, cults of personality.

Belief in the nation—*we, the people*—is much deeper and durable than belief in one figurehead. Moreover, belief in *us* is more compatible with Marion's account of idolatry, since it is a kind of collective narcissism, a self-love writ large. At the same time, however, nationalism qualifies as a kind of splendid idolatry because it also calls forth real, though limited, virtues: fidelity to something larger than oneself, devotion to one's fellow citizens, and willingness to sacrifice oneself for the good of others. "Splendid idolatry" is a phrase that Marion uses in passing and does not develop into a full-blown concept. I am going to make use of the phrase in this chapter, nevertheless, because it helpfully suggests both the positive and the negative aspects of a phenomenon like nationalism. Nationalism splendidly draws upon what is best in *homo liturgicus*, while simultaneously directing lethal levels of devotion toward what is not God. We once again become subject to gods of our own making, gods that are constituted by the mirrors we hold up to our collective self.

The present chapter takes the case of nationalism to illustrate what I argued in the first two chapters: we do not live in a disenchanted world, but one in which forms of worship may have migrated but are still pervasive. As in Weber, there are modern gods that are not simply chosen but rather *given* to us. This chapter furthermore uses nationalism as a contemporary example of the dynamics of idolatry examined in chapters 3 through 5: the common human impulse to worship is often self-directed, and often with dire consequences. Nevertheless, I also want to use the notion of nationalism as "splendid idolatry" to display the sympathetic aspects of idolatry critique I have explored in the previous chapters. In the first section of this chapter, I explore the phenomenon of nationalism through the concept of "religion." Is nationalism a type of idolatrous religion? In the second section, I look at theories about the origins of nationalism and argue that Western forms of nationalism come about through a migration of the holy from the church to the nation. The third section addresses the virtues of nationalism. In the fourth section, I examine the vices of nationalism and argue that it tends toward an idolatry at odds with worship of the Christian God. The fifth and final section is a brief exposition of the scriptural notion of the People of God.

6.1. Nationalism as Religion

Anthony D. Smith defines nationalism as "an ideological movement for the attainment and maintenance of autonomy, unity, and identity on behalf of a population some of whose members deem it to constitute an actual or potential 'nation.'" Smith defines "nation" in turn as "a named human population occupying a historic territory and sharing common myths and memories, a public culture, and common laws and customs for all members."[4] By these definitions, nationalism does not seem to qualify as a religion in competition with other religions like Christianity. Religions, we generally assume, are systems of belief and practice whose object is a god or gods. The object of nationalism is a nation, not a god. Nationalism is therefore a secular phenomenon, not a religion. To ask "Is nationalism a religion?" is like asking "Is Buddhism a sport?"

But there are many scholars of nationalism writing over the past century who are convinced that nationalism *is* a religion. Carlton Hayes, professor of history at Columbia University, published a book in 1960 titled simply *Nationalism: A Religion*. That judgment has been echoed by other scholars of nationalism. If they are right, it has profound implications for the question of idolatry. Most Christians, for example, already claim to have a religion, and religion is the kind of thing of which most people think a person can have only one. If a person were to say "I'm a Mormon and a Muslim," most people would think that something has gone very wrong. Such a person would be seen as confused at best, and judged unfaithful and perhaps harmful by both Mormons and Muslims alike. A person who is both a Christian and a nationalist would be similarly confused, unfaithful, and potentially harmful. They would be, in Christian terms, an idolater, someone who directs loyalty to a false god.

It is clear that those who see nationalism as a religion use the term "religion" differently than it is usually used in the modern West. Generally, the term is used to refer to beliefs and practices organized around a God or gods or transcendence or some such concept. Such definitions of religion are called "substantivist" because they define religion based on the substance of adherents' beliefs. Those who see nationalism as a religion, however, tend to use a "functionalist" definition, whereby religion is defined according to how it functions to order people's lives. The substance of the beliefs matters less than how people behave. Émile Durkheim is the primary source for this kind of theorizing about religion. He writes in his classic *The Elementary Forms of the Religious Life*, "Religious force is only the sentiment inspired by the group in its members, but projected outside of the consciousnesses that experience them, and objectified. To be objectified, they are fixed upon some object which thus becomes sacred; but any object might fulfill this function."[5] Here we see that the object of religion—or, to put it another way, the substance of the beliefs—is a matter of relative indifference; it can be a god or it can be a flag. We also see that religion is not a private matter but is generated by a group. Religion can be explained sociologically, thought Durkheim, not as a human response to a transcendent reality or god but as a dynamic inherent in collectivities. Religion, according to Durkheim, is in fact the self-worship of the group. The idea of nationalism, devotion to one's own nation, fits easily within Durkheim's concept of religion. Durkheim asks rhetorically, "What essential difference is there between an assembly of Christians celebrating the principal dates of the life of Christ, or of Jews remembering the Exodus from Egypt or the promulgation of the Decalogue, and a reunion of citizens commemorating the promulgation of a new moral or legal system or some great event in the national life?"[6] The implied answer is "none."

Durkheim, like Weber, has a reductive account of the gods, which are human creations: "[T]he idea of society is the soul of religion. Religious forces are therefore human forces, moral forces."[7] Durkheim can have no critique of idolatry as such, because he recognizes no true God from whose worship people can deviate. Nevertheless, he puzzles over the same thing the book of Isaiah puzzles over: How can mere human creations come to have power over their creators? Unlike in Isaiah, however, for Durkheim the power of created divinities is a mark not of stupidity but of collective intelligence.[8]

Durkheim critiques the work of predecessors like Friedrich Max Müller, for whom religion was a primitive way of dealing with a nature we cannot control, "this overwhelming sensation of an infinity which surrounds us and dominates us."[9] For Max Müller, primitive peoples responded to this sensation by imagining natural forces as personal agents, thinking beings who took the form of gods to be worshiped and entreated, thus making it possible to make such forces work for human ends. Durkheim, however, thinks this naturalistic account fails to explain the utility of religion, even for primitive people. They would have figured out soon enough that all their prayers and fasting had no effect on nature, and they would have dropped religion as useless.[10] Durkheim, in contrast, attributes the persistence of religion to its fulfilling a genuine and necessary social function rather than to some kind of primitive error. Though "[t]he reasons with which the faithful justify them may be, and generally are, erroneous," there are in fact "no religions which are false," because they all answer to certain defined social needs.[11]

Durkheim's positive account of religion centers on the totem, a name or an emblem that comes to represent a social group. In so-called primitive groups, an animal or plant becomes the symbol of the clan, and its emblem is inscribed on shields, clothing, and human bodies. The totem, furthermore, is sacred and is rigidly separated from mere profane things by elaborate rules governing who may touch it, when, and how. Such rules give order to a social group, delineating who has power, under what circumstances others can access that power, and where boundaries lie. Violations of taboos harm the entire community, while maintaining the separation of sacred from profane preserves the order of the social group and the cosmos. Religion, therefore, is founded in a collective feeling of belonging to a group that is objectified in a sacred object, which then serves as the basis of social order. Society is based on fellow-feeling or compassion, sentiments of belonging to a larger group, not in the first place on exclusion and violence. What is really being worshiped in religion is the group, ourselves; as in theological accounts of idolatry, religion is a kind of self-worship. "The god of the clan, the totemic principle, can therefore be nothing else than the clan itself, personified and represented to the imagination under the visible form of the animal or vegetable which serves as totem."[12] This self-worship is disguised as the worship of some other object, but for Durkheim, as we have already seen, "any object can play this role"; he sees flags, for example, as a modern national version of the totem.[13]

What remains to be explained, however, is how mere human creations come to have power over their creators. Durkheim's account of the origins of society emphasizes cooperation, not violence, but his is not a social contract theory by which people consciously agree to abide by certain necessary rules. He argues, rather, that "it is unquestionable that a society has all that is necessary to arouse the sensation of the divine in minds, merely by the power that it has over them; for to its members it is what a god is to his worshipers."[14] The individual has to submit to the rules of society whether they want to or not. Though the rules of order are made by the society, and the society is made of individual human beings, the individual experiences the rules as something imposed upon them, something vastly transcending the will and power of any individual.[15] The collective representations have the power of all the individuals combined, because they are elaborated in common. The common voice is loud enough to silence any individual voice. This common action, though it can and does resort to physical violence, is in its source purely psychical; it imposes itself on common opinion "by the simple radiation of the mental energy which it contains."[16] This social pressure Durkheim also describes as "spiritual"; people understand that they are subject to invisible powers on which they depend. Were the mechanisms of society simple (as in social contract theory, which, I would note, is itself a mythological account), people might be able to get by without myth. "But social action follows ways that are too circuitous and obscure, and employs psychical mechanisms that are too complex to allow the ordinary observer to see when it comes."[17] And so people invent gods and mythological accounts of the abstract forces that both empower and dominate them.

Durkheim makes clear that his account of religion applies equally to so-called primitive societies and modern societies alike. Although modernity dissolves some ethnic ties, modern societies are still "moral" societies, attached to the collective by sentiments that are often stronger than those of their primitive counterparts.[18] The effervescence which produces collective revolutionary or creative action relies on the same mental processes that produced primitive religion.[19] "This aptitude of society for setting itself up as a god or for creating gods was never more apparent than during the first years of the French Revolution. . . . A religion tended to become established which had its dogmas, symbols, altars, and feasts."[20] The Fatherland, Liberty, and Reason were elevated to sacred status. But Durkheim contends that it is not only under exceptional circumstances that such a religion is created. As members of a society, we are always surrounded by forces, both imperious and helpful, that no individual created and to which each individual is subject. We still have our leaders who are elevated to sacred status.[21] We have our taboos; anyone who questions free speech would be accused of sacrilege.[22] And we have our totem. "It is this which is loved, feared, respected; it is to this that we are grateful; it is for this that we sacrifice ourselves. The soldier who dies for his flag, dies for his country; but as a matter of fact, in his own consciousness, it is the flag that has the first place."[23] Despite the strategic uselessness of a piece of cloth, a soldier will die to save a flag, having substituted the sign for the reality.[24]

Although Durkheim wrote little on nationalism as such,[25] it is clear that for him the sentiments and rituals that bind the nation together are a modern species of religion, in which the real object of worship is the nation itself. Durkheim's account of the nation is thus similar to theological accounts of idolatry as self-worship, though it is the collective, not individual, self that worships its reflection in the mirror. As in biblical evaluations of idolatry, Durkheim sees that people have a need to worship, and their worship falls upon all sorts of objects. Though there is a strict distinction between the sacred and the profane in both the Bible and in Durkheim, the religious/secular distinction applies to neither; there is no separate secular realm of government and business and so on to which worship does not apply. Likewise, Durkheim provides an account of how people come to be subjected to the power of their own creations, a dynamic which is also central to theological critiques of idolatry.

Durkheim does not, however, engage in idolatry critique as such. Idolatry is not a relevant category for Durkheim, because he does not acknowledge a true God to be contrasted to the many gods of human creation. And critique is not his purpose in analyzing the social genesis of religion. In contrast to Max Müller and other naturalists, Durkheim sees religion not as a primitive error but as a necessary binding agent for any social group. There is something splendid in dedication to the *patrie*. Such collective self-worship is not mere narcissism because the individual is caught up in something larger than themselves. Religion is not simple alienation. After giving his account of how our creations come to have power over us, Durkheim adds, "But a god is not merely an authority upon whom we depend; it is a force upon which our strength relies. The man who has obeyed his god and who for this reason believes the god is with him, approaches the world with confidence and with the feeling of an increased energy."[26] The god does not simply stand over against us, demanding sacrifice. The collective force is both larger than us and within us; it penetrates us and becomes part of our being, thus ennobling the individual.[27] Self-sacrifice is not simply the alienation of the self to some other outside force; it is sacrifice of the individual self to and for the larger, social self, which thereby elevates the individual to participation in the divine.

Durkheim's *Elementary Forms of the Religious Life* was published in 1912, on the eve of World War I. Durkheim was convinced that traditional religions like Christianity were fading because their supernatural claims were incompatible with science, but new secular religions like devotion to the nation would take their place.[28] Durkheim was a French patriot, who saw the deification of France as a response to basic impulses of human sociality. Robert Bellah called Durkheim "a theologian of the French civil religion."[29] Carlton Hayes was harsher in his judgment, crediting Durkheim with laying the groundwork for the totalitarianism that came after his death in 1917:

> It must not be imagined that the sowers of totalitarian nationalism were all anti-semites. Some Jews were effective planters—for example, Emile Durkheim, who started out to be a rabbi and ended up as a world famous sociologist. He taught that the national state, the *patrie*, is a "psychic being," that of all "societies"—family, class, church, etc.—it is the most basic and by right the most powerful, and that, as its function is the supreme one of directing and giving harmony to the ideal "corporative society," so its members owe it supreme allegiance and the highest public worship.[30]

The more charitable judgment of Josep Llobera is probably more accurate: Durkheim distinguished between patriotism and nationalism, attributing to the former a healthy balance between love for one's own nation and respect for the broader universal *patrie* of humanity.[31] Nevertheless, Durkheim was not a cosmopolitan, and he condemned "anti-patriot internationalists."[32] Like other French thinkers of his generation, he was searching for a renewed sense of national identity and strength in the wake of the humiliating defeat at the hands of the Prussians in 1870. The sense of loss comes through in the conclusion to *Elementary Forms*, where Durkheim laments, "The great things of the past which filled our fathers with enthusiasm do not excite the same ardour in us."[33] As in Marion, splendid idolatry is feared lost. Both Christianity and the revolutionary spirit of 1789 have faded, and there is nothing yet evident which is capable of replacing them. "In a word, the old gods are growing old or already dead, and others are not yet born."[34] But Durkheim is convinced that the situation will change, because the gods answer to a basic human need. Though no gods last forever, humans are constantly inventing new ones: "A day will come when our societies will know again those hours of creative effervescence."[35] That creative effervescence returned two years after he wrote those lines with the outbreak of World War I, but the resurgence of national pride would be fed into a senseless slaughter that was considerably less splendid than anyone in France anticipated. Durkheim's own son was killed in battle in 1915, a blow from which Durkheim never recovered.

Hayes was compelled by the unhinged zealotry and carnage of World War I to begin his investigations into nationalism as a form of religion, resulting in his seminal 1926 essay, "Nationalism as a Religion." Like Durkheim, Hayes was not a cultured despiser of religion, but thought rather that empirical observation of human behavior revealed that all of humanity shared a "religious sense":

> From the dawn of his history man has been distinguished by what may be called a "religious sense," that is, a mysterious faith in some power outside of himself, a faith always accompanied by feelings of reverence and usually attended by external acts and ceremonial. Everywhere, under the most diverse forms, you find its expression. . . . It may be worship of Christ or Buddha; it may be worship of totem or fetish; it may likewise be worship of science or humanity—provided these concepts are written in his mind with capital letters.[36]

Homo religiosus is also *homo liturgicus*, with feelings of reverence accompanied by rites. The rise of skepticism in the Enlightenment, according to Hayes, did not signal the loss of the religious sense but rather its relocation. The post-Enlightenment rise of the worship of the national state at the same time that Christianity was in decline was not a coincidence but instead illustrates the perdurance of the religious sense, which does not disappear but migrates to other objects. The French Revolution was a milestone in this migration, writes Hayes, as the rites and doctrines formerly belonging to the church were transferred, in mutated form, to the cult of the nation. The Declaration of the Rites of Man was promulgated as the new "national catechism." The written national Constitution became scripture, and those who refused to swear by it faced civil excommunication. At the first session of the French Legislative Assembly in 1791, twelve men slowly processed in with the Book of the Constitution, as the deputies reverently bared their heads. Rites of civic baptism, marriages, and funerals were soon invented.[37] At the National Convention in 1793, Marie-Joseph Chenier proposed replacing Catholicism with a "single universal religion, which has neither sects nor mysteries, of which the only dogma is equality, of which our law-makers are the preachers, of which the magistrates are the pontiffs, and in which the human family burns its incense only at the altar of la Patrie, common mother and divinity."[38]

Hayes continues on to discuss the many characteristics that nationalism shares with other things that are called religions. Here he is thinking primarily of Christianity; given that nationalism arises first in traditionally Christian lands, he finds it unsurprising that national cults would have borrowed much from the church. Nationalism has first a god, the nation, on whom the citizen must acknowledge dependence through acts of homage and adoration, for the sake of the salvation of the entire community. Nationalism, like any religion, involves not only the intellect and the will but also the imagination and the emotions. To the nation are due faith, hope, and filial love, ecstatic joy, thankfulness for benefits bestowed and protection from foreign devils, fear of causing offense, and reverence for the fatherland's power and wisdom. The role of the nation is not primarily economic or transactional; "it is primarily spiritual, even otherworldly, and its driving force is its collective faith, a faith in its mission and destiny, a faith in things unseen, a faith that would move mountains."[39]

Around this faith in the national god is built an entire system of formation that Hayes likens to medieval Christendom. One does not join the nation voluntarily but is registered as a citizen at birth, as one was previously baptized. Membership in one nation or another is compulsory. The educational system inculcates reverence for the stories of national holiness and a proper awe for sacred national symbols like the flag. Owing to its relative youth, the rituals of nationalism are not yet as developed as those of medieval Christendom, but "curious liturgical forms" have been developed for handling the flag, which must never, for example, be profaned by contact with the ground. Schoolchildren are "required to recite daily, with hierophantic voice and ritualistic gesture, the mystical formula," pledging allegiance to the flag and to the nation. The national anthem is "the Te Deum of the new dispensation," and proper care must be shown not to blaspheme during its performance. Nationalism has its processions, pilgrimages, and holy days. Just as Christians borrowed elements from pagan feasts, so now nationalists borrow freely from Christian celebrations: Flag Day substitutes for Corpus Christi, Memorial Day is the new All Souls Day for remembering the faithful departed, Presidents Day replaces saints' feast days, the Capitol building is the new cathedral. Catholic veneration of images, icons, and relics is considered superstitious paganism by many Americans, but their attitude is quite different when confronted with a statue of a Founding Father or a tattered battle flag lovingly preserved. When the Liberty Bell was transported to San Francisco by train in 1915, Hayes reports, throngs of women bestowed pious kisses upon it at stops along the way, just as Catholics on Good Friday venerate the wood of the Cross.[40]

In addition to all the formative ritual elements nationalism shares with other religions, according to Hayes, nationalism also shares high regard for sacrifice and for the myths on which such sacrifice is based. The essential holiness and salvific destiny of the nation are constantly propagated, especially through tales of those who bravely gave their lives on behalf of the nation. Such stories express faith in the eternal goodness of the nation and must not be tainted by doubt and the ambiguity of historical fact. Nationalism is beset by the fear common to religious zealots that the masses are always on the verge of losing their faith, and so only edifying stories that will support their faith should be allowed to reach them. In a passage that could have been written today rather than a century ago, Hayes quotes a 1922 report on textbooks in New York City schools that declares, "The textbook must contain no statement in derogation or in disparagement of the achievements of American heroes. It must not question the sincerity of the aims and purposes of the founders of the Republic or of those who have guided its destinies."[41] Governments and parties can be criticized, and even government as such can be vilified, but the eternal nation and its heroes rise above mere historical events that can be critiqued, just as the Church Triumphant must never be confused with the Church Militant.

Possibly because he considers the point too obvious to belabor, Hayes spends only one paragraph on what he calls "perhaps the surest proof of the religious character of modern nationalism [which] is the zeal with which all manner of its devotees have laid down their lives on battlefields of the last hundred years."[42] Sacrifice is a common feature of religion, and the supreme sacrifice, Hayes writes, is paid willingly not for merely mundane purposes or economic gain, but most often in response to the "religious sense." This explains why there are fields of hundreds of thousands of little white crosses in France bearing the inscription *Mort pour la Patrie*. Hayes notes laconically that such deaths from the four years of World War I dwarf the carnage from four centuries of Crusades.[43]

In closing his essay, Hayes makes clear that he does not condemn nationalism because it is a manifestation of the common human religious sense. He does aver, however, "Some forms of religion are superior to others," and he clearly thinks that nationalism is not what we need more of.

In addition to being one of the most prominent twentieth-century scholars of nationalism, Hayes was also a convert to Catholicism, and the two interests were related.[44] He understood nationalism as a rival to Christian humility—nationalism is "tribal selfishness and vainglory"[45]—to Christian peaceableness, and to the international and catholic nature of the Church: "Nationalism as a religion represents a reaction against historic Christianity, against the universal mission of Christ."[46] Nationalism is idolatry.[47] Despite such normative judgments, however, Hayes was as capable of distinguishing the Church Militant from the Church Triumphant as his nationalist counterparts were. As president of the Catholic Association for International Peace, Hayes often criticized his fellow Catholics for subordinating their loyalty to Christ to their loyalty to the nation.[48] Though he was convinced that "the final great bulwark of mankind against the errors and evils of nationalism is the Catholic Church," he nevertheless chastised his fellow Catholics, past and present, who "put nationalism above our faith and thus give aid and comfort to our most persistent and insidious foe."[49]

Hayes did not see nationalism as yet replacing Christianity, at least not in the United States. The situation was rather one of syncretism, in which Christianity and American nationalism were mixed, increasingly to the benefit of the latter and the detriment of the former. Hayes thought such syncretism was inevitable, given the divided nature of Christianity in the United States. Catholicism was a minority faith, and Protestants were scattered into hundreds of denominations, none strong enough to establish a common American faith. "Consequently the spiritual unity, which almost everyone deems desirable, must be sought in nationalism."[50] Hayes appears to believe that the religious sense cannot remain private but must be manifested at the level of the community as a whole; in this he shows his Catholic influence. Christian churches and denominations are free to argue over theological doctrines like biblical interpretation and sacraments, but they agree on the one central tenet of homage to the nation.[51]

Since Hayes's first explorations of this theme, many other scholars have used the idea of religion to describe nationalism. I will not try to present a comprehensive history of this discourse, but I will examine a few of the more significant interventions.[52] One of the most influential was sociologist Robert Bellah's 1967 essay "Civil Religion in America," which argued that Christianity is not the national faith of the United States but exists alongside a "well-institutionalized civil religion" which "has its own seriousness and integrity and requires the same care in understanding that any other religion does."[53] Bellah's subject is not nationalism as such but the particular national faith of and in America. As did Hayes, Bellah recognized American civil religion and Christianity operating on two parallel tracks, one public and the other private. The separation of church and state relegated the churches to the private sphere, but the separation of church and state was not the separation of religion and politics. While Christianity was privatized, "the separation of church and state has not denied the political realm a religious dimension."[54] Indeed, though Bellah does not say so explicitly, it may be the case that the separation of church and state has paved the way for the development of a religion of the state, precisely by clearing Christianity out of the way. This observation lends credence to Hayes's idea that the religious sense abhors a vacuum, and new objects to worship publicly will inevitably substitute for those that have been displaced.

Bellah gives many examples of reference to a generic "God" in solemn American political discourse. While some are inclined to discount such references as vacuous window dressing, Bellah says that we now know enough about how ritual functions in various societies that we should not dismiss something as "only a ritual."[55] Societies live by ritual and can hold together only if people are united by a sentiment that transcends themselves. In a democracy, the will of the people is the source of political authority, but, writes Bellah, "it is deprived of ultimate significance." The people can be wrong, and so their will cannot be the ultimate criterion of right and wrong. The immanent belief in "we, the people" must be supplemented by a transcendent belief that the will of the people is rooted in, guided by, and judged by a transcendent power. There must be a higher criterion; Bellah quotes John F. Kennedy saying that "here on earth God's work must truly be our own."[56]

This "God" is not the Trinitarian God of Kennedy's Catholic faith, but a Unitarian God. Stretching back to the discourse of the founders, Bellah finds a consistent absence of any appeal to Christ or any more specific modifier for the Deity. Bellah doubts that the founders would have meant to spare the feelings of the tiny non-Christian minority. "Rather," Bellah writes cryptically, "the civil religion expressed what those who set the precedents felt was appropriate under the circumstances."[57] American civil religion was not Christian, but it was not simply a generic "religion in general" either. Bellah notes that "the civil religion was specific enough when it came to the topic of America."[58] America has a special salvific role to play in human history, and American civil religion freely borrows biblical themes: Americans as the Chosen People given a new land; the Civil War as death, sacrifice, and rebirth; American war dead as martyrs; and so on. But while such symbolism is biblical, it "is Christian without having anything to do with the Christian church."[59] American civil religion is not meant to replace Christianity, but between church and state there is a clear division of labor; Christianity is private, while civil religion, with all its attendant rituals and feast days, is public.[60]

In contrast to Hayes and other critics, Bellah does not regard American civil religion as inherently idolatrous: "Against these critics, I would argue that the civil religion at its best is a genuine apprehension of universal and transcendent religious reality as seen in or, one could almost say, as revealed through the experience of the American people."[61] It is not clear what function the "almost" plays in this sentence; throughout the article, Bellah treats civil religion as a genuine religion, not a quasi- or almost-religion.[62] Like Hayes, Bellah seems to acknowledge the existence of a "universal and transcendent religious reality" which expresses itself in different forms. Unlike Hayes, Bellah does not think that civil religion is a lesser form of religion than Christianity or any other traditional faith. Bellah contrasts American civil religion with that of revolutionary France. Jean-Jacques Rousseau, from whom Bellah borrows the phrase "civil religion," intended the French civic cult to replace Christianity, but American civil religion was never hostile to Christianity. "On the contrary, it borrowed selectively from the religious tradition in such a way that the average American saw no conflict between the two. In this way, the civil religion was able to build up without any bitter struggle with the church powerful symbols of national solidarity and to mobilize deep levels of personal motivation for the attainment of national goals."[63] Bellah credits the civil religion with pushing for a "humane solution" to the problem of "the treatment of the Negro American." It remains to be seen, Bellah writes, if the American civil religion will have a similarly benign influence on the war in Vietnam.[64] Here Bellah tacitly acknowledges the ambivalence of the quote from Kennedy: if God's work is our work, then either we subject our work to judgment by a higher standard, or we simply come to identify whatever we are doing with the will of God.[65] Bellah exudes confidence that the former is more generally the case, and even holds open the possibility that American civil religion could be subsumed into a larger "new civil religion of the world":

Fortunately, since the American civil religion is not the worship of the American nation but an understanding of the American experience in the light of ultimate and universal reality, the reorganization entailed by such a new situation need not disrupt the American civil religion's continuity. A world civil religion could be accepted as a fulfillment and not a denial of American civil religion.[66]

Bellah thinks that this international civil religion has been the "eschatological hope" of American civil religion since its beginning. "To deny such an outcome would be to deny the meaning of America itself."[67]

For Bellah, then, the reason that people who follow Christianity can have a second religion and see no conflict between the two is that "American civil religion is not the worship of the American nation" and therefore is not the idolatrous worship of a false god, despite the different ways the "God" of each is specified. Both religions, Christianity and civil religion—one for private consumption, the other for public use—are manifestations of a larger ultimate and universal religious reality. One puzzle remains for Bellah, however, which he addresses in a footnote. America has a civil religion that is the equal of any other religion. "Why something so obvious should have escaped serious analytical attention is in itself an interesting problem."[68] If American nationalism is so obviously a religion, in other words, why do we deny it? Bellah posits that conservative religious groups deny it because they believe that Christianity is, in fact, the national religion. As recently as the 1950s they proposed a constitutional amendment recognizing the sovereignty of Jesus Christ. Secularists deny that America has a civil religion because they do not believe the nation-state does or should have anything to do with religion. Those in between these two extremes have simply missed "the positive institutionalization with which I am concerned." Part of the problem, Bellah concludes, is that the usual Western concept of "religion" is such that a person can have only one. "The Durkheimian notion that every group has a religious dimension . . . is foreign to us,"[69] so we miss the religious dimensions of our own society. Bellah seems to rule out idolatry critique by allowing more than one religion to any one person.

Carolyn Marvin and David Ingle take an explicitly Durkheimian approach to the question of civil religion, and, like Bellah, they recognize an American national religion that is distinct from Christianity or any other traditional faith. Marvin and Ingle state categorically that "nationalism is the most powerful religion in the United States, and perhaps in many other countries."[70] Their response to the question of why we deny this fact is, however, quite different from Bellah's answer.

Marvin and Ingle think that civil religion has not been properly understood. In most discourse, civil religion is a pale imitation of traditional or "sectarian" religion.[71] American civil religion borrows its fundamental elements—myths, rituals, feasts, sacraments, sacrifices, and so on—from Christianity, and so civil religion is seen as derivative, a mere simulacrum of the real thing. According to Marvin and Ingle, the opposite is in fact the case: American civil religion is the real religion of American society, because it controls and directs violence. The worship of killing authority is central to religion; the god is the one that commands life and death. Belonging to a sectarian religion is optional, and Americans have very rarely killed or died for Methodism, Catholicism, Lutheranism, Judaism, Islam, Buddhism, and so on. Doing obeisance to the civil religion, however, is not optional, and Americans consider killing and dying for their country to be necessary and laudable: "Though denominations are permitted to exist in the United States, they are not permitted to kill, for their beliefs are not officially true. What is really true in any society is what is worth killing for, and what citizens may be compelled to sacrifice their lives for."[72] Marvin and Ingle, like Bellah, recognize the division in the United States between public civil religion and private traditional religion. Unlike Bellah, they do not think that civil religion and sectarian religion coexist amicably, each expressing a different facet of the universal religious sense. There can be only one that controls the means of violence; the modern state, as Weber saw, seeks a *monopoly* on the legitimate use of violence. And that monopoly depends on the exclusive loyalty of its devotees. "Only nationalism motivates the sacrificial devotion of citizens, without which there can be no effective governance. In relation to *that* faith, sectarian religion is best understood as a jealous competitor."[73] *Pace* Bellah, one cannot have more than one true religion. Religions that claim to be true in some objective and public way must compete. For Marvin and Ingle, the waxing of nationalism and the waning of Christianity in the West is due to the transfer of killing authority from the church to the nation-state.[74] Christianity is still practiced by millions in the West, but it is optional, private, not officially true, and allowed to operate only insofar as it does not interfere with the worship of the national god.

Marvin and Ingle reject a tendency, since Weber, to associate violence with the state and sharply to distinguish the state from the nation, to which people have a benign and sentimental attachment. Violence is not accidental to nationalism; the nation as imagined community must be formed and reformed by violent sacrifice, expressed through a religion of patriotism that is organized around the flag.[75] Civil religion establishes the identity of the nation by determining who may kill and what for, and it is propagated through myths, images, and rituals. "In our scheme, civil religion and nationalism are synonymous terms for the sacralized agreement that creates killing authority and specifies the relationship of group members to sacrificial death."[76] Marvin and Ingle add considerable detail to Hayes's insight that "perhaps the surest proof of the religious character of modern nationalism" is the zeal with which millions have sacrificed their lives for a flag.

In America, we prefer to think of the nation as having overcome blood as the basis for social order. We are a melting pot made up of many different races, ethnic groups, and faith communities. We have overcome ethnic nationalism, that is, basing social cohesion on blood ties. This narrative is at the basis of American exceptionalism: called out from among all the other nations, we created a new nation that is pluralistic, inclusive, and peace-loving. The facts, Marvin and Ingle argue, are quite different from this comforting myth. In fact, the United States has had an extraordinarily bloody history, both within and outside its own borders. The nation that spends more on its military than the next ten largest militaries combined bases its group identity on violence. The production and reproduction of the nation are based on defending borders with blood. The nation is the shared memory of blood sacrifice, which must be constantly refreshed; new threats must be found, new sacrifices made to defend ourselves against those threats, and rituals must be performed to keep the memory of those sacrifices alive. We think that we are a secular and modern society, well past the religious violence of more primitive societies. But we have not in fact overcome the organization of society around blood sacrifice. "Patriotism is a religion of the borders organized around a myth about the violence that begets them. This religion is as necessary to the American nation-state as its standing armies, its police and its administrative apparatus."[77]

The idea that group identity is formed around violent sacrifice is by no means original to Marvin and Ingle. They draw on theorists like René Girard, for whom social order is maintained by the various factions of society uniting against a singular scapegoat. "Religion" is the ritualized commemoration of how that sacrifice saved the society from division and ruin.[78] Girard is right, Marvin and Ingle argue, that the victimization process must be unanimous. War must be popular to be ritually successful. Where they depart from Girard, however, is in their emphasis on the death of beloved members of the community. Enemies must be scapegoated, but sacrifice is effective only if our own die. The cult of the martyred hero soldier is crucial to the refreshing of the imagined borders of the community: "The ritual victim, the scapegoat, makes our anger and killing acceptable and disguises its real target. Our rage at the scapegoat provides a pretext to kill the savior."[79] The "ultimate sacrifice" is not the killing of the other but the death of one of our own, our best: "To die for others is the ultimate expression of faith in social existence."[80] Self-sacrifice is the key to the religion of nationalism, and it is precisely what makes nationalism "splendid": it does not appear to be a kind of narcissism but is instead the giving of oneself wholly over to one's fellow citizens, even to the point of death.

As Marvin and Ingle point out, it is this impulse that fuels laments that we have lost the "greatest generation," those who were willing to sacrifice themselves for the good of the nation. World War II is seen wistfully as "the good war," when we were united against a common enemy and willing to give our lives for each other. The nation is imperiled because we no longer have a common enemy against whom to sacrifice ourselves. Marvin and Ingle quote Mario Cuomo, a former governor of New York, giving a representative version of this lament: "We found strength in this common commitment, this commonality, community, family, the idea of coming together was best served in my lifetime in the Second World War." Now, however, we search in vain for such a spirit. "Where are our heroes, great causes? No cause. No hero. No heroine. Nothing big to believe in. Nothing to wrap your arms around."[81] Similar laments can be heard now about the time after the 9/11 attacks in 2001, when the country was similarly united by the deaths of our own. We no longer seem capable of such a splendid idolatry.

Marvin and Ingle distinguish their own approach from those of other scholars of nationalism who emphasize texts. For Benedict Anderson, a sense of national belonging among people vastly distant and different from one another is created through "print capitalism," through the media of newspapers and novels. The reinforcement of a national language is crucial to this process. For Ernest Gellner, devotion to the nation is inculcated through schooling. According to Marvin and Ingle, this type of textual approach cannot account for the willingness of people to kill and die for a country. Shared textual experience could never suffice for this type of devotion; "nationalism is a community of blood and not text."[82] It is not by accident that war and the commemoration of the dead play such a central role in patriotic ritual. Armies and nations are organized around bodies, not texts. The social body is constructed of individual bodies; bodies are the raw material of society, and organizing them, using them, and disposing of them is society's most basic task.[83]

The various individual human bodies, however, do not signify the nation in and of themselves. They must be organized around a totem symbol; here Marvin and Ingle draw directly from Durkheim. Just as so-called primitive tribes adopted a sacred animal or plant as a totem to symbolize the group, so do modern nations adopt a flag as the totem under which one is born and for which one must be willing to sacrifice: "Sacrifice for the flag establishes a blood kinship that is stronger than the familial bond."[84] Marvin and Ingle apply Durkheim's parsing of the essential properties of the totem to the American flag. The flag signifies the nation as a whole, and occupies a considerable place in American culture. The flag is surrounded by taboos that regulate how it is handled; it must not be "desecrated," which indicates its sacred character. The flag is numinous; people respond emotionally to the presence of the flag. The flag, like other totems, wards off evil and offers protection. The flag is surrounded by certain rituals that govern communication with the totem as the only way to ensure its blessing.

One does not have to look far to find examples of the flag as sacred totem in American society. One such example is the controversy ignited by professional football players, starting with Colin Kaepernick in 2016, deciding to take a knee rather than stand for the singing of the national anthem in order to protest systemic racism in the United States. President Trump responded with horror: "There are other things you can protest, but not our Great American Flag—NO KNEELING!" For Trump, kneeling before the flag was enough potentially to disqualify one from membership in the nation: "You have to stand proudly for the national anthem or you shouldn't be playing, you shouldn't be there. Maybe you shouldn't be in the country."[85] The protests were often linked by critics to disrespecting the military and the soldiers who had died for the flag. At a rally of Gold Star mothers, the mother of a soldier killed in Afghanistan slammed the NFL players and, pointing to her grandchildren, said, "These two children right here—you can look at a flag and say that's Uncle Jacob," in reference to her deceased son.[86]

Marvin and Ingle put great emphasis on this type of identification of the flag with the bodies of those slain for the nation. The flag, they claim, is a body, not a text. The flag is treated as both a living body that must be handled with delicacy and reverence, and as the sacred embodiment of the dead. We tend to regard texts as subject to free speech—why did Muslims get so upset at a mere novel by Salman Rushdie?—but flag burning is a matter of the body and entirely more serious.[87] When Gold Star mothers are handed the flag from their child's coffin, they cradle it like a baby, one observer notes. The flag represents the body of the dead soldier.[88] It must be treated as sacred. Sometimes the flag even substitutes for a particular sacred body, the crucified body of Jesus Christ. At the 2020 Republican National Convention, Vice President Mike Pence—an evangelical Christian—ran together two scripture verses, while substituting the flag for Jesus Christ: "So let's run the race marked out for us. Let's fix our eyes on Old Glory and all she represents. Let's fix our eyes on this land of heroes and let their courage inspire. And let's fix our eyes on the author and perfecter of our faith and our freedom and never forget that where the spirit of the Lord is, there is freedom. That means freedom always wins."[89] In Hebrews 12:1–2, the source, almost verbatim, of the first part of this quote, we are encouraged to run the race with our eyes fixed on Jesus. On location at Fort McHenry, where the lyrics to the "Star-Spangled Banner" were written, Pence substitutes the flag and military heroes for Jesus Christ. Pence does invoke some sort of god, quoting from II Corinthians 3:17 in the second part of the passage, but rather than the God of Jesus Christ, in whom, Paul says later in same letter, "power is made perfect in weakness" (12:9), Pence invokes a god who "always wins." This is a god who is identified with "our freedom."

The distinction between texts and bodies is crucial for Marvin and Ingle because it is a key to addressing the denial of the religious nature of nationalism that so puzzled Bellah. For Marvin and Ingle, the body/text distinction explains *how* we deny that nationalism is a religion: bodily ritual gestures make very clear that nationalism is a religion; it is only in language, texts, that we deny it. *Why* we deny it is explained by the Durkheimian notion of taboo: what is sacred is powerful and must be set apart:

> If nationalism is religious, why do we deny it? Because what is obligatory for group members must be separated, as holy things are, from what is contestable. To concede that nationalism is a religion is to expose it to challenge, to make it just the same as sectarian religion. By explicitly denying that our national symbols and duties are sacred, we shield them from competition with sectarian symbols. In so doing, we embrace the ancient command not to speak the sacred, ineffable name of god. The god is inexpressible, unsayable, unknowable, beyond language. But that god may not be refused when it calls for sacrifice.[90]

Here Marvin and Ingle give two different answers to the question they ask, one I find convincing, the other not. The first is that we deny nationalism is a religion to keep it from competition with sectarian religions like Christianity. The second is that we deny nationalism is a religion in order to respect the ineffable name of the god. This second answer does not seem plausible to me. The Israelites did not pronounce the name of YHWH, but they did not deny that YHWH was God and the explicit object of their worship. They did, however, deny that relying on the Egyptians for military help constituted idolatry. They denied that they were thereby worshiping false gods by putting their reliance on anyone or anything other than YHWH to defend them. Marvin and Ingle's first answer explains why Christians in the United States deny that American nationalism is a religion: so that they can deny that American nationalism and Christianity are in competition, and thereby avoid the charge of idolatry. Putting one's faith in America and its military might can be placed in a different category from Christianity, which is about the explicit worship of God. Christians can give their bodies over to the nation-state while continuing to express in textual terms that worship belongs to God alone. If language sometimes strays over the line that separates religious from secular, as in Pence's case, one can either claim that he was only speaking metaphorically, and thus keep the religious/secular distinction intact, or one can claim that American nationalism is in fact Christian, thus eliminating any competition between the two. In either case, however, one would need to deny that American nationalism is in fact a separate religion with its own distinct "seriousness and integrity," as Bellah puts it.

For Bellah, American civil religion is clearly not Christian but a distinct public religion in its own right that exists parallel to Christianity. Bellah believes Americans deny civil religion either because they want to say that the national religion is Christianity or because they want to say there is no national religion in a secular country. He thinks neither party should be so worried; there can be a secular national religion that does not compete with sectarian religions like Christianity. Marvin and Ingle agree that American civil religion is not Christian, but they think that competition between Christianity and American civil religion is unavoidable. Only one god can be true, and that is the god that controls life and death. What is really sacred, what is officially true in any society, is that for which one can be compelled to sacrifice one's life.[91] As President Biden has said, "We've a lot of obligations as Americans. . . . But only one sacred obligation, and that's prepare those we send to war and care for them and their families when they come home from

238 THE USES OF IDOLATRY

war."[92] According to Marvin and Ingle, the difference between Christianity and nationalism is not in the relative importance of blood sacrifice, which is crucial to both; it is in social location. Christianity used to be able to organize killing energies in the West; now, only the nation-state can do so. If Christianity is widely recognized as a religion, then nationalism cannot be a mere religion; nationalism rises above mere sectarianism.[93]

Marvin and Ingle cite a 1989 opinion by Supreme Court Justice William Rehnquist supporting state laws against "desecration" of the flag as evidence that what is sacred must be set apart: "The flag is not simply another 'idea' or 'point of view' competing for recognition in the marketplace of ideas. Millions and millions of Americans regard it with an almost mystical reverence regardless of what sort of social, political, or philosophical beliefs they may have."[94] Here, Rehnquist signals that the flag is a bodily reality, not simply a textual idea, and it stands above mere sectarian beliefs. But the word "almost" in this passage indicates that—at least in language—Rehnquist feels compelled to subordinate flag worship to "real" religion, "real" mystical reverence as would be accessed through a sectarian religion. In language we continue to affirm that nationalism does not quite rise to the level of a real religion, while in bodily gesture we acknowledge that the flag, and not any sectarian God, is what we really worship, what we would kill and die for. As we saw in chapter 2 with Charles Taylor, the "almost" is crucial for avoiding the charge of idolatry, but idolatry, as we saw in chapter 3, is primarily not about what we say we believe but about what our bodily actions reveal our true beliefs to be.

Marvin and Ingle's analysis is thus helpful for our exploration of nationalism as idolatry, though idolatry is not a relevant concept for them. Like Durkheim, they have no true God against which to contrast idolatrous gods. They make no ontological claims; a god is true only insofar as it is officially recognized as true by a society in organizing killing energies around that god. Like Girard, they see the origins of religion and society in violence. According to Girard, societies channel the centrifugal tendencies of violence by focusing it on a single victim, a scapegoated individual or group, against whom the society can unite. Just as Marvin and Ingle think societies must disguise the fact that we want and need our own to die, so Girard thinks societies cohere through an act of hiding our own violence from ourselves in the unanimity in which we agree that the scapegoated victims get what they deserve. Unlike Girard, however, Marvin and Ingle do not recognize the possibility of a nonviolent God. For Girard, in the death and resurrection of Jesus Christ we see a God who takes the place of the scapegoated victims and thereby reveals the injustice of the scapegoating mechanism. In Christ, God reveals the violence on which societies build a tenuous peace to be a lie. The killing that is "officially true," in Marvin and Ingle's terms, is revealed as false by a God who is aligned not with the officially true but with the onto-logically true. For Girard, the self-sacrifice of Jesus Christ is meant to end the sacrifice of all the victims whose bodies are used up by officially sanctioned violence.[95] Marvin and Ingle, however, make no distinction between Jesus's self-sacrifice and the self-sacrifice by which we kill our own. There does not seem to be any escape from officially true violence. For Girard, by contrast, the officially true god is an idolatrous god, and that concept of idolatry allows the possibility that violence does not necessarily have the final word.

In the face of evidence of the religious nature of nationalism, some scholars attempt to distinguish between religious and secular types of na-tionalism, or ethnic and civic nationalisms. Scholarship on nationalism often focuses on "bad" nationalism, which incorporates ethnic, cultural, and re-ligious elements and is therefore prone to exclusiveness and violence. It is inherited, not chosen. "Good" nationalism is civic, secular, pluralistic, and liberal; it is a matter of rational choice. Civic nationalism is the idea that the nation is constituted not by ethnic, cultural, or religious belonging but by shared legal or institutional traditions.[96] As Bernard Yack argues, how-ever, the civic/ethnic distinction is itself an example of ethnocentrism. The idea that the French headscarf ban, for example, upholds purely civic values ignores a heavy dose of French national chauvinism and orien-talism which sees Muslims as foreign contaminants of the sacred French identity. As Yack comments, the claim of civic—as opposed to ethnic or religious—nationalism for one's own devotion to the nation is "a mixture of self-congratulation and wishful thinking."[97] Atalia Omer and Jason Springs likewise reject the distinction between religious and nonreligious forms of nationalism. Nationalisms of all kinds employ language, ritual, and imagery invoking divinity, providence, mythic narratives, sacred texts, sacred spaces, faith, sacrifice, and chosenness, often coupled with an evangelistic zeal to spread these blessings to other lands.[98] As Omer and Springs point out, the deeper and more pervasive are the practices of civil religion, the more incon-spicuous they tend to be. In a supposedly "civic" nationalism, the national anthem at a sporting event is routine and barely noticed. Let such rituals be challenged, however, especially during times of national crisis, and one quickly sees how essential they are to forging national identity and therefore how sacred they are. Kneeling for the national anthem is decried as an abomination, and burning the flag is an act of "desecration," literally "violating the sacredness."[99]

Omer and Springs conclude that "nationalism functions as a form of religion."[100] They explicitly adopt a functionalist definition of religion.[101] One of the advantages of the functionalist over the substantivist approach is that functionalism is based on empirical observation of how people actually behave, not solely on what they claim to believe. If someone claims to believe in the Christian God but would not allow the Sermon on the Mount to interfere with the imperative to kill for their country, then the functionalist would regard their true religion as nationalism. Functionalism allows us to recognize a distinction between belief and behavior. Functionalism is less useful, however, if it maintains the religious/secular distinction and tries to determine once and for all what belongs in each category. For my purposes, it is not necessary to decide once and for all what is a religion and what is not. The more interesting question—just as with enchantment and disenchantment in the first chapter—is under what circumstances and why some things are called religions and others are not. I favor an approach that can be labeled "constructivist," examining the history of the religious/secular distinction and the political purposes to which it has been put.[102] Rather than move nationalism from the secular to the religious category, I want to question the religious/secular distinction altogether, which posits a dramatic division between two things, like Christianity and nationalism, that are really quite similar. Why do some people want to call nationalism a religion, and others want to deny it and say that it is secular? There can be many different answers to this question, depending on who is doing the affirming or denying and under what circumstances. Secularists will deny that nationalism is a religion in order to maintain the distinction between religious and secular that is fundamental to their worldview. For many secularists, what is religious is irrational and dangerous, and the secular is what is rational and saves us from religion, so the border between the categories must be strictly policed. Secular patriots can see their devotion to the nation as rational and natural rather than as irrational and supernatural. For Christians and others commonly labeled "religious," there is another reason for denying that nationalism is a religion, and it gets to the heart of the question of idolatry: the religious/secular distinction allows people who think they can have only one religion to practice both nationalism and their sectarian "religion" at the same time, without acknowledging any competition between them. Christians, for example, can be ardent American nationalists without exposing themselves to the charge of idolatry, provided that nationalism occupy an entirely different, "secular" category of pursuit.

Secularist scholars resist the idea of nationalism as a religion. The sharp divide between secular rationality and religious irrationality or nonrationality is crucial for such scholars of religion. Summing up this line of thought, José Santiago, writing in the *Journal for the Scientific Study of Religion*, contends that functionalist definitions of religion are "controversial" and that the choice of either a substantivist or a functionalist definition of religion reflects different conceptualizations of social life. Denial or affirmation of the status of nationalism as a religion depends in part on the conceptualization of integration and differentiation in modern societies. Santiago divides sociological analyses of this question into Durkheimian and Weberian strands: Durkheim thought that social integration came about through cultural cohesion, that is, shared standards and values that serve as "final signifiers that act as the Sacred Center of society," whereas for Weber

the process of rationalization has created a world where social integration is no longer the result of consensus over religious standards and values. In the modern world, the coordination of social action may be the result of the mechanics of political domination or of the economic constraints of capitalism, neither of which need a cultural or religious framework. Social integration, therefore, does not require a shared "sacred center."[103]

Santiago sides with Weber, for whom modernity is characterized by conflicting values, not unity of values: "It is in this sense that we can conclude after all that modern societies are secular societies."[104] Nationalism is not a religion because there is no "civil religion" that unites a modern society. Modern societies are integrated by political or economic mechanisms, not religious ones, and nationalism is called "religious" only by using an overly broad and imprecise definition of religion.

There are several problems with Santiago's analysis. First, if my reading of Weber in chapter 1 is correct, then the gulf between Durkheim and Weber is not as broad as Santiago thinks. Weber's account of rationalization is not an account of secularization, and Weber regards the gods that rise from their graves in the form of impersonal forces as no more or less sacred than the gods of old, all of which he thought were human inventions intimately tied to the process of rationalization. Weber put conflicting values and the decision of which of the many gods to follow against the backdrop of an overriding system of domination that was impossible to escape. This type of social integration, in Weber's view, was "entirely transcendental and absolutely irrational";[105] the society disciplined by capitalism does not lack for a sacred center. Second, regardless of what Weber himself thought, Santiago's distinction between political domination and economic constraints on the one hand, and religious factors on the other, simply begs the question of how and why we make such distinctions between "religion" on the one hand and "politics" or "economics" on the other. Santiago assumes that we know what "real" religion is; other things are religions only metaphorically or analogically. He provides no defense of the substantivist view of religion, which is just as "controversial" as the functionalist view, nor does he recognize that the religious/secular distinction is a modern Western invention which is itself dependent on how power is exercised.[106] His analysis has done nothing more than simply declare that nationalism and capitalism are not religions, despite the similarities.

When Durkheim uses the term "religion," he is employing it in the original sense in which the Romans used it. Religion for Durkheim is the glue that holds a society together; the very etymology of the word—*religio* from *re* + *ligare*, to re-bind—suggests as much. Santiago does not deny that modern societies continue to be integrated; he simply declares that such integration is not religious. For Hayes, however, as for Durkheim, nationalism is religious in part precisely because it is what integrates all other loyalties into one. In modern nation-states, Hayes writes, individuals have many different loyalties to political parties, churches, fraternal lodges, unions, colleges, and so on, and sometimes those loyalties come into conflict with one another. "But nowadays, and herein lies the fundamental difference between us and our ancient and mediaeval and early modern forebears, the individual is commonly disposed, in case of conflict, to sacrifice one loyalty after another, loyalty to persons, places and ideas, loyalty even to family, to the paramount call of nationality and the national state."[107] As we saw with the biblical concept of idolatry, loyalties can be a matter of degree, and it is not always clear when loyalty to God is being sacrificed to loyalty to the nation. What is clear, to my mind, is that nationalism and Christianity (and Judaism, Islam, etc.) do not belong in essentially separate categories—one secular, the other religious—and that they do in fact compete for the primary loyalty of Christians. Splendid or not, nationalism is one of the most significant of modern idolatries.

6.2. Migration of the Holy

If Christianity and nationalism are similar enough to compete, and if, as Hayes suggests, nationalism is winning the competition, we will need to get some historical perspective on the emergence of nationalism out of a prenational or international Christian order. If nationalism develops as a new sacred center of many modern societies, was the sacred appropriated from the old Christian order? If it was, then the theme of idolatry comes into sharper focus, because we can point to a contest over both the manner and the object of public worship.

Ernest Gellner, one of the most influential theorists of nationalism, explained the phenomenon as a response to the erosion of traditional social structures following in the wake of industrialization. Preindustrial societies were stratified horizontally with layers of royal, clerical, and military castes that had little sense of shared culture with the large peasantry over whom they ruled. Peasants' loyalties were mostly local, and mobility was very limited. There was a collection of societies rather than a unified society. Speakers of different local languages and dialects were often mutually incomprehensible.[108] Industrialization, in contrast, demanded mobility, context-free communication, and the breakdown of linguistic barriers. Political and economic elites engineered a common national culture, primarily through state control of education, in order to create a compliant and homogeneous workforce made up of interchangeable individuals without fixed social roles. The segmented nature of preindustrial society had to be overcome so that the flow of capital and labor could move where necessary. The process of industrialization also produced conflicts, especially between capitalists and the working class, which needed to be overcome by a wider sense that all classes belonged to one united group. Nationalism produced a relatively homogeneous culture, and people began to think of themselves as belonging to a nation. Nationalism is not simply natural or ancient, thought Gellner. The state produced the nation, and not the other way around.[109]

Although medieval Christendom was certainly marked by an overarching Christian identity, Gellner thought that identity was not sufficient to overcome all the political and caste and linguistic segmentation. There was a shared doctrine but not a shared culture. According to Gellner, industrialization and economic growth required a new type of thinking, the de-absolutization of doctrine and the rise of a secularized, neutral public reason: "An absolute doctrine for all and a high culture for *some*, becomes an absolute culture for *all*, and a doctrine for some. . . . In general, what had once been an idiom for some and an obligatory prescribed faith for all, becomes an obligatory idiom for all, and a watered-down, non-serious, Sunday-suit faith for some."[110] The obligatory idiom is the civil religion, though Gellner does not use that term, and Christianity is privatized. Gellner continues, "The Church must surrender and dissolve itself if it is to capture the entire society."[111] The church gives way to the nation-state; the nation-state, in effect, becomes the new church, through its superior ability to unite the society into a common culture. In Europe, the transition happens in two stages: "[T]he Reformation universalized the clerisy and unified the vernacular and the liturgy, and the Enlightenment secularized the now universalized clerisy and the now nation-wide linguistic idiom, no longer bound to doctrine or class."[112] The nation-state transcends doctrine and class and unites all into one universal culture.

Although Gellner describes the replacement of the church by the nation-state as a process of secularization, he nevertheless adopts Durkheim's language of worship to describe nationalism. Gellner, however, departs from Durkheim in one significant way: "Durkheim taught that in religious worship society adores its own camouflaged image. In a nationalist age, societies worship themselves brazenly and openly, spurning the camouflage."[113] For Durkheim, the camouflage meant that groups thought they were worshiping a god or some other object, but were really worshiping the group. Nationalism, thought Gellner, is straightforward group self-worship with no pretense of worshiping something else, no matter if God is occasionally invoked as being on our side. In Gellner's view this does not mean, however, that nationalism is any more veridical than Durkheimian self-worship. "The basic deception and self-deception practised by nationalism is this: nationalism is, essentially, the general imposition of a high culture on society, where previously low cultures had taken up the lives of the majority, and in some cases of the totality, of the population."[114] Nationalism sees nations as natural and ancient, often as the gift of a providential God; nationalism appeals to the pristine purity of the national past and its sacred traditions. In actual fact, nationalism invents nations and their traditions by selectively using and distorting preexisting bits of low culture to invent a largely fictitious past and present sense of belonging. "It is nationalism which engenders nations, and not the other way round."[115]

Gellner's work has been critiqued on many fronts, especially for being too simple and neat. There are cases of nationalism without industrialization, and industrialization without nationalism. Industrialization in many cases did not require mass education; in Britain, for example, mass education came later. Gellner does not sufficiently account for ethnic minorities within nations. He does not explain the persistence of nationalism in postindustrial settings. His narrative overemphasizes the top-down imposition of culture by an elite. In his theory, economics drives everything else in deterministic fashion; nationalism is not contingent or accidental but required by industrialization.[116] All of these critiques have merit, but none diminishes the importance of Gellner's genealogy for our exploration of nationalism as idolatry. Gellner gives a plausible account of how group self-worship can maintain its utility in a secularized society; if God becomes unbelievable, we can still believe in our collective self as a way of occluding class conflict and facilitating economic modernization. Gellner furthermore gives a plausible explanation for the waxing of nationalism and the waning of the church as a public authority in the West at the same historical juncture. It was not a mere coincidence, but rather a result of the migration of public worship from the church to the nation-state.

Following in Gellner's wake are other modernists who emphasize the invention of the nation and the replacement of Christianity by nationalism in the modern era. Eric Hobsbawm, in his books *The Invention of Tradition* and *Nations and Nationalism since 1780*, sees the nation as an invented tradition and nationalism as the "new secular religion."[117] Benedict Anderson's *Imagined Communities* is probably the best known of the modernist works, largely because of its fertile image of nations as realities that are not found but conjured by the imaginations of people who sense a connection to other people they cannot know. Anderson, like Gellner and Hobsbawm, sees nationalism as a successor to Christianity. Nationalism was the answer to the decline of certainties like a sacred language and sacred kingship that had given people a sense of solidarity with each other and with the cosmos. Religion has always been concerned with the contingency of life and death; it transforms fatality into continuity by linking the living with the dead and the not yet born. What to do when "in Western Europe the eighteenth century marks not only the dawn of the age of nationalism but the dusk of religious modes of thought"?[118] The loss of heaven makes another kind of continuity necessary. "What then was required was a secular transformation of fatality into continuity, contingency into meaning."[119] The nation was the answer to this problem, for nations ensure continuity between the national heroes who have gone before us and their eternal destiny that stretches into the future.

Modernist scholars like Gellner, Hobsbawm, and Anderson offer explanations of why and how public worship in the West came to be focused on the nation instead of on the Christian God. In different ways, they track the migration of the holy from the church to the nation-state, buttressing the argument that "secularization" is not the disappearance of worship but merely its relocation. For Gellner nationalism brings the self-worship at the heart of all religion into the open; from a Christian point of view, his historical narrative shows the idolatry at the heart of modern nationalism. However, the migration story the modernists tell, though compelling, is incomplete, for it is largely a story of the replacement of Christianity by nationalism.[120] This narrative does not account either for the Christian tools used to construct nationalism or for the kind of syncretism of Christianity and nationalism that can be found in places like Poland, Ireland, and the United States. The modernist story ignores the ongoing relevance of Christianity well after the rise of nationalism, but it also in some ways lets Christians off the hook too easily. Christianity largely disappears from the story of nationalism, conveniently making the charge of idolatry, from a Christian point of view, a problem for *them*, not *us*. The real story is more complicated.

To tell a more complete story we need to turn to Gellner's student Anthony D. Smith, whose ethnosymbolic approach is an important supplement and corrective to the modernist approach of his mentor. Like the modernists, Smith agrees that nationalism is in many ways a creation of modernity and not something natural and ancient. Unlike the modernists, Smith shows how Western nationalism is constructed from preexisting elements mined from Jewish and Christian traditions. Gellner agrees that nationalism uses such elements, but he regards their content as mostly indifferent: "The cultural shreds and patches used by nationalism are often arbitrary historical inventions. Any old shred and patch would have served as well."[121] For Smith, by way of contrast, there is a limit to the malleability of the theological resources nationalism uses, and therefore more continuity between Christianity and nationalism than modernists like Gellner allow.[122] Christianity does not simply fade away with the rise of nationalism; the process is more one of the reconfiguration of Christian elements to fit within a nationalist framework. When the holy migrates from the church to the nation-state, the church does not disappear but generally takes a supporting role to the creation of national identities.

As Smith writes, "Nationalism did not appear as a *deus ex machina*, nor as a totally new ideological artefact and culture embodying a radical discontinuity from all that had gone before."[123] Rather, nationalists drew selectively from religious symbolism, stories, doctrines, and rituals to legitimate loyalty to the nation, ignoring some, adopting others, and always adapting such resources to their own purposes. The history Smith narrates is therefore one of both continuity and change, for the preexisting religious elements nationalists used were inevitably altered in the process. Smith rejects both modernist approaches that ignore religion and neotraditional approaches that see nationalism as a return to religion. He is more drawn to approaches that see nationalisms as rivals of or surrogates for traditional religions that sometimes borrow traditional practices but also undermine them. The nation-state, for example, can take the place of God as the object of worship, thus both adopting and undermining traditional forms of worship. Smith counsels care in using this approach, noting that the process of appropriation is rarely simple continuity or displacement. Nationalisms might, for example, take on the language of salvation from Christianity but reject the idea that salvation is to be sought from some otherworldly source. At the same time, secular heroes and saints can be held up using both the form and some of the content of Christianity.[124] Wilbur Zelinsky tellingly calls such figures *eidolons*, the same word that Paul uses for "idols." In the United States, George Washington was the original public *eidolon*;[125] *The Apotheosis of Washington* in the dome of the Capitol rotunda depicts the "becoming god" (*apo-theosis*) of Washington as he ascends to the heavens surrounded by mythical figures. The content is pagan, but the form is familiar from Christian art; the artist, Constantino Brumidi, came from the Vatican, where he had worked for years under Pope Gregory XVI. Other *eidolons* would incorporate more of the content of Christianity; Abraham Lincoln, shot on Good Friday, would take on explicit Christlike qualities in the national imagination.[126]

Smith identifies four types of "sacred foundations" that nationalisms draw on for "deep cultural resources": community, territory, history, and destiny.[127] Nationalism romanticizes the community in the form of "the people," especially common folk who are the repository of truth and virtue. Smith shows how nationalism often draws on motifs of election and covenant borrowed from the Bible, conferring the status of "chosen people" and "a priestly kingdom and a holy nation" (Ex. 19:6) on the nation, which is thereby entrusted with a mission to the world.[128] Territory takes on sacred status in nationalism; Smith notes a "spiritual fusion between the land and its people" that often includes a return to nature and rootedness in the land, which is not just an economic resource and political unit but takes on moral qualities.[129] Smith shows how the Romantic notion of sacred homeland draws on the biblical motif of the Promised Land, flowing with milk and honey.[130] History is sacralized in the commemoration and romanticization of the past, a Golden Age of creativity and virtue that gives the nation a (usually distorted) vision of its authentic self against which to judge the present. The present is commonly found wanting in relation to the past; nationalists always want to make the country great again. The connection with Jewish and Christian narratives of a Fall from a pristine Eden is obvious.[131] Finally, the sacred destiny of the nation is found in salvation narratives that revolve around fallen heroes who have selflessly sacrificed on behalf of the nation. The nation is guided by providence, but only the sacrifice of its members can ensure the nation's ultimate destiny.[132] This "destiny through sacrifice," as Smith calls it, draws easily on the story of Jesus Christ and the martyrs who imitate him, but as Smith shows throughout his analysis, nationalism worldwide draws on religious resources well beyond Christianity. Furthermore, the appropriation of such symbols did not wait until the modern rise of nationalism in the eighteenth century. Armenians saw their native land as the "true Israel" already in the fifth century,[133] and fourteenth-century English proto-nationalism was already drawing on the Arthurian legend of a past Golden Age.[134]

Smith's work is helpful in that it explains how nationalism emerged not *ex nihilo* but in commerce with previous forms of belonging—Christianity in the West—that were not simply jettisoned but appropriated and changed. Smith also improves over previous accounts that overemphasized the role of state elites in inventing national identities. He does not ignore the role of the state, but recognizes also the role of the church. People's deeply held beliefs were not simply manipulated through top-down programs of social engineering; Christians often actively syncretized their traditional religious beliefs with new and robust national allegiances.[135] The result is what Smith calls "the belief-system of nationalism, or what we may term a new *religion of the people*. It is not a religion of the people because it has emerged from the common people, but because the people alone constitute the object of this new religion. . . . [I]ts object of worship is all the people of every class and region."[136] Nationalism for Smith is collective self-worship, what Augustine would recognize as idolatry. Smith is not a theologian, and he has no stake in trying to sort out idolatry from the proper worship of God. He does recognize, however, that nationalism and Christianity are competing forms of worship. Nationalism is "a powerful religion of the people, which parallels and competes with traditional religions."[137]

As Braden Anderson points out, Smith himself is not always consistent in identifying competing elements in the two faiths. Smith presents a rather Pelagian account of chosen nations choosing to be chosen and effecting their own salvation through self-sacrifice, and he does not comment on the obviously heretical misappropriation of Christian beliefs and symbols.[138] Despite identifying the competition between nationalism and traditional religions, he sometimes presents them as generally complementary, as when he writes that nationalisms "did not generally disrupt, or abolish, pre-existing beliefs, sentiments, and symbols," or when he claims that the nationalist cult of authenticity "complements, [and] does not supplant, the old ideas of the sacred in religious traditions."[139] Smith is not a theologian, and therefore does not have a stake in naming idolatry or even naming what counts as Christianity and what does not. When he says that nationalism did not disrupt or abolish or supplant preexisting religious elements, he is likely simply observing— unlike the modernists—that Christian elements like election and covenant are still in use and that many people still identify themselves as Christians. Braden Anderson, however, is a Christian theologian and wants to press the question of *authentic* Christian belief and practice. It is not enough to observe that nationalism incorporates Christian elements and Christians adopt nationalism. The real question is whether or not they are right to do so. If nationalism is a "new religion," as Smith contends, can a Christian adopt it and still be a Christian?

There are many Christians in the United States who see their nationalism as flowing from and indeed required by their Christian faith. Christianity and nationalism are often densely intertwined in practice. To cite one of many possible examples, many American Catholic dioceses have incorporated the "Patriotic Rosary" into their "Fortnight for Freedom" campaigns promoted by the U.S. Conference of Catholic Bishops.[140] The Patriotic Rosary associates the fifty beads with the fifty U.S. states.[141] Each Hail Mary is prefaced by pleading the blood of Jesus over a U.S. state. Patriotic songs like the "Battle Hymn of the Republic" and the "Star-Spangled Banner" are sung between decades. The Mysteries before each decade consist of quotes from the Fathers of the nation such as George Washington and John Adams. The devotees of the Patriotic Rosary are apparently unaware that Adams once wrote contemptuously of Catholics as "[t]he poor wretches fingering their beads, chanting Latin, not a word of which they understood" or that Adams railed in print against the Catholic Church's "direct and formal design on foot, to enslave America."[142] Speaking of slavery, the Fifth Mystery is a quote by General Robert E. Lee from 1863, exhorting his Confederate troops to beseech "the aid of the God of our forefathers in the defense of our homes and our liberties," one liberty of which was the right to buy and sell other human beings.[143]

Braden Anderson examines Christian nationalism in the United States and finds the narrative of America interwoven with the biblical narrative. America is the "city on the hill," a nation covenanted to God and founded on "Judeo-Christian principles," with a mission to spread those principles throughout the world. But America has strayed from that calling and must be made great again by returning to the principles held dear by those who sacrificed on behalf of the nation. Nationalism is a theological virtue in this worldview.[144] To Anderson, this is syncretism, the adulteration of the Christian faith by its admixture with another religion, American nationalism. Unlike other theopolitical critiques that focus on the contest between the church on the one hand and the state and the market on the other, Anderson points out that nationalism is independent of the state—indeed, many ardent nationalists view the state with suspicion—and eagerly adopted by many Christians themselves.[145] Nationalism does not simply pick up and adopt Christian themes and symbols and stories; it adopts Christians too, and thus changes the identity of the church. In other words, when the holy migrates from the church to the nation-state, it brings a lot of the church along with it. When nationalism becomes the new religion, the nation-state becomes the new church. *Pace* Gellner, however, the Christian church does not simply surrender and dissolve itself. It persists, but as a transformed system of formation that prepares Christians for service to the real theopolitical body, the nation-state, which alone has the power to require blood sacrifice.[146]

6.3. Splendid Virtues

Medieval Christians classified *religio* as a virtue, that is, a good habit. Virtue names the way in which voluntary repetition of good acts over time changes the actor by instilling habits that become second nature. Virtues rely on communal disciplines to inculcate habits in people; though their will remains free, it is conformed to the good. Aquinas treats *religio* as a subvirtue of justice, which entails giving to each their due. For Thomas, *religio* is the embodied habit of giving to God his due.[147]

If nationalism is a religion, then, it cannot be a virtue in the same sense that Aquinas says religion is a virtue, because it does not explicitly render worship to God. But although nationalism does not share the end of religion, which is God, it does share what Aquinas calls the "matter" or "object" of religion, which is *latria*, often translated "worship," which includes what we would call reverence or piety and the external rites and sacrifices associated with it.[148] Aquinas writes that, in one sense, *latria* can be applied univocally to all kinds of worship. The definition of *latria* is the human act of worshiping a god; the definition says nothing about the truth or falsity of the god. "Taken thus *latria* is applied univocally, whether to true religion or to idolatry, just as the payment of a tax is univocally the same, whether it is paid to the true or to a false king."[149] So nationalism can share the matter or object of religion, though it does not share the same end, by Aquinas's definition.

Although Aquinas has more to say about *latria*, as we will see further on, I want to take his observation at this point as a recognition that the virtue of religion is echoed in other dispositions, rites, and sacrifices. The love of one's country, for example, calls forth many of the same interior dispositions and external actions that the love of God calls forth. Love for one's country is not just self-love but loyalty to one's place and care for the common good, a way to love one's neighbor as oneself. Indeed, nationalism calls forth one of the most publicly compelling forms of self-sacrifice, which is military service. People in the military take great risks on behalf of others, and they often undergo rigorous discipline and make significant sacrifices that echo the self-sacrifice at the heart of the story of Jesus Christ. Above all, nationalism calls forth a love of something bigger than oneself, a sense of being part of a common project to which one's own wants must be subordinated. The "greatest generation" that sacrificed on behalf of the United States during World War II was composed overwhelmingly of churchgoers whose sense of duty extended to both God and country.

A lot of nationalist discourse in the United States plays on the theme of virtue. One variation popular among Christian nationalists is what Andrew Murphy calls the "American jeremiad," which is "a vindication of the American past and the virtues of previous generations."[150] Once upon a time, the story goes, America was a Christian nation, steeped in the virtues of faithfulness to God. America is subject to a unique covenant that God made with this exceptional nation. Today, however, America has strayed from its calling. Since the 1960s especially, secularism, the loss of moral absolutes, sexual immorality, and a host of other ills have sapped our ability to obey our divine mission. What is needed is the renewal of a sense of God's covenant with the American nation, and this renewal can come only from a willingness to sacrifice on behalf of others. In this view, nationalism, as Braden Anderson writes, "is a theological virtue, since it recalls the nation's divine mission, whose enactment constitutes Christian faithfulness."[151]

While such militant nationalism is generally associated with the Christian Right in the United States, there are also Christian defenses of the virtues of nationalism from other parts of the theopolitical spectrum.[152] Such defenses can be sophisticated and not easily dismissed. Jesuit scholar Dorian Llywelyn's book *Toward a Catholic Theology of Nationality*, for example, argues that love of one's nation is a natural virtue upon which grace can build. National belonging evokes the natural virtues of love, sympathy, and unity with one's fellows. Llywelyn follows Smith and other ethnosymbolists' contention that nationalism has ancient roots; he suggests that belonging to a group larger than one's immediate kin group is a natural and fundamental human experience that is never simply imagined or invented.[153] Furthermore, "the experience of feeling national identity remains partly ineffable,"[154] which touches on the religious dimensions of national identity. Llywelyn suggests that in addition to being *homo religiosus*, human beings are also *homo nationalis*, with a natural affection for the values of one's own particular group and culture.[155]

While the key theological locus for the nationalism of the Christian Right tends to be covenant, for Llywelyn it is the Incarnation of Jesus Christ. The Incarnation indicates God's appreciation for what Llywelyn calls "the value of thisness," the worthiness of particularity. More than an affirmation of generic humanity, God took on the very particular flesh of a Jewish carpenter's son two millennia ago. In the hypostatic union of divinity and humanity, God takes up and saves all that is constitutively human, including social identity, for there is no one who is not located in a particular community.[156] Llywelyn adopts John Duns Scotus's minority opinion that the Incarnation was not contingent on human sin but a part of God's plan from the beginning of creation. Rather than a response to a problem, the Incarnation is the culmination of God's plan to extend divine life to the entirety of creation. From the affirmation of the full and real humanity of Jesus of Nazareth, Llywelyn derives God's love for the particular thisness of every created thing and moves from there to the affirmation of the belonging of each person to their own particular nation.[157]

Llywelyn is by no means blind to the dangers of excessive nationalism, and he acknowledges that nationalism can be a form of self-worship instead of worship of God.[158] Nevertheless, he appeals to the Thomist principle of *gratia naturam supponit*—grace supposes nature and builds on it—to suggest that the natural love of one's nation can be taken up and transformed by the grace of God into a love that is rooted in the particular but open to the universal love of all.[159] Given that nationality is natural, Christianity cannot simply repudiate the natural love that people feel for their homeland. To do so would relegate Christianity to an otherworldly irrelevance. Christianity cannot be simply anational or supracultural, but nor should it be absorbed into national belonging. Llywelyn suggests instead a "*perichoresis* of nationality and religion," which need each other to keep nationality from chauvinism and religion from otherworldliness.[160] The universality of Christianity does not destroy but perfects the particularity of nations.[161]

Like Llywelyn, Catholic scholars Michael and Kenneth Himes have also mounted a defense of national belonging based on the particularism of the Incarnation. The Himeses begin, however, by making a distinction between patriotism and nationalism: "By patriotism we mean a combination of affections for a nation-state." These affections include, most importantly, loyalty and devotion to a nation-state and its people. Patriotism is essentially defensive, while nationalism is aggressive: patriotism seeks to protect the genuine goods of a particular community, by legitimate force if necessary, but nationalism is prone to aggressive war to redress past grievances or advance the national interest against competing nation-states.[162] "Patriotism seeks the elements of the human good to be found in localism. Nationalism seeks the advancement of one group even at the expense of others and the greater common good."[163] The Himeses reject nationalism but endorse patriotism as a good which is necessary for the promotion of virtue.

The distinction between patriotism and nationalism is common, but it can mean different things. In a 2019 statement, the Pontifical Academy of Social Sciences declared:

> [T]he Social Doctrine of the Church distinguishes between patriotism and nationalism to signal two different attitudes: patriotism—defined as love in one's homeland and the willingness, derived from this love, to contribute to its development and to defend it—is a noble sentiment, since it is the affirmation of a community's legitimate desire for self-determination and self-government. . . . Nationalism that is exclusive and imperialistic is a

perversion of patriotism. There are three forms of nationalism that should be rejected on moral and political grounds: Nationalism manifested in unjustified secessionist activities; manifested in the oppression of ethnic minority rights; and aggressive nationalism that can lead to armed conflict.[164]

From this statement it is hard to judge whether, for example, Kurds are being patriotic in pursuing their "legitimate desire for self-determination" or nationalistic by engaging in "unjustified secessionist activities." When patriotism and nationalism are distinguished as two different "attitudes," the determination of which is which is rather subjective. I am not sure that the Himeses' affective definition and distinction between defensive and aggressive is any easier to adjudicate. "Patriotism" and "nationalism" are words used to approve of some things and disapprove of others; the shift from "nationalism" to "patriotism" can be little more than an exercise in rebranding. The distinction between patriotism and nationalism is often nothing more than the distinction between what *we* do and what *you* do. When Turks have a military parade, it is nationalistic; when it is done in the United States, it is patriotic.

There are other uses of the two terms, however, that distinguish them based not on subjective affections and attitudes but on the objects of those affections and attitudes. For Hayes, patriotism is a natural and instinctive human affection for and loyalty to familiar places and people. Just as the French distinguish between *pays* and *patrie*, Hayes distinguishes between his natural loyalty to his homeland, the south-central part of upstate New York, and the artificial extension of this loyalty to unfamiliar places like Alaska and Oklahoma, while simultaneously withholding such affection from nearby Canada. According to Hayes, patriotism is natural when applied to familiar places, but one must be taught to apply it to an entire nation. "Patriotism, therefore, while instinctive in its origin and root, is much more naturally and readily associated with a small community in a restricted area than with a large nationality in a broad expanse of territory. Only through an intensive and extensive educational process will a local group of people become thoroughly aware of their entire nationality and supremely loyal to it."[165] Hayes adds that nationalism, while admitting of degrees, becomes the supreme loyalty "when national emotion is fused with religious emotion, and nationalism itself becomes a religion."[166] For Hayes, then, patriotism is not a natural devotion to the nation-state, and devotion to the nation-state is not, as in the Himeses, a type of localism: the opposite is in fact the case.

The Himeses nevertheless, like Llywelyn, treat patriotic devotion to the nation-state under the rubric of the "scandalous particularism" of the Incarnation.[167] That the God of all would choose one particular people and then become incarnate in a Jew of one time and place seems like an unfair truncation of the universality of God's redemption. Jesus himself seems "wedded to the particularism of nationhood" in his preference for the lost sheep of Israel (Mt. 10:5–6). But Jesus is both particular and universal; just as salvation is through the Jews but for all, so Jesus is the "concrete universal" who opens salvation to all nations. The Incarnation is extended by the church through the sacramental principle, by which concrete material things and persons and actions are vehicles of grace for all. As in Llywelyn, the Himeses defend devotion to the nation-state by appealing to the Thomistic principle of grace working with nature to bring it to perfection.[168]

According to the Himeses, patriotism follows from Aquinas's teaching that it is natural and good to love some more than others. Such love is in fact a requirement of the virtue of charity, which is the form of the virtues. Aquinas says that we should love those who are good more than those who are close to us but not as good, since love is the object of loving, and the good are more loving. Nevertheless, Aquinas acknowledges that we love those who are closer more intensely, since we have more ways to love them, more kinds of friendships, and complete "charity requires the realization of every other kind of friendship. . . . And thus, by both the prompting and the requirement of charity, we love in more ways those who are more closely related to us."[169] The Himeses expand on Aquinas's insight to expound on the loyalty we owe to our fellows. Especially in Catholicism, community is valued; we are who we are as moral persons only by interacting with others. We do not experience ourselves as human beings in the abstract, but as occupying different roles in community: daughters, sons, neighbors, fellow citizens, and so on. Moral development comes from responding to those with whom we find ourselves; we respond to God in loving our neighbor. The preferential love of friendship schools us in the virtues because it draws us out of our small selves and into relationship with concrete others. Patriotism—like parenting, marriage, and friendship—is a moral discipline that develops character.[170] "Patriotism, the love of one's community, nation and heritage, is a good to be fostered by the gospel precisely because it is a locus of our experience of love for others."[171]

The Himeses acknowledge the dangers in such particularism. "[V]ices are virtues taken to extremes," they write, and the absolutizing of a relative good like the nation can lead to the idolatry of nationalism. Devotion to the nation, nevertheless, seems to respond to something deep within human nature. The Himeses trace nationalism to the reaction against Enlightenment universalism, which aimed at throwing off the particular attachments of tradition and place in favor of universal goals of human life accessible to everyone through reason. Enlightenment anthropology is essentially individualistic: each individual is entitled to certain rights and freedoms as a human being, not as a member of a particular community. The liberal contractarian model that issues from this anthropology views society as a contract entered into by individuals for mutual benefit. Patriotism is simply holding up one's end of the bargain. But the Himeses argue that the contractarian model misunderstands the origins of nations. The only reason we enter into mutual benefit structures is because we already see ourselves as belonging to a people.[172] The communitarian model, in contrast to the liberal contractarian model, understands that the ties among people are spontaneous and natural. "Membership in a nation-state is not so much a reasoned judgment as an emergent reality beginning with experiences of kinship."[173] The Himeses acknowledge, however, that there are "elements of invention" in the creation of national patriotism, and one of the obstacles to patriotism in a large country like the United States is the fact that we do not experience relations of intimacy and kinship with the vast majority of our fellow citizens. To overcome this obstacle, we must acknowledge that public life is fundamentally impersonal, and reject the "ideology of intimacy." Recognizing our social interdependence and shared decision-making should be enough to produce devotion to the nation-state.[174] In this way, the Himeses embrace what is elsewhere labeled "civic" nationalism.

Having argued that a nation-state can be a proper object of loyalty, the Himeses address the conflict between the particular duties due to one's own country and the universal obligations one owes to all humankind. While acknowledging the universalist warning against the narrowness of patriotism, the Himeses argue that incarnated beings neither can nor should abandon the personal bonds of the dense web of human relations in which we are each enmeshed. As Aquinas argued, special relations are required by the virtue of charity. We love the universal good in particular persons, but we love it *in them*. We cannot love humanity but overlook actual persons. Catholic social teaching combines both the universalist and the particularist positions.[175] According to the Himeses, therefore, "[t]here is no inherent contradiction between patriotism and a deep attachment to the well-being of all people."[176]

Both Llywelyn and the Himeses give, in balanced and measured prose, theological warrants for the popular sense that devotion to one's country is one of the most admirable and virtuous traits a person can manifest. To be a patriot is to be a person for others. It is to recognize the deeply human reality of our interconnection with other people, not mere humanity in the abstract but particular incarnated people with names and faces. It is to want what is best for those people, to want to promote the common good. Patriotism is a school of the virtues because it instills the moral discipline of putting others before oneself. Beyond a merely contractual relationship, in which I do a cold cost-benefit analysis of my interactions with others, patriots are willing to serve others without calculating the cost, because they feel part of something larger than the individual self. What is "splendid" about devotion to one's nation-state, in Marion's terms, is precisely this urge to give the self over to something larger than the self, to overcome the mere narcissism of narrow self-mirroring and self-interest. Self-sacrifice is the summit of such devotion. The Incarnation of God in Jesus Christ points not only to God's love of creation and love of the particular but also to God's willingness to be poured out, emptied into the form of a slave, crucified for our sake. The self-sacrifice of the American soldier is assimilated to the self-sacrifice of Jesus Christ in countless memes. According to a popular one, "Only two defining forces have ever offered to die for you: Jesus Christ and the American Soldier." While we should not press the analogy too far—Jesus never offered to kill for you—there can undoubtedly be something splendid in the risks, hardships, and disciplines the soldier willingly undergoes on behalf of something larger than the self.

What is the identity of that "something larger"? What is the community which mediates the Christian's ultimate loyalty? Consideration of the church, the body of Christ, is simply absent from the Himeses' chapter on Incarnation and patriotism. Llywelyn acknowledges "the obvious fact that the New Testament is not interested *prima facie* in the role of ethnicity in the economy of salvation. Salvation is dependent solely on adherence to Christ, and being 'in Christ' involves membership in a new society which transcends the limits of family, class, gender, ethnic group, or nation."[177] That new society is the church. As Llywelyn writes, "According to Catholic theology, the Church, not any one nation, inherits the blessings of Sinai, the original covenant being restated and fully revealed in the Paschal mystery."[178] The New Testament, he notes, presents the church—at least metaphorically—as a "nation" (I Pet. 2:9) set apart not by ethnicity but by allegiance to Christ, but that allegiance would inevitably come to combine with Christians' membership in other social groups.[179] Llywelyn is convinced that Christians cannot simply reject "natural" categories of belonging nor, at the opposite pole, deify the natural world. So, like the Himeses, he eschews ecclesiology and turns toward Incarnation, which, he says, unites the orders of salvation and creation, the particular and the universal.[180] In both the Himeses and Llywelyn, the church simply drops out of consideration as a possible category for the Christian's primary belonging. There is no consideration of how the church, both local and catholic, might help reconcile the particular and the universal. Reconciliation is found instead in a "healthy patriotism" that combines love of one's country—and a willingness to kill and die for it—with a love of all.

There are reasons to think, however, that devotion to the modern nation-state promotes neither a healthy localism nor a true universalism. To consider the former, there are problems with the straight line that Llywelyn and the Himeses draw from love of neighbor to devotion to the nation-state. They associate the nation-state with particularity and localism, but as Hayes points out, the opposite is in fact the case: devotion to the nation-state is in tension with local forms of loyalty. The nation-state arises by usurping local forms of authority, self-governance, and loyalty. In Robert Nisbet's words, "the rise and aggrandizement of political States took place in circumstances of powerful opposition to kinship and other traditional authorities."[181] The fundamental conflict of modernity, says Nisbet, is not between state and individual but between state and social group.[182] Rather than incarnation, national belonging is a type of what Charles Taylor calls "excarnation," the replacement of communion and embodied belonging with abstract "nomolatry" and bureaucracy.[183] Llywelyn's work is especially concerned with defending local forms of cultural particularity against the homogenizing onslaught of globalization, but the nation-state is in many respects an agent of homogenization and the destruction of local forms of belonging. As David Albertson and Jason Blakely put it, "Nationalist consciousness is not a local or natural affection but a monoculture engineered by modern states."[184] At the end of his book, Llywelyn laments the disappearance of thousands of threatened languages in the face of the global hegemony of English, French, Spanish, Arabic, Chinese, and Russian.[185] But the process of nation-building is the enemy of linguistic and cultural diversity; the consolidation of French identity and the dominance of the French language in France required the ruthless suppression and death of Breton, Occitan, Provençal, and other regional languages. The *pays* is increasingly assimilated to the *patrie* through the cult of the French nation-state, the kind of civil religion of which Durkheim was a vocal booster. Nationalism, as Hayes points out, becomes the supreme loyalty over more local forms of belonging only through a long educative process and a kind of catechism in the nationalist religion.

If devotion to the nation is not the kind of localism the Himeses and Llywelyn seek to promote, neither does it become a kind of benign universalism simply by declaring it so. Aquinas presents the virtue of charity as radiating outward in concentric circles from those nearest us to those more remote, but devotion to the nation halts that process abruptly at the borders of the nation-state. It is unclear why German and French Christians in the world wars should have considered their membership in the nation to supersede their membership in the universal body of Christ, or why American Christians should have considered Iraqi Christians bomb-worthy, or why neighbor-love should demand that the citizens of El Paso build a wall to keep those of Ciudad Juárez on their side of the border.

Part of the problem is the way that national ideologies appeal to the strongest, most local and natural bonds but apply that sentiment to the weakest and most abstract types of belonging. We can see this dilemma in the Himeses' account. On the one hand, they present patriotism as a type of localism and reject cold contractarian accounts of national belonging in favor of the communitarian sense that patriotism is rooted in spontaneous and natural feelings of kinship. On the other hand, however, faced with the fact that it is hard to feel kinship with 300 million other people spread across a continent, they urge us to eschew the "ideology of intimacy" and accept the fundamentally impersonal nature of public life in a modern nation-state. If we understand this, we can develop some affection for the nation-state. "Nation-states *can* be seen as formative communities capable of inducing loyalty, if we understand that communities include groups of people who are socially interdependent, who share certain practices that define the group, and who participate in the decision-making of the group."[186] But is this cold understanding enough to produce the kind of people who are willing to go through the discipline and sacrifice necessary to kill and die for the nation? Here we see the contradictory nature of the modern nation-state, so well summed up by Alasdair MacIntyre:

The modern nation-state, in whatever guise, is a dangerous and unmanageable institution, presenting itself on the one hand as a bureaucratic supplier of goods and services, which is always about to, but never actually does, give its clients value for money, and on the other as a repository of sacred values, which from time to time invites one to lay down one's life on its behalf.... [I]t is like being asked to die for the telephone company.[187]

How does one convince people to kill and die for the telephone company? How does one convince a farm boy from Iowa to travel to the other side of the world to kill people he knows little about? Hayes's explanation seems most plausible to me: the only way to transfer people's natural and strong loyalties from intimate relationships with people and places to an abstraction like the modern nation-state is to make national belonging into a "religion." Rousseau intuited this; his social contractarianism included what he called a "civic religion." According to Rousseau, Christians, being focused on the next world, make lousy soldiers; they do their duty but "they do it without the lust for victory: they know how to die but they do not know how to win.... Your true Christians are born slaves. They know this themselves, but—this brief life being of so little moment in their eyes—give it hardly a second thought."[188] Christians can believe what they like in private, but in public what is needed is "a purely civil *creed, or* profession of faith" that establishes as dogma "the sanctity of the social contract and the laws."[189] The sole means to encourage individuals to kill and die for the artificial entity created by contract is to make the nation into something sacred. Nationalism as religion is the only way to gin up the necessary energies to produce sacrifice on a grand scale on behalf of a fairly recently constructed political configuration that is distant from the strong and intimate attachments of kinship and locality.

MacIntyre's essay "Is Patriotism a Virtue?" remains an important reflection on the contradictions of modern nation-states. According to MacIntyre, patriotism is *not* the claim that my particular nation demands my highest loyalty because it represents the highest universal values, that is, not because it just happens to be my nation by the accident of birth.[190] This is a disingenuous assertion akin to claiming to love my mother not because she is my mother but because she meets certain objective criteria of superior lovability. For MacIntyre, patriotism is particularistic, like loving your mother just because she is your mother. Patriotism belongs to a class of loyalties—like those of family, kin, friendship, school, and cricket club—based on a particular historical relationship. The Enlightenment tradition out of which liberal democracy emerges, on the other hand, is universalistic. For the liberal tradition, "to judge from a moral standpoint is to judge impersonally. It is to judge as any rational person would judge, independently of his or her interests, affections and social position. And to act morally is to act in accordance with such impersonal judgments. Thus to think and to act morally involve the moral agent in abstracting him or herself from all social particularity and partiality."[191] Patriotism, says MacIntyre, could only be a vice, not a virtue, in liberal thought.

But MacIntyre, of course, is not a liberal and thinks that Enlightenment universalism is incoherent. Moral discernment must be based in a particular community:

> If first of all it is the case that I can only apprehend the rules of morality in the version in which they are incarnated in some specific community; and if secondly it is the case that the justification of morality must be in terms of particular goods enjoyed within the life of particular communities; and if thirdly it is the case that I am characteristically brought into being and maintained as a moral agent only through the particular kinds of moral sustenance afforded by my community, then it is clear that deprived of this community, I am unlikely to flourish as a moral agent. . . . Loyalty to that community, to the hierarchy of particular kinship, particular local community and particular natural community, is on this view a prerequisite for morality.[192]

On such an argument, MacIntyre says, one can make the case for patriotism as a virtue. For MacIntyre as for Hayes, patriotism is the kind of loyalty to a particular, local, natural community on which virtue depends.

The problem, MacIntyre contends, is that the modern nation-state is not that kind of community. Patriotism is possible only in certain types of national community under certain circumstances. It is not possible where a nation has substituted a largely fictional historical narrative for its real history, or where the bonds deriving from history have been replaced by the bonds of reciprocal self-interest: "Since all modern bureaucratic states tend towards reducing national communities to this condition, all such states tend towards a condition in which any genuine morality of patriotism would have no place and what paraded itself as patriotism would be an unjustifiable simulacrum."[193] At the root of the problem is the conflation of universal and particular claims. On the one hand, both revolutionary France and the

United States have claimed to express in their institutional forms the impersonal and impartial aspirations of all rational beings. On the other hand, such a polity demands soldiers who will sacrifice their lives for the nation without measuring the justifiability of their country's cause on the basis of some impartial moral standard.[194] MacIntyre suggests that one could write "the political and social history of modern America as in key part the living out of a central conceptual confusion."[195] "For a morality of particularist ties and solidarities has been conflated with a morality of universal, impersonal and impartial principles in a way that can never be carried through without incoherence."[196]

What MacIntyre describes as "conceptual confusion" should not be misunderstood as simply an intellectual mistake that some influential people have made. Devotion to the modern nation-state is better understood as a necessary mistake; such strong devotion is necessary to defend the far-flung borders of a large and unwieldy bureaucratic organization. No one willingly dies for such an abstraction. To create willing soldiers one must tap into real virtues which dispose people to give their lives for the sake of their neighbors and something larger than themselves. To detach such splendid virtues from their natural locus in intimate forms of community, however, requires an object of devotion that is super-natural. And so the development of nationalism as a religion is not simply a matter of conceptual confusion, of the wrong philosophical moves, nor is it a historical accident. Where the basis of unity is territory rather than worship of the same God, a large, heterogeneous, and unwieldy polity attempting to unify culturally distinct people within territorial borders needs a strong glue to bind people together (religion = re + ligare, to rebind), as Gellner intuited. It needs the new territorial entity itself to take the place of the old God. This is especially true in a polity like that of the United States, where a new nation of immigrants is formed without shared history and without a shared church.

The virtues of neighbor-love and self-sacrifice and devotion to something larger than oneself that are commonly associated with devotion to the nation merit our respect. Augustine, as we saw in chapter 4, acknowledged the selflessness of pagan Roman statesmen and soldiers who sacrificed their own material interests for the common good. Such pagan virtue should check Christian pride, thought Augustine, though ultimately, if directed toward an object other than the true God, such virtues were vices. Christian patriots solve this problem by worshiping the true God while serving their country. As we saw in chapter 3, the Bible recognizes the temptation of political idolatry, of putting one's trust in human power and military might rather than in the LORD, but such trust is on a sliding scale of more to less. The Bible recognizes the limited authority of earthly kings provided they remain subordinate to the LORD. There is a significant gray area within which accusations of idolatry operate. Llywelyn is right that to be human is to have all kinds of natural attachments—to family, for example—that can, but do not necessarily, distract from the worship of God. We cannot simply reject all earthly attachments to worship God; to do so would be inhuman. So we claim a healthy patriotism rather than a vicious nationalism, keeping our devotion to the nation in check by our devotion to God.

The problem with such an attractively balanced account is that it relies on interior dispositions simply to will away broader social dynamics. Devotion to the nation is not less than a religion if the individual simply wills it to be so. More is involved than the individual simply choosing to be a patriot rather than a nationalist, or choosing to make God primary and the nation secondary. At issue is the social imaginary, how social and political stories, rituals, and symbols operate to form people—soul and body—and the world they live in. At issue, in other words, are the gods that are not simply chosen but given to us. For the question of idolatry, what is publicly true matters. Marvin and Ingle suggest a simple and pointed way of determining what is publicly true: it is that for which we are willing to kill. In the case of the United States and other modern nation-states, that for which we are willing to kill is the nation-state itself. As Weber put it, the state has achieved a monopoly on the legitimate use of violence, and the idea of the nation wedded to the state provides the motivating passion for such lethal energies. There is a reason that the soldier is the quintessential exemplar of devotion to the nation. The soldier exhibits not only exemplary willingness to self-sacrifice but also and necessarily the willingness to kill. The goal of military service to the nation is not self-sacrifice, but the sacrifice of the other. As General George S. Patton famously said, "No dumb bastard ever won a war by going out and dying for his country. He won it by making some other dumb bastard die for *his* country."[197] This is the most splendid type of devotion, the willingness to kill and, if necessary, die for the flag. The nation cannot live without it. Allowing God to keep our patriotism in check is a threat to the nation. Jesus offered to die for you; soldiers are trained to kill for you. This is not a small difference. Willingness to allow the Sermon on the Mount to override the demands of military preparedness and action is ultimately intolerable to the nation. The more splendid devotion to the nation becomes, the more it approaches the realm of what is commonly called "religion," and therefore idolatry. It is precisely the moral seriousness of this type of devotion that makes it dangerous.

6.4. Splendid Vices

In Aquinas's terms, as we have seen, devotion to the nation shares the same matter with religion, in terms of both reverence and external rites. But although Aquinas allows that, in one sense, *latria* can be applied univocally to either true or false worship, in another sense, he says, it is applied equivocally, because those things that share the object of religion—the reverential rites and sacrifices—but not religion's end, are vices, not virtues.[198] The vice contrary to the virtue of religion by excess, according to Aquinas, is superstition, "not that it offers more to the divine worship than true religion, but because it offers divine worship either to whom it ought not, or in a manner it ought not."[199] What appears to be a virtue, no matter how splendid, is in fact a vice if it is directed to the wrong end; *latria* is a vice if it is directed toward anything other than the true God. Idolatry, which is giving worship to something created, is a species of the vice of superstition. Aquinas notably includes under idolatry Augustine's category of "civil theology," the deification of the Roman *civitas*.[200]

The question of which god is being worshiped is raised most acutely by R. R. Reno's 2019 book *Return of the Strong Gods: Nationalism, Populism, and the Future of the West*. Reno is a former professor of theology at Creighton University and the editor of *First Things*, which, under his leadership, has become a vehicle of Christian support for nationalism. In March 2019, for example, *First Things* published a manifesto, signed by Catholic scholars such as Patrick Deneen and C. C. Pecknold, announcing, "We embrace the new nationalism insofar as it stands against the utopian ideal of a borderless world that, in practice, leads to universal tyranny. Whatever else might be said about it, the Trump phenomenon has opened up space in which to pose these questions anew. We will guard that space jealously."[201]

The thesis of Reno's book is easily summarized. In the wake of the world wars, the West rejected strong beliefs and loyalties in favor of an "open society." The postwar consensus is now breaking down, and rightly so, as people return to the "strong gods," powerful loyalties that bind people to their homeland and to one another. A key figure for the postwar consensus is Karl Popper, whose book *The Open Society and Its Enemies* set a course for the

West to move away from the kind of tribalism and deference to authority that produced Nazism and communism. Against the comforting collectivism that deifies the nation, Popper argued, we need to uphold the freedom of the individual. Against the notion of unchanging metaphysical truths, we need critical thinking and the courage to create our own meanings; as Popper writes, "Facts as such have no meaning; they gain it only through our decisions."[202] Truth is limited to value-free facts; values and meaning are the realm of opinion. In the hopes of not exciting violent passions again, what Reno calls "strong gods" like truth, religious faith, patriotism, and the marriage covenant are under attack.[203] "The strong gods are the objects of men's love and devotion, the sources of the passions and loyalties that unite societies."[204] Reno recognizes that the strong gods can be beneficent or destructive; truth and patriotism are strong gods, but so are fascism and racism. In the attempt to do away with the latter, we have attacked the former with openness, disenchantment, and the "gods of weakening."[205] We have bought into the false notion that strong loves lead to oppression and weak loves are necessary for liberty and prosperity. This conviction is not Popper's alone but is embraced in one way or another by a host of intellectuals who promote individualism and attack the notion that we have access to transcendent metaphysical truth. Reno critiques Milton Friedman, Gianni Vattimo, Jacques Derrida, Richard Rorty, Joseph Fletcher, Harvey Cox, Karl Rahner, Martin Heidegger, and others as prophets of the weak gods.

The consequences of this embrace of the weak gods are dire:

[O]ur societies are dissolving. Economic globalization shreds the social contract. Identity politics disintegrates civic bonds. A uniquely Western anti-Western multiculturalism deprives people of their cultural inheritance. Mass migration reshapes the social landscape. Courtship, marriage, and family no longer form our moral imaginations. Borders are porous, even the one that separates men from women. Tens of thousands die of heroin overdoses. Hundreds of thousands are aborted.[206]

The antidote to this devastation is the "virtue of solidarity—the sense of fraternity and common destiny among all members of a society," which is based on shared convictions that unite rather than diversify. We cannot truly consolidate around shared devotion to a weak god like "diversity."[207] For Reno, then, the "fundamental question" is "What is the role of the nation in the twenty-first century?"[208] Devotion to the nation is the main antidote to the dissolution of society. The need for a home is an indelible aspect of human nature, and nationalism is among the most significant expressions of that need. To say that the nation is a recent invention, writes Reno, "is not an intellectually serious claim."[209] Reno thus simply dismisses modernist scholarship on nationalism and cites the Israel of biblical times and the English people of the Magna Carta as evidence that devotion to the nation is a primordial need embedded in the human heart. It is, in fact, a manifestation of a basic Augustinian theme: people are united by shared loves.

We are made for love, and love breaks down the barriers that surround the self:

> It impels us outside ourselves, breaking the boundaries of me-centered existence. Love seeks to unite with and rest in that which is loved. This outflowing of the self makes love the engine of solidarity. The strong gods of public life are quite simply the objects of our shared loves. They are whatever arouses in us an ardor to wed our destinies to that which we love.[210]

Reno calls upon Augustine's definition of the *res publica* as rational creatures bound together by common agreement on the objects of their love.[211] According to Reno's Augustine, the Romans' dual love of freedom and honor set the template for the modern West's love of self-government: "If it is 'nationalist' to cherish self-government, then we should be nationalists. The strong god of self-government and sovereignty, which calls upon us to use our freedom and reason, is ennobling."[212] Devotion to the nation, like all shared loves, draws us outside of our individual selves; in precisely this sense is it splendid: "The strong god of the nation draws us out of our 'little worlds.' Our shared loves—love of our land, our history, our founding myths, our warriors and heroes—raise us to a higher vantage point."[213]

Two things are notable here: the focus on "us" and "ours" and the transcendence associated with that collective self. As Reno puts it, "the 'we' touches on sacred things."[214] The "miracle of the 'we'" makes group solidarity more precious than our universal humanity, such that we will gladly sacrifice our lives for our fellow citizens. The "we" transcends our biological families and incorporates us into a larger political entity. Because the "we" is not simply biological, it must constantly be reinforced and defended. "The 'we' is an end in itself that asks us to do what is necessary to sustain and promote our shared loves, all of which harken to the call of strong gods."[215] But at the same time Reno wants to guard against social contract theories that see the "we" as a merely artificial matter of consent and choice. Just as we do not consent to our parents, "[t]he objects of our loves in a real sense choose us, not we them."[216] The nation transcends the individual. Truth must once again ascend from the human-made to the divinely given: "The twentieth century will end only when we entertain new metaphysical dreams, dreams of strengthening rather than weakening."[217] Reno borrows theological language from Augustine to describe such longing for what transcends us: "Our hearts remain restless. They seek to rest in loyalty to strong gods worthy of love's devotion and sacrifice."[218]

Of course, when Augustine famously stated that our hearts are restless, he added "until they rest in You," not "us." Augustine's statement took the form of a confession and prayer to God, the God of Jesus Christ, not any of the many strong gods on offer. It is hard to see that Reno is any less post-metaphysical than those he critiques. What seems to matter is not the identity of the god or gods to be worshiped, but rather their relative strength or weakness; it is a matter of degree, not kind. Reno relegates metaphysical claims about which of the many available gods is true to the realm of "religious belief": "Let us leave aside religious leadership, which is explicitly ordered to the service of the divine, and focus on political leadership and the sacred sources of the civic 'we.'"[219] Like Bellah, Reno divides American piety into private religious expressions like Christianity and the public cult of the nation. The God of Jesus Christ, the God whose power is made perfect in weakness (II Cor. 12:9), makes virtually no appearance in the book among the strong gods. Reno confesses himself a Catholic, but Christianity appears only as a prop to the social order: "I'd like to see a widespread revival of Christianity in the West. Until that happens, unbelievers need to wake up to the perils of a faithless society."[220] A healthy political culture depends on the moral discipline that faith communities provide. Religious faith provides a home, resting in God's arms, that makes believers "stable and stalwart citizens," resistant to ideology. Religious faith prepares people to endure trials. Faith communities have "pinioned the nation from above," equipping people to sacrifice on its behalf. "The solidarities of domestic life and religious community are not at odds with the civic 'we.' On the contrary, the strong gods can reinforce each other, preparing our hearts for love's many devotions. A man who makes sacrifices for his family or for his faith is likely to be ready to give the full measure of devotion to his country."[221] Despite Reno's call for adherence to metaphysical Truth, God is reduced to God's usefulness for the social order, and theology is reduced to sociology.

Reno makes no secret of the provenance of this reduction. The first section of the final chapter of the book is a laudatory reading of Durkheim's *Elementary Forms of Religious Life*. The unity of society, says Durkheim, draws upon the power of the sacred, and according to Reno, the Bible agrees. Reno cites Romans 13—in which Paul admonishes his addressees to be subject to the governing authorities, for they are instituted by God—and contends, "In Judeo-Christian tradition, governing powers are not deities, but their dictates are tinctured with divine legitimacy."[222] Though they are not deities, and civic rituals and monuments are "not religious in the sense in which we now use the term," they nevertheless "reach for the transcendent"; though modern gods can be false idols, "the sacralizing impulse in public life is fundamental. Our social consensus always reaches for transcendent legitimacy."[223] The disclaimers are Reno's version of the "almost"; as a Christian, Reno knows that the "strong gods" must always remain "just a metaphor" if he is to avoid explicit idolatry. But once the crucial "almost" is acknowledged, he goes on to praise Durkheim's analysis of the essentially religious nature of social unity: "Durkheim was right. To be human is to seek transcendent warrants and sacred sources for our social existence."[224] As a Christian, Reno would not accept Durkheim's reduction of the divine to nothing but social processes; Reno sees the social reaching for the divine rather than the divine being grounded in the human. In this sense, we could read nationalism in a sympathetic, Augustinian way; even idolatry is a tacit acknowledgment that we are *Homo liturgicus*, groping beyond ourselves, searching for God, even if we don't realize it. But treating the "we" as "an end in itself," in Reno's words, is pure Durkheim. In the absence of a theological account of idolatry, and in the absence of anything but a sociological account of "transcendence" and "the sacred," Reno's book effectively reduces the divine to the social dynamics that constitute the "we." In the absence of any Christian theology or Christian God, the strong gods take over and become much more than a mere metaphor.

Reno is especially appreciative of Durkheim's diagnosis of the weakness of the West. He quotes from Durkheim's passage, discussed above, that laments the passing of the old gods that "filled our fathers with enthusiasm," while the new gods have yet to be born. Reno agrees with Durkheim that neither Christianity nor Enlightenment devotions can be restored to their former place in the West:

> Biblical religion can surely endure and its soulcraft will continue. It may
> even see a season of revival that enlarges its influence. I certainly hope it

does. But it cannot resume its old place in society. The same is true for naïve Enlightenment pieties. "But neither is there any reason," Durkheim continued, "for believing humanity is incapable of inventing new ones." The death of old gods in no way means the death of the sacred. We are social animals, and public life requires the aroma of the sacred.[225]

The apparent death of the Christian God, in public anyway, has left us no choice but to create new gods. They can be destructive and evil gods, like fascism and communism, or they can be benevolent gods, like the shared love of the American nation, but we cannot live without strong gods, even if we have to invent them. The only difference between this conviction and Popper's post-metaphysical belief that humans create their own meanings is that for Popper the individual is the main meaning-making agent, while for Reno it is the "we."

The fact that Donald Trump, the very embodiment of the posttruth society, appears as something of a hero in Reno's book—a flawed hero, but a hero nonetheless[226]—only amplifies the Durkheimian message that the divine is whatever gives strength to the "we." Reno's Trump is the rejection of the postwar consensus on weakening. His border wall is a symbol of closure, the opposite of openness. He violates the canons of political correctness, "the police arm of cultural openness." He is unabashedly nationalist.[227] Reno highlights a speech Trump gave in Warsaw in 2017. Instead of decrying the horrors of war, Trump praised the heroism of the Warsaw Uprising, saying, "Let us all fight like the Poles—for family, for freedom, for country, and for God."[228] Reno continues, "The Polish inheritance, he said, was sanctified with the blood of sacrifice. . . . His praise of national reconsolidation was a call for the strengthening of Being, not its weakening."[229] In Reno's telling, Trump's victory in 2016 was the revenge of the people against elites, a reckoning with the basic need for strong borders, advantageous trade, and patriotism instead of open borders, open trade, and open minds.[230]

Reno never tries to explain the relationship of Being to the God of Jesus Christ. To Jean-Luc Marion, entrapping God in Being is idolatry. Would Reno dismiss Marion's analysis of God beyond the metaphysical category of Being as another attempt at postwar weakening? Reno also never spells out the relationship of the strong gods to God. Reno would no doubt contend that "strong gods" is just a metaphor, and he acknowledges that strong gods can be false idols.[231] He never discusses how to tell the difference between devotion to idolatrous strong gods and devotion to benign strong gods, however, and advocating devotion to gods that are not God is not a very helpful metaphor if one is trying to sort out idolatry from true worship. Given the almost complete absence of the Christian God from his narrative, and given his Durkheimian identification of the divine with social unity, "strong gods" appears less as a metaphor and more as simply a frank recognition of the idolatry of nationalism. In this sense, Reno is right: devotion to the nation is devotion to a god, a strong one. But this god is not the true God; the strong gods are the wrong gods. Rather than a return to Truth, the strong gods continue to tell what World War I poet Wilfred Owen called "The old Lie: *Dulce et decorum est/Pro patria mori*." That is, it is sweet and fitting—let us say splendid—to die for one's country. As Aquinas makes clear, a virtue directed to the wrong end is a vice. *Religio* directed to a false god is idolatry.

Christian patriots can always rebuff the charge of idolatry by claiming that their own devotion to the nation is tempered by, and secondary to, their belief in the biblical God. As we saw in chapter 3, political idolatry in the Bible is a matter of degree. One can be loyal to an earthly king and be loyal to YHWH at the same time as long as the king is subordinate to God and one's loyalty to the king is weaker than and subordinate to one's loyalty to God. Loyalty to the king is not idolatrous if it is kept in check by loyalty to God. The problem for Reno is that loyalty to God in this biblical view appears as yet another agent of weakening the bonds of solidarity. He wants to push for strengthening such bonds, for strong loyalties. But in the biblical view, the stronger the loyalties to created things that are not God, the more they tend toward idolatry. Reno's language of "strong gods" captures this dynamic precisely: the stronger the loyalties to group solidarity, the more such loyalties tend to become gods for people, false idols that violate the first commandment to worship only the LORD.

The only way to get around this dilemma is to identify the true God with the nation; worshiping God will not distract from social solidarity if social solidarity is identified with God. Reno knows better than to attempt to provide biblical warrants for such an identification, for there are none. He turns instead to Durkheim for a universal account of how divinity is identified with the strong loyalties that bind groups together. But the identification of God with the "we" is a blatant form of idolatry: it is collective narcissism. As we saw in chapters 4 and 5, Augustine and Marion, building on biblical critiques of idolatry, analyze idolatry in terms of individual narcissism, the self-love that can see only its own reflection in created things. Devotion to the nation seems to break one out of the confines of the idolatrous self by calling forth a kind of self-giving and neighbor-love, to the point of self-sacrifice for others. It is "splendid" in the sense I have been using the term, to indicate the giving of oneself to something larger than oneself. When that something larger is nothing more than the "we" of the group, however, it is still narcissism, but narcissism writ large, a collective narcissism. Religion, Durkheim thought, is just the self-worship of the group. For Durkheim, a French patriot and a nonbeliever in God, this was not a problem; it provided a tidy explanation for why groups of people invented gods who don't actually exist. For someone who believes that there is one true God, however, the self-worship of the group is simply idolatry, a violation of the paramount commandment to have no other gods. It might be splendid idolatry, but it is idolatry nonetheless.

In a 2020 article titled "Nationalism as Collective Narcissism," social psychologists Aleksandra Cichocka and Aleksandra Cislak apply earlier, more general work on collective narcissism to the current resurgence of nationalism around the globe.[232] They point out that political ideologies have become less important than ethnic and national identities. The nationalist demand for respect fits the concept of collective narcissism, which they define as "a grandiose in-group image that is contingent upon external recognition of the in-group's worth."[233] Like Narcissus, the nationalist falls in love with an image of the nation, that is, not simply the reality of the nation but an idealized image of it, often based on a fictionalized history of the nation. Collective narcissism, like individual narcissism, is driven by perceived shortcomings: a lack of self-esteem, unmet needs, and a lack of control. Under such conditions, people derive their sense of self-worth from the respect accorded to the group. If the group is not respected, collective narcissism actually increases with resentment about the status of the in-group.[234] As an example, Cichocka and Cislak quote Trump's calls for other countries to respect the United States: "For many years other countries that are allies of ours . . . have not treated our country fairly, so in that sense I am absolutely a nationalist and I'm proud of it."[235] The nationalist demand for respect can lead to violence linked to an exaggeration of threats and a propensity for hostile responses to such threats.[236] Nationalism is not just about the "we," in other words, but needs a "they" to oppose to the "we," an out-group to oppose to the in-group.

Cichocka and Cislak recognize forms of dedication to an in-group that are relatively free of defensive narcissism, and they distinguish between a healthy patriotism and an unhealthy nationalism.[237] We certainly should acknowledge that there are many different forms of national projects, and like many forms of idolatry they occupy a spectrum from toxic to benign. Russian nationalism and Ukrainian nationalism are not the same, and we might recognize in postapartheid South African nationalism, for example, an attempt to create a larger "we" that would encompass and reconcile previously antagonistic subgroups, Black and white. We cannot ignore, however, the effect of collective narcissism on intragroup relations. As Cichocka and Cislak's study points out, nationalism commonly does not simply promote a sense of group solidarity, a sense of the "we" for everyone within the borders of the nation-state. Instead, insecurity and concern for the in-group image often lead to scapegoating others within the group, especially minorities, for negatively affecting the image of the in-group. To maintain the positive image of the in-group, historical accounts that reflect negatively on the group must be denied or suppressed. Internal dissenters from the positive national narrative must be attacked and discredited.[238] This analysis goes a long way toward explaining the frequent connection between nationalism and racism. In the United States, for example, the nation is frequently identified either with the enterprising white people who supposedly built it, or with the "melting pot" that overcomes racial and ethnic differences to make one large "we" who are all in this together. People who tell a different story—about the nation being built on the backs of enslaved African Americans, or about the ongoing structural barriers that relegate minorities to second-class citizenship—are labeled internal enemies. Equally relevant are the real divisions that nationalism encourages us to ignore, especially class divisions. The idea that Mexicans are taking our jobs unites owners and workers against a common enemy. The resentments of working-class whites are stoked, but they are directed against racially coded members of the same working class, while the wealthy help themselves to a greater portion of the national pie.

For Reno, antiracism, multiculturalism, the search for microaggressions, and the emphasis on inclusion are all signs of weakening that oppose the strong gods of group loyalty.[239] Identity politics based on race, sexual orientation, and so on accentuate differences and are an ersatz solidarity, a substitute for strong national identity.[240] Reno does not, however, accept the association of racism with the strong gods; in fact, he argues, the opposite is the case: "When racial tensions increased during Obama's eight years as president, commentators assumed the cause was white backlash. This is always the pattern of the postwar consensus: social problems stem from closed-society vices. Our leadership class is unable to countenance the obvious explanation: *They are dysfunctions of an open society*."[241] The emphasis on diversity and focus on racism only serves to exacerbate racial tensions, according to Reno. The solution to such divisiveness is more devotion to the group solidarity of the nation, in which all are regarded equally: "That mandate of justice, which is a strong god, requires race-blind policies, not the race-conscious policies with which universities recruited black students."[242]

Reno's "obvious explanation" of racism is not obvious to everyone, to put it mildly. American nationalism has a history of deeply embedded racism that long predates the Obama administration: the genocide of First Nations peoples, the denial of citizenship and full humanity to enslaved Blacks, the Mexican War, the nativist treatment of Jewish and Catholic immigrants as unwhite and un-American,[243] the Chinese Exclusion Act, Jim Crow segregation and denial of full citizen rights to African Americans, the internment of Japanese Americans in World War II, the fear of the "invasion" of Mexican immigrants, the removal of African American men from American society through incarceration, and more. The resurgence of nationalism under Trump began with the scapegoating of Mexicans as rapists and criminals and has included an attempted ban on Muslims entering the country, closing the door to refugees from nonwhite countries, the separation of children from their parents at the Mexican border, white supremacist rallies, an admonition by the president to some congresswomen of color to "go back" to the "crime infested places from which they came," the suppression of the Black and Latino vote, and much more. Some advocates of the new nationalism have tried to distance themselves from the racially charged messaging of Trump and some of his supporters. Matthew Peterson and Kevin Stuart, signers of the *First Things* manifesto, stress that theirs is not an ethnonationalism but a civic nationalism, open to all from "any" race and "many" creeds who would embrace the fundamental principles of the American founders.[244] They deny that ethnonationalism is even a coherent possibility in a country as diverse as the United States. David Albertson and Jason Blakely respond that white nationalism is a troubling historical reality in the United States that cannot be theorized away by good intentions. To Albertson and Blakely, this is not an accidental but a necessary feature of nationalism. Civic nationalism, shared traditions of law and political procedure, will never be a strong enough glue to bind a huge and disparate nation together, especially when it is a nation composed mainly of immigrants. Civic nationalism will inevitably slide toward more primordial ways of belonging, like race and religion. "The more 'civic' they become, the less 'nationalist,' but the more 'nationalist,' the less civic."[245] This is why Reno insists that national belonging is not simply assent to laws, but more like belonging to a family or a religion of strong gods. The kind of energies that Trump has unleashed depend on more than mutual recognition of equals under the law; the law in fact can become an obstacle to national destiny if it is associated with a minority of elites who use their privileged operation of the levers of legality to thwart the will of the people. Nationalism, as Cichocka and Cislak point out, tends not only toward strong group solidarity but the stoking of grievances against both external and internal enemies.[246] Racism is a natural companion of the collective narcissism of nationalism: those whose very presence diversifies rather than unites must be excluded, but the story of that exclusion is itself a threat to the heroic narrative that nationalism needs to maintain its glorious self-image.

Etienne Balibar makes the connection between nationalism and racism by means of the concept of "neoracism." Since the biological language of "race" has fallen into disrepute, the more sociological language of "culture" has taken its place; the nationalist discourse around "immigration" has replaced that of "race." Neoracism stresses the need for borders, which are supposedly an expression of the deep and natural differences between different peoples and cultures. Like race, "*culture can also function like a nature, and it can in particular function as a way of locking individuals and groups a priori into a genealogy, into a determination that is immutable and intangible in origin.*"[247] Nationalism confines people into a pseudo-biological belonging, as if to a family; attempts to overcome such differences evoke a "natural" defensiveness. Overt racism as such can then be blamed, as in Reno, on the attempt to abolish differences.[248] But as Balibar points out, "'peoples' do not exist naturally any more than 'races' do";[249] they are contingent attempts to construct a national unity against other possible unities. One such unity is that of class; there is no need for laborers to practice class solidarity because there is no class conflict—we are all Americans, shareholders and minimum-wage workers alike.[250] At the same time that nationalism promotes this *we are all in this together* kind of imagination, it simultaneously creates racially coded enemies, both internal and external, who seek to dilute our cohesiveness. Muslims can never be true French because they are not universalist enough; the "browning of America" through immigration is a threat to our (white) national identity. Mere civic nationalism is too weak; what is needed is a pseudo-biological cultural belonging, the fetishization of an "us" that is defined over against a "them."[251]

Racism is collective narcissism, the love of those who look like us and the perceived threat of those who do not. As species of collective narcissism, both racism and nationalism are idolatries. Martin Luther King Jr. saw the connection clearly. For King, both racism and nationalism are idolatrous because they cut divinity down to the size of one limited social group. In a sermon titled "The False God of Nationalism," King denounced an age in which affirming the "brotherhood of man" was considered a heresy. People had "turned away from the eternal God of the universe, and decided to worship at the shrine of the god of nationalism."[252] Both nationalism and racism make a god in our own image, a god limited by our own limits, our own desires, our own fears:

> Will we continue to serve the false god that places absolute national sovereignty first or will we serve the false god of imperialistic greed or will we serve the God who makes love the key which unlocks the door of peace and security? Will we continue to serve the false god of racial prejudice or will we serve the God who made of one blood all men to dwell upon the face of the earth?[253]

6.5. The People of God

If nationalism tends toward idolatry, are there other kinds of collective belonging that lend themselves to the faithful worship of God? The Bible tells the story of the people chosen by God, Israel, to which the church later claims to become engrafted. Many Christian nationalists have seen the election of Israel as a kind of proto-nationalism, biblical support for modern claims that the United States or some other nation-state has been chosen by God for some divine mission. In fact, however, the biblical narrative provides resources for resisting nationalism; belonging to the people of God cuts against the restriction of one's loyalty to any nation, any mere "us" that truncates the whole human family.

The election of Israel and the covenant God makes with Israel are central to the biblical narrative. The Bible deliberately contrasts Israel's story, however, with those of other nations and their gods. The gods of the surrounding ancient Near Eastern peoples were national gods; there was no sense that one people's deities would apply to another people, unless the latter were conquered by the former. The God of Israel, YHWH, is different. The Exodus narrative sets up a contest between, on the one hand, Pharaoh and his imperial pantheon, who are wedded to the political and social order of Egypt, and on the other hand, YHWH, the self-existent God who transcends all human societies and categories (3:14). In the book of Exodus, the contest between YHWH and Pharaoh, as Walter Brueggemann writes, is a battle that is both theological and political, contrasting an order of freedom and justice to an order of oppression and exploitation.[254] In this contest, YHWH chooses a people, but the election of Israel is not for its own sake but for the sake of the world. Election is not for the aggrandizement of Israel (Israel First!), but for the blessing of all the peoples of the world (Gen. 12:3). In Gerhard Lohfink's reading of the biblical narrative, God elects to change the world not by force but by choosing one relatively insignificant people to exemplify God's love and justice to the world, for the world's salvation.[255] Far from aggrandizement, Israel more often faces God's chastisement for failure to live up to the covenant.

As a unique covenant community, Israel's mandate was to be unlike other nations. Kingship was a relatively short experiment in Israel's history, and not the norm by which all previous and subsequent history should be judged. The fact that Israel was a loose confederation of tribes with no king before Saul is theologically significant.[256] The Israelite request for a king in order to "be like other nations" (I Sam. 8:20) is granted only reluctantly, and as a form of punishment for the Israelites (8:11–18), for the desire for a king is the rejection of YHWH and the serving of other gods (8:7–8). Nationalism is an imitation of Israel's *un*faithfulness, insofar as it seeks consolidation of national power and turns away from faithfulness to God.[257] The biblical narrative is one of decline and divine punishment after the kingship of David. By the eighth century BC, throne and altar had been fused to such an extent that, as Lohfink puts it, "YHWH became a state god."[258] As YHWH says through the prophet Hosea (8:4), "They made kings, but not through me; they set up princes, but without my knowledge. With their silver and gold they made idols for their own destruction." Israel became like the other nations, making alliances based on *realpolitik* rather than faithfulness to God, alliances that, as we saw in chapter 3, the prophets denounced as idolatry (e.g., Hos. 7:11, 11:5). Royal theology assumed that the covenant with David was unconditional and security was assured, but prophets like Jeremiah punctured the attempt to base security on anything other than faithfulness to God. Braden Anderson sums up the importance of the Old Testament material for nationalism as follows: "[N]ationalist appropriations of Israel as the forebear of the current nation are off base from the start, given that Israel's identity is theopolitically unique and constituted in contrast with the world's political systems."[259]

As we look at how the New Testament builds on the Old Testament narrative, Anderson writes, "it is the church that is uniquely engrafted onto Israel's identity and mission, such that no state and no other nation can be considered divinely chosen to this end."[260] The church are the followers of Jesus of Nazareth, the one who Christians believe definitively fulfills the covenant with Israel. Jesus comes to inaugurate a new kingdom, the kingdom of God (Mk. 1:15), which is not restricted to any one nation but encompasses all nations (Matt. 28:19). In Jesus, YHWH reassumes the throne of the kingdom on earth, over against human usurpation.[261] Jesus is killed by those who claim no king but Caesar (John 19:15), but he rises from the dead and is vindicated, given all authority in heaven and on earth (Matt. 28:18). The crucified King is not a mere extension or restoration of the Davidic monarchy, however, but the inauguration of a new type of kingdom, a new humanity capable of living lives of peace and justice and reconciliation.

The kingdom of God is in this world, but not of this world (John 18:36). The kingdom is not reduced to the afterlife, or to merely spiritual and immaterial realities. Rather, the people of God who live according to the kingdom are meant to live differently from the fallen world, to "not conform to the structures of this world" but to stand as a contrast to the world's "structures of domination."[262] Christians have a new type of citizenship (Eph. 2:19). As N. T. Wright describes Paul's missionary work, the church "claims to be the reality of which Caesar's empire is the parody; it claims to be modeling the genuine humanness, not least the justice and peace, and the unity across traditional racial and cultural barriers, of which Caesar's empire boasted."[263] The people of God are concerned with embodying the new social order of the kingdom of God, but they are not a nation-state with borders to defend.[264] The church is the body of Christ (I Cor. 12), the sacramental embodiment of Christ's sovereignty over the world; in this sense the church is a "theopolitical" reality. Christ's sovereignty is a very peculiar type of sovereignty, however, one displayed in the self-sacrificial love of Jesus on the cross. The church is called to be a visible, sacramental participant in Christ's paradoxical sovereignty. As Douglas Harink puts it, "the church enacts and makes visible its 'lordly' freedom in the patience, suffering, and 'witness' (*martyrion*) it shows in the face of enmity and oppression."[265] Unlike the nations of the world, the church can refuse self-assertion because it claims to rely on the love and power of God alone, not weaponry or worldly coercive power. The church's identity is not created by the will of *we, the people*, but is received from God only insofar as it is faithful to the Gospel. Its security can come only from God.

As we saw in chapter 3, political loyalty is on a sliding scale; it is not always clear at what point one's loyalty to one's community and its leaders becomes idolatrous. It is not usually the case that one must make a stark, either/or choice between one's nation and God, or one's nation-state and the church. There are all kinds of cooperation at many different levels of political community that are not inherently idolatrous. There are, in addition, many different kinds of nation-states, with varying degrees of justice and peaceableness; there is no one "nation-state" as such. Modern nationalism, nevertheless, is often not content with a modest coordination of different communal identities; it pushes some nation-states toward becoming both a substitute church and a substitute god, the narcissistic church that worships itself. The temptation to idolatry becomes most acute when violence is at issue; most nation-states not only demand sacrifice on their behalf but also demand to be the only authority to decide when and how and whom to kill. The church as a process of independent communal discernment of when, if ever, a war is just constitutes an intolerable threat to nation-states, which is why the United States does not legally recognize selective conscientious objection.

When we talk about what the church is or does, however, we need to distinguish carefully between normative and empirical judgments. To say that the church receives its identity from God is a normative theological statement, not an empirical statement about the actual behavior of Christians. Christians, like the Israelites denounced by the prophets, are often unfaithful. To say that the Christian's *primary* communal belonging should be in the church and not the nation-state is not to say that the church is good and the nation-state is bad. The church on earth is often manifestly idolatrous. Indeed, the point is that nationalism is one of the primary means of the church's idolatry; the resurgence of Christian nationalism in Russia, the United States, and elsewhere has made that abundantly clear. As Anderson puts it, "when a nation or state appropriates elements of the stories of Israel and the church for its own purposes—'projecting its national ego into the world of the divine'—and especially when such a nationalist move emanates from within the church itself, ecclesial identity and mission is clearly corrupted. The church in that context ceases to be the church, and becomes something decidedly other."[266] The problem for Christians, however, is not confined to explicitly Christian nationalism; nationalism that is not explicitly Christian but is practiced by Christians is very much a problem for the church. The nation-state becomes a false church when the strong god of the nation is worshiped, and the Christian church withers into an idolatrous parody of the people of God. The point is not that Christians should place their primary communal loyalty in the Body of Christ because the church is better than the nation; the point is that resisting nationalism is one way that Christians can repent of the idolatry of the church.

For Reno, the return of the strong gods is the antidote to Derrida's deconstruction, which is meant, at least in part, as a therapy against idolatry.[267] Derrida's Jewish roots show in his attempt to banish idolatry once and for all by disclaiming stable knowledge of any universal truth or anything transcendent. In the attempt to banish idolatry, God is erased as well. But Reno's solution—strong gods—invites idolatry. The choice between no gods and strong gods is a false choice. The scriptures present us a better solution in the weak God, Jesus Christ, the one whose very self-emptying (Phil. 2:7) is the universal Truth, the manifestation of his Lordship (2:9–11). To worship such a paradoxical God is to cultivate the virtues that make nationalism splendid—the self-sacrificial dedication to something larger than oneself—but to direct them toward the service of the true God, the one who absorbed the violence of the world and inaugurated a new type of kingdom, one of reconciliation, justice, and peace.

I will discuss worship of the weak God in the final chapter. Before we get there, I will examine in the next chapter another kind of contemporary god that is given to us and helps structure our lives both private and public.

7

The Unsplendid Idolatry of Consumerism

After exploring nationalism as a type of splendid idolatry—that is, one that invites self-sacrifice and devotion to something larger than oneself—I will explore in this chapter a more apparently "unsplendid" type of idolatry, consumerism, which seems to invite nothing more noble than stuffing the self with things. By "consumerism" I mean the global capitalist economic order that emphasizes ever-increasing production and consumption of commodities, and the accompanying cultural system that emphasizes the consumption of commodities as an important key to happiness and well-being. Keynesian economics sees consumer spending as the main driver of economic growth, but I am primarily interested in the *culture* of consumerism, the way we are formed to spend much of our lives pursuing or thinking and dreaming about commodities. Rather than inspire devotion to something larger than oneself, as in nationalism—an imagined community and a cause that transcends the generations—consumerism seems to inspire devotion to small and petty things, not just material objects themselves but the desires that seek to indulge the self.

The apparently self-oriented nature of consumerism makes it both harder and easier to analyze in terms of idolatry. Consumerism as idolatry is a harder case to make than that of nationalism as idolatry. Consumerism is not a strong god; commodities are generally considered banal and mundane, not divine. In consumerism, there is no single object of devotion like the nation that rivals God. Indeed, many objects compete for our attention, and we seem to be living among fragments rather than directed toward a sacred center. There is no demand for self-sacrifice, and no doctrine that might rival those of Christianity or other faiths. Consumerism is apparently devoid of its own content; increased consumption is the goal, not consumption of anything in particular. Consumerism does not present itself as a rival to any particular faith system, and indeed has shown its adaptability to marketing all kinds of faiths with equal enthusiasm. Idolatry in the biblical sense implies devotion and attachment to false gods, but consumerism encourages detachment from particular things, the constant dissatisfaction of desire and the

The Uses of Idolatry. William T. Cavanaugh, Oxford University Press. © Oxford University Press 2024.
DOI: 10.1093/oso/9780197679043.003.0008

perpetual movement of desire to the next object and the next. Indeed, the restlessness of the human heart that Augustine pointed to is present in consumerism in equal measure.

It is simultaneously easier to analyze consumer culture in terms of idolatry because, as we have seen in chapters 3 through 5, idolatry can be described as the replacement of the worship of God with the worship of the self. As Pope Francis has said, "Worship means concentrating on what is essential: ridding ourselves of useless things and addictions that anaesthetize the heart and confound the mind. In worship, we learn to reject what should *not* be worshiped: the god of money, the god of consumerism, the god of pleasure, the god of success, the god of *self*."[1] Not just material things but the desire for them become gods, because they take the place of the worship of the true God. Francis italicizes the word "self" here, it seems, as a way of summarizing the various other kinds of gods on offer in our society. Unlike splendid idolatry, a consumer-driven economy seems oriented toward the self and its desires; there is no incentive toward self-sacrifice for the greater good. The very notion of consumption seems to indicate the ingestion of material things into the self, where they are used up for the enjoyment of the self, often at the expense of the earth and the workers who make our stuff. If there is any sacrifice, it is the sacrifice of others. Consumerism is a type, therefore, of what Augustine calls "self-love," which is opposed to the love of God. Consumerism is often seen as a type of narcissism, in which the material world is only a mirror to the self and its desires. As we saw in both Augustine and Marion, the more the person tries to aggrandize and deify the self, the more the self is alienated from its true being in God, and the person ends up dominated by material things of human creation.

Consumerism, nevertheless, is not a simple matter of individuals having bad values and turning away from God to feed their own desires. Consumerism is embedded in a whole capitalist system—economic, cultural, and spiritual—in which we are all enmeshed. Capitalism is a decentered center, a hegemony that presents an infinity of choices, a god that is no god. If we are to understand it, we must understand it as something much larger than the choices of the individual self. The concept of idolatry may be helpful for this analysis because, as we have seen, idolatry describes a whole technology of human desire that is larger than the individual. In this chapter, I will return to the analysis of idolatry in chapters 3 through 5, beginning with the notion of idolatry as the search for meaning in created things, which will be the topic of the first section. As we have seen, idolatry critique can

282 THE USES OF IDOLATRY

have a certain sympathy with the plight of material creatures in search of an immaterial God. As Augustine makes clear, we are called to delight in God's material creation insofar as its beauty aids us in our journey back to God. Nevertheless, in the process of "misrecognition," to use Charles Taylor's word, the pursuit of material things becomes an end in itself. In the second section of this chapter, I will explore the way that people invest divinity in things. The pursuit of material goods becomes a kind of substitute for more traditional faiths. To explain how and why this happens, I will turn to Karl Marx's analysis of the commodity fetish in the third section. Capitalism has changed our whole way of relating to the material world, in ways that we saw anticipated in the biblical critique of idolatry discussed in chapter 3. Material things take on life, while life is drained away from human persons. The magic of commodities is the flip side of the ruthless rationalization of human labor. I will show how consumer culture leads to the domination and oppression of both workers and consumers by the products of human making. In the fourth and final section, I will address the question of narcissism, which was highlighted by Augustine and Marion. I will argue ultimately that consumer culture lends itself to a kind of unsplendid idolatry, but it is an idolatry that is not simply inevitable.

7.1. Looking for Meaning in Things

It would be easy for any examination of consumer culture in the light of idolatry critique to turn immediately to jeremiad. The indictment of consumer culture as idolatry seems straightforward: we have put our trust in things rather than in God, in creation rather than the Creator. To begin with this stark opposition between things and God would be unhelpful, however, for reasons that have been spelled out in previous chapters. Idolatry critique should contain within it a kind of sympathy that sees idolatry as a manifestation of the basic human search for meaning, as Weber would have it, or for fullness, in Taylor's terms. The Bible witnesses to this search as a search for God, the Creator of all things. As Augustine and Marion attest, for creatures like us the way to the Creator is mediated by the creation. The beauty of God is visible in the beautiful things of God's creation. We are naturally drawn outside of ourselves to find God in the things God has made, for we are material creatures with no direct access to an immaterial God. The human employment of things can become idolatrous if God is neglected in favor of things, but material culture is not necessarily idolatrous. Indeed, as Augustine contends, the entire creation was made for our salvation, and we are invited to delight in it, to seek and find God therein. It is possible to see in human material culture a search for meaning, and ultimately for God, in the use of the things we material creatures have at hand.

Anthropologist Daniel Miller thinks an overly negative view of material things is not just typical of critiques of consumerism but typical of religion more generally. In his book *Stuff*, Miller writes, "There is an underlying principle to be found in most of the religions that dominate recorded history. Wisdom has been accredited to those who claim that materiality represents the merely apparent, behind which lies that which is real."[2] Miller cites the Hindu belief that the material world is mere illusion, *maya*, as representative of religion's take on materiality. Paradoxically, material culture has been a key means to expressing this belief; Hinduism and other religions are thick with attention to materiality, though mostly as a route to the immaterial: "In religion the main purpose of the material is to express the immaterial."[3] As a result of this paradox, according to Miller, most of what we take for morality emphasizes flight from the material, while we simultaneously seek to accumulate more things.

The late twentieth-century anthropological turn toward the study of material culture is in part an attempt to correct an overly negative view of materiality that is often associated in the West with Christianity. Catholic anthropologist Mary Douglas's work is a landmark in the study of material culture. Her 1979 book *The World of Goods*, co-authored with economist Baron Isherwood and updated in 1996, attempted to move beyond understanding goods as primarily needed for subsistence plus competitive display ("conspicuous consumption"). For Douglas and Isherwood, things are mediating materials for relating to other people. They make statements about the hierarchy of values to which the owner subscribes. "Goods in their assemblage present a set of meanings. . . . They are read by those who know the code and scan them for information."[4] Concern for things is not an illegitimate and crass turn from the realm of meaning and value to the merely material; rather "consumption is a ritual process whose primary function is to make sense of the inchoate flux of events."[5] As much as Weber recognized the necessary human search for meaning, Douglas and Isherwood ground that search in materiality. Things "are needed for making visible and stable the categories of culture,"[6] and the authors make clear that this means *any* culture; they are looking for an anthropology of consumption that applies to both modern capitalist societies and tribal societies with little or no commerce.[7] The recognition that the material realm is not inherently illusory or oppressive, however, does not preclude making judgments about truth and falsehood. Once Douglas and Isherwood establish their point about the social function of objects, they go on to ask, "How do we distinguish construction of reality from fantasy?"[8] One way of doing so is by making moral judgments about the ways that people are organized, especially the principles of exclusion that are used.[9]

Miller recognizes that Douglas's work was an important step forward for the study of material culture. Miller is concerned nevertheless that Douglas's work does not sufficiently refute the putatively religious view of the material as merely expressing a more basic immaterial reality. For Douglas, according to Miller, relationships with objects are ultimately reducible to previously existing social relations.[10] Miller worries that Douglas tends to treat the self as the real reality behind merely material things, which then uses things like clothes to communicate with other selves. For Miller, there is no true inner self lurking behind material things. Things actually make us who we are—the clothes do make the man—or more accurately, persons and things mutually make one another.[11] For Miller the objects in our world are frames that provide settings for our action as humans. They tell us what kinds of activity and speech are suitable in each room of the house. Objects gently tell us how to act appropriately, and they are most effective when we don't consciously pay attention to them. Objects help constitute what Pierre Bourdieu refers to as our *habitus*, a term he borrows from medieval scholastics, the second nature that forms our disposition to behave in certain ways without consciously choosing to do so. Not individual things but the whole system of things makes us the people we are, and the more we fail to notice them, the more powerful they are.[12]

Miller is after a theory that does not reduce the relations between persons and things to a mere representation of the former. For this he looks to Hegel and Marx and their conceptions of "objectification," the process by which human creations react back upon us. The law, for example, is a human creation, but one which we often experience as an external force that acts on us. This force can be experienced by the individual as oppressive, but for Hegel it need not be so. The process of objectification, or self-alienation, is the process by which we achieve self-consciousness and the process by which reason manifests itself in history, as it continually undergoes a dialectical process of development. For Hegel, self-alienation is a positive and necessary condition of our development, though Miller acknowledges that every time we enhance our human capacity through this process we also create a contradiction, the possibility that our creations will oppress us. Marx elaborates Hegel's concept of objectification in the realm of the material world, seeing the products of human labor as the expression of the species-being of humans. According to Miller, however, Marx sees the process of self-alienation in capitalism as entirely negative. The product of human labor is attributed to capital rather than to the workers. Lost is the workers' consciousness of themselves as those who communicate themselves in the material world by means of their labor. For Marx, writes Miller, "things are no longer fluid, but harden themselves against us to become the instruments of our oppression."[13] Marx's goal is for humans to reclaim our subjectivity, to control objects rather than be controlled by them. In contrast, Miller favors a theory in which "ultimately there is no separation of subjects and objects";[14] objects make us in the same process by which we make them. Miller sees the creative potential in private property and prefers to see oppression as "a contradiction, rather than the only way to characterize our relationship to things."[15] Contradiction, furthermore, "is not just a new feature of modern capitalism. . . . It is intrinsic to the very process we describe as culture."[16] An aboriginal person can find their own native material culture as oppressive as a modern suburbanite can find consumer culture.[17]

The emphasis in both Douglas and Miller, then, is on the continuity between pre- and postindustrial material cultures, between Western consumers and isolated indigenous peoples. Both Douglas and Miller, as anthropologists, are after a theory of material culture as such, and so they stress the continuities among all the different ways that human beings relate to the material objects in their lives. Both are trying to counter typical critiques of modern Western consumerism as an aberrant materialism; both present a more positive account of the role that material objects play in human communication and the construction of meaningful lives, while also acknowledging the exclusion and oppression that can be established and reinforced by material culture. For Miller, the emphasis on continuity also relativizes the boundary between material and immaterial, and between the secular and the religious. According to Miller, we think we have a good grasp of the distinction between the material and the immaterial, especially in a supposedly secular world in which things have been disenchanted. "But our secular world is just as haunted today by shadowy spirits that seem to perform strange magical feats that conjure vast powers out of the dross."[18] As an example, Miller points to anthropological studies of traders in derivatives markets. The traders begin by reconceptualizing potential future profit streams into something that can be traded. Derivatives are formed by trading the risk involved in speculating what the future profit will be. In arbitrage, trades are made based on the tiny discrepancies between how models say the markets should be functioning and how they actually are functioning. Values are created on the basis of tacit agreement to act as though they existed. Before the crisis of 2008, the notional value of derivative contracts exceeded the size of the entire world economy. Such value existed in some sense, says Miller, but determining the boundary between the material and the immaterial here is very difficult. "The point is merely that the relationship between materiality and immateriality is no more straightforward in secular than in religious domains."[19] The material world will always grope toward the transcendent, and the immaterial conversely cannot do without things. In Miller's words, "The more humanity reaches towards the conceptualization of the immaterial, the more important the specific form of its materialization."[20]

The kind of anthropological studies done by Douglas and Miller can help us to appreciate the positive work that material objects do in mediating human communication and forming human persons. Blurring the lines between the material and the immaterial, the secular and the religious, can also open possibilities for seeing God at work in material culture. As Eugene McCarraher writes, "another way to say that the world is 'enchanted' is to say that it is sacramental."[21] In Christian practice and thought, the presence of God is mediated through the material world. I will have much more to say about sacraments and sacramentality in the final chapter. For now it suffices to note that there is nothing inherently idolatrous about material culture as such, and we need to avoid simplistic denunciations of materialism, as opposed to a supposedly more salutary spirituality or religion or transcendence. Indeed, idolatry is in some ways opposed to mere materialism, for it is the investing of the material with the divine.

It is precisely here that Douglas and Miller are less helpful to our investigation. They are after a general theory of material culture, and so they emphasize the continuity between capitalist culture and forms of culture that stand prior to or outside of capitalist modes of production. But clearly the advent of consumer culture does mark a substantially different way of dealing with the material world. The sheer proliferation and ubiquity not only of manufactured goods but of marketing for those goods is unprecedented, as is the amount of time and energy that we spend thinking and dreaming about and looking at images of commodities. Douglas emphasizes the ways that we express ourselves through material items, but she understates the ways in which material things make us, to use Miller's language. But Miller also, in his critique of Marx, mitigates the control of things over us with the control of us over things, an attractively balanced account of mutual making that leaves us with considerable agency. I am not sure, however, that this account does justice to the realities of either consumption or production in a late capitalist economy. People in consumer culture are in the thrall of commodities at the same time that most people do not experience themselves as makers.

Though there is continuity in the ways that people make meaning through material goods, we need to examine the distinctive features of the contemporary economy, specifically the theme I used to open chapter 1 on Max Weber: the connection between the magic of consumption and the rationalization of production. For the consumer with sufficient money, the world of commodities is magical. The experience of shopping is no longer limited to the stores that one can visit in person. With online shopping, the consumer can be immersed twenty-four hours a day in a virtually unlimited ocean of images portraying products available for sale. From the comfort of one's own home—or anywhere else, for that matter—consumers can be fascinated and delighted by these images and the imagination of possessing the products they depict. With a few simple clicks, the products can then be summoned to appear at one's doorstep, in some cases within hours. No interactions with people, or even images of people, need ever intervene between the consumer and the commodity. The consumer merely clicks on the image of the product and—*Abracadabra!*—the product appears at their home, seemingly materializing out of thin air. And the prices that the consumer pays are often extraordinarily low.

What makes this magic possible for the consumer is what Weber would recognize as the "rationalization" of production. Amazon warehouses, ironically named "fulfillment centers," illustrate the lengths to which retail has been subjected to a ruthless drive toward efficiency. In a fulfillment center, as opposed to a typical store, there is no down time, no waiting for customers to come, no fraternizing with co-workers or chitchat with customers. Worker productivity is tracked by the scanners workers use to retrieve and package products. Bathroom breaks and other drags on productivity are strictly monitored and punished. According to court documents filed by Amazon, around 10% of warehouse workers are fired annually for falling behind in productivity, and the terminations are issued according to computer algorithms, with no input from supervisors, although supervisors can manually override that process.[22] As an extensive *New York Times* report documents, human resources at Amazon are highly automated, with humans ironically absent from most decisions to hire, manage, discipline, and fire workers.[23] The automated human resource system has repeatedly led to workers on medical or parental leaves being summarily fired, having their benefits cut off, and being shortchanged in their paychecks.[24] People are both supervised by and treated like robots. According to James Bloodworth, who worked at an Amazon fulfillment center, "It was all obsessed with productivity. . . . People were told off for taking five minutes to go to the bathroom. They started treating human beings as robots, essentially. If it proves cheaper to replace humans with machines, I assume they will do that."[25] One advantage of machines is that they do not suffer injuries; the injury rates at Amazon warehouses are double the industry average,[26] and vending machines at Amazon warehouses have been stocked with free painkillers.[27]

The point of this dehumanization of workers is to increase convenience and lower prices for consumers and to increase the salaries and profits of managers and owners of the means of production. Consumers are attracted by cheap goods and ease of purchase. Why drive to the mall and pay more for something when I can stay home and have it come to me for less money? The managerial class and shareholders reap great monetary rewards; Amazon CEO Jeff Bezos's net worth increased by $67 billion in 2020—over $183 million *per day*—in a year when a quarter of Americans reported that someone in their household was laid off. In the same year, Amazon disclosed that its workers' median annual salary was $28,848, meaning half of its workers made less than that amount.[28] Amazon has successfully fought off almost all attempts to unionize its workers. Bezos's founding vision included high worker turnover; data showed that workers become less eager over time, and Bezos believed people were inherently lazy, so they were encouraged not to stick around. Before the COVID-19 pandemic, Amazon turnover was already 150% per year, almost double the U.S. average in retail and logistics.[29] A third of Amazon workers qualify for SNAP food assistance; food vouchers, meanwhile, can be used online, which is one of many ways that Amazon profits from government money.[30] As Alec MacGillis's book *Fulfillment: Winning and Losing in One-Click America* documents, the rise of Amazon has exacerbated the trend toward increasing concentration of wealth and power. Thousands of stores and other small businesses have either gone out of business or have been forced to sell through Amazon, surrendering a portion of their profits to the behemoth. Wealth continues to flee the heartland and become concentrated in a few coastal cities, where it is further concentrated in the managerial class of the online economy.[31]

To explore the question of contemporary idolatry, then, we will need to examine both the enchantment of material goods in consumer culture and the related rationalization of production, in which people become subordinated to their own creations. We have explored the elevation of things and the subordination of humans in previous chapters. I will now try to make those explorations more concrete by showing, first, how products have taken on life, and then how life has been drained from their makers.

7.2. Charged Objects

What Frank Trentmann calls "a historic shift in humans' relations with things"[32] and Jean Baudrillard calls a "fundamental mutation in the ecology of the human species"[33] begins with a monumental increase in the sheer quantity of commodities beginning in the nineteenth century. A typical German today, Trentmann reports, owns ten thousand objects. Baudrillard comments, "Strictly speaking, the humans of the age of affluence are surrounded not so much by other human beings, as they were in all previous ages, but by *objects*."[34] These objects are not things that we made, as they primarily were in previous ages, but almost entirely things that we bought. This is a profound difference in the way that we relate to the material world, so much so that our identity as consumers has become our primary—though not our only—identity. We are not primarily warriors or workers or prayers, but consumers, and we define who we are and who we aspire to be through consumption.[35]

The heightened importance of things in our lives is therefore not merely quantitative but qualitative. So much of who we are and what our highest aspirations are for ourselves is caught up with consumption that to identify consumerism with materialism misses the mark rather widely. Human life has not simply been reduced to the level of base materiality. The material world has instead been elevated above the merely material. I cannot make this point any more effectively than the following peroration to a convention of store display designers in 1923:

Sell them their dreams. . . . Sell them what they longed for and hoped for and almost despaired of having. Sell them hats by splashing sunlight across them. Sell them dreams—dreams of country clubs and proms and visions of what might happen if only. After all, people don't buy things to have things. They buy things to work for them. They buy hope—hope of what your merchandise will do for them. Sell them this hope and you won't have to worry about selling them goods.[36]

Hopes and dreams and visions that transcend mundane life have typically been considered under the rubric of "religion," but there is an ever-growing body of scholarship exploring the religious—and related themes of magic, the sacred, transcendence, liturgy, animism, fetishism, and the like—in the practices of consumer culture. In other words, one way that consumer culture approaches idolatry is as a substitute technology of divinity.

Baudrillard compares modern consumer culture to the supposedly more primitive Melanesian natives who were fascinated by the flying machines that occasionally crossed the sky above them. They noticed that the machines would descend for white people, but not for them, so they built a simulacrum of an airplane and landing strip out of branches and vines and waited for the planes to descend. For Baudrillard, modern consumers are not essentially different: "The beneficiary of the consumer miracle also sets in place a whole array of sham objects, of characteristic signs of happiness, and then waits (waits desperately, a moralist would say) for happiness to alight."[37] According to Baudrillard, "consumption is governed by a form of *magical thinking*":[38] we accumulate objects as the signs of happiness that are meant to call down the miracle of satisfaction from on high. "Consumer goods thus present themselves as a *harnessing of power*, not as products embodying work."[39] The abundance of goods is seen as a kind of manna from heaven, unrelated to the whole system of production via human labor and dispensed by "a beneficent mythological agency."[40]

Rather than critique magical thinking in consumer culture, other scholars view it more sympathetically as a meaningful cultural practice that allows people to cope with various social stresses. Magic has been vilified or ridiculed both as a primitive stage superseded by religion and as a threat to a scientific worldview. Some studies of consumer behavior, on the other hand, see magic—defined as acts people perform to influence unseen forces[41]— as an integral and potentially beneficial aspect of modern consumer society. Cele Otnes and Linda Scott, for example, note the way that advertised products promise magical transformation to those who properly complete the ritual: a diamond engagement ring is a ritual artifact that transports the woman to a "shining land where love is ever new and magical."[42] Yannik St. James, Jay M. Handelman, and Shirley F. Taylor argue that consumerism is thoroughly imbued with the three defining principles of magic: creative persuasion, retribution, and efficient causality. Creative persuasion operates when people see no sharp boundary between themselves and the mysterious, sacred forces of nature. That environment is a moral one, where good deeds are rewarded and bad ones punished (retribution). Magic operates as efficient causality when ritual artifacts promise to deliver gains. The authors use the "magic-in-a-bottle" of beauty creams and weight-loss products to illustrate the enchantment imbued in products. Consumer magic breaks down the boundaries between natural and supernatural, scientific and religious. Rather than see consumers as irrational dupes, St. James and colleagues see consumers as exercising agency via magical thinking to find meaning and hope in consumer goods that promise transformation. They conclude that "by engaging in play that blurs the domains of reality and fantasy, consumers find agency in a cultural context which otherwise affords them very little."[43]

In an influential article Russell Belk, Melanie Wallendorf, and John Sherry argue, "For many, consumption has become a vehicle for experiencing the sacred."[44] Consumer items are a way of tapping into something more powerful and extraordinary than the self. The authors did extensive fieldwork, interviewing people at swap meets, flea markets, festivals, grocery stores, restaurants, museums, homes, and other venues. They found that people spontaneously made distinctions between the sacred and the profane among the objects that they possessed and used. The authors define the sacred/profane dichotomy based on the work of Émile Durkheim, Mircea Eliade, and others. According to Belk et al., there are twelve properties that can mark something as sacred: rather than our creating a thing as sacred, it manifests itself to us as sacred; sacred items exhibit power, of attraction both and repulsion; the sacred is set apart from the profane and the ordinary; objects can become imbued with sacredness through contact; acts of sacrifice and asceticism reinforce sacredness; the sacred requires commitment; sacredness is objectified in things; it is ritualized; it is surrounded by myth; it is imbued with mystery; the sacred creates community; it is experienced as ecstasy and flow.[45] It is easy enough to see how these characteristics of the sacred are found in what is usually labeled "religion," but Belk and colleagues note that in modern Western society the boundaries between the sacred and the profane have shifted in the process of secularization. They argue that the diminishment of what is generally considered "religion"—church attendance and the like—has been accompanied by a movement of the sacred to the "secular" realm. There has been both a "secularization of religion"—decline in traditional church services and family sacred rituals, commercialization of Christmas, profanization of religion through televangelism—and a "sacralization of the secular," that is, a seeking out of the sacred in areas of life previously regarded as profane. As the church lost political power, the nation became sacred; as Christianity declined, science became the repository of sacred truth; as charismatic preachers receded in importance, charismatic rock stars became increasingly idolized.[46] Belk et al. see the same migration of the holy to consumer culture. They describe the various ways that people sacralize their lives by employing consumer items ritually, especially in the home. Being surrounded by the right things is crucial to expressing one's identity and one's place in the cosmos. Even mass-produced items can attain sacred status if they have the right "quintessence": one becomes a "Chevy man" or a "Ford man" by tapping into the quintessential qualities of a product that are irreducible to the physical qualities or use-value of an item. Items that are given or added to a collection take on sacramental qualities that did not exist when they were simple commodities for sale. Experiences such as a trip to Disneyworld or Graceland share many of the sacred qualities of pilgrimages.[47]

For Belk and colleagues, the sacralization of consumption has both benefits and drawbacks. For the individual, sacred consumption can provide meaning, stability, and even joy and ecstasy, as well as connections with other people. For society, maintaining boundaries between the sacred and the profane provides social cohesion and integration, as Durkheim thought. But Belk et al. recognize that sacralized consumption can operate as just another opiate for the masses, a way of keeping the revolutionary spirit distracted, channeling the desire for transcendence and transformation into the collecting of butter dishes. They quote Michael Harrington wondering if a noble project like democratic socialism could replace the Judeo-Christian transcendental values now fading in Western civilization: "According to Harrington . . . Western society *needs* transcendence. Like it or not, to our benefit or peril, consumption has become such a transcendental vehicle for many."[48] They appear to acknowledge that the sacred does not simply disappear in modernity but migrates to places where the religious/secular dichotomy has trained us not to see it.

In the wake of this work by Belk et al., there has been a proliferation of research on the sacred in supposedly mundane consumer culture. Scholars have examined consumer behavior as liturgical and shopping malls as cathedrals.[49] Scholars have explored product loyalty as a type of religious devotion, sacred motifs in retail spaces, and certain consumer experiences as transcendent.[50] For example, in their ethnography of Harley Davidson riders, John Schouten and James McAlexander write, "Harley consumption experience has a spirituality derived in part from a sense of riding as a transcendental departure from the mundane."[51] There is a vast literature on types of consumer behavior as transcendence of the mundane, using Victor Turner's idea of antistructure, a liminal space that departs from the mundane and is therefore sacred.[52] Bernard Cova, Antonella Carù, and Julien Cayla have tried to supplement such work by moving the focus from dramatic departures from structure—extreme sports like whitewater rafting, for example—to flight within more mundane types of consumer behavior, such as watching TV or escaping work and home by going to Starbucks. What these various types of escape have in common, according to the authors, is weariness of being a self and an attempt to transcend the singular self into multiple selves, especially in an age in which we must constantly curate and market ourselves.[53]

Recognizing sacred motifs in such mundane activities depends on a willingness to question the religious/secular and the material/spiritual dichotomies. In their study "Religiosity in the Abandoned Apple Newton Brand Community," for example, Albert Muñiz and Hope Jensen Schau contend, "Religion is fundamental to human existence. It endures"—even in highly secularized societies.[54] They view the supposed disenchantment of the secularized modern world as a displacement of religion, not its destruction: "Also fundamental to human existence is the meaningfulness of material objects."[55] In every time and place, they contend, material objects have borne meaning beyond their use-value: "The intersection of religious and material is neither unusual nor unimportant to understanding consumers and their consumption."[56] Religious narratives, they contend, are "highly accessible and highly portable templates for human understanding."[57] This explains why the language of the community that doggedly held onto the Apple Newton long after its discontinuation is so full of references to the supernatural, to martyrdom, to faith, to eschatology, to the miraculous, and to resurrection.[58] Muñiz and Schau find nothing unusual about the gathering of a community based on reverence for particularly powerful "charged objects," to use Charles Taylor's phrase. Though Muñiz and Schau do not completely erase the boundaries between the religious and the secular, they write of a spillover effect between the two, whereby they "contaminate" each other. Leigh Eric Schmidt comes to a similar conclusion in his book *Consumer Rites* about the commodification of American holidays. Schmidt tries to avoid jeremiads against the commercialization of Christmas and other holidays, noting that material goods have always been imbued with religious and cultural meaning: "In this story the sacred and secular have often reversed themselves, the marketplace becoming a realm of religious enchantment and the churches a site of material abundance and promotional gimmicks. What one sees finally in these modern holiday rituals is this: how secular much of the sacred is, and how sacred much of the secular is."[59]

I don't find this language of two substances or realms—the religious and the secular—spilling over and contaminating each other very helpful. I don't know how one could identify something as secular if it is so sacred, or how one could identify something as sacred if it is so secular. What interests me about this scholarship on consumerism as religious is simply that it shows that the reverence accorded to commodities in a consumer culture is similar to the reverence accorded to the divine in other types of cultures. In this scholarship, the shift from the latter to the former is said to be one of the markers of modernity. If this is true, the shift is inadequately characterized as "secularization" if that term is meant to indicate the diminution of "religion." Indeed, the religious/secular distinction becomes pointless except as a way to obscure what is really going on, to maintain that there is a sharp difference between reverence for commodities and reverence for God, even though there is no such sharp divide. There are various reasons one could want to maintain that distinction. For a Christian, it could help shield one from suspicion of idolatry. Just as in the first chapter I found it uninteresting to try to decide whether or not the modern world is really enchanted or disenchanted, I am equally uninterested here in trying to sort out the really religious from the secular. What interests me is the work that the religious/secular or enchanted/disenchanted distinctions do to obscure the way that power operates in the modern world.

The question of power is crucial to our analysis because the investment of divinity in commodities, while certainly involving the agency of consumers, is also accomplished by a well-organized and well-funded system of persuasion in which we are almost uninterruptedly immersed. We are well past critiques of marketing—and advertising more specifically—that present

consumers as mindless dupes manipulated according to the will of the producer. Consumers can and do exercise agency when they invest material
objects with sacred meaning. But there is also an entire industry dedicated to
selling people their dreams and, in so doing, helping to shape those dreams,
often using images and language borrowed from Christianity. As one ad man
wrote to his peers in the trade journal *Advertising and Selling* in 1932, "I'm
tired of looking at things as they are. . . . You are entrusted with the responsibility of showing others what they cannot see for themselves. If your eyes
see only what is seen by others, from where will the vision come?"[60] Grant
McCracken and Richard Pollay note, "If goods have a symbolic aspect it is
largely because advertising gives them one. They plainly do not spring from
the factory fully possessed of their ability to communicate."[61]

To understand the investment of commodities with divinity, then, we
will need to understand the history of advertising. One of the most authoritative accounts of that history is in the textbook *Social Communication in
Advertising* by William Leiss, Stephen Kline, Sut Jhally, Jacqueline Botterill,
and Kyle Asquith, now in its fourth edition (2018) after first appearing in
1986. The authors lay out the history of advertising in five stages: idolatry
(1890–1925), iconology (1925–45), narcissism (1945–65), totemism (1965–
90), and mise-en-scène (1990–present). The stages are an elaboration of the
four stages Sut Jhally, one of the co-authors, laid out in his 1987 book *The
Codes of Advertising*. The authors caution that the stages are not meant to
convey a regimented historical march from one style to another; the different
styles of advertising commingle in different stages. The chronology is meant
to convey the dominant cultural frame for goods in each period, with a cumulative effect in which earlier frames are incorporated in the later stages
into a more complex ensemble of strategies.[62] What is most interesting for
our purposes is that Jhally has chosen terms for his four stages that we have
already encountered in our study of idolatry. Although, as we will see, Jhally
uses the terms differently than I do and as a critic of religion, not a theologian, Jhally sees advertising as a type of "old-time religion" or "polytheism" of
powerful forces imputed to material things.[63] It is not by accident that he uses
the term "idolatry" to analyze advertising. Nor are Jhally and colleagues the
only ones to suggest that advertising is a kind of "religion"; such is the main
theme that James Twitchell, a defender of consumerism, explores in his book
Adcult USA.[64]

Leiss et al. label the first stage in modern advertising "idolatry" because the focus is on the veneration of the product. The mass production

of consumer goods that accelerated in the late nineteenth century was accompanied by a confidence that new devices and products could deliver significant improvements to daily life. Advertisements in this first stage, 1890 to 1925, tended to consist primarily of densely worded text meant to convey the virtues and uses of the product. Vague forms of sacred symbolism were used to show the enhancement, awe, and rapture that products could bring, but the emphasis was on the use-value of the product. An early advertisement would explain why the physical qualities of the product in question made it superior to others on the market. Although many products were fraudulent—patent medicines with cocaine in them promised cures for all sorts of ailments—the persuasive appeal tended to be rational: use this product to achieve these marvelous results. Ads at this stage promised that products would help people better accomplish the tasks they were already accustomed to doing, but did not challenge social or gender roles. Ads were, most important, focused on the product and not on the person using the product.[65]

The second stage of advertising, from 1925 to 1945, Leiss et al. label "iconology" because the focus began to shift away from the product itself toward more abstract qualities and values, such as status, elegance, familial affection, and love. "Icon" for the authors indicates a symbol, something that represents something else. The focus has shifted from the veneration of the product to the meaning of the product within a social context. There was a movement away from utility and toward meaning: automobiles are not just for getting from point A to point B but for expressing a "modern outlook" on life. Products were increasingly presented as capturing some potent unseen force, what the authors label "white magic." As an ad in *Printers' Ink Monthly* noted in 1926, advertisements were "beginning to occupy the place in inspiration that religion did several hundred years ago."[66] Appeals were less rationalistic and more impressionistic, with a decrease of text and an increase of images. The shift from the product to the person had begun, but people in advertisements were still less autonomous individuals and more exemplars of reigning social values.[67]

The third stage, "narcissism," 1945–65, completed the shift from the product to the person. People now appeared in ads as real, concrete individuals with emotions and psychological depth. Advertising agencies increased their use of psychological research to understand what makes people buy. This stage introduced "mirror ads," in which a face—usually female—gazed out at viewers and invited them to see themselves in the scene in relationship to the product, which fulfilled some longing. "Having been admitted to the innermost recesses of the psyche, the product reciprocated by placing its powers at the individual's disposal."[68] Consumers were now encouraged to think about the self, to imagine what the product could do for them as individuals. The consumer could now also wield the product's power to sway the judgment of other people, what the authors label "black magic": the right perfume or the right shoes would cause a stranger to fall head over heels in love with the wearer. Products became essential elements to interpersonal relationships, such that the products themselves became personalized.[69] Jhally notes that this stage could therefore also be labeled "fetishism."[70]

The term the authors use for the fourth stage of advertising, roughly 1965 to 1990, is "totemism," borrowed from Durkheim. As we saw in the previous chapter, Durkheim understood the totem as a natural sign, often an animal, that served as a representation of a social group. It was the way a group represented itself to itself, and was therefore "religious," in Durkheim's view. In the totemic stage of advertising, products became badges of group membership. For Leiss et al. this stage marks the gathering of people into communities on the basis of symbolic displays of consumption.[71] Instead of appealing to mass audiences in which all consumed the same things, this stage is marked by market segmentation in which marketers appealed to subgroups gathered around certain preferences and patterns of consumption.[72] Advertisers presented authoritative representations of consumption in different subgroups, especially based on income, indicating a rather fixed hierarchy of social differentiation which nevertheless encouraged the individual's aspiration to move from a lower to a higher level.[73]

In the third and fourth editions of the book, the authors have added a fifth stage, mise-en-scène, which they think captures the post-1990 moment in advertising. The French term means "put into the scene" and comes from the world of theater and film. Commodities in advertisements are props arranged in a theatrical production. The "directors" are consumers themselves, who use commodities to convey an extremely varied set of meanings, values, and stories. This new era is characterized by what Leiss et al. call "demassification" because—although products are mostly mass-produced by a dominant set of corporations—individuals are encouraged to see themselves as the true agents of meaning-creation and to use commodities to stand out from the crowd. At the same time, what corporations know about consumers has increased exponentially, down to detailed knowledge of the habits and preferences of individual consumers. Surveillance of individuals' habits while using their electronic devices now allows the targeting of advertising to individuals rather than to whole groups. At the same time that we are encouraged to write our own scripts, Google "has assumed control, much as Julius Caesar did in Rome in 48 B.C."[74] We are vaguely aware of the concentrated power of a few corporations, but the same corporations simultaneously encourage us to set ourselves apart from the crowd. As Leiss et al. remark, "Advertising addresses the central anxiety of how to maintain individuality under the pressures of the massifying forces of the market and media, while at the same time contributing to that very anxiety." The result, the authors say, is "often fantastically mythic."[75]

Although various details of this history of advertising are debatable, what emerges is a clear picture of what Jhally calls "advertising as religion."[76] Advertising invests commodities with deep human aspirations for transcendence. McCarraher notes that both critics and boosters of marketing have seen it as appealing to the deepest wells of human desire. Marketers "knew that consumers desired more than an accumulation of objects; they studied and captured the immortal longing for an enchanted, beloved community."[77] McCarraher's magisterial history *The Enchantments of Mammon: How Capitalism Became the Religion of Modernity* rejects the idea that Western culture has ever been disenchanted. He argues instead that we have been "misenchanted." He calls consumer culture both a "counterfeit beatific vision" and a parody of a sacramental way of being in the world.[78]

As we look at the overall contours of the history of advertising since the late nineteenth century, we see how products gradually take flight from the mundane and the material to the transcendent. I illustrate this dynamic for my students with a series of shoe advertisements. The first, a 1909 ad from Regal Shoes of Boston, explains in several paragraphs of dense text the advantages of the new kind of last they invented for the manufacturing process: "All other ready-to-wear shoes are built on old-style lasts, large enough at the 'waist' to allow the broad part of the last to be withdrawn. That is why they are so apt to wrinkle over the instep and under the arch and allow the foot to slide forward." The second is a 1972 ad for Weyenberg Shoes of Milwaukee, showing a naked woman lying on the floor admiring a man's shoe; the only text is the five-word caption "Keep her where she belongs." The third, from 2010, is a black square with nothing but the words "Write the future" and the Nike swoosh in white. There is no description of a shoe or image of a shoe or indeed any mention of shoes at all. Over the course of a century, the focus has gone from the material qualities of the shoe to the association of the shoe with pathetic male fantasies of sex and power to the disappearance of the shoe altogether into a gaseous cloud of transcendent aspirations to be the author of the world to come. This sequence illustrates the way that material goods have taken flight as consumer culture has spread and intensified. Consumer culture is in many ways the opposite of materialism; it is instead a form of excarnation, an attempt to transcend the material by making material goods vehicles for the highest of human aspirations.

Leiss et al. link this transcendence of the material with the broader "dematerialization" of economic activity in late capitalism. There has been a significant shift from industrial society, focused on the manufacture of material goods, to a postindustrial society in which information, financial services, and other kinds of services now make up well more than half of the economy. Manufacturing has largely been shifted to poorer countries of the Global South, while the service and information economy is dominated by the wealthier nations of the North. The companies that dominate the culture now make images instead of things. As Phil Knight of Nike has said, "There is no value in making things anymore. The value is added by careful research, by innovation and by marketing."[79] Manufacturing is largely left to subcontractors in poorer countries, where wages, working conditions, and environmental impact are subject to lax oversight by the parent company. Naomi Klein describes this movement as a kind of excarnation: "After establishing the 'soul' of their corporations, the superbrand companies have gone on to rid themselves of their cumbersome bodies, and there is nothing that seems more cumbersome, more loathsomely corporeal, than the factories that produce their products."[80]

As Leiss et al. explain, in the latter decades of the twentieth century it became harder for products to distinguish themselves from competitors on the basis of innovation alone, because advanced techniques of production and communication allowed competitors to replicate innovations quickly. Brands became increasingly important as companies unable or unwilling to distinguish themselves on the basis of quality or price sought to compete on the basis of symbolic distinctions.[81] Brands sought to sell people not just products but an image of a style of life that transcends their own mundane life. As Klein mordantly puts it, "liberated from the real-world burdens of stores and product manufacturing, these brands are free to soar, less as the disseminators of goods and services than as collective hallucinations."[82] In the era of branding, "the product always takes a back seat to the real product, the brand, and the selling of the brand acquired an extra component that can only be described as spiritual. . . . Branding, in its truest and most advanced incarnations, is about corporate transcendence."[83]

If Klein seems to be exaggerating here, Douglas Atkin makes essentially the same argument in his book *The Culting of Brands*, but with a positive spin. Atkin is not a cultural critic but is himself a partner in a marketing firm. When he compares brands to cults, he defines cults broadly and nonpejoratively as communities of exclusive devotion gathered around the making of meaning, that is, an interpretation of the world and one's purpose in it, and a picture of how the world should be.[84] Atkin explores the many ways that people make meaning through symbolic expression in both cults and cult brands like Apple, Harley Davidson, Saturn, the Body Shop, and many others. Such people are not duped, says Atkin; they are aware of what they are choosing to join.[85] Cults and brands gather communities around them in part by making people feel special and set apart from the crowd of nonbelievers. Both cults and brands have shared symbols, rituals, narratives of persecution, distinctive clothing or logos, and "metaphysics" or worldviews. Atkin quotes a loyal Snapple drinker: "Because things are so crazy out there, people like to find out if they see the world in the same way as other people. People will believe in anything . . . if it makes them feel that they belong to something bigger than themselves."[86]

According to Atkin, this important aspect of human life was carried, until the 1960s, by cults and traditional religions like Catholicism. Today, however, brands supply symbolic meaning to the majority of global citizens;[87] "corporations are arguably the most powerful meaning engines today."[88] Today we enjoy "a consumer culture arguably more Catholic than the symbolical world of organized religion."[89] Brands began as a way to authenticate products, Atkin writes, but today they authenticate the consumer. They are markers of human identity. Atkin exhorts marketers—the primary intended audience for his book—to embrace their vocation as priests in this new religion:

> Companies must offer more than a stand-alone product that conveys meaning like some solitary crucifix. Cult-brand marketers know that they must colonize every single moment of everyday life. Their mission is to brand a living *experience*, to create a unified meaning system that transforms every possible touch-point between the company and the customer into [a] symbol that refers back to a single idea or belief.[90]

Atkin admonishes his marketing colleagues to transcend the material world and focus on their role as idol-makers:

> Get over your products. Get an integrated symbolic system. Get over the plastic, the wires, the fillers, and the ingredients. . . . Think about the symbol system you're making possible instead—that is where you'll find true and lasting differentiation. What kind of environment are you providing that will allow your customers a place to commune with their fellow believers and the distinct symbols of their belief? What Temple to what god are you creating?[91]

Lest we be tempted to dismiss all this as marketing hyperbole, there is in fact empirical evidence that brands can indeed substitute for traditional faiths. A paper in the journal *Marketing Science* by a team of U.S. and Israeli researchers demonstrates that—in products like clothes that are related to self-expression—attachment to brands is inversely proportional to attachment to what is traditionally considered religion. The article, titled "Brands: The Opiate of the Nonreligious Masses?," lays out the data from four different empirical studies, all of which demonstrate that the less traditionally religious consumers are, the more loyalty they exhibit to brands; conversely, more religious consumers are less interested in brands. The authors of the study theorize that the reason religions and brands can substitute for each other is that both are important ways that people express their self-worth.[92]

As much as we take brands for granted today, the phenomenon is relatively recent. Until the Industrial Revolution, most of the things people had were made by themselves or by people they knew. It would have seemed odd for people to name their breakfast or the shirt they wore or the chair they sat on. As people moved from subsistence farming to wage labor and a cash economy, stores still mostly consisted of generic goods: the shopkeeper would scoop oats and pickles out of barrels, sell nameless shirts and chairs. Tobacco and patent-medicine sellers were the first to use brand names, but it was not until the 1880s that packaged and branded goods largely came to replace locally produced goods sold in bulk. One of the first successfully branded and mass-marketed products was Quaker Oats, first packaged with the image of a Quaker man in 1888. Breakfast cereal now had a name, and a face to go with it.[93]

Aunt Jemima, Tony the Tiger, Michael Jordan, the iconic Oscar Mayer commercial ("My baloney has a first name . . .") and a host of other attempts to animate products would follow. Once people no longer knew the people who made their goods or the shopkeeper who sold them, advertising encouraged people to develop relationships instead with products and brands.[94] There is an extensive literature exploring brand personality, animism, and anthropomorphism in brands.[95] To cite just a couple of examples, Jennifer Aaker has developed an influential typology of brand personalities that attempts to understand how and why certain brands are perceived as "sincere," others as "exciting," and so on.[96] Susan Fournier has explored theories of animism to understand how people invest humanlike personalities in brands and develop relationships with them.[97]

Work on animism in consumer culture is complemented by studies of fetishism in consumer culture, a theme that has its origins in Marx's *Capital*, as discussed below. The term comes from the Portuguese *feitiço*, used by seventeenth-century traders to describe the charms and talismans used on the Guinea coast of Africa. The word became a term of art among European anthropologists from the eighteenth century onward, who used it to describe a supposedly primitive stage of religion in which independent powers were attributed to material objects made by humans; the Portuguese word comes from the Latin *facticius*, meaning "artificial," that is, made by human hands. In the nineteenth century, the use of "fetishism" overlapped with "animism," in which spirits were thought to be installed temporarily in material objects, which allowed the objects to see, hear, understand, and act. Such actions include curing sickness, warding off evil, bringing rain, assisting in catching fish, making their users brave, and much more. By the end of the nineteenth century, the term "fetishism" had come to be applied so loosely—including for the worship of spirits, ancestors, and natural forces resident in material objects—that some more recent anthropologists prefer to restrict the term to a certain class of magical objects in West Africa. But anthropologists and cultural theorists have continued to use the term to describe aspects of consumer culture, specifically the attribution of independent powers to a material object.[98]

One important feature of fetishism to note is that power comes from outside an object and is invested in the object. As in Marion's account of the idol and the icon, there is nothing intrinsic in the material thing that qualifies it as a fetish. The imposition of a spirit on an object is performed by a priest or other ritual figure, but the occupation of the object by the spirit is not necessarily permanent. The fetish must perform the powerful acts of which it is said to be capable. If it fails, then the fetish is discarded, and new fetishes are invested and deployed. Fetishes are not gods but operate at the level of everyday life to realize supernatural power in the mundane.[99]

The anthropological literature is full of analyses of fetishism in contemporary consumer culture.[100] For example, in his 2013 book *Tourism Art and Souvenirs* David Hume argues that "tourism—with its developmental base in the religious pilgrimage, holy days and the desire to discover oneself and its associated artefacts—must be seen as a type of secular, post-modern, religious practice, a practice that includes the investment of magical powers in inanimate objects and animals."[101] Hume reads tourism as an attempt to escape to a transcendent and sacred realm of pure consumption beyond work.[102] The souvenir, as a fetish, serves as the material anchor for such a narrative. The souvenir is a fetish object that substitutes for the finite experience of the destination.[103] Hume maintains a careful ambiguity as to agency in the relationship between the tourist and the souvenir. On the one hand, the tourist invests their own narrative into the object. On the other hand, the object is invested with its own aura, either from its exotic producer or from the natural surroundings of the tourist site, that works on the individual tourist. Hume argues "that souvenirs construct the experience of the collector and are endowed with the same supernatural powers of the fetish."[104]

The aura of the fetish is not only attached to what Catholics would call first- or second- class relics,[105] that is, souvenirs with a claim to authenticity, such as an item handcrafted by a local artisan or a rock from an exotic locale. In an article titled "Making Magic: Fetishes in Contemporary Consumption," Karen Fernandez and John Lastovicka show how even mass-produced replicas can become fetish objects. Drawing on the work of Roy Ellen, they describe four cognitive elements of fetishism: (1) concretization, for example, a baseball glove used by a famous player that embodies the player's aura; (2) animation, allowing one to talk to the glove; (3) conflation, whereby the glove becomes a causative agent of good play; and (4) ambiguity of control, whereby it becomes unclear whether the possessor plays well because of their own ability or because of the glove.[106] Implicit in the magical thinking of fetishes is the transferability of power, in the above case from the star player to the glove to the new owner of the glove. Fernandez and Lastovicka use this transferability to explore how even mass-produced replicas that have had no physical contact with a famous person can take on that person's aura. Magic is both imitative and contagious, such that things that resemble one another share properties. The closer a replica resembles the original prototype, the more the power of the original can be transferred to the copy and to its user.[107] Fernandez and Lastovicka conduct an empirical study of guitar players, all of whom would prefer to play a beat-up guitar played by a star rather than a brand-new version of the same model. But because such first-class guitar relics are rare and expensive, most often players opt for a replica of a guitar played by their favorite virtuoso, and they report increased ability and self-confidence in their playing because even the mass-produced replica takes on the aura of the star performer. Players name their guitars, talk to them, describe them as "singing." The animation of the guitar, even a replica, comes with ambiguity of control, where it is not clear if it is the human player or the guitar itself that is responsible for the enhanced performance.[108]

The ready transferability of power even to mass-produced objects indicates that, for all its obsession with objects, fetishism is not permanent and is often fleeting. Objects do not possess power of themselves; power is invested in them by people, and once invested, power can be disinvested. Consumer items, like fetishes, can be discarded if they fail to satisfy. Consumer culture encourages both fascination with material things and the constant pursuit of newer and better things, what an internal General Motors memo referred to as the "organized creation of dissatisfaction," in reference to annually changing car models.[109] Consumer culture encourages attachment to material things, but it is what we might call a serial attachment, the constant pursuit of new and different objects in which to invest spiritual power. As Augustine famously noted, our hearts are restless. As Augustine also saw, serial attachment to material things that are not God is a technology of the self, a type of self-love that ultimately fails. I noted above that the stage of advertising Jhally labels "narcissism" could also be called "fetishism."[110] The obsession with material objects is simultaneously an obsession with the self and its image. The stage of narcissism in advertising for Jhally, Leiss, and their co-authors represents the completion of the movement from the centrality of the product to the centrality of the self. But the concept of fetishism allows us to see that the product is not simply left behind. In its attempts to create its own self-image, the self is constantly investing divinity in things. Particular things matter less than the ongoing pursuit of particular things; people fall in and out of love with Snapple and the Body Shop. But fetishized objects and brands remain essential to the construction of the consumer self. The array of fetishized objects continually changes, but the goal remains the construction of the self through the consumption of powerful things and the transcendent aspirations invested in them. We can acknowledge that Snapple does not look much like a god, and—as I suggested at the end of chapter 5—our claim that we obey only our own desires erases our sense that we are obeying at all. But the unsplendid nature of this type of idolatry may only make it more difficult to resist because it does not look like idolatry.

All of this should suffice to call the narrative of disenchantment into question. When someone is willing to pay $3 million for the baseball Mark McGwire hit for his seventieth homerun in 1998—despite the ball being physically identical to every other ball used that season—the world of "charged objects" is not consigned to the past, as it is for Charles Taylor. I see no reason to say, with Taylor, that consumerism is "almost" a "stronger form of magic." The "almost" responds to a felt need to reinforce the boundaries between enchanted and disenchanted, religious and secular, and related dichotomies which, I have argued, are of little help here. They mostly serve to obscure, not reveal, the true dynamics of consumer culture. As I argued in the first two chapters, modernity is not the condition of being disenchanted but the condition of learning to say that we are disenchanted.

There is nevertheless an objection to this analysis that has affinities with Taylor's presentation of modern people as "buffered selves." Modern people are aware of the fantastic and mythic characteristics of consumer culture, the objection goes, but embrace it anyway, with a certain spirit of irony and detachment. One devoted Snapple drinker admiringly told the marketer Atkin, "We've been bamboozled by The Man and we know it."[111] According to Michael Saler, whose work we engaged with in chapter 1, consumers are delighted but not deluded. Saler cites James W. Cook's study of nineteenth-century hucksterism. Cook argues that P. T. Barnum and other showmen in fact promoted Enlightenment rationality by challenging their audiences to spot their artful deceptions and thus distinguish between fantasy and reality. Simon During similarly argues that "secular magic" creates illusions rather than accessing the supernatural, showing the capacity of modern people to be simultaneously enchanted and disenchanted; that is, they embrace the wonders of modernity with delight, while maintaining the critical distance to tell truth from fiction. For Saler, it is elitist to think that mass culture is under what Klein would call "collective hallucinations"; people enjoy the delights of mass culture with a certain ironic distance. They remain buffered selves. "It may not provide the transcendent meanings and purposes of a religious world view, but that does not mean that the modern world is bereft of wonders, enchantment defined as 'delight.'"[112] The delighted/deluded binary allows one to acknowledge the enchantments of consumer culture while keeping the rational/irrational and secular/religious dichotomies intact, and locating consumer culture safely on the left side of these binaries.

I do not think that this appeal to irony and buffered selves adequately responds to the evidence I have summarized above. In quantitative terms, it does not deal with the sheer ubiquity of commodities and marketing in our lives. It is hard to take ironic distance from marketing and images of commodities when one is immersed in them like a fish in water. In qualitative terms, the evidence that consumerism has to some extent replaced what is traditionally considered religion or at least is capable of substituting for it would indicate that consumer culture responds to fairly deep human longings from which it is difficult to take ironic distance. The history of advertising and branding shows the extent to which the self is not buffered from material goods but is rather constructed in and through engagement with them. People see their longings reflected in products and images and fantasies of their possession and use, at the same time that those longings are under construction by those images and fantasies.

As I noted in chapter 3, the real issue in idolatry is not mere belief but behavior. As Slavoj Žižek argues, "the fetishist illusion resides in our real social life, not in our perception of it—a bourgeois subject knows very well that there is nothing magic about money, that money is just an object which stands for a set of social relations, but he nevertheless acts in real life as if he believed that money is a magical thing."[113] What is decisive is what people actually do, not simply how they learn to describe their experience; it is not that belief is irrelevant, but rather that belief and behavior are inseparable, such that what people actually believe is more accurately reflected by what they do than by what they claim to believe. The fact that a consumer can admit to being "bamboozled by The Man" does not suffice to determine either that the consumer has in fact been bamboozled or that they adopt an ironic distance from consumerism. What is decisive is how the consumer actually behaves with regard to material goods, the time and effort spent in the quest for them, the amount of mental energy consumed in thinking about them, the sacrifices made to attain them, the seriousness with which they are regarded, the extent to which one's identity and vision of the future are built around them, the activities and prayers forgone because of them, the communities created around them and the people excluded from such communities, the politics one adopts to defend them, the working and environmental conditions ignored in pursuit of them.

I do not think, however, that Žižek gets it right when he says that the consumer "knows very well" that commodities are not really magic. Žižek draws on Freud's concept of "disavowal," in which a given state of affairs is simultaneously acknowledged and denied because of the formation of a fetish—a sexual fetish, in Freud's case—which preserves an anterior and more comforting belief. Commodity fetishism, however, is not an individual psychological state but a generalized condition of living in a consumer culture, "our real social life," in Žižek's words. And that condition is not one of "knowing very well" but being suspended in a world in which our aspirations to transcendence are constantly being activated. As Francis Mulhern puts it, commodity fetishism "plunges the subject into a primary condition of unknowing, from which neither theoretical elucidation nor social point of vantage can redeem it."[114] For this reason, Mulhern sees commodity fetishism not as knowing acknowledgment of reality accompanied by contradictory behavior, but rather as a state of "fascination." Fascination shares everything with curiosity except for the will to find out more, to get "behind" the object to explore the social relations in which it is embedded. Curiosity is transitive, wanting to move to a better state of knowledge, whereas fascination is intransitive, "fulfilled in the presence of an object that is compelling but opaque."[115]

Mulhern's language here is very close to Marion's in analyzing the idol. In Marion's terms—as discussed in chapter 5—the gaze of idolatry is intransitive. Rather than "transpiercing" an object, it settles and becomes fascinated with it. In so doing, the viewer, Marion says, is not duped but ravished, not fooled but dazzled, so that the gaze settles on an object, and whatever is not aimed at drops out of view. Marion, like Mulhern, gives us a way of articulating the experience of the consumer gaze as something which is neither simply irony nor gullibility. Consumer culture is neither an enlightened state in which we control our enchantment nor a state of simply being manipulated and deluded by marketers. We do not have to choose between seeing the consumer as a rational, buffered self adopting a stance of ironic distance from material goods on the one hand, and seeing the consumer as an easily manipulated chump on the other. The idolization of things, in Marion's terms, invests things with our longings for the divine. In so doing, we subject the divine to the human conditions for experience of the divine, and thus distort the divine, but the experience might not be entirely devoid of some inchoate participation in the divine.

To explore the theme of idolatry in consumer culture is not therefore necessarily to engage in simple jeremiad, to denounce the entire culture as either deluded or willfully sinful. If, as we have seen, all people construct meaning through things, the mere fact that people in consumer culture take goods seriously and use them to construct identities and meaning does not necessarily equate all such activities with the worship of a false god. As I will show in the next chapter, if fetishism is the investment of transcendent power in things, then Christian sacraments have something in common with fetishism. In its original context in African traditions, fetishism is compatible with belief in a supreme being or high god above myriad spirits. Fetishes and their spirits are involved in the day-to-day practicalities of life, and so fetishism may indicate a relative indifference to a high god at the level of everyday life. The mere fact that power is invested in material objects does not necessarily constitute a challenge to the worship of the supreme god. In the Catholic tradition, the location of power in relics can, but does not necessarily, distract from the worship of God. It can be a way of opening daily life and the material world to the reality of transcendence, of recognizing portals to the grace of God in the most mundane incarnations.

Here it is important to remember the point first made in chapter 3, that idolatry is usually a matter of degree. Except in cases where one is deliberately worshiping a named god other than YHWH, idolatry is inordinate devotion to some created thing instead of the Creator. When devotion becomes inordinate is often difficult to discern. There is no simple scale on which to measure at what point one's devotion to a political ideology or to one's retirement account becomes idolatrous. The present analysis is not intended as a how-to guide for discerning when one has crossed the line into idolatry, nor is it intended as a blanket condemnation of an entire culture, with the implication that followers of the true God must flee consumer culture and set up pure enclaves untainted by commodification and marketing, as if that were either possible or desirable. People will of course take all kinds of different stands toward and within consumer culture, immersing themselves in it uncritically, adopting ascetic practices, creatively appropriating different aspects of material culture into a faithful life. The point of the current chapter is to analyze some of the prevailing dynamics of our present consumer culture theologically, both to challenge the common narrative of the secularization of Western culture and to allow for awareness and discernment about how to follow God more faithfully within that culture.

To do so, we need an understanding of the peculiar dynamics of the present moment in history, to understand what has and has not changed. If the simultaneous rise of consumer culture and the decline of Christianity in the

West is not a mere coincidence, then it is worth exploring whether the holy has disappeared or rather migrated from the latter to the former. In this section, I have presented evidence that, for many, consumer culture has invested products and brands with aspirations toward the transcendence of the mundane and the material; that the material has been animated and personalized, as were the gods of old; and that material goods and brands have become a focus of devotion for many people, whether they recognize it or not. Whether or not these types of behavior amount to idolatry depends in part on what has been *displaced* through them. Both the Bible and Augustine, as we saw in chapters 3 and 4, describe our relation to material objects in terms of at least a potential conflict between devotion to them and devotion to God. In Jesus's words, "No one can serve two masters; for a slave will either hate the one and love the other, or be devoted to the one and despise the other. You cannot serve God and wealth" (Mt. 6:24). In Augustine's terms, one must choose between love of God and love of the self. To seek salvation for the self through the things of the world is to neglect the Creator of those things and to condemn both things and the self to nothingness. For Augustine, we may delight in beautiful earthly things, but if we invest eternal longings in them, they will fail to save us. The displacement of God constitutes idolatry. If, therefore, the worship of God has been displaced by devotion to material goods, as many of the above scholars have suggested, then idolatry is a frame on consumer culture worth investigating.

7.3. Dominated by Our Own Creations

So far in this chapter we have explored the investing of divinity in things and the waning of more traditional types of "religious" practice in consumerist culture. What has not been adequately explained, however, is why that movement has taken place. Why does my baloney have a first name? To answer that question I will now turn to Marx's idea of commodity fetishism, which explains the exaltation of commodities in terms of the degradation of human labor, what Marx calls "the conversion of things into persons and the conversion of persons into things," or what Alexandra Dobra calls the symmetrical deification of commodities and reification of human beings.[116] In this section, I will explore another crucial aspect to idolatry that we have discussed in previous chapters: the way in which things react upon their makers and oppress them. In chapter 3 we saw how the Bible depicts an exchange in which idols made of wood and stone take on life while life is drained away from those who make them. Above we discussed the animation of commodities. We will now explore the way that commodification depersonalizes those who make those commodities appear to us.

For Marx, commodities exhibit a dual aspect, as use-values and as exchange-values. A table can be used to write on, and it can also be exchanged for other commodities through the medium of money; I can sell the table for money and buy shoes with the money. How many shoes I can get for a table is a matter of quantitative equivalence. "As use-values, commodities differ above all in quality, while as exchange-values they can only differ in quantity, and therefore do not contain an atom of use-value." Once a thing enters the market, what matters is what it can be exchanged for, not its use-value. Its materiality is, in a sense, transcended:

> It is no longer a table, a house, a piece of yarn or any other useful thing. All its sensuous characteristics are extinguished. Nor is it any longer the product of the labor of the joiner, the mason or the spinner, or of any other particular kind of productive labour. With the disappearance of the useful character of the products of labour, the useful character of the kinds of labour embodied in them also disappears.[117]

In the market, what matters is not what things are used for or the conditions of labor that went into making them; what matters is only what they can be exchanged for. In the market, commodities enter into relationships with each other, and the workers who made them disappear from view.

Marx's expression "fetishism of the commodity" is not a moral judgment about people putting too much importance on material things; rather it is a way of analyzing the manner in which inert material goods are invested with a power of their own that appears to give them agency independent of human control. Marx notes that a commodity at first thought seems to be a mundane and trivial thing, "[b]ut its analysis brings out that it is a very strange thing, abounding in metaphysical subtleties and theological niceties."[118] As a use-value, Marx writes, a table is an ordinary thing made out of wood for human use. "But as soon as it emerges as a commodity, it changes into a thing which transcends sensuousness. It not only stands with its feet on the ground but, in relation to all other commodities, it stands on its head, and evolves out of its wooden brain grotesque ideas far more wonderful than if it were to begin dancing of its own free will."[119]

The exchange-value is an expression of the human labor that went into its production; in capitalism, value—which determines how many tables equal how many shoes—is the "socially necessary labour-time" for the production of a commodity.[120] In the market, however, the social relations of production—who is laboring for whom, under what conditions, and for what pay—are all hidden. All one sees are products that enter into relations of exchange with each other and with consumers. "The mysterious character of the commodity-form consists therefore simply in the fact that the commodity reflects the social characteristics of men's own labour as objective characteristics of the products of labour themselves, as the socionatural properties of these things."[121] In other words, the fetishism of commodities naturalizes properties that are in fact social.

> It is nothing but the definite social relation between men themselves which assumes here, for them, the fantastic form of a relation between things. In order, therefore, to find an analogy we must take flight into the misty realm of religion. There the products of the human brain appear as autonomous figures endowed with a life of their own, which enter into relations both with each other and with the human race. So it is in the world of commodities with the products of men's hands.[122]

Marx explains that producers come into social contact with each other only in the act of exchange, and so social relations "do not appear as direct social relations between persons in their work, but rather as material [*dinglich*, or 'thingly'] relations between persons and social relations between things."[123] Another way he puts this is that in capitalism "persons exist for one another merely as representatives and hence owners, of commodities"—not as persons.[124] Note the inversion of Douglas's analysis, in which things represent human relationships rather than humans appearing as representatives of things. For workers, the result of this inversion of persons and things is that commodities buy people and not vice versa:

> The objective conditions essential to the realization of labour are *alienated* from the worker and become manifest in *fetishes* endowed with a will and soul of their own. *Commodities*, in short, appear as the purchasers of *persons*. . . . It is not the worker who buys the means of production and subsistence, but the means of production that buy the worker to incorporate him into the means of production.[125]

In capitalism, then, we see the kind of inversion that we saw in biblical critiques of idolatry in chapter 3: things are personified, while persons are reified. The flight of commodities into the "misty realm of religion" is accompanied by the simultaneous degradation of human persons through their disappearance from view. From the point of view of the consumer, the whole process has been excarnated. When shopping on Amazon, one enters into a strangely dehumanized world populated only by commodities. One is immersed in a sea of images of products, all beckoning for our attention, but there are no humans; the workers who make the products and deliver them to our doorsteps are invisible. It is extremely difficult to find out anything about the wages people earn, the conditions under which they work, the environmental impact of the manufacturing process, and so on. Human social relations have been replaced with relations among commodities, while workers are often treated like things—watched over by robots—from which the maximum of productivity must be extracted.

Exploitative economic relations are nothing new in history. As Marx points out, the serf in medieval times worked for the lord in a relationship of personal dependence. "But precisely because relations of personal dependence form the given social foundation, there is no need for labour and its products to assume a fantastic form different from their reality."[126] Serfs knew exactly how much of their crop was due to their lord, and how much of their own personal labor-power they expended in producing that crop. "Whatever we may think, then, of the different roles in which men confront each other in such a society, the social relations between individuals in the performance of their labour appear at all events as their own personal relations, and are not disguised as social relations between things, between the products of labour."[127] Relations were exploitative, but serfs knew for whom they were working and the lord knew whence the produce on his table came. Today, by contrast, warehouse or factory workers are often managed anonymously, according to algorithms, have their hours and pay set by impersonal "market forces," and the fruits of their labors accrue to anonymous shareholders unknown and unknowable to the worker.

As Marx points out, however, in a capitalist market control of the system also eludes the owners of capital. Exchange-value—one ton of iron for two ounces of gold, for example—is beyond the will and actions of the exchangers: "Their own movement within society has for them the form of a movement made by things, and these things, far from being under their control, in fact control them."[128] This arrangement is, furthermore, thought to be subject to certain iron-clad economic "laws" that must be obeyed as if they were simply natural laws, like that governing gravity. Fetishism comes with a certain kind of fatalism; we believe we are fated to obey forces beyond our control, and we cannot change them. Marx writes of the labor theory of value under capitalism:

> These formulas, which bear the unmistakable stamp of belonging to a so-cial formation in which the process of production has mastery over man, instead of the opposite, appear to the political economists' bourgeois con-sciousness to be as much a self-evident and nature-imposed necessity as productive labour itself. Hence the pre-bourgeois forms of the social organ-ization of production are treated by political economy in much the same way as the Fathers of the Church treated pre-Christian religions.[129]

Again and again, Marx has recourse to the analogy between capitalism and religion: "Just as man is governed, in religion, by the products of his own brain, so, in capitalist production, he is governed by the products of his own hand."[130] Marx sees the supposed laws of capitalism in the same way as he sees the laws handed down by the biblical God: as the contingent self-alienation of human consciousness and the oppression of human beings by our own creations. Marx believes that we will be liberated from the oppres-sion of idolatry when no gods are worshiped; the followers of the Abrahamic traditions believe we will be liberated from the oppression of idolatry when no gods are worshiped but the one true God.

Just as we saw in Weber in chapter 1, for Marx it is not capitalists but capital that dominates. In addition to the fetishism of commodities, Marx identifies the fetishism of capital, that is, the attribution of independent and transcendent power to what is in fact a creation of human labor. In a capitalist economy, surplus value is the product of surplus physical produc-tion, that is, the creation of more use-value than is consumed in the process of production. New things are made by human labor employing the means of production and sold at a profit.[131] Both the means of production (as con-stant capital) and labor power (as variable capital) are available only as cap-ital.[132] Because labor power is activated only by capital, which hires labor and thereby "creates" jobs, the whole process of the production of goods appears to be owed to capital, rather than capital being the product of human labor. The extra productive power that comes from the combination of many laborers together is attributed to capital: "Because this power costs capital nothing, while on the other hand it is not developed by the worker until his labour itself belongs to capital, it appears as a power which capital possesses by its nature—a productive power inherent in capital."[133] This is the fetishism of capital, the attribution of autonomous productive power to capital which in fact derives from labor. In capitalism, labor appears powerless outside its relationship with capital, because workers have nothing but the labor of their own bodies to sell in the market. And so there is a strange inversion in the meaning of the word "manufacture," which derives from the Latin for "made" (*factum*) "by hand" (*manu*). The "manufacturer" is now the capitalist, who makes nothing by hand, and the worker is nothing more than an instrument or tool of capital.[134] Interest-bearing capital takes this fetishism to a higher level, because capital appears to multiply itself without any involvement of labor. "In interest-bearing capital, therefore, this automatic fetish, self-expanding value, money generating money, are brought out in their pure state and in this form it no longer bears the birthmarks of its origin."[135]

Marx describes interest-bearing capital in biblical language as a god who devours humans: "In its capacity of interest-bearing capital, capital claims the ownership of all wealth which can ever be produced, and everything it has received so far is but an instalment for its all-engrossing appetite. By its innate laws, all surplus-labour which the human race can ever perform belongs to it. Moloch."[136] With one word Marx identifies interest-bearing capital with the Canaanite god associated with child sacrifice (Lev. 18:21, 20:2–5; II Kings 23:10; Jer. 32:35; Acts 7:43). In choosing this image, Marx no doubt had in mind the conditions for child laborers he quotes in detail from British government reports on the matter: children as young as eight labored in brutal conditions, some working eighteen-hour shifts daily for weeks at a time, with factories employing children around the clock. Presiding over this sacrifice is the god capital, for whom capitalists act as mere spokespersons. "Let us now hear how capital itself regards this 24-hour system. The extreme forms of the system, its abuse in the 'cruel and incredible' extension of the working day, are naturally passed over in silence. Capital only speaks of the system in its 'normal' form."[137] The reports quote the voice of capital speaking through factory owners: child labor employed twenty-four hours a day was necessary to avoid the waste of fuel and loss of time involved in restarting the furnaces. "[T]he furnaces themselves would suffer from the changes of temperature," one factory owner reports, while Marx notes that the waste, loss, and suffering of human children go unnoticed.[138] Both the furnaces and capital itself are personified, while both capitalists and workers are turned into instruments, with the workers bearing the pain.

Marx has frequent recourse to Christian, often biblical, language to describe the miraculous powers of the money god. Money is transcendent and
eternal because it permits the real social wealth produced by human labor
to be captured and hoarded, where—Marx says, quoting Jesus (Mt. 6:20)—
"neither moth nor rust could destroy."[139] Money's power is absolute, for everything is convertible into money, everything can be bought and sold; there
are no holy things beyond human commerce, and even "the bones of the
saints cannot withstand it." As a result, Marx quotes Christopher Columbus,
"Gold can even enable souls to enter Paradise."[140] And so the bourgeois
puts his trust in this new god to save him; sardonically paraphrasing Psalm
42, Marx writes, "As the hart pants after fresh water, so pants his soul after
money, the only wealth."[141] The pursuit of money becomes a replacement
for Christianity: "It was the 'strange God' who perched himself side by side
with the old divinities of Europe on the altar, and one fine day threw them all
overboard with a shove and a kick. It proclaimed the making of profit as the
ultimate and sole purpose of mankind."[142] Marx does not lament the loss of
the Christian God, but he does not like the looks of the new god either. He
equates money with the beast of the book of Revelation, quoting in Latin
both Revevlation 17:13, "These are united in yielding their power and authority to the beast," and 13:17, "So that no one can buy or sell who does not
have the mark, that is, the name of the beast or the number of its name."[143]

Starting in the 1970s, Marx's analysis of commodity, capital, and money
fetishism was taken up by Latin American liberation theologians into a theological critique of capitalism as idolatry.[144] While the Catholic Church in
Latin America had long considered atheistic Marxism a threat, liberation
theologians made common cause with Marxists by arguing that atheism
is not the problem in Latin America; the problem is instead the worship of
a false god, capitalism.[145] It is the idolatry of capitalism that keeps the majority of people in Latin America poor and oppressed. Liberation theologians
argue that Christians need to learn from Marx to denounce false religion, including certain dominant manifestations of Christianity, that serves merely
as an opiate for the masses. In this sense, writes Victorio Araya, Christians
need to be atheists.[146] Liberation theologians go beyond Marx, however, in
recognizing a true God who liberates from the oppression of the false gods.
The Bible is read as a contest between the God of life and the idols of death.[147]
Hugo Assmann rejects Marx's reliance on Feuerbach, for whom God is a
mere projection of human aspirations. The capital god is not a simple projection, writes Assmann, but is in fact a *deus absconditus*, a hidden god whose

quintessence is its invisibility.[148] Assmann contrasts the absolute, abstract, and spiritual god of the rich with the unpredictable, incarnate, and material-istic God of Jesus Christ.[149]

Perhaps the most significant engagement of Latin American libera-tion theology with the theme of commodity fetishism and idolatry is Franz Hinkelammert's 1977 book *The Ideological Weapons of Death*. Through a close reading of Marx, Hinkelammert emphasizes the way that commodities take on life in the market economy: in Latin America, coal battles oil, ar-tificial nitrate defeats natural nitrate, corporations marry one another, and so on.[150] Behind this apparent polytheism, however, there is a more basic monotheism of capital, the unifying force behind all commodities.[151] The life or death of the worker is in the hands of capital; workers die, but cap-ital is immortal. When artificial nitrate defeats natural nitrate, thousands of workers are thrown into misery, relegated to poverty, nonhuman status, and death.[152] Hinkelammert emphasizes, however, that when commodities do battle, it is not because they are under the control of their owners: "Even if the commodity character of production is a human product, it is a product that gets beyond the control of human beings."[153] The sense that capital owns the worker is most intensely experienced in the confrontation of worker and machine:

> Here the confrontation is not experienced as being with the capitalist, who is usually not there to be seen, but with the machinery itself. Only in the machine is capital present as owning the worker. Although it is really only a tool it becomes something different—that is, a mechanism of pro-duction, whose organs are human beings. . . . The worker who belongs to capital undergoes the experience of being converted into a part of some machinery. It is now the machinery that exercises the right to decide over the worker's life or death.[154]

Does all this emphasis on the rule of capital, not capitalists, let capitalists off the hook? Are capitalists, then, just as powerless as workers in the face of capital or the "laws" of the market? Hinkelammert is not trying to ab-solve capitalists of responsibility; indeed idolatry is the refusal to accept responsibility for the consequences of the whole human-made apparatus. Hinkelammert sees subjection to the capital god as "a situation in which human beings have delegated the decision-making power over their own life or death to a commodity mechanism for whose results they do not accept responsibility—even though this mechanism is the work of their own hands."[155] As with biblical idolatry, human beings are both dominated by their own creations and culpable for their own subjection. As Gustavo Gutiérrez writes, not only the oppressed but the oppressors as well need to be liberated. Class struggle is better understood in terms of the universality of Christian love: "Universal love is that which in solidarity with the oppressed seeks also to liberate the oppressors from their own power, from their ambition, and from their selfishness. . . . One loves the oppressors by liberating them from their inhuman condition as oppressors, by liberating them from themselves."[156] As Augustine emphasizes, idolatry is essentially being entrapped in the self, from which one must be liberated by a love that comes from without.

Marx wrote in the context of laissez-faire industrialization in England, before laws were passed to restrict child labor, limit the workweek, and protect collective bargaining. The first generation of liberation theologians wrote in the context of vast inequality in Latin America between the small minority who owned the means of production—land and factories—and the large majority of poor laborers. Those of us now living in the Global North might be tempted to consign the critique of idolatry in capitalism to other times and other places. But if we look at some of the major developments in capitalism since Marx wrote—the deskilling of labor, globalization, financialization and the growth of debt, the ubiquity of marketing, surveillance capitalism, and the commodification of the self—we see that the basic twinned dynamic of the personification of commodities and capital on the one hand and the instrumentalization of human beings on the other applies in every case. As in biblical idolatry, material things are empowered, while human beings are disempowered and made subject to their own creations.

7.3.1. Deskilling of Labor

Beginning in the 1890s, Frederick Taylor spread the gospel of "scientific management" in industry. Taylor had determined that manufacturing was inefficient; skilled laborers held too much power over production and did not work as hard as they could for maximum productivity. Taylor's solution was to break the manufacturing process into discrete elements and remove, as he said, "all possible brain work from the shop." Instead, management would gather "all of the traditional knowledge which in the past has been possessed by the workmen"[157] and direct production scientifically. Breaking down the manufacturing process into brainless operations made for greater efficiency and allowed the manager to work the laborers harder, since unskilled labor occupied an inferior negotiating position. But the rewards of consumer culture could also be used to incentivize more work. Taylor tells the story of "Schmidt," a pig-iron worker with sufficient energy remaining at the end of the workday to work on his own house. Taylor incentivized a 400% increase in Schmidt's workload with a 60% increase in pay. Now, with more money and less energy remaining after work, the home became a locus of consumption rather than production, and demand for manufactured goods increased. At the same time, craft traditions in the workplace were largely eliminated.[158]

The deskilling of labor is not just a past episode in the history of capitalism; it continues to mark the way most of us deal with the material world. As Matthew Crawford points out, the goal of management continues to be the transfer of knowledge, skill, and decision-making from employee to manager, even in white-collar work. Consumer culture simultaneously diminishes our agency: what we once made we now buy, and what we once fixed ourselves we now either hire someone to fix or we throw the item out and buy a new one. Cars and appliances are increasingly engineered to hide their inner workings from the curious. Shop class as a standard feature of high school is largely gone, in favor of "a vision of the future in which we somehow take leave of material reality and glide about in a pure information economy."[159] As a result of this excarnation, we have a more passive and dependent relationship with things. "Both as workers and as consumers, we feel we move in channels that have been projected from afar by vast impersonal forces."[160] As consumers we are in the thrall of things, while as workers we are tools to be used to generate profit for others.

7.3.2. Globalization

The exploitation of human labor that Marx detailed has been ameliorated in many places in the West, but since the 1970s production has been moved to places—Asia especially—where Moloch still devours those whose desperation leaves them with few other choices but to take sweatshop employment. As of 2021, the minimum wage for garment workers in Sri Lanka was $54 *a month*, about one-eighth of the estimated living wage in that country.[161] Low wages, abusive and dangerous working conditions, and environmental degradation are the norm in many places that manufacture the goods consumed in the West, but the situation of workers is largely hidden from our view, both by the geographical distance between us in the West and the people who manufacture our stuff, and by the fetishism of commodities by which we see things rather than people. There has been no shortage of exposés of low wages, brutal conditions, and child labor in overseas production over the past several decades.[162] The Rana Plaza garment factory collapse in Bangladesh in 2013 that killed over eleven hundred workers was bad enough to garner some notice in the West, but the attention span of those who enjoy cheap consumer products has not yet been long enough to demand and achieve significant change.[163]

7.3.3. Financialization

The "financialization" of the world economy since the 1980s seems to support the illusion Marx pointed out more than a century earlier, that capital can simply create more capital, even if none of it is used productively. Profit is made increasingly by debt and financial instruments like futures and derivatives rather than by production of commodities. For a variety of reasons, in recent decades the rate of profit to be made by producing goods has fallen below the rate of profit to be made through finance. General Motors can make more money from car loans than from the manufacture of cars.[164] Profit has been pursued increasingly by inflating the prices of already existing assets, such as real estate and stocks, which produces speculative bubbles and increasing inequality between the owners of capital and workers.[165] Because profit can appear without the production of anything new, the tendency to fetishize capital as if it were itself inherently productive is increased.

The financialization of the economy intensifies the disciplining effects of the market. The only goal of the corporation is to increase its stock price and thus reward shareholders. It is not good enough to make sufficient profit to pay workers and overhead costs with enough left over to invest in future equipment needs. Profit must be maximized to keep shareholder value high and prevent hostile takeovers. Workers are pressed toward maximum efficiency, jobs are outsourced to places where wages and working conditions are poor, and the economy replaces good-paying and stable jobs with demands for worker "flexibility." While Taylor incentivized hard work through increased pay, finance capitalism prefers to do so through fear of being replaced, either by cheaper, part-time workers or by automation.[166] Workers are increasingly trying to get by with multiple jobs without benefits. In such a situation, workers are more likely to take on debt, which increases their servitude to finance capitalism, which thrives on loans. Unlike an economy geared toward the production of goods and services, finance capitalism can thrive amid recession and high unemployment, as desperate people turn to loans in order to get by. Governments are less likely to help if they have heeded corporate demands for ever lower taxes, which leaves governments without the money necessary to provide a social safety net and, increasingly, needing money to service their own debt.[167] In finance capitalism, individuals turn to debt to attain what corporations and governments no longer provide: a living wage, education, and healthcare. The result of taking on debt, as Kathryn Tanner puts it, is that "workers are chained to the past even as their employers are freed from it."[168]

In his *Theology of Money*, Philip Goodchild writes, "A market based on debt money is an immanent system of credits and liabilities, of debts and obligations, and it is capable of unlimited growth. It ensures participation and cohesion, with promises of wealth and threats of exclusion, through a system of social obligations. Debt takes over the role of religion in economic life."[169] Debt is a system of social obligations in which money takes the role that God played in medieval life: as the guarantor of value. Money and God compete for worship, and also for the way that time, attention, and devotion are socially organized.[170] One essential difference between the two faiths is modernity's lack of consciousness of the transcendence of money.[171] We think of money as mundane and immanent, but in fact the value of money is a promise, taken on faith. "Being transcendent to material and social reality, yet also being the pivot around which material and social reality is continually reconstructed, financial value is essentially religious."[172] The two faith traditions also differ in substance: "Where God offers himself as grace, money offers itself as a loan."[173] The value of money in the debt economy is furthermore backed by contracted servitude, the exploitation of human labor and of the earth. Excarnation is only from the point of view of the consumer. "The value of money is still paid for in flesh and blood."[174]

7.3.4. Marketing

The disciplining of workers is accompanied by the disciplining of consumers. As I have already indicated, it is possible to exaggerate the power that marketing has over consumer choice, to present consumers as if they were puppets controlled by others. Some scholarship since the 1980s has emphasized the agency that consumers employ in constructing diverse identities through material things. As I noted in chapter 2, however, such studies tend to focus on the micro level to the exclusion of the macro level. As even a sympathetic critic like Roberta Sassatelli acknowledges, there is an asymmetry of power between consumers and producers: "If it is true that consumption is subjectively more important than production for many people, it is also true that, at the systemic level, producers and distributors are more powerful than consumers. In other words, private rebels may not become public revolutionaries."[175] Marketing is not robotic control but rather sets the parameters in which individual choices are made.

Marketing presents itself in two mutually contradictory ways. To consumers, it sells the idea of "consumer sovereignty," the idea that the consumer is in control and that consumer demand drives production. Marketing is simply a way of connecting consumers with the products they want. To businesses, marketing touts its power to influence consumers to do what businesses want them to do. A study of articles in the *Journal of Marketing* shows this dual approach, extolling the consumer as king while simultaneously selling marketers' ability to control consumer behavior. Consumers are defined as "targets" rather than sovereigns.[176] This dual self-presentation may seem like a contradiction, but convincing consumers that they are in control is essential to influencing them. Marketing works in part because none of us thinks it works on *me*.

Some critics have noted that the scientific management techniques that Taylorism applied to workers have been applied by marketing firms to consumers. The goal and procedure are similar: apply scientific technique to control human behavior for the benefit of the producer.[177] Consumers, however, are not under the same direct control by producers as workers are. To describe the kind of power that marketing exerts over consumers, therefore, many scholars refer to Michel Foucault's concept of "governmentality," a diffuse form of control that works through a complex constellation of institutions and procedures through which people are formed.[178] In Foucault's concept, freedom and power are not mutually opposed; power operates through the choices that people make. It is not a matter of seeing consumers either as puppets or as fully sovereign choosers. It is rather a matter of people becoming self-disciplining by choosing within a matrix of different techniques of power. Marketing encourages people, above all, to define themselves as consumers, to take their position in a capitalist economy through the mechanism of their own free choices, putting together a lifestyle and an identity through the purchase of goods in a way that feels, at the micro level, like freedom and self-expression.[179] There is, as I discussed in chapter 2, a hegemony of optionality; one has no choice but to be a consumer.

There is a sense in which the consumer is not just the passive target of marketing but in fact is actually working for marketers. Jhally argues that watching television is a form of labor which produces surplus-value for media companies, with the nonadvertising programming as the "wages" of the audience.[180] More recently, the line between work and consumption has been blurred by viral ads, which depend on our free choice to send them on to others, which again produces surplus-value for marketers and producers. Brand communities—fans of a particular brand who gather online or in person to celebrate their devotion to a brand of products—are another unpaid way that consumers actively create surplus-value for corporations.[181] The concept of governmentality captures this dynamic of being willing participants in our own discipline.

7.3.5. Surveillance Capitalism

Foucault famously used the image of Jeremy Bentham's Panopticon to illustrate how governmentality works through surveillance. Bentham's model for a prison arranged the cells in a circular configuration around a central guard tower from which the guard could see into any cell at any time. The prisoners could not see each other or see whether or not they were being watched, so they would learn to become self-disciplining, internalizing the guard in the tower.[182] The same kind of surveillance and self-discipline characterize marketing today. Marketers gather information on individual consumers in an attempt to understand their motivations and desires in order to influence their purchases. Though the purchases remain subject to free choice, they are channeled into predetermined routes for consumption based on the marketers' surveillance of the consumer's habits. The feedback loop of surveillance and choice becomes a kind of panoptical self-discipline as the consumer responds to stimuli directed by the marketer's superior knowledge of the consumer. Through marketing, producers do not simply respond to consumer desire but help produce it.[183] The effect is less like brainwashing, as Michael Budde remarks, and more like playing poker against an opponent who can see your hand.[184]

Surveillance of our habits has become increasingly sophisticated. Crude instruments like surveys and focus groups—which rely on people's willingness and ability to communicate their preferences—have been eclipsed by "neuromarketing," which records various kinds of emotional and cognitive brain activity in response to various brands and products. Neuromarketing, however, is so far limited to laboratory settings. Big data tracking, on the other hand, now allows for the monitoring of what millions of people actually do in the real world, and at an individual level, allowing marketers to target people in ways tailored to their individual profiles. In-store retailer tracking has moved from cameras to the use of customers' Wi-Fi–enabled smartphones, Bluetooth, and GPS to track customers inside and outside the store. Downloading a retailer's app and joining their loyalty program allows further gathering of information. The most pervasive and thorough form of surveillance, of course, is the data mining carried out on individuals' internet browsing habits, cellphone use, and social media interactions. The business model of Google, Facebook, and other gargantuan media companies is generally to provide their services for "free," making billions in profits only by selling individuals' data to marketers.[185]

In her important work on the rise of "surveillance capitalism," Shoshana Zuboff has argued that the mining of personal data for sale by Google, Facebook, Verizon, and others is the most recent mutation of primitive accumulation.[186] Human experience is like "virgin" land was to the colonists. Without our knowledge or consent, our online habits—and increasingly our movements in the world of things—are tracked and mined to establish behavioral profiles of individual users that are then sold to marketers who target us with increasingly successful attempts at behavior modification. Each individual's behavior, tracked through online activity and "smart" devices and spaces, becomes a kind of behavioral surplus that is expropriated by powerful others for the sake of profit. The process is marked by a drastic asymmetry of knowledge and power; they know all about us, but their operations are unknowable to us. Whereas industrial capitalism thrived at the expense of nature, surveillance capitalism thrives at the expense of human nature. Humans are the "sources of raw-material supply" for surveillance capitalism;[187] "ownership of the new means of behavioral modification eclipses the ownership of the means of production as the fountainhead of capitalist wealth and power in the twenty-first century."[188]

7.3.6. The Commodification of the Self

As commentators have noted with regard to "free" services like Google and Facebook, if you are not paying for the product, you *are* the product. The data of your life are being sold to marketers so that producers can sell you products. In ways that Marx never foresaw, the reification of human beings applies not only to workers but to consumers. We are constantly encouraged to curate our image on social media.[189] There is an entire industry of helping people brand themselves. As Alison Hearn comments, "Here we see the self as a commodity for sale in the labour market, which must generate its own rhetorically persuasive packaging, its own promotional skin, within the confines of the dominant corporate imaginary."[190] Zygmunt Bauman notes that people are not seen as belonging by birth to a community that cares for them in a circle of mutual responsibility; in a market society, they belong by making themselves marketable.[191] Humans are increasingly defined as entrepreneurs of the self. One has capital in one's person, and one must use it to earn profit in the marketplace, where one is responsible for oneself. The self has become a commodity.[192]

In this section of the chapter I have tried to show the flip side of the exaltation of material things in the subjection of human beings to their own creations. The human labor that produces commodities and capital is hidden, and commodities and capital take on a life of their own, as if they were the creators of work for humans, instead of the other way around. Workers are thus subject to exploitation, and even capitalists feel that they must bow before and obey the "laws" of the market. Consumers as well are subject to various forms of surveillance and discipline, to the point that the human person is defined not only as a consumer of commodities but as a commodity itself. The basic biblical theme of idolatry is everywhere manifest: the investing of divinity in created things leads to the subjection of human beings.

The root of the ecological crisis is often said to be anthropocentrism; figures as different as Lynn White and Pope Francis agree on this diagnosis.[193] The critique of anthropocentrism is not without merit: humanity in the aggregate has certainly assumed a position of domination and exploitation of the world's resources, with devastating consequences for the other living things on the planet, both animals and plants. Nevertheless, there is something important missing in this critique. In the first place, the critique of anthropocentrism treats humanity, or "man," in the aggregate and does not distinguish among (1) the captains of industry whose constant search for shareholder value drives ecological degradation; (2) the relatively affluent consumers whose lifestyle demands the continued exploitation of natural resources; (3) the billions whose levels of consumption barely rise above subsistence; and (4) the workers whose labor constitutes another resource to be exploited. The critique of anthropocentrism, in other words, tends to avoid class analysis, and is therefore too blunt an instrument.[194] In the second place, even people in affluent consumer cultures often experience the contemporary economy not as domination but as powerlessness; we feel like cogs, not masters. In some ways, the critique of commodity fetishism reveals the opposite of anthropocentrism; it is things, not people, that have been put at the center.

7.4. Unsplendid Idolatry

It is possible that this emphasis on subjection lets consumers off the hook too easily. Are we simply caught in a matrix over which we have no control? Does the above analysis encourage fatalism, a sense that we are subject to powers beyond our comprehension and ability to manage, so we might as well just keep clicking on Amazon.com? Or is it rather the case that our subjection is just the flip side of our narcissism? Is our subjection to idols not a consequence of our culpable self-love and self-worship, as in Augustine and Marion?

Unlike the splendid idolatry of nationalism, which invites the virtues of self-sacrifice for others and for a cause larger than oneself, consumer culture is focused on the self and one's own desires. As management guru Peter Drucker has written, the consumer's "only question is—and should be: 'What does this do for *me*?'"[195] Bernd Wannenwetsch has argued that the self—not any material object—is the true idol of consumer culture. As material things have taken flight, as advertising has focused on identifying with a brand rather than on the products themselves, it has become increasingly apparent that the self and its desires are the true object of worship: "Actual products are reduced to mere footnotes in a drama which features desire as a one-man show."[196] Created things are not as important as the self's desire, the desire for desire. The covetousness that Paul (Rom. 7:7) condemns without mentioning any particular object of desire is now the central virtue of our political economy: the need for desire to move restlessly from one object to another in order to keep the wheels of production moving. For capitalism, then, "the secret idol of its economy of desire has always been man him-self."[197] As we saw with Augustine in chapter 4, the love of money and things is not desired for their own sake but as a means for the aggrandizement of the self.

There is a significant amount of scholarly work connecting consumer culture to narcissism. In a review of such scholarship, a team of British psychologists notes that, in general, studies of consumer behavior no longer depict consumers as rational choosers doing cost-benefit analyses. Consumers do often choose for utilitarian reasons, but the preponderance of studies done over the past few decades has emphasized the importance of consumer behavior for constructing the self. Consumer behavior is based more on the symbolic than on the functional features of commodities, though the latter are not unimportant. The authors cite numerous studies showing that consumers "purchase products as means to define and express themselves, to regulate their moods or emotions, to bolster their self-esteem or gain social status, and to fulfil their needs for self-efficacy or mastery. Thus, self-oriented considerations often underlie consumer decision and behavior."[198] They go on to cite studies in self-congruity theory showing that consumers use products and brands that are seen to have personality traits that mirror those of the consumer's preferred self-image, and often use purchases to compensate for self-image impairment.[199]

This mirroring effect is relevant to the British team's main goal, which is to study the connection between narcissism and consumer behavior. Narcissism is defined as an "agentic, egocentric, self-aggrandizing, domi-nant, and manipulative orientation" that is accompanied by a lack of regard for others.[200] Narcissism has a very high correlation with conspicuous con-sumption in an effort to boost social status and self-esteem. Narcissists are fo-cused on the symbolic, rather than functional, importance of commodities, and the symbolism of the products they purchase is often used to compen-sate for fragile egos and fluctuating self-esteem. The British team is interested in studying the consumer behavior of narcissists, but they are also interested in the narcissism of consumer behavior more broadly. They write, "[I]t has been suggested that the emphasis on consumerism prevalent in contempo-rary society sparks increases in narcissism." They cite evidence that narcis-sism is on the rise in both Western cultures and China, point to the emphasis of advertising on self-regard, and argue that consumerism "may exacer-bate the signature narcissistic characteristics: self-sufficiency or autonomy, egocentricity, competitiveness, unwillingness to help, and poor interpersonal relationships."[201]

Matthew Crawford connects consumer culture and narcissism in terms of our relationships with the material world. Being engaged with material reality—making things and having to learn how to fix them—means taking a humble and attentive stance before the material world, being schooled by it. Virtue requires this act of "unselfing." Consumer culture, on the other hand, fosters a type of infantile narcissism in which the individual is encouraged to see the world of objects as extensions of their will. We try to put our stamp on the world by buying things. Consumerism invites magical thinking and delusions of omnipotence, with freedom and fulfillment of our wants available at the click of the mouse. When things break or otherwise fail to deliver freedom, it is an affront to our self-absorption, and we find ourselves increasingly dependent on objects that we cannot fix and do not understand:[202] "The growing dependence of individuals in *fact* is accompanied by ever more shrill invocations of freedom in *theory*, that is, in the ideology of consumerism. Paradoxically, we are narcissistic but not proud enough."[203] As in Augustine, attempts to aggrandize oneself through the material world only lead to the subservience of the self to created reality. Narcissism and idolatry are two sides of the same coin, and they lead to the diminution of the self. True freedom is found in service to the Creator of that material world; a healthy engagement with the material world requires humility. Crawford expresses the paradox this way:

> There seems to be an ideology of freedom at the heart of consumerist material culture; a promise to disburden us of mental and bodily involvement with our own stuff so we can pursue ends we have freely chosen. Yet this disburdening gives us fewer occasions for the experience of direct responsibility. I believe the appeal of freedomism, as a marketing hook, is due to the fact it nonetheless captures something true. It points to a paradox in our experience of agency: to be master of your own stuff entails also being mastered by it.[204]

Or as Augustine might put it in more explicitly theological terms, being free of idolatrous subservience to created things requires doing service to the presence of God in all things. Once we humbly see that the true purpose of material reality is not the aggrandizement of the self at the expense of others, we can penetrate to the true nature of things and use them in service to their Creator and to our fellow creatures.

While Crawford concentrates on the way consumer narcissism distorts our relationship to things, we need also to consider what it does to our relationships with other people. Why do consumers continue to take advantage of the inequalities in power that deliver products to us cheaply and conveniently at the expense of low wages and miserable working conditions for laborers and the ongoing destruction of the environment? For Marx, as we have seen, commodities hide the conditions of their production; we see the gleaming products and the price and have no idea of how the materials to make them were sourced, where and how they are made, how much the people who make them and bring them to us are paid, and so on. But today we do not simply stand behind a veil of ignorance about the conditions of production. We now know that our clothes are made in sweatshops, and we buy them anyway. To be aware of and troubled by the conditions of production makes little difference.

Michael Billig suggests that we need to supplement Marx's analysis of commodity fetishism with Freud's concept of repression, the willful forgetting of what we know about the social relations of production. My enjoyment of my stuff would be spoiled if I thought too long and hard about the young Thai girls who made my things or the use of fossil fuels in their manufacture and delivery, so I repress that knowledge. In Freud, repression is society's way of keeping the pleasure principle in check, but consumer culture depends on the pleasure principle to perpetuate itself. Repression today, then, is something different from what Freud imagined: we repress the knowledge that would ruin our pleasure. Freud had a rigid distinction between the conscious and the unconscious in the individual, but capitalism transcends this difference. Repression is a routine, collective ideological practice, social and not individual. We are not completely unaware of labor conditions and environmental destruction, but we keep ourselves distracted from making any significant changes by busyness and the volume of information and entertainment we receive through media. We buy a few Fair Trade products and tell ourselves that we have done our part to solve the problem.[205]

Robert Cluley and Stephen Dunne go further in exploring the dark side of consumer narcissism. Like Billig, Cluley and Dunne turn from Marx's concept of fetishism to Freud's. For Freud, a fetish is a substitute that helps one cope with traumatic reality; it is not ignorance but a refusal to know, motivated by our desires and wishes.[206] There is no benevolent and sovereign consumer subject who becomes self-contradictory in a capitalist society; rather the human subject as such is self-contradictory, both altruistic and selfish, aware and unaware, rational and irrational. Freud connects consumerism to narcissism directly in his discussion of how parents shower their children with gifts as a way to satisfy their own narcissistic desires, while simultaneously thinking of themselves as altruistic.[207] Cluley and Dunne inflate Freud's account of parental narcissism into a general theory of narcissism and consumption, understood as inherently cruel to others: "The knowledge of other people's suffering that our consumption perpetuates is precisely what satisfies our destructive and narcissistic desires, in this sense. This sadistic pleasure, according to Freud, is precisely what affords 'the narcissistic satisfaction of being able to think oneself better than others.'"[208] According to Cluley and Dunne, we consume *in order to* deprive and harm others, so that we can express our narcissistic desire to elevate ourselves above the herd. Freud says that it is impossible for a human to live with others without occasionally giving in to "the temptation to ill-treat his neighbour."[209] Though narcissism is the key concept here, fetishism remains relevant, in the sense that we need to refuse to know this unpleasant fact about ourselves, and so we continue to come up with alternative explanations for why we consume in ways that harm others, despite our professed concern for them.

Adam Smith famously wrote, "It is not from the benevolence of the butcher, the brewer, or the baker that we expect our dinner, but from their regard to their own self-interest. We address ourselves not to their humanity but to their *self-love*, and never talk to them of our own necessities, but of their advantages."[210] Cluley and Dunne want to extend Smith's analysis of the narcissism of the producer to that of the consumer as well, and they want to include an element of malevolence, not simply a lack of benevolence. In their words, commodity narcissism is not simply an "other-denying self-interest" but an "other-abasing self-love."[211] By invoking Freud, Cluley and Dunne suggest that the sadism of consumerism is not simply a structural feature of the capitalist economy, but is part of the psychological makeup of the human person as such.[212]

A Christian account of the human person will be more skeptical of the idea that sadism is simply hardwired into human psychology; the human condition is more ambivalent. People communicate with each other through material goods, as they always have, for better and for worse. In this chapter, I am interested less in a transhistorical human anthropology and more in the particularities of our contemporary society and economy. Today, more than in the past, we communicate through purchases, but it is clearly not the case that every purchase is an act of narcissism, nor is it the case that every commodity is the product of exploited labor. There is no single monolithic culture that one must either accept or reject, and, although it is accurate to talk about a dominant consumer culture in many societies, people adopt all kinds of different practices within those societies. Idolatry, as I have argued throughout, is on a sliding scale of more and less and requires case-by-case discernment.

Nevertheless, there are, as I have argued in this chapter, good grounds for identifying the particular ways the dominant consumer culture as such lends itself to idolatry. Consumer culture both encourages investing divinity in human creations and has structural features which allow those creations to subject us to their rule. Consumer culture also promotes a type of unsplendid idolatry, a narcissism that does not encourage self-sacrifice for others but rather encourages the sacrifice of others for our own desires. Cluley and Dunne's analysis is helpful for its focus on malevolence. We like to tell ourselves that we would never intentionally make other people suffer for our comfort, but in fact other people *do* suffer for our comfort, and the reality is so widespread, systemic, and brutal that it is worth inquiring whether or not there is culpable malevolence involved rather than mere unwitting complicity. There is an ugly violence in the exploitation of workers and the destruction of God's creation; we need to view clearly the effects on others of how our desires are stoked and satisfied in the contemporary economy. Consideration of the malevolent side of consumer narcissism at least does not allow us to minimize or excuse the damage that our actions do. We are not simply innocents with no knowledge of or responsibility for the misery and devastation that fall on the backs of the billions of people who make possible the comfortable lives of the few. Both the Bible and Augustine make clear that idolatry is culpable. Those whose loves are not referred to the true God are in fact guilty of self-love, which is not a true care for the person that God loves but a self- and other-destructive isolation from the common good.

At the same time, and without minimizing the seriousness of our collective sin, the concept of idolatry that we have explored allows for a certain sympathetic take on the human condition. Augustine and Freud might not agree on much, but they both see the human person as divided and self-contradictory. Sadism mingles with altruism in the human soul. We do what we do not intend. We lie to ourselves and repress our true desires. For Augustine, our true desire is God, and we restlessly move from one created thing to another, searching for God in all the wrong places. We try to find love by loving our-selves, fleeing from the truth that we can find love only by accepting the love that comes from outside the confines of the self. Idolatry, as Augustine sees it, is rooted in our restless search for God, a search that gets sidetracked by the very beauty of God's creation. Augustine might even acknowledge some-thing splendid buried deep in our attempts to reach out to God and to one another through our purchase and display of material things.

As I have already noted, Marion also allows for a sympathetic approach to idolatry. We do not simply have bad values and choose to follow Mammon rather than God. We are instead fascinated, overwhelmed, dazzled, ravished by the attractive things of this world, and they blot out the visibility of all else, including, Marx suggests, the social conditions of their production. As we saw in chapter 5, however, in his later work on Augustine Marion presents the idol as that which resists the truth, the saturated phenomenon that demands a response. Here Marion considers the possibility that we culpably resist, repress, or evade the truth. We might be confronted, for ex-ample, with the Rana Plaza sweatshop disaster, and the truth of the exploita-tive system of commodity production might come upon us in the undeniable reality of the lifeless bodies of innocents pulled from the rubble. The pain of acknowledging the way we benefit from their labor seems too great to bear, so we get some relief by recoiling from the truth and denying its status as truth. But ultimately I have to choose either to bear the truth and change or refuse the truth and remain in my habitual self. The latter choice, an act of self-love, becomes its opposite; because I hate the truth, I will love myself only as deformed, which is ultimately an act of self-hatred. As we have seen, this is what Marion calls the "law of idolatry."

Vincent Miller has rightly emphasized that consumer culture is not about adopting bad values or ideas; it is about behavior, not simply belief. He also emphasizes that people do not simply choose to exploit others but rather choose within a system that hides the consequences of their actions from them. Capitalism has a way of capturing even our attempts to resist and making a profit off them—think Che Guevara T-shirts. Miller is rightly trying to counter moralistic Christian approaches to consumerism that scold people for having bad values without considering the larger systems that form those values.[213] In correcting this approach, however, we need to be careful not to relieve ourselves too easily of culpable responsibility, nor to see the overarching system of consumer culture as simply inexorable and inevitable. The conditions of production are not *entirely* hidden from us, and—as long as we believe in a God, whose love will ultimately overtake any idolatry—we cannot draw too pessimistic an account of the powers and principalities of this world. To attempt to counter idolatry, we will need to avoid the extremes—either try to escape to some imagined space of purity or simply give in to the inevitable—and instead search for material practices that embody a sacramental relationship between humans and created things. I will take up that search in the next and final chapter.

8

Incarnation and Sacrament

The previous chapter ended with a discussion of the question of human agency, a theme that has been present since the first chapter, on Weber. If idolatry in some of its many forms—including, I have argued in the previous two chapters, nationalism and consumer culture—involves humans being dominated by their own creations, to what extent can humans break free of idolatry? Does that domination make us powerless to rebel? As we discussed in the first chapter, Weber was pessimistic: the complexity of the iron cage that humans had built was too great to overcome by altruistic human effort. Marx was more optimistic that humans could create a truly anthropocentric world once the gods—all of them false—could be overthrown. Once the world was divested of divinity, the merely material could be returned to its proper place as instruments to be used toward human happiness. As the authors of *The God That Failed* recognized, however, postrevolution Marxism erected a new god that was even more ruthless in devouring its subjects.[1] And the instrumentalization of the material world seems unlikely to forestall ecological death. If the analysis of the previous chapter is correct, then the enchantment of the material world responds to a deep human need to interact with the material world in sacramental ways. The reduction of the world to the merely material does not correspond to the lived experience of being a creature in the world, and it does not produce the kind of reverence for creation that will compel us to make the world livable for all its creatures.

From the point of view of the Bible, Augustine, and the Christian tradition more generally, the solution is not anthropocentrism but theocentrism, the restoration of harmonious relationships between and among Creator and creatures. Only God can save us from our own distorted use of the world. Once people acknowledge that they are not self-creators but dependent on a Creator who loved them into being, they can see their fellow creatures not as threats or saviors or objects to be exploited but as reflections of the glory that made them. And if they can thus see the presence of God in creation, they can adopt a new way of living that respects the value and integrity of their fellow humans, animals, plants, and the rest of the material world. As Pope

The Uses of Idolatry. William T. Cavanaugh, Oxford University Press. © Oxford University Press 2024.
DOI: 10.1093/oso/9780197679043.003.0009

Francis has written in *Laudato Si'*, "The ultimate purpose of other creatures is not to be found in us. Rather, all creatures are moving forward with us and through us towards a common point of arrival, which is God, in that transcendent fullness where the risen Christ embraces and illumines all things."[2]

The task at hand, then, is simultaneously to see God in things and not to make a god of things. Given that we are material creatures living in a material world, how are we to do that without falling into idolatry? Most of this book has been taken up with the analysis and critique of idolatry. In this final chapter, we turn to a more positive account of how idolatry can be healed. What can we say about how we are to navigate the material world while worshiping an immaterial God? Are there practices we can point to that neither attempt to reject the created world nor idolize it or some aspect of it?

In what follows, I sketch out a sacramental vision—rooted in Christian belief in the Incarnation of God in Jesus Christ—of a theocentric creation that both reveals God and is not identified with God. In the biblical tradition, idolatry critique is not a general statement about materiality and divinity; it is a response to an encounter with the living God. The fact that not everyone is a Christian does not mean that all non-Christians will find the following account of an incarnate God irrelevant; there are many bridges between the Christian tradition and other traditions, with traffic moving in both directions, though I can't begin to explore them here. It is also obviously not the case that Christians, by virtue of these core beliefs, are free in practice from idolatry. Far from it. If idolatry, as I have argued, is not just a matter of belief but a matter of the beliefs implicit in practice, I will need to explore the practices that make these beliefs operative.

In this final chapter, I first consider the question of sacramentality, the notion that divinity is found in creation. Having found that *Which divinity?* is a crucial question, I turn in the second section to a consideration of the Incarnation of Jesus Christ as an antidote to idolatry. In the third and fourth sections, I consider icons and sacraments proper as remedies for idolatry. In the fifth and final section of the chapter and book, I reflect on what resisting idolatry by living sacramentally might mean in practice.

8.1. Sacramentality

In his brilliant book *The Enchantments of Mammon*, Eugene McCarraher has argued that capitalism has not disenchanted the world but rather "misenchanted" it; capitalism is "a parody or perversion of our longing for a sacramental way of being in the world."[3] McCarraher examines management theory, academic defenses of capitalism, and in-house marketing discourse to show how corporate America adopted and adapted the aspirations to transcendence, metaphysical implications, and sacramental practices traditionally embedded in Christianity, turning them toward the end of making a profit. The antidote to the idolization of things, McCarraher suggests, is not stripping them of all reference to the divine—as Marx would have it—but rather seeing them as mediating the presence and power of God, the creator and sustainer of all. All enchantments—even misbegotten ones—draw their power by tapping into our deepest and truest desire, which is to experience the world sacramentally, to uncover "the dearest freshness deep down things," as McCarraher quotes Gerard Manley Hopkins. "Hence the importance of theology for this book, as I root my affirmation of the persistence of enchantment in a theological claim about the world: that the earth is a sacramental place, mediating the presence and power of God, revelatory of the superabundant love of divinity,"[4] a love which calls us into communion with other humans and with all creation. McCarraher does not develop this insight theologically, but in the closing pages of *Enchantments of Mammon* he gestures toward a "Romantic, sacramental radicalism" that would build an economy around a vision of "superabundant love as the ontological architecture of creation, harmoniously blending unfathomable power and gracious, immeasurable munificence."[5] The Romantic ideal of work aims at workers' control of production and measures economy based not on efficiency but on what kinds of labor and what kinds of goods best contribute to human flourishing.[6]

McCarraher uses the term "sacrament" to refer beyond the boundaries of the Christian tradition; there is warrant within the Christian tradition for such an expansive view of sacramentality. In McCarraher's Catholic tradition, there are seven recognized sacraments—paradigmatic practices such as baptism and Eucharist that confer the grace of the Holy Spirit—but there are also "sacramentals," objects or actions such as holy water, blessed palms, ashes, crucifixes, and more that dispose people toward receiving grace. According to the Vatican II document *Sacrosanctum Concilium*:

[F]or well-disposed members of the faithful, the liturgy of the sacraments and sacramentals sanctifies almost every event in their lives; they are given access to the stream of divine grace which flows from the paschal mystery of the passion, death, the resurrection of Christ, the font from which all sacraments and sacramentals draw their power. There is hardly any proper use of material things which cannot thus be directed toward the sanctification of men and the praise of God.[7]

It is notable that this passage, while privileging sacraments and sacramentals, locates their power not in themselves but in the paschal mystery of Jesus Christ. The universal nature of the event of Christ thus allows "almost every event" in the lives of ordinary people to be sanctified, and there is furthermore "hardly any proper use of material things" that cannot be used for the sanctification of people and the praise of God. Sacraments and sacramentals are part of a series of concentric circles whose center is Jesus Christ but whose power extends through to the ordinary events of human life and the ordinary use of material things. Not every event or thing is as privileged a locus of divine grace as the sacraments; there are degrees of more and less. But some degree of sacramentality clearly extends far beyond the sacraments proper and connects the life-giving power unleashed by Christ to the most mundane of human events and human use of material things. Insofar as Vatican II also sees the presence of grace far beyond the boundaries of the visible Church,[8] there is a sense that sacramentality extends to a more general attitude toward the material world, such as McCarraher has located in the Romantics.

For Vatican II, the recognition of shared human experience is centered in a theology of Jesus Christ. Both because he is trying to appeal to a broader audience and because he is a historian, not a theologian, McCarraher largely leaves theological reflection to others. He is trying to be as ecumenical as possible, acknowledging that "Christians are not alone in perceiving a sacramental quality in ordinary things," citing the Maori and the *mana* they see lurking in all things.[9] Admittedly, McCarraher writes, Christian, Jewish, and Muslim theology "asserts that things in themselves have no power apart from God. Still, material life has sacral significance, and how we make and use material goods has a sacramental and moral dimension; there are sacramental— as well as perversely sacramental—ways of being in the world."[10] Without theological criteria, however, it is not clear how we are to separate good from perverse sacramentality. Is seeing power lurking in all material things a sufficient condition for the practice of good sacramentality? Clearly not, because, as McCarraher shows, advertisers infuse their own version of *mana* in the products they sell. McCarraher holds up Romanticism as the antidote to capitalism because "Romanticism's passionate vision sees the presence of divinity throughout the material universe."[11] But corporate ideologues do too; the hard question is *Which divinity*? Communists and capitalists follow, respectively, the god that failed and the god that sucked.[12] An account of the God that, ultimately, neither fails nor sucks becomes necessary at some point.

The closest McCarraher gets to spelling out this ontological and theological vision is in his treatment of the Romantics:

> Whether they believed in some traditional form of religion or translated it into secular idioms of enchantment, such as "art" or "beauty" or "organism," Romantic anticapitalists tended to favor direct workers' control of production; the restoration of a human scale in technics and social relations; a sensitivity to the natural world that precluded its reduction to mere instrumental value; and an apotheosis of pleasure in making sometimes referred to as *poesis*, a union of reason, imagination, and creativity, an ideal of labor as a poetry of everyday life, and a form of human divinity.[13]

This list of Romantic convictions goes some way toward specifying *which divinity* is to be found in material creation; a properly sacramental economy, broadly conceived, would indeed contain these elements, and people with many different theological or ontological points of view could potentially agree on this broad vision. But surely it makes some difference whether people believe in "some traditional form of religion" or translate it into "secular idioms of enchantment." There is a difference between the Christian God and "organism," for example. Surely a lot depends on how one specifies "a form of human divinity"; is this a reference to the Incarnation or some more Enlightenment-friendly exaltation of the human? If McCarraher's analysis really is about competing theologies, then theology cannot be one of the *adiaphora* we can safely ignore so that we can concentrate on economics or ethics or politics or some other "secular" discipline. I worry that, despite McCarraher's radical challenge to the religious/secular distinction, by shying away from theology it will have ended up reinscribing that distinction.[14]

If the problem we are addressing is disenchantment, then appealing to Romanticism's "passionate vision" of the "presence of divinity throughout the material universe" makes sense. But if the problem is misenchantment— the passionate visions of divinity in material realities like the nation and consumer items that I explored in the previous two chapters—then the appeal to Romanticism is inadequate. As is well-known, Romanticism was one of the principal drivers of nationalism from the late eighteenth century onward, led by figures such as Rousseau, Herder, and Fichte. In the words of Fichte in his thirteenth address in *To the German Nation*, "Only when each people, left to itself, develops and forms itself in accordance with its own peculiar quality, and only when in every people each individual develops himself in accordance with that common quality, as well as in accordance with his own peculiar quality—then, and then only, does the manifestation of divinity appear in its true mirror as it ought to be."[15] Adam Zamoyski's comprehensive account of Romantic nationalism argues that it served as a substitute for Christianity: "God had been superseded by 'Our Lord Mankind.'"[16] With regard to consumer culture, Colin Campbell's acclaimed book *The Romantic Ethic and the Spirit of Modern Consumerism* argues that consumerism emerged out of Romanticism; finding pleasure in daydreaming about consumer goods developed as an unintended consequence of the Romantic emphasis on feeling, imagination, and self-expression.[17] None of this discounts the positive forms of Romanticism that McCarraher alludes to; "Romanticism" is a broad category that applies to many different kinds of thought and practice. Countering misenchantment, however, will require some work to separate the good from the perverse forms of sacramentality.

I affirm that there is a good argument to be made for expanding the notion of sacramentality beyond the visible borders of Christianity and its sacraments. David Brown, like McCarraher, rightly wants to reach out beyond those who are churched to find common ground in the everyday experience of the sacred in human life. In his contribution to the *Oxford Handbook of Sacramental Theology*, Brown writes of the need to build bridges between the secularized world and the church, "even without appeal to revealed theology."[18] The birth of a child, the daily reception of food, the encounter with beauty, and more are all experiences of the world as gift, even if the term "grace" is not used. Works of imagination, even by artists hostile to talk of God, are using the same tools—metaphors, symbols, images,—that make talk of God possible. All are manifestations of a sacramental world.[19]

How we talk about this broader sense of sacramentality, however, depends on what problem we think we are trying to solve. Brown wants to recover a sacramental sense of the world from "'the disenchantment of the world'— that is, the way in which modern society tends to value only what is a means to something else, and so turns aside from what appears mystical or magical, and thus without further purpose."[20] Brown cites both sociologists and intellectual historians to explain how God was distanced from ordinary human experience in the West, and how a sense of sacramentality could help bridge the gap: "Yet in much more recent writing on this wider sense of sacramentality, indeed perhaps most, the story is told almost entirely from the inside out, as it were, that is, with the assumption that such a reading of the world has validity only if it starts with Christ and his church."[21] Brown cites the influential work of Alexander Schmemann as an example: "But the problem then becomes that there is no easy way of dialoguing with all those who in some sense 'believe without belonging' or for Christians themselves to comprehend how sacramentality might effectively bridge the gap between the two worlds, the earth that is ours, and heaven, God's space, since on this analysis the latter seems to belong firmly on the other side of the great divide."[22]

Brown does not shy away from theological language, but he tries to show how theology builds on what is encountered by everyone in our daily encounters with material reality. "So the incarnation was not simply a thunderbolt out of the blue"; Jesus used the images and metaphors already there in his culture to bridge the gap between God and the mundane, while simultaneously transforming them. This is why his life is sacramental. The sacraments proper likewise use what is already there; the Eucharist builds on the prior reality of human sharing of food and drink. Brown argues that "unless the Incarnation builds on the way human beings are actually situated, it is hard to see why its message should be relevant to socially conditioned beings such as ourselves."[23]

I appreciate Brown's pastoral approach here. There is no point in starting a conversation with someone alienated from Christian practice by talking about the centrality of Christ and the church. One does not have to look far to find good reasons that many people are wary of the church and Christianity more generally. Relating to people on the basis of common experiences of life as a gift, with or without the term "grace," is a good way to appreciate our common humanity and common experiences. If the God Christians believe in is who we say God is, then God sheds grace prodigally well beyond the boundaries of the visible church. As I understand Brown, he is not suggesting that a dialogue with those who are alienated from Christian practice should end before we talk about Christ and the church, only that it need not start there. I think that's right. But building bridges is best done from both sides of the river. As I read Schmemann, he is also trying to bridge the gap between Christ and common experience, but he does it starting from the side of Christians who worship Christ in the liturgy but do not have a good sense of what that has to do with the rest of their lives. Like Brown, Schmemann wants to light up the mundane with sacred significance, but he does so by tapping into what Christians already claim to believe. The difference between Schmemann and Brown here might simply be the difference in the audiences—churched and unchurched—they are trying to reach.

I do not think, however, that Brown is well served by the narrative of disenchantment, for reasons that I hope to have made clear in earlier chapters. The narrative of disenchantment gives the impression that many or most people have simply lost belief in a transcendent realm of meaning; people have stopped recognizing another world and focus exclusively on this one. If that is the case, then it is hard to see where a dialogue with those who don't believe in such an invisible realm would go; if I already experience the world as full of gift and imagination without reference to God or anything transcendent, why would I need such a belief? I seem to be doing fine with nothing to worship. If, on the other hand, our predicament is better described as misenchantment, if we are *homo liturgicus*, worshiping beings who encounter divine presence in all sorts of created realities for good and for ill, then the question *Which divinity?* is necessary to address not necessarily at the start, but sooner rather than later. Idolatry is a different thing from disenchantment. We are not talking only about a beautiful world in which people have forgotten to thank the invisible God for the visible gifts they receive. We are also living in a broken world in which people are oppressed and slaughtered by gods of human creation. If sacramentality is not to become sentimentality—*Look at all the pretty flowers!*—then the hard questions of which gods are being encountered in things must be addressed.

Brown believes that the Incarnation is a true account of what kind of divinity we are dealing with. Care must be taken, however, with language of the Incarnation "building on" creation as it stands. Brown, I think, simply wants to point to the fact that Jesus does not come upon first-century Jewish culture as an alien dropped out of the sky. The very idea of Incarnation means that Jesus takes on, while also transforming, the particulars of human life in a particular time and place. This is right. But care should be taken so that the idea of the Incarnation building on what is already there does not underwrite the two-tiered view of the universe that I critiqued in chapter 2, in which transcendence simply adds another layer above and beyond the immanent. If the Incarnation merely adds an exclamation point to the more general sacramentality of matter, then the dialogue Brown envisions with the disenchanted person is likely to leave such a person unconvinced that belief in the Christian God adds anything significant to a general sense of the value of gift, imagination, metaphor, and so on. Sooner, rather than later, a

Christian must claim and witness to the notion that the Incarnation reveals something essential at the heart of creaturely existence. The Incarnation is not something to get around to eventually if the dialogue goes well; it is at the core of creaturely life. The Incarnation is not simply the beginning or the end of reflection on life as a creature; a fully sacramental life is a recurring back and forth between Jesus and the most mundane details of everyday life.

McCarraher and Brown are right to tap into the recovery of a wider notion of sacramentality in the twentieth and twenty-first centuries. In the post-Tridentine Catholic Church, sacramentality was largely reduced to discussion of the seven official sacraments, their proper performance and efficacy. Since the work of Henri de Lubac and others in the twentieth century, the notion of sacrament has expanded in Catholic theology beyond the seven sacraments to embrace the prior realities of Jesus Christ and the church. As de Lubac writes, "The Church is a mystery; that is to say that she is also a sacrament. She is 'the total locus of the Christian sacraments,' and she is herself the great sacrament which contains and vitalizes all the others. In this world she is the sacrament of Christ, as Christ Himself, in His humanity, is for us the sacrament of God."[24] Christ is the sacrament of God, the one who reveals God in material form, and the church is the sacrament of Christ, the people who mediate Christ to the world. This emphasis on Christ as the sacrament of God pushes the concept of sacramentality not only wider than the seven sacraments but also deeper, back to the origin of the sacraments, the origin of the church, and even creation itself, insofar as all is dependent on Christ, through whom all things were made (John 1:3). The sacramentality of the world—the notion that all nature is graced—is not a general principle about the nature of matter but is rooted in Jesus Christ, who mediates God to all creation.

Building on the work of de Lubac and others, Vatican II embraced the idea of a grace-soaked nature as a consequence of the Incarnation. *Gaudium et Spes*, for example, sees the grace of the Incarnation well beyond the visible confines of the church: "Since human nature as He assumed it was not annulled, by that very fact it has been raised up to a divine dignity in our respect too. For by His incarnation the Son of God has united Himself in some fashion with every man."[25] Indeed, the unity of the church presumes a unity of the human race in its natural condition. As de Lubac writes, "the unity of the Mystical Body of Christ, a supernatural unity, supposes a previous natural unity, the unity of the human race."[26] This unity of all humankind is what should prevent the church from being just another "we" versus "they."

Karl Rahner likewise extended the sacramental presence of the Incarnation to the whole of humanity, not just the church, as the "people of God": "By the gracious coming of the Logos in the flesh, in the unity of the race, in the one history of humanity, mankind as a whole has become a consecrated humanity, in fact the people of God."[27] The Incarnation elevates humanity to a heightened intimacy with God. As Paul McPartlan comments, Rahner here is not trying to dissolve the church into humanity; "rather he is emphatically wanting to anchor the Church in the reality of a consecrated humanity, as the ongoing public presence in the midst of humanity that calls humanity to recognize the head and savior it already has."[28]

As much as he approves of expanding the focus of sacramentality beyond the seven sacraments, Kevin Irwin worries that language of Jesus and the church as "sacraments" still puts too much emphasis on the seven sacraments themselves as the paradigm of God's transmission of grace rather than the broader sacramentality of the world that underlies the sacraments. The sacraments are based on the principle of sacramentality, that all reality "is potentially or in fact the bearer of God's presence and the instrument of God's saving activity."[29] The word "potentially," says Irwin, rescues the principle of sacramentality from being overly optimistic; any emphasis on the goodness of creation must still recognize the distorted condition of creation in the presence of sin. Nevertheless, in order not to dichotomize the sacred and the mundane by privileging the sacraments as special moments of escape from the world, Irwin's argument is that "Jesus, the church and the seven sacraments are best appreciated as particular and privileged expressions of a sacramental world in which God has revealed and continues to reveal God's very self through the material of human existence, set within the world as itself regarded as sacramental."[30]

I value Irwin's attempt to recognize the sacramental potential of all creation and to prevent the splitting off of sacraments to a sacred sphere removed from everyday life. I worry, however, that making Jesus a particular and privileged expression of a more general sacramentality will unwittingly accomplish the same splitting by making the Incarnation an afterthought to creation and the sacraments just a nice but not strictly necessary reminder or intensification of what we already experience elsewhere.[31] What we need is a way to express the uniqueness of the God of Jesus Christ—again the question is *Which divinity?*—as simultaneously embedded deeply in the structure of all creation. Schmemann articulates a broader concept of sacramentality in the following terms:

It is then the "natural" symbolism of the world—one can almost say its "sacramentality"—that makes the sacrament *possible* and constitutes the key to its understanding and apprehension. If the Christian sacrament is *unique*, it is not in the sense of being a miraculous exception to the natural order of things created by God and "proclaiming His glory." Its absolute newness is not in its ontology as sacrament but in the specific "res" which it "symbolizes," i.e., reveals, manifests, and communicates—which is Christ and His Kingdom. But even this absolute newness is to be understood in terms not of total discontinuity but in those of fulfillment. The "mysterion" of Christ reveals and fulfills the ultimate meaning and destiny of the world itself.[32]

For Schmemann, the sacraments are in deep continuity with the broader sacramentality of all creation not because Christ is a particular manifestation of the more general principle—the Incarnation as the icing on the cake of creation—but because Christ is the one in whom and for whom all is created, and Christ is the ultimate destiny of the world. Again, how we articulate a concept of sacramentality depends on what problem we think we are solving. If the problem is disenchantment, then a more general concept of sacramentality is perhaps sufficient. If the problem is misenchantment, then the specification of *which divinity* will take on a greater urgency.[33]

8.2. Incarnation

I have argued so far for both a wider concept of sacramentality that moves beyond the seven sacraments and a deeper concept of sacramentality that is rooted in a theology that specifies which God is being worshiped when we reverence creation. It is not enough to talk about divinity in creation; specifying *which divinity* makes all the difference. To be clear, however, to proclaim triumphalistically "the Christian God" does not solve our problems. With regard to non-Christians, I take for granted that truth and goodness and beauty are found well beyond the Christian tradition and that God is at work everywhere. Interreligious dialogue and comparative theology are necessary and important and far beyond my competence. I am a Christian theologian attempting to develop a set of protocols for resisting idolatry using Christian tools. My understanding of idolatry is Christian, and the tools of resistance I can muster are Christian. I cannot begin to respond from within other faith traditions, and I cannot cobble together some universal theological Esperanto that hovers above them all. With regard to Christians, I hope to have made it clear by now that there is no guarantee that Christians are actually worshiping the God they claim to worship. We Christians often practice idolatry. I am trying to develop a Christian theological framework in which discernment about which gods we are in fact serving can properly take place. My analysis is intended primarily as a remedy for idolatrous Christians, not a triumphalistic claim that *our* worship is true and *yours* are all false.

For a Christian, the specification of *which divinity* centers on the Incarnation of Jesus Christ. Any affirmation of the goodness of creation must be rooted in the goodness of the Creator, and Christians affirm that creation is through (John 1:3) and in and for (Col. 1:16) the Word of God, Jesus Christ. "He himself is before all things, and in him all things hold together" (Col. 1:17). Any account of the sacramental quality of the world will need to draw its specificity from the particular contours of the story of a God who became incarnate and dwelt among us in the person of Jesus of Nazareth. Christians have long understood the Incarnation as the antidote to idolatry. How and why this might be so will need some careful unpacking.

As we have explored in the previous two chapters, current manifestations of idolatry in the West are related to a dynamic that Charles Taylor has labeled "excarnation," a movement that has its roots in changes in sacramental practice and theology in the early modern period. For Taylor, excarnation begins with "the transfer of our religious life out of bodily forms of ritual, worship, practice, so that it comes more and more to reside 'in the head.'"[34] A key move toward secularization in Taylor's *A Secular Age* is the attack on the medieval sacramental system, particularly the Eucharist, but including the whole system of sacramentals, devotional objects, and pilgrimages. Reformers objected to the capture of God's power in the material world, which they routinely labeled idolatry. Reformers wanted to do away with the magical view of the sacraments, such that the changes that the Eucharist effected became less in the bread and wine and more in the interior of the human person. John Calvin, for example, could not countenance the idea that God had let loose his saving action into the material world at the mercy of sinful human actors. And so the world was disenchanted, stripped of both bad and good magic; the body was ignored while God was increasingly confined to the mind and the heart.[35] The critique of idolatry, in Taylor's account, leads directly to disenchantment and the excarnation of Christian life.

Excarnation does not remain confined to the "religious" realm, however: "the direction of this Reform was towards a far-reaching excarnation; that is one of the main contentions of this book."[36] Taylor uses the term to describe the separation of pure Reason from embodied feeling,[37] the reduction of morality to correct propositional truths,[38] our captivity in the world of media images,[39] and the denial of the lived body through virtual reality.[40] Excarnation is also apparent in the two forms of idolatry I examined in chapters 6 and 7. Nationalism, I have argued, is a form of abstraction from embodied and rooted local communities to an "imagined community." Excarnation is manifested in the nation-state, according to Taylor, in its "code fetishism," the way law and bureaucracy have replaced communion and embodied care for one another.[41] In the dominant consumer culture as well, there is a tendency to use material goods as a way to transcend and escape materiality, to take flight from the material world into a realm of fantasy and enchantment. It is not difficult to see excarnation in the dematerialization of the economy and the disappearance of the bodies involved in the production of goods.

Taylor's identification of excarnation as a key feature of modern life seems to me right and important. Taylor, however, links excarnation to disenchantment and the creation of "buffered" selves; I think excarnation is better understood as a crucial feature of misenchantment. The more disembodied our culture becomes, the more closely it is aligned not with sober reason but with fantasy. The apparent materialism of the "American Dream" and the apparent bodiliness of internet pornography are both profoundly excarnated and deeply imbued with fantasy and flight from material and bodily reality. Excarnation is best understood as an attempt to escape human finitude, to transcend the limits of creatureliness. In that respect, it is a version of the primordial sin identified in Genesis 3:5, the sin that is at the heart of idolatry: the attempt to reach out, grasp, and be like gods.

The term "excarnation" is obviously an inversion of a key Christian term, and Taylor himself makes the connection "Christians today . . . live in a world where objectification and excarnation reign, where death undermines meaning, and so on. We have to struggle to recover a sense of what the Incarnation can mean."[42] What is needed is a profound reflection on and practice of the Incarnation, but this cannot mean nostalgia for the past. We could respond to the change of epochs polemically, writes Taylor, either celebrating the present and condemning the past, or chastising ourselves for having gone astray. Taylor rightly urges us instead to see both the gains and the losses of the present era, and see that neither medieval nor modern people understand the whole picture: "None of us could ever grasp alone everything that is involved in our alienation from God and his action to bring us back."[43] Central to the Incarnation is a profound sense of communion, both with our contemporaries and with those who have gone before us. What we need is to be "open to a conversation that ranges over the whole of the last 20 centuries (and even in some ways before)."[44]

With his characteristic charity and openness to dialogue, Taylor invites everyone, Christians and non-Christians, to a conversation about the ills of excarnation and the profound communion that an openness to Incarnation offers. He capitalizes "Incarnation" and clearly means something more than a generic principle of relating to reality bodily; as a Christian, he suggests that the Incarnation of Jesus Christ reveals something true about the world and makes possible a different way of living in the world. The Incarnation, he suggests, opens possibilities not just for Christians but for the world more generally. As a philosopher and not a theologian, Taylor does not develop a theology of the Incarnation. At some point, however, any Christian contribution to the conversation to which he invites us will have to explore what exactly Incarnation means and how it can be a remedy for the excarnation that ails us.

For a Christian, the conversation begins in the Old Testament. As discussed in chapter 3, the rejection of idolatry and the emphasis on aniconism in Israelite worship does not indicate the rejection of the divine presence in the created world. God's "sacramental" presence is found in the Tabernacle and its furnishings, including the Ark of the Covenant and the table of the Bread of the Presence (Ex. 25–31, 35–40). The detailed prescriptions of the Law governing the mundane minutiae of life—from personal hygiene to animal husbandry, from clothing to pots and pans—indicate that God is to be found in everyday interactions with the material world, which, as Genesis 1 repeatedly reminds us, is good in God's eyes. Though Judaism and Christianity differ on the reality of the Incarnation of Jesus Christ, the movement of God in both is in the same downward direction: the life of the faith is not essentially the challenge of climbing a ladder to transcend the material world; rather it is responding to God's descent into concrete human life. As Rabbi Joseph Soloveitchik writes:

> When the righteous sit in the world to come . . . they occupy themselves with the study of the Torah, which treats of bodily life in our lowly

world. . . . The Creator of worlds, revealed and unrevealed, the heavenly
hosts, the souls of the righteous all grapple with halakhic problems that are
bound up with the empirical world—the red cow, the heifer whose neck is
to be broken, leprosy, and similar issues. They do not concern themselves
with transcendence, with questions that are above space and time, but with
the problems of earthly life in all its details and particulars. . . . The universal
homo religiosus proclaims: the lower yearns for the higher. But halakhic
man, with his unique mode of understanding, declares: The higher longs
and pines for the lower.[45]

The story of creation and salvation is the story of God's longing to be with
God's creation. This ecstatic movement does not leave the world unchanged;
the lower is lifted by the descent of the higher. As Soloveitchik writes, "A
lowly world is elevated through the halakha to the level of a divine world."[46]
Soloveitchik's student Michael Wyschogrod emphasizes the incarnational
aspect of the election of Israel. Wyschogrod's book *The Body of Faith: God
in the People Israel* argues that Judaism is a "religion of the body." God chose
Israel to be a vessel for God's Indwelling (*shekhinah*) in the world.[47]

Encountering God in the material world, at first sight, seems more like a
temptation to idolatry than a remedy for it. The problem is compounded in
Christianity, where God is identified with one flesh-and-blood human being.
To Jews, the identification of one man with God is practically the definition of idolatry.[48] As discussed in chapter 3, the New Testament writers who
proclaimed Jesus as Lord were not unaware of this obvious objection. They
nevertheless thought that worshiping Jesus as the *eikōn* of God is in continuity with the aniconism of the Old Testament, and is in fact the remedy for
idolatry. Paul uses *eikōn* both for pagan idols (Rom. 1:23) and for Jesus Christ
(Col. 1:15; II Cor. 4:4), the "image of the invisible God." Paul contrasts the
multiplicity and lifelessness of pagan idols with the oneness of Christ with
God and the manifestation of the living God in the living Christ. The living
God cannot be fully present in mute statues, but only in the living figure
of Jesus Christ. At the same time, since the image of Christ is borne by the
believer (Rom. 8:29; I Cor. 11:7, 15:49; II Cor. 3:18), at least in eschatological anticipation, God's likeness can be found in the movable icons that are
one's brothers and sisters in Christ. Rather than render gods in the image of
humans, God renders humans in the image of God by restoring that image
through Jesus Christ. God thus provides a path for the undoing of idolatry.
The key to undoing idolatry is again a matter of direction. Idolatry tries to

reach up and seize divinity, to bring it within human grasp; in contrast, God offers participation in God's life as a gift to be received. In Paul's speech to the Athenians in Acts 17, he critiques the pagans for trying to read god off the face of humanity, and thus build a ladder to ascend to the divine. The movement of God is instead one of descent, restoring the image of God in humanity by the Incarnation, which can be received only as a gift.

Nowhere is the descending motion of the Incarnation clearer than in the Christ-hymn of Philippians 2:5–8:

> Let the same mind be in you that was in Christ Jesus,
>   who, though he existed in the form of God,
>   did not regard equality with God
>   as something to be grasped,
>   but emptied himself,
>   taking the form of a slave,
>   assuming human likeness.
> And being found in appearance as a human,
>   he humbled himself
>   and became obedient to the point of death—
>   even death on a cross.

From the heights of existing in the form of God (*morphē Theou*), Christ emptied (*ekenōsen*) and humbled (*etapeinōsen*) himself. What he empties himself of is the desire for *harpagmon*, something to be seized or grasped. John Barclay argues that we should understand the phrase not as "he did not view equality with God as something to use for his own advantage" but rather as "he did not consider seizing to be a manner of existence equal to God." Seizing or grasping is what the pagan rulers do. The contrasting term in Paul's letters is "giving," which is what God does. Christ identified the divine nature with giving, not using creation but giving himself for its sake.[49]

The point of Christ's kenosis, however, is not—as for some kenotic theologies—to divest Christ of his divinity.[50] Kenosis is not the loss or concealment of divine power but the manifestation of a kind of divine power that is not like human power. In the Philippians hymn, the exaltation of Christ follows his humiliation:

> Therefore God exalted him even more highly
>   and gave him the name
>   that is above every other name,

so that at the name given to Jesus
every knee should bend,
    in heaven and on earth and under the earth,
  and every tongue should confess
    that Jesus Christ is Lord,
    to the glory of God the Father. (Phil. 2:9–11)

The reason Jesus's exaltation follows from his kenosis is that God's descent into a broken creation heals that creation, according to Paul. God works within an alienated creation to absorb sin. Christ takes the form of a slave (*morphēn doulou*) and assumes human likeness to subject himself to the constraints imposed on the human condition and the entire creation post-Fall. The whole creation is subject to the "slavery of decay" (Rom. 8:21). Christ is fully present as God within the human condition. His triumph over death thus becomes ours. As Barclay puts it, "Christ participates in our condition so that we might participate in his."[51]

Paul's language of bent knees and confessing tongues is a reference to Isaiah 45:22–3:

Turn to me and be saved,
    all the ends of the earth!
    For I am God, and there is no other.
By myself I have sworn;
    from my mouth has gone forth in righteousness
    a word that shall not return:
"To me every knee shall bow,
    every tongue shall swear."

The text is explicitly antiidolatry; the prophet's words are directed to "those who carry about their wooden idols and keep on praying to a god that cannot save" (45:20). Paul's message is clear: worshiping Jesus Christ is worshiping the one God of Israel, the same God who declares "there is no other." Worshiping Jesus Christ as Lord is not idolatry, but is in fact the antidote to idolatry.

If idolatry is a matter of behavior and not simply belief, as I have been arguing throughout this book, how should we respond to the Incarnation, in Paul's view? It would be easy to contrast the narcissism of idolatry with the loss of self that Christ manifests, but kenosis as the loss of self is not the goal. Theologies of kenosis have been criticized for valorizing vulnerability, fragility, and suffering as goods in themselves, something that can be damaging, especially for people on the receiving end of abuse and unjust uses of power.[52] Christ's humility is not an end in itself to be imitated but rather a means toward the "solidarity"—Barclay's translation of *koinōnia*—of the community in Christ. This is the frame for understanding Paul's preface to the hymn: "[B]e of the same mind, having the same love, being in full accord and of one mind. Do nothing from selfish ambition or empty conceit, but in humility regard others as better than yourselves. Let each of you look not to your own interests but to the interests of others" (Phil. 2:2–4). The choice is not between selfishness and selflessness, narcissism and the annihilation of the self, but rather the creation of a larger self that incorporates all things in Christ. The person becomes a person only in communion with others; the self, as Barclay puts it, must be a "self-with," just as Christ is fully with humanity. The goal, however, is not simply a harmonious community for its own sake. The goal is the unification of all things under the lordship of Jesus Christ. The community participates in this drama of salvation insofar as it becomes a community of solidarity, living with and for one another. We do not grasp divinity through our own efforts but are incorporated into the divine life through the descent of Christ into human life.

The notion of the Incarnation as remedy for idolatry is found most explicitly in infralapsarian theologies of the Incarnation, that is, theologies that see the Incarnation as God's response to human sin. Athanasius's *On the Incarnation*, for example, begins with a reference to Athanasius's previous refutation of idolatry in his *Contra Gentes* and promises to show that "what men, in their conceit of wisdom, laugh at as merely human, He by His own power demonstrates to be divine, subduing the pretensions of idols by His supposed humiliation."[53] Athanasius locates the motive for the Incarnation in human sin: "[T]he reason of His coming down was because of us, and that our transgression called forth the loving-kindness of the Word."[54] Athanasius gives two explanations for the Incarnation. In the first, humans were summoned out of nothingness at creation and are descending back into nothingness and death through sin. The image of God in humans was being effaced. Christ, the very image of God, took on a corruptible human body and underwent death on behalf of all—and resurrection on behalf of all—in order to rescue us from corruption.[55] The second reason has to do with the corruption of human knowledge and is more directly related to idolatry. According to Athanasius, humans were made in the image of the Word to know the Word, but had turned instead to idols and served creatures rather than the Creator. Humans' attention descended to "lower things," and even the law and prophets sent by God were not enough to raise their vision to God.[56] God then, like a good teacher, descended to their level and took material form, since that is where their attention lay:

> For seeing that men, having rejected the contemplation of God, and with their eyes downward, as though sunk in the deep, were seeking about for God in nature and in the world of sense, feigning gods for themselves of mortal men and demons; to this end the loving and general Saviour of all, the Word of God, takes to Himself a body, and as Man walks among men and meets the senses of all men half-way, to the end, I say, that they who think that God is corporeal may from what the Lord effects by His body perceive the truth, and through Him recognize the Father.[57]

Though humans' eyes are fixed on base material things, Athanasius assumes that what they are really looking for is God. Looking for God among created things has only led them to idolatry so far; creation itself is not enough. What is needed is the Word, who "gives movement to all things in creation, and by them makes known the Father."[58] Christ both reveals the Father and restores the image of God in humans, for he is the original image of God; when the likeness painted on a panel becomes faded, the one whose likeness it is must come and sit for the portrait to be restored.[59]

And so God's descent into the material world in the Incarnation is not the abasement of God but the elevation of creation. The Incarnation is not idolatry but the very opposite of idolatry, the remedy for all idolatry. The key difference between Incarnation and idolatry is once again the direction of the movement between God and creation. Humans had attempted to make themselves the creators of God, having set out "to fashion for themselves one invention after another."[60] This is again the primordial sin, wanting to be like God by bringing God within our grasp. The antidote to this upward movement of self-aggrandizement is the downward movement of God's self-giving; the only source of all creation descended through "the loving-kindness of the Word" into creation in order to return humans to true knowledge of God. God accommodates Godself to the finite condition of human beings, redeeming our senses by appearing to them.[61] Athanasius sums up the two motives of the Incarnation as the movement of love: "For by His becoming Man, the Saviour was to accomplish both works of love; first, in putting away death from us and renewing us again; secondly, being unseen and invisible, in manifesting and making Himself known by His works to be the Word of the Father, and the Ruler and King of the universe."[62]

For Augustine as well, the Incarnation is God's response to human sin and the remedy for idolatry. As we saw in chapter 4, for Augustine there is an ambivalence to the beauty of creation. With proper vision we can see the beauty of the Creator through the things that God has created, all of which participate in God. The problem is that people have a tendency to become entangled in the temporal world of beautiful things and turn to idolizing them. The ambivalence of beauty is not because of an ambivalence in created things themselves, but because of sin. People fail to see God's beauty shining through created things, and thus direct their love toward those things, making idols of them. The beauty of creation is not sufficient to lead people to God. Great pagan philosophers have discerned the things of God in the created order, but still they have fallen short, because they lacked belief in the Incarnation:

> But those distinguished philosophers of the Gentiles, who were able to perceive that the invisible things of God are understood by those things that are made, yet held back the truth in wickedness, as it was said of them, because they philosophized without the Mediator, that is, without the man Christ. . . . For placed as they were in these lowest things, they could not but seek for some means whereby they might reach those sublime things which they had understood; and so they fell into the power of these deceitful demons, who brought it about that they changed the glory of the incorruptible God into the likeness of an image of corruptible man, of birds, of four-footed beasts, and of serpents. For in such forms they even set up or worshiped idols.[63]

Though God has liberally shown Godself in the beauty of created things, in our fallen condition we continually divinize those things themselves. The Incarnation is necessary because, as for Athanasius, there must be an accommodation to our lowly status, some way of mediating between our lost and confused condition and the lofty and eternal truths that we need to attain for salvation:

> Since we were, therefore, incapable of grasping eternal things, and the stains of sin, contracted by our love of earthly things and implanted in us, as it were, from the root of our mortality, pressed heavily upon us; it was necessary for us to be cleansed. But we could not be cleansed so as to be tempered

with eternal things, except by means of the temporal things with which we had already been tempered and held fast. For there is an immense distance between health and disease, and unless the healing process, through all the intermediate stages, is adapted to the disease, it does not lead to perfect health.[64]

As the doctor adapts the cure to the disease, so God adapts to the human condition in a way that we are capable of understanding.

Though Augustine puts the emphasis on human sin, part of the reason that we fail to see God in things is that God's presence is veiled in things. God is not immediately available in creation; there is no beatific vision of God face to face in the temporal world. A tree can reveal something of God, but perhaps we can be forgiven if sometimes a tree just seems like a tree. The Incarnation is necessary because Christ, as begotten, not made, is able to reveal the nature of divine Form; Christ is the very image of the invisible God (Col. 1:15), but in a manner that humans can fathom. Christ is the Incarnation of supreme Form or Beauty. What we love in loving Christ, even in his human form, is no created thing but divine Beauty itself, "beauty so old and so new."[65] And yet even in Christ we encounter God sacramentally; we are not given a direct vision of God. No one has ever seen God, but Christ has made God known (John 1:18). We can only respond with faith, hope, and love, and thus witness to the restoration of the image of God in ourselves.

For Augustine the very temporality and mutability of created things have a providential role in guarding against things being taken as ends in themselves. As we saw in chapter 4, things proclaim, "We are not your God, look beyond us."[66] The fact that they are beautiful, but their beauty is fleeting, compels us to look beyond them to their Creator. As Carol Harrison notes, in certain passages Augustine takes this insight further and develops an aesthetic of the ugly, with the idea that unsightly things are less likely to be idolized.[67] Things of physical beauty tempt us to seek rest in them, to look no further for the spiritual beauty beneath the surface. Ugly things are free of this temptation. This principle applies to the interpretation of difficult scripture passages: "[I]n order to exercise us, the divine word has caused us to inquire with greater zeal, not into those things that lie openly at hand, but into those that are to be searched out in the depths, and brought to light from the depths."[68] It applies to the Incarnation as well. There God appears in human flesh, with all its limitations, and is crucified on the cross. Augustine juxtaposes two seemingly contradictory scripture passages: Christ is both the "fairest of the sons of men" (Ps. 45:2) and the suffering servant "who had no form or comeliness" (Is. 53:2). The deep spiritual beauty of the divine is veiled by the ugliness of the cross, and yet it is simultaneously revealed in Christ's self-sacrificial love. Christ is deformed in his suffering by the sins of others, yet his deformity makes us aware of our deformity by sin and God's offer of love to heal that deformity. We respond not to physical beauty but to a deeper spiritual beauty that allows our deformity to be reformed. As Harrison puts it, "It is as if the breaking down of corporeal beauty allows spiritual beauty to be seen more clearly. It is a sort of breaking of idols so that the reality of God might be grasped."[69] In this way, Augustine turns the apparent scandal of Jesus's divinity on its head. It is not idolatry to proclaim this one broken and humiliated man to be God; it is in fact the key to healing our vision and our actions of their idolatry.

Although Incarnation as remedy for idolatry is articulated most explicitly in infralapsarian accounts, such as those of Athanasius and Augustine, more recent supralapsarian accounts of the Incarnation in significant ways drive the logic of Incarnation deeper into the structure of creation and thereby illuminate pathways for the avoidance of idolatry. Supralapsarian accounts do not make the Incarnation contingent on human sin, but rather see the Incarnation as revealing the very goal of creation. I will not here try to adjudicate the debate between infralapsarian and supralapsarian accounts; I will only briefly suggest ways in which some supralapsarian accounts drive the sacramental nature of the world not only wider, into all creation beyond the church, but deeper, into the very structure and logic of creation, in part by accentuating the basic dynamic of God's giving as opposed to the grasping of idolatry.

Supralapsarian accounts contend that seeing the Incarnation as a solution to a human-caused problem is too narrow a lens from which to view it. As Edwin van Driel puts it, supralapsarian accounts contend "that in the incarnation we gain a richness in divine intimacy and creational transformation that cannot be explained simply as a divine countermeasure to sin, but rather, that in this event is revealed to us the goal of creation."[70] According to Colossians 1:15–7, Christ is the "image of the invisible God," and "all things have been created through him and for him. He himself is before all things, and in him all things hold together." Supralapsarian accounts do not deny that God deals with human sin through the birth, life, death, and resurrection of Jesus Christ. As the same passage in Colossians continues, "through him God was pleased to reconcile to himself all things, whether on earth or in heaven, by making peace through the blood of his cross" (1:20). Supralapsarians contend only that "the need to take care of sin is not the only, and not even the deepest, word that can be said about incarnation and election."[71] In this passage, there is a priority of Incarnation to creation and redemption. God's first intention was to become incarnate; Christ is the one for whom all things are created. For van Driel, there is an ecstatic movement to Incarnation and creation; for God to become incarnate as a human being is

> a form of divine self-giving. It is, in general, to "reach outside" of Godself and to participate in that which is not God. And it is, specifically, to assume a human nature, to identify with this nature as being God's very own, as an extension of God's own life and an expression of God's own being. To become incarnate is for God to give Godself to what is not God. It is a decision to be a God for others. This is, of course, what the whole biblical narrative drives at: God is not just the Creator, the one who calls that which is not God into being, but God is the one who commits to this creation, who sees it through, who is creation's eschatological consummator. The insight of supralapsarian Christology is that this commitment is embedded in the ultimate act of divine self-giving: the decision to be Jesus Christ. Everything else is subsequently called into being for him.[72]

Van Driel applies this logic to the election of Israel, arguing that to be incarnate is to be a particular, historically situated human being. To elect this particular human nature is to elect a people. Love is the driving force of election; other creatures are called into being to provide the incarnate one with a large family. We exist in order to be friends of the incarnate God.[73]

Similarly for Samuel Wells, God's first intention is to be in relationship, to be with that which is not God. The Incarnation is prior to human sin and prior to creation. The Son is not a response to a deficit; he is not defined primarily as Savior, as doing something *for* us, but is first Immanuel, the God who is *with* us: "God is with us not primarily to do things for us, even to secure our salvation; God is with us because that is the purpose of creation."[74] Wells calls the book from which this quote comes *The Nazareth Manifesto* because he makes much of the thirty-some years that Jesus spent in Nazareth before starting his active ministry. In this long period, the presence of God in the everyday and the mundane is quietly apparent. This time is "an extended window into heaven," for although there was certainly good work and learning and celebrating during this period, it was most fundamentally

God simply being with us: "This is Sabbath—the crown of creation; simply being with God."[75] Human sin is certainly a reality, and Christ's passion and resurrection do redeem us, but sin is not the original motivation for the Incarnation. Sin is best understood as our resistance to being with God, our preference to be gods instead. The Cross, then, is not the satisfaction of God's wrath but rather the evidence of God's commitment to be with us no matter what the cost. Jesus remained with us even when we had abandoned him. His forgiveness of us opens the possibility for a new way of being together.[76] The Kingdom of God is the full realization of this communion of God with God's creation. The Kingdom indicates "a rejoining of such relationship, a restoration of community, a discovery of partnership, a sense of being in the presence of another in which there is neither a folding of identities that loses their difference nor a sharpening of difference that leads to hostility, but an enjoyment of the other that evokes cherishing and relishing."[77]

For my present purposes, supralapsarian accounts of the Incarnation do not necessarily cancel out infralapsarian accounts. A supralapsarian account does not necessarily deny that the figure of Jesus Christ is particularly well-suited to our sinful and confused condition, God meeting us in material form to teach us exactly how to look for God in the created world. Supralapsarian accounts need not simply reject Athanasius's and Augustine's accounts of how the Incarnation heals idolatry; they need only claim that the Incarnation is more deeply embedded in the logic of creation than fixing the problem of human sin. Paul's hymn in Philippians 2 seems to assume an infralapsarian account of Christ taking on the fallen human condition in order to heal it. But a supralapsarian account could and should affirm the Incarnation as the self-giving of God's presence to us, God's reaching down to offer participation in divine life rather than the human attempt to reach up and seize divinity. Paul's understanding of *koinonia* and the "self-with," in Barclay's terms, certainly affirm van Driel's and Wells's understandings of Incarnation as God's being-with us that enables a new type of human communion that overcomes our tendencies to narcissism and our tendencies to be oppressed by our own creations. Finally, all of the accounts of the Incarnation I have so briefly summarized form a basis for the affirmation of a sacramental view of creation, the idea that God is found in the creation but is not identical with it. Just as in Jesus Christ we encounter God, but veiled in human flesh, so God is present to God's creation, but always simultaneously veiled in material form. Therefore, we are to reverence creation, but not idolize it.

I have capitalized the word "Incarnation" in order to make clear that I am talking about the Incarnation of God in Jesus of Nazareth, not a more general notion of the incarnation of divinity in the material. There are theologians who want to resolve the scandal of particularity—the God of the universe in this one particular human being—by making incarnation a more general principle of how God is present to the world. In this view, incarnation is a statement about the inherent revelatory properties of created things rather than a statement about how God has chosen to reveal Godself in material reality. However, as Ian McFarland—who also presents a supralapsarian account of the Incarnation—explains, to see incarnation as God's normal way of being in the world means that God is either equally perceptible everywhere, so God is insufficiently different from the world to effect its salvation, or God is not directly perceptible anywhere, so God is insufficiently present in the world to effect salvation.[78] Without the claim that God is uniquely present in and as the life of Jesus Christ, the gospel is devoid of meaning. Another way of saying this is that if everything is a sacrament, then nothing is.

The Incarnation invites us to see God's elective act of self-giving in all of creation; it is not simply a statement about the inherently divine properties of all material things. Trevor Hart writes, "The Nicene *homoousion* is not a metaphysical principle, but a factual claim about God's action in the world at a particular time and place."[79] The Incarnation does indeed tell us much about the world and about God; it tells us that God has used the material to figure the transcendent reality of God, and that God can do so in other ways. God can enter into fruitful union with all sorts of physical realities to draw us into relationship with God and with each other. But this has to do with God's action and our response, not the intrinsic qualities of physical things. The most brilliant creations of human art and ingenuity can be idolatrous; the most banal and kitschy artifacts can and do mediate human worship of God, especially for people without much money.[80] Augustine's aesthetic of the ugly makes a similar point. The theology of the Incarnation is fundamentally a statement about how God wants to have a relationship with us, how God wants to be with us, and how God wants to use material reality to forge relationships with us as material creatures. The Incarnation is the action of God's self-gift; it is not a statement about the inherent qualities of material reality as such. As Jean-Luc Marion stresses, any material thing can be either an icon or an idol.

8.3. Icons

So far, I have rooted a sacramental view of the world in the Incarnation of Jesus Christ. In Christ we encounter the God who undoes idolatry by offering healing for our relationships with God, with each other, and with the material world. Christ is God come among us as gift, descending to us to defuse our desire to climb to the place of God. Christ establishes communion among people based on self-gift, not oppression by gods of our own making. And in the Incarnation God sanctifies creation without identifying it with God. The Incarnation, however, establishes a delicate dynamic interaction of visibility and invisibility, presence and absence. The Gospel of John proclaims both "No one has ever seen God" (1:18) and "Whoever has seen me has seen the Father" (14:9). The Incarnation opens the possibility of seeing the invisible God, but without identifying God with what is visible. The Incarnation thus also opens the possibility of seeing the world as icon and sacrament of the presence of God. The goal of both is to present the invisible God in visible form, but without thereby reducing God to something that can be grasped and manipulated. God makes Godself accessible to humans, but on God's terms, not ours. If idolatry is reaching out to seize divinity (Gen. 3:5), then avoiding idolatry can only be the reception of the true God as God gives Godself.

Not everyone is convinced, of course, that finding the invisible in the visible is possible. For the stereotypical Platonist, the goal is ascent; we begin with the visible, material world but then attempt to leave it behind, given that the visible world is inherently inferior to—a mere copy of—the transcendent realm of ideas.[81] This is a type of iconoclasm, a suspicion of all images. Another possibility is to reject the reality of the invisible altogether. In an article titled "Every Religion Is Idolatry," Stathis Gourgouris adopts a Marx-inspired materialism for which the creation of an invisible, transcendent source of absolute alterity is an ideological form of covering over the groundlessness of society, the fact that society is self-created and based on nothing. Religion tries to conceal this abyss by naming it as unnamable, but naming it as unnamable is still an act of naming, and therefore idolatrous. Every religion is idolatrous because it tries to perform the impossible act of representing the unrepresentable, but in fact nothing is unrepresentable.[82] From a different position, Nietzsche also does away with the invisible prototype; there is no original that stands behind and governs the sensible world. Nietzsche embraces the manufacture of idols as the liberation of the image from any prototype. In all of the above, there is a mimetic rivalry between the visible and the invisible, such that deprecating the one is required to exalt the other.

For Marion, both transcending the visible and doing away with the invisible fail. The Platonist cannot do justice to the visible, which is always an untrustworthy copy of the invisible prototype. The Nietzschean gaze stops at the visible and meets nothing but itself in the ceaseless manufacture of images. The image is subjected to the will to power of the viewer, and the creation of images becomes nothing more than self-deification, not doing away with divinity but rather the creation of impoverished little gods living among impoverished images: "[H]ere we have a self-idolatry, where man, as estimator of all values, can or should, as regards the world, live only on images of his obsessed will to power."[83] Marion's task, then, is to articulate a way in which the invisible can give itself in the visible without ceasing to be invisible. He wants to move beyond both iconoclasm and idolatry.[84] Marion also expresses this search in terms of distance. If idolatry "arranges a presence of the divine without distance,"[85] then the antidote to idolatry must somehow retain the distance between God and creatures and yet bring them into noncompetitive relationship.

In chapter 5, we examined Marion's analysis of the idol. We need now to examine his phenomenology of the icon, which he pairs with the idol as two contrasting modes of aiming at the divine. The idol reduces the invisible to visibility and thus to the conditions provided by the human gaze; "[t]he icon, on the contrary, attempts to render visible the invisible as such, hence to allow that the visible not cease to refer to an other than itself, without, however, that other ever being reproduced in the visible."[86] We encounter the invisible not apart from the visible, as the iconoclasts thought, but within it. At the same time, however, the icon is nonmimetic. Painted icons in the Eastern tradition are not meant to be "life-like" or representational art. Icons are painted without reference to the viewer's perspective. Indeed, while the idol is characterized by a dazzling excess of visibility, "the icon shows, strictly speaking, nothing."[87] The image effaces itself. Marion emphasizes the kenotic nature of the icon; just as Christ yields to the will of the Father and becomes an icon to the Father, so the icon empties itself so the viewer can be grasped by God: "The self-affirmation of the image, like all others, yields only in front of an abandonment: it is precisely because the icon is not given for itself, but rather undoes its own prestige, that it perhaps demands veneration— veneration that it does not seize but rather lets pass through it to the invisible prototype."[88]

For Marion, the icon painted on wood is determined not by the hand of the painter but by the infinite depth that crosses it. Both the idol and the icon are defined by the gaze, but in the icon the intention of the gaze belongs to the icon itself. In other words, the intention comes to the icon from elsewhere, "whose invisible strangeness saturates the visibility of the face with meaning."[89] In the icon, unlike the idol, there is no gaze that comes to rest on a visible, since the visible is saturated by the invisible. An icon is a saturated phenomenon according to modality, that is, as a phenomenon that cannot be looked at; in other words, the gaze is not stopped by the image on the icon itself but encounters another gaze from beyond the image.[90] The icon does not re-present Christ or the saints but invites one into a relationship with them. The icon is a site of communion, not an object.

Traditional icons are not painted with the vanishing point that, since the Renaissance, has characterized Western art. Objects farther in the background of an icon do not get smaller, as in Western painting.[91] Rather than attempt to produce a three-dimensional effect from the point of view of the observer, the focal point is in front of the image, such that the gaze comes from behind the image. We do not find ourselves simply gazing at the icon; rather the icon gazes at us. Marion likens the experience to that of meeting another person face to face. What captures our gaze are the pupils of the other person's eyes, in which we see nothing; the pupils are empty spaces, "black holes." We do, however, feel ourselves being seen, and indeed put into question.[92] The visible is interrupted by an invisible look; the invisible is included within the visible. Just as in the face-to-face meeting with another person, the icon opens a space of potentially "erotic" attraction: "The exchange of gazes (the one aiming in the way of the prayer, the other aiming in the way of benediction), in effect by crossing the visible, opens up to an extremely erotic face-to-face relation: two invisible gazes crossing themselves through the visible witness of their bodies."[93]

The icon thus inverts the mirroring effect of the idol. Whereas the idol is a mirror that reflects back to us our own desires, in the icon we encounter its desires, or rather the desires of God's gaze that come from beyond it. Rather than imposing our vision on the divine, we are called to a more receptive attitude to what is being given to us. If the idol cuts the divine down to human measure, the icon opens us up to the infinite excess of God's love. Marion quotes from Paul: "And all of us, with unveiled faces, seeing the glory of the Lord as though reflected in a mirror, are being transformed into the same image [eikona] from one degree of glory to another, for this comes from the Lord, the Spirit" (II Cor. 3:18). Here, rather than the idol mirroring our desires back to us, we become reflections of God's glory; "our gaze becomes the optical mirror of that at which it looks only by finding itself more radically looked at: we become a visible mirror of an invisible gaze that subverts us in the measure of its glory."[94] It would be inadequate to suggest that whereas the idol is a mirror, the icon is a window, because the icon does not make God visible. The icon is more like a door, a portal into which we are invited to walk, to follow where God is leading us.[95] The icon is not to be seen, but venerated. It "summons one to travel through the (invisible) mirror, and to enter, so to speak, into the eyes of the icon—if the eyes have that strange property of transforming the visible and the invisible into each other."[96]

Overcoming idolatry requires overcoming the rivalry between the visible and the invisible. As we have seen, the Incarnation opens the possibility of seeing the invisible without reducing the invisible to the visible. According to Marion, the icon maintains the visible and the invisible in a noncompetitive relationship; the union of the two terms increases paradoxically along with the distance between them.[97] While the idol seeks to render the divine visible, the icon exposes us to the divine while simultaneously maintaining the invisibility of the divine, or the "distance" between us and God. As we saw in chapter 5, for Marion distance is not simply spatial; God's transcendence does not mean that God is far away. On the contrary, divine distance is what makes the union of the invisible and the visible possible. As creator of all, God is wholly other to creation, and precisely therefore God is not another thing competing for space with created things. As the ground of all being, God is innermost to all beings.[98] God is both wholly transcendent and wholly immanent in all things. One does not have to leave the world behind to experience transcendence. As Ola Sigurdson wonderfully puts it, "Transcendence makes up the luster of the world."[99] For Marion, painted icons are a paradigmatic instance of encountering God in the visible without reducing God to the visible. This does not mean, however, that painted icons as found in Eastern Christianity are the only privileged means of access of the invisible through the visible. The icon for Marion is not an object but a way of appearing in the world. Marion makes clear that concepts can also be icons, if they receive the incomprehensible without trying to reduce the incomprehensible to our conceptual grasp of it. "Valid as icon is the concept or group of concepts that reinforces the distinction of the visible and the invisible as well as their union, hence that increases the one all the more that it highlights the other. Every pretension to absolute knowledge therefore belongs to the domain of the idol."[100] Iconicity is a way of appearing that allows the divine to appear through things without reducing things to idols; it allows the person to receive the world in a new way, not as an object to be grasped and used and hoarded but as a gift from a gracious God, which opens the person to true noncompetitive communion with God, fellow humans, and the whole created order.

Icons are an antidote to idolatry not because they are magical objects that connect us to God but rather because of their relationship to the Incarnation. In Christ, John of Damascus writes, we are now able to overcome the fear that all images are idolatrous and to discern what can and cannot be depicted: "What therefore is this that is revealed and yet remains hidden? For it is now clear that you cannot depict the invisible God. When you see the bodiless become human for your sake, then you may accomplish the figure of a human form; when the invisible becomes visible in the flesh, then you may depict the likeness of something seen."[101] In the controversies leading up to the Second Council of Nicaea in 787, the defenders of icons from iconoclasm held both that the painted depiction could not be confused with the prototype and that the prototype and the depiction could not be separated so as to make the presence of God in the image impossible. In so doing, they were very consciously building on the decree of Chalcedon that Christ's two natures, divine and human, could be neither confused nor separated.[102] Christ himself is the paradigm of the icon,[103] which is why iconicity is not confined to painted icons but is rooted deeper in what God has revealed about Godself and about creation in Christ. The hypostatic union of divinity and humanity in Christ is a paradigm of the universe; God is present in all creation while not confused with it.[104] The invisible divinity is given to appear in the visible humanity of Jesus Christ, but divinity is not directly visible in Christ any more than it appears as a spectacle in the painted icon. The Incarnation both conceals and reveals God; nowhere is this more operative than in the cross. Marion writes:

The difficulty of recognizing on the painted wood of the icon the invisible gaze of Christ precisely reproduces the absolute difficulty of confessing that on the wood of the Cross the divine nature of the Son of God dies according to his humanity, the mortal sufferings of invisible holiness in the horror of visible sin. But the hypostatic union guarantees the intentional unity only by the strictly divine equivalence that enables Christ to say "The one who has seen me has seen the Father" (John 14:9).[105]

The human flesh of Christ both conceals and reveals God. On the cross, it is hard to recognize the invisible and all-powerful God in the tortured body of Jesus. At the same time, God is manifested in the self-sacrificial love that the cross reveals. This kenotic love, Marion notes, is founded in the perichoretic relations of love in the Trinity; "the ultimate icon is thus revealed as a 'living icon of charity.' "[106]

Marion has been criticized for overemphasizing the kenotic aspect of the icon to the point of disparaging images. Graham Ward has accused Marion of a "Gnostic logic" that denies the full reality of the Incarnation; the cross appears in Marion as a rupture in creation, reducing the only valid exception to idolatry to images that efface themselves.[107] John Milbank has written that "Marion's account of the icon is in fact iconoclastic."[108] More recently, James K. A. Smith has accused Marion of fundamentally devaluing finitude by equating it with sinfulness, concluding that "Marion's supposedly 'iconic' rescuing of images still, in the end, negates a positive role for images and harbors a logic of prohibition which can affirm only those images which erase themselves—that is, precisely those images that cease to be images."[109]

I find these critiques of Marion less persuasive than Stephanie Rumpza's defense of Marion's phenomenology of icons.[110] Rumpza asks what it would mean for an image to "efface itself," and she points—as I did in chapter 5—to the middle voice in Marion, the way that what the icon "does" is neither entirely the image's action nor entirely my action but stands in the in between space where the icon's self-effacement is related to the conditions of my reception of it. The kenosis of the image requires the kenosis of the viewer. In neither case is kenosis meant to be understood as self-destruction, though, as Rumpza admits, Marion's own language sometimes risks misleading his readers. As in Barclay's analysis of the Christ-hymn in Philippians 2, Marion identifies the fundamental contrast between *kenosis* and *harpagmon*, self-emptying and grasping or seizing. Kenosis is a way of relating to God, a receptive openness to being filled by God, as opposed to the idolatrous reaching out and grasping God, subjecting God to the limits of our understanding. *Pace* Ward, Marion's kenosis is not a rupture in creation but simply the nature of the Trinitarian relations, in which the Father's self-gift to the Son and the Son's abandonment to the Father is performed in the Spirit.[111] The violence of the cross is the violence done not by God's command but by those who cannot accept with humility God's loving self-gift. The kenosis of the image is not a judgment against finitude or against material creation, but is rather an invitation to love as God loves, not by grasping but by receiving.

The conditions for seeing the icon—that is, the conditions for receiving the gift of the icon—depend on the kenosis of the viewer. In *The Crossing of the Visible*, Marion does not contrast the self-effacing icon with images or finitude as such, but with "the modern tyranny of the image,"[112] the sea of advertising and clickbait and memes in which we are immersed that both give us what we want to see and train us what to want. "Icons" are now something we click on. As we saw in the previous chapter, on consumer culture, such images aim to make the divine accessible to our grasp, to put the divine on display for our viewing pleasure. Marion regards as paradigmatic the icons of Eastern Christianity, but he does not reject other kinds of beautiful or delightful images from being icons, only those that are self-referential, marked by manipulation and possession. When this is the case is not simply an aesthetic question, however, but an "ethical" one, we might say, that is, a question of how the person interacts with the image. An image is iconic if the person encounters God through it, if it reveals its relation to God, and the person receives that gift and enters into communion with God. Once again, the middle voice is crucial: the initiative belongs to God, such that the person does not reach out idolatrously and grasp God, but neither is the person wholly passive. Both person and image pour themselves out kenotically, giving themselves over to a love that transcends them both. And that love is not only between God and the individual but opens out, as in the Philippians Christ-hymn, into *koinonia* or communion, being a self-with-others. Marion's analysis of the icon is not a mere aesthetics: the point is to become, as Marion says, a living icon of charity. The condition of receiving charity is the ability to pass it along to others.

The point here is not to defend Marion against criticism, but to make the broader point that resisting idolatry is more than a matter of aesthetics. To see God poured out in the beauty of creation is simultaneously to refuse to reduce the divine to creation and subject creation to our control and manipulation. That refusal can come only from a response to God's loving self-gift to creation by offering ourselves in self-gift to others. If idolatry is to cut God to the measure of the self, then the antidote to idolatry is to lose the small self by gaining a much larger communion with God and with our fellow creatures. Sacramentality is not simply seeing the divine in things, but an imitation of the sacrament of God, Jesus Christ, who emptied himself so that we might share divine life.

8.4. Sacraments

Beyond a general sense of sacramentality, a Christian antidote to idolatry will need to consider the sacraments proper as the paradigm of how the Incarnation is extended in historical time. By "sacraments proper" I am referring to the seven sacraments identified as such in the Catholic tradition, though I will concentrate on the Eucharist since, along with baptism, the Eucharist is recognized by virtually all Christian traditions as central. In addition to having more ecumenical reach than icons, sacraments are also more commonly linked with practices of charity and a broader sense of communion. Nevertheless, the basic dynamic of the sacraments and that of icons is the same: making contact with the immaterial God in the material world without reducing God to the material. Following the basic logic of the Incarnation, sacraments, like icons, both reveal and conceal. In them God gives Godself in the ordinary without ceasing to be God.[113]

Just as there are good reasons not to reduce incarnation to a general principle of which the Incarnation of Jesus Christ is one important instance, we also need to explore the sacraments as significant beyond mere exemplars of a more general sacramentality. Creation is not simply radiant with the divine; it is fallen and redeemed. Beyond a simple appreciation for the beauty of creation, sacraments are meant to have a restorative effect on a creation that is often distorted because of the idolatry of human action. Both people and things are sinned against by being treated as mere objects for the use of others; the abuse of people and environmental degradation do not completely destroy their ability to refer to God, but obscure the revelatory function of creatures. Through the agency of others, the ability of creatures to refer to God is obstructed and distorted. Junius Johnson writes that sacrament is the "general rubric for the divine restorative action toward those things that have been made ugly by the agency of another."[114] The Eucharist, for example, insofar as it takes the creatures of bread and wine into real personal identity with God, affirms God's intention to dwell with creatures and even be borne by them, and thus returns them to the original glory of creation.[115] The Eucharist is not simply the recognition of a more general sense of the sacramentality of created things; sacramentality flows from the sacrament. As Schmemann writes, "The world was created as the 'matter,' the material of one all-embracing eucharist, and man was created as the priest of this cosmic sacrament."[116] In other words, sacramentality should be rooted in the liturgy, meaning not just the rites that humans celebrate but the eternal liturgy that Christ works to heal a broken world.[117]

As discussed above, sacramentality is a vision of the ecstatic nature of finite reality, the way that God can reveal Godself through all of creation. Sacramentality in this broad sense is not the proprietary insight of the Christian tradition but applies to any worldview that properly recognizes a noncompetitive, analogical relationship between the finite and the infinite, as in forms of Platonic and Hindu thought. From within the Christian tradition, nevertheless, there is a case to be made for a special relationship between sacramentality and the practice of the sacraments. One finds God not just everywhere in general but in the particular, a particular that is specified cultically. Jonathan Ciraulo refers to the relationship between the principle of sacramentality and liturgical practice as a double helix; the two are ordinarily intertwined. Although it is possible to give notional assent to a principle of sacramentality without a sacramental practice, and it is possible to participate in a sacramental cult while denying the principle, in the ordinary course of events the two rise and fall together. Beyond mere notional assent, real assent to God in things takes place in some particular here and now. As Maurice Blondel argued, a metaphysics is realized in action. More than a general principle, sacraments attest that God and creation meet in harmonious action: "This providential ordering is seen most tangibly, and perhaps noticed for the first time, in sacramental action, where the primary causality of God provides the capacity for finite creatures to cause spiritual effects that totally exceed their native powers."[118]

Christian theology centers Christology, such that Christ is not just one example of a more general principle, but rather a whole picture of reality can be read off the Christ-event. But Christology is unlikely to bear such a load unless it is complemented by the continuation of the Incarnation in the church's sacramental practice. Sacraments ratify and concretize Christology by showing how finite actions cooperate with divine action. The Incarnation is not a one-off exceptional event; it is continued through time in sacramental practice. Chalcedonian metaphysics is applied in the present tense through sacramental action. Ciraulo recognizes the general consensus that ritual actions help to inscribe values on the bodies of those who perform them, as the whole field of liturgy and ethics attests, but he is primarily concerned with the ways that rituals also inscribe metaphysical commitments—for example, the idea that God prefers to act via finite causes—on the bodies of those who perform them. Convictions about secondary causality are unlikely to have much purchase in the absence of concrete, cultic instances where God's action and human action coincide. Ciraulo does not thereby dismiss the "ethical" implications of cultic practice but rather emphasizes how an abstraction like "ontological participation" can become a concrete way of life through sacramental *koinonia*: "Without some theurgical outlet, philosophical notions such as secondary causality or participation are stillborn, and conversely, Eucharistic *koinonia* is ultimately incoherent without a basis in a metaphysics of participation."[119]

Like Charles Taylor, as discussed in chapter 2, Ciraulo traces the eclipse of Christian theology in the West to the rejection of the efficacy of the sacraments. For an Enlightenment figure like Immanuel Kant, the idea of sacramental efficacy was a mere superstition, a futile attempt to capture the transcendent within the limits of human action. Sacraments as Catholics understood them were an attempt to manipulate God by the means of nature rather than please God by moral means; sacraments were a type of idolatry.[120] For Kant, superstition named any supernatural effect from finite means, such that the rejection of sacramental efficacy was at the same time a rejection of a more general sacramentality, the harmonious cooperation of matter with God. Like Taylor, Ciraulo implies that changes in sacramental practice preceded and helped cause changes in belief: "[W]ithout a need or a desire to uphold a theophanic and sacramental view of the cosmos, and without any convincing examples of real sacramental efficacy that would advocate for such a position, the philosophical mind quite naturally will exclude it as an unproven and overly complicated hypothesis."[121]

Ciraulo is primarily concerned with atheist, mechanistic, or Idealist philosophies that reduce matter to *mere* matter and rule out the notion that the finite could express what is more than finite, that matter could be ecstatic. My concern, however, is less with disenchantment and more with misenchantment, the perdurance of practices that continue to seek the infinite in the finite, even if they often end up as little more than mirrors of our own desires and fears.[122] The importance of Ciraulo's analysis for my present purpose is the way he underscores and explains the grounding of a more general principle of sacramentality in sacraments. Sacraments of course do not operate automatically to bear fruit in human lives; sacramental practice, as will be made clear below, does not make Christians immune to idolatry, to put it mildly. But without a concrete sacramental practice of the presence of God in particular things, it is easier either to reduce creation to mere matter to be manipulated by godlike humans, or conversely to divinize creation. To encounter God in things is to move past the abstraction of "things" in general and to encounter God in a particular thing. Jesus Christ is God in one particular human person who left with us particular signs of his continued presence. If the Incarnation of Jesus Christ is central to healing human idolatry, and if the Incarnation is continually made present to us in the action of God in the sacraments, then something important is lost when we do not avail ourselves of God reaching out to us in the particularity of the sacraments.

The importance of the sacraments in remedying idolatry is not only that they are a concrete and particular practice of God's presence, but that they are divinely instituted. Cathal Doherty's work on Blondel is helpful here. Blondel is well-known for his work on action and his contention that it is concrete practices, not mere speculation, that brings the supernatural into the interstices of everyday life. Doherty applies this basic insight to the sacraments, but uses Blondel to address the further question of what distinguishes sacraments from superstitious practices. Blondel turns Kant's critique of superstition back against Kant himself. For Blondel, superstition arises from the genuine human need to worship, but short-circuits it. Superstition is the human attempt to absorb what escapes us infinitely, to reduce the universal absolute to a particular object of the will. The result is the fabrication of gods that do not have the capacity to receive the homage we give, but which precisely therefore satisfy our felt need both to create gods and to try to master them. As in Marion, the object of the cult is a mirror of the self, a fruitless attempt at human self-sufficiency. Enlightenment figures like Kant wanted to rise above this human tendency to create rituals when coming up against human limits, but Blondel sees this as nothing more than a heightened form of superstition. The attempt to reduce religion to the limits of human reason while rising above those limits in order to mark them is simultaneously a diminution of God and an apotheosis of human beings. It is another form of idolatry.[123]

What separates sacrament from superstition is their origins, divine in the former case and human in the latter. Blondel does not reduce sacramentality exclusively to the sacraments. He recognizes the symbolic nature of created things. Revelation does not come entirely from outside the natural order, or else it would be unintelligible to human creatures. Revelation must be expressed in sensible signs, but sensible signs are not necessarily efficacious. For Blondel, the sacraments differ from the way that natural signs reveal God not only by degree but by the fact that the sacraments are divinely instituted, and therefore guaranteed by divine authority to be efficacious.[124] It is God's action, not the correctness of our execution nor our ability to interpret signs, that marks a sacrament. The sacraments are not a help that humans administer to themselves, or else they would be another form of superstition. They are a divinely instituted gift from God whose fruitfulness depends on how we receive them but whose reality does not.[125] The contrast with idolatry is again one of direction, the contrast between bringing God within human grasp and receiving God as gift, between humans reaching up to seize God and God descending to give Godself.

Marion explores what it means for God to give Godself in the sacrament. Like an icon, a sacrament—Marion treats the Eucharist as the paradigm—makes the invisible manifest in the visible. As the Council of Trent declares, the sacraments are "the visible form of an invisible grace."[126] For Marion, this marks sacraments apart from worldly phenomena, and therefore sacramental theology goes beyond and marks the limits of phenomenology, which deals with the relationship between the appearance and that which appears, a "first visible" and a "second visible," neither of which is invisible. The sacrament is the invisible in the visible, and it draws its legitimacy from the Incarnation, in which the Word assuming flesh marks the transition from the invisible to the visible. Marion understands the manifestation of God in the Son through the Spirit as eternal and intrinsic to God as Trinity, not achieved only in the earthly ministry of Jesus. The sacrament, therefore, draws its legitimacy from "the eternal involvement of the God of Jesus Christ in the process of manifesting and showing *himself*. The sacrament is sent by the dispensation of God himself, not only as one of his effects, nor even of one of his gifts, but also of Himself. When he gives, God never gives less than himself. God causes in person."[127] Marion rejects a merely semiotic account of a visible sign and invisible referent. The only way to make a *necessary* connection between invisible referent and visible sign is if the referent comes in person to validate the sign and act as its guarantor.[128] As for Blondel, the givenness of the sacrament depends on its divine institution by Christ in the Spirit.

Marion acknowledges some continuity between the sacramentality of all created things and the sacraments proper. When allowed to show themselves truly, beyond our fleeting utilitarian encounters with them, things of this world show more than mere materiality or utility. Water cannot help but show itself as something that saves my life or threatens it, bread as what maintains my strength, wine as what rejoices and also blurs my spirit. Things are already imbued with sense and promise: "Anything already shows infinitely more than its materiality."[129] It therefore also manifests something invisible. The sacrament "thus implements a determination of the phenomena in general in a simply more radical mode."[130] Marion does not discount the role that humans play in receiving the sacrament: "Here, as in all cases, that which the thing shows, at least when one allows it the freedom to show *itself*, depends on the width of our reception and the meaning it carries with it."[131] But he insists that the crucial question is who or what gives; he wants to resist the notion that we ourselves determine the gift by accepting it as given. In the sacraments, Marion argues, God gives Godself so radically that all the invisible it promises to give is guaranteed, by the authority of the Holy Spirit, to be really shown. The sacrament shows itself by the authority of God who gives Godself in it. Christ's *kenosis* on the Cross, his radical self-abandonment in love, qualifies the elements of bread and wine in the sacrament as Christ himself.[132]

Christina Gschwandtner's critique of Marion's phenomenology of the sacraments, the Eucharist in particular, is helpful for clarifying the ways in which sacraments are or are not a remedy for idolatry. Gschwandtner's book *Degrees of Givenness* argues that Marion's distinction between poor and saturated phenomena is too binary and needs an account of degrees of saturation and givenness; in many ways Gschwandtner's argument complements my argument that idolatry is usually a matter of degree. Gschwandtner's chapter on Eucharist and sacrament shows how Marion, especially in his early work, presented the Eucharist as what he would later call a saturated phenomenon—indeed the paradigm of all saturated phenomena—that comes to the human subject in kenotic abandon and overwhelms the subject, the gaze unable to contain it. Because of human sin, not merely because of finitude, the subject contributes nothing to this gift, but can only receive it or reject it. The Eucharist provides its own correct interpretation, its own "absolute hermeneutic." Marion has little to say about the human experience of the Eucharist; the emphasis is entirely on God's self-revelation.[133]

Gschwandtner asks if Marion has really done justice to the actual human experience of the Eucharist and the degrees of givenness therein. Marion's emphasis is on the way the Eucharist overwhelms the subject with excess; the intentionality of the experience flows in one direction, from the Eucharist to the recipient. But does excess actually describe the experience of bored and distracted churchgoers? If we are not completely overwhelmed by the experience, it may not simply be because of our sin. Our experience of sin and brokenness does not simply prevent us from receiving the Eucharist well, but may be what brings us to the Eucharist in the first place. Besides degrees of brokenness, we also experience the Eucharist in different ecclesial and liturgical contexts. The experience of the Eucharist in a fifteen-minute weekday mass in Ireland may not be the same as the experience of the Eucharist in a three-hour Sunday celebration in a Nigerian village. An evangelical Protestant communion service with grape juice in individual plastic cups may not be the same experience as the Easter Vigil in the Orthodox tradition. The phenomena are not identical. "What the phenomenon means," Gschwandtner writes, "does not impose itself entirely from itself, but emerges through the ways it is practiced and enacted."[134] The phenomena, though they may have much in common, may be differently saturated, or saturated to different degrees. There is one Christ, but the Eucharist is not a monolithic phenomenon that gives itself always in the same way. Marion's account is largely disembodied, paying no attention to the corporeal gestures through which the Eucharist is celebrated and enacted. Marion's account is also primarily focused on the experience of the individual before God, patterned on his account of the individual praying before an icon. But the experience of receiving the Eucharist in a hospital bed is different from receiving the Eucharist in the communal setting of the Mass, and the practices of different communities affect the performance of the Eucharist as well.[135]

For Gschwandtner, all of this points to the need for hermeneutics that the Eucharist does not in and of itself provide. Gschwandtner's critique here is like those we discussed in chapter 5: experiences do not simply impose themselves on us but depend on how they are received. In his analysis of the Eucharist, Marion is trying to make the theological point that God is truly present there in a way that does not depend on our interpretation or reading of signs. As we have seen above, Marion does recognize the importance of human reception: what a thing shows depends on allowing it "the freedom to show *itself*," which "depends on the width of our reception and the meaning it carries with it."[136] Gschwandtner wants to push Marion farther, to acknowledge that "phenomena in themselves are neither poor nor saturated, but that this is an interpretation imposed on them by the consciousness that experiences them as such."[137] For good theological reasons, I think, Marion resists this conclusion with regard to the Eucharist, in which Christ's presence does not depend on our consciousness of it. Gschwandtner wants to separate phenomenological analysis from theological claims,[138] a separation which I think we do well to avoid. Nevertheless, Gschwandtner points out that when Marion does acknowledge the importance of hermeneutics, he tends to see hermeneutics as what takes place after the phenomenon has been encountered. He emphasizes the surprising ways that saturated phenomena can jar us out of our preconceptions. In so doing, he neglects the ways that the Eucharist requires attention to context and ascetic preparation. The question of how we are opened to receive the Eucharist need not imply the reduction of the Eucharist to human effort.[139]

Again, I am not so much interested in determining whether or not Marion has said all that needs to be said. As I write in chapter 5, I think Marion recognizes the pitfalls in trying to divide up a phenomenon into God's activity and human passivity, or vice versa. If God is both wholly other and therefore innermost in creatures, then the remedy to idolatry is precisely to avoid seeing the God-creatures relationship as zero-sum. Nevertheless, Gschwandtner's critique is important because it underscores the inadequacy of simply appealing to the Eucharist to solve the problem of idolatry. There is one Christ, but there are many ways of celebrating the Eucharist and many different contexts in which the Eucharist is celebrated.

Gschwandtner focuses on the liturgical experience itself, but the way that Eucharistic communities live out their faith outside the liturgy adds an even deeper layer of complexity to any appeal to the Eucharist or sacraments more generally. In other words, there is an ethical dimension to the Eucharist that demands attention in any attempt to remedy idolatry. To put a sharper point on it, there are not only different celebrations of the Eucharist, but there are idolatrous ones. The line between genuine and perversely sacramental ways of being in the world does not run between Christian and non-Christian practices; that line runs through the church as well.

Katie Grimes has made this point forcefully with regard to the racism of the church in the United States. Baptism became perverse in the churches of slaveholders, ushering Black people from freedom into bondage. The Eucharist in segregated parishes has likewise operated perversely. The Eucharist has not failed to bind white people into a corporate body, but it has helped to reinforce the racist identity of local congregations by effectively excluding Black people from the celebration of this sacrament of unity.[140] Grimes warns against "sacramental optimism," defined as "the belief that the church's practices, if enacted and understood properly, possess a demonstrable capacity to resist the atomizing individualism of the modern nation-state."[141] Grimes identifies the main culprits as Stanley Hauerwas and me. We are accused of putting forth an ecclesiology of "battened-down hatches," in which a virtuous church, fortified by sacramental practices, stands against a vice-filled world. I am said to believe that the church's failures are due to contamination by the world, so I appeal to the Eucharist as a discipline that builds a new kind of social body that is visible and efficacious.[142] Grimes rebukes my "confidence" in the Eucharist and remarks, "Perhaps the cultic Eucharist ought to act as Cavanaugh claims it does. But at least in its relation to antiblackness supremacy, it does not."[143] The cultic Eucharist, in "purporting to operate more or less magically and medicinally," allows us to ignore the social conditions surrounding it: "As long as the priest bears valid ordination, recites the correct formula, and distributes the holy bread to hands unsoiled by mortal sin, we believe the sacrament efficacious. It does not seem to matter whether black people are barred, either explicitly or indirectly from the Mass at which the Eucharist occurs."[144] Grimes sheds light on the social conditions under which the Eucharist is received and argues that the Eucharist is received only when performed properly.[145] The Eucharist does not work by "realigning the church's corporate body automatically."[146] Grimes recommends "transforming the cultic Eucharist back into a real meal,"[147] because a real meal would bring to light social conditions; who has food and who does not, who is welcome to eat with us and who is not. "Christian communities need to subject themselves to the diagnostic capacities of the real meal. Precisely because the real meal considers what takes place in, through, and among the human bodies it gathers together, the real meal positions us to discern this body more perspicaciously and therefore receive it more worthily."[148]

Grimes's critique is an opportunity to clarify some issues in the relationship between the sacraments and practice. Grimes rightly wants Christians to scrutinize the link—or lack thereof—between the sacraments and our concrete political, social, and economic practices; this is what I have tried to do in analyzing the Eucharist in the context of torture in Pinochet's Chile and in the context of American consumerism.[149] Grimes faults me for underemphasizing the sinfulness of the church, which is probably a fair criticism, though the idea that I want a church of battened-down hatches sealed off from the world is an unwarranted caricature.[150] I have been focused on what Christianity has to offer the world, rather than focused on critiques of the church, which are plentiful enough. But part of what the church has to offer the world is a penitential way of living; I have argued in the present book that idolatry critique is first and foremost self-critique. If we wish to remedy idolatry, we need to shine a harsh light on our own sins, which Grimes so effectively does in the case of anti-Black racism.

The question then becomes not about the status of the church—which is manifestly sinful, sometimes more and sometimes less—but about whether and how God offers us a remedy. If the sacraments really do convey God's presence in an efficacious way, does that affirmation really make any difference in the world? It should first be clear that no responsible theological voice holds that the sacraments work "automatically" or "magically." The classical distinction that arises out of the Donatist controversy is between the validity and the fruitfulness of the sacraments. The *Catechism of the Catholic Church* puts the distinction this way: "From the moment that a sacrament is celebrated in accordance with the intention of the Church, the power of Christ and his Spirit acts in and through it, independently of the personal holiness of the minister. Nevertheless, the fruits of the sacraments also depend on the disposition of the one who receives them."[151] In the traditional formulation, the sacrament is valid *ex opere operato*, regardless of the merits of the minister, but it does not therefore necessarily bear fruit in the recipient's life. Grimes is saying nothing new in insisting that the Eucharist must be embodied and lived out. When she writes "A real meal would make the reconciliation required to ensure that 'a true Eucharist takes place' not just possible but necessary,"[152] the internal quote is from my book *Theopolitical Imagination*, where I write, "Where peace is lacking, the Eucharist appears as an eschatological sign of judgment requiring that people reconcile before a true Eucharist can take place."[153] We need to be careful here, however, neither to make the presence of Christ in the Eucharist dependent on our actions, nor to see the Eucharist as automatically achieving social reconciliation regardless of human sin. The valid/fruitful distinction avoids both extremes. We can go further, as Grimes insists, and acknowledge that the Eucharist can be perversely and idolatrously performed; this can happen by exclusion, as in segregated white parishes, or by inclusion, as in Pinochet's Chile, when tortured and torturers were for a time welcomed to the same altar without requiring that torture stop.[154] Where reconciliation is lacking, Christ appears in the Eucharist, but in the form of judgment on our failure to enact a full and "true Eucharist." It should be clear that our Eucharistic celebrations are never pure but are always tainted by sin, to greater and lesser degrees; the Eucharist is a "damaged gift."[155]

The fundamental issue here is the same one that Marion and his critics are wrestling with: to what extent does God freely act on us in the sacraments, and to what extent does their efficacy depend on our response? In my early work, I had the tendency to write about the Eucharist as an agent: the

Eucharist reconciles, challenges, knits together, and so forth. As we have seen, Grimes also uses such language of the Eucharist as agent when writing about the Eucharist as real meal,[156] though she recognizes that the Eucharist does not operate automatically.[157] Language of the Eucharist as agent makes a connection between the liturgy and real life and emphasizes that God acts in history through the sacraments. Such language can resist idolatry; if it is taken as emphasizing God's action, not ours, it refuses to reduce the Eucharist to our performance of it and does not reduce the Eucharist to something over which we have control. To speak of the Eucharist as agent is not to speak of humans as agents; however, it is also not to speak explicitly of God as agent. The danger of speaking of the Eucharist, not the Holy Spirit, as agent is that it leaves the door open to a Pelagian account that centers human action. Such language also blurs the distinction between empirical and normative claims. To say that the Eucharist reconciles, for example, is a normative theological claim, but it can be taken in the indicative as an empirical claim that this is in fact what the Eucharist accomplishes in any given circumstances. This can cause confusion and give the impression that the Eucharist acts "automatically."[158]

For these reasons, it is probably best to avoid speaking of the Eucharist doing this or that without qualification. What we are seeking is what we have identified in this chapter and in chapter 5 as the "middle voice," in which humans are neither simply active nor passive in the face of God's action. The *Catechism* says of the sacraments, "They are *efficacious* because in them Christ himself is at work,"[159] but the "fruits of the sacraments also depend" on human disposition.[160] As I emphasized in chapters 4 and 5, idolatry imagines the relationship between human action and divine action as zero-sum; in a nonidolatrous relationship the human response to God is always God's response in us, without thereby ceasing to be our response. The sacraments invite us into participation in divine life, into the circulation of love that includes oneself, one's neighbor, and God. Such love must be lived out in an embodied way. But determining how to do this and when it is being done right depends on highly specific discernment about our practices.

There is, however, another type of objection to the appeal to sacraments as a remedy for idolatry that questions the urge to bring our social, political, and economic practices into congruence with what we claim about the Eucharist. To do so, goes the objection, is to reduce the Eucharist to ethics, ignore the way God is already at work in the structures of the world, and overstate our ability to change the world. According to Antonio Alonso's book *Commodified Communion,* calls for Christian resistance to consumer culture—in works by Geoffrey Wainwright, Vincent Miller, Kathryn Tanner, myself, and others—set up an impossible goal of separation from consumer culture, another form of Grimes's "battened-down hatches." Such theological critiques rest on the presumption that "[s]ome Christian practices, and the Eucharist in particular, have the ability to support Christian resistance against the distortions of consumer culture."[161] Such accounts present a "stark and total opposition"[162] between the Eucharist and "consumerism as something corrupt to the core."[163] In such accounts, commodified products "mediate nothing but deception" about both the conditions of production and the desires of those who buy them. "Individual desires for commodified goods are destructive, dangerous, or blasphemous. They threaten Christian thought and practice at their deepest levels."[164] Christianity therefore must escape the market. "True Christianity, so many arguments go, is something that should be isolated from and opposed to the market."[165]

Such arguments fail, according to Alonso, for two different kinds of reasons: they fail to appreciate the presence of grace in the market, and they fail to reckon with the inescapability of the market. In the first place, consumer culture is a place of grace, despite the manipulation of desire, unjust labor practices, and environmental degradation.[166] Alonso emphasizes that people live their theology through commodities: candles, holy cards, statues, hymnals, and much more, which testify to theology embedded in culture even in their commodified state. Such objects express the desires, hopes, joys, fears, and faith of people in ways that are neither merely ancillary to faith nor unsullied by market forces.[167] Alonso includes a section on his Cuban grandmother's *altarcito,* a small devotional space in her home littered with campy holy cards, prayer books, newspaper clippings, scapular medals, crucifixes, vials of holy water, and the like. Most of the objects had been cheaply mass-produced. As such, her altar "was deeply entangled in the processes of consumer culture. . . . [T]here are no objects on her altar unmystified by the machinations of the market. Indeed, my grandmother's *altarcito* testifies to the modern market's ability to commodify everything, even the material of a premodern devotional Catholicism."[168] And yet, her contact with God was mediated by such things.

The second type of reason that Christian theological critiques of consumer culture fail, according to Alonso, is that they present calls for resistance that do not appreciate the inescapability of the market. In addition to his grandmother's *altarcito,* Alonso includes sections on the commodification of hymnals and even mass-produced communion wafers.[169] One reason to resist calls to resistance is "the ease with which the market co-opts *any* form of resistance."[170] As an example, Alonso offers Apple computers and their "Think Different" marketing campaign, which presents Apple users as rebels who resist and transcend corporate conformity. Here it is easy to see the way that putative rebellion against consumer capitalism is being used as just another way to sell merchandise. The irony is that Christian resistance to consumer culture adopts the same form; the telos of Christian resistance might be different, but the promise, logic, and deep structure are the same. "Theological conviction around the need for Christian resistance to consumer culture rests on the presumption that some meaningful contrast can and must be drawn between consumer culture and Christianity."[171] The logic of *thinking differently* permeates Christian calls for resistance:

> At a time when everything worth doing, buying, or praying promises a revolution, far from resisting the market, *thinking differently*—even when it is informed by the gospel, the Eucharist, or the pope—is the orthodoxy of a market logic. And so remedies for Christian tactical resistance end up looking a lot like the strategies they seek to resist. . . . But these merely confirm in us a revised version of a fantasy that will never finally deliver the salvation it promises in this world, even with the purchase of the right computer, even with the most sincere and committed forms of gospel-centered efforts at cultural resistance, even with desires that claim their truth because they are more properly directed toward the living God.[172]

Rather than conclude that Apple's claims of transcendence are an idolatrous imitation of Christianity, Alonso goes in the opposite direction and concludes that Christianity is merely imitating Apple. "The market" is the real thing, and even Christian attempts at resistance cannot escape its gravitational pull.

Alonso continues on to reassure the Christian reader that "even in the mess of a world where our deepest hopes for transformation are sold back to us in the form of a product or a prayer, the activity of God is never fully absent."[173] But the implication seems to be that God is *mostly* absent. For a theology of God's absence, Alonso turns to Michel de Certeau. Certeau's work, especially his distinction between strategies and tactics in *The Practice of Everyday Life*, has been used by critics of consumer culture to suggest the possibility of resistance within and despite the apparent hegemony of capitalism. Strategies are the totalizing grids of power that structure society, and tactics are the creative and subversive ways that people take everyday opportunities to turn those structures to their advantage, without overthrowing the dominant system. Alonso offers a reading of Certeau's tactics that sees them not as "signs of resistance" but as "signs of absence," that is, "signs of living realities that pulse within and against systems of strategies that can never quite contain them."[174] According to Alonso, Certeau rejects naïve and impossible attempts to withdraw from the strategic grid of power. The only way we become legible to others is by conforming to the codes of the grid. But this assimilation is never total. At the limit of our conscription, a cry breaks out, a deviation, ecstatic revolt, or flight in the margins of everyday life that insinuates itself into language. "And this cry is one that does not seek out ways to consciously resist the grid but one that insists that though we are necessarily conscripted into it, something escapes that resists assimilation."[175] We do not seek, identify, or create this resistance; it simply exists between the cracks in the system and in the losses and absences we experience.

For Certeau, God's absence is generative, not something simply to be overcome. In his book *The Mystic Fable*, Certeau describes mysticism as the kind of speech born of the apparent absence of God, in a situation where the authority of the Christian sacraments, scriptures, and institutions has broken down; "mystics do not reject the ruins around them but remain there."[176] The absence of God is not simply a historical accident associated with the collapse of Christendom but a central theological theme in Christianity, attached to the disappearance of the body of its founder. For Certeau, the ascension of Jesus is where Christian speech begins. Jesus's self-effacement authorizes a pluralism of performances that do not repeat the Christ-event but would be impossible without it. Because "absence is the mode of Christ's presence," we must resist the temptation "to appropriate this insight to strategically identify, create, or define tactical practice." Tactics must remain "inventive, anonymous, and unidentifiable diversions and displacements." "Only new departures testify to the presence of the absence of the ascended Lord."[177] Since the collapse of Christendom especially, Christianity speaks not through the church but through the forms of the world. "Christians, [Certeau] argues, must abandon not only their strategic quest for an immanent Christian utopia but also their efforts to identify, fabricate, or explain practices as specifically Christian."[178] Alonso critiques theologies—by Virgil Michel, Aidan Kavanagh, Mark Searle, and others—that either invest the Eucharist with power to form people or reduce the Eucharist to ethics, making God's grace depend on us doing right.[179] Letting go of attempts to identify Christian practices with which to resist consumer culture is not an abandonment of hope, Alonso says, but an expression of the hope that God is still at work in consumer culture.[180] We should see "commodities not *only* as monuments to false desire but also as objects that bear collective hopes, if only indirectly visible through their cracks."[181] There we trust that God remains active, in and through God's apparent absence.

Alonso's work is in some ways a helpful theological extension of Mary Douglas's and Daniel Miller's anthropological appreciation of material culture. Our desires and longings for meaning, fullness, transcendence, salvation, God—all take shape in our relationships to the material world. Catholicism especially finds deep expression through material things and gestures, sacraments and sacramentals; the *altarcito* of the *abuela* can be a place of profound grace and a source of theological reflection, even if the items there are mass-produced. Alonso is right as well to appreciate the way that grace can inhabit even the displaced theological motifs that show up in commercials, art, and other nonecclesial spaces. Consumer culture is surely not simply a place abandoned by God or cut off from the higher aspirations of human desire. In this sense, Alonso elaborates a key theme I have been exploring in this book: even idolatry is an expression of the longing for God.

Beyond the general affirmation that God is not entirely absent from consumer culture, however, I find Alonso less helpful in identifying where and how God's presence can be recognized. Another theme I have been exploring in this book is the notion that idolatry is usually a matter of degree; there are more and less faithful material practices that we can identify. But Alonso, on the one hand, discourages attempts to identify tactical practices, emphasizing the futility of resistance and, on the other hand, admonishes theological critics of consumer culture for supposedly rejecting consumer culture as a whole, not allowing for degrees, as if they called for Christianity to be "isolated from and opposed to the market"[182] or "utterly pure or entirely other to this world."[183] I know of no one who actually calls for such a wholesale and frankly impossible escape from the market or the world.[184] The concrete economic practices that Vincent Miller[185] or I suggest in conversation with sacramental practices are part of a "theological vision of economics [that] cannot help but engage at the micro level, where particular kinds of transactions—those that really enhance the possibility of communion among persons and between persons and God—are to be enacted."[186] I see in such practices a

Christianity deeply engaged in the world, not trying to remain isolated from or "entirely other to" the world.

A critique of some of the prevalent dynamics of a consumer culture is not necessarily a condemnation of every type of material engagement that takes place within contemporary culture. Finer distinctions would be helpful here. Alonso refers to the water his *abuela* brought home from Lourdes in a jar that she filled herself as one of her most "transcendent and valuable commodities,"[187] but it is not a commodity, because it was not bought, sold, or otherwise exchanged in a market. Some of the other items on the *altarcito* were, but is the *abuela* praying at her *altarcito* "entangled in the processes of consumer culture" to the same degree as one shopping on Amazon? Can we not distinguish between Fair Trade clothing and that produced by sweatshop labor? Alonso is right to stress the goodness of material culture generally and the fact that God's grace can still be found in a consumer culture, and he is obviously correct that there is no way simply to escape the interconnected world economy and create enclaves of purity. Alonso wants to recognize the ambiguity in even our most heroic attempts to fix the world. All this is salutary. But without any more specific ways of making distinctions and identifying God's activity in the world, we seem left with fatalism about the inescapability of "the market" on the one hand, and a vague assurance that God is still present despite God's apparent absence on the other.

I am not convinced that Alonso is well served by Certeau's emphasis on the inevitability of the strategic grid and our "necessary conscription" into it, and his rejection of any attempt to "identify, fabricate, or explain practices as specifically Christian."[188] I agree with Certeau's critics who worry about his tendency to erase Christian practices and to ignore robust continuing forms of Christian community that incompletely but genuinely embody alternative ways of life. Rather than see the transition from Christ's historical body to his sacramental body as one of the extension of Christ in history by our incorporation and participation in that body, Certeau describes it in terms of loss, lack, and absence; the church and the Eucharist are mere substitutes. There is an almost total lack of Incarnation and sacrament in Certeau's preference for ascension and absence, and Certeau allows God to intrude only on the margins of history.[189] Alonso resists these kinds of charges against Certeau and emphasizes how absence makes something new possible. I remain unconvinced, however, that Certeau could do justice to the *abuela*'s thick Catholic devotional practices that have been largely swept aside by consumer culture and its constant emphasis on something new. And I continue to wonder if Alonso's Certeauian emphasis on the co-optation of all forms of resistance could do justice to the activists working to ameliorate the plight of the sweatshop laborers who produce many of the commodities we consume.

Alonso is right to remind us that God works mysteriously in and despite the sinful structures of the world and our own muddled practices. I am afraid, however, that his reliance on Certeau leaves us without much guidance on how to connect our material practices with our sacramental practices in ways that do not simply leave the world or ourselves as they are. The danger is that we end up simultaneously with an overly positive view of consumer culture on the one hand and an overly fatalistic view of it on the other; God must be at work in there somewhere, we hope, because there's not much we can do about it anyway. Alonso's emphasis on the futility of resistance is a sobering reminder of our limits, but it can also cut short our imagination and our urgency to confront massive injustice. Without a specific sacramental practice of the material world, fatalism can lead not to reliance on God but to resignation to the rule of Moloch.

8.5. Living Sacramentally

Alonso rightly wants to appreciate God's sacramental presence-in-absence despite the idolatrous systems we have created. But if, as I have argued throughout this book, idolatry is the human creation of systems that react back upon us and come to dominate us as false gods, then healing idolatry cannot be resignation to the inevitability—the godlike nature—of such systems. The acceptance of the inescapability of false gods is itself a type of idolatry; it imputes to them too much reality. If the Incarnation of Jesus Christ is in fact God's answer to idolatry, then we must be able to hope in something more than God's furtive and endless nibbling at the edges of history. To acknowledge God as God, and therefore to turn from idolatry, is to acknowledge that God is Lord of history, despite human sin. It is because Jesus Christ has somehow saved the world that we are called to and enabled to participate in that salvation, to live sacramental, though imperfect, lives. If, as I have argued, idolatry is not simply a matter of belief but rather of how our true beliefs are manifested in our behavior, then—while not reducing the sacraments to ethics—we are called to let our lives be conformed to the sacrament of God's presence in the world. I don't think we can abstain from seeking to identify and create less idolatrous tactical practices.

What would it mean to practice the worship of the incarnate God? To say that remedying idolatry is a matter of practice, not simply belief, is not thereby to suggest that we can provide a complete ethical roadmap to which our worship must be conformed. Idolatry can be healed only by encounter with the living God, an encounter that cannot be programmed in advance according to ethical criteria. We cannot reduce worship to ethics, or bring God within our grasp. To worship the incarnate God is to participate in God's kenosis; rather than grasp God, we allow ourselves to be poured out in the encounter with God, to receive the presence of God as a gift. Participation in Christ allows us to break through the boundaries of the small self and become a self with others, to participate in a wider body of solidarity or *koinōnia*. While the false gods fail to come to life, the true God is made visible in God's human image; we seek God in our fellow humans—movable icons made in God's image—and in all of God's creatures that bear traces of their Creator's presence. To see the world iconically or sacramentally is not just an aesthetic act; it requires conforming our daily lives to our worship, which means entering into solidarity with one another as we participate in God's life. In what follows, I will suggest what sacramental living might look like, first in relation to nationalism, then in relation to consumer culture.

The idolatrous danger in nationalism that we encountered in chapter 6 is that the "we" will be divinized. If idolatry is often reducible to self-love, nationalism tends toward self-love writ large, a kind of collective narcissism. The "strong god" of the "we" must furthermore define itself over against a "they," enemies both external and internal. Rather than solidarity with all, narcissism tends toward insecurity, a mirror that reflects our own fears back to us. The sense of "we" does not apply to minorities and dissenters who threaten the positive national narrative, so they are often scapegoated. Another way of dealing with internal division is to unite against external enemies, hence the strong link between nationalism and blood sacrifice. In both ways, humans become dominated by gods of our own making.

Paul sketches a very different vision of a divinized "we" in his first letter to the Corinthians (10:14-6): "Therefore, my beloved, flee from the worship of idols. I speak as to sensible people; judge for yourselves what I say. The cup of blessing that we bless, is it not a sharing in the blood of Christ? The bread that we break, is it not a sharing in the body of Christ?" As I argued in chapter 3, Paul in I Corinthians 8–10 sets Eucharistic fellowship with Christ against table fellowship with idols, but he does not envision a community of the pure set apart from the rest of society. "If an unbeliever invites you to a meal and you are disposed to go, eat whatever is set before you without raising any question on the ground of conscience," though Paul recommends abstaining if the host specifically points out that the food was offered in sacrifice to false gods (10:27–8). The community Paul envisions is one that tries carefully to discern how to live out true solidarity in Christ amid an idolatrous world and given Christians' own sinfulness. For Paul, living Eucharistically means sharing food with the hungry (11:17–34) as we are all members of the same body because of our Eucharistic fellowship (12:4–31). That body is no merely immanent "we" because its head is one who is wholly Other, the very Lord Jesus Christ, whose Spirit activates all of the various gifts given to the community (12:11). Because the life of the body is received as a gift from God, not self-generated, the individual members must look beyond the individual self to the others gathered by the Other. More than simply diversity, the body of Christ lives on interdependence, each member recognizing the gifts conveyed by the others and the indispensability of each (12:14–21). Far from being scapegoated, the weakest members are in fact regarded as most indispensable and given the greatest honor (12:22–4). The community receives its identity not by looking in a mirror narcissistically but by looking toward the weakest among them, who are icons of the self-emptying God whose "power is made perfect in weakness," as Paul says elsewhere (II Cor. 12:9). Such is the circulation of love through the body of the weak God that the difference between self and other is relativized: "If one member suffers, all suffer together with it; if one member is honored, all rejoice together with it" (12:26). Paul thus makes the connection between encountering Christ sacramentally in the bread and wine and encountering Christ sacramentally in the poor and weakest among us.

We examined this circulation of love in Augustine's work in chapter 4. If idolatry is self-love, writ small or writ large, then the remedy for idolatry is breaking down the barriers between ourselves and God, and between ourselves and our neighbors. Rather than see in creation—both other people and things—a mirror of our own desires and fears, we should see creation iconically as mediating the presence and love of God. All of creation is caught up in the movement of God's self-giving love; we journey together with our neighbors and created things toward our eternal home, though we often frustrate our enjoyment of God and one another in God by reducing things to the measure of our own wants and neglecting the love of others. Self-love inevitably turns autonomy into heteronomy, as we become dominated by our own inventions. Augustine sees the sacraments as part of the pedagogy that draws us away from narcissism and into the circulation of charity. Christ, offered in the Eucharist, is the mediator between God and creation, drawing all into participation in God. We humans become the Eucharist offered on the altar, participating in the body of Christ in the Spirit, and thus offer ourselves to feed others as bread for the world. In the sacraments more generally, the things of this world are used toward the participation of people in the body of Christ and the lives of one another.

The divinized "we" of nationalism is different from the divinized "we" of the body of Christ because nationalism has no true ontological participation in anything higher than we the people, and because nationalism erects barriers between "us" and "them," both external and internal others. To live sacramentally is to break down the barriers between us and God and between us and them by basing a love for all people and all creation in an ontological participation in the Creator of all. In the Gospel accounts, the Eucharist is a foretaste of the eschatological banquet in which all will be gathered and eat and drink equally well. In Luke's narrative of the institution of the Eucharist, Jesus refers to the eschatological banquet three times (22:16, 18, 30; see also Mk. 14:25; Mt. 26:29). There are clear echoes here of the vision of the eschatological banquet in the book of Isaiah, where "all peoples" will be gathered for a rich feast on God's holy mountain (25:6). Isaiah 56:3–8 makes clear that foreigners will be gathered to God's mountain along with Israel. The Eucharist is meant to gather a community of peoples from all parts of the globe, a healing of the divisions that plague the world. In the Didache the bread of the Eucharist is linked to the gathering of the people: "Even as this broken bread was scattered over the hills, and was gathered together and became one, so let Your Church be gathered together from the ends of the earth into Your kingdom."[190]

The violence of nationalism is also turned upside down in Jesus's words at the institution of the Eucharist: "This cup that is poured out for you is the new covenant in my blood" (Lk. 22:20; see also I Cor. 11:25; Mk. 14:24). Matthew's account adds "for the forgiveness of sins" (26:28). Rather than scapegoating others to promote our sense of "we," Jesus offers himself as a sacrifice of reconciliation and a new covenant that will gather the nations. The mercy of God will be renewed, and unjust death will end. "For as often as you eat this bread and drink the cup, you proclaim the Lord's death until he comes" (I Cor. 11:26). Proclaiming the Lord's death is not to stoke fantasies of revenge for his unjust death but to look forward to the Lord's coming when death is brought to an end, "when he hands over the kingdom to God the

Father, after he has destroyed every ruler and every authority and power. For he must reign until he has put all his enemies under his feet. The last enemy to be destroyed is death" (15:24–6). Christ triumphs over the rulers not by dealing out more death but by dying. The cross disarms the rulers and makes a spectacle of them (Col. 2:15). The story ends not in death, but in resurrection.[191] The body of Christ the Eucharist incorporates us into is a resurrection body, one in which "death has been swallowed up in victory" (I Cor. 15:55). We are called to live resurrected lives in the resurrected body of Christ, in which division, exclusion, and violence are healed.

For a glimpse of what this might look like in practice, I suggest Pope Francis's approach in his address for the 2021 World Day of Migrants and Refugees, titled "Towards an Ever Wider 'We.'" Francis recounts how God created all in God's image, a communion in diversity, and how that image, tarnished by sin, has been restored in the mystery of Christ. God "wished to offer us a path of reconciliation, not as individuals but as a people, a 'we,' meant to embrace the entire human family, without exception." Today, however, our sense of "we" embracing all humanity is broken by "myopic and aggressive forms of nationalism" and individualism. "And the highest price is being paid by those who most easily become viewed as *others*: foreigners, migrants, the marginalized, those living on the existential peripheries." To the church, Francis exhorts us to remember our baptism into one body and one Spirit (Eph. 4:4) and embrace diversity within that unity, tending especially to migrants, refugees, displaced persons, and victims of trafficking. To the world, Francis encourages us to dream an "even more beautiful creation" into reality; "we can transform borders into privileged places of encounter, where the miracle of an ever wider 'we' can come about."[192]

This encounter, as Pope Francis makes clear in his 2019 address for World Day of Migrants and Refugees, is not just a matter of intramundane ethics; it is about our relationship with God. Fear of those seeking our protection, security, and a better life not only deprives me of encountering the other; "it deprives me of an opportunity to encounter the Lord."[193] In other addresses for the same occasion, Francis has invoked the flight into Egypt, where Jesus begins life as a refugee,[194] and Matthew 25:31–46, where Christ identifies himself with the stranger looking for welcome.[195] The worship of the God who became incarnate is not reducible to policy or ethical codes; worshiping this God and not some other god requires being vulnerable to the presence of God in the weakest who come uninvited seeking our aid. This encounter with God is not programmable; it must be received rather than controlled.

We need to supplement Marion's overwhelming encounter with Christ in the Eucharist with the overwhelming encounter with Christ incarnated in the marginalized. Poor persons are not a problem to be solved but a locus of God's unmanageable presence, and the unmanageability of the encounter with God is precisely what rescues us from idolatry. Pope Francis writes that the fruitfulness of the encounter "depends above all on our openness to being touched and moved by those who knock at our door. Their faces shatter and debunk all those false idols that can take over and enslave our lives; idols that promise an illusory and momentary happiness blind to the lives and sufferings of others."[196] Francis continues on to name some of the idols that produce migrants and refugees to begin with: markets favoring wealthier countries; wars and weapon selling by countries which then refuse to accept refugees from the wars they have fueled; an attitude by nations and individuals of "Me first!" when the Gospel commands us to put the last first. The remedy to the ills of nationalism—compassion, sharing the sufferings of others, striving to widen our sense of "we"—is not just an ethical program but a rejection of idolatry and an encounter with the true God. It is an expansion of the body of Christ, God-with-us, and a participation in the circulation of love that is God's life.

The idolatrous danger in consumer culture that we encountered in chapter 7 is simultaneously investing divinity in things while objectifying people. While there is a basic human desire to encounter the material world sacramentally, consumer culture often distorts that longing by severing the link between creation and Creator. Things become a mirror of narcissistic desire rather than a means of participation in the life of God. Devotion to things replaces devotion to God, and while things take on greater visibility and importance in our lives, the capitalist economy that drives the production of things hides the destruction of human lives and ecosystems necessary to bring cheap goods to our doorstep. As in biblical idolatry, life is imputed to material things while life is drained away from people, animals, and plants. As in biblical idolatry, we become dominated by our own creations; we pin our hopes to the divinity we ascribe to things, while that god is sustained by human sacrifice, the consumption of lives.

Once again, scripture and tradition offer resources for living sacramentally rather than idolatrously. Paul's multiple uses of the image of Christ's body have the effect of turning the act of consumption inside out. We consume Christ's body in the sacramental form of bread, and we thereby become Christ's body, which the Pauline literature identifies with the church (Col.

1:18, 1:24; I Cor. 12:27; Rom. 12:4–5; Eph. 1:23, 5:29–30). Rather than the consumption of material things serving to construct and buttress our narcissistic self-images, the consumption of Christ's body in the form of bread offers to pull us out of our small selves and into participation in the cosmic Christ who encompasses all creatures in love. Augustine puts God's word to us in this way: "I am the food of the fully grown; grow and you will feed on me. And you will not change me into you like the food your flesh eats, but you will be changed into me."[197] Instead of pulling divinity into the small self, that self is called to participate in God's life. We are consumed by God and called to offer ourselves to be consumed as food for the hungry. Rather than this being a threat to our autonomy or our well-being, as we saw in chapter 4 it is a call to participation in a much larger self, where the zero-sum relationship of self and other is superseded by the circulation of love in which the weakest are shown the greater honor, and all suffer and rejoice together. Our relationship with things is therefore reintegrated into our relationship with God and with other people. As opposed to looking at things and seeing reflections of our own divinized wants, we see things in relation to the laborers who made them, the marginalized who lack necessary goods, and the God who makes creation possible and wants it to be shared.

The Eucharist is meant to be an economy of gift; the name, Greek for "thanksgiving" (*eucharistia*), indicates as much. The elements of bread and wine—"fruit of the earth and work of human hands," in the words of the Catholic Mass—are received both from God's creation and from the laborers who fashioned wheat and grapes into their current form. Christ takes these gifts and makes them the form of his own self-giving. Our task is to receive them gratefully and continue the circulation of gifts by giving to others. Circulation, not accumulation, is the point of a gift economy. Abundant life is not defined as possessing more things but as participation in the common good, the circulation of goods to all. The offertory is not giving to God what we possess but a recognition that all belongs to God, and we can bring only the gifts we have received; bringing up "the gifts" at the offertory is not simply our gift to God but our participation in the circulation of gifts that God inaugurates. Offertory processions by the laity have a long history and have often included other fruits of the earth besides bread and wine.[198] I have attended Mass in a Nigerian village in which people processed one by one to the altar bearing yams, bowls of rice, cash, even live chickens. All of the people's material lives are included in the Eucharist; the Incarnation is a blessing of all creation. Though from the eleventh century onward the offertory was increasingly reduced to the offering of money, the inclusion of monetary offerings is still a sign that all our economic life is meant to be subject to what we celebrate in the Eucharist. All that we have belongs to God; private property is subject to a "social mortgage," the use of goods for the benefit of all.[199] According to Acts of the Apostles, the early church community broke bread in the context of communal ownership of property (Acts 2:44–7; see also 4:32–7). This is why Paul chastised the Corinthians for failing to discern the body when they did not share their food at the Lord's Supper (I Cor. 11:17–34).

Those hidden by our system of production and consumption are not only included in this sacramental economy; they are themselves sacraments of God's presence, in the broader sense of "sacrament." The fetishism of commodities is countered by the sacramentalization of the exploited and hidden people who produce commodities for our consumption. The marginalized as sacrament of Christ is revealed in Jesus's telling of the last judgment in Matthew 25:31–46. There the Son of Man identifies himself not with those who do good but with the "least of these brothers and sisters of mine," those who were hungry, thirsty, strangers, naked, sick, or imprisoned. God comes to us in material form in people, especially the most vulnerable, who are living icons of Jesus Christ. Those who did not care for them were unaware that they were in fact the Lord, and most likely went about their lives without paying attention to the suffering at all. But those who cared for them were also unaware that the least were identified with Christ. As with all sacraments, the presence of God is not simply visible in the material elements but can be perceived only with the eyes of faith. Jesus's story of the last judgment is a challenge to see the people who have been marginalized and hidden. Despite their failure to recognize the Son of Man in the weakest, the behavior of those who cared for them was rewarded in the last judgment as revealing their implicit belief. Idolatry and its opposite again are about more than what one claims to believe; they are what one's life reveals about *which divinity* one really worships. Note as well that there is no indication that either the least or those who cared for them are limited to members of the church; indeed, "all the nations" are summoned to judgment before the Son of Man (Matt. 25:32). There is, nevertheless, a strong congruence between the sacrament of the Eucharist and the story Jesus tells here; those who would be assimilated to Christ's body in the Eucharist must see the weakest as the most honored members of Christ's body, and therefore as part of their very own body.

Certeau, writing for a supposedly secularizing Europe after the "death of God," emphasized the absence of Christ's body from history, his "founding disappearance."[200] As we saw in the previous chapter, Latin American theologians have identified the modern problem not as the death of God but as the proliferation of false gods, especially the national security state and the market; the problem is not atheism but idolatry. Likewise, Latin American theologians have emphasized the presence of Jesus Christ in the bodies of those who suffer from the depredations of the false gods. Solidarity with those who suffer is based in the presence of Jesus in the bodies of the oppressed. The physical body of Jesus Christ may be gone from history, but one place his body is still present is in those who suffer deprivation, persecution, and isolation from the centers of power in human society. Ignacio Ellacuría and Jon Sobrino have emphasized the theme of the crucified people, focusing especially on Matthew 25 and the suffering servant song in Second Isaiah. Despite being despised and oppressed by the sins of others (Is. 53:2–8), despite being unseen (53:2–3), the servant has salvific importance: we are made whole and healed by the servant's suffering (53:5), and he shall make many righteous (53:11). The crucified people are not fully identified as Christ in history, but they participate in Christ's crucifixion and have an important role to play in the salvation of the world. They demonstrate the reality of sin and offer opportunities for the conversion in history of those who participate in their oppression. They offer values such as solidarity, hope, forgiveness, and faith that point toward the possibility of a better world. Not all the marginalized are virtuous, of course; poverty and oppression can kill the spirit as well as the body. But Ellacuría and Sobrino both insist that salvation must be historical or it is just another myth, and among the marginalized is the concrete historical location where the salvation offered by the suffering servant can be found.[201] It is perhaps best to think of marginalized people as a sacrament of Christ in the world, showing the presence of Christ in the world and yet pointing beyond themselves to him. Their sacramental presence offers the possibility of healing the idolatry that contributes to their suffering.

To encounter Christ in marginalized people is not simply to emphasize God's presence over God's absence in history. Incarnation is always an interplay between presence and absence; God is both hidden and manifest in creation. To truly encounter God in a person is not thereby to efface the person, to see past the person and reduce them to a conduit for the encounter with God. The person retains their own integrity—and their own defects—while simultaneously offering a portal to participation in God. To encounter God in the marginalized is to encounter God amid sin and chaos, amid God's apparent absence from the unjust structures of the world and human wretchedness. Yet the Incarnation teaches us that it is by entering into the very vulnerability and chaos of this encounter that we meet God, shorn of our own attempts to make a God according to our own wants. Sacraments of all kinds encompass both the already of God's presence and the not yet of God's absence. We encounter God in kenosis, in God's self-emptying into vulnerable material reality, but that encounter offers hope for the coming of God's healing Kingdom, which is already among us. We cannot overlook the eschatological dimension of the Eucharist. It is what we do to "proclaim the death of the Lord until he comes" (I Cor. 11:26). In the Eucharist, we confront both the powers of death and the absence of the Cross, and the present and future hope of the resurrection.

What would a sacramental economy look like in practice? Without trying to give a full and detailed account, I will suggest a few pathways for avoiding idolatry. Production and consumption must be oriented to avoid the fetishization of things and the dehumanization of people. Consumers often pay more for Fair Trade products, with the understanding that the additional cost goes to pay a living wage for the workers who make the products. The Fair Trade movement also attempts to inform the consumer about the actual people who labor to produce things for us. Fair Trade is an attempt to demystify commodities by revealing their source in human labor, and thereby invite consumers to support dignified lives for the people who produce the products they consume. Clothes are no longer items that simply appear to the consumer, at the store or online, offering identity and fulfillment for a price; Fair Trade clothing reminds consumers that actual people made the clothes and tries to tell their story, inviting consumers into a type of communion with producers and inviting consumers to make sure that laborers and the environment are not exploited. Fair Trade is, potentially, both the defetishization of commodities and the concrete enactment of the kind of solidarity that Paul's image of the body of Christ envisions.

We have to be cautious here, however, because Fair Trade cannot counter fetishization if we imagine that our consumption of a few luxury items like coffee and chocolate can reverse the problems inherent in our current economic system. Ethical consumerism has in fact been critiqued as a new layer of fetishization in which commodities are granted magical powers to change the world, when they do no such thing. The main problem with Fair Trade and other kinds of ethical consumerism, argues Ryan Gunderson, is that it depoliticizes individuals by making them believe they can effect change just by consuming, rather than by concerted political action. The wealthy are encouraged to believe they can effect positive change in the world just by buying more stuff. Fair Trade products must compete for profits in the market, and so farms in the Fair Trade system, for example, continue to base food production on profit, not need. The Amazon-owned Whole Foods, for example, operates under the imperative to pursue and increase profitability. What is needed, argues Gunderson, is planned production meant to meet basic human needs, not private profit.[202]

This type of critique is a sobering reminder that Fair Trade items are currently seen as luxury items; those with more disposable income should not congratulate themselves on their purchases of higher-priced items from Whole Foods that are inaccessible to others with less disposable income. Consumption of fine clothing and food is not in and of itself solidarity with the poor. The scale of Fair Trade production and consumption is still quite small, and the expansion of a just economy depends on building different kinds of businesses and concerted political action—supporting trade unions and anti-trust action, or weaning federal policy away from agribusiness, for example—that is not taken care of by consumption alone. In fact, the very way we now think of ourselves above all as consumers rather than producers or citizens with a common good has been encouraged by deliberate U.S. government policies that favor cheap imported goods, suppress worker power, and give free rein to corporate consolidation. We have been encouraged to accept disempowerment as a fair exchange for cheap consumer goods.[203] The confluence of government with the interests of ever-larger corporations cannot be overcome by mere consumption; more systemic action is required. McCarraher has repeatedly objected that critiques of *consumerism* can distract from critiques of *capitalism*, which is the fundamental problem.[204] Consumption of a few Fair Trade items without deeper attention to production is not getting at the systemic root of the issue. Though my emphasis here is on consumer behavior, the above analysis should make clear that restructured consumption is inseparable from restructured relations of production and politics.

If the root of the issue is in fact a type of idolatry, then we will not simply be able to buy our way out of it. But Catholic social teaching has also been wary of putting faith in state-controlled planned production of the kind favored by Gunderson, which has not proven effective at producing a sacramental economy. Pope Benedict XVI's encyclical *Caritas in Veritate* seeks an economy of gift based in *caritas*, love: "[T]he *principle of gratuitousness* and the logic of gift as an expression of fraternity can and must *find their place within normal economic activity*."[205] Benedict rejects the "binary model of market-plus-State" which combines "*giving in order to acquire* (the logic of exchange) and *giving through duty* (the logic of public obligation, imposed by State law)."[206] What is needed is an economy based in gratuitousness and communion. "The market of gratuitousness does not exist, and attitudes of gratuitousness cannot be established by law."[207] An economy of gift can be created only by people encountering one another in the love of God. Benedict recommends attention, therefore, to the scale of enterprises, recommending the logic of subsidiarity, whereby both economic and political decisions are made by the most local community possible in order to facilitate the visibility of human persons and their mutual encounter. The goal, however, is not to create niches of ethical economic activity but to evangelize the entire economy. This will happen neither through the exclusive pursuit of profit for its own sake nor through the imposition of state planning, but through the creation of enterprises based on mutualist principles and pursuing social ends, in which labor can be re-imagined as a gift.[208] Benedict neither dismisses state intervention nor wants to abolish markets, but rather wants to see the market as "the economic institution that permits encounter between persons."[209] Examples of economic spaces that facilitate this encounter include cooperatives, worker-owned and worker-governed enterprises, microfinance, credit unions, and the Focolare Movement's Economy of Communion.[210]

Part of the difficulty of this language of gift is that it can privilege those who begin with more to give. As a relatively wealthy consumer, I can imagine my purchases at Whole Foods as gifts to the poor, but they are gifts from my excess, they directly benefit me in the fine foods I consume, and the question of justice—how did the disparity of purchasing power come about to begin with?—is not raised. In order to answer critiques of Fair Trade like those of Gunderson, our practices of consumption must be embedded in acts of solidarity with those disadvantaged by our current economic system. This means not only that our acts of consumption must be accompanied by concrete political solidarity with the oppressed, for example, defending indigenous people in the Amazon and elsewhere subject to the enclosure and privatization of their common lands. It means also that our consumption will need to include an element of penance and asceticism. Solidarity with the icons of the incarnate Christ in our world is not a frictionless act of luxury consumption; paying more for Fair Trade products should be understood as an act of penance, which in the Catholic tradition is also a sacrament. Those of us who have benefited from an economy of exclusion should see our efforts to create alternative spaces of inclusion as penance for the injustice in which we have participated. If "penance" sounds much harsher than "gift," the goal of solidarity is the same. The sacrament of penance is also called the sacrament of reconciliation because the goal is the healing of broken relationships between the penitent and God and between the penitent and other people. I prefer the language of penance in this context because it can deflate the idolatry of the self as giver that can accompany the economy of gift. The point of the economy of gift is that God is the original giver; a nonidolatrous economy is one where we recognize ourselves as recipients of God's munificence, and we strive to keep the circulation of gifts in motion until they reach all those currently excluded. Participating in the circulation of gifts requires recognizing and repenting of our participation in the circulation of injustice in which we are all enmeshed.

An anti-idolatrous economy of gift requires a certain kind of asceticism, a willingness to forgo *amor sui* in Augustine's sense of withdrawal from the circulation of love in order to stuff the self. Asceticism requires work; *ascesis* in its original Greek context referred to the kind of training that athletes undergo in order to perform at the optimal level. Learning about where products come from, how workers and the environment are treated, and to whom the profits go takes work, especially in an economy designed to hide such facts from the consumer. Avoiding some businesses—especially ubiquitous ones like Amazon—can be an inconvenience. Creating and investing in businesses that allow work to be reconfigured as the gift of necessary labor also takes effort, as does consuming less and giving the excess to those suffering poverty. Work is required to puncture a magical world of products that simply appear on our doorstep without work. But as Sut Jhally has pointed out (see the previous chapter) we are already working for marketers, creating surplus value for them and for producers by consuming ads, wearing branded clothing, passing on viral ads, allowing our data to be harvested, and participating in "brand communities." We freely pay a price premium for items associated with famous brands or celebrities: 20% of the wholesale cost of Nike's shoes endorsed by LeBron James goes to James for lending his name and image. People who willingly pay this "brand premium" balk at Fair Trade goods as too expensive; some would rather pay wealthy celebrities and wealthy corporations than the local organic farmer at the farmer's market.

David Cloutier suggests that instead of paying a "brand premium" for items, we pay a "sacramental premium" that directs money not toward the delight of the self through the magic of branding but to the flourishing of those who labor to produce the things we consume. More generally, rather than the work involved in "smart shopping," finding what we want for the lowest price, Cloutier suggests "sacramental shopping," figuring out how to do the most good and connect with the most people through our purchases. This is most easily done where the scale of businesses allows for encounter with real people.[211]

Penance and asceticism are commonly misunderstood as types of masochism; to be against self-love is to promote self-hatred. As we saw in chapter 4, the opposite is the case. The remedy for idolatry is not the denigration of the self and creation via the exaltation of God, as if God and creation were locked in a zero-sum contest. The remedy for idolatry is opening the self to participation in God with all of creation. The point of asceticism is to loosen our grip on the illusion of the isolated self and on the things that separate that self from God and from creation. The Trappist monk Thomas Merton sees this detachment, if understood as detachment from the small self, as a remedy for idolatry:

> Detachment from things does not mean setting up a contradiction between "things" and "God" as if God were another "thing" and as if His creatures were His rivals. We do not detach ourselves from things in order to attach ourselves to God, but rather we become detached *from ourselves* in order to see and use all things in and for God. . . . There is no evil in anything created by God, nor can anything of His become an obstacle to our union with Him. The obstacle is in our "self," that is to say in the tenacious need to maintain our separate, external, egotistic will. It is when we refer all things to this outward and false "self" that we alienate ourselves from reality and from God. It is then the false self that is our god, and we love everything for the sake of this self. We use all things, so to speak, for the worship of this idol which is the imaginary self.[212]

Another way of putting this is simply to say that the opposite of idolatry is joy. Joy is not the same as security or pleasure: "those who enjoy life most are those who leave security on the shore and become excited by the mission of communicating life to others."[213] Joy requires vulnerability. Joy is a kind of ecstasy that pulls us out of the confines of our fears and wants, and brings us into communion with God and with other creatures. There is a risk involved in this kind of vulnerability, a risk that is obvious in attempts to welcome strangers from beyond our national borders or to step out from behind our commodities to prioritize encounter with those excluded from such consumption. As Pope Francis has written:

> [T]he Gospel tells us constantly to run the risk of a face-to-face encounter with others, with their physical presence which challenges us, with their pain and their pleas, with their joy which infects us in our close and continuous interaction. True faith in the incarnate Son of God is inseparable from self-giving, from membership in the community, from service, from reconciliation with others. The Son of God, by becoming flesh, summoned us to the revolution of tenderness.[214]

The incarnate God is the key to healing idolatry. Rather than humans reaching up to grasp at divinity—and becoming oppressed by gods of our own making—the true God descends and pours Godself out into creation in order to invite all into participation in divine life. All creation is a sacrament of God's presence without reducing God to creation. The sacraments proper are the divinely instituted actions that celebrate that fact and incorporate us into participation in God and one another. We are called not just to celebrate rituals but to live sacramentally, to practice the love of God we find in created things and in our unmanageable encounters with other people. Healing idolatry is not so much a matter of self-discipline, of getting our worship right, of coloring within the lines. It is rather an act of thanksgiving—*eucharistia*—for all the good gifts God has lavished upon us. Healing idolatry is finally an act of grateful reception, a joyful response to being loved into being by God.

Notes

Introduction

1. David Foster Wallace, "Transcription of the 2005 Kenyon Commencement Address," May 21, 2005, https://web.ics.purdue.edu/~drkelly/DFWKenyonAddress2005.pdf, 8.
2. Ibid., 9.
3. Paul Gifford, *The Plight of Western Religion: The Eclipse of the Other-Worldly* (Oxford: Oxford University Press, 2019), x.
4. William T. Cavanaugh, *The Myth of Religious Violence: Secular Ideology and the Roots of Modern Conflict* (New York: Oxford University Press, 2009).
5. As will become apparent in later chapters, I am indebted to both James K. A. Smith, *Cultural Liturgies*, vol. 1: *Desiring the Kingdom: Worship, Worldview, and Cultural Formation* (2009), vol. 2: *Imagining the Kingdom: How Worship Works* (2013), and vol. 3: *Awaiting the King: Reforming Public Theology* (2017) (Grand Rapids, MI: Baker Academic); and Eugene McCarraher, *The Enchantments of Mammon: How Capitalism Became the Religion of Modernity* (Cambridge, MA: Harvard University Press, 2019).
6. Carl Schmitt, *Political Theology: Four Chapters on the Concept of Sovereignty*, trans. George Schwab (Cambridge, MA: MIT Press, 1985).
7. Paul Kahn, *Political Theology: Four New Chapters on the Concept of Sovereignty* (New York: Columbia University Press, 2011), 116–7. Idolatry critique depends on the idea that there is one true God beyond the myriad false ones, but Kahn seems to think this idea impossible. Kahn has a thoroughly pragmatist view of truth. We decide among "models of order" not by their approximation to or distance from some "independent facts of the matter"; they become true as we use them to convince ourselves and others (111). Kahn's book was published in 2011. Perhaps in the wake of Donald Trump and "alternative facts," the idea of objective truth does not look so bad after all.
8. Ibid., 124. See my response to Kahn's book in "Am I Impossible? A Political Theologian's Response to Kahn's *Political Theology*," *Political Theology* 13, no. 6 (2012): 735–40.
9. Robert A. Yelle, *Sovereignty and the Sacred: Secularism and the Political Economy of Religion* (Chicago: University of Chicago Press, 2018), 124.
10. Ibid., 5.
11. Ibid., 169. See my appreciative critique of Yelle's book in "Peeling Away the Cellophane: Political Theology and the Exceptional God," *Journal of Law and Religion* 36, no. 3 (2021): 538–46.
12. Max Weber, "Science as a Vocation," in *From Max Weber: Essays in Sociology*, ed. and trans. H. H. Gerth and C. Wright Mills (New York: Oxford University Press, 1946), 149.

13. Charles Taylor, *A Secular Age* (Cambridge, MA: Harvard University Press, 2007), 376.
14. Ibid., 768.
15. McCarraher, *Enchantments of Mammon*, 5.

Chapter 1

1. There exist multiple accounts of life in an Amazon warehouse. One of the most prominent is James Bloodworth, *Hired: Six Months Undercover in Low-Wage Britain* (London: Atlantic Books, 2018). You can buy it on Amazon.com: save 24% off the list price!

2. Amazon spokesperson, quoted in Thuy Ong, "Amazon Patents Wristbands That Track Warehouse Employees' Hands in Real Time," *The Verge*, February 1, 2018, https://www.theverge.com/2018/2/1/16958918/amazon-patents-trackable-wristband-warehouse-employees.

3. As Hans Joas notes, these different meanings of *Entzauberung* are rarely disambiguated, and often *Entzauberung* is treated as if it were a single concept. Hans Joas, *Die Macht des Heiligen: Eine Alternative zur Geschichte von der Entzauberung* (Berlin: Suhrkamp, 2017), 11, 220–32.

4. Aimee Picchi, "Inside an Amazon Warehouse: 'Treating Human Beings as Robots,'" CBS News, April 19, 2018, https://www.cbsnews.com/news/inside-an-amazon-warehouse-treating-human-beings-as-robots/.

5. Though it is commonly assumed that Weber borrowed the phrase from Schiller, it is not found in Schiller's writings. Weber read Schiller, and Schiller does write of an *entgotteten Natur*, a "de-deified nature," so the general idea is not foreign to Schiller. But the earliest known version of Weber's phrase comes from the philosopher Jakob Friedrich Fries in 1837, who writes of *die Entzauberung dieser Welt*. See Jason Josephson-Storm, *The Myth of Disenchantment: Magic, Modernity, and the Birth of the Human Sciences* (Chicago: University of Chicago Press, 2017), 271.

6. As Peter Ghosh comments on the term *Entzauberung* in Weber, "there is an excellent headline and very little body of material beneath it"; Peter Ghosh, *Max Weber and the Protestant Ethic: Twin Histories* (Oxford: Oxford University Press, 2014), 271.

7. Charles Taylor, "Western Secularity," in *Rethinking Secularism*, ed. Craig Calhoun, Mark Juergensmeyer, and Jonathan VanAntwerpen (New York: Oxford University Press, 2011), 38.

8. Joshua Landy and Michael Saler, "Introduction: The Varieties of Modern Enchantment" in Joshua Landy and Michael Saler, *The Re-enchantment of the World: Secular Magic in a Rational Age* (Stanford, CA: Stanford University Press, 2009), 3–4. An extended use of this typology is found in Michael Saler, "Modernity and Enchantment: A Historiographic Review," *American Historical Review* 111, no. 3 (June 2006): 692–716.

9. See Karl Marx, *Capital* (Harmondsworth: Penguin Classics, 1990), I.165.

10. Max Horkheimer and Theodor W. Adorno, *Dialectic of Enlightenment*, trans. John Cumming (New York: Herder and Herder, 1972), 3.

11. "On the road to modern science, men renounce any claim to meaning" (ibid., 5).
12. Ibid.
13. Ibid., 6.
14. "The awakening of the self is paid for by the acknowledgement of power as the principle of all relations. In view of the unity of this *ratio*, the divorcement between God and man dwindles to the degree of irrelevancy to which unswervable reason has drawn attention since even the earliest critique of Homer. The creative god and the systematic spirit are alike as rulers of nature. Man's likeness to God consists in sovereignty over existence, in the countenance of the lord and master, and in command" (ibid., 9).
15. Ibid., 4.
16. Ibid., 16.
17. Ibid., xiii.
18. Ibid. The full passage is worth reading: "The dilemma that faced us in our work proved to be the first phenomenon for investigation: the self-destruction of the Enlightenment. We are wholly convinced—and therein lies our *petitio principii*—that social freedom is inseparable from enlightened thought. Nevertheless, we believe that we have just as clearly recognized that the notion of this very way of thinking, no less than the actual historic forms—the social institutions—with which it is interwoven, already contains the seed of the reversal universally apparent today. If enlightenment does not accommodate reflection on this recidivist element, then it seals its own fate. If consideration of the destructive aspect of progress is left to its enemies, blindly pragmatized thought loses its transcending quality and its relation to truth. In the enigmatic readiness of the technologically educated masses to fall under the sway of any despotism, in its self-destructive affinity to popular paranoia, and in all uncomprehended absurdity, the weakness of the modern theoretical faculty is apparent. We believe that these fragments will contribute to the health of that theoretical understanding, insofar as we show that the prime cause of the retreat from enlightenment into mythology is not to be sought so much in the nationalist, pagan and other modern mythologies manufactured precisely in order to contrive such a reversal, but in the Enlightenment itself when paralyzed by fear of the truth" (xiii–xiv).
19. Some examples cited by Landy and Saler include Jean Comaroff and John Comaroff, eds., *Modernity and Its Malcontents: Ritual and Power in Postcolonial Africa* (Chicago: University of Chicago Press, 1993; Fernando Coronil, *The Magical State: Nature, Money, and Modernity in Venezuela* (Chicago: University of Chicago Press, 1997); and Peter Geschiere, *The Modernity of Witchcraft: Politics and the Occult in Post-colonial Africa*, trans. Janet Roitman (Charlottesville: University of Virginia Press, 1997). More recent books include Gurminder Bhambra, *Rethinking Modernity: Postcolonialism and the Sociological Imagination* (New York: Palgrave, 2007); Kwame Gyekye, *Tradition and Modernity: Philosophical Reflections on the African Experience* (New York: Oxford University Press, 2011).
20. Landy and Saler, "Introduction," 7, italics in the original.
21. Ibid., 3.
22. Saler, "Modernity and Enchantment," 714.

23. Ibid.

24. For a review of this scholarship, see chapter 2 of my book *The Myth of Religious Violence: Secular Ideology and the Roots of Modern Conflict* (New York: Oxford University Press, 2009). See also Brent Nongbri, *Before Religion: A History of a Modern Concept* (New Haven, CT: Yale University Press, 2013).

25. "Modernity is defined less by binaries arranged in an implicit hierarchy, or by the dialectical transformation of one term into its opposite, than by contradictions, oppositions, and antinomies: modernity is messy" (Landy and Saler, "Introduction," 7).

26. Ibid., 13.

27. Ibid., 14; see R. Lanier Anderson, "Nietzsche on Redemption and Transfiguration," in Landy and Saler, *Re-Enchantment of the World*, 225–58.

28. Jane Bennett, *The Enchantment of Modern Life: Attachments, Crossings, and Ethics* (Princeton, NJ: Princeton University Press, 2001).

29. Margaret J. Wiener, "Hidden Forces: Colonialism and the Politics of Magic in the Netherlands Indies," in *Magic and Modernity: Interfaces of Revelation and Concealment*, ed. Birgit Meyer and Peter Pels (Stanford, CA: Stanford University Press, 2003), 140.

30. Ibid.

31. Bruno Latour, *We Have Never Been Modern*, trans. Catherine Porter (Cambridge, MA: Harvard University Press, 1993).

32. Ibid., 10–11. Wiener puts it this way: "Indeed, colonial rulers, depending as they did upon enlisting the cooperation of native populations, could not maintain in practice the purity of their rejection of magic in theory. In attempting to act effectively in ways they thought would be meaningful to those they ruled, they tangled themselves in contradictions" ("Hidden Forces," 149).

33. Quoted in Wiener, "Hidden Forces," 147.

34. Wiener, "Hidden Forces," 149.

35. Ibid.

36. Ibid., 158.

37. This Gallup poll from 2005 is reinforced by the Baylor Religion Survey of 2005 and 2007 and by Pew research data from 2007; Josephson-Storm, *Myth of Disenchantment*, 23–30.

38. Josephson-Storm, *Myth of Disenchantment*, 29.

39. Ibid., 30–4.

40. Ibid., 18, 34.

41. Ibid., 275–7, 288–97.

42. Josephson-Storm traces the idea of a disenchanted modern world to the German Romantics, who lamented the supposed fact of the loss of myth. They thought disenchantment had to happen so that a higher enchantment could take place. What began among German philosophers in the early nineteenth century became a historians' trope in the middle of the century. Josephson-Storm credits Jacob Burckhardt with retroactively assigning disenchantment to the Renaissance, when "man" awoke from the childish illusions of the medieval period to become "objective." Weber read Burckhardt, though Weber assigned the birth of modern rationality to the Reformation, not the Renaissance (ibid., 63–93).

43. At Galileo's trial, it was not Galileo but his opponents who thought that the scriptural revelation could not be reconciled with heliocentrism.

44. Peter Harrison, *The Territories of Science and Religion* (Chicago: University of Chicago Press, 2015).

45. Josephson-Storm, *Myth of Disenchantment*, 13–6.

46. Ibid., 314.

47. See Latour, *We Have Never Been Modern*, and Hans Robert Jauss, "Modernity and Literary Tradition," trans. Christian Thorne, *Critical Inquiry* 31, no. 2 (2005): 329–64.

48. Josephson-Storm, *Myth of Disenchantment*, 7.

49. Ibid., 8.

50. William T. Cavanaugh, *Migrations of the Holy* (Grand Rapids, MI: Eerdmans, 2011). I borrow the phrase "migration of the holy" from historian John Bossy, *Christianity in the West 1400–1700* (Oxford: Oxford University Press, 1985).

51. Josephson-Storm, *Myth of Disenchantment*, 316. He continues, "By challenging this narrative, I have been aiming to take up modernity and postmodernity together and exit both. This will not be an exodus into a mythless future. Contra Lyotard, I see no end to metanarratives. But I also see no reason to flee from them. Reason is historical. Thought is narrative" (316).

52. Ghosh, *Max Weber*, 264.

53. Max Weber, "Confucianism," *Archiv für Sozialwissenschaft und Sozialpolitik* 41 (1915): 372, quoted in Ghosh, *Max Weber*, 260.

54. Max Weber, "The Social Psychology of the World Religions," in *From Max Weber: Essays in Sociology*, ed. and trans. H. H. Gerth and C. Wright Mills (New York: Oxford University Press, 1946), 293. The title given this essay by the translators is not inaccurate as a description of the essay's contents, but it is a far stretch from the actual German title, "Die Wirtschaftsethik der Weltreligionen," which means "The Economic Ethic of the World Religions."

55. Ibid., 293–4.

56. Max Weber, *Economy and Society*, ed. Guenther Roth and Claus Wittich (Berkeley: University of California Press, 1978), 26.

57. This is not a quote from Weber, but my way of summarizing his gist. For a discussion of the types of rationality in Weber, see Stephen Kalberg, "Max Weber's Types of Rationality: Cornerstones for the Analysis of Rationalization Processes in History," *American Journal of Sociology* 85, no. 5 (1980): 1145–79; Josephson-Storm, *Myth of Disenchantment*, 272–3.

58. Max Weber, *The Sociology of Religion*, trans. Ephraim Fischoff (Boston: Beacon Press, 1963), 1.

59. Hans Joas, *Die Macht des Heiligen*, 242–8 argues that Weber has no basis for thinking that the instrumental rationality of magic is the most elementary level of religion. Joas compares Weber's understanding with that of Durkheim, for whom communal rituals of the sacred provide the prerequisite for the emergence of magic.

60. Weber, "Social Psychology," 283.

61. Weber, *Sociology of Religion*, 27.

62. Ibid., 4.

63. Ibid., 5.
64. Ibid., 9.
65. "The proliferation of symbolic acts and their supplanting of the original naturalism will have far-reaching consequences. . . . Every purely magical act that had proved successful in a naturalistic sense was of course repeated in the form once established as effective. This principle extended to the entire domain of symbolic significances, since the slightest deviation from the ostensibly successful method might render the procedure inefficacious. Thus, all areas of human activity were drawn into this circle of magical symbolism" (ibid., 7).
66. Ibid., 1. "To define 'religion,' to say what it *is*, is not possible at the start of a presentation such as this. Definition can be attempted, if at all, only at the conclusion of the study. The essence of religion is not even our concern, as we make it our task to study the conditions and effects of a particular type of social behavior" (1). Weber does not explain how he can study the conditions and effects of religion if he has no working definition of what counts as religion and what does not.
67. Ibid., 28.
68. Ibid., 25.
69. Ibid., 25–31.
70. Ibid., 1.
71. As quoted above in Weber, "Social Psychology," 293.
72. Weber, *Sociology of Religion*, 2.
73. Ibid., 27–8.
74. Ibid., 44.
75. "The process of rationalization (*ratio*) favored the primacy of universal gods; and every consistent crystallization of a pantheon followed systematic rational principles to some degree, since it was always influenced by professional sacerdotal rationalism or by the rational striving for order on the part of secular individuals" (ibid., 22).
76. Ibid.
77. Ibid., 36.
78. Weber, "Social Psychology," 281. Similarly, "all religions have demanded as a specific presupposition that the course of the world be somehow *meaningful*, at least in so far as it touches upon the interests of men" (Max Weber, "Religious Rejections of the World and Their Directions" in *From Max Weber*, 353).
79. Weber, "Social Psychology," 271–5.
80. Weber, "Religious Rejections," 327.
81. Ibid., 328.
82. The title means "Intermediate Reflections," so named because it occupies a place between Weber's sections on the religion of China and the religion of India in volume 1 of his *Collected Essays on the Sociology of Religion* (*Gesammelte Aufsätze zur Religionssoziologie*). Gerth and Mills title the English translation of the essay "Religious Rejections of the World and Their Directions," which is the subtitle of the essay in its original version.
83. Weber, "Religious Rejections," 328, italics in the original.
84. Ibid., 328–30.
85. Ibid., 331.

86. Ibid.

87. Ibid., 334.

88. "It is absolutely essential for every political association to appeal to the naked violence of coercive means in the face of outsiders as well as in the face of internal enemies. It is only this very appeal to violence that constitutes a political association in our terminology. The state is an association that claims the monopoly of the *legitimate use of violence*, and cannot be defined in any other manner. The Sermon on the Mount says 'resist no evil.' In opposition, the state asserts: 'You *shall* help right to triumph by the use of *force*, otherwise you too may be responsible for injustice'" (ibid., italics in the original). See also Weber's definition of the state in terms of a monopoly on the legitimate use of violence in his "Politics as a Vocation," in *From Max Weber*, 77–8.

89. Weber, "Religious Rejections," 335.

90. Ibid.

91. Ibid.

92. Ibid., 336.

93. Ibid. Weber regards these two approaches as typifying the difference between Western (worldly asceticism) and Eastern (mysticism) approaches to religion. For a representative example of the critique of Orientalist stereotyping of the East as "mystical," see Richard A. King, *Orientalism and Religion: Post-Colonial Theory, India, and the Mystic East* (London: Routledge, 1999).

94. Weber, "Religious Rejections," 333.

95. Ibid., 326.

96. Ibid., 332, 336.

97. Ibid., 339.

98. Ibid., 350–1, italics in the original. The sense in which empirical science is an *Entzauberung der Welt* can be seen in the following quote in which Weber describes the magical world as unified and modernity as binary: "The unity of the primitive image of the world, in which everything was concrete magic, has tended to split into rational cognition and mastery of nature, on the one hand, and into 'mystic' experiences, on the other" ("Social Psychology," 282).

99. "In principle, the empirical as well as the mathematically oriented view of the world develops refutations of every intellectual approach which in any way asks for a 'meaning' of inner-worldly occurrences" (Weber, "Religious Rejections," 351).

100. Ibid.

101. Ibid., 351–3.

102. Ibid., 357.

103. Max Weber, *The Protestant Ethic and the Spirit of Capitalism*, trans. Talcott Parsons (New York: Charles Scribner's Sons, 1958), 105.

104. Ibid., 117.

105. Ibid.

106. On this point, see Joas, *Die Macht des Heiligen*, 228–9.

107. Weber, *Protestant Ethic*, 105.

108. Ibid., 149–50, 121.

109. Ibid., 149. Elsewhere, Weber contends that the magical or sacramental character of the means of grace must be abandoned by the worldly ascetic, because they devalue action in the world as merely secondary ("Social Psychology," 290).
110. Weber, *Protestant Ethic*, 111–5.
111. Ibid., 117.
112. Ibid., 154.
113. Weber, *Sociology of Religion*, 173: "The ascetic, when he wishes to act within the world, that is, to practice inner-worldly asceticism, must become afflicted with a sort of happy stupidity regarding any question about the meaning of the world, for he must not worry about such questions. Hence, it is no accident that inner-worldly asceticism reached its most consistent development on the foundation of the Calvinist god's absolute inexplicability, utter remoteness from every human criterion, and unsearchableness as to his motives."
114. Weber, *Protestant Ethic*, 176.
115. Ibid., 75; see also 181.
116. "In fact, [the capitalistic system] no longer needs the support of any religious forces, and feels the attempts of religion to influence economic life, in so far as they can still be felt at all, to be as much an unjustified interference as regulation by the State" (ibid., 72). Or again, "The ability to free oneself from the common tradition, a sort of liberal enlightenment, seems likely to be the most suitable basis for such a business man's success. And to-day that is generally precisely the case. Any relationship between religious beliefs and conduct is generally absent, and where any exists, at least in Germany, it tends to be of the negative sort. The people filled with the spirit of capitalism to-day tend to be indifferent, if not hostile, to the Church. The thought of the pious boredom of paradise has little attraction for their active natures; religion appears to them as a means of drawing people away from labour in this world" (70).
117. Max Weber, "Science as a Vocation," in *From Max Weber*, 143.
118. Ibid., 139, italics in the original. The advent of quantum theory, it seems, would require at least a nuancing of Weber's claim. According to quantum theory, there are certain things that we cannot know, not only in practice but *in principle*. The modern person's claim, then, would need to be that "if one but wished one *could* know all that could be known." Whether or not the randomness of quantum behavior would qualify as "mysterious incalculable forces" depends on how one defines "mysterious"; they are certainly "incalculable forces."
119. Ibid.
120. Ibid., 142.
121. Ghosh, *Max Weber*, 285: "Hence this statement in the essay on 'Objectivity' of the *only* explicit a priori commitment on which his thinking relies: 'The transcendental presupposition of every *science of Kultur* is . . . that we are persons of *Kultur*, equipped with ability and the will to take up a conscious *position* in relation to the world and endow it with *meaning*'" (italics in the original). Here Ghosh is quoting from Max Weber, "Objecktivität" (1904), in *Gesammelte Aufsätze zur Wissenschaftslehre*, ed. J. Winckelmann (Tübingen: Mohr Siebeck, 1968), 180. For an English translation of this article, see Max Weber, "'Objectivity' in Social Science and Social Policy,"

in *Max Weber on the Methodology of the Social Sciences,* trans. and ed. Edward A. Shils and Henry A. Finch (Glencoe, IL: Free Press, 1949), 49–112. The quote is on 81. According to Ghosh, "There has been a striking absence of discussion of the 'problem of meaning' throughout the history of Weberian reception" (*Max Weber,* 277n131).

122. Weber, "Science as a Vocation," 143. Weber continues, "[S]till less can it be proved that the existence of the world which these sciences describe is worth while, that it has any 'meaning,' or that it makes sense to live in such a world. Science does not ask for the answers to such questions" (144).

123. Ibid., 155.

124. Ibid., 140–1, 143. Weber notes, nevertheless, "No science is absolutely free from presuppositions, and no science can prove its fundamental value to the man who rejects these presuppositions" (153).

125. Ibid., 155.

126. Ibid., 155–6. He also holds them in higher regard than those academics who use the classroom to impose their own personal values on students: "In my eyes, such religious return stands higher than the academic prophecy, which does not clearly realize that in the lecture-rooms of the university no other virtue hold but plain intellectual integrity" (155–6). See also 145–7.

127. I use this phrase with deliberate irony to note the way that Weber's account is gendered. The modern scientific man chooses values as an act of sheer will; he stands above givenness and materiality. The manly man is juxtaposed with the feminine figure of the compassionate old churches waiting with open arms. For an analysis of the feminization of the churches in the nineteenth century, see Ann Douglas, *The Feminization of American Culture* (New York: Farrar, Strauss and Giroux, 1998). Douglas analyzes churches in the American context, but the analysis applies, *mutatis mutandis,* to Weber's context as well.

128. Weber, "Science as a Vocation," 153.

129. Ibid., 147. Weber credits the notion to James Mill.

130. Ibid., 152–3.

131. Ibid., 147.

132. Ibid., 148.

133. Ibid., 149.

134. On this point, see Ghosh, *Max Weber,* 284.

135. Max Weber, "The Meaning of 'Ethical Neutrality' in Sociology and Economics" in *Max Weber on the Methodology of the Social Sciences,* 17–8.

136. Weber, "Science as a Vocation," 152.

137. Weber, "'Objectivity' in Social Science and Social Policy," 57, italics in the original.

138. Alkis Kontos, "The World Disenchanted, and the Return of Gods and Demons," in *The Barbarism of Reason: Max Weber and the Twilight of Enlightenment,* ed. Asher Horowitz and Terry Maley (Toronto: University of Toronto Press, 1994), 227: "Not the right choice, not the right path matter in and of themselves, but *the making* of the right choice, *the choosing* of the right path; and to do so time and again."

139. Ibid., 238–41.

140. Susan Hekman, "Max Weber and Post-Positivist Social Theory," in Horowitz and Maley, *Barbarism of Reason*, 272–5.
141. Weber, "Science as a Vocation," 156.
142. Ghosh, *Max Weber*, 284.
143. Ghosh makes this argument: "Above all, charisma and the idea of grace that accompanies it are magical qualities, but these qualities are *precious* to Weber in a modern context, because they are the last vestige of 'free' behavior that has not fallen prey to the 'steel housing' or 'causal mechanism' of cumulative rationalization.... The associations of magic may be peasant and primitive; but in the contexts of modern capitalism and political leadership, they may also be liberating" (ibid., 263–4).
144. Of course, my argument is that the distinction between charisma and rationality is blurred, even in Weber. The burden of S. N. Eisenstadt's introduction to the collection of Weber's writings titled *Max Weber on Charisma and Institution Building* (Chicago: University of Chicago Press, 1968) is to show that for Weber charisma is essential to institution building. Eisenstadt uses the work of another Weber scholar, Edward Shils, to note that every society has a "central power" that partakes of a charismatic quality, whether it be God or the ultimate principles of law. According to Shils, "The central zone partakes of the nature of the sacred. In this sense, every society has an 'official' religion, even when that society or its exponents and interpreters conceive of it, more or less correctly, as a secular, pluralistic, and tolerant society" (quoted in Eisenstadt, "Introduction," in *Max Weber on Charisma*, xxx).
145. Weber, *Protestant Ethic*, 181. Richard Baxter (1615–1691) was an English Puritan theologian.
146. Ibid.
147. Eyal Chowers, *The Modern Self in the Labyrinth: Politics and the Entrapment Imagination* (Cambridge, MA: Harvard University Press, 2004), 1–19.
148. Mary Shelley, *Frankenstein*, quoted in ibid., 34.
149. Max Weber, *Selections in Translation*, trans. E. Matthews (Cambridge: Cambridge University Press, 1978), 281. This passage is from Weber's 1906 text "Zur Lage der bürgerlichen Demokratie in Russland." Weber continues, "It is utterly ridiculous to suppose that it is an 'inevitable' feature of our economic development under present-day advanced capitalism, as it has now been imported into Russia and as it exists in America, that it should have an elective affinity with 'democracy' or indeed with 'freedom' (in *any* sense of that word), when the only question to be asked is: how are all these things, in general and in the long term, *possible* where it prevails?" (282, italics in the original).
150. Weber defines "personality" as "a concept which entails a constant and intrinsic relation to certain ultimate 'values' or 'meanings' of life, 'values' and 'meanings' which are forged into purposes and thereby translate into rational-teleological action." Max Weber, *Roscher and Knies: The Logical Problems of Historical Economics* (New York: Free Press, 1975), 192, quoted in Chowers, *Modern Self*, 69.
151. Gilbert Germain, "The Revenge of the Sacred: Technology and Re-enchantment," in Horowitz and Maley, *Barbarism of Reason*, 248–54, 258–60. Germain makes this

argument in more detail in his book *A Discourse on Disenchantment: Reflections on Politics and Technology* (Albany, NY: SUNY Press, 1993), 25–42.

152. Germain illustrates this point with a number of examples from contemporary life. We no longer eat to enjoy good food, for example, but as a means toward the end of "health." We are absorbed in achieving techniques, such as "parenting skills" and even "life skills," rather than simply raising children and living life ("Revenge of the Sacred," 262–3).

153. Ibid., 255–7, 261. Elsewhere Germain comments, "Although Weber himself does not use the term, we could say that our technological environment has acquired 'magical' qualities to the extent that we count on processes whose behavior we are at a loss to explain" (*Discourse on Disenchantment*, 42).

154. Max Weber, "Bureaucracy," in *From Max Weber*, 228.

155. Weber, *Economy and Society*, 1401.

156. Weber, "Bureaucracy," 228.

157. Max Weber, "Socialism," in *Political Writings*, ed. Peter Lassman and Ronald Speirs (Cambridge: Cambridge University Press, 1994), 260, quoted in Chowers, *Modern Self*, 54.

158. Weber, "Bureaucracy," 215–6.

159. Although he does not directly discuss Feuerbach, Weber took for granted that in their origins "the various kinds of gods and demons . . . are determined quite directly by the economic situation and historical fortunes of individual peoples above all" (*Max Weber Gesamtausgabe* I/22–2.137–8, quoted in Ghosh, *Max Weber*, 91). Ghosh notes that "Weber does not mention Feuerbach, but he was by no means a forgotten man, and is a frequent presence in the writings of the day" (91n31). Weber, however, did not think that the human origins of Christianity should mean its dismissal. He thought that Christianity was the very foundation of German culture.

160. Chowers, *Modern Self*, 79.

161. Weber, *Economy and Society*, 1402.

162. Weber, "Science as a Vocation," 149.

163. Weber, "Religious Rejections," 334.

164. Ibid., 335.

165. Ibid.

166. Ibid., 336.

167. Weber makes this argument in his famous "Politics as a Vocation," in *From Max Weber*, 77–128. The quote is from 121. Anthony Carroll situates Weber's insistence on the proper "objectivity" of politics within the context of German Protestant anti-Catholicism. In politics, objectivity was most threatened by confessional parties, especially the Catholic Center Party. Anthony Carroll, "Disenchantment, Rationality and the Modernity of Max Weber," *Forum Philosophicum* 16, no. 1 (2011): 117–37.

168. Weber, "Religious Rejections," 331.

169. Max Weber, *Die Börse I*, *Max Weber Gesamtausgabe* I/5.148, quoted in Ghosh, *Max Weber*, 300.

170. Ghosh, *Max Weber*, 285, italics in the original.

171. Weber, *Protestant Ethic*, 70.

172. Ibid., 53. The language here is reminiscent of papal social teaching. See, for example, John Paul II's warning of the "onesided subordination of man to material goods alone" in his 1979 address to the UN General Assembly, https://w2.vatican.va/content/john-paul-ii/en/speeches/1979/october/documents/hf_jp-ii_spe_19791002_general-assembly-onu.html, §16.

173. Weber, *Protestant Ethic*, 181.

174. Ibid., 54. He continues, "It forces the individual, in so far as he is involved in the system of market relationships, to conform to capitalistic rules of action."

175. Ghosh, *Max Weber*, 290.

176. As Lawrence Scaff puts it, with apologies to Hegel, for Weber "[w]hat is rational is not actual, and what is actual is irrational." Lawrence A. Scaff, "Fleeing the Iron Cage: Politics and Culture in the Thought of Max Weber," *American Political Science Review* 81, no. 3 (September 1987): 740.

177. Lawrence A. Scaff, *Max Weber in America* (Princeton, NJ: Princeton University Press, 2011), 45–6.

178. See Ghosh, *Max Weber*, 305–17.

179. Weber, *Protestant Ethic*, 194n9.

180. Alan Jacobs, "On the Myth of Disenchantment," *New Atlantis*, May 9, 2018, http://text-patterns.thenewatlantis.com/2018/05/on-myth-of-disenchantment.html.

181. L.M. Sacasas, "Are We Really Disenchanted?," *Frailest Thing*, May 15, 2018, https://thefrailestthing.com/2018/05/15/are-we-really-disenchanted/.

182. Weber, *Protestant Ethic*, 181.

183. Weber, *Sociology of Religion*, 206, italics mine.

184. John Evans and Michael Evans make a helpful distinction between sociological analyses of religion and science that are "symbolic" and those that are "social-institutional." They argue that the common Western narrative of an implacable conflict between religion and science is based on seeing them exclusively as opposing truth claims about the natural world; this is the "symbolic" approach. When viewed from a "social-institutional" lens, however, religion and science are seen as meaning systems that are institutionalized in different ways and rarely come into conflict. See John H. Evans and Michael S. Evans, "Religion and Science: Beyond the Epistemological Conflict Narrative," *Annual Review of Sociology* 34 (2008): 87–105. Evans and Evans seem to put Weber in the former "symbolic" camp, but I am arguing that Weber was in fact more interested in the latter approach.

185. See, for example, Robert W. Scribner, "The Reformation, Popular Magic, and the 'Disenchantment of the World,'" *Journal of Interdisciplinary History* 23, no. 3 (Winter 1993): 475–94. Historians have questioned the idea that the Reformation was a significant agent of disenchantment to such an extent that Alexandra Walsham in 2008 declared the revisionist thesis as "something approaching the current historical consensus." Alexandra Walsham, "The Reformation and 'The Disenchantment of the World' Reassessed," *Historical Journal* 51, no. 2 (2008): 500. Walsham points to many ways in which Protestants continued to see objects, places, and times as saturated with the presence of the sacred. Zwinglian Eucharistic theology and Calvinist iconoclasm did indeed promote a distance between nature and God, but the Protestant world was populated by angels, devils, and witches. The rationality of the Protestant

world over against the superstition of the medieval Catholic predecessor culture was, in the first instance, a product of Protestant polemics. At the same time,
Walsham writes that in historical scholarship, "[t]he idea of an enchanted middle
ages is gradually evaporating" (504). Weber's understanding of sacrament as magic,
for example, is crude and ignores the role that the disposition of the recipient played
in determining the fruitfulness of the sacrament. Patrick Sherry likewise observes,
"Since [Weber] does not really take into account the ways in which God is believed to
work through the ordinary chains of cause and effect in nature, he tends to construe
God's agency in terms of special interventions." Patrick Sherry, "Disenchantment,
Re-Enchantment, and Enchantment," *Modern Theology* 25, no. 3 (July 2009): 381.
Walsham suggests that any narrative of linear progression from enchantment to
disenchantment be replaced by thinking in terms of cycles of desacralization and
resacralization ("The Reformation," 527). Weber himself might not be averse to such
a reading of history. He seems to have seen the relationship between charisma and
rationalization not as one giving way inexorably to the other but as a dialectic that
continues into the modern world; see Raymond L. M. Lee, "Weber, Re-enchantment
and Social Futures," *Time & Society* 19, no. 2 (2010): 180–92; Sam Whimster and
Scott Lash, "Introduction," in *Max Weber, Rationality and Modernity* (London: Allen
and Unwin, 1987), 13. However, I am less interested in merely rearranging the chronology of enchantment and disenchantment, or sacralization and desacralization,
than in questioning our confidence that the two members of each pair—in any era—
are clearly separable.

186. Weber, *Sociology of Religion*, 205–6. Here he emphasizes the irrelevance of changes
in metaphysical belief to the behavior of historical subjects in the West, which
manifests continuity. In his historical narratives crossing over into modernity,
Weber is consistently captivated by what has not changed.

187. Asher Horowitz and Terry Maley, "Introduction," in Horowitz and Maley, *Barbarism
of Reason*, 1.

188. Alison Stone, "Adorno and the Disenchantment of Nature," *Philosophy and Social
Criticism* 32, no. 2 (2006): 238.

189. In addition to the sources mentioned in note 19, see Robert Yelle, *The Language
of Disenchantment: Protestant Literalism and Colonial Discourse in British India*
(New York: Oxford University Press, 2012).

190. Robert Yelle, "The Trouble with Transcendence: Carl Schmitt's 'Exception' as
a Challenge for Religious Studies," *Method and Theory in the Study of Religion* 22
(2010): 191.

191. Carl Schmitt, *Political Theology: Four Chapters on the Concept of Sovereignty*, trans.
George Schwab (Cambridge, MA: MIT Press, 1985), 36.

192. Carl Schmitt, *Political Theology II: The Myth of the Closure of Any Political Theology*,
trans. Michael Hoelzl and Graham Ward (Cambridge, UK: Polity, 2008), 74.

193. Yelle, "The Trouble with Transcendence," 203. If my argument in this chapter is correct, however, Weber himself may not have repressed this thought to the complete
extent that both Schmitt and Yelle appear to think.

Chapter 2

1. Taylor indicates that he did walk away from the Church at one point in his life, but came back. "But for people coming out of the present predicament of the immanent frame, and the search for meaning, this historic order doesn't have the same meaning. How to recover contact with the Gospel today? For most of us (I speak for myself again), we went through some period of break with the faith we were brought up in (if we were brought up Christian at all), before returning through a different route. We are 'believing again,' rather than 'believing still' (W. H. Auden). We are very aware of the fragility of historical constructions supposed to resolve the problems of mankind once and for all, supposed to resist the forces of decay and loss of direction, whether these be communist or liberal, or whatever." Charles Taylor, "Shapes of Faith Today," in *Renewing the Church in a Secular Age*, ed. João Vila-Chã, Charles Taylor, José Casanova, and George McLean (Washington, DC: Council for Research in Values and Philosophy, 2016), 278.
2. Charles Taylor, "Western Secularity," in *Rethinking Secularism*, ed. Craig Calhoun, Mark Juergensmeyer, and Jonathan VanAntwerpen (New York: Oxford University Press, 2011), 38.
3. Charles Taylor, *A Secular Age* (Cambridge, MA: Harvard University Press, 2007), 1.
4. Charles Taylor, "Disenchantment-Reenchantment," in *The Joy of Secularism: 11 Essays for How We Live Now*, ed. George Levine (Princeton, NJ: Princeton University Press, 2011), 57.
5. Taylor, *Secular Age*, 376.
6. See Shmuel Eisenstadt, "Introduction: The Axial Age Breakthroughs—Their Characteristics and Origins," in *The Origins and Diversity of Axial Age Civilizations*, ed. Shmuel Eisenstadt (Albany, NY: SUNY Press, 1986), 1–28.
7. Taylor, *Secular Age*, 147. To put the matter this way already assumes that there is something called "religion" which is distinct from social life; though the two are inseparably linked, they are two. I will address the problems with this concept of "religion" later in the chapter.
8. Ibid., 147–50.
9. Ibid., 150.
10. Ibid., 150–5.
11. Taylor remarks, "Weber is obviously one of my sources" (ibid., 156).
12. Ibid., 73–4. The episode is in I Kings 18:16–45. I discuss this episode in the next chapter.
13. Taylor, *Secular Age*, 154–5.
14. Ibid., 61–75.
15. Ibid., 34–5.
16. Ibid., 70–4.
17. Ibid., 79.
18. Ibid., 80–4.
19. Ibid., 84.
20. Ibid., 29–30.

21. Ibid., 35.
22. Ibid.
23. Ibid., 31–6.
24. Ibid., 36–40.
25. Ibid., 85–6, 99–112. What Taylor is describing here is often discussed by historians under the rubric "confessionalization." See, for example, John M. Headley, Hans J. Hillerbrand, and Anthony J. Papalas, eds., *Confessionalization in Europe, 1555–1700: Essays in Honor of Bodo Nischan* (Aldershot: Ashgate, 2004); James D. Tracy, ed., *Luther and the Modern State in Germany* (Kirksville, MO: Sixteenth Century Journal Publishers, 1986); and R. Po-Chia Hsia, *Social Discipline in the Reformation: Central Europe 1550–1750* (London: Routledge, 1989).
26. Taylor, *Secular Age*, 97–9, 113.
27. Ibid., 130–6.
28. Ibid., 136, 309–10, 475.
29. Ibid., 1–3.
30. Ibid., 539.
31. Ibid., 540.
32. Ibid., 541.
33. Ibid., 542.
34. Ibid., 553.
35. Ibid., 554.
36. See ibid., 426–8. Taylor refutes Steve Bruce's idea that technology tends to turn modern people away from religion; why, Bruce asks, would people pray to protect cattle from ringworm when they can buy a drench to solve the problem? Taylor comments, "But this seems to me to confound disenchantment with the decline of religion, and thus to fudge again the complex, sometimes contradictory relation between the religions dominant in our civilization, Judaism and Christianity, and the enchanted world which I referred to above" (ibid., 428).
37. Ibid., 143–5.
38. Ibid., 16. He continues, "In which case, the highest, most real, authentic or adequate human flourishing could include our aiming (also) in our range of final goals at something other than human flourishing. I say 'final goals,' because even the most self-sufficing humanism has to be concerned with the condition of some non-human things instrumentally, e.g., the condition of the natural environment. The issue is whether they matter also finally" (16).
39. Ibid., 17.
40. Ibid.
41. Ibid., 17–8.
42. Ibid., 20.
43. Ibid., 430–1.
44. Ibid., 18.
45. Ibid.
46. Taylor does not think it was never available before; he thinks ancient Epicureanism was a self-sufficient humanism, with gods that were irrelevant to human life. He

also does not think that religion and exclusive humanism are the only alternatives on offer today; he cites various kinds of Nietzschean nonreligious antihumanisms (ibid., 19).

47. Ibid., 19–20.
48. Ibid., 543–4.
49. Ibid., 15.
50. Ibid.
51. Ibid.
52. Ibid.
53. Ibid., 15–16.
54. Ibid., 427.
55. Ibid., 429.
56. Ibid., 430: "Another thing that I like about Bruce's definition is that it includes the 'impersonal powers,' and thus recognizes the important place of what I called in Chapter 2 'moral forces' in our 'enchanted' religious past." I have not been able to locate where in his second chapter Taylor uses "moral force" as a term of art, but I think he is referring to the hazy line between personal agency and impersonal force that he discusses in chapter 1 of his book. Such spiritual but impersonal forces might include the power issuing from a relic or a blessed candle (see 32–3, 42).
57. Ibid., 429–30.
58. Ibid., 430.
59. Peter B. Clarke and Peter Byrne, *Religion Defined and Explained* (New York: St. Martin's Press, 1993), 7.
60. Taylor, *Secular Age*, 818n21. He makes a similar comment in a footnote to the introduction; he claims not to be taking a stand in the abstract between functional and substantive definitions of religion, only ruling out the functionalist definition for his present purposes (see 780n19).
61. Ibid., 430–1.
62. Commenting on Bruce's prediction that modern people will simply become indifferent to religion, Taylor writes, "This, of course, might be right, but it seems to me deeply implausible. But this is because I cannot see the 'demand for religion' just disappearing like that. It seems to me that our situation (the perennial human situation?) is to be open to two solicitations. One (in our civilization, anyway) is the draw to a transformation perspective. The other comes from a congeries of resistances to this kind of solicitation" (ibid., 435).
63. Ibid., 437.
64. Taylor tells this story in chapter 12 on "The Age of Mobilization" (ibid., 423–72).
65. "Thus my own view of 'secularization,' which I freely confess has been shaped by my own perspective as a believer (but that I would nevertheless hope to be able to defend with arguments), is that there has certainly been a 'decline' of religion. Religious belief now exists in a field of choices which include various forms of demurral and rejection; Christian faith exists in a field where there is also a wide range of other spiritual options. But the interesting story is not simply one of decline, but also of a new placement of the sacred or spiritual in relation to individual and social life. This

new placement is now the occasion for recompositions of spiritual life in new forms, and for new ways of existing both in and out of relation to God" (ibid., 437).

66. Taylor makes this point explicit in Charles Taylor, "Afterword," in *Working with* A Secular Age, ed. Florian Zemmin, Colin Jager, and Guido Vanheeswijck (Berlin: Walter de Gruyter, 2016), 369–70.

67. Taylor, *Secular Age*, 13.

68. Ibid., 21.

69. See Charles Taylor, *Sources of the Self* (Cambridge, MA: Harvard University Press, 1989), ch. 7. I have used "reflectivity" as the title of this section instead of "reflexivity" because Taylor consistently contrasts "naïve" with "reflective" in *A Secular Age*.

70. Taylor, *Secular Age,* 30.

71. Ibid.

72. Hent de Vries, "The Deep Conditions of Secularity," *Modern Theology* 26, no. 3 (July 2010): 393.

73. Ibid., 392.

74. Taylor, *Secular Age*, 171.

75. Ibid., 172.

76. Ibid.

77. Ibid.

78. Ibid., 175.

79. Ibid., 39.

80. Ibid., 252.

81. Ibid., 325. See Taylor's similar comments about experience on 543.

82. Ibid., 729–30. Taylor's comments here are brief and cryptic, but I think he means the contrast to work something like the following: In modernity, feelings are spontaneous and interior. They might be aroused by an external object, but they are independent of that object and belong to the agent alone. The same object might arouse entirely different feelings in another agent. Feelings, furthermore, are independent of the agent in the sense that they are generated within the agent but do not change the long-term dispositions of the agent. For Aquinas, by way of contrast, love is not a feeling but a virtue, and therefore a habit, a disposition that is built up within the agent by repeated loving interactions with the world.

83. Ibid., 543.

84. Ibid., 728.

85. Ibid., 376.

86. Taylor is referencing Weber's lecture "Science as a Vocation," which I discussed in the previous chapter, in *From Max Weber: Essays in Sociology*, trans. H. H. Gerth and C. Wright Mills (New York: Oxford University Press, 1946), 155.

87. Taylor, *Secular Age*, 551. Taylor goes on to say that those who think that God's existence can be "proven" suffer from the same kind of disability, but since their numbers are few, he will direct his arguments against the secularists, who currently enjoy intellectual hegemony.

88. Ibid., 768. The passage continues, "They are shutting out crucial features of it. So the structural characteristic of the religious (re)conversions that I described above, that

one feels oneself to be breaking out of a narrower frame into a broader field, which makes sense of things in a different way, corresponds to reality" (768).

89. Ibid., 732; see also 375–6.
90. Ibid., 351–2.
91. For a summary of these moves, see ibid., 486–7.
92. Ibid., 483.
93. Ibid., 474.
94. Ibid., 483.
95. Ibid.
96. Ibid., 484.
97. Ibid., 492.
98. Max Weber, *The Protestant Ethic and the Spirit of Capitalism*, trans. Talcott Parsons (New York: Charles Scribner's Sons, 1958), 181.
99. Taylor, *Secular Age*, 483.
100. Ibid., 493.
101. Ibid., 483.
102. Ibid.
103. Ibid., 479–80.
104. Juliet B. Schor, "In Defense of Consumer Critique: Revisiting the Consumption Debates of the Twentieth Century," *Annals of the American Academy of Political and Social Science* 611 (May 2007): 25.
105. Charles Taylor, interview with James K. A. Smith, "Imagining an 'Open' Secularism," *Comment* (Fall 2014), https://www.cardus.ca/comment/article/4645/imagining-an-open-secularism/.
106. Taylor, "Afterword," 370. The other development is "unbundling," a term Taylor does not, to my knowledge, use in *A Secular Age*, but which encompasses most of what he calls "disembedding" in the book.
107. See the quote referenced in note 2 in this chapter.
108. Taylor, "Afterword," 374.
109. Ibid.
110. Ibid.
111. Ibid., 375.
112. Ibid.
113. Ibid., 375–6n2.
114. See chapter 1, and Jason Josephson-Storm, *The Myth of Disenchantment: Magic, Modernity, and the Birth of the Human Sciences* (Chicago: University of Chicago Press, 2017), 22–37.
115. The ambiguity of the terms Taylor uses to describe disenchantment guarantees that the concept will expand beyond the narrow corral he sometimes wants to limit it to. What qualifies as the loss of "moral forces" or "meaningful causal forces" or "the atrophy of earlier ideas of cosmic order," all of which Taylor identifies as disenchantment? Taylor wants to limit the concept of disenchantment to rebut the idea that the loss of magic necessarily means the loss of God, but the ambiguity of the term "spirits" threatens to expand the notion of disenchantment to include the loss of God. Is God not a spirit? Belief in which spirits qualifies one as still enchanted?

Taylor himself seems to use "disenchantment" more broadly to include disbelief in God in the following passage: "I argued that our understanding of ourselves as secular is defined by the (often terribly vague) historical sense that we have come to be that way through overcoming and rising out of earlier modes of belief. That is why God is still a reference point for even the most untroubled unbelievers, because he helps define the temptation you have to overcome and set aside to rise to the heights of rationality on which they dwell. That is why 'disenchantment' is still a description of our age which everyone understands, centuries after the practitioners of magic have ceased to be indispensable figures in our social life" (Taylor, *Secular Age*, 268).

116. Taylor, "Afterword," 376: "Moreover, if like me one is on the 'Romantic' side in this question of re-enchantment, one can discern a continuity here. One of the convictions powering post-Romantic poetry, as well as a good part of contemporary ecological concerns, is that the kinship with the universe exists, and that living in attunement with the world is a profound human need/aspiration."

117. "The art and thought of the Romantic period gave voice to this kind of unease and dissatisfaction with modern identity. It is not surprising that since that period, people have been tempted to view disenchantment as a loss, rather than an achievement, and even to call for a 're-enchantment' of the world" (ibid., 375).

118. Ibid., 376.

119. See, for example, Taylor, *Secular Age*, 541, where he identifies the decline of ideas of cosmic order and teleology as "another facet of disenchantment."

120. Quoted in ibid., 490.

121. Ibid.

122. Taylor, *Secular Age*, 490.

123. Taylor, "Afterword," 374.

124. Another way of putting this is Colin Jager's recommendation that we "consider disenchantment performatively rather than empirically." Colin Jager, "This Detail, This History: Charles Taylor's Romanticism," in *Varieties of Secularism in a Secular Age*, ed. Michael Warner, Jonathan VanAntwerpen, and Craig Calhoun (Cambridge, MA: Harvard University Press, 2010), 186.

125. Courtney Bender, "'Every Meaning Will Have Its Homecoming Festival': *A Secular Age* and the Senses of Modern Spirituality," in Zemmin, Jager, and Vanheeswijck, *Working with* A Secular Age, 299–300.

126. Taylor, *Secular Age*, 376.

127. Taylor refers in another context to "products promoted to the status of icons" in modern consumer culture (ibid., 552).

128. William Desmond, "The Porosity of Being: Toward a Catholic Agapeics. A Response to Charles Taylor" in Vila-Chã et al., *Renewing the Church*, 289–91. On Desmond and porosity, see also William Desmond, *God and the Between* (Oxford: Wiley-Blackwell, 2008) and Renée Köhler-Ryan, *Companions in the Between: Augustine, Desmond, and Their Communities of Love* (Eugene, OR: Pickwick, 2019), 35–59.

129. Taylor, *Secular Age*, 772.

130. In *Sources of the Self*, Taylor comments on these perennial spiritual needs: "Adopting a stripped-down secular outlook, without any religious dimension or radical hope in

history, is not a way of *avoiding* the dilemma, although it may be a good way to live with it. It doesn't avoid it, because this too involves its 'mutilation.' It involves stifling the response in us to some of the deepest and most powerful spiritual aspirations that humans have conceived" (520).

131. Taylor, *Secular Age*, 16.

132. I will leave it to Buddhists to comment on the accuracy of Taylor's portrayal of Buddhism.

133. Thanks to Renée Köhler-Ryan for her comments to this effect on an earlier draft of this chapter.

134. Taylor, *Secular Age*, 17.

135. Taylor, "Afterword," 380–1.

136. William E. Connolly, "Belief, Spirituality, and Time," in Warner, VanAntwerpen, and Calhoun, *Varieties of Secularism*, 131.

137. Ibid., 129.

138. Martha Nussbaum, *Love's Knowledge* (New York: Oxford University Press, 1990), 286–313; Taylor, *Secular Age*, 626–32.

139. Gilles Deleuze and Félix Guattari, *A Thousand Plateaus: Capitalism and Schizophrenia*, trans. Brian Massumi (Minneapolis: University of Minnesota Press, 1987). An excellent overview of philosophies of pure immanence can be found in Patrice Haynes, *Immanent Transcendence: Reconfiguring Materialism in Continental Philosophy* (London: Bloomsbury, 2012). I agree with Haynes that such philosophies of pure immanence are not successful. They appeal to a quasi-transcendental condition such as life (Deleuze) or history (Adorno) that ends up dematerializing or idealizing an aspect of actual, lived material reality. See 152–5. Haynes more positively articulates a "theological materialism" that overcomes the antinomy of transcendence and immanence.

140. Taylor, *Secular Age*, 632.

141. Ruth Abbey, "*A Secular Age*: The Missing Question Mark," in *The Taylor Effect: Responding to a Secular Age*, ed. Ian Leask with Eoin Cassidy, Alan Kearns, Fainche Ryan, and Mary Shanahan (Newcastle: Cambridge Scholars), 13–14.

142. Peter E. Gordon, "The Place of the Sacred in the Absence of God: Charles Taylor's *A Secular Age*," *Journal of the History of Ideas* 69, no. 4 (October 2008): 654.

143. Taylor, *Secular Age*, 676.

144. Ibid., 726.

145. Charles Taylor, "Disenchantment-Reenchantment," in Levine, *The Joy of Secularism*, 71–3. Taylor gives as an example physicist Douglas Hofstadter's claim to find "in reductionism the ultimate religion" (66).

146. Taylor, *Secular Age*, 517–8.

147. L. Oeing-Hanhoff, "Immanent, Immanenz," in *Historisches Wörterbuch der Philosophie*, vol. 4: *I–K*, ed. Joachim Ritter (Basel: Schwabe, 1995), quoted in Marc Rölli, "Immanence and Transcendence," *Bulletin de la Société Américaine de Philosophie de Langue Français* 14, no. 2 (2004): 71n2.

148. Ola Sigurdson comments, "The doctrine of the incarnation in Christian theology thus treats the question of how transcendence and immanence may be related to each

other in a way that respects both their integrity and their affinity." Ola Sigurdson, *Heavenly Bodies: Incarnation, the Gaze, and Embodiment*, trans. Carl Olsen (Grand Rapids, MI: Eerdmans, 2016), 7.

149. Thomas Aquinas, *Summa Theologiae*, I.8.1: *in omnibus rebus, et intime.*

150. As Eoin Cassidy points out, the relationship of interior and exterior is complicated in Augustine, for whom the return to God is simultaneously a return to our interiority, for God is *interior intimo meo*, closer to me than I am to myself. Eoin G. Cassidy, "'Transcending Human Flourishing': Is There a Need for a Subtler Language?," in Leask et al., *Taylor Effect*, 31–2.

151. Taylor, "Afterword," 380–1.

152. Taylor gives both reasons—that the transcendence/immanence distinction is part of the modern Western social imaginary and it is universal—in his response to a critique by Romand Coles and Stanley Hauerwas. Taylor recognizes that the transcendent/immanent distinction is not absolute, but he claims that some such terminology is indispensable because some distinction between the everyday world and the higher world is part of "every civilization" and because without the distinction "we couldn't understand our dominant social imaginary, and hence the world it helps constitute." Charles Taylor, "Challenging Issues about the Secular Age," *Modern Theology* 26, no. 3 (July 2010): 411–2.

153. Charles Taylor, "Concluding Reflections and Comments," in *A Catholic Modernity? Charles Taylor's Marianist Award Lecture*, ed. James L. Heft (New York: Oxford University Press, 1999), 105–6.

154. Jonathan Sheehan accuses Taylor of smuggling his own normative views into what is supposed to be a descriptive account, but Taylor responds that, although the quote about exclusive humanism "misrecognizing" reality is indeed his own position, it is not the conclusion of the book. Taylor is happy to let his own view be known, but the point of the book is to spur sympathy with positions other than one's own and to build friendships with people with whom one disagrees. Charles Taylor, "Afterword: Apologia pro Libro suo," in Warner, VanAntwerpen, and Calhoun, *Varieties of Secularism*, 318–20.

155. Rosemary Luling Haughton argues that Taylor's description of the extraordinary as transcending mundane flourishing devalues the sacramental quality of everyday life. Sacraments break down the transcendent/immanent binary and establish things as a locus of divinity. See Rosemary Luling Haughton, "Transcendence and the Bewilderment of Being Modern" in Heft, *A Catholic Modernity?*, 74–8. I will take up the subject of sacraments in the final chapter.

156. Ruth Abbey notes that Taylor's use of the concept of "religion" is addressed by few commentators, despite its importance for Taylor ("*A Secular Age*: The Missing Question Mark," 10).

157. Taylor, *Secular Age*, 437.

158. Ibid., 454.

159. Ibid., 486. See also Taylor's summary of the differences between the paleo- and neo-Durkheimian dispensations on 459–60.

160. Ibid., 459.

161. Ibid., 521.

162. Ibid., 606.

163. See, for example, Junaid Quadri, "Religion as Transcendence in Modern Islam: Tracking 'Religious Matters' into a Secular(izing) Age," in Zemmin, Jager, and Vanheeswijck, *Working with* A Secular Age, 331–47. Quadri shows how the religious/secular and transcendence/immanence distinctions fit the Muslim world only after it had been colonized by Western powers. Quadri describes how the British imposed a separation between "religion" and law in Egypt, which instigated an Islamic reaction against Western "materialism" which only reinforced the distinction between the now-transcendent "religion" and the secular/natural/immanent world.

164. See Saba Mahmood, "Can Secularism Be Other-wise?," in Warner, VanAntwerpen, and Calhoun, *Varieties of Secularism*, 282–99; Peter van der Veer, "Is Confucianism Secular?," in *Beyond the Secular West,* ed. Akeel Bilgrami (New York: Columbia University Press, 2016), 117–34.

165. Taylor, *Secular Age*, 147–51.

166. Ibid., 151–8.

167. For example, ibid., 79.

168. Ibid., 147. José Casanova has disputed the notion that every Axial development involved the emergence of "transcendence," and he points out that every form of transcendence does not necessarily imply "religion." José Casanova, "Religion, the Axial Age, and Secular Modernity in Robert Bellah's Theory of Religious Evolution," in *The Axial Age and Its Consequences*, ed. Robert N. Bellah and Hans Joas (Cambridge, MA: Harvard University Press, 2012), 191–221. For a similar disambiguation of the conceptual pairs sacred/profane, transcendent/immanent, and religious/secular, see Hans Joas, *Die Macht des Heiligen: Eine Alternative zur Geschichte von der Entzauberung* (Berlin: Suhrkamp, 2017), 253–5.

169. Émile Durkheim, *The Elementary Forms of Religious Life,* trans. Carol Cosman (Oxford: Oxford University Press, 2001), 46.

170. See Timothy Jenkins, "Why Do Things Move People? A Sociological Account of Idolatry," in *Idolatry: False Worship in the Bible, Early Judaism, and Christianity,* ed. Stephen C. Barton (Edinburgh: T. & T. Clark, 2007), 294.

171. Taylor, *Secular Age*, 458: "My 'neo-Durkheimian' category can even be expanded to include a founding of political identity on an anti-religious philosophical stance, such as we saw with the long-standing 'republican' French identity."

172. See chapter 2 of my book *The Myth of Religious Violence: Secular Ideology and the Roots of Modern Conflict* (New York: Oxford University Press, 2009), where I provide an extensive genealogy of the religious/secular distinction.

173. I will give only a few examples here: Brent Nongbri, *Before Religion: A History of a Modern Concept* (New Haven, CT: Yale University Press, 2013); Timothy Fitzgerald, *Discourse on Civility and Barbarity: A Critical History of Religion and Related Categories* (New York: Oxford University Press, 2007); Tomoko Masuzawa, *The Invention of World Religions: Or, How European Universalism Was Preserved in the Language of Pluralism* (Chicago: University of Chicago Press, 2005); Daniel

Dubuisson, *The Western Construction of Religion: Myths, Knowledge, and Ideology*, trans. William Sayers (Baltimore, MD: Johns Hopkins University Press, 2003); Derek R. Peterson and Darren R. Walhof, eds., *The Invention of Religion: Rethinking Belief in Politics and History* (New Brunswick, NJ: Rutgers University Press, 2002).

174. John Bossy, "Some Elementary Forms of Durkheim," *Past and Present* 95 (May 1982): 3–18.

175. Taylor, *Secular Age*, 15.

176. Abbey applauds Taylor's "inclusive and generous approach" to religion that allows him to "avoid invidious distinctions and decisions about what does and does not qualify as religion." But she also notes that Taylor often deviates from his broad use of "religion" to use it more narrowly as meaning "belief in God" ("*A Secular Age*: The Missing Question Mark," 11, 16).

177. Jan N. Bremmer, "Secularization: Notes toward a Genealogy," in *Religion: Beyond a Concept*, ed. Hent de Vries (New York: Fordham University Press, 2008), 433. As John Milbank has pointed out, Taylor should have made more of the fact that secularization is not an entirely benign process but one deeply implicated with the growth of state power and the establishment of the state as a quasi-church operating an economy of salvation. John Milbank, "A Closer Walk on the Wild Side," in Warner, VanAntwerpen, and Calhoun, *Varieties of Secularism*, 73–6.

178. It is worth noting that the sacred/profane distinction does not track the religious/secular distinction in the way that Taylor seems to think it does. As Casanova puts it, "the modern secular is by no means synonymous with the 'profane,' nor is the 'religious' synonymous with the modern 'sacred.' . . . In this respect, modern secularization entails a certain profanation of religion through its privatization and individualization and a certain sacralization of the secular spheres of politics (sacred nation, sacred citizenship, sacred constitution), science (temples of knowledge), and economics (through commodity fetishism). But the truly modern sacralization, which constitutes the global civil religion in Durkheim's terms, is the cult of the individual and the sacralization of humanity through the globalization of human rights." José Casanova, "The Secular, Secularizations, and Secularisms" in Calhoun, Juergensmeyer, and VanAntwerpen, *Rethinking Secularism*, 65.

179. Taylor, "Western Secularity," 51.

180. Taylor, *Secular Age*, 148. The internal quotation is from Godfrey Lienhardt.

181. Mark Twain, *The Mysterious Stranger* (1910), Goodreads, accessed October 22, 2018, https://www.goodreads.com/work/quotes/908563-the-mysterious-stranger.

182. Of course, it is inadequate simply to say "Everyone believes in something" and not to go on to the harder question of what beliefs are truer than others. The problem is illustrated by Ronald Dworkin's posthumously published *Religion without God*. Dworkin argues that everyone has a religion; we all seek a sense of coherent meaning in our lives. Religion is "deeper than God." Ronald Dworkin, *Religion without God* (Cambridge, MA, Harvard University Press, 2013), 1. The law must protect religion, but if religion is flattened out, the law has no reason to recognize churches over Chicago Cub fan clubs. What appears as a consistent application of liberal neutrality in fact privileges a practice of religion as consumerism; Dworkin likens the search for one's personal religion to the free market in goods. We have no choice but to be

choosers. The god that is a consumer item is different from the God of Christianity. The struggle among the gods, as Weber would put it, is unavoidable, and so ultimately we must do theology to sort out, insofar as possible, the real God from the false ones. Thanks to Joel Harrison for pointing me toward this problem in Dworkin's work. See Joel Harrison, "Dworkin's Religion and the End of Religious Liberty," in *Research Handbook on Law and Religion*, ed. Rex Ahdar (Cheltenham: Edward Elgar, 2018), 79–102.

Chapter 3

1. The sixteen official documents of the Council cover 1,001 pages in the Flannery edition; see Austin P. Flannery, ed., *The Documents of Vatican II* (Grand Rapids, MI: Eerdmans, 1975). The three mentions of idolatry are as follows. In *Lumen gentium*, the Church is said to rescue people "from the slavery of error and of idols" (no. 17). In the Decree on the Apostolate of the Laity, *Apostolicam actuositatem*, we are warned that "those who have trusted excessively in the progress of the natural sciences and the technical arts have fallen into an idolatry of temporal things and have become their slaves rather than their masters" (no. 7). In *Gaudium et spes* we are assured that, because of our belief in Christ's incarnation, cross, and resurrection, "the Church can anchor the dignity of human nature against all tides of opinion, for example those which undervalue the human body or idolize it" (no. 41).
2. Pope Francis, *Lumen fidei*, June 29, 2013, §13, http://w2.vatican.va/content/francesco/en/encyclicals/documents/papa-francesco_20130629_enciclica-lumen-fidei.html.
3. Pope Francis, *Evangelii gaudium*, November 24, 2013, §55, http://w2.vatican.va/content/francesco/en/apost_exhortations/documents/papa-francesco_esortazione-ap_20131124_evangelii-gaudium.html. I give many more examples of Francis's use of the language of idolatry in "Return of the Golden Calf: Economy, Idolatry, and Secularization since *Gaudium et Spes*," *Theological Studies* 76, no. 4 (December 2015): 698–717.
4. See, for example, the essays collected in Pablo Richard, ed., *The Idols of Death and the God of Life: A Theology* (Maryknoll, NY: Orbis, 1983).
5. Eduardo Galeano, quoted in Lawrence Wechsler, *A Miracle, a Universe: Settling Accounts with Torturers* (New York: Pantheon Books, 1990), 147.
6. James K. A. Smith, *Desiring the Kingdom: Worship, Worldview, and Cultural Formation* (Grand Rapids, MI: Baker, 2009), 25.
7. Ibid., 52.
8. Ibid., 39–73.
9. Ibid., 86. Smith uses "liturgy" and "worship" synonymously (25n8).
10. Charles Taylor, "Western Secularity," in *Rethinking Secularism*, ed. Craig Calhoun, Mark Juergensmeyer, and Jonathan VanAntwerpen (New York: Oxford University Press, 2011), 51. See my analysis of this passage in Taylor near the end of chapter 2.

11. Smith offers a tour of "one of the most important religious sites in our metropolitan area." Pilgrims flock to the soaring building, a space of vertical transcendence and light cut off from the normal space of the city. The building is full of rich iconography, promises of salvation through sacramental objects, and a kind of exchange and communion that ritually unites the faithful. The building is, of course, a shopping mall. By using liturgical language, Smith is able to suggest that the reader sees the mall with new eyes (*Desiring the Kingdom,* 19–22).

12. Ibid., 93.

13. Ibid., 94.

14. The philosophical anthropology is laid out in part 1 of *Desiring the Kingdom,* followed by an explication of the Christian life and worship in part 2. See Smith's comments on philosophical anthropology as a prolegomenon to his discussion of Christian worship (134).

15. Smith does allude briefly to idolatry in citing Calvin's contention that "even idolatry is a testament to humanity's essentially religious, liturgical nature" (ibid., 123).

16. Alexander Schmemann, *For the Life of the World* (Crestwood, NY: St. Vladimir's Seminary Press, 2002), 14, quoted in Stephen Fowl, *Idolatry* (Waco, TX: Baylor University Press, 2019), 64.

17. See Fowl's comments on this passage in *Idolatry,* 64–5.

18. Here I disagree with Fowl's otherwise excellent analysis when he writes, "The second half of Wisdom 14 seems to indicate that idolatry is not some sort of original failure. That is, idolatry is not directly connected to the first sin narrated in Genesis 1–3. Rather, it arises over time in the course of repeated human error (14:13–14)" (ibid., 7). Wisdom 14:12–4 reads, "For the idea of making idols was the beginning of fornication, and the invention of them was the corruption of life; for they did not exist from the beginning, nor will they last for ever. For through human vanity they entered the world, and therefore their speedy end has been planned." It seems to me that "the beginning" the verse refers to is an echo of Genesis 1:1, pre-Fall. There was no idolatry before the Fall, but when "human vanity" entered the scene in the Fall, so did idolatry.

19. Fowl, *Idolatry,* 7.

20. Paul does not use the term *eidōlolatria* here, but he does use *eikonos* (1:23), a Septuagint term for idol. On Paul's use of Septuagint terminology for idolatry in Romans 1, see Bertil Gärtner, *The Areopagus Speech and Natural Revelation,* trans. Carolyn Hannay King (Uppsala: Gleerup, 1955), 75n1.

21. Fowl, *Idolatry,* 8.

22. Thanks to Gary Anderson of Notre Dame for pointing me toward these passages.

23. Fowl, *Idolatry,* 27.

24. Brian S. Rosner, *Greed as Idolatry: The Origin and Meaning of a Pauline Metaphor* (Grand Rapids, MI: Eerdmans, 2007), 142.

25. Ibid., 21.

26. Ibid., 61. The internal quotes are from Janet Soskice, *Metaphor and Religious Language* (Oxford: Clarendon, 1985), 41.

27. Rosner, *Greed as Idolatry,* 65–6. Rosner takes this point from Richard Hays.

28. Ibid., 167–8.

29. Ibid., 168.
30. Ibid.
31. Ibid., 148, italics in the original.
32. Ibid., 129, italics in the original.
33. I understand the objections to using the term "Old Testament" for the first part of the Christian Bible. Some reject the term as hopelessly supersessionist, as if the old had been superseded by the new, and so they substitute "Hebrew Scriptures" and "Christian Scriptures" for "Old Testament" and "New Testament." I think the substituted terms merely compound the problem. In the first place, for a Catholic the term "Hebrew Scriptures" is not accurate, since the seven deuterocanonical books were written in Greek, not Hebrew. More crucially, to distinguish between "Hebrew" and "Christian" scriptures is to imply that the Hebrew scriptures are not Christian scriptures, which is precisely what Marcion thought. There could be no clearer statement of supersessionism. There is an obvious and ugly history of supersessionism in Christian history, but I do not think supersessionism necessarily clings to the terms "old" and "new." Indeed, in Catholic circles what is new is often what is suspect; Réginald Garrigou-Lagrange could think of no more pejorative term for Henri de Lubac's thought than calling it the "nouvelle théologie." I will continue to use the traditional terms "Old Testament" and "New Testament" until I am convinced of a better alternative.
34. The NRSV translates *teraphim* as "household gods."
35. Josh Ellenbogen and Aaron Tugenhaft, "Introduction," in *Idol Anxiety*, ed. Josh Ellenbogen and Aaron Tugenhaft (Stanford, CA: Stanford University Press, 2011), 3–4; Robert Hayward, "Observations on Idols in Septuagint Pentateuch," in*Idolatry: False Worship in the Bible, Early Judaism and Christianity*, ed Stephen C. Barton (London: T. & T. Clark, 2007), 40–57.
36. M. G. Easton, *Illustrated Bible Dictionary*, accessed July 24, 2023, https://www.bibl estudytools.com/dictionary/idol/.
37. See the discussion in G. K. Beale, *We Become What We Worship: A Biblical Theology of Idolatry* (Downers Grove, IL: IVP Academic, 2008), 84–6, including 84n37. Some authors resolve the ambiguity by arguing that the calf is not a cult image of another god but is an improper means for worshiping YHWH. For example, see Michael D. Coogan, *A Brief Introduction to the Old Testament: The Hebrew Bible in Its Context* (Oxford: Oxford University Press, 2009), 115.
38. In the first section, the document declares that "the council professes its belief that God Himself has made known to mankind the way in which men are to serve Him, and thus be saved in Christ and come to blessedness. We believe that this one true religion subsists in the Catholic and Apostolic Church, to which the Lord Jesus committed the duty of spreading it abroad among all men." *Dignitatis humanae*, December 7, 1965, §1, http://www.vatican.va/archive/hist_councils/ii_vatican_council/docume nts/vat-ii_decl_19651207_dignitatis-humanae_en.html.
39. Thomas Jefferson, *Notes on the State of Virginia*, query XVII, accessed July 24, 2023, http://avalon.law.yale.edu/18th_century/jeffvir.asp.

40. Timothy Gorringe, "Idolatry and Redemption: Economics in Biblical Perspective," *Political Theology* 11, no. 3 (2010): 369.

41. Ibid., 369–73.

42. Ibid., 371. Here Gorringe is drawing on Ton Veerkamp, *Die Vernichtung des Baal* (Stuttgart: Alektor, 1981).

43. Veerkamp, *Die Vernichtung*, 51, quoted in Gorringe, "Idolatry and Redemption," 372.

44. For another example, see chapter 3 of the book of Daniel. King Nebuchadnezzar erects an enormous golden statue and commands that all worship it or suffer death. The act is not merely "religious" but also reinforces Nebuchadnezzar's "political" power. The refusal of Shadrach, Meshach, and Abednego was simultaneously an act of obedience to YHWH and an act of disobedience to the king. As Daniel 2:21 has already made clear, the LORD "changes times and seasons, deposes kings and sets up kings." There is no distinction between "religion" and "politics" in either idolatry or its refusal.

45. Mark S. Smith, *God in Translation: Deities in Cross-Cultural Discourse in the Biblical World* (Grand Rapids, MI: Eerdmans, 2010), 6. Thanks to Rachelle Gilmour for pointing me toward Smith's book.

46. Ibid., 160. Smith is here arguing against the necessary link of monotheism to violence posited by Jan Assmann in *Moses the Egyptian: The Memory of Egypt in Western Monotheism* (Cambridge, MA: Harvard University Press, 1997) and other works.

47. Smith, *God in Translation*, 28.

48. Walter Brueggemann, *Israel's Praise: Doxology against Idolatry and Ideology* (Philadelphia, PA: Fortress Press, 1988), 8–15.

49. Ibid., 49ff.

50. Ibid., x.

51. Ibid., 11.

52. Ibid., 128. See also 105, 113.

53. Ibid., 124–5.

54. Ibid., 126.

55. Ibid., 127.

56. Ibid.

57. Jan Assmann, "What's Wrong with Images?," in Ellenbogen and Tugendhaft, *Idol Anxiety*, 22–3.

58. Moshe Halbertal and Avishai Margalit, *Idolatry*, trans. Naomi Goldblum (Cambridge, MA: Harvard University Press, 1992), 180–4.

59. Ibid., 22–3.

60. Ibid., 31.

61. Halbertal and Margalit note the frequent association in Jewish commentary on the Bible between sexual immorality and idolatry. Many interpreters regard sexual license to be one of the attractions of idolatry. Idolatry is part of a lifestyle and is not simply about metaphysical beliefs; see ibid., 23–5.

62. Ibid., 9–36.

63. Ibid., 220.

64. Ibid., 216–8.

65. Isaiah 2:6–9 similarly connects military alliances and idolatry:

> You have forsaken your people,
>   the house of Jacob,
> for they are full of diviners from the East
>   and of soothsayers like the Philistines,
> and they clasp hands with foreigners.
>   Their land is filled with silver and gold,
> and there is no end to their treasures;
>   their land is filled with horses,
> and there is no end to their chariots.
>   Their land is filled with idols;
> they bow down to the work of their hands,
>   to what their own fingers have made.
> And so people are humbled,
>   and everyone is brought low.

66. See Halbertal and Margalit, *Idolatry*, 223–4.

67. The laws governing relationships are not symmetrical in the Old Testament, which forbids a woman to have more than one husband but permits a man to have multiple wives. God is therefore depicted as the husband in the relationship with Israel. See ibid., 215.

68. Ibid.

69. Ibid., 220; Henri Frankfort, *Kingship and the Gods: A Study of Ancient Near Eastern Religion as the Integration of Society and Nature* (Chicago: University of Chicago Press, 1978).

70. Hosea 8:4 also links the desire for a king with idolatry: "They made kings, but not through me; they set up princes, but without my knowledge. With their silver and gold they made idols for their own destruction." Here YHWH does not give even grudging approval to the creation of human kings.

71. Jotham's parable of the trees in Judges 9 makes the same point. The good and useful trees and vines—olive, fig, and grape—refuse the trees' request to be king over them. Only the thorn bush, which represents Abimelech, accepts the offer to be king (9:7–20). The consequences are plain to see in Abimelech's murder of his seventy brothers and the subsequent violence and mayhem. Judges prefaces the account of Abimelech's brief reign by noting the Israelites' relapse into idolatry, taking Baal-Berith for their god (8:33–5).

72. See also Exodus 14:13–4, where the emphasis is entirely on God's action in securing military victory for the Israelites, and the Israelites are ordered to do nothing: "But Moses said to the people, 'Do not be afraid, stand firm, and see the deliverance that the Lord will accomplish for you today; for the Egyptians whom you see today you shall never see again. The Lord will fight for you, and you have only to keep still.'" Another parallel is found in the David and Goliath story, where David—armed only with five smooth stones—declares that "the Lord does not save by sword and spear; for the battle is the Lord's and he will give you into our hand" (I Sam. 17:47).

73. For example, Helen K. Bond, "Standards, Shields, and Coins: Jewish Reactions to Aspects of the Roman Cult in the Time of Pilate" in Barton, *Idolatry*, 102–4.

74. For example, Ched Myers, *Binding the Strong Man: A Political Reading of Mark's Gospel* (Maryknoll, NY: Orbis Books, 1988), 310–4.

75. I find Bond's conclusions in this light unsatisfactory. She attempts to put off the choice between God and Caesar to the time when the Kingdom of God is fully established: "Until that comes about, however, Jesus accepts that Caesar does have some authority and that, therefore, the Judeans are obliged to pay their taxes" ("Standards, Shields, and Coins," 104).

76. Myers notes that the only other time the word "inscription" (*epigraphē*) appears in Mark is to describe the writ of conviction affixed to the cross, which read, "The King of the Jews" (Mk. 15:26). The contest between the two kings would have been obvious to the reader (Myers, *Binding the Strong Man*, 311).

77. Rosner, *Greed as Idolatry*, 22–3.

78. Stephen C. Barton, "Food Rules, Sex Rules and the Prohibition of Idolatry: What's the Connection?," in Barton, *Idolatry*, 143.

79. See Rosner's commentary on these passages in *Greed as Idolatry*, 73–9.

80. Fowl, *Idolatry*, 58–68.

81. Herbert Niehr, "In Search of YHWH's Cult Statue in the First Temple," in *The Image and the Book: Iconic Cults, Aniconism, and the Rise of Book Religion in Israel and the Ancient Near East*, ed. Karel van der Toorn (Leuven: Peeters, 1997), 73–95. The idea that there were cult statues of YHWH in pre-exilic Israel and Judah has also been advanced by, e.g., Brian Schmidt, "The Aniconic Tradition: On Reading Images and Viewing Texts," in *The Triumph of Elohim: From Yahwisms to Judaisms*, ed. Diana V. Edelman (Grand Rapids, MI: Eerdmans, 1996), 75–105 and Christopher Uehlinger, "Israelite Aniconism in Context," *Biblica* 77 (1996): 540–9.

82. B. J. Diebner, "Anmerkungen zum sogenannten 'Bilderverbot' in der Torah," *Dielheimer Blätter zum Alten Testament* 27 (1991): 46–57.

83. Niehr, "In Search of YHWH's Cult Statue," 73.

84. Of Niehr's claim that the ban on images presupposes their existence, Weeks writes, "[O]n such a basis, we would have to assume also that the Israelites had frequently to be restrained from eating creepy-crawlies and sleeping with their stepmothers." Stuart Weeks, "Man-made Gods? Idolatry in the Old Testament," in Barton, *Idolatry*, 13n16. For more skepticism about claims that aniconism was a late innovation among the Jews, see the contributions of Tryggve Mettinger and Ronald Hendel in van der Toorn, *The Image and the Book*, 173–228.

85. Weeks, "Man-made Gods?," 7–12.

86. Karel van der Toorn, "The Iconic Book: Analogies between the Babylonian Cult of Images and the Veneration of the Torah," in van der Toorn, *The Image and the Book*, 229–48. Van der Toorn argues that the wide separation between book religions and ritual religions was in many ways a creation of Protestant scholars like Friedrich Max Müller, intent on demonstrating the superiority of Christianity over other religions, and Protestantism over Catholicism (230–2). Halbertal and Margalit also say the Israelites treated the Ark as a fetish (*Idolatry*, 48–9).

87. "Then King David rose to his feet and said: 'Hear me, my brothers and my people. I had planned to build a house of rest for the ark of the covenant of the LORD, for the

footstool of our God; and I made preparations for building'" (I Chron. 28:2). See also Psalms 99:5 and 132:7 for additional references to God's footstool.

88. Weeks, "Man-made Gods?," 14–21. On the thorny question of the existence of other gods—monotheism versus henotheism—Weeks tentatively concludes that the prophetic literature does not so much reject their existence as demotes them to the status of demons.

89. According to Sommer, "the God with many bodies remains woundable and alterable, but this deity can nevertheless be omnipotent. In short, the fluidity model manages, to a greater extent than the traditions that posit a single divine body, to preserve God's freedom and transcendence even as it maintains the divine personhood and vulnerability so central to biblical and rabbinic literature." Benjamin D. Sommer, *The Bodies of God and the World of Ancient Israel* (Cambridge: Cambridge University Press, 2011), 142.

90. Ibid., 67.

91. Ibid., 85. See also C. M. McCormick, "From Box to Throne: The Development of the Ark in DtrH and P," in *Saul in Story and Tradition*, ed. C. S. Ehrlich and M. C. White (Tübingen: Mohr Siebeck, 2006), 174–86. I am grateful to Rachelle Gilmour for pointing me to these sources.

92. Assmann, echoing Weber, calls the Israelite ban on images "a radical disenchantment of the world" ("What's Wrong with Images?," 20).

93. Nathan MacDonald, "Recasting the Golden Calf: The Imaginative Potential of the Old Testament's Portrayal of Idolatry," in Barton, *Idolatry*, 26–34.

94. See the comments on this aspect of the Israelite ban on images in Roger Burggraeve, Johan de Tavernier, Didier Pollefeyt, and Jo Hanssens, "True Faith in God and Forms of Religious Idolatry," in *Desirable God? Our Fascination with Images, Idols and New Deities*, ed. Roger Burggraeve, Johan de Tavernier, Didier Pollefeyt, and Jo Hanssens (Leuven: Peeters, 2003), 21–3.

95. Halbertal and Margalit, *Idolatry*, 40, 52.

96. Weeks notes that Heraclitus warned against mistaking images for the deities themselves, but Weeks thinks that ancient people were sufficiently sophisticated to distinguish between the localizable presence of a god and the totality of the god ("Man-made Gods?," 9–10). Assmann concurs, arguing that "no Egyptian or Babylonian would mistake a statue for a god. An image becomes a medium for establishing contact with the divine only after complex rites of consecration and investiture, only temporarily, and only within the special, temporal and social frames of the cultic scene" ("What's Wrong with Images?," 27). Kavin Rowe, on the other hand, recommends that we not conflate the more sophisticated views of pagan writers with the views of the general populace, and he gives several examples of ancient people treating statues as gods. C. Kavin Rowe, *World Upside Down: Reading Acts in the Graeco-Roman Age* (Oxford: Oxford University Press, 2009), 35–6.

97. Halbertal and Margalit, *Idolatry*, 47–8.

98. Assmann, "What's Wrong with Images?," 28.

99. Ibid., 21.

100. "People create idols for themselves because they actually cannot deal with the idea of God's invisibility" (Burggraeve et al., "True Faith in God," 34; see also 26–8).

101. Joel Marcus, "Idolatry in the New Testament," *Interpretation* 60, no. 2 (April 2006): 160–2.

102. C. Kavin Rowe, "New Testament Iconography? Situating Paul in the Absence of Material Evidence," in *Picturing the New Testament: Studies in Ancient Visual Images*, ed. Annette Weissenrieder (Göttingen: Mohr Siebeck, 2005), 289–312.

103. Marcus, "Idolatry in the New Testament," 162.

104. For a discussion of this theme, see Marcel Poorthuis, "The Prohibition of Idolatry: Source of Humanity or Source of Violence?," in Burggraeve et al., *Desirable God?*, 54–7.

105. Martin Dibelius, "Paul on the Areopagus," in *The Book of Acts: Form, Style, and Theology*, ed. K. C. Hanson (Minneapolis, MN: Fortress, 2004), 95–128.

106. Rowe, *World Upside Down*, 38.

107. See Trevor Hart's essay "'Goodly Sights' and 'Unseemly Representations': Transcendence and the Problems of Visual Piety" in Barton, *Idolatry*, 198–212.

108. The negative theology of Maimonides represents this trend in Judaism for Halbertal and Margalit, *Idolatry*, 108–36.

109. MacDonald, "Recasting the Golden Calf," 33–4.

110. Fowl, *Idolatry*, 44–6.

111. Ibid., 46.

112. Ibid.

113. Halbertal and Margalit, *Idolatry*, 42: "A fetish is an object to which people attribute powers that it does not have. But not every error in the attribution of powers transforms an object into a fetish. Although such errors occur all the time, we can call an object a fetish only if the error gives the object some control over its worshipers."

114. Beale's *We Become What We Worship* is an exhaustive examination of the theme of people coming to resemble idols in the Bible.

115. Ibid., 86–92.

116. Ibid., 204–16.

117. Gärtner, *The Areopagus Speech*, 197.

118. Beale, *We Become What We Worship*, 196–8. Later in Acts (28:25–8), Paul quotes from Isaiah 6:9–10 on those who hear but do not understand, who see but do not perceive. Beale thinks it probable that the mirroring effect is in the background here as well. Just as the living God is reflected in living people, those who follow inert idols will become inert and lifeless (*We Become What We Worship*, 198–200).

119. Beale, *We Become What We Worship*, 284. Although there is much of value in Beale's book, and I find the overall argument persuasive and important, there are aspects of the analysis that I find distorted and unhelpful. Beale's treatment of the New Testament presents Jesus and Paul as foes of the Jews' dead traditions and rituals, in a way that smacks of supersessionism; for example, "Apparently, there were professing Jewish Christians who could not leave behind the essence of their Jewish past: they still insisted on keeping Jewish traditions as a necessary part of being a true child of God" (287–8). See also the chapter on the Gospels, 161–83. It is not hard to detect anti-Catholicism in the same dismissal of dead tradition and ritual. So, "both in non-Christian and Christian religions, worshipers can direct the focus of their

worship to created objects. For example, some Christians may be tempted to worship icons, saints, and the elements of the Eucharist" (311).

120. Max Weber, "Science as a Vocation," in *From Max Weber: Essays in Sociology*, trans. H. H. Gerth and C. Wright Mills (New York: Oxford University Press, 1946), 149.

121. On the ambiguity of the term, see Rowe, *World Upside Down*, 33–4.

122. This at least is John Chrysostom's understanding of this passage in his *Catena on the Acts of the Apostles*, 17.23.

123. See also Acts 14:15–7, where Paul heals a man in Lystra and the locals try to assimilate Paul and Barnabas to pagan gods: "We are mortals just like you, and we bring you good news, that you should turn from these worthless things to the living God, who made the heaven and the earth and the sea and all that is in them. In past generations he allowed all the nations to follow their own ways; yet he has not left himself without a witness in doing good—giving you rains from heaven and fruitful seasons, and filling you with food and your hearts with joy." Again, despite their pagan worship, God is available to them in the good things of God's creation.

124. Fowl, *Idolatry*, 4.

125. Another way of putting the matter is illustrated by Mary Douglas's treatment of belief and practice in her study of the "Bog Irish" after Vatican II. Douglas argues that Catholics did not lose faith and then stop practicing abstinence on Fridays during Lent, but the reverse. Their beliefs were embedded in practices, so that their faith collapsed when practices such as eating fish on Fridays were no longer central to their experience of being Catholic. Mary Douglas, *Natural Symbols*, 2nd ed. (London: Routledge, 1996), 39–56.

126. See Scott Schauf, *The Divine in Acts and in Ancient Historiography* (Minneapolis, MN: Fortress, 2015), 95–6.

127. David G. Horrell, "Idol Food, Idolatry and Ethics in Paul," in Barton, *Idolatry*, 139.

128. Christopher Rowland, "Living with Idols: An Exercise in Biblical Theology," in Barton, *Idolatry*, 164.

129. Ibid., 168.

Chapter 4

1. Augustine, *City of God*, IV.11, trans. Henry Bettenson (Harmondsworth: Penguin, 1972), 152.

2. Ibid., IV.8, 144. I will cite the *City of God* giving the book and chapter numbers, followed by the page number(s) in the Bettenson translation.

3. Ibid., IV.11, 148–52.

4. Ibid., IV.15, 154.

5. Ibid., IV.20, 158–9.

6. On this point, see Gregory W. Lee, "Republics and Their Loves: Rereading *City of God* 19," *Modern Theology* 27, no. 4 (October 2011): 560.

7. Augustine, *City of God*, IV.16, 155.

8. Ibid., III.14, 104–5. The biblical quote is Psalm 10:23.

9. Ibid., XVIII.22, 787.

10. Lee, "Republics and Their Loves," 560.

11. Augustine, *City of God*, XVIII.54, 842.

12. Ibid., XIV.28, 593–4. The interior quote is from Romans 1:21ff.

13. Hermes Trismegistus, quoted in Augustine, *City of God*, VIII.24, 334. For Nietzsche on god-making, see chapter 5 on Marion.

14. Augustine, *City of God*, VIII.23, 332.

15. Ibid. The interior quote is from Psalm 49:20.

16. Ibid., VIII.24, 335.

17. Ibid.

18. Ibid.

19. Ibid., XII.6, 477.

20. See Luigi Alici, "The Violence of Idolatry and Peaceful Coexistence: The Current Relevance of *civ. Dei*," *Augustinian Studies* 41, no. 1 (2010): 212–3.

21. Augustine, *City of God*, VII.27, 288.

22. Ibid. Augustine makes clear that it is possible both to worship the wrong god ("worshipping an unworthy object") and to worship the right God badly ("worshipping the proper object of worship by improper means").

23. Ibid., VIII.28, 290.

24. Augustine, *On Christian Doctrine*, III.7.11, trans. D. W. Robertson Jr. (Indianapolis, IN: Bobbs-Merrill, 1958), 85–6. Latin text Sancti Aurelii Augustini, *De Doctrina Christiana*, Corpus Christianorum, Series Latina, vol. 32 (Turholt: Brepols, 1962).

25. Augustine, *On the Trinity*, I.6.13, trans. Stephen McKenna, The Fathers of the Church: A New Translation, vol. 45 (Washington, DC: Catholic University of America Press, 1963), 17. Latin text "Augustine de Trinitate, Liber I," Latin Library, accessed July 26, 2023, http://www.thelatinlibrary.com/augustine/trin1.shtml.

26. "But that the Holy Spirit is not a creature shines forth with sufficient clarity in that passage particularly, where we are commanded to serve not the creature but the Creator, not in the sense in which we are commanded to serve one another through charity, which in Greek is *douleúein*, but that in which we render service to God alone, which in Greek is *latreúein*. Wherefore they are called idolaters who pay to images that service which is due to God. For it was said with regard to this service: 'The Lord your God shall you adore and him only shall you serve,' and this is brought out more clearly in the Greek Scriptures for they have *latreúseis*. Moreover, if we are forbidden to serve a creature with such a service, since it was said: 'The Lord your God shall you adore and him only shall you serve,' and the Apostle also detests those who have worshiped and served a creature rather than the Creator, then the Holy Spirit is certainly not a creature to whom such service is shown by all the saints as the Apostle says: 'For we are the circumcision, serving the Spirit of God,' which in Greek is *latreúontes*." Augustine, *On the Trinity*, I.6.13, 17–18. I will cite *On the Trinity* giving the book and chapter numbers, followed by the page number(s) in the McKenna translation.

27. Ibid., XIII.19.24., 406.

28. Augustine, *On Christian Doctrine*, II.20.30, 55. I will cite *On Christian Doctrine* giving the book and chapter numbers, followed by the page number(s) in the Robertson translation.

29. Ibid., II.23.36, 59–60.

30. Augustine, *City of God*, V.14, 204.

31. Augustine, *Confessions*, IV.6.11, trans. Henry Chadwick (Oxford: Oxford University Press, 1991), 58.

32. Ibid., IV.7.12, 60. I will cite *Confessions* giving the book and chapter numbers, followed by the page number(s) in the Chadwick translation.

33. Ibid., IV.10.15., 61–2.

34. Ibid., IV.10.15, 62.

35. Ibid., IV.10.15, 61.

36. "They flee away and cannot be followed with the bodily senses. No one can fully grasp them even while they are present. Physical perception is slow, because it is a bodily sense: its nature imposes limitations on it. It is sufficient for another purpose for which it was made. But it is not adequate to get a grip on [*teneat*] things that are transient from the moment of the intended beginning to their intended end (cf. Ps. 138:7). In your word, through which they are created, they hear: 'From here as far as there' (Job 38:11)" (ibid., IV.10.15, 62).

37. Ibid., VII.16.22, 126.

38. Ibid., VII.17.23, 127.

39. Ibid., II.2.3, 25.

40. Ibid., IV.13.20, 65.

41. Ibid., X.27.38, 201.

42. Ibid., X.6.8, 183.

43. Ibid., X.6.9, 183.

44. "There is no alteration in the voice which is their beauty. If one person sees while another sees and questions, it is not that they appear one way to the first and another way to the second. It is rather that the created order speaks to all, but is understood by those who hear its outward voice and compare it with the truth within themselves" (ibid., X.6.10, 184).

45. Ibid.

46. Ibid., X.6.8, 183.

47. Ibid., IV.12.18, 63.

48. Unfortunately, not all translations are consistent in their renderings of these terms. In Henry Bettenson's translation of the *City of God*, for example, Augustine describes the heavenly city as that which, in this life, "does not depend on hope in shifting and transitory things." The denizens of the heavenly city are "schooled for eternity. They enjoy their earthly blessings in the manner of pilgrims [*bonisque terrenis tamquam peregrina utitur nec capitur*] and they are not attached to them." Here Bettenson's use of "enjoy" instead of "use" to render *utitur* gives the term the precise opposite of Augustine's intended meaning. Augustine, *City of God*, I.29, 41.

49. Augustine, *On Christian Doctrine*, I.4.4, 9.

50. Ibid., I.3.3, 9.

51. Ibid., I.22.20, 18.

52. "The things which are to be enjoyed are the Father, the Son, and the Holy Spirit, a single Trinity, a certain supreme thing common to all who enjoy it, if, indeed it is

a thing and not rather the cause of all things, or both a thing and a cause" (ibid., I.5.5, 10).

53. Ibid., I.22.20, 18. Augustine concludes this section "But 'cursed be the man that trusteth in man'" (Jer. 17:5).

54. Augustine, *On Christian Doctrine*, I.4.4, 9–10. Augustine then cites Romans 1:20 again to suggest that the visible things God has made be used toward the enjoyment of the invisible things of God.

55. Oliver O'Donovan, *The Problem of Self-Love in St. Augustine* (New Haven, CT: Yale University Press, 1980); Oliver O'Donovan, "*Usus* and *Fruitio* in Augustine, *De Doctrina Christiana* I," *Journal of Theological Studies* 33 (1982): 361–97.

56. Anders Nygren, *Agape and Eros*, trans. Philip S. Watson (Philadelphia: Westminster Press, 1953).

57. O'Donovan, "*Usus* and *Fruitio*," 393.

58. Among many examples, see Helmut David Baer, "The Fruit of Charity: Using the Neighbor in *De doctrina christiana*," *Journal of Religious Ethics* 24, no. 1 (Spring 1996): 47–64; Sarah Stewart-Kroeker, "Resisting Idolatry and Instrumentalisation in Loving the Neighbour: The Significance of the Pilgrimage Motif for Augustine's *Usus–Fruitio* Distinction," *Studies in Christian Ethics* 27, no. 2 (2014): 202–21; Rowan Williams, "'Good for Nothing'? Augustine on Creation," *Augustinian Studies* 25 (1994): 9–24; John Bowlin, "Augustine Counting Virtues," *Augustinian Studies* 41, no. 1 (2010): 277–300; Raymond Canning, *The Unity of Love for God and Neighbour in St. Augustine* (Leuven: Augustinian Historical Institute, 1993); Kevin Corrigan, "Love of God, Love of Self, and Love of Neighbor: Augustine's Critical Dialogue with Platonism," *Augustinian Studies* 34, no. 1 (2003): 97–106.

59. See Baer, "The Fruit of Charity," 48–9. Baer is drawing on the Oxford Latin Dictionary.

60. See Baer's comments on O'Donovan's perplexity in ibid., 50n9.

61. Augustine, *On Christian Doctrine*, I.14.13, 15.

62. Ibid., I.34.38, 29.

63. Ibid., I.11.11, 13.

64. Ibid., I.17.16, 16.

65. Ibid., I.14.13, 14–5.

66. Ibid., I.14.13, 15.

67. Ibid., I.31.34, 27.

68. Ibid., I.32.35, 27.

69. Baer, "Fruit of Charity," 60.

70. Augustine, *On Christian Doctrine*, I.33.36, 28.

71. Ibid., I.30.32, 26.

72. Ibid., I.30.31, 26.

73. Ibid., I.30.33, 26.

74. Ibid., I.22.21, 19.

75. It is clear that for Augustine the enjoyment of God is a communal reality and not an individual achievement: "Among those who are able to enjoy God with us, we love some whom we help, some by whom we are helped, some whose help we need and whose wants we supply, and some on whom we bestow no benefits and from whom

we await none ourselves. Be that as it may, we should desire that all enjoy God with us and that all the assistance we give them or get from them should be directed toward this end" (ibid., I.29.30, 24).

76. Ibid., I.32.35, 27–8.

77. The vision here is echoed in the *City of God*, where Augustine describes the citizens of the heavenly city as those "who form a community where there is no love of a will that is personal and, as we may say, private, but a love that rejoices in a good that is at once shared by all and unchanging—a love that makes 'one heart' out of many, a love that is the whole-hearted and harmonious obedience of mutual affection" (XV.3, 599).

78. Ibid., I.23.22, 19: "Not everything which is to be used is to be loved, but only those things which either by a certain association pertain to God, like a man or an angel, or pertain to us and require the favor of God through us, like the body."

79. Ibid., I.35.39, 30.

80. As we have seen in *City of God*, Augustine designates improper self-love as *amor sui*. On the different kinds of love in *De doctrina christiana*, see Stewart-Kroeker, "Resisting Idolatry," 210n24.

81. Augustine, *On Christian Doctrine*, I.33.36, 28.

82. Ibid., I.38.42, 32.

83. Stewart-Kroeker, "Resisting Idolatry," 203.

84. Augustine, *City of God*, XIV.28, 593.

85. Augustine, *Confessions*, II.5.10, 29–30.

86. Augustine, *City of God*, V.15, 204–5. In a similar vein, see also V.12–7, 196–207. In books IV and V Augustine contrasts the earlier Romans positively to his pagan contemporaries, for whom virtue had given way to *libido dominandi*.

87. Ibid., V.17, 206: "Let us consider all the hardships these conquerors made light of, all the sufferings they endured, and the desires they suppressed to gain the glory of men. They deserved to receive that glory as a reward for such virtues. Let this thought avail to suppress pride in us."

88. Ibid., XIV.13, 573.

89. Ibid.

90. Ibid.

91. Augustine, *The Spirit and the Letter*, 18.11, in *Augustine: Later Works*, trans. John Burnaby (Philadelphia, PA: Westminster Press, 1955), 207–8.

92. Ibid., 19.12, 208.

93. Ibid., 19.12, 209.

94. Augustine, *The Literal Meaning of Genesis*, XI.15.19, in *On Genesis*, trans. Edmund Hill, vol. 13 of *The Works of St. Augustine*, part I (Hyde Park, NY: New City Press, 2002).

95. Ibid. Robert Markus contends that this emphasis on privacy becomes an increasingly important concern for Augustine after 400: "He now searched for the roots of human sin in man's liability to close in on himself." Robert Markus, *The End of Ancient Christianity* (Cambridge: Cambridge University Press, 1990), 51.

96. Richard B. Miller, "Evil, Friendship, and Iconic Realism in Augustine's *Confessions*," *Harvard Theological Review* 104, no. 4 (October 2011): 391.

97. Augustine, *Confessions*, IV.4.7, 56. Augustine says he turns him away from the true faith in which he was raised and toward pagan mythologies. The friend is baptized while sick, and when Augustine teases him about it, he objects sharply. Augustine resolves to wait until his friend is well to convince him to turn away from his baptism: "Then I would be able to do what I wished with him" (ibid., IV.4.8, 57).

98. Ibid., IV.6.11, 59.

99. Ibid.

100. Ibid., IV.9.14, 61.

101. Ibid., IV.7.12, 60.

102. Ibid., IV.6.11, 58.

103. Richard Miller points out that Augustine's failure to mention his friend's name—a key marker of individuation—is another telling sign of Augustine's narcissism at this stage ("Evil, Friendship, and Iconic Realism," 391).

104. Augustine, *Confessions*, IV.4.7, 56.

105. Ibid., II.8.16, 33.

106. Ibid., II.4.9, 29.

107. Ibid., II.6.13, 31.

108. Ibid., II.6.14, 32.

109. Ibid.

110. Ibid., I.1.1, 3.

111. Ibid., VIII.5.10, 140.

112. Augustine, *Sermon 90A*, in *Works of Saint Augustine: A Translation for the 21st Century*, III/11, ed. John E. Rotelle, trans. Edmund Hill (Hyde Park, NY: New City Press, 1997), 80.

113. Ibid., 81–2.

114. Ibid., 81.

115. Augustine, *Confessions*, III.6.11, 43. The more complete phrase is "*interior intimo meo et superior summo meo*," or, as Chadwick renders it, "more inward than my most inward part and higher than the highest element in me." On the importance of the noncompetitive Creator/creation distinction, see Robert Sokolowski, *The God of Faith and Reason: Foundations of Christian Theology* (Washington, DC: Catholic University of America Press, 1995), 21–40.

116. See Taylor's chapter on Augustine in Charles Taylor, *Sources of the Self: The Making of the Modern Identity* (Cambridge, MA: Harvard University Press, 1992), 127–42.

117. John C. Cavadini, *Visioning Augustine* (Oxford: Wiley Blackwell, 2019), 144. Cavadini points out that part of the difficulty is that reflexive pronouns in English like "myself" encourage the idea that there is a separate self that is mine.

118. Augustine, *Sermon 90A*, 80–1.

119. Augustine, *On Christian Doctrine*, I.23.23, 20. The interior quote is from a Latin translation of Psalm 11:5.

120. Carol Harrison has an excellent exposition of this point in her essay "Taking Creation for the Creator: Use and Enjoyment in Augustine's Theological Aesthetics," in *Idolatry: False Worship in the Bible, Early Judaism and Christianity*, ed. Stephen C. Barton (London: T. & T. Clark, 2007), 179–84.

121. Augustine, *The Spirit and the Letter*, 19.12, 208–9, as cited above.

122. Plato, *Republic*, 597a–e, 598a, trans. G. M. A. Grube and C. D. C. Reeve (Indianapolis, IN: Hackett, 1992), 266–8. My discussion here relies on Natalie Carnes, "How Love for the Image Cast Out Fear of It in Early Christianity," *Religions* 8, no. 20 (2017), 1–15.

123. Plato is apprehensive about human-made images in the *Republic*, but positive about the images crafted by the Demiurge in *Timaeus*.

124. See Augustine, *City of God*, II.8–14, 56–65. In II.14, Augustine applauds Plato for banning poets and theatrical performances from his city for spreading fictions instead of truth.

125. Augustine, *Confessions*, III.2.2.

126. Ibid., III.2.2, 36.

127. Ibid.

128. Ibid., III.2.4, 37.

129. Carnes, "How Love for the Image," 8.

130. Augustine, *On the Trinity*, VI.10.11, 213. As we have seen, Augustine tends to use the term *simulacrum*, rather than *imago*, when referring to idolatrous images. *Simulacra* are copies of appearances; as Augustine uses it here, *imago* translates the Greek *eikōn*, used in II Corinthians 4:4 and Colossians 1:15 to describe Christ as the perfect Image of God, not a mere copy of appearances but one who instantiates the entirety of the original.

131. Augustine acknowledges nevertheless that there is nothing automatic about humans reading the Image of God rightly. In his homilies on the First Letter of John, Augustine writes that evil people will see only the fleshly Jesus, not the eternal Word: "To see Christ in this sort, Christ in the form of God, Word of God, Only-Begotten of the Father, equal with the Father, is to the bad impossible. But in regard that the Word was made flesh, the bad also shall have power to see Him: because in the day of judgment the bad also will see Him; for He shall so come to judge, as He came to be judged. In the selfsame form, a man, but yet God: for cursed is every one that puts his trust in man." Augustine, *Homilies on the First Epistle of John*, 4.5, trans. H. Browne, in *Nicene and Post-Nicene Fathers, First Series*, vol. 7, ed. Philip Schaff (Buffalo, NY: Christian Literature, 1888), revised and edited for New Advent by Kevin Knight, http://www.newadvent.org/fathers/170204.htm.

132. Augustine, *On the Trinity*, VI.10.12.

133. Augustine, Sermon 51, in *Works of Saint Augustine: A Translation for the 21st Century*, III/3, ed. John E. Rotelle, trans. Edmund Hill (Brooklyn, NY: New City Press, 1991), 19–21.

134. Augustine, *City of God*, II.27–28, 84–6. See also Carnes, "How Love for the Image," 9; Chanon Ross, *Gifts Glittering and Poisoned: Spectacle, Empire, and Metaphysics* (Eugene, OR: Cascade, 2014), 43–60.

135. Augustine, *City of God*, X.20, 400–1.

136. Augustine, Sermon 277A, in *Works of Saint Augustine: A Translation for the 21st Century*, III/8, ed. John E. Rotelle, trans. Edmund Hill (Hyde Park, NY: New City Press, 1994), 47.

137. Augustine, *Sermon* 272, in *Works of Saint Augustine*, III/7, ed. John E. Rotelle, trans. Edmund Hill (New Rochelle, NY: New City Press, 1993), 300–1.
138. Augustine, *Sermon* 227, in *Works of Saint Augustine*, III/6, ed. John E. Rotelle, trans. Edmund Hill (New Rochelle, NY: New City Press, 1993), 254.
139. David Vincent Meconi, "Becoming Gods by Becoming God's: Augustine's Mystagogy of Identification," *Augustinian Studies* 39, no. 1 (2008): 61–74.
140. Ibid., 62–3.
141. Ibid., 63–7.
142. Augustine, *Sermon* 15.2, quoted in ibid., 70.
143. Meconi, "Becoming Gods," 72–3. The reference is to *Sermon* 23B.

Chapter 5

1. Joeri Schrijvers counts up the mentions of Augustine in Marion's work before *Au lieu de soi* was published in 2008 and is surprised to find only a very few scattered references, mostly relegated to the notes. See Joeri Schrijvers, "In (the) Place of the Self: A Critical Study of Jean-Luc Marion's *Au lieu de soi. L'approche de Saint Augustin,*" *Modern Theology* 25, no. 4 (October 2009): 662–3. Schrijvers nevertheless thinks that Augustine's influence on Marion is decisive: "The facts and figures listed above should, however, not confuse readers of Marion, for the few times that Marion has hinted at Augustine's thought reveal much more than their sheer scarcity seems to suggest. Indeed, it is more than likely that the innermost workings of the phenomenology of givenness is already oriented towards the theology of the saint" (663).
2. Jean-Luc Marion, *In the Self's Place: The Approach of Saint Augustine*, trans. Jeffrey L. Kosky (Stanford, CA: Stanford University Press, 2012).
3. Jean-Luc Marion, *The Idol and Distance: Five Studies*, trans. Thomas A. Carlson (New York: Fordham University Press, 2001), 3. On this point, see also Jean-Luc Marion, *God without Being: Hors-Texte*, trans. Thomas A. Carlson (Chicago: University of Chicago Press, 1991), 29.
4. Marion, *Idol and Distance*, 2.
5. Ibid., 9.
6. Friedrich Nietzsche, *Will to Power*, §55, quoted in Marion, *God without Being*, 30.
7. Marion, *God without Being*, 33.
8. Friedrich Nietzsche, *Thus Spoke Zarathustra*, trans. G. Parkes (New York: Oxford University Press, 2005), 158.
9. Marion, *God without Being*, 38.
10. In the original edition of *God without Being*, Marion implicates Thomas Aquinas in the subordination of God to Being (see 73–83). He has since walked back that criticism of Aquinas and medieval thought more generally. The second edition of *God without Being*, which appeared in 2012, is identical to the first, except that Marion's essay "Thomas Aquinas and Onto-theo-logy" is added as its eighth chapter, in which Marion absolves Thomas of the original charge. In his book *On*

the Ego and on God: Further Cartesian Questions, trans. Christina M. Gschwandtner (New York: Fordham University Press, 2007), Marion finds that Descartes was the first to posit God as *causa sui,* and the first to engage fully in metaphysics as ontotheology; "the medieval thinkers could, at least partially, be removed from the onto-theological constitution of metaphysics and hence from an idolatrous interpretation of God" (160).

11. Marion, *God without Being,* 33–7; Marion, *Idol and Distance,* 9–19.
12. Martin Heidegger, *Identity and Difference,* quoted in Marion, *God without Being,* 35.
13. Marion, *God without Being,* 37–45.
14. On this point, see Christina Gschwandtner, *Marion and Theology* (London: Bloomsbury, 2016), 39.
15. Marion, *God without Being,* 36–7, 45–9. The influence of Hans Urs von Balthasar is evident here.
16. Ibid., 48.
17. Ibid., 12.
18. Ibid., 8.
19. Marion defends his broader use of the term "idol" by noting that the Bible regards even representation of the true God to be idolatrous (ibid., 8).
20. Ibid.
21. Ibid.
22. Ibid., 9.
23. Marion, *Idol and Distance,* 5.
24. Ibid., 6.
25. Marion, *God without Being,* 9–12.
26. Ibid., 13.
27. Ibid.
28. Marion, *Idol and Distance,* 6.
29. Marion, *God without Being,* 28.
30. Ibid., 14.
31. Ibid., 28–9. In a similar vein, "The idol always marks a true and genuine experience of the divine, but for this very reason announces its limit: as an experience of the divine, starting in this way with the one who aims at it, in view of the reflex in which, through the idolatrous figure, this aim masks and marks its defection with regard to the invisible, the idol always must be read on the basis of the one whose experience of the divine takes shape there" (27–8).
32. Ibid., 49–50.
33. Ibid., 18.
34. Marion, *Idol and Distance,* 198.
35. Thomas Aquinas, *Summa Theologiae,* I.8.1.
36. Marion, *Idol and Distance,* 215.
37. On the influence of Balthasar's interpretation of Pseudo-Dionysius on Marion's notion of distance, see Tamsin Jones, "Dionysius in Hans Urs von Balthasar and Jean-Luc Marion," in *Re-Thinking Dionysius the Areopagite,* ed. Sarah Coakley and Charles M. Stang (Oxford: Wiley-Blackwell, 2009), 218–9.

38. Marion, *Idol and Distance*, 214–5.

39. Robyn Horner, *Jean-Luc Marion: A Theo-logical Introduction* (Aldershot: Ashgate, 2005), 57–60.

40. Marion, *Idol and Distance*, 153.

41. "This means that distance does not separate us from the Ab-solute so much as it prepares for us, with all its anteriority, our identity. It denotes, therefore the positive movement of the Ab-solute, which, through its being set in distance, is ecstatically disappropriated from Itself in order that man might receive himself ecstatically in difference. In receiving himself from distance, man comprehends not only that distance comprehends him, but that it renders him possible. Distance appears, then, as the very disappropriation through which God creates—not the break of alienation, but the ecstatic place that saves irreducible alterity" (ibid., 153–4).

42. Marion has asserted a sharp distinction between phenomenology and theology in his work: phenomenality describes only the possibility of revelation, not the actuality or historicity, which is the realm of theology. Many of the most prominent commentators on Marion seem to find this assertion, if not entirely unconvincing and unnecessary, then at least more complicated than Marion lets on. See, for example, Robyn Horner, "Translator's Introduction," in Jean-Luc Marion, *In Excess: Studies of Saturated Phenomena* (New York: Fordham University Press, 2002), ix–x; Thomas A. Carlson, "Translator's Introduction," in Marion, *Idol and Distance*, xi–xxxi; and Gschwandtner, *Marion and Theology*, 1–2. I side with Marion's critics here; I do not share Marion's apparent anxiety to reinforce a sharp divide between phenomenology and theology.

43. It might be the case that Marion is not entirely fair to Husserl; see Shane Mackinlay, *Interpreting Excess: Jean-Luc Marion, Saturated Phenomena, and Hermeneutics* (New York: Fordham University Press, 2010), 57–74.

44. For a good summary of Marion's saturated phenomenon as it relates to Husserl, see Gschwandtner, *Marion and Theology*, 55–64.

45. Ibid., 61–3.

46. Marion, *In Excess*, 57–62.

47. Ibid., 58.

48. Ibid., 60–1.

49. Marion, *God without Being*, 10.

50. Ibid.

51. Marion, *In Excess*, 60.

52. Ibid., 61. This is similar to Augustine's "My weight is my love"; Augustine, *Confessions*, XIII.9.10., trans. Henry Chadwick (Oxford: Oxford University Press, 1991), 278. Thanks to Scott Moringiello for pointing me to this passage.

53. Marion, *In Excess*, 61.

54. Ibid., 59.

55. Ibid., 63.

56. Ibid.

57. Ibid., 66.

58. Ibid., 68.

59. Ibid., 69.

60. It is not clear if Marion has painting alone in mind here, or if other types of idols also impose their fascination on society. Surely an individual artist like Picasso has helped change the way we see. But in a society now inundated by images, the "reign" of great art is questionable. See chapter 7 on consumer culture.

61. Marion, *In Excess*, 61.

62. Ibid., 70.

63. Ibid., 70-1.

64. Jean-Luc Marion, *Being Given: Toward a Phenomenology of Givenness,* trans. Jeffrey L. Kosky (Stanford, CA: Stanford University Press, 2002), 234-41.

65. On this point, see Peter Joseph Fritz, "Black Holes and Revelations: Michel Henry and Jean-Luc Marion on the Aesthetics of the Invisible," *Modern Theology* 25, no. 3 (July 2009): 424-5.

66. Marion, *In Excess*, 75-81, 104-27.

67. Gschwandtner, *Marion and Theology*, 51.

68. Jean-Luc Marion, *The Crossing of the Visible*, trans. James K. A. Smith (Stanford, CA: Stanford University Press, 2003), 34, quoted in Mackinlay, *Interpreting Excess*, 122.

69. Mackinlay, *Interpreting Excess*, 122-4.

70. Ibid., 68.

71. Ibid., 58-9. In *Being Given*, Marion writes, "My entire project, by contrast [to metaphysics], aims to think the common-law phenomenon, and through it the poor phenomenon, on the basis of the paradigm of the saturated phenomenon, of which the former two offer only weakened variants, and from which they derive by progressive diminishment. For the saturated phenomenon does not give itself apart from the norm, by way of exception to the definition of phenomenality. . . . What metaphysics rules out as an exception (the saturated paradox), phenomenology here takes for its norm" (227, quoted in Mackinlay, *Interpreting Excess,* 58-9).

72. Mackinlay, *Interpreting Excess*, 175.

73. Ibid., 217.

74. Ibid., 218.

75. Jean-Luc Marion, "The Banality of Saturation," trans. Jeffrey L. Kosky, in Marion, *The Visible and the Revealed* (New York: Fordham University Press, 2008), 174n7, quoted in Mackinlay, *Interpreting Excess*, 69. Marion adds, "The devoted [*l'adonné*] operates according to the call and response and manages the passage of what gives itself to what shows itself: neither the one nor the other corresponds to these categories. 'Passivity' and 'activity' intervene only once the characteristics of the devoted are misconstrued" (174n7).

76. Marion, *In Excess*, 33n3.

77. Ibid., 33.

78. Marion, *In the Self's Place*, 84.

79. Augustine, *Sermon* 34, 2, quoted in ibid., 96.

80. Marion, *In the Self's Place*, 96.

81. Ibid., 93.

82. Ibid., 98.

83. Ibid., 102–3.

84. Ibid., 107.

85. Ibid., 108.

86. Ibid., 108–10.

87. Augustine, *Confessions*, X.23.34, 199–200. I have used Chadwick's translation of Augustine here rather than Kosky's translation of Marion's translation of Augustine, which I find awkward and confusing; for example, "Is it not because [everyone] loves truth in such a way that [all] those who love something else [besides this very truth] want for this other thing that they love to be [also] the truth, and, as they do not want to suffer any illusions, they do want [any more to admit] to be deceived?" There seems to be a "not" missing from the phrase "they do want . . . to be deceived." I also don't find the added glosses in brackets to be helpful.

88. Marion, *In the Self's Place*, 125.

89. Ibid., 112.

90. Ibid., 115–20.

91. Ibid., 113.

92. Ibid., 122.

93. Ibid., 276–8.

94. Ibid., 124.

95. Schrijvers, "In (the) Place of the Self," 672.

96. Schrijvers is critical of Marion's unapologetic turn to theology here. Schrijvers is unhappy that Marion has not at least brought theology into explicit dialogue with other disciplines, and he is unconvinced that theology is the only resource that can adequately describe the interpenetration of the self and the other. Schrijvers, finally, thinks Marion is tainted by Augustine's disdain for the finite world, and thus remains captured by metaphysics. He writes, "[O]ntotheology indeed seems to haunt Marion's thinking when it sets out its Manichean-like opposition between God (love) and the world" (ibid., 681). I do not think such a judgment is fair to either Augustine or Marion. As I laid it out in chapter 4, in exploring Augustine's thinking on finite creation, an iconic view of the world does not result in a depreciation of the world unless one understands the relationship between God and creation as zero-sum. I will have more to say about this in the final chapter.

97. Marion, *God without Being*, 14–5.

98. Ibid., 15.

99. Ibid.

100. Ibid., 16.

101. Ibid., 210n10.

102. Marion, *In Excess*, 71.

103. Marion, *God without Being*, 111–4.

104. Ibid., 114.

105. Marion, *Idol and Distance*, 6.

106. Ibid.

107. Ibid., 7.

Chapter 6

1. Jean-Luc Marion, *God without Being: Hors-Texte*, trans. Thomas A. Carlson (Chicago: University of Chicago Press, 1991), 15.

2. Jean-Luc Marion, *The Idol and Distance: Five Studies*, trans. Thomas A. Carlson (New York: Fordham University Press, 2001), 6.

3. In the introduction to *Chosen Peoples*, his important 2003 book on nationalism, Anthony D. Smith finds himself having to explain why such a study is still relevant, despite the common belief that people's loyalties to nations were dissipating in a globalized world. Anthony D. Smith, *Chosen Peoples: Sacred Sources of National Identity* (Oxford: Oxford University Press, 2003), 1–3.

4. Both quotes are from ibid., 24.

5. Émile Durkheim, *The Elementary Forms of Religious Life,* trans. Joseph Ward Swain (New York: Free Press, 1965), 261.

6. Ibid., 475.

7. Ibid., 466.

8. See Timothy Jenkins, "Why Do Things Move People? A Sociological Account of Idolatry," in *Idolatry: False Worship in the Bible, Early Judaism, and Christianity*, ed. Stephen C. Barton (London: T. & T. Clark, 2006), 289.

9. Durkheim, *Elementary Forms*, 93.

10. "If, then, religion's reason for existence was to give us a conception of the world which would guide us in our relations with it, it was in no condition to fulfil its function, and people would not have been slow to perceive it: failures, being infinitely more frequent than successes, would have quickly shown them that they were following a false route, and religion, shaken at each instant by these repeated contradictions would not have been able to survive" (ibid., 98).

11. Ibid., 14–5.

12. Ibid., 236.

13. "Now the totem is the flag of the clan" (ibid., 252). See also 236 and 264.

14. Ibid., 236–7.

15. "In the same way, finally, the causal relation, from the moment when it is collectively stated by the group, becomes independent of every individual consciousness; it rises above all particular minds and events" (ibid., 491).

16. Ibid., 238.

17. Ibid., 239.

18. On this point, see Joseph Llobera, "Durkheim and the National Question," in *Debating Durkheim*, ed. Hermino Martins and William Pickering (London: Taylor and Francis, 1994), 135.

19. Durkheim, *Elementary Forms*, 242.

20. Ibid. 244–5.

21. Ibid., 242–4.

22. Ibid., 244.

23. Ibid., 251–2.

24. Ibid., 252.

25. Smith writes that although "Durkheim wrote little directly about nationalism or nationality problems, he became increasingly interested in the subject, and not only with the drift towards world war." Anthony D. Smith, "Nationalism and Classical Social Theory," *British Journal of Sociology* 34 (1983): 29.

26. Durkheim, *Elementary Forms*, 240.

27. Ibid.: "For the collective force is not entirely outside of us; it does not act upon us wholly from without; but rather, since society cannot exist except in and through individual consciousness, this force must also penetrate us and organize itself within us; it thus becomes an integral part of our being, and by that very fact this is elevated and magnified."

28. As Robert Bellah comments, Durkheim "believed that traditional religion was on its way out, essentially because it conflicts with science. But the concept of the sacred would remain: without this basis of moral respect society itself is impossible. But what would be the referent to which sacred symbols refer? Durkheim replied 'society,' and as the most comprehensive functioning society 'the nation.'" Robert N. Bellah, "Durkheim and History," in *Emile Durkheim: Critical Assessments*, vol. 7, second series, ed. Peter Hamilton (London: Routledge, 1995), 47.

29. Robert N. Bellah, "Introduction," in *Emile Durkheim on Morality and Society*, ed. Robert N. Bellah (Chicago: University of Chicago Press, 1973), xvii.

30. Carlton J. H. Hayes, *A Generation of Materialism 1870–1900* (New York: Harper, 1941), 247.

31. Llobera, "Durkheim and the National Question,"145–58.

32. Ibid., 149.

33. Durkheim, *Elementary Forms,* 475.

34. Ibid.

35. Ibid.

36. Carlton J. H. Hayes, "Nationalism as a Religion" (1926), §2, Panarchy, https://www.panarchy.org/hayes/nationalism.html. This essay can also be found in Carlton J. H. Hayes, *Essays on Nationalism* (New York: Russell & Russell, 1966), 93–125.

37. Ibid., §3.

38. Marie-Joseph Chenier, quoted in ibid.

39. Hayes, "Nationalism as a Religion," §4.

40. Ibid.

41. Ibid., §5.

42. Ibid., §6.

43. Ibid.

44. Hayes's essay "Nationalism as a Religion" was serialized in the progressive Catholic magazine *Commonweal* when it first appeared in 1926. For more background on Hayes, see Arthur Hughes, "Carlton J. H. Hayes: A Christian Historian Confronts Nationalism," *Records of the American Catholic Historical Society of Philadelphia* 100, no. 1 (March–December, 1989): 39–54.

45. Hayes, "Nationalism as a Religion," §8.

46. Ibid.

47. On Hayes and idolatry, see H. Vincent Moses, "Nationalism and the Kingdom of God according to Hans Kohn and Carlton J. H. Hayes," *Journal of Church and State* 17, no. 2 (Spring 1975): 259–74.

48. Hughes, "Carlton J. H. Hayes," 46.

49. Both quotes are from the closing paragraph of Carlton J. H. Hayes, "The Church and Nationalism: A Plea for Further Study of a Major Issue," *Catholic Historical Review* 28, no. 1 (April 1942): 12. The point of the article is to show that Catholics were far from blameless in fostering nationalistic attitudes. Hayes cites examples dating back to the medieval period, beginning with national primates and vernacular translations. The constant Catholic ideal, by contrast, is Christian internationalism, as expressed by Pope Pius XI and quoted by Hayes: "All must remember that the peoples of the earth form but one family in God" (12).

50. Hayes, "Nationalism as a Religion," §7.

51. Ibid.

52. For more examples, see Josep Llobera, *The God of Modernity: The Development of Nationalism in Western Europe* (Providence, RI: Berg, 1994); Conor Cruise O'Brien, *God Land: Reflections on Religion and Nationalism* (Cambridge, MA: Harvard University Press, 1998); Talal Asad, "Religion, Nation-State, Secularism," in *Nation and Religion: Perspectives on Europe and Asia*, ed. Peter van der Veer and Hartmut Lehmann (Princeton, NJ: Princeton University Press, 1999), 178–96; Wilbur Zelinsky, *Nation into State: The Shifting Symbolic Foundations of American Nationalism* (Chapel Hill: University of North Carolina Press, 1988).

53. Robert N. Bellah, "Civil Religion in America," *Daedalus* 96, no. 1 (Winter 1967): 1.

54. Ibid., 3.

55. Ibid., 2.

56. Ibid., 4.

57. Ibid., 8.

58. Ibid.

59. Ibid., 10.

60. Ibid., 8.

61. Ibid., 12. Bellah does not name Hayes or any other critics.

62. In the last paragraph of the article, Bellah notes that Abraham Lincoln called Americans an "almost chosen people." Bellah uses the "almost" in this phrase to note the moral ambiguity of American action in the world, not to signal, à la Charles Taylor (see chapter 2), that civil religion is almost, but not really, a religion (ibid., 19).

63. Ibid., 13. On the subject of the relative empirical performance of the two religions, Bellah writes, "I am not at all convinced that the leaders of the churches have consistently represented a higher level of religious insight than the spokesmen of the civil religion" (12). Hayes, given his critiques of the Catholic bishops' capitulation to nationalism, might ruefully agree.

64. Ibid., 15. Bellah worries, "We have in a moment of uncertainty been tempted to rely on our overwhelming physical power rather than on our intelligence, and we have, in part, succumbed to this temptation" (17).

65. In the debate that followed the publication of his seminal article in 1967, Bellah defended himself against charges of idolatry by arguing, as he does in his original article, that American civil religion is subordinate to higher ethical principles and is not simply self-worship. He recognized the danger of idolatry more clearly than he did in the original article, but was nevertheless convinced that American civil religion has the resources to guard against it. Bellah professed himself "convinced that every nation and every people come to some form of religious self-understanding.... Rather than simply denounce what seems in any case inevitable, it seems more responsible to seek within the civil religious tradition for those critical principles which undercut the ever present danger of national self-idolization." Robert N. Bellah, *Beyond Belief: Essays on Religion in a Post-Traditionalist World* (New York: Harper & Row, 1970), 168.
66. Bellah, "Civil Religion in America," 18.
67. Ibid.
68. Ibid., 19n1.
69. Ibid.
70. Carolyn Marvin and David Ingle, "Blood Sacrifice and the Nation: Revisiting Civil Religion," *Journal of the American Academy of Religion* 64, no. 4 (Winter 1996): 767.
71. Carolyn Marvin and David W. Ingle, *Blood Sacrifice and the Nation: Totem Rituals and the American Flag* (Cambridge: Cambridge University Press, 1999), 11.
72. Ibid., 9.
73. Ibid., 10. Peter Berger argues that civil religion promotes civil unity in order to guarantee pluralism at the level of sectarian religions. Peter Berger, "From the Crisis of Religion to the Crisis of Secularity," in *Religion and America: Spiritual Life in a Secular Age*, ed. Mary Douglas and Stephen M. Tipton (Boston: Beacon Press, 1983), 18. Marvin and Ingle think that civil religion has vanquished its rivals and keeps them under watchful control (*Blood Sacrifice*, 18).
74. Marvin and Ingle, *Blood Sacrifice*, 25.
75. "We say the nation is the shared memory of blood sacrifice, periodically renewed" (ibid., 4).
76. Ibid., 11. David Ingle writes about violence from the perspective of one who served in special operations in the U.S. Army and as an antisubmarine warfare specialist in the U.S. Navy.
77. Ibid., 66.
78. Girard writes, "Any phenomenon associated with the acts of remembering, commemorating, and perpetuating a unanimity that springs from the murder of a surrogate victim can be termed 'religious.'" René Girard, *Violence and the Sacred*, trans. Patrick Gregory (Baltimore, MD: Johns Hopkins University Press, 1977), 315.
79. Marvin and Ingle, *Blood Sacrifice*, 79.
80. Ibid., 15.
81. Mario Cuomo, quoted in ibid., 153.
82. Marvin and Ingle, *Blood Sacrifice*, 27.
83. Ibid., 20–1.
84. Ibid., 20. For the flag as totem in Durkheim, see Durkheim, *Elementary Forms*, 236.

85. Donald Trump, quoted in Andrew Naughtie, "Trump Furious after NFL Chief Admits He Was Wrong to Oppose Colin Kaepernick," *The Independent*, June 8, 2020, https://www.independent.co.uk/news/world/americas/trump-roger-good ell-nfl-colin-kaepernick-twitter-take-knee-a9554496.html.

86. Amanda Jacobs, quoted in Nicholas Ballasy, "Gold Star Mothers Condemn Socialism, Slam Kaepernick," PJ Media, July 8, 2019, https://pjmedia.com/news-and-politics/nicholas-ballasy/2019/07/08/gold-star-moms-condemn-socialism-slam-kaepernick-n66998.

87. Marvin and Ingle, *Blood Sacrifice*, 46. Marvin and Ingle note that the contest between texts and bodies is often played out along class lines. The educated classes skilled at using texts are generally shielded from having to use their bodies on behalf of the nation. It is the working classes, those identified more closely with the body, who do the preponderance of killing and dying on behalf of the nation (42).

88. Ibid., 45, 149.

89. Mike Pence, quoted in Michael Peppard, "Old Glory to God," *Commonweal*, September 1, 2020, https://www.commonwealmagazine.org/print/41341. In the NIV version, the relevant passage in Hebrews 12:1–2 reads, "And let us run with perseverance the race marked out for us, fixing our eyes on Jesus, the pioneer and perfecter of faith." II Corinthians 3:17 reads, "Now the LORD is the Spirit, and where the Spirit of the LORD is, there is freedom."

90. Marvin and Ingle, "Blood Sacrifice," 770.

91. Marvin and Ingle do not appear to recognize the possibility of a religion that could be both true and nonviolent: "Champions of nationalism see sectarianism as dangerous to nationalism's healthiest aspirations. Sectarianism, they fear, introduces passions that may manifest themselves in violence. They wish to separate church and state by subordinating the claims of the former to the latter. Champions of sectarianism see nationalism as threatening to religious values, especially non-violence. The state, they say, is profane because it engages in violence. . . . Perhaps nationalism and sectarianism recognize something about each other that they hesitate to recognize about themselves. Each fears that members of the other community are willing to kill and die for truth as they understand it. For what is really true in any community is what its members can agree is worth killing for, or what they can be compelled to sacrifice their lives for. The sacred is thus easily recognized. It is that set of beliefs and persons for which we ought to shed our own blood, if necessary, when there is a serious threat. Rituals that celebrate this blood sacrifice give expression and witness to faith. Sacrificial death thus defines both sectarian and national identity. This is the first sense in which both are species of religion" (ibid., 769).

92. The full quote is "And, you know—and we have a—my colleagues have heard me say this for a long, long time. We've a lot of obligations as Americans. But we only have one sacred obligation. Obligations of the old and the young to educate, to take care. But only one sacred obligation, and that's prepare those we send to war and care for them and their families when they come home from war. And I mean that. And I know my colleagues mean that from the bottom of our heart." "Remarks by

President Biden at a Delaware Veterans Summit and PACT Act Town Hall," White House, December 16, 2022, https://www.whitehouse.gov/briefing-room/speeches-remarks/2022/12/16/remarks-by-president-biden-at-a-delaware-veterans-sum mit-and-pact-act-town-hall-new-castle-de/. Biden has spoken in nearly identical terms about Americans' "only truly sacred obligation" before; see, e.g., "Biden Says U.S. Has Sacred Obligation to Fallen Service Members," U.S. Department of Defense News, May 30, 2022, https://www.defense.gov/News/News-Stories/Article/Article/ 3047003/biden-says-us-has-sacred-obligation-to-fallen-service-members/.

93. Marvin and Ingle, "Blood Sacrifice," 768–9.

94. William Rehnquist, quoted in Marvin and Ingle, *Blood Sacrifice*, 30. Rehnquist was writing for the minority in a case, *Texas v. Johnson* (1989), that struck down the laws in forty-eight of fifty states criminalizing the "desecration" of the flag.

95. For Girard's single-volume account of the scapegoating mechanism and its unmasking by the Gospel, see René Girard, *I See Satan Fall Like Lightning*, trans. James G. Williams (Maryknoll, NY: Orbis Books, 2001).

96. One example of this distinction is Michael Ignatieff, *Blood and Belonging: Journeys into the New Nationalism* (New York: Farrar, Straus and Giroux, 1993), 5–9.

97. Bernard Yack, "The Myth of the Civic Nation," in *Theorizing Nationalism*, ed. Ronald Beiner (Albany: State University of New York Press, 1999), 105. For further critiques of the civic/ethnic distinction, see Erika Harris, *Nationalism: Theories and Cases* (Edinburgh: Edinburgh University Press, 2009), 28–38, who argues that all nationalisms are both civic and ethnic; Atalia Omer and Jason A. Springs, *Religious Nationalism: A Reference Handbook* (Santa Barbara, CA: ABC-CLIO, 2013), 60–3.

98. Omer and Springs, *Religious Nationalism*, 43–60.

99. Ibid., 52–3.

100. Ibid., 67. Likewise "nationalism is a kind of religion" (76).

101. Ibid., 51.

102. For examples of this approach, see Timothy Fitzgerald, *Discourse on Civility and Barbarity: A Critical History of Religion and Related Categories* (Oxford: Oxford University Press, 2010); Richard King, ed., *Religion, Theory, Critique: Classic and Contemporary Approaches and Methodologies* (New York: Columbia University Press, 2017).

103. José Santiago, "From 'Civil Religion' to Nationalism as the Religion of Modern Times: Rethinking a Complex Relationship," *Journal for the Scientific Study of Religion* 48, no. 2 (June 2009): 399.

104. Ibid.

105. Max Weber, *The Protestant Ethic and the Spirit of Capitalism*, trans. Talcott Parsons (New York: Charles Scribner's Sons, 1958), 53.

106. A full genealogy of the religious/secular distinction and its construction by Western forms of power can be found in my book *The Myth of Religious Violence: Secular Ideology and the Roots of Modern Conflict* (New York: Oxford University Press, 2009), ch. 2.

107. Hayes, "Nationalism as a Religion," §1. Whereas Durkheim sees primitive societies as unified, Hayes emphasizes the decentralized nature of ancient and medieval life. Medieval Christendom, for example, was a jumble of overlapping personal loyalties to guilds, cities, local nobility, kings, ecclesiastical authorities, and emperors.

108. Ernest Gellner, *Nations and Nationalism*, 2nd ed. (Ithaca, NY: Cornell University Press, 2006), 8–18.

109. Ibid., 19–51.

110. Ibid., 76. See also 135, where Gellner writes, "By contrast, an industrial high culture is no longer linked—whatever its history—to a faith and a church. Its maintenance seems to require the resources of a state co-extensive with society, rather than merely those of a church superimposed on it. A growth-bound economy dependent on cognitive innovation cannot seriously link its cultural machinery (which it needs unconditionally) to some doctrinal faith which rapidly becomes obsolete, and often ridiculous."

111. Ibid., 76. According to Gellner, "in the agrarian world, high culture co-exists with low cultures, and needs a church (or at least a clerkly guild) to sustain it. In the industrial world high cultures prevail, but they need a state not a church, and they need a state *each*. That is one way of summing up the emergence of the nationalist age" (71).

112. Ibid., 76.

113. Ibid., 55.

114. Ibid., 56.

115. Ibid., 54.

116. For summaries of critiques of Gellner, see D. V. Kumar, "Gellnerian Theory of Nation and Nationalism: A Critical Appraisal," *Sociological Bulletin* 59, no. 3 (September–December 2010): 392–406; Harris, *Nationalism*, 54–6; and John Breuilly's "Introduction" to Gellner, *Nations and Nationalism*, xiii–liii.

117. Eric Hobsbawm and Terence Ranger, eds., *The Invention of Tradition* (Cambridge: Cambridge University Press, 1983), 303. See also Eric Hobsbawm, *Nations and Nationalism since 1780: Programme, Myth, Reality* (Cambridge: Cambridge University Press, 1990). Hobsbawm resists Gellner's top-down approach and emphasizes the willing participation of people at all levels of society in the construction of national sentiment.

118. Benedict Anderson, *Imagined Communities: Reflections on the Origin and Spread of Nationalism*, revised ed. (London: Verso, 2006), 11.

119. Ibid.

120. Anderson denies his is a replacement story: "Needless to say, I am not claiming that the appearance of nationalism toward the end of the eighteenth century was 'produced' by the erosion of religious certainties, or that this erosion does not itself require a complex explanation. Nor am I suggesting that somehow nationalism historically 'supersedes' religion. What I am proposing is that nationalism has to be understood by aligning it, not with self-consciously held political ideologies, but with the large cultural systems that preceded it, out of which—as well as against which—it came into being" (ibid., 12). But if religion "precedes" nationalism, as he says in the last sentence, how is it that nationalism does not "supersede" religion?

Anderson would no doubt recognize that plenty of people still consider themselves to be religious, but in the story he tells, religion more or less drops out after the Enlightenment.

121. Gellner, *Nations and Nationalism*, 55.

122. Smith notes that it is not only Gellner, Hobsbawm, and Anderson who regard religion as a residual and declining phenomenon, worth mentioning only as part of the "traditional society" out of which nationalism emerged and against which it reacted. Other modernist scholars of nationalism, such as Michael Hechter, Tom Nairn, John Breuilly, and Michael Mann, likewise ignore religion as a continuing phenomenon (Smith, *Chosen Peoples*, 10).

123. Ibid., 6.

124. Ibid., 17–8.

125. Zelinsky, *Nation into State*, 20–1, 30–5. Zelinsky comments, "In describing Washington's symbolic import, the only appropriate term is deification, not as a mere figure of speech but as a soberly realistic assessment" (34).

126. Ibid., 46–8.

127. Smith, *Chosen Peoples*, 31.

128. Ibid., 44–130.

129. Ibid., 36.

130. Ibid., 131–65.

131. Ibid., 166–217.

132. Ibid., 218–53.

133. Ibid., 66–73.

134. Ibid., 179–83.

135. Ibid., 34.

136. Ibid., 42, italics in the original.

137. Ibid. Smith recognizes both the substantivist and functionalist definitions of religion and says that they are both necessary and useful (28). He oscillates between them, depending on his purpose. Smith uses a substantivist definition of religion when he writes about "traditional religion." Things like Christianity are religious because they have certain beliefs in salvation; they have a sense of the sacred and generate sentiments of binding unity. Official nationalist discourse presents itself as nonreligious, or secular, while at the same time it borrows religious elements from traditional religion. At a deeper level, however, Smith sees nationalism as a religion because it draws on the same deep wells of sentiment and on the same separation of the sacred from the profane. Here Smith explicitly draws on Durkheim and employs a functionalist definition of religion, such that there is no *essential* difference in form between the cult and the faith of nationalism and, say, Christianity (3–5, 24–30).

138. Braden Anderson, *Chosen Nation: Scripture, Theopolitics, and the Project of National Identity* (Eugene, OR: Cascade Books, 2012), 56–7.

139. Smith, 6 and 205, as quoted in ibid., 58.

140. The Fortnight for Freedom was a campaign initiated by the U.S. Conference of Catholic Bishops in 2012 to highlight matters of religious liberty. The Fortnight was meant to run annually for the two weeks leading up to July 4. A Google search finds the Patriotic Rosary as part of Fortnight for Freedom celebrations in the (arch)

dioceses of Baltimore, Dallas, Wichita, Rockville Centre, Fort Wayne–South Bend, Albany, Washington, DC, Orlando, Yankton, Camden, Milwaukee, and elsewhere.

141. The Catholic television network EWTN sells a Rosary for America with the abbreviation for each state printed on the beads, an image of the Virgin Mary superimposed on a map of the United States, and a crucifix with the stars and stripes on the front; https://www.ewtnreligiouscatalogue.com/blessed-is-the-nation-rosary-for-amer ica/p/ROSTHM19183.

142. John Adams, quoted in Steven Waldman, "Was John Adams an Anti-Catholic Bigot?," Beliefnet, April 2004, http://www.beliefnet.com/columnists/stevenwald man/2008/04/was-john-adams-an-anticatholic.html.

143. Instructions for the Patriotic Rosary can be found at http://www.patrioticrosary. com/patriotic-rosary.html. The Patriotic Rosary comes from Caritas of Birmingham, a site in Alabama that promotes the reported Marian apparitions at Medjugorje. The founder of Caritas of Birmingham, Terry Colafrancesco, claims that one of the young people reporting visions at Medjugorje continued to have visions on a visit to the Caritas site in Alabama; see http://www.patrioticrosary.com/. The Medjugorje visions are under investigation by the Vatican, and the Diocese of Birmingham has forbidden diocesan priests from performing services for Caritas of Birmingham; see https://www.bhamwiki.com/w/Caritas_of_Birmingham.

144. Anderson, *Chosen Nation*, 156–9.

145. Ibid., xiv. Anderson's excellent book is in part framed as a corrective to my previous work, which is both too directed against the state, to the neglect of nationalism, and not sufficiently critical of the church's complicity with nationalism. See his critique of my work on 12–30 and 73–6, and my response in "Is Catholicism a Religion? Catholics and Nationalism in America," in *Beyond the Borders of Baptism: Catholicity, Allegiances, and Lived Identities*, ed. Michael L. Budde (Eugene, OR: Cascade Books, 2016), 262–78.

146. For a recent example, see the sermon by Patriarch Kirill, the head of the Russian Orthodox Church, on September 25, 2022, a few days after Vladimir Putin ordered the mobilization of 300,000 more troops for the war against Ukraine. After reflecting on Christ's sacrifice as the greatest manifestation of love of neighbor, Kirill went on to say, "But at the same time, the Church realizes that if somebody, driven by a sense of duty and the need to fulfill their oath . . . goes to do what their duty calls of them, and if a person dies in the performance of this duty, then they have undoubtedly committed an act equivalent to sacrifice. They will have sacrificed themselves for others. And therefore, we believe that this sacrifice washes away all the sins that a person has committed." J.-P. Mauro, "Patriarch Kirill Says Russian Soldiers Who Die in Ukraine Have Sins Washed Away," *Aleteia*, September 27, 2022, https://aleteia. org/2022/09/27/patriarch-kirill-says-russian-soldiers-who-die-in-ukraine-have-sins-washed-away/.

147. Thomas Aquinas, *Summa Theologiae*, II-II.81.1.

148. Ibid., II-II.81.5, II-II.84.2.

149. Ibid., II-II.94.1.ad2.

150. Andrew R. Murphy, *Prodigal Nation: Moral Decline and Divine Punishment from New England to 9/11* (Oxford: Oxford University Press, 2009), 10.

151. Anderson, *Chosen Nation*, 159.

152. Focusing on right-wing Christian nationalism tends to let Christians who practice other types of nationalism off the hook. Although the nationalism of the evangelical Christian Right is important and dangerous, in what follows I will focus my analysis on more sophisticated and scholarly Christian defenses of devotion to the nation that are not so easily dismissed. Right-wing Christian nationalism has been extensively critiqued elsewhere, for example, Philip S. Gorski and Samuel L. Perry, *The Flag and the Cross: White Christian Nationalism and the Threat to American Democracy* (New York: Oxford University Press, 2022); Paul D. Miller, *The Religion of American Greatness: What's Wrong with Christian Nationalism* (Downers Grove, IL: IVP Academic, 2022); Bradley Onishi, *Preparing for War: The Extremist History of White Christian Nationalism—and What Comes Next* (Minneapolis, MN: Broadleaf, 2023); Katherine Stewart, *The Power Worshippers: Inside the Dangerous Rise of Religious Nationalism* (New York: Bloomsbury, 2019).

153. Dorian Llywelyn, *Toward a Catholic Theology of Nationality* (Lanham, MD: Rowman and Littlefield, 2010), 56–8. In his second chapter, titled "Longtime Companions," Llywelyn tries to make the case that Christianity and nationalism have historically been linked, but almost all the examples of Christian nationalism he gives are modern, and most are Protestant. See especially 78–94.

154. Ibid., 57.

155. Ibid., 48.

156. Ibid., 185–92. Although in the first chapter Llywelyn tries carefully to discuss the various meanings of "nation" and its relationships to other terms, like "culture" and "ethnicity," in the latter chapters the terms "nation," "culture," "particularity," "cultural belonging," and a host of others that are significantly broader than "nationality" are run together. In chapter 4 Llywelyn writes, "[B]y nationality we mean at the least a socio-cultural identity wider than that of the family or the immediate kin-group and which extends beyond the immediate generation" (201).

157. Ibid., 185–223.

158. Ibid., 68. Here Llywelyn quotes John Breuilly, who writes that "nationalists celebrate themselves rather than some transcendent reality, whether this be located in another world or in a future society, although the celebration also invokes a concern with the transformation of present reality."

159. Ibid., 4, 58. Llywelyn notes that Pope Leo XIII commended patriotism as a virtue. In an article titled "Nationalism without Idolatry," Catholic sociologist Slavica Jakelić has also called upon Leo XIII to present a defense of love of country without the dangers of extreme nationalism. She quotes from Leo's encyclical *Sapientiae christianae* to the effect that love of country is "natural," and we are "bound . . . to love dearly" the country in which "we had birth, and in which we were brought up." Slavica Jakelić, "Nationalism without Idolatry: How Christians Can Purify Their Civic Attachments," *Commonweal*, October 22, 2019, https://www.commonwealm agazine.org/nationalism-without-idolatry. It is worth noting, however, that the country in which Leo XIII was born in 1810 was not Italy, which did not exist until

1860, when it was created by forcibly taking the Papal States in which Leo was born from his predecessor, Pope Pius IX. Leo continued Pius IX's policies of refusing to recognize Italy, maintaining self-imposed incarceration in the Vatican, and admonishing Catholics not to vote in Italian elections or hold office in Italy.

160. Llywelyn, *Toward a Catholic Theology of Nationality*, 119–21.

161. Ibid., 142.

162. Michael J. Himes and Kenneth R. Himes, *Fullness of Faith: The Public Significance of Theology* (New York: Paulist Press, 1993), 125.

163. Ibid., 125–6.

164. "Final Statement" in *Nation, State, Nation-State*, Pontifical Academy of Social Sciences Acta 22, eds. Vittorio Hösle and Marcelo Sánchez Sorondo (Vatican City: Libreria Editrice Vaticana, 2020), 482–3, https://www.pass.va/content/dam/casinapioiv/pass/pdf-volumi/acta/acta22pass.pdf. The *Catechism of the Catholic Church* recognizes the providential division of humanity into nations as a check on the pride of Babel, but says that "because of sin, both polytheism and the idolatry of the nation and of its rulers constantly threaten this provisional economy with the perversion of paganism" (§57).

165. Carlton J. H. Hayes, *Nationalism: A Religion* (New York: Macmillan, 1960), 10. Hayes's point here can be illustrated by the fact that the Italian word *paese* can mean both "country" or "nation" and "town"; the latter was its original meaning before Italy was created in the nineteenth century and the affections for one's local *paese* were harnessed for the new nation-state.

166. Ibid.

167. The Himeses' analysis of nationalism and patriotism comes from a chapter called "Incarnation and Patriotism." After the first introductory chapter, the rest of the chapters of their book pair a theological doctrine with a "secular" reality of public life (e.g., "The Trinity and Human Rights") in an attempt to show the public relevance of Christian theology.

168. Himes and Himes, *Fullness of Faith*, 126–32.

169. Thomas Aquinas, *Summa Theologiae*, II-II.26.7, quoted in ibid., 132–3. Aquinas's full reasoning is as follows: "For those who are not related to us we have no other friendship save that of charity. But for those who are related to us we have various other friendships according to the ways they are related to us. But since the good on which is based every possible kind of true friendship is directed as its end to the good on which charity is based, it follows as a consequence that charity requires the realization of every other kind of friendship, as the art which concerns an end requires the art which concerns those things which are necessary for that end. And so loving someone because he is of the same blood or related to us or because he is a fellow-countryman or for any other reason whatever which is ordinarily in accord with the end of charity, can be required by charity. And thus, by both the prompting and the requirement of charity, we love in more ways those who are more closely related to us." The Latin word that is rendered "fellow-countryman" in the translation the Himeses use is *concivis*, which is more accurately rendered "fellow-citizen," since in Aquinas's time there were no "countries" in the modern sense of nation-states.

A *concivis* in the thirteenth century would most likely be a citizen of the same city or locality.

170. Himes and Himes, *Fullness of Faith*, 133–5.

171. Ibid., 136.

172. Ibid., 138–43.

173. Ibid., 144.

174. Ibid., 145–7.

175. Ibid., 147–50.

176. Ibid., 151.

177. Llywelyn, *Toward a Catholic Theology of Nationality,* 129. Llywelyn goes on to claim that the scriptures accept nationality as a category of classification, but admits the "porosity" of the various biblical terms that we translate as "nation," "people," "tribe," "clan," and so on and says that there "is not sufficient evidence, however, to support a claim that Christianity holds or does not hold nationality as a good" (129–31).

178. Ibid., 186.

179. Ibid., 143.

180. Ibid., 186–7. He works this out in the rest of his chapter "The Value of Thisness" and 185–223.

181. Robert Nisbet, *The Quest for Community* (London: Oxford University Press, 1969), 100.

182. Ibid., 109.

183. Taylor, *Secular Age*, 704–7, 741–3.

184. David Albertson and Jason Blakely, "Whose Nation? Which Communities? The Fault Lines of the New Christian Nationalism," *America*, September 19, 2019, https://www.americamagazine.org/politics-society/2019/09/19/whose-nation-which-communities-fault-lines-new-christian-nationalism.

185. Llywelyn, *Toward a Catholic Theology of Nationality*, 298.

186. Himes and Himes, *Fullness of Faith*, 146.

187. Alasdair MacIntyre, "A Partial Response to My Critics," in *After MacIntyre: Critical Perspectives on the Work of Alasdair MacIntyre*, ed. John Horton and Susan Mendus (Notre Dame, IN: University of Notre Dame Press, 1994), 303.

188. Jean-Jacques Rousseau, *The Social Contract*, trans. Willmoore Kendall (South Bend, IN: Gateway, 1954), 157–8.

189. Ibid., 159–60.

190. As MacIntyre notes, this is not really patriotism because the ideal and not the nation is the object of devotion, and the reasons provided for allegiance to one's country would apply not just to fellow citizens but to anyone in any country. Nationalists frequently try to give their particular attachments universal significance: Weber said the world should support Germany in World War I because it was the defender of universal *Kultur*, while Durkheim simultaneously saw France as the defender of universal *civilisation*. Alasdair MacIntyre, "Is Patriotism a Virtue?," 3–4. The essay is the published version of MacIntyre's Lindley Lecture at the University of Kansas in 1984. It is available at https://kuscholarworks.ku.edu/bitstream/handle/1808/12398/Is%20Patriotism%20a%20Virtue-1984.pdf;sequence=1.

191. Ibid., 5.

192. Ibid., 10–11.

193. Ibid., 17.

194. Ibid., 17–9.

195. Ibid., 19.

196. Ibid. The Himeses quote several times from MacIntyre's essay to buttress their claim that patriotism is a loyalty-exhibiting virtue and that virtue must be embedded in particular historical relationships. They ignore the rest of MacIntyre's argument, which contends that patriotism toward modern nation-states is incoherent and dangerous. Himes and Himes, *Fullness of Faith*, 136–7, 148–9.

197. Various versions of the quote exist. This one is as reported by General James M. Gavin in his book *War and Peace in the Space Age* (New York: Harper, 1958), 64.

198. "The term latria may be taken in two senses. On one sense it may denote a human act pertaining to the worship of God: and then its signification remains the same, to whomsoever it be shown, because, in this sense, the thing to which it is shown is not included in its definition. Taken thus latria is applied univocally, whether to true religion or to idolatry, just as the payment of a tax is univocally the same, whether it is paid to the true or to a false king. On another sense latria denotes the same as religion, and then, since it is a virtue, it is essential thereto that divine worship be given to whom it ought to be given; and in this way latria is applied equivocally to the latria of true religion, and to idolatry: just as prudence is applied equivocally to the prudence that is a virtue, and to that which is carnal." Thomas Aquinas, *Summa Theologiae*, II-II.94.1ad2.

199. Ibid., II-II.92.1.

200. Ibid., II-II.94.1. Aquinas concludes in II-II.94.3 that idolatry is the gravest of sins, but he distinguishes between objective and subjective senses of gravity. Objectively, idolatry is the gravest of sins, but subjectively, on the part of the sinner, idolatry committed through ignorance is a less grave sin than heresy committed knowingly. In the following article, II-II.94.4, Aquinas considers the causes of idolatry and presents a somewhat sympathetic account of why humans become idolaters. Humans commit idolatry because of inordinate affections, natural pleasure in representations, and ignorance of the true God.

201. "Against the Dead Consensus," *First Things*, March 21, 2019, https://www.firstthings.com/web-exclusives/2019/03/against-the-dead-consensus.

202. Karl Popper, quoted in R. R. Reno, *Return of the Strong Gods: Nationalism, Populism, and the Future of the West* (Washington, DC: Regnery Gateway, 2019), 8. Likewise, Popper writes, in italics, "Although history has no meaning, we can give it meaning" (8).

203. Reno, *Return of the Strong Gods*, 51.

204. Ibid., xii.

205. Ibid., xiii. Reno writes that Weber regarded disenchantment as an iron cage, but the postwar consensus embraces it as liberating and redemptive; disenchantment will save us from the return of the strong gods (40).

206. Ibid., ix.

207. Ibid., 120.

208. Ibid., 144.

209. Ibid.

210. Ibid., 139.

211. Ibid., 150.

212. Ibid., 154.

213. Ibid., 154–5.

214. Ibid., 148.

215. Ibid., 150.

216. Ibid., 157. Elsewhere Reno has said that "citizenship is akin to membership in a family. It is a given, not a choice." Quoted in Albertson and Blakely, "Whose Nation?"

217. Reno, *Return of the Strong Gods*, 158.

218. Ibid., 152.

219. Ibid., 150.

220. Ibid., 160.

221. Ibid., 160–1.

222. Ibid., 135.

223. Ibid., 136.

224. Ibid., 139.

225. Ibid., 137.

226. "Donald Trump, Viktor Orbán, and other populist challengers are not choirboys or immaculate liberals. But their limitations are not nearly as dangerous to the West as the fanaticism of our leadership class, whose hyper-moralistic sense of mission— *either us or Hitler!*—prevents us from addressing our economic, demographic, cultural, and political problems. The growth of these problems stokes further discontent and greater polarization, to which our leadership class responds with an amplified anti-fascist or anti-racist rhetoric. Convinced that only they can save the West and beholden to the postwar consensus, the rich and powerful, not populist voters, will shipwreck our nations" (ibid., xvi).

227. Ibid., 131. Trump has in fact said, "You know what I am? I'm a nationalist, O.K.? I'm a nationalist. . . . Use that word." Donald Trump, quoted in Albertson and Blakely, "Whose Nation?"

228. Donald Trump, quoted in Reno, Reno, *Return of the Strong Gods,* 132.

229. Reno, Reno, *Return of the Strong Gods,* 132.

230. Ibid., 133. In Reno's mind, it is the elite opposition to Trump and not Trump himself who is a danger to democracy: "In the United States, the antidemocratic future of the postwar consensus is foreshadowed in the coalition of establishment Republicans and Democrats that has worked overtime to delegitimize the Trump presidency, by legal means or otherwise. These people are convinced that they are not partisans. Rather, they see themselves as guardians of the open society, saving us from authoritarianism, fascism, racism, or some other moral evil" (125).

231. Ibid., 136. "We can critique these modern gods—and we should; they are often false idols—but the sacralizing impulse in public life is fundamental" (136). Elsewhere Reno acknowledges that the strong gods can be destructive (xii, 150).

232. The concept of collective narcissism appears first in Theodor W. Adorno, *Critical Models: Interventions and Catchwords* (New York: Columbia University Press, 1963) and Erich Fromm, *The Anatomy of Human Destructiveness* (New York: Holt, Rinehart & Winston, 1973). More recent work by social psychologists includes Agnieszka Golec de Zavala, Aleksandra Cichocka, Roy Eidelson, and Nuwan Jayawickreme, "Collective Narcissism and Its Social Consequences," *Journal of Personality and Social Psychology* 97, no. 6 (December 2009): 1074–96.

233. Aleksandra Cichocka and Aleksandra Cislak, "Nationalism as Collective Narcissism," *Current Opinion in Behavioral Sciences* 34 (August 2020): 69.

234. Ibid., 71–2.

235. Donald Trump, quoted in ibid., 69.

236. Cichocka and Cislak, "Nationalism as Collective Narcissism," 70–1.

237. Ibid., 72.

238. Ibid., 71.

239. For examples, see Reno, *Return of the Strong Gods*, viii, xiii–xvi.

240. Ibid., 121.

241. Ibid., 122. The italics are Reno's.

242. Ibid., 116.

243. Noel Ignatiev's book *How the Irish Became White* (London: Routledge, 1995) illustrates one way that racism and nationalism intersect. Irish Catholics became white and joined the American national project by outdoing nativists at anti-Black racism. For a similar argument about Jews, see Karen Brodkin, *How the Jews Became White Folks and What That Says about Race in America* (New Brunswick, NJ: Rutgers University Press, 1998).

244. David Albertson, Jason Blakely, Matthew Peterson, and Kevin A. Stuart, "A Dialogue on the 'New Nationalism,'" *America*, October 22, 2019, https://www.americamagaz ine.org/politics-society/2019/10/22/dialogue-new-nationalism#:~:text=This%20 is%20a%20dialogue%20among%20thinkers%20who%20have,further%20explain ing%20their%20concerns%20about%20the%20new%20nationalism. Peterson and Stuart are signatories of the *First Things* manifesto, and Albertson and Blakely are critics. In their exchange, Peterson and Stuart write, "As such our definition of nationalism is obviously open to people of all races and many religious traditions." The shift from "all" races to "many" religions raises interesting questions about which religious traditions would be excluded.

245. Albertson and Blakely, in ibid. "Ethnonationalism" is, as I have already noted, a slippery term that often means *the kinds of nationalism that I don't like*. Peterson and Stuart use the term in a more restrictive sense that would exclude the United States, as a nation of immigrants, from being ethnonationalist by definition. Albertson and Blakely appear to use the term in a broader sense to indicate the kind of strong attachments that usually accrue to families, races, ethnic groups, and faith traditions.

246. Anthony W. Marx explores this dynamic in "The Nation-State and Its Exclusions," *Political Science Quarterly* 117, no. 1 (Spring 2002): 103–26.

247. Etienne Balibar, "Is There a 'Neo-Racism'?," in Etienne Balibar and Immanuel Wallerstein, *Race, Nation, Class: Ambiguous Identities*, trans. Chris Turner (London: Verso, 1991), 22, italics in the original. See also 20–2, and Etienne Balibar, "Racism and Nationalism," in Balibar and Wallerstein, *Race, Nation, Class*, 37.

248. Balibar, "Is There a 'Neo-Racism'?," 22.

249. Balibar, "Racism and Nationalism," 49.

250. Ibid., 48; see also Balibar, "Is There a 'Neo-Racism'?," 2–4. Immanuel Wallerstein makes the connection between racism and capitalism in the following way: "It is precisely because racism is anti-universalistic in doctrine that it helps to maintain capitalism as a system. It allows a far lower reward to a major segment of the work force than could ever be justified on the basis of merit." Immanuel Wallerstein, "The Ideological Tensions of Capitalism: Universalism versus Racism and Sexism," in Balibar and Wallerstein, *Race, Nation, Class*, 34.

251. Balibar, "Is There a 'Neo-Racism'?," 24–5; Balibar, "Racism and Nationalism," 59–60. Balibar allows that there can be liberative types of nationalism, as in Gandhi's India, but he thinks that racism is *"a supplement internal to nationalism"* ("Racism and Nationalism," 54, italics in the original). The history of nationalism shows how often it is linked to anti-Semitism (Spain, Russia, Germany, Romania, etc.) and other kinds of racism (United States, India, Algeria, Israel, etc.) (52–3).

252. Martin Luther King Jr., quoted in Vaughn A. Booker, "The False God of Nationalism," in *#Charlottesville: White Supremacy, Populism, and Resistance*, ed. Christopher Howard-Woods, Colin Laidley, and Maryam Omidis (New York: OR Books, 2018), 121.

253. Ibid., 123–4.

254. Walter Brueggemann, *The Prophetic Imagination* (Minneapolis, MN: Fortress Press, 1978), 16–9.

255. Gerhard Lohfink, *Does God Need the Church? Toward a Theology of the People of God* (Collegeville, MN: Liturgical Press, 1999), 27.

256. Ibid., 107.

257. For a detailed account, see Braden Anderson's book *Chosen Nation*, chs. 4 and 5.

258. Lohfink, *Does God Need the Church?*, 110.

259. Anderson, *Chosen Nation*, 126.

260. Ibid., 127.

261. Ibid., 138.

262. Lohfink, *Does God Need the Church?*, 49–55.

263. N. T. Wright, "Paul's Gospel and Caesar's Empire," in *Paul and Politics: Ekklesia, Israel, Imperium, Interpretation*, ed. Richard A. Horsley (Harrisburg, PA: Trinity Press International, 2000), 182–3.

264. For an exploration of "ecclesial solidarity" as a Christian's primary loyalty that contextualizes loyalties to nation, state, and class, see Budde, *The Borders of Baptism*, 3–42.

265. Douglas Harink, *1 & 2 Peter* (Grand Rapids, MI: Brazos Press, 2009), 72–3, quoted in Anderson, *Chosen Nation*, 139.

266. Anderson, *Chosen Nation*, 148.

267. See Reno's critique of Derrida in *Return of the Strong Gods*, 64–8.

Chapter 7

1. Pope Francis, "Homily on the Solemnity of the Epiphany of the Lord," Vatican, January 6, 2020, https://www.vatican.va/content/francesco/en/homilies/2020/documents/papa-francesco_20200106_omelia-epifania.html.

2. Daniel Miller, *Stuff* (Cambridge, UK: Polity Press, 2010), 69.

3. Ibid., 72.

4. Mary Douglas and Baron Isherwood, *The World of Goods: Toward an Anthropology of Consumption*, revised ed. (London: Routledge, 1996), ix.

5. Ibid., 43. Similarly, "the essential function of consumption is its capacity to make sense" (40).

6. Ibid., 38.

7. "To speak sensibly of consumption here, in industrial society, in terms that also apply without strain to distant tribal societies that have barely seen commerce, still less capitalism, is indeed a challenge. But unless we make the attempt there can be no anthropology of consumption" (ibid., 36).

8. Ibid., xxii.

9. Ibid., xxiii. For the point that organizing social relations through things always involves *moral* judgments, see 37.

10. Miller blames this tendency ultimately on Durkheim, who employed a secularism that reduced God to a mere projection of more basic human social processes. In this view, human society is the real thing, so attention to material things can distract from attention to persons; objects need to be reduced to subjects. Miller writes, "The question is, after a couple of hundred years of secularism, whether we still need such a highfalutin ideal of society to help deal with the trauma of replacing the divinity. Indeed perhaps keeping that aura of the divine and attributing it to society has been more a problem than an asset? Personally I would rather have a divine God than pay obeisance to society as a kind of divine-lite" (*Stuff*, 77).

11. Ibid., 12–3, 48.

12. Ibid., 50–4.

13. Ibid., 60.

14. Ibid.

15. Ibid., 61.

16. Ibid., 68.

17. Ibid., 64–7.

18. Ibid., 74.

19. Ibid., 74–5.

20. Ibid., 75.

21. Eugene McCarraher, *The Enchantments of Mammon: How Capitalism Became the Religion of Modernity* (Cambridge, MA: Harvard University Press, 2019), 11.

22. Colin Lecher, "How Amazon Automatically Tracks and Fires Warehouse Workers for 'Productivity': Documents Show How the Company Tracks and Terminates Workers," *The Verge*, April 25, 2019, https://www.theverge.com/2019/4/25/18516004/amazon-warehouse-fulfillment-centers-productivity-firing-terminations.

23. Jodi Kantor, Karen Weise, and Grace Ashford, "The Amazon That Customers Don't See," *New York Times*, June 15, 2021.

24. Jodi Kantor, Karen Weise and Grace Ashford, "Inside Amazon's Worst Human Resources Problem," *New York Times*, October 24, 2021. "The extent of the problem puts in stark relief how Amazon's workers routinely took a back seat to customers during the company's meteoric rise to retail dominance. Amazon built cutting-edge package processing facilities to cater to shoppers' appetite for fast delivery, far outpacing competitors. But the business did not devote enough resources and attention to how it served employees, according to many longtime workers."

25. James Bloodworth, quoted in Aimee Picchi, "Inside an Amazon Warehouse: 'Treating Human Beings as Robots,'" CBS News, April 19, 2018, https://www.cbsnews.com/news/inside-an-amazon-warehouse-treating-human-beings-as-robots/.

26. Will Evans, "How Amazon Hid Its Safety Crisis," *Reveal,* September 29, 2020, https://revealnews.org/article/how-amazon-hid-its-safety-crisis/.

27. Emily Guendelsberger, *What Low-Wage Work Did to Me and How It Drives America Insane* (New York: Little, Brown, 2019).

28. Benjamin Romano, "Amazon Discloses Median Pay, Plans Virtual Shareholder Meeting Due to Coronavirus, Climate Concerns," *Seattle Times*, March 27, 2020, https://www.seattletimes.com/business/amazon/amazon-discloses-median-pay-plans-virtual-shareholder-meeting-due-to-coronavirus-climate-concerns/.   The amount cited is the global median compensation for Amazon employees for the year 2019.

29. Kantor, Weise, and Ashford, "The Amazon That Customers Don't See." According to David Niekirk, the former Amazon vice president for human resources, Bezos encouraged turnover: "What he would say is that our nature as humans is to expend as little energy as possible to get what we want or need" (quoted in article).

30. Vauhini Vara, "Amazon Has Transformed the Geography of Wealth and Power: Understanding America in the Giant Company's Shadow," *The Atlantic*, March 2021, https://www.theatlantic.com/magazine/archive/2021/03/alec-macgillis-fulfillment-amazon/617796/.

31. Alec MacGillis, *Fulfillment: Winning and Losing in One-Click America* (New York: Farrar, Straus and Giroux, 2021).

32. Frank Trentmann, *Empire of Things: How We Became a World of Consumers, from the Fifteenth Century to the Twenty-First* (New York: HarperCollins, 2016), 1.

33. Jean Baudrillard, *The Consumer Society: Myths and Structures* (London: Sage, 1998), 25.

34. Ibid., italics in the original.

35. Trentmann, *Empire of Things*, 1.

36. Helen Landon Cass, quoted in William Leach, *Land of Desire: Merchants, Power, and the Rise of a New American Culture* (New York: Pantheon Books, 1993), 298. Cass was a popular radio personality in the 1920s.

37. Baudrillard, *Consumer Society,* 31.

38. Ibid., italics in the original.

39. Ibid., 32, italics in the original. As we will see below, the way that commodities hide their origin in human work is an important Marxist theme.

40. Ibid.

41. Yannik St. James, Jay M. Handelman, and Shirley F. Taylor, "Magical Thinking and Consumer Coping," *Journal of Consumer Research* 38 (December 2011): 633.

42. Cele Otnes and Linda M. Scott, "Something Old, Something New: Exploring the Interaction between Ritual and Advertising," *Journal of Advertising* 25, no. 1 (Spring 1996): 37.

43. St. James, Handelman, and Taylor, "Magical Thinking," 646.

44. Russell W. Belk, Melanie Wallendorf, and John F. Sherry Jr., "The Sacred and the Profane in Consumer Behavior: Theodicy on the Odyssey," *Journal of Consumer Research* 16, no. 1 (June 1989): 1.

45. Ibid., 6–8.

46. Ibid., 8–9.

47. Ibid., 14–21.

48. Ibid., 32, italics in the original. Michael Harrington was a democratic socialist activist and chronicler of poverty in the United States, whose book *The Other America* (New York: Macmillan, 1962) is credited with inspiring the anti-poverty efforts of the Kennedy and Johnson administrations.

49. Part 1 of Baudrillard's book *The Consumer Society* is titled "The Formal Liturgy of the Object." On shopping malls as sacred spaces, see Michael Kearl, "Temples of Consumption: Shopping Malls as Secular Cathedrals," Trinity University, accessed July 28, 2023, http://faculty.trinity.edu/mkearl/temples.html; James K. A. Smith, *Desiring the Kingdom* (Grand Rapids, MI: Baker, 2009), 19–22; and Scott W. Gustafson, *At the Altar of Wall Street: The Rituals, Myths, Theologies, Sacraments, and Mission of the Religion Known as the Modern Global Economy* (Grand Rapids, MI: Eerdmans, 2015), 25–8.

50. For a partial bibliography of such work, see Diego Rinallo and Pauline Maclaran, "Conversations on the Sacred and Spirituality in Consumer Behavior," *Advances in Consumer Research* 40 (2012): 1094–5.

51. John W. Schouten and James H. McAlexander, "Subcultures of Consumption: An Ethnography of the New Bikers," *Journal of Consumer Research* 22, no. 1 (June 1995): 50.

52. Such research is summarized in Bernard Cova, Antonella Carù, and Julien Cayla, "Re-conceptualizing Escape in Consumer Research," *Qualitative Market Research* 21, no. 4 (2018): 445–64. The authors include an extensive bibliography of such studies.

53. Ibid., 455.

54. Albert M. Muñiz Jr. and Hope Jensen Schau, "Religiosity in the Abandoned Apple Newton Brand Community," *Journal of Consumer Research* 31 (March 2005): 737. The authors do not deny that disenchantment has occurred but see it as a suppression of basic human longings that then surface elsewhere: "Modernity might force the religious and magical to emerge in different contexts, displacing rather than destroying them."

55. Ibid.

56. Ibid.

57. Ibid.

58. Ibid., 739–46.

59. Leigh Eric Schmidt, *Consumer Rites: The Buying and Selling of American Holidays* (Princeton, NJ: Princeton University Press, 1995), 297.

60. Rene Clarke, quoted in McCarraher, *Enchantments of Mammon*, 408.

61. Grant McCracken and Robert Pollay, "Anthropology and the Study of Advertising," unpublished manuscript, quoted in Sut Jhally, *The Codes of Advertising: Fetishism and the Political Economy of Meaning in Consumer Society* (New York: Routledge, 1990), 11.

62. William Leiss, Stephen Kline, Sut Jhally, Jacqueline Botterill, and Kyle Asquith, *Social Communication in Advertising*, 4th ed. (New York: Routledge, 2018), 305; Sut Jhally, "Advertising as Religion: The Dialectic of Technology and Magic," in *Cultural Politics in Contemporary America*, ed. Lan Angus and Sut Jhally (New York: Routledge, 1989), 217–29.

63. Jhally, *Codes of Advertising*, 199, 203.

64. James Twitchell, *Adcult USA: The Triumph of Advertising in American Culture* (New York: Columbia University Press, 1996).

65. Leiss et al., *Social Communication in Advertising*, 15, 114–5, 154–5. The stage that Leiss et al. label "idolatry" is in some ways the least idolatrous of the stages, since products in the initial "idolatry" stage are still presented primarily in terms of their use-value. It is only in later stages that products really take flight into the realm of the transcendent.

66. Quoted in Roland Marchand, *Advertising the American Dream: Making Way for Modernity, 1920–1940* (Berkeley: University of California Press, 1985), 265.

67. Leiss et al., *Social Communication in Advertising*, 15, 115, 156–60.

68. Ibid., 161. As McCarraher notes, this period saw the intensification of research meant to lend products a "halo of psychological meanings." The point was to mystify rather than explain the commodity, or as Pierre Martineau, one of the most prominent proponents of "scientific" marketing in the 1950s put it, to construct "a powerful symbol capable of lifting the brand completely out of the long, long parade of faceless products" (quoted in McCarraher, *Enchantments of Mammon*, 560).

69. McCarraher, *Enchantments of Mammon*, 116, 160–5.

70. Jhally, *Codes of Advertising*, 202.

71. Leiss et al., *Social Communication in Advertising*, 166–9.

72. Ibid., 117–9.

73. Ibid., 305–6.

74. Siva Vaidhyanathan, quoted in ibid., 315.

75. Leiss et al., 308.

76. Jhally, "Advertising as Religion."

77. McCarraher, *Enchantments of Mammon*, 226.

78. Ibid., 5, 227.

79. Phil Knight, quoted in Naomi Klein, *No Logo* (New York: Picador, 2000), 197.

80. Klein, *No Logo*, 196. As McCarraher illustrates extensively, the invention of a soul for corporations dates back to the 1870s, to a large extent in reaction to critiques of the soullessness of corporate entities that had names but were at the same time artificial and impersonal (*Enchantments of Mammon*, 196–209).

81. Leiss et al., *Social Communication in Advertising*, 199. Randall Rothenberg notes, "In a world of increasingly commoditized products and services, the only sustainable differentiation lies in the values, esthetics and information content of the brand, and the originality with which they are communicated to consumers." Randall Rothenberg, "Before It Goes 'Hollywood': Some Cautions for Mad Ave," *Advertising Age*, March 4, 2002, 32.

82. Klein, *No Logo*, 22.

83. Ibid., 21. The priority of the brand to the product came home to me in an article from a student newspaper about a college senior who started her own skincare company. The article described the name of the product line and the marketing around it, designed to make young women feel confident in themselves, encouraged and empowered. After describing in great detail the aura surrounding the brand, the article eventually mentioned that the young woman had come up with the mythos surrounding the brand first, and then found a product to associate with the brand, contracting with a manufacturer of skincare products in another state to make the actual product. Until finding a manufacturer, the college senior knew almost nothing about how skincare products are actually made or the ingredients that go into them.

84. Douglas Atkin, *The Culting of Brands: When Customers Become True Believers* (New York: Portfolio, 2004), xiii–xix, 102.

85. Ibid., 4.

86. Charlene, quoted in ibid., 95. For more about supernatural motifs and the mythologization of brands, see Maria Kniazeva and Russell W. Belk, "Packaging as a Vehicle for Mythologizing the Brand," in *Brands: Interdisciplinary Perspectives*, ed. Jonathan E. Schroeder (London: Routledge, 2015), 34–53.

87. Atkin, *Culting of Brands*, 112.

88. Ibid., 96.

89. Ibid., 115.

90. Ibid., 116. Atkin quotes a speech by Steve Jobs to software developers and dealers: "Marketing is about values. . . . What we're about is not making boxes for people to get their jobs done, although we do that very well. Apple is about more than that. What Apple is about, its core value is that we believe that people with passion can change the world for the better. That's what we believe" (133).

91. Atkin, *Culting of Brands*, 119.

92. Ron Shachar, Tülin Erdem, Keisha M. Cutright, and Gavan J. Fitzsimons, "Brands: Opiate of the Nonreligious Masses?," *Marketing Science* 30, no. 1 (January–February 2011): 92–110.

93. Juliann Sivulka, *Soap, Sex, and Cigarettes: A Cultural History of American Advertising* (Belmont, CA: Wadsworth, 1998), 48–52.

94. "Familiar personalities such as Dr. Brown, Uncle Ben, Aunt Jemima, and Old Grand-Dad came to replace the shopkeeper, who was traditionally responsible for

measuring bulk foods for the customers and acting as an advocate for products....
[A] nationwide vocabulary of brand names replaced the small local shopkeeper as
the interface between customer and product." Ellen Lupton and J. Abbott Miller,
Design Writing Research: Writing on Graphic Design (New York: Kiosk, 1996), 177.
McCarraher notes that early on advertisers recognized that animating products
increased their monetary value (*Enchantments of Mammon*, 231).

95. In addition to Aaker's and Fournier's work mentioned below, see, for example,
Traci H. Freling and Lukas P. Forbes, "An Empirical Analysis of the Brand
Personality Effect," *Journal of Product & Brand Management* 14, no. 7 (2005): 404–
13; Marina Puzakova, Hyokjin Kwak, and J. F. Rocereto, "Pushing the Envelope
of Brand and Personality: Antecedents and Moderators of Anthropomorphized
Brands," *Advances in Consumer Research* 36 (January 2009): 413–20; Artyom
Golossenko, Kishore Gopalakrishna Pillai, and Lukman Aroean, "Seeing Brands
as Humans: Development and Validation of a Brand Anthropomorphism Scale,"
International Journal of Research in Marketing 37, no. 4 (February 2020): 737–55;
Pankaj Aggarwal and Ann L. McGill, "Is That Car Smiling at Me? Schema Congruity
as a Basis for Evaluating Anthropomorphized Products," *Journal of Consumer
Research*, 34, no. 4 (2007): 468–79.

96. Jennifer L. Aaker, "Dimensions of Brand Personality," *Journal of Marketing Research*
34, no. 3 (August 1997): 347–56.

97. Susan Fournier, "Consumers and Their Brands: Developing Relationship Theory in
Consumer Research," *Journal of Consumer Research* 24, no. 4 (March 1998): 343–
73. For a follow-up study, see Susan Fournier, "Lessons Learned about Consumers'
Relationships with their Brands," in *Handbook of Brand Relationships*, ed. Deborah
J. MacInnis, C. Whan Park, and Joseph R. Priester (London: Routledge, 2015), 5–23.

98. I take this summary of the history of the term "fetish" from Jhally, *Codes of
Advertising*, 53–6. By "independent" I mean that fetishism sees power and meaning
as inherent in the physical object, not as coming from a system of power and
meaning in which the item is embedded. See 29.

99. Ibid., 54–6.

100. For more examples of work on fetishism and consumer culture—in addition to
the work cited in the next section—see Tim Dant, "Fetishism and the Social Value
of Objects," *Sociological Review* 44, no. 3 (1996): 495–516; Roy Ellen, "Fetishism,"
Man 23, no. 2 (1988): 213–35; George Gmelch, "Baseball Magic," in *Conformity
and Conflict*, ed. James Spradley and David W. McCurdy (Upper Saddle River,
NJ: Prentice-Hall, 2008), 322–31; Jonathan E. Schroeder and Janet L. Borgerson,
"Dark Desires: Fetishism, Representation and Ontology in Contemporary
Advertising," in *Sex in Advertising: Perspectives on the Erotic Appeal*, ed. Tom Reichert
and Jacqueline Lambiase (Mahwah, NJ: Erlbaum, 2003), 65–87; Amber M. Epp and
Linda L. Price, "The Storied Life of Singularized Objects: Forces of Agency and
Network Transformation," *Journal of Consumer Research* 36, no. 5 (2010): 820–37.

101. David Hume, *Tourism Art and Souvenirs: The Material Culture of Tourism*
(London: Routledge, 2013), 74.

102. Ibid., 53.

103. Ibid., 52, 59.

104. Ibid., 53.

105. In Roman Catholicism, a first-class relic is an item directly associated with Christ's earthly life, such as a piece of the True Cross, or a part of a saint's body, such as a fragment of bone. A second-class relic is an item used by a saint, such as a shirt or rosary. A third-class relic is something that has been in physical contact with a first- or second-class relic.

106. Karen V. Fernandez and John L. Lastovicka, "Making Magic: Fetishes in Contemporary Consumption," *Journal of Consumer Research* 38 (August 2011): 279–80.

107. Ibid., 280–1. In making this argument, the authors are refuting Walter Benjamin, who thought that mass-produced replicas lack aura and are mere shadows of the original. See Walter Benjamin, "The Work of Art in the Age of Mechanical Reproduction," in *Illuminations: Essays and Reflections*, ed. Hannah Arendt, trans. Harry Zohn (New York: Schocken, 1968), 219–53.

108. Fernandez and Lastovicka, "Making Magic," 282–97.

109. Quoted in Erik Larson, *The Naked Consumer: How Our Private Lives Become Public Commodities* (New York: Henry Holt, 1992), 20.

110. Jhally, *Codes of Advertising*, 202.

111. Quoted in Atkin, *Culting of Brands*, 4. This quote appears to come from a different Snapple drinker than Charlene, quoted above.

112. Michael Saler, "Modernity and Enchantment: A Historiographic Review," *American Historical Review* 111, no. 3 (June 2006): 714. Cf. James W. Cook, *The Arts of Deception: Playing with Fraud in the Age of Barnum* (Cambridge, MA: Harvard University Press, 2001) and Simon During, *Modern Enchantment: The Cultural Power of Secular Magic* (Cambridge, MA: Harvard University Press, 2002).

113. Slavoj Žižek, *The Universal Exception:* vol. 2 of *Selected Writings*, ed. Rex Butler and Scott Stephens (London: Continuum, 2006), 254–5.

114. Francis Mulhern, "Critical Considerations on the Fetishism of Commodities," *ELH* 74, no. 2 (Summer 2007): 483.

115. Ibid., 482.

116. Karl Marx, *Capital*, vol. 1, trans. Ben Fowkes (New York: Vintage, 1977), 209; Alexandra Dobra, "What Does Marx Mean by the 'Fetishism of Commodities,'" *E-Logos* 7 (2010): 4. Marx's words are "personifizierung der Sachen und Versachlichung der Personen." Although I think the symmetry of reification and deification expresses something important about Marx's concept, it is perhaps too much to say that commodities are "deified," that is, made into gods, rather than, in various ways, participating in divine life. It is really capital that takes the place of God, as discussed below.

117. Marx, *Capital*, 128.

118. Ibid., 163.

119. Ibid., 163–4.

120. "Socially necessary labour-time is the labour-time required to produce any use-value under the conditions of production normal for a given society and with the average degree of skill and intensity of labour prevalent in that society" (ibid., 129).

The value of a commodity is not determined simply by the labor-time that went into its production, or else commodities produced by lazy or incompetent workers who take twice as long as they should to make a product would have twice the value.

121. Ibid., 164–5.
122. Ibid., 165. Marx continues, "I call this the fetishism which attaches itself to the products of labour as soon as they are produced as commodities, and is therefore inseparable from the production of commodities" (165).
123. Ibid., 166.
124. Ibid., 178–9.
125. Ibid., 1003–4.
126. Ibid., 170.
127. Ibid.
128. Ibid., 167–8.
129. Ibid., 174–5. David Harvey points to the way that Marx stresses the contingency of the laws that capitalism treats as natural. People misunderstand Marx as adhering to the labor theory of value, that is, that the only source of value is from labor inputs. Marx in fact sees the labor theory of value as socially contingent, a product of capitalism that he wants to replace with an alternative way of determining value. See David Harvey, *A Companion to Marx's* Capital (London: Verso, 2018), 48.
130. Marx, *Capital,* 772.
131. Profit, according to Marx, derives from the expropriation of the surplus value produced by the worker. There would be no profit for the capitalist if workers were paid the full value of their work. Because the worker is paid for only a portion of the value they produce, the surplus value appears as if it were the product of capital. On this point, see G. A. Cohen, *Karl Marx's Theory of History: A Defence* (Princeton, NJ: Princeton University Press, 1978), 124.
132. Marx, *Capital,* 307–19.
133. Ibid., 451.
134. Cohen, *Karl Marx's Theory of History,* 122n2.
135. Karl Marx, *Capital,* vol. 3, trans. Ernest Untermann (New York: International Publishers, 1967), 392.
136. Ibid., 397.
137. Marx, *Capital,* 1: 370–1.
138. Ibid., 1: 374.
139. Karl Marx, *A Contribution to the Critique of Political Economy* (Moscow: Progress, 1970), 158. See Matthew 6:20: "[B]ut store up for yourselves treasures in heaven, where neither moth nor rust consumes and where thieves do not break in and steal."
140. Marx, *Capital,* 1: 229.
141. Ibid., 1: 236.
142. Ibid., 1: 918.
143. Ibid., 1: 181.
144. For a few additional examples to the sources cited below, see Jon Sobrino, "Reflexiones sobre el significado del ateísmo y la idolatría para la teología," *Revista Latinoamericana de Teología,* no. 7 (January 1986): 50–62; Hugo Assmann, ed., *Sobre Ídolos y Sacrificios: René Girard con Teólogos de la Liberación* (San José, Costa

Rica: Departamento Ecuménico de Investigaciones, 1991); Enrique Dussel, *Las Metáforas Teológicas de Marx* (Estella: Editorial Verbo Divino, 1993); Jung Mo Sung, "Idolatry: A Reading Key to the Market Economy?," *Dialog* 55, no. 1 (Spring 2016): 25–30; Jung Mo Sung, *Neoliberalismo y derechos humanos: Una crítica teológica y humanista al nuevo mito del capitalismo*, trans. Néstor O. Míguez (Buenos Aires: La Aurora, 2019). The most prominent Latin American thinker who has kept alive the liberationist critique of capitalism as idolatry is certainly Pope Francis. See William T. Cavanaugh, "Return of the Golden Calf: Economy, Idolatry, and Secularization since *Gaudium et Spes*," *Theological Studies* 76, no. 4 (December 2015): 698–717 and Allan Silva Coelho, "A Idolatria e o Papa Francisco: Radicalidade na Crítica ao Capitalismo," *Estudos de religião* 33, no. 1 (April 2019): 203–30.

145. Pablo Richard, "Introduction," in *The Idols of Death and the God of Life*, ed. Pablo Richard, trans. Barbara E. Campbell and Bonnie Shepard (Maryknoll, NY: Orbis Books, 1983), 1.

146. Victorio Araya G., "The God of the Strategic Covenant," in Richard, *Idols of Death*, 106.

147. See, e.g., J. Severino Croatto, "The Gods of Oppression," in Richard, *Idols of Death*, 26–45. Joan Casañas, however, identifies God so closely with the historical struggle for liberation that he argues God will exist only in a just world; we will make God exist by creating a just world. So "the other side of the threshold between finitude and infinitude is not a You, but All of Us." Joan Casañas, "The Task of Making God Exist," in Richard, *Idols of Death*, 141. This strikes me as replacing one type idolatry with another, in which the collective "we" substitutes for God, yet another example of collective narcissism, as I discussed in chapter 6.

148. Hugo Assmann, *La Idolatría del Mercado* (San José, Costa Rica: Departamento Ecuménico de Investigaciones, 1997), 49.

149. Hugo Assmann, "The Faith of the Poor in Their Struggle with Idols," in Richard, *Idols of Death*, 204–18.

150. Franz J. Hinkelammert, *The Ideological Weapons of Death: A Theological Critique of Capitalism*, trans. Phillip Berryman (Maryknoll, NY: Orbis Books, 1986), 6.

151. Ibid., 10.

152. Ibid., 30–1.

153. Ibid., 7.

154. Ibid., 29.

155. Ibid., 15.

156. Gustavo Gutiérrez, *A Theology of Liberation: History, Politics and Salvation*, trans. Caridad Inda and John Eagleson (Maryknoll, NY: Orbis Books, 1973), 275–6. These sentences do not appear in the 1988 revised edition of the book. In response to criticism, including from the Vatican, Gutiérrez rewrote the section in chapter 12 called "Christian Brotherhood and Class Struggle" in the original edition. In the revised version, it is called "Faith and Social Conflict," and in it Gutiérrez bends over backward to soften language of taking sides in the class struggle, though he still maintains that "social conflict" is a fact and it is impossible for a Christian to remain neutral. See Gustavo Gutiérrez, *A Theology of Liberation: History, Politics and Salvation*,

revised ed., trans. Caridad Inda and John Eagleson (Maryknoll, NY: Orbis Books, 1988), 156–61.

157. The Taylor quotes are from Frederick Winslow Taylor, *Shop Management* (New York: Harper & Row, 1947), 98 and Frederick Winslow Taylor, *Principles of Scientific Management* (New York: Harper & Row, 1947), 36, as quoted in Vincent J. Miller, *Consuming Religion: Christian Faith and Practice in a Consumer Culture* (New York: Continuum, 2004), 40. I am indebted to Miller's excellent discussion of Taylor on 39–42.

158. Miller, *Consuming Religion*, 41–2.

159. Matthew B. Crawford, *Shop Class as Soulcraft: An Inquiry into the Value of Work* (New York: Penguin, 2009), 3.

160. Ibid., 7.

161. "Sri Lanka: Impacts of COVID-19 on Sri Lanka's Garment Sector," Business and Human Rights Resource Center, accessed October 8, 2021, https://www.business-humanrights.org/en/from-us/covid-19-action-tracker/sri-lanka/.

162. For just a few of many possible examples, see Robert J. S. Ross, *Slaves to Fashion: Poverty and Abuse in the New Sweatshops* (Ann Arbor: University of Michigan Press, 2004) and Alessandra Mezzadri, *The Sweatshop Regime: Labouring Bodies, Exploitation, and Garments Made in India* (Cambridge: Cambridge University Press, 2016). For a realistic but hopeful account that resists fatalism, see Ashok Kumar, *Monopsony Capitalism: Power and Production in the Twilight of the Sweatshop Age* (Cambridge: Cambridge University Press, 2020).

163. This is not to say that resistance is futile. For an account of how garment manufacturing can be done successfully while paying workers well, allowing unions, and maintaining high health and safety standards, see the account of the Alta Gracia factory in the Dominican Republic in Sarah Adler-Milstein and John M. Kline, *Sewing Hope: How One Factory Challenges the Apparel Industry's Sweatshops* (Berkeley: University of California Press, 2017).

164. Kathryn Tanner provides a helpful summary of the dynamics of finance capitalism in *Christianity and the New Spirit of Capitalism* (New Haven, CT: Yale University Press, 2019), 11–25.

165. A useful and accessible resource on financialization is *Financialisation: A Primer*, Transnational Institute, 2018, https://www.tni.org/en/publication/financialisation-a-primer.

166. Tanner, *Christianity and the New Spirit of Capitalism*, 64–5.

167. Ibid., 19–24.

168. Ibid., 38.

169. Philip Goodchild, *Theology of Money* (Durham, NC: Duke University Press, 2009), xiv.

170. Ibid., 6.

171. We are taught that money is a mere means, not an end. Goodchild remarks, "It is in modern life that alienation is complete and the consciousness of humanity departs entirely from the conditions of its existence. It is in modern life, rather than religious life, where ideology is most fully instantiated" (ibid., xv). Tanner similarly

comments, "Every way of organizing economic life is flawed. Besides having especially egregious faults . . . what is unusual about the present system is the way
its spirit hampers recognition of those faults" (*Christianity and the New Spirit of
Capitalism*, 7).

172. Goodchild, *Theology of Money*, 12.

173. Ibid., 11.

174. Ibid., 236.

175. Roberta Sassatelli, *Consumer Culture: History, Theory and Politics* (Los Angeles,
     CA: Sage, 2007), 105.

176. Emily Beth Hill, *Marketing and Christian Proclamation in Theological Perspective*
     (Lanham, MD: Lexington/Fortress, 2021), 71–2. Mark Tadajewski discusses the
     study of *Journal of Marketing* articles in "Critical Reflections on the Marketing
     Concept and Consumer Sovereignty," in *The Routledge Companion to Critical
     Marketing*, ed. Mark Tadajewski, Matthew Higgins, Janice Denegri-Knott, and Rohit
     Varman (London: Routledge, 2018), 196–224.

177. For example, Frank Cochoy, "Another Discipline for the Market Economy: Marketing
     as a Performative Knowledge and Know-How for Capitalism," in *The Laws of the
     Markets*, ed. Michel Callon (Oxford: Blackwell, 1998), 194–221.

178. Michel Foucault, "Governmentality," in *The Foucault Effect: Studies in Governmentality*,
     ed. Graham Burchell, Colin Gordon, and Peter Miller (Chicago: University of
     Chicago Press, 1991), 102.

179. Hill, *Marketing and Christian Proclamation*, 74–7. For more on marketing as
     governmentality, see Peter Miller and Nikolas Rose, "Governing Economic Life,"
     Economy and Society 19, no. 1 (1990): 1–31; Damian Hodgson, "'Know Your
     Customer': Marketing, Governmentality and the 'New Consumer' of Financial
     Services," *Management Decision* 40, no. 4 (2002): 321; Per Skålén, Markus Fellesson,
     and Martin Fougère, "The Governmentality of Marketing Discourse," *Scandinavian
     Journal of Management* 22 (2006): 275–91; Detlev Zwick, Samuel Bonsu, and
     Aron Darmody, "Putting Consumers to Work: 'Co-Creation,' and New Marketing
     Governmentality," *Journal of Consumer Culture* 8, no. 2 (2008): 164–96.

180. Jhally, *Codes of Advertising*, 83–90.

181. Leiss et al., *Social Communication in Advertising*, 344, 358–9.

182. Michel Foucault, *Discipline and Punish: The Birth of the Prison*, trans. Alan Sheridan
     (New York: Vintage, 1995).

183. Christopher E. Hackley, "The Panoptic Role of Advertising Agencies in the
     Production of Consumer Culture," *Consumption Markets & Culture* 5, no. 3
     (2002): 221–9.

184. Michael Budde, *The (Magic) Kingdom of God: Christianity and Global Culture
     Industries* (Boulder, CO: Westview Press, 1997), 42.

185. For a summary of big data tracking, see Hill, *Marketing and Christian Proclamation*,
     91–5, 112–6.

186. Shoshana Zuboff, *The Age of Surveillance Capitalism: The Fight for a Human Future
     at the New Frontier of Power* (London: Profile, 2019), 99–100.

187. Ibid., 69–70.

188. Ibid., 11.

189. Jonathan E. Schroeder, "Introduction," in Schroeder, *Brands*, 7; Adam Arvidsson, "Public Brands and Entrepreneurial Ethics," *Ephemera: Theory and Politics in Organization* 14, no. 1 (2014): 119–24; Leiss et al., *Social Communication in Advertising*, 360–2.

190. Alison Hearn, "'Meat, Mask, Burden': Probing the Contours of the Branded 'Self,'" *Journal of Consumer Culture* 8, no. 2 (2008): 201.

191. Zygmunt Bauman, *Consuming Life* (Cambridge, UK: Polity Press, 2007), 52–81.

192. For further commentary on the commodification of the self, see Michel Foucault, *The Birth of Biopolitics*, trans. Graham Burchell (New York: Picador, 2008), 224–6 and Tanner, *Christianity and the New Spirit of Capitalism*, 74–6.

193. As Pope Francis puts it near the beginning of *Laudato Si'*, "We have come to see ourselves as [the earth's] lords and masters, entitled to plunder her at will" (§2): https://www.vatican.va/content/francesco/en/encyclicals/documents/papa-francesco_201 50524_enciclica-laudato-si.html. Rather than seeing humans as part of nature, anthropocentrism elevates humans to a uniquely privileged position while simultaneously reducing the natural world to mere raw material to be used for our benefit. The natural world is instrumentalized and disenchanted, reduced to inert matter. Anthropocentrism thereby leads to the exploitation of nature and the breakdown of natural systems, what Pope Francis calls the "tyrannical and irresponsible domination of human beings over other creatures" (§83). Lynn White's famous article "The Historical Roots of Our Ecologic Crisis" similarly lays the blame on Western anthropocentrism. He declares, "Especially in its Western form, Christianity is the most anthropocentric religion the world has seen. . . . Christianity . . . not only established a dualism of man and nature but also insisted that it is God's will that man exploit nature for his proper ends." Lynn White, "The Historical Roots of Our Ecologic Crisis," *Science* 155, no. 3767 (1967): 1205. Where Francis and White differ is on the biblical roots of the crisis. White traces anthropocentrism to the biblical creation story that directs humans to subdue the earth, giving them dominion over the fish of the sea and the birds of the air: "God planned all of this explicitly for man's benefit and rule: no item in the physical creation had any purpose save to serve man's purposes" (1205). Francis, on the other hand, blames a misreading of the Bible and sees the creation story as God-centered, not human-centered: "Clearly, the Bible has no place for a tyrannical anthropocentrism unconcerned for other creatures" (*Laudato Si'*, §68).

194. This is not to say that those who critique anthropocentrism *always* avoid consideration of class inequality. Pope Francis, for example, notes that "twenty percent of the world's population consumes resources at a rate that robs the poor nations and future generations of what they need to survive" (*Laudato Si'*, §95).

195. Peter F. Drucker, *Managing for Results: Economic Tasks and Risk-Taking Decisions* (London: Heinemann, 1964), 90, italics in original.

196. Bernd Wannenwetsch, "The Desire of Desire: Commandment and Idolatry in Late Capitalist Societies," in *Idolatry: False Worship in the Bible, Early Judaism and Christianity*, ed. Stephen C. Barton (London: T. & T. Clark, 2007), 320.

197. Ibid., 322.

198. Sylwia Z. Cisek, Constantine Sedikides, Claire M. Hart, Hayward J. Godwin, Valerie Benson, and Simon P. Liversedge, "Narcissism and Consumer Behavior: A Review and Preliminary Findings," *Frontiers in Psychology* 5, no. 232 (March 2014): 2.

199. Ibid.

200. Ibid., 3.

201. Ibid.

202. Crawford, *Shop Class as Soulcraft*, 16, 56–68, 99–100.

203. Ibid., 70–1.

204. Ibid., 56–7.

205. Michael Billig, "Commodity Fetishism and Repression: Reflections on Marx, Freud, and the Psychology of Consumer Capitalism," *Theory and Psychology* 9, no. 3 (1999): 313–29.

206. Robert Cluley and Stephen Dunne, "From Commodity Fetishism to Commodity Narcissism," *Marketing Theory* 12, no. 3 (2012): 251–7.

207. Ibid., 258–60.

208. Ibid., 260. The internal quote is from Sigmund Freud, "Civilization and Its Discontents," in *The Standard Edition of the Complete Works of Sigmund Freud*, vol. 21, ed. J. Strachey (London: Hogarth, 1994), 143.

209. Freud, "Civilization and Its Discontents," 113, quoted in Cluley and Dunne, "From Commodity Fetishism," 260.

210. Adam Smith, *The Wealth of Nations* (London: Penguin, 1986), 119, quoted in Cluley and Dunne, "From Commodity Fetishism," 260, italics added by Cluley and Dunne.

211. Cluley and Dunne, "From Commodity Fetishism," 253.

212. For further reflections on consumerism as sadism, see James Fitchett, "Marketing Sadism: *Super-Cannes* and Consumer Culture," *Marketing Theory* 2, no. 3 (2002): 309–22.

213. Miller, *Consuming Religion*, 15–31. As examples of Christian jeremiads against the bad values of consumerism, Miller cites Pope John Paul II's critique of consumerism in his 1999 "World Day of Peace" address and John Kavanaugh's book *Following Christ in a Consumer Society*, revised ed. (Maryknoll, NY: Orbis, 1991).

Chapter 8

1. Richard Crossman, ed., *The God That Failed* (New York: Harper, 1949). The book is a collection of reflections by former sympathizers with communism, including Arthur Koestler, Ignazio Silone, Richard Wright, André Gide, Louis Fischer, and Steven Spender.

2. Pope Francis, *Laudato Si'*, Vatican, May 24, 2015, §83, https://www.vatican.va/content/francesco/en/encyclicals/documents/papa-francesco_20150524_enciclica-laudato-si.html#_ftnref74.

3. Eugene McCarraher, *The Enchantments of Mammon: How Capitalism Became the Religion of Modernity* (Cambridge, MA: Harvard University Press, 2019), 5.

4. Ibid., 11.

5. Ibid., 675.

6. Ibid., 676.

7. Pope Paul VI, *Sacrosanctum Concilium* (Constitution on the Sacred Liturgy), Vatican, December 4, 1963, §61, https://www.vatican.va/archive/hist_councils/ii_vatican_council/documents/vat-ii_const_19631204_sacrosanctum-concilium_en.html.

8. See Pope Paul VI, *Lumen Gentium* (Dogmatic Constitution on the Church), Vatican, November 21, 1964, §14–16, https://www.vatican.va/archive/hist_councils/ii_vatican_council/documents/vat-ii_const_19641121_lumen-gentium_en.html. "All men are called to be part of this catholic unity of the people of God which in promoting universal peace presages it. And there belong to or are related to it in various ways, the Catholic faithful, all who believe in Christ, and indeed the whole of mankind, for all men are called by the grace of God to salvation" (§13). The next three sections then unfold a series of concentric circles of grace, moving from the Catholic Church to all Christians to Jews, Muslims, others who believe in God, and finally to those who have not yet arrived at an explicit knowledge of God but strive to live a good life.

9. McCarraher, *Enchantments of Mammon*, 11–12.

10. Ibid., 12.

11. Ibid., 675.

12. I take the latter phrase from Thomas Frank's article "The God That Sucked," *The Baffler*, no. 14 (April 2001), https://thebaffler.com/salvos/the-god-that-sucked.

13. McCarraher, *Enchantments of Mammon*, 17.

14. These comments are made in the context of a deep appreciation for the outstanding work McCarraher has done in his monumental book. I am not so much complaining about McCarraher's book as pointing to the work ahead that remains to be done. McCarraher is a historian, not a theologian, and he cannot be faulted for writing history instead of theology. Indeed, I find it immensely significant that a historian, in a major work published by Harvard University Press, would underline the significance of theology and at least gesture in the right direction. And McCarraher's gestures toward sacramental theology—found scattered in the prologue and the last five pages of the epilogue—are enormously suggestive. For my full response to *The Enchantments of Mammon*, see the book symposium published by *Syndicate* online in December 2020: https://syndicate.network/symposia/theology/the-enchantments-of-mammon/.

15. Johann Gottlieb Fichte, "Thirteenth Address," in *Addresses to the German Nation*, trans. Reginald Foy Jones, Wikisource, accessed July 29, 2023, §204, https://en.wikisource.org/wiki/Addresses_to_the_German_Nation/Thirteenth_Address.

16. Adam Zamoyski, *Holy Madness: Romantics, Patriots, and Revolutionaries 1776–1871* (New York: Viking, 2000), 2.

17. Colin Campbell, *The Romantic Ethic and the Spirit of Modern Consumerism*, new extended ed. (London: Palgrave McMillan, 2018).

18. David Brown, "A Sacramental World: Why It Matters," in *The Oxford Handbook of Sacramental Theology*, ed. Hans Boersma and Matthew Levering (Oxford: Oxford University Press, 2015), 605.

19. Ibid., 608–11.

20. Ibid., 604.

21. Ibid., 605.

22. Ibid.

23. Ibid., 612.

24. Henri de Lubac, *The Splendor of the Church*, trans. Michael Mason (San Francisco, CA: Ignatius, 1986), 203.

25. Vatican II, *Gaudium et Spes (Pastoral Constitution on the Church in the Modern World)*, §22. https://www.vatican.va/archive/hist_councils/ii_vatican_council/documents/vat-ii_const_19651207_gaudium-et-spes_en.html.

26. Henri de Lubac, *Catholicism: Christ and the Common Destiny of Man*, trans. Lancelot C. Sheppard and Elizabeth Englund (San Francisco, CA: Ignatius, 1988), 25.

27. Karl Rahner, *The Church and the Sacraments*, trans. W. J. O'Hara (London: Burns & Oates, 1974), 13.

28. Paul McPartlan, "Catholic Perspectives on Sacramentality," *Studia Liturgica* 38 (2008): 227.

29. Kevin W. Irwin, "A Sacramental World—Sacramentality as the Primary Language for Sacraments," *Worship* 76, no. 3 (May 2002): 202. Here Irwin is quoting the definition of sacramentality from Richard P. McBrien, ed., *The HarperCollins Encyclopedia of Catholicism* (San Francisco, CA: HarperCollins, 1995), 1148.

30. Irwin, "A Sacramental World," 202–3.

31. Irwin tends to describe the sacraments in cognitive terms of the meaning that we take from them: "[T]hrough sacramental liturgy human persons put their lives and the world itself into perspective" (ibid., 206). "To my mind, then, among the things which the enactment of the Eucharist accomplishes is that bread and wine, taken and shared, are the regular ritual reminders of what it means to share in God's grace in all of human life" (208). "Sacramental liturgy thus provides the lens we need through which to view all of reality—a reality which is both sacred and secular, fully divine and fully human" (208).

32. Alexander Schmemann, *For the Life of the World* (Crestwood, NY: St. Vladimir's Seminary Press, 1988), 139–40.

33. Regina Schwartz and others have critiqued monotheism as being intolerant and violent by nature because it demands exclusive loyalty to one God. See Regina Schwartz, *The Curse of Cain: The Violent Legacy of Monotheism* (Chicago: University of Chicago Press, 1998). I doubt that the problem can be solved quantitatively; it is not a question of *how many gods* but a question of *which gods, which divinity* is being worshiped.

34. Charles Taylor, *A Secular Age* (Cambridge, MA: Harvard University Press, 2007), 613.

35. See ibid., 70–9, and my discussion in chapter 2.

36. Ibid., 614.

37. Ibid., 288, 554–5.

38. Ibid., 613–5.

39. Ibid., 740.

40. Ibid., 741.

41. "Nomolatry" is another term Taylor uses for the same phenomenon. See ibid., 704–7, 741–3.

42. Ibid., 753.

43. Ibid., 754.

44. Ibid.

45. Joseph B. Soloveitchik, *Halakhic Man*, trans. Lawrence Kaplan (Philadelphia, PA: Jewish Publication Society of America, 1983), 38–9. Similarly, Martin Buber writes that the purpose of the Bible is to "make the spirit incarnate and sanctified in everyday life": Martin Buber, *On the Bible* (New York: Schocken Books, 1968), 3.

46. Soloveitchik, *Halakhic Man*, 38.

47. Michael Wyschogrod, *The Body of Faith: God in the People Israel* (Lanham, MD: Rowman and Littlefield, 2000).

48. See, for example, Meir Y. Soloveichik, "No Friend in Jesus," *First Things*, January 2008, https://www.firstthings.com/article/2008/01/no-friend-in-jesus. Soloveichik writes, "Christians embrace the concept of the Incarnation; but, from the Jewish perspective, a human God is the equivalent of a four-sided triangle. . . . If we deny his divinity, then we can respond with nothing short of shock and dismay when we read the words of a man who puts himself in the place of God." Meir Soloveichik is the great nephew of Joseph B. Soloveitchik, quoted above.

49. John M. G. Barclay, "Kenosis and the Drama of Salvation in Philippians 2," in *Kenosis: The Self-Emptying of Christ in Scripture and Theology*, ed. Paul T. Nimmo and Keith L. Johnsons (Grand Rapids, MI: Eerdmans, 2022), 7–23.

50. The notion of a vulnerable God who divests Godself of power has been employed as a response to an overemphasis on Jesus's divinity and as a response to the problem of theodicy and human suffering. Such notions often create more theological problems than they solve. For critiques of this type of kenoticism or theologies of a vulnerable God, see, inter alia, Ian A. McFarland, *The Word Made Flesh: A Theology of the Incarnation* (Louisville, KY: Westminster John Knox, 2019), 4–6; Linn Tonstad, "On Vulnerability," in *Suffering and the Christian Life*, ed. Karen Kilby and Rachel Davies (London: T. & T. Clark, 2020), 175–88.

51. Barclay, "Kenosis and the Drama of Salvation." Paul points to the same dynamic in Philippians 3:10–11, in which Paul seeks conformity with Christ's death in order to participate in his resurrection.

52. For example, Karen Kilby, "The Seductions of Kenosis," in Kilby and Davies, *Suffering and the Christian Life*, 163–74.

53. Athanasius, *On the Incarnation of the Word*, trans. Archibald Robertson, in *Nicene and Post-Nicene Fathers*, second series, vol. 4., ed. Philip Schaff and Henry Wace (Buffalo, NY: Christian Literature, 1892), revised and edited for New Advent by Kevin Knight, accessed July 29, 2023, http://www.newadvent.org/fathers/2802.htm.

54. Ibid., 4.2.

55. Ibid., 4.4–10.

56. Ibid., 12.2.

57. Ibid., 15.2.

58. Ibid., 14.6.

59. Ibid., 14.1–2.

60. Ibid., 11.4.

61. For more on accommodation, see Tobias Tanton, "Accommodating Embodied Thinkers," *Modern Theology* 37, no. 2 (April 2021): 316–35.

62. Athanasius, *On the Incarnation*, 16.5.

63. Augustine, *On the Trinity,* XIII.19.24, trans. Stephen McKenna, The Fathers of the Church: A New Translation, vol. 45 (Washington, DC: Catholic University of America Press, 1963), 406.

64. Ibid., IV.18.24, 160. The last number is the page number in the McKenna translation.

65. Augustine, *Confessions*, X.27.38, trans. Henry Chadwick (Oxford: Oxford University Press, 1991), 201.

66. Ibid., X.6.9, 183. The last number is the page number in the Chadwick translation.

67. Carol Harrison, "Taking Creation for the Creator: Use and Enjoyment in Augustine's Theological Aesthetics," in *Idolatry: False Worship in the Bible, Early Judaism, and Christianity*, ed. Stephen C. Barton (London: T. & T. Clark, 2007), 195.

68. Augustine, *On the Trinity*, XV.17.27, 491.

69. Harrison, "Taking Creation for the Creator, 195. See also Carol Harrison, *Beauty and Revelation in the Thought of Saint Augustine* (Oxford: Clarendon, 1992), 230–8.

70. Edwin van Driel, "Incarnation and Israel: A Supralapsarian Account of Israel's Chosenness," *Modern Theology* 39, no. 1 (January 2023): 9. For a more thorough defense of a supralapsarian account of the Incarnation, see Edwin Chr. van Driel, *Incarnation Anyway: Arguments for Supralapsarian Christology* (Oxford: Oxford University Press, 2008).

71. Van Driel, "Incarnation and Israel," 12. According to van Driel, "Once creation wanders away from God, God decides that the One for whom all things were called into being, the One who is the eschatological goal of everything that exists, also will be the One through whom God draws back creation—'so that he might have first place in everything' (Col. 1:18)" (12).

72. Ibid., 10.

73. Van Driel argues that to say Israel is elected for the sake of the Incarnation is not supersessionism but rather universalizes the election of Israel, embedding it in creation's eschatological goal (ibid., 13–8).

74. Samuel Wells, *A Nazareth Manifesto: Being with God* (Malden, MA: Wiley Blackwell, 2015), 232–3.

75. Ibid., 27.

76. Ibid., 243.

77. Ibid., 44.

78. McFarland, *Word Made Flesh*, 201. Here McFarland is critiquing in particular Paul Knitter, Catherine Keller, and Sallie McFague.

79. Trevor Hart, " 'Goodly Sights' and 'Unseemly Representations': Transcendence and the Problems of Visual Piety," in Barton, *Idolatry*, 211. Hart's comment about the particular time and place of the Incarnation of Jesus Christ should not, however, lead us to think of God's embrace of creation as episodic. A supralapsarian account of the Incarnation sees the logic of the particularity of Jesus of Nazareth as the same logic as that of the universal desire of God to be with creation.

80. Ibid.

81. Whether or not this stereotype is fair to Plato is not my concern here. For the view that it is not fair to Plato, see Ola Sigurdson, *Heavenly Bodies: Incarnation, the Gaze, and Embodiment in Christian Theology*, trans. Carl Olsen (Grand Rapids, MI: Eerdmans, 2016), 272–3.

82. Stathis Gourgouris, "Every Religion Is Idolatry," *Social Research* 80, no. 1 (Spring 2013), 101–28. "The sacred prohibition of the name *is a name*, an act of naming, of localizing in an immanent sense, the Abyss that must—and does by virtue of this naming which is the unnaming of the Name—remain shielded" (119). "The obvious—and I think indisputable—point is that nothing is unrepresentable because whatever signifies it as unrepresentable must configure its unrepresentability in some form, even if entirely in the realm of the sayable" (123).

83. Jean-Luc Marion, *The Crossing of the Visible*, trans. James K. A. Smith (Stanford, CA: Stanford University Press, 2004), 81. See Marion's contrast of Plato and Nietzsche as the two extremes on 79–83.

84. Natalie Carnes similarly wants to explore both presence and absence, visibility and invisibility, in images, but rather than rejecting iconoclasm, she argues that there is both good and bad iconoclasm. Every image presents what it is not, and so negation is at the heart of imaging; every image carries a kind of iconoclasm. Carnes chides Marion for failing to appreciate good iconoclasm and thus setting up a dynamic of us versus them, Christians versus Muslims, for example. See Natalie Carnes, *Image and Presence: A Christological Reflection on Iconoclasm and Iconophilia* (Stanford, CA: Stanford University Press, 2018), 6–13.

85. Jean-Luc Marion, *The Idol and Distance: Five Studies*, trans. Thomas A. Carlson (New York: Fordham University Press, 2001), 9.

86. Jean-Luc Marion, *God without Being: Hors-Texte*, trans. Thomas A. Carlson (Chicago: University of Chicago Press, 1991), 18.

87. Ibid.

88. Marion, *Crossing of the Visible*, 62.

89. Marion, *God without Being*, 21.

90. Marion, *In Excess*, 112.

91. Jeana Visel, *Icons in the Western Church: Toward a More Sacramental Encounter* (Collegeville, MN: Liturgical Press, 2016), 10–11.

92. Marion, *Crossing of the Visible*, 21. As Visel points out, in icons one sees but is also seen, precisely because the holy person depicted is also understood to be present (*Icons in the Western Church*, 2–3).

93. Marion, *Crossing of the Visible*, 21.

94. Marion, *God without Being*, 22.

95. The eighth-century text *The Life of St. Stephen the Younger* (PG 100.1113) refers explicitly to the icon as a door; see John Chryssavgis, *Creation as Sacrament: Reflections on Ecology and Spirituality* (London: T. & T. Clark, 2019), 119.

96. Marion, *God without Being*, 19.

97. Ibid., 23; Marion, *Crossing of the Visible*, 86.

98. Thomas Aquinas, *Summa Theologiae*, I.8.1.

99. Sigurdson, *Heavenly Bodies*, 272.

100. Marion, *God without Being*, 23.

101. St. John of Damascus, *Three Treatises on the Divine Images*, trans. Andrew Louth (Crestwood, NY: St. Vladimir's Seminary Press, 2003), 88–9.

102. See Sigurdson, *Heavenly Bodies*, 260–1.

103. Marion writes that "the formula that Saint Paul applies to Christ, *eikōn tou theou tou aoratou*, icon of the invisible God (Col. 1:15), must serve as our norm; it even must be generalized to every icon" (*God without Being*, 17).

104. John of Damascus writes that he reverences matter, but reserves veneration for God: "Of old, God the incorporeal and formless was never depicted, but now that God has been seen in the flesh and has associated with human kind, I depict what I have seen of God. I do not venerate matter, I venerate the fashioner of matter, who became matter for my sake and accepted to dwell in matter and through matter worked my salvation, and I will not cease from reverencing matter, through which my salvation was worked. I do not reverence it as God" (*Three Treatises*, 29).

105. Marion, *Crossing of the Visible*, 84.

106. Ibid., 85. The internal quote is from Maximus the Confessor. In a footnote Marion comments, "If the Incarnation offers an icon of charity, it would also be necessary conversely to conclude that Christ, by being made charity for men, is given as an icon only by accomplishing charity. Thus charity alone would render the icon possible" (99n19).

107. Graham Ward, "The Beauty of God," in John Milbank, Graham Ward, and Edith Wyschogrod, *Theological Perspectives on God and Beauty* (Harrisburg, PA: Trinity Press International, 2003), 35–65.

108. John Milbank, "The Gift and the Mirror," in *Counter Experiences: Reading the Work of Jean-Luc Marion*, ed. Kevin Hart (Notre Dame, IN: University of Notre Dame Press, 2007), 272.

109. James K. A. Smith, *The Nicene Option: An Incarnational Phenomenology* (Waco, TX: Baylor University Press, 2021), 209.

110. This paragraph and the next rely on Stephanie Rumpza, "Crossing the Visible or Crossing It Out? Jean-Luc Marion's Icon as Window into Heaven," *Horizons* 49, no. 1 (June 2022): 21–48.

111. Marion sets this out most clearly in Jean-Luc Marion, "À partir de la Trinité," *Communio* 40, no. 6 (2015): 23–38.

112. Marion, *Crossing of the Visible*, 58.

113. There are certainly differences between icons and sacraments. Junius Johnson outlines them as follows. Though both are creaturely signs, sacraments follow natural signification (bread, wine, water, etc.), whereas icons follow traditional signification. Sacraments bring divine things "down" to us, whereas icons are meant to send the viewer "up" to God's glory. Icons thus reference divine realities as they are in heaven, whereas sacraments are *viaticum*, strength for the journey on earth. Sacraments are instituted by Christ, but icons lack such a moment of institution. The Eucharistic elements become what they signify, whereas icons are more a portal to Christ. See Junius Johnson, *The Father of Lights: A Theology of Beauty* (Grand Rapids, MI: Baker, 2020), 172–5.

114. Ibid., 36.

115. Ibid., 36–7.

116. Schmemann, *For the Life of the World*, 15.

117. Joris Geldhof points out a lamentable *Liturgievergessenheit* in theologies of sacramentality, a neglect of the liturgical shape of the sacraments: "The sacramental is not what *is* sacred, but what *sanctifies*: it is what participates in the divine dynamics and the economy of salvation." Joris Geldhof, "Liturgy: The Sacramental World par Excellence and the Church's True Politics: A Response to David Brown," *Louvain Studies* 39, no. 2 (Summer 2015–6): 179.

118. Jonathan Ciraulo, "The Sacramental Principle," *Communio* 50, no. 1 (Spring 2023): 72.

119. Ibid., 81.

120. On Kant and the superstition of sacraments, see Cathal Doherty, *Maurice Blondel on the Supernatural in Human Action: Sacrament and Superstition* (Leiden: Brill, 2017), 25–9.

121. Ciraulo, "Sacramental Principle," 96–97.

122. Ciraulo does have one sentence where he gestures toward misenchantment: "There is of course the decision between the sacramental principle and the anti-sacramental principle, but there are also a whole host of ersatz sacramental principles, from Hegel's Joachimite sacramentology to the sacramental longings of Romanticism, which often enough never allow nature itself to be intrinsically theophanic, but merely theophanic as a site for the projection of the longing heart" (ibid., 101).

123. Doherty, *Maurice Blondel on the Supernatural*, 102–10.

124. For a similar argument, see Johnson, *Father of Lights*, 145–7. Sacraments are not mere signs; they effect what they signify. They are a matter of presence, not mere semiotics. God must give God's presence freely, and so what is a sacrament can be instituted only by Lordly authority.

125. Ibid., 152–95. Doherty makes his case by contrasting Blondel with Karl Rahner's and Marie-Louis Chauvet's approaches to the sacraments, which Doherty thinks assign too much of sacramental efficacy to human effort of interpretation. I will leave the question of whether his readings of Rahner and Chauvet are fair to others more qualified to judge.

126. Quoted in Jean-Luc Marion, "The Phenomenality of the Sacrament—Being and Givenness," in *Words of Life: New Theological Turns in French Phenomenology*, ed. Bruce Ellis Benson and Norman Wirzbas (New York: Fordham University Press, 2010), 89.

127. Ibid., 99. Marion continues, "[T]he sacrament accomplishes and reduces the intrinsic manifestation of the Son, the transition in it from the Father's invisibility to Christ's visibility spread by the Spirit in its Church" (99).

128. Ibid., 94.

129. Ibid., 101.

130. Ibid.

131. Ibid.

132. Ibid., 101–2.

133. Christina Gschwandtner, *Degrees of Givenness: On Saturation in Jean-Luc Marion* (Bloomington: Indiana University Press, 2014), 170–6. Gschwandtner is primarily focused on chapters 5 and 6 of *God without Being* and Marion's *Prolegomena to Charity*, trans. Stephen E. Lewis (New York: Fordham University Press, 2002). She acknowledges that in the later essay I discuss above, "The Phenomenality of the Sacrament," Marion more carefully backs away from claims that we might move over to God's hermeneutical point of view, and Marion acknowledges the possibility of different approaches to the Eucharist (*Degrees of Givenness,* 181).

134. Ibid., 184.

135. Ibid., 181–6.

136. Marion, "The Phenomenality of the Sacrament," 101.

137. Gschwandtner, *Degrees of Givenness,* 189.

138. "[I]t might make more sense to examine the phenomenality of the sacramental event as it appears in the experience of human beings instead of first and foremost as a manifestation of the invisible—without implying that this may not also be the case or that the two are not intimately connected to each other. That is to say, phenomenology can validly examine the experiences of religious believers as they practice religious rites and experience religious events and thereby reach some conclusions about the meaning of these rites and events without thereby degenerating *either* into mere 'psychologizing' interpretations *or* making theological claims about God's activity in the event" (ibid. 191).

139. Ibid., 192, 197–9.

140. Katie Walker Grimes, *Christ Divided: Antiblackness as Corporate Vice* (Minneapolis, MN: Fortress Press, 2017), 190–200.

141. Ibid., 205.

142. Ibid., 205–22.

143. Ibid., 222.

144. Ibid., 231.

145. In language that contrasts with Marion's language of being overwhelmed by the Eucharist, Grimes writes, "[W]e do not suffer the sacraments passively like a slap in the face. We instead receive them by performing them; that is, we receive them only if we perform them" (ibid., 227).

146. Ibid., 229.

147. Ibid., 226.

148. Ibid., 230.

149. As in my books *Torture and Eucharist: Theology, Politics, and the Body of Christ* (Oxford: Blackwell, 1998) and *Being Consumed* (Grand Rapids, MI: Eerdmans, 2008).

150. Grimes sums up her two main criticisms—refusing to accept that the body of Christ is porous, and failing to put the church's vice, particularly racism, at the center of the analysis—in *Christ Divided,* 209. I will relegate to this endnote the tedious and ego-tainted task of defending myself from being caricatured; Stanley Hauerwas can defend himself. For my analysis of the sinfulness of the church, see *Migrations of the Holy* (Grand Rapids, MI: Eerdmans, 2011), particularly chapter 5, "How to Do Penance for the Inquisition," and chapter 8, "The Sinfulness and Visibility of the

Church: A Christological Exploration"; also chapter 2 of *Torture and Eucharist*, and my "The Church among Idols: How My Mind Has Changed," *Christian Century* 138, no. 12 (June 16, 2021): 26–31. On the porous boundaries between the church and the world, see *Migrations of the Holy*, chapter 2, and chapter 2 of my *Field Hospital: The Church's Engagement with a Wounded World* (Grand Rapids, MI: Eerdmans, 2016). Grimes accuses me of a stark "Augustinian" opposition of the two cities, the *civitas terrena* and the *civitas Dei*, but I show in the former chapter how the two cities are intermingled performances on the stage of history. In the latter chapter I show that Vatican II uses the term "world" in four different senses, and in only one of them are church and world opposed. Grimes quotes me saying that the Eucharist has been used to reinforce negative social hierarchies and exclude others, especially the Jews, but nevertheless says of me that "this fact does not shake his confidence in the cultic Eucharist's capacity to resist political evil as long as it is performed correctly" (Grimes, *Christ Divided*, 212). On the Eucharist as judgment against the church for its failure to overcome social divisions, see *Torture and Eucharist*, chapter 5, especially 234–52.

151. *Catechism of the Catholic Church* (Washington, DC: U.S. Catholic Conference, Libreria Editrice Vaticana, 1994), §1128.

152. Grimes, *Christ Divided*, 233.

153. William T. Cavanaugh, *Theopolitical Imagination: Discovering the Liturgy as a Political Act in an Age of Global Consumerism* (Edinburgh: T. & T. Clark, 2002), 52. Grimes footnotes my book here; her quote omits the word "can."

154. Cavanaugh, *Torture and Eucharist*, 253–64.

155. The phrase is that of Lauren Winner, who levels a critique very similar to that of Grimes in her book *The Dangers of Christian Practice: On Wayward Gifts, Characteristic Damage, and Sin* (New Haven, CT: Yale University Press, 2018).

156. In addition to what is quoted above: "Unfortunately, however, the cultic Eucharist limits the ability of the church to recognize itself. The real meal, on the other hand, makes the body of Christ visible to itself in a way that the cultic meal cannot. While the cultic Eucharist obscures the damage corporate vice inflicts upon the body of Christ, the real meal brings the sacramental impact of these bad habits to the surface" (Grimes, *Christ Divided*, 229).

157. "Indeed, like cultic feasts, real meals can reinforce unjust social hierarchy just as they can improperly exclude. But, while the cultic meal easily obscures this interrelation between sacramental integrity and worldly justice, the real meal can illuminate it. Rather than realigning the church's corporate body automatically, a return to the real meal as advocated by the Apostle Paul enables us to more perspicaciously recognize when it is broken" (ibid.).

158. As an example of such confusion, Grimes writes, "Hauerwas retains his sacramental optimism even in the face of racism. According to Hauerwas, once a person acknowledges 'the absolute sovereignty of God . . . that person can no longer be a racist.' History refutes this: Iberian Christians first Africanized slavery in fulfillment of their sincere belief in God's absolute sovereignty" (ibid., 210–1). It appears here that Hauerwas is making a normative theological claim that Grimes takes as

an empirical claim. Hauerwas does not think that anyone who claims to acknowledge the absolute sovereignty of God is immune to racism; he thinks that if you are a racist, you are not in fact acknowledging the absolute sovereignty of God. You are, in other words, an idolater.

159. *Catechism of the Catholic Church*, §1127, italics in original.
160. Ibid., §1128.
161. Antonio Eduardo Alonso, *Commodified Communion: Eucharist, Consumer Culture, and the Practice of Everyday Life* (New York: Fordham University Press, 2021), 41.
162. Ibid., 30.
163. Ibid., 53.
164. Ibid., 53–4.
165. Ibid., 52.
166. Ibid., 1–2.
167. Ibid., 4. Beyond commodified items produced specifically for the religious market, Alonso also looks positively on the ways that "Christianity is poured into the forms of the world." Christian traditions, symbols, and motifs reappear in art, music, and media, on talk shows and at the unveilings of new technological devices, in Instagram memes and hot-yoga classes. "This transfer often reveals consumer culture doing one of the things it does best: abstracting sacred objects and faithful practices from the communities in which they were formed and putting them to new use" (4). Alonso adds that there is much to lament about such abstraction and its effects on the communities from which such material is taken. But moving beyond resistance, he says, helps us to appreciate the genuine cravings for redemption that appear in consumer culture, even in misshapen form.
168. Ibid., 16.
169. Ibid., 45–52, 107–14. Both traditionalist and progressive hymnals "are equally captive to the logic of the market. Both have depended on market strategies to carry into the world a theological brand marked by a consumer culture that they often claim to transcend" (51–2).
170. Ibid., 2, italics in the original.
171. Ibid., 40.
172. Ibid., 84.
173. Ibid.
174. Ibid., 54, and identically on 57.
175. Ibid., 61.
176. Ibid., 65.
177. Ibid., 67.
178. Ibid., 68.
179. Ibid., 86–106.
180. Ibid., 69.
181. Ibid., 125.
182. Ibid., 52.
183. Ibid., 54.

184. The whole point of the first chapter of my book *Being Consumed* is in fact to argue that there is no such thing as "the market"; Christian economic reflection is to discern if and when a market is free or not, that is, if and when any particular transaction contributes to the flourishing of the parties involved—including the environment and the factory workers who make the products—and if and when it is exploitative, gluttonous, polluting, and so on. Fair Trade businesses are not trying to escape "the market"; they are trying to create other, freer kinds of markets. William T. Cavanaugh, *Being Consumed: Economics and Christian Desire* (Grand Rapids, MI: Eerdmans, 2008), 1–32.

185. See Vincent J. Miller, *Consuming Religion: Christian Faith and Practice in a Consumer Culture* (New York: Continuum, 2004), 179–94.

186. This is from the introduction to Cavanaugh, *Being Consumed*, viii–ix.

187. Alonso, *Commodified Communion*, 14.

188. Ibid., 68, and again on 69.

189. Graham Ward's appreciative critique of Certeau is relevant here. Ward argues that Certeau's work can be read within a dualism between alterity and sameness: discourse of the other is possible only as discourse of the lost and irrecuperable other, because to be other, the other must be pure and untouched by the same. Graham Ward, "Michel de Certeau's 'Spiritual Spaces,'" *New Blackfriars* 79, no. 932 (October 1998): 432. Rational space (sameness) is opposed by mystical space (otherness), univocity by equivocity. Certeau wants to open a space for analogy, for otherness within sameness, for presence within absence. Ward calls this a "eucharistic spacing," because Certeau himself sees his work, particularly in *The Mystic Fable*, as a sequel to de Lubac's history of the theology and practice of the Eucharist. For both de Lubac and Certeau, the doctrine of creation opened a sacramental space in which God could be read in the material reality that God had called into being and sustained. Before the thirteenth century, an analogical relationship held, in which the church as Eucharist held together the Word in the world by means of liturgical and sacramental actions. Nominalism and later modernity opened up a distrust in the transparency of the Word in creation, a split between God and the world. The analogical view of the world was eclipsed by the duality of univocity and equivocity (434–5). Ward nevertheless points to two important differences between de Lubac's and Certeau's understanding of eucharistic spacing. First, the movement from Jesus's historical body to the sacramental body of Christ in the Eucharist is described by de Lubac as extension, incorporation, and participation, whereas Certeau describes it in terms of lack, loss, bereavement, and substitution. For de Lubac, Ward writes, "[t]he Eucharist is not a sign of the presence of Christ's body, it *is* Christ's body" (436). For Certeau, the Eucharist is an attempt to recover the lost original body of Christ, so the Eucharist and the church are substitutes, signs of absence. As Ward points out, this is awkward, because Certeau regards the economy of loss and lack as manifestations of the eclipse of analogy with the advent of nominalism. Second, de Lubac has a theology of history as the grace-filled time given for the salvation of the world. Certeau is critical of grand historical narratives, and so he has no theology of history. Though he seems to want to recognize the importance and coherence

of an analogical and sacramental worldview, his narration of time is arbitrary, and meaning lies outside of history. The endless, mystical wandering in exile leans toward nihilism. According to Ward, Certeau wants to resist this conclusion; while the church as institutional place must collapse, eucharistic spaces of communal living can go on. But such sites remain utopic, a transcendental horizon. Instead of a theological account of history that includes such spaces, Certeau pushes them to the margins of history and maintains a modern binary logic: secular and sacred, visible and hidden, here and there. It amounts to a denial of incarnation. Despite his analysis of everyday practices, he fails to engage directly with Christian practices. "He is evidently interested in the everyday practices of secular believing—that which 'creates opinion.' He is, furthermore, concerned about the ideologies and politics of such a creating something believable. But what is the status of the observations he makes if he fails to relate these 'beliefs' to practices of the faith (in fact fails to examine contemporary practices of the faith at all), even though these practices are the benchmark for judging what ideal practising and belief is?" (440). In short, the possibility of sacramental practices haunts Certeau's account, but his emphasis on absence renders a sacramental worldview utopic, in the sense of no-place.

190. The Didache, trans. M. B. Riddle, from Ante-Nicene Fathers, vol. 7, ed. Alexander Roberts, James Donaldson, and A. Cleveland Coxe (Buffalo, NY: Christian Literature, 1886), revised and ed. for New Advent by Kevin Knight, 9:4, accessed July 29, 2023, https://www.newadvent.org/fathers/0714.htm. For reflections on the Eucharist and the eschatological banquet, see Andrea Bieler and Luise Schottroff, The Eucharist: Bodies, Bread, and Resurrection (Minneapolis, MN: Fortress, 2007), 53–6, 65–7.

191. Bieler and Schottroff, The Eucharist, 56–65.

192. "Message of His Holiness Pope Francis for the 107th World Day of Migrants and Refugees 2021: Towards an Ever Wider 'We,'" Vatican, September 26, 2021, https://www.vatican.va/content/francesco/en/messages/migration/documents/papa-francesco_20210503_world-migrants-day-2021.html.

193. "Message of His Holiness Pope Francis for the 105th World Day of Migrants and Refugees 2019: It Is Not Just about Migrants," Vatican, September 29, 2019, https://www.vatican.va/content/francesco/en/messages/migration/documents/papa-francesco_20190527_world-migrants-day-2019.html.

194. "Message of His Holiness Pope Francis for the 106th World Day of Migrants and Refugees 2020: Like Jesus Christ, Forced to Flee. Welcoming, Protecting, Promoting and Integrating Internally Displaced Persons," Vatican, September 27, 2020, https://www.vatican.va/content/francesco/en/messages/migration/documents/papa-francesco_20200513_world-migrants-day-2020.html.

195. "Message of His Holiness Pope Francis for the 108th World Day of Migrants and Refugees 2022: Building the Future with Migrants and Refugees," Vatican, September 25, 2022, https://www.vatican.va/content/francesco/en/messages/migration/documents/20220509-world-migrants-day-2022.html.

196. "Message of His Holiness Pope Francis for the 105th World Day of Migrants and Refugees 2019."

197. Augustine, *Confessions*, VII.16, 124.

198. Bieler and Schottroff, *The Eucharist*, 91–122.

199. The term "social mortgage" was first used by Pope John Paul II; see *Sollicitudo rei socialis*, §42: "Private property, in fact, is under a 'social mortgage,' which means that it has an intrinsically social function, based upon and justified precisely by the principle of the universal destination of goods." Pope John Paul II, *Sollicitudo rei socialis*, Vatican, December 30, 1987, §42, https://www.vatican.va/content/john-paul-ii/en/encyclicals/documents/hf_jp-ii_enc_30121987_sollicitudo-rei-socialis.html#-27. The idea is consonant with scripture and tradition. Thomas Aquinas, for example, writes that "man ought to possess external things, not as his own, but as common, so that, to wit, he is ready to communicate them to others in their need" (*Summa Theologiae*, II-II.66.2).

200. Michel de Certeau, *The Mystic Fable,* vol. 1, trans. Michael B. Smith (Chicago: University of Chicago Press, 1992), 81.

201. Ignacio Ellacuría, "El Pueblo Crucificado," in *Mysterium Liberationis: Conceptos fundamentales de la teología de la liberación*, ed. Ignacio Ellacuría and Jon Sobrino (San Salvador: UCA Editores, 1991), 2: 189–216; Jon Sobrino, *Jesus the Liberator: A Historical-Theological Reading of Jesus of Nazareth*, trans. Paul Burns and Francis McDonagh (Maryknoll, NY: Orbis Books, 1993), 254–71.

202. Ryan Gunderson, "Problems with the Defetishization Thesis: Ethical Consumerism, Alternative Food Systems, and Commodity Fetishism," *Agriculture and Human Values* 31 (2014): 109–17.

203. For an overview of the scholarship on this exchange, see Regina Munch, "Let Them Eat TVs: How We Traded Away Our Democracy for Cheap Stuff," *Commonweal* 150, no. 6 (June 2023): 32–8.

204. For example, "In short, talking about consumerism is often just a way of *not* talking about capitalism." Eugene McCarraher, "The Storm Cloud of the Twenty-First Century: John Ruskin, Pope Francis, and Global Warming," *Commonweal* 149, no. 10 (November 2022): 31.

205. Pope Benedict XVI, *Caritas in Veritate*, Vatican, June 29, 2009, §36, https://www.vatican.va/content/benedict-xvi/en/encyclicals/documents/hf_ben-xvi_enc_20090629_caritas-in-veritate.html, italics in the original. The encyclical continues, "This is a human demand at the present time, but it is also demanded by economic logic. It is a demand both of charity and of truth."

206. Ibid., §39, italics in the original.

207. Ibid. Pope Francis likewise rejects the market/state binary: "The principle of the maximization of profits, frequently isolated from other considerations, reflects a misunderstanding of the very concept of the economy. . . . An instrumental way of reasoning, which provides a purely static analysis of realities in the service of present needs, is at work whether resources are allocated by the market or by state central planning" (*Laudato Si'*, §195). In both cases, the problem is the corporate manager or state bureaucrat looking down from on high and deciding the fates of people,

animals, and the land—none of which the manager really knows—on the basis of what Francis calls the "technocratic paradigm" that treats them as resources to be manipulated. The technocratic paradigm exalts a rational subject who sees from above and gains power by "possession, mastery, and transformation" of the world (§106).

208. See especially *Caritas in Veritate*, §37–8.

209. Ibid., §35.

210. Pope Francis has a similar vision of a sane economy. In *Laudato Si'* he writes, "Liberation from the dominant technocratic paradigm does in fact happen some-times, for example, when cooperatives of small producers adopt less polluting means of production, and opt for a non-consumerist model of life, recreation and community" (§112). For a much fuller analysis of *Caritas in Veritate*, see chapter 6 of my book *Field Hospital*.

211. David Cloutier, *The Vice of Luxury: Economic Excess in a Consumer Age* (Washington, DC: Georgetown University Press, 2015), 132–8. Cloutier's excellent book contains a final chapter contrasting luxury and sacrament, with a finely nuanced account of the proper ordering of different kinds of surplus goods.

212. Thomas Merton, *New Seeds of Contemplation* (New York: New Directions, 1961), 21.

213. Pope Francis, *Evangelii Gaudium*, Vatican, November 24, 2013, §10. https://www. vatican.va/content/francesco/en/apost_exhortations/documents/papa-france sco_esortazione-ap_20131124_evangelii-gaudium.html. This sentence is quoted from the Fifth General Conference of the Latin American and Caribbean Bishops, Aparecida document, 2007, which Francis had a hand in drafting.

214. Pope Francis, *Evangelii Gaudium*, §88.

Index of Scripture passages

For the benefit of digital users, indexed terms that span two pages (e.g., 52–53) may, on occasion, appear on only one of those pages.

Index of subjects and names

For the benefit of digital users, indexed terms that span two pages (e.g., 52–53) may, on occasion, appear on only one of those pages.